Object-Oriented Programming in Visual Basic .NET

PEARSON
Education

We work with leading authors to develop the
strongest educational materials in computer science,
bringing cutting-edge thinking and best
learning practice to a global market.

Under a range of well-known imprints, including
Addison-Wesley, we craft high-quality print and
electronic publications which help readers to understand
and apply their content, whether studying or at work.

To find out more about the complete range of our
publishing, please visit us on the World Wide Web at:
www.pearsoned.co.uk

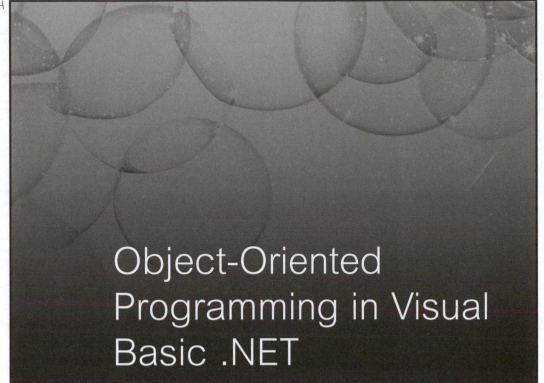

Object-Oriented Programming in Visual Basic .NET

Alistair McMonnies

University of Paisley

PEARSON

Addison
Wesley

Harlow, England • London • New York • Boston • San Francisco • Toronto • Sydney • Singapore • Hong Kong
Tokyo • Seoul • Taipei • New Delhi • Cape Town • Madrid • Mexico City • Amsterdam • Munich • Paris • Milan

Pearson Education Limited
Edinburgh Gate
Harlow
Essex CM20 2JE
England

and Associated Companies throughout the world

Visit us on the World Wide Web at:
www.pearsoned.co.uk

First published 2004

ISBN 0 201 78705 9

Screenshots reprinted by permission from Microsoft Corporation

British Library Cataloguing-in-Publication Data
A catalogue record for this book is available from the British Library

Library of Congress Cataloging-in-Publication Data
A catalog record for this book is available from the Library of Congress

10 9 8 7 6 5 4 3 2 1
08   07   06   05   04

Typeset in 10/12pt Times by 35
Printed in Great Britain by Henry Ling Ltd., at the Dorset Press, Dorchester, Dorset
The publisher's policy is to use paper manufactured from sustainable forests.

To Jack, Betty and Margaret

Contents

Introduction: What is Visual Basic .NET?

Visual Basic was first released by Microsoft in the early 1990s. At that time, Visual Basic Version 1 (VB1) was a revolutionary product that introduced a new style of computer programming to the world.

Previously, computer programs were most commonly written as lines of text which were instructions to the computer describing how to perform some task. Every part of a program was written as one or more lines of text that described some aspect of the task to be performed. This was regardless of whether the program was created in C, Pascal (popular programming languages of the time) or any other programming language.

Microsoft had introduced Windows version 3.0 (the first popular version of Windows) a few years before this, and was determined to make it the standard operating environment for IBM PC compatible computers. To improve the popularity of Windows, Microsoft knew that a wide range of software products would need to become available as quickly as possible.

However, it was difficult to write Windows programs because of the complex ways in which users could interact with them: a good Windows program would allow the user to control it with a mouse, selecting commands from menus, moving easily between interactive screen elements and, above all, move between several programs apparently running simultaneously in a single system. All of these requirements imposed a heavy burden on programmers, who for the first time had to concede that the user of a program was entitled to exercise a degree of flexibility and control that was previously not attainable.

Visual Basic was introduced as the saviour of Windows, making it possible to create programs that reacted to user interactions in a way that was natural for the programmer to incorporate. Two key elements gave Visual Basic its power and ease of adoption: the 'Visual' element of the language, which allowed a programmer to design a user-interface by drawing its appearance on the computer screen and configure it interactively, and a new model of programming which allowed the programmer to write 'scripts', or mini-programs that were activated as a response to the user interacting with the user-interface.

Over several versions, Visual Basic gradually grew in power and popularity to become the world's most widely used programming system. It also became Microsoft's standard scripting language for its range of office products, its web browser and servers and a number of third party products such as AutoCAD.

By the release of VB6 a few years ago, it was possible to do almost anything in Visual Basic that Microsoft programmers would normally use Visual C++ (Microsoft's industrial strength programming language) for, and in most situations, Visual Basic was far easier to work with and led to quicker development timescales.

However, Visual Basic has always had its detractors. It was a derivation of BASIC, an early programming language (circa 1963) developed in Dartmouth Naval College in the U.S. to teach programming. As such, it lacked the powerful numerical processing capabilities of FORTRAN, and the powerful data storage, retrieval and manipulation capabilities of COBOL. The development of Pascal and the C programming language in the late 1960s and their widespread adoption in the 1970s led to a new model of programming, known as structured programming. Structured programming features were retro-fitted to BASIC and other languages over the next few years, but not before C and Pascal became the de-facto programming languages for systems development. By the introduction of Microsoft Windows, BASIC was already frowned upon by many programmers due to its lack of power, limited features and 'mongrel' lineage.

The initial version of Visual Basic was dismissed as a toy language by many programmers of the time, and the subsequent years of development work that went into Visual Basic did not do much to change the opinions of a fair proportion of them. There was also a community of Microsoft detractors who refused to see any good in anything that Microsoft did, and to these, Visual Basic was just a good reason for saying "I told you so". As new powers and features were added to VB (as many have come to know it), they would be derided as poor cousins of features in 'grown-up' languages, poor copies of good programming language practice, or "just another attempt by Microsoft to railroad the development of programming languages and environments in their direction".

Many of the accusations of these detractors were founded on good points, but it is fair to say that while Microsoft have never been purely philanthropic in their motives, they have rarely been the unmitigated devils that many make them out to be. Most of the software development community would probably agree that Visual Basic 6 and earlier, for all their faults, did open up Windows programming to a huge number of people who would never have got on with C or C++. Visual Basic version 6.0 was and remains a highly capable programming environment that any other software company would be proud of, and is used by a huge community of software developers who simply could not do what they do without it. Even hard-core C++ programmers can admit that their language has power at the expense of a very steep learning curve, and that Visual Basic can always be a language for 'the rest of us'.

In 2000, Microsoft announced a new addition to Windows; the .NET software environment. This was to be the foundation of their new strategy for program development; a software 'platform' that could be tailored to run on a range of different computers and operating systems and that provided a programming model that could host many different programming languages seamlessly.

The .NET (pronounced "dot-net") environment is effectively a 'virtual computer' that runs on a real computer, with the advantage that any program written for it will run on any computer that is running .NET. This is not a new idea, having been pioneered by UCSD (University of California San Diego) Pascal in the 1970s, and brought to modern computing by the Java language. However, .NET is different in that it can support almost any language (to date there are as many as 30 programming languages available for it, most of which were released in its first year of Beta testing), and integrates seamlessly with Microsoft Visual Studio to provide a true 'Visual' development environment for any of these. It also provides integral services for database and Internet programming, and can be used to extend the visual model shipped with Visual Studio without any need for additional tools.

The first version of Visual Studio .NET is without doubt the best programming environment I have ever worked with, and Visual Basic .NET has finally become a grown-up language, by anyone's measure. If you're learning to program for the first time, Visual Basic will give you a previously unheard of mix of ease of use, power and flexibility. Whether you are an expert or among the rest of us, Visual Basic .NET is a language that you can use to release your full potential as a programmer.

Software Development and .NET

By the end of this chapter, you should be able to:

- describe the life-cycle approach to creating software;
- outline the main features of object-oriented programming;
- describe a specific form of software life-cycle suitable for use in developing object-oriented programs in Visual Basic;
- develop a simple software requirements specification;
- describe the key features of an algorithm;
- decompose a statement of software requirements into a detailed step-by-step task description;
- describe the role of .NET in supporting software and the development process.

1.1 Software Development

1.1.1 Learning to program

Learning to use a programming language is not the same as learning to develop software. Well, it is in a way, since when you are developing software you will certainly have to use a programming language to finish the job. However, there is more to developing software than writing programs. Most professionally developed software is hugely complex, and as such it has to be constructed in an environment that takes account of that complexity. No matter who you are, if you are learning how to program you should be aiming to do it to a professional standard.

Programming, the act of writing computer software to add some function to a computer system, is one part of software development. However, in many cases it may be only a small part. The other things that are done during software development are there to support the act of programming in the same way that architecture, surveying and civil engineering are there to support building. Sometimes, we need this additional support to make the act of programming safe and accurate. At other times we do not.

The aim of this book is to show you how to write programs in Microsoft Visual Basic .NET. If it is successful in this, you may go on to write large, best-selling programs, but not unless you pick up a lot of other skills as well. Nevertheless, the subject of this book is programming in Visual Basic .NET, and you can expect the vast majority of the material in here to be just about those things – programming first, programming in Visual Basic .NET as a close second. However, it would be doing everyone a great disservice if some time was not spent laying the foundations for programming.

Probably the first thing that needs to be explained to those new to programming is that it is never as hard as it seems. It may take you a while to tune into the various bits of vocabulary, the idioms used and even the downright technical stuff, but nothing hard is ever being done – complex in the sense that programming can involve many different components yes, but not hard. A program is simply a set of instructions to a very dumb servant (a computer of course) to get it to do something. Most often, that something is to manipulate information, but there are certainly some computer systems where manipulating information is just one part of the job. Controlling an industrial robot, or a car engine, for example, may require a program to manipulate information, but that is not the goal.

For our purposes in this book, everything we do will be to manipulate information (it would not be sensible to unleash a novice programmer on an industrial robot control system or car engine management). The good thing about this is that there is no danger involved. The really good thing is that when you are learning to program, there are no simulators – you just do it and the results are (normally) immediate. Your program works, and you go on to the next program, or it doesn't, and you get to try to find what is wrong with it. Either way you will have learned something practical. I can think of no other skill to learn where the results are so immediate and so satisfying (of course the down side of this is that frustration can figure quite highly as well).

1.1.2 Programming and Complexity

Creating a computer program can be incredibly easy or immensely difficult. The range of factors that affect this include: the type and size of program to be created; the skill of the designers and programmers involved in the work; the environment the program will execute on (the 'platform'); the programming language used; and the way the programming tasks are organized. If you have never done any computer programming, a lot of the job of building a program can look like a mixture of complex mathematics and black magic. Newcomers to programming are often bewildered at the apparent complexity of the tasks involved, and this bewilderment is never helped when those who can already program blandly state that it is 'easy'. The biggest obstacle barring the path of many newcomers to programming is the perception that software springs, fully formed, from the typing fingers of programmers. The perception is often that people who can casually work with such complexity must be very clever. This perception is wrong.

1.1.2.1 Building and Complexity

To understand why this is so, we need only compare the potential range of tasks involved in software development with that of building. If you were to decide to build a shed in the garden, you could probably calculate the amount of wood and other materials you need on the back of an envelope, go out and buy these and proceed to build the shed. You might finish the whole job in a weekend.

If instead you decided to build a house, you would have to put a lot more effort into calculating the materials needed, planning the construction phases so that the foundations were built before the walls went up, organizing bricklayers and carpenters and so on. Without detailed plans, it is very likely that there would be serious errors – forgetting to lay drains, omitting to provide access for delivery lorries and hundreds of other important, but easy to forget requirements.

If you were building a multi-storey block of flats, there is no doubt that a great deal of effort would have to be put into planning, scheduling, organizing and designing before any building work was done at all, and the overall job would certainly involve many specialists whose work would have to be carefully coordinated.

The same principles hold for software development. However, since the effects of the equivalent errors in programming are less visible than they would be in building, many naïve software developers are happy to start the building work almost as soon as they have a rough idea of what is expected written on the back of an envelope. For small projects, this approach can work. For larger projects it can seem to work for a time. An ill-defined system development can continue until so much effort has been expended that the only realistic way of putting it right is to start again from the beginning, just as would happen if having just finished the foundations of a house you discovered that you had forgotten to lay the drains.

In this book on programming, you may consider a whole chapter on the organization of the software development environment and practices to be superfluous. For most of the programs you will learn to create while reading the book, this chapter *will* be superfluous. However, it is as well to realize from the outset that at some point, programming will become only a minor part of the job that you, as a programmer, will have to do. Consider this chapter to be an overview of what you may have to do in the future.

1.2   The Life-Cycle Approach

The *software development (SD) life-cycle* is an idealized model of the processes of software development. It is used to define the various distinct phases of development, and the sequence in which these are organized. Without a life-cycle approach, software development is done in a style sometimes called 'code-and-fix', where a programmer starts writing program code almost immediately the job commences, and deals with the problems that occur as they are discovered. This approach can work for small projects involving one or possibly two programmers, but for large projects it can involve a lot of wasted time, thrown away work and re-starting the whole project. Code-and-fix is a development process that has hung-over from the 'heroic' period in the early days of computer programming when computer and software systems were small and simple enough to be understood by an individual. It has no place in the development of large applications involving teams of programmers.

There are almost as many variations of the SD life-cycle as there are software developers. This is less a feature of the richness of the available knowledge about software development as it is an indication of how immature the field is. As yet, no one has been able to demonstrate unequivocally that one approach to organizing the software development process is any better than the many alternatives. The only real consensus is that software development follows a life-cycle. That is, a software project is born, goes through a number of distinct stages, and finally comes to an end (or dies).

Contrary to what you might expect, the act of programming is only a small portion of the SD life-cycle. Most formal software projects go through a number of phases before programming begins, and then continue through several other phases after programming has been completed. Even in an unstructured environment where undisciplined developers go directly to the programming phase, much of the time will be spent doing things other than programming. The remainder of the life-cycle involves activities that are at least as important as, and often more important than, programming. Most practitioners agree that a life-cycle will involve some or all of the following phases:

- feasibility study/concept analysis
- requirements gathering and analysis
- requirements specification
- software specification
- structural design/architectural design
- detailed design
- implementation/coding and debugging
- testing
- installation
- maintenance

Some of these phases will contain sub-phases (e.g. testing will often be implemented as a number of phases: specification testing, unit testing, integration testing, pre-acceptance testing, acceptance testing). Functionally, the list of phases can be broken down into five broad steps:

- finding out what the software is to do (*requirements analysis*);
- designing a system to do it (*system design*);
- building the system (*programming*, or *implementation*);
- verifying that what has been built does what is required (*testing*); and finally
- installing, maintaining and supporting the system during its operational life (*maintenance*).

Whatever type of software system we develop, and whatever development style we choose to use, we will have to consider all of these stages in some form or other. It is the aim of this book to describe *object-oriented programming* in some detail, and to describe enough of an *object-oriented design method* to allow you to take a specification and develop software to fulfil it. We should start by putting these activities into a context.

1.2.1 Software Life-Cycle Models

Once we have agreed that software development is a process that involves a number of activities, we need some way of deciding what each activity will contain and of organizing the separate activities to make the move from one to the next as effortless as possible. A software life-cycle model is an idealized description of how the activities relate to each other. We could, for example, decide that the correct way to develop software is to complete each activity in turn, moving to the next once the current activity has been completed. A diagram of this might appear as shown in Figure 1.1.

While this approach would certainly work, it is perhaps not the optimal one. In a large software project, the people who do the requirements analysis are not usually the same people who do design, the designers do not implement software, those who implement the system do not test it and the testers do not perform any maintenance. It does not make sense to have all but one group of software developers standing by idle while one group works feverishly. In a large development team, we would wish to overlap these activities as much as possible, which can usually be done since any individual stage in the life-cycle can be broken up into sections as shown in Figure 1.2.

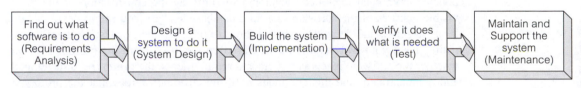

Figure 1.1 A simple software life-cycle

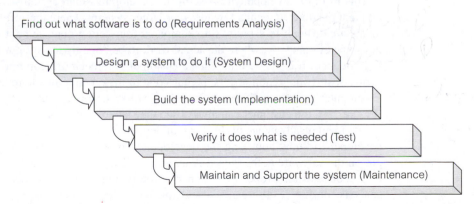

Figure 1.2 A software life-cycle with overlapping phases

Neither of these models may be very effective if software development is to be done by an individual or a small team of multi-skilled individuals who will take part in some or all of the activities. For one thing, it is very difficult for an individual to perform more than one of these activities simultaneously. For another, these life-cycle models are organized to allow the information that has been compiled, developed or uncovered in each of the phases to be communicated to the developers who will do the next phase. For a sole developer or a small team, much of this communication would be extraneous.

Instead of concentrating on communications, a small team of developers would probably find a life-cycle that concentrated on ensuring that software requirements were correctly interpreted more effectively. This is because determining software requirements is by far the most difficult and error prone activity.

1.2.1.1 The Evolutionary Prototyping Life-Cycle

In this life-cycle model, the system concept is developed progressively as the project proceeds. I'm suggesting it as a good model for building your first few real programs (i.e. those you create beyond this book). When you are new to a language or programming environment, it is a good idea to develop a few prototype programs to see how everything can fit together. It is also useful to build small example programs that let you try out various techniques in isolation, since you are less likely to get bogged down in unnecessary complexities.

As the name of this life-cycle suggests, the software system evolves from a very primitive version to the final release version. Once the essential requirements of the software (what it must do) have been determined and the major software components have been identified, development starts by the construction of the most visible features of the software (e.g. in a database system, you might develop data input screens), and demonstrations of these to the customer, or testing them to see if they meet your own requirements. Based on feedback from the customer, or on whether the software meets your personal requirements, the prototype is developed and demonstrated, and this continues until the customer agrees that the prototype system is adequate or you are happy with it. Any remaining work is completed and the system is handed over to the customer.

This form of development is useful for developing small systems where there is no great risk to trying out a few ideas, or larger systems where the software requirements are difficult to capture; for example, a transaction management system for a new type of company, where the actual work to be done by the system has not been fully defined. It is also useful when a customer is reluctant to commit to any statements of software requirements, perhaps due to them being unable to envisage how a computer system will be used in their work. Using evolutionary prototyping (Figure 1.3), the customer can always see the state of progress.

The main disadvantage of this form of development is that it is impossible for the developer to know how long the development process will take. No price can be put on the software at the outset. A major risk is that the development can devolve into code-and-fix. Proper evolutionary prototyping requires proper requirements analysis, design, well-organized and maintainable program code, etc. The main differences from the general form of life-cycle discussed earlier are that the work

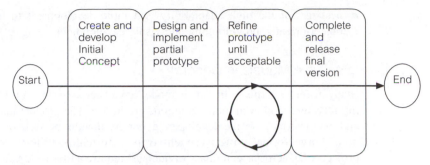

Figure 1.3 Evolutionary prototyping

progresses in smaller increments, and that requirements analysis, design and implementation are interleaved within each incremental phase as successive prototypes evolve into the final product.

1.2.1.2 Factors that Affect the Software Life-cycle

For our purposes, we are interested in planning the life-cycle phases of a system developed in an object-oriented style in general, and one suited to the special facilities available to Visual Basic in particular. Different forms of life-cycle are used in different circumstances, the variations being due to a number of factors, including:

- the size of the software project;
- the number of people involved in the project;
- the size of the company employing the developers;
- the level of formality adopted by the company;
- the type of software being developed;
- the expertise and experience of the developers;
- the knowledge that the customer or end-user has about software and software development.

None of these factors will have any great effect on the projects you will work on as exercises while working through this book, but all have great importance to practising software professionals.

From our perspective, a suitable life-cycle model will have the following features:

- support for an object-oriented development model;
- support for the 'Visual' development model espoused by Visual Basic (and several other development systems);
- scalability – that is, a facility to enable the use of the life-cycle model for projects in a range of sizes;
- ease of use – we have no wish to wrap up an already complex task in layers of bureaucracy;

■ best use of the high adaptability and rapid-development features inherent in object-oriented programming and visual development.

1.2.1.3 Life-Cycle Models in General

Many different forms of life-cycle model have been described in software engineering literature, and even more variations are in use. The product under development and the experience of the developers generally dictate the style of life-cycle model used. Large formal projects benefit from a formalized life-cycle. Safety-critical projects (e.g. aerospace, military or nuclear) require a life-cycle that reduces risk and favours quality assurance.

While it is true to say that a large number of software development houses use a seemingly undisciplined form of development we could call 'code-and-fix', with the addition of one or two formal stages for requirements capture and final testing, this should not be treated as an endorsement of a code-and-fix approach. Code-and-fix is used successfully by small developers working on small projects with little risk, but this pattern does not translate to larger projects. Big successful software companies use formal life-cycle models; the bigger and more complex the software is to be, the more important it is to use a standardized development cycle.

Exercises 1.1

1. Any software life-cycle must address the different stages in software development, these being: requirements analysis, design, implementation, testing and maintenance. Using books or the Internet, find out what is involved in each of these activities and try to place the following list of terms into the most appropriate life-cycle activity:

   class diagram, use-case, validation, configuration management, structure diagram, indefinite loop, test-harness, regression test, subroutine, actor

2. Object-oriented programming is a term that has specific implications for the analysis and design phases of a software project. Look up these other terms used to describe a style of programming and find out what order they appeared in the history of programming languages:

   visual programming, structured programming, imperative programming, assembly-language programming, spaghetti programming

1.2.2 Object-Orientation in the Life-Cycle

Object-oriented development involves designing and implementing software systems as an assembly of 'objects'. In this context, an object is a package of program code which models an item that has specific attributes and capabilities. There are numerous advantages to be gained using this style of development. At the software analysis and design stages, it is usually easier to describe a system accurately in terms of the objects that it is composed of, than to describe it in terms of the processes that it will perform.

Real-world systems are full of 'objects' that interact to accomplish tasks. For example, a travel agency office is populated with travel agents, brochures, holidays, foreign currency, airline bookings, etc. If we were to develop software for managing a travel agency, we would find it natural to describe the software in terms of the roles that parts of it played; a holiday package, a booking clerk, an airline booking, etc. It would also be easier to discuss the functions the software will perform with the customer (the travel agency staff) by describing system components that perform analogous roles to their real-world counterparts.

Life-cycle models do not usually contain features that make them specifically object-oriented or not. Object-orientation is an organizational principle rather than the use of any specific programming tools or management methods. Life-cycle models are simply used by developers to organize the various development phases. Any life-cycle model is simply a framework into which we can incorporate any development style we choose.

All of the life-cycle phases will be influenced in some way by the decision to use object-oriented design and development techniques. At the requirements specification phase, effort will be concentrated on determining what objects there will be in the system and which forms of interaction between them we might expect. At the design phase, how the objects should be connected to each other and the organizational structure will be most under consideration. Implementation will be done in an object-oriented style (probably using the specific features of an object-oriented language). System testing will be centred on trying to determine whether the objects developed behave as they are supposed to. Finally, system maintenance will involve identifying the objects and services that need to be amended or upgraded, and working on these.

All of these tasks could be done using a more established style of development, such as structured system design and development. The life-cycle model would probably remain the same.

1.2.3 Modelling and Designing Software

Having decided on a life-cycle model to use, we need to adopt a set of tools that, where possible, will assist us at each phase. The obvious phase in which to employ a tool is the implementation phase, and here we will use our programming language, Visual Basic .NET, to create the program code that will be delivered to the customer. However, within the other phases it would be useful to have tools and techniques to use to document the system requirements and designs.

Over the years in which software development has grown into a major industry, a variety of development methods have come into fashion. Many have since gone out of fashion (who remembers OODLE?) as new, refined methods have been developed. The *Unified Modeling Language* or *UML* is a set of techniques used to develop software and has in recent years gained widespread industrial acceptance. It is now the industry standard for a wide range of types of software project. The range of methods that make up UML form a framework that covers the software development life-cycle, providing specific methods for performing all of the necessary analysis, design, construction and quality-assurance tasks for software projects of any size.

UML provides us with five distinct views of a system, sometimes referred to as the 4+1 view model.

- The *use-case view* allows us to depict the behaviour of a system from the perspective of an external observer. It defines the requirements of the system, and is of particular interest to software analysts, testers and end-users (normally considered to be the customer we are developing for).
- The *design view* describes the logical structures that support the software requirements, and consists of class definitions and how classes interact and relate to each other.
- The *implementation view* describes the physical components of the system, such as program code files and assemblies, databases and configuration files.
- The *process view* depicts the ways that elements of a software system interact over time, and gives us a way of modelling the behaviour of a system that dynamically changes its structure as it performs its job.
- The *deployment view* describes how the physical components of a system (the objects and assemblies of objects) are organized within their physical environment, such as a computer network, a workstation or the Internet.

UML provides a very detailed description of a computer software system from every useful perspective. To do this, it employs mainly diagrams, although textual annotation is used to add detail that would be cumbersome to put into a diagram. The aim of a UML model of a system is to create a paper (or screen) model of the system that is complete and unambiguous, and in doing so to make it easy to design a system, communicate the designs to other interested parties (such as co-developers and end-users) and change the model of the system as anomalies or changes in requirements become apparent. We will use a subset of UML consistent with the sizes and types of program we will develop through this book.

1.3 Software Requirements Specification

The first real stage of development involves identifying what the software has to do. This is generally considered to be the most difficult part of software development. The problem is that programmers and end-users do not speak the same language – even when both speak English. A seemingly simple request, like "I would like to record a log of all of the communication we have with each customer" is likely to be interpreted differently by each software developer that is asked it. The usual way to overcome this difficulty is to maintain a constant dialogue with the software end-users or customers. In this way ambiguities can be resolved before too much development work is done on wrongly interpreted requirements. Evolutionary prototyping can help here by allowing the end-user to see and work with an early version of the software and correct any misconceptions.

On the face of it, stating software requirements is a simple process; look at the work the software is to do, divide it up into statements of specific functions, list these. In practice, the process is strewn with ambiguities, misconceptions, misunderstandings, variations on the use of jargon and even basic vocabulary, leading to misrepresentation, subterfuge and, in some cases, lawsuits. It is difficult for technical developers to fully understand a customer's description of what may be the basic tasks of their business – every business has its own vocabulary and many business vocabularies re-use common words to mean different things.

In most cases, it is even more difficult for a customer to fully appreciate what a software developer is explaining to them. For a start, their immediate concerns are steeped in their own domain of business, and anything they are told by developers will be interpreted according to this. The term storage, for example, means filing cabinets, cupboards and box rooms to most people, and presents a fairly simple set of concepts to comprehend. To a software developer, storage represents a set of software and hardware mechanisms involving a complex set of trade-offs between quantity and speed of access, and in which structure can be paramount. No wonder communication is difficult.

Of course, it is the job of the software developer to understand the customer's requirements – the customer should not have to work too hard to follow the developer's explanations. For a big project, this may mean the developers becoming expert in the customer's subject domain – many software developers are expert in accounting, physics, defence models, etc., simply because they have worked in that area over a long period.

Here's an example of the initial requirements statement for a system:

> A new software system for a travel agency is to incorporate facilities for booking holidays, including accommodation and travel, exchanging foreign currency and billing customers. Agency workers should be able to record the details of customers and their holiday requirements, book package holidays, individual flights and accommodation, issue invoices for these to the customers and exchange local currency for foreign money.

From the outset, developers will know that this feature will have exacting technical requirements. Speed of access will be a factor (quick retrieval of information will be essential if customers on the phone are not to be kept waiting), as will storage capacity, integration with the rest of the system and several other factors. However, at the requirements specification phase, technical constraints are to be actively ignored; *what is to be done* is the only question that should be pursued. Otherwise, the software design will be locked into a number of assumptions that have little to do with what is required and everything to do with the personal preferences and technical ability of designers and developers. Other constraints, such as efficiency in speed and storage, compatibility with other systems, etc. are important, but not compared to the basic job of finding out what is necessary.

The first stage of requirements specification is simply to list all of the user-interactions that this facility might involve, normally in conference with the customer (travel agent). In UML, these are referred to as *use-cases*. For example:

The travel agency system will enable the user to . . .

1. enter details (name, address, phone) of a new **customer** on to the system
2. enter proposed package holiday bookings

3. retrieve bookings information for a package holiday or customer

4. exchange currency

5. generate an invoice for a customer's holiday

This first cut at a requirements specification can be used in discussions with the customer, so that points can be corrected, additional requirements inserted, ambiguities resolved and extraneous features removed. It is normal to take each statement, or use-case, and expand it into a paragraph that describes a scenario describing how the user and system will interact to accomplish each requirement. It is easier for an end-user to understand a use-case explained in this way. For example:

1. To enter the details of a new **customer** on to the system, the user selects the New Customer menu item from the main screen and when the customer details entry screen appears, fills in the customer's name, address and telephone number into the appropriate fields. The user presses the OK button to commit the new customer's details to the system database, or the Cancel button to abort the operation.

Note that the use-case description starts with the form 'To . . .'. This is normal for use-cases and is the format that is likely to produce less ambiguous descriptions.

After a few consultations with the customer, the list can be regarded as complete and clear, and at this point, it is usual and desirable to get the customer to sign the list off. Any further additions or changes will then be regarded as extra (with a possible extra development cost).

Exercise 1.2

Read the following description of a system's requirements:

A Driving School booking system is required to enable operators to register new customers, book customers for driving lessons, practice tests and tests, calculate and issue customer billing based on lessons taken. Customer records should include the customer's personal information (Name, Address, Telephone Number, Gender) and details of preferences for instructors (Male or Female, Standard or Advanced) and car types (Manual or Automatic shift). Records also need to be kept of lessons taken and the number of tests taken to date. Lessons and Practice Tests are booked for a specific time, date and instructor. Driving Tests are booked at a predefined time by the testing authority (by the customer) and the driving school provides a car for the customer to be tested in.

Write a list of use-cases for this system.

A use-case diagram is available in UML to depict this information graphically. The use-case diagram for the travel agency is shown in Figure 1.4. This introduces the notion of the system (within the box labelled Travel Agency System), and a system actor (the Travel Agent – some external entity that interacts with the system).

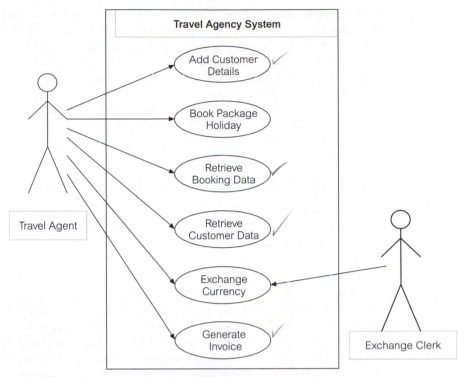

Figure 1.4 Use-case diagram for a Travel Agency

To refine a system's requirements specification, it is usual to take each use-case and describe it more fully. This involves adding indications of the source of any data required, the destination of any results and spelling out details of any processing to be done (i.e. what is to be done to the data). By the end of this phase, there should be no doubt *what* the system will do.

Exercise 1.3

Draw a use-case diagram for the Driving School system from the use-cases you listed in the previous exercise.

1.3.1 Objects in the Requirements Phase

Software requirements tend to be expressed as *operations*, since they are descriptions of tasks. In describing the way that an invoice is generated in his or her business, a client will probably set out all of the steps followed in getting the job done. The people doing the job (such as an invoicing clerk), or the items used in getting the job done (such as invoice forms, price catalogues, etc.) may be mentioned, but the emphasis will most likely be on the work done.

If we are to design an object-oriented system, our first job will be to express the system requirements in terms of objects and the services that they provide. These will either be the actors involved in doing the work (the invoice clerk) or the items used (the forms, catalogues, etc.). The translation from a description of processes to an identification of objects can be fairly straightforward or extremely difficult, depending on the system, the client and, most of all, experience of object-oriented systems.

One simple method is to go through the requirements descriptions, identifying the actors and items. These will usually appear as nouns or phrases describing specific items in the text. We can start with a rigorous list, taken from each requirement statement:

1. enter **details** (**name**, **address**, **phone**) of a new **customer** on to the **system**
2. enter proposed **package holiday bookings**
3. retrieve **bookings information** for a **package holiday** or **customer**
4. exchange **currency**
5. generate an **invoice** for a customer's holiday

We would now go through the compiled list of objects, vetting each as candidates for objects in the system being developed. For example, we could remove those that did not describe items that had responsibility for specific actions, since these will probably be attributes of some of the other objects rather than objects in their own right. 'Name', 'address', 'phone', 'booking information' and 'customer's holiday' would go on this basis. Vague items, such as 'details', have no place in the final list.

Our refined list would therefore be reduced to:

system

customer

package holiday

currency

invoice

This simple analysis of the initial requirements results in a list of potential objects that we can validate in consultation with the customer or end-user. By returning to the initial requirements statements, we can attach responsibilities to each of these objects. For example, a Package Holiday object must retain details such as destination, date of travel, accommodation type, etc., and must also refer to a specific customer. Using this combination of items and their responsibilities, we can go on to construct detailed scenarios that show how objects will be required to interact in the system and hopefully add more detail to the requirements statements. Once we have compiled a complete and correct list of objects and their responsibilities, we have a system specification, which is a full description of what the system must do.

A system specification will probably consist of the details of a large number of objects and tasks that they must perform. Normally, these are inter-related, in that an object's task may need to perform some work requiring the information contained in another object. For example, an insurance record object will be related to some customer object and may need to interact with it in order to process an insurance quote.

Exercise 1.4

Compile a list of objects that the Driving School system will include. Refine this list in the same way that the list for the Travel Agency system was refined.

The system architecture indicates how these objects and tasks are related in terms of the information they must share and the ways in which they affect each other. However, a more fundamental problem is simply how to encode each task so that it can be performed by a computer. We refer to this as *algorithm design*.

1.4 Algorithms

Algorithms are at the core of computer programs and software systems. Before an object can perform a task in a computer program, a designer needs to express the task in terms of statements in a programming language, and this is one form that an algorithm can take. Described formally, an algorithm is:

A systematic (mathematical) procedure, which enables a problem to be solved in a finite number of steps

Key points in this description are that it involves a step-by-step procedure, and that the number of steps must be finite. From this, we can see that an algorithm is similar to a recipe; describe an overall task as a sequence of steps leading to its completion. Since its completion is necessary, the number of steps can not be infinite. You would be hard pressed to find a food recipe that contained an infinite number of steps, but there is a whole class of mathematical procedures that can be shown to have no definite ending point, making them computationally useless.

Algorithms are related to objects, since objects have responsibilities, or tasks that they must be able to perform. Most object-oriented systems are composed of large numbers of objects, and each object can be responsible for several tasks. Therefore, an object-oriented program could involve dozens, hundreds or even thousands of algorithms.

Algorithms can be used to describe any number of processes:

Algorithm for making a cup of instant coffee:
1. Add water to kettle and switch on
2. Add required amount of coffee to a cup
3. Add sugar if required
4. Wait till kettle boils
5. Pour water from kettle into cup
6. Add milk to taste if required
7. Look for Hob-Nobs

Algorithm for finding the greatest-common divisor of two numbers (m & n):
1. Let quotient = m / n, disregarding any fractional part of quotient
2. Let Remainder = m- (quotient * n)
3. Let m = n

   4. Let n = quotient
   5. If Remainder is not zero, go to step 1
   6. Greatest-common divisor is m.

Algorithm to calculate fuel use in miles per litre (MPL)
   1. Fill the fuel tank
   2. Let initial = milometer reading
   3. Run the car for a period
   4. Fill the fuel tank – Let F = amount of fuel in litres
   5. Let final = new milometer reading
   6. MPL = (final-initial) / F

Note that although all three of the algorithms shown above are step-by-step procedures, only two of them start at step 1 and continue to the final step without deviation. The middle algorithm (Euclid's algorithm for finding the greatest common divisor of two numbers) includes a stage that may involve going back to an earlier step and continuing from there. This *iteration* is a common feature of many algorithms where continued processing depends on some condition being met. It is important in these cases that the algorithm is known to lead to a solution (a finite number of steps); in this case, Euclid's algorithm is well known and guaranteed to produce a result in a finite number of steps.

Although many algorithms depend on a mathematical process (particularly the more interesting ones), most algorithms that are incorporated into computer programs are ordinary sequences of steps that are followed by humans in clerical, administrative and technical tasks. As such, they are easy to identify and easy to encode as operations performed by objects in computer programs. The vast majority of computer programming involves directing a computer to perform routine humdrum tasks that humans find mind numbing (the name 'computer' was first used to describe humans who performed repetitive arithmetic calculations for the creation of navigational or ordinance tables). Therefore, most algorithms used in computer programs are easy to develop. The key requirement is to be able to break down a task into a sequence of steps (see the first sample algorithm above).

Exercises 1.5

Write algorithms (in numbered step-by-step format):

1. To add sales tax (at 17.5%) to the price of a single purchase (refer to the price as P)
2. To calculate the cost per person of a meal for 10 where the total price is £150.00 plus sales tax (at 17.5%), including a gratuity of 15%.

1.4.1 Approaches to Task Decomposition

Of course, breaking a task into a sequence of steps may not be as innocuous as it sounds. Given a complex problem, it is not always a trivial job to deconstruct it into a sensible sequence of smaller problems. To get around this, software designers tend to use well-tried recipes (which are themselves algorithms) for task decomposition. The two most common approaches are known as top-down decomposition and bottom-up composition.

1.4.1.1 Top-Down Task Decomposition

Top-down task decomposition is done by examining an overall task and dividing it into a few (commonly somewhere between two and eight) smaller sub-tasks. It is also known as *stepwise-refinement* and *top-down design*. It is characterized by a move from a general statement of what an operation is to do towards detailed statements describing how information is to be processed.

To perform a top-down decomposition of a task:

- start with the overall task description and divide this into the first level decomposition by breaking it into a number of steps;
- treat each step in the first level decomposition as a whole task, and decompose as for the top level;
- continue this until each step is computationally trivial.

Using this approach, it is possible to make almost any complex task easier to do. Since programming languages will allow us to perform only relatively simple operations, top-down decomposition is a necessary requirement if we are to do useful work with them.

During the top-down decomposition process, it is necessary to follow some simple guidelines to make sure that the task is well defined. Among these are:

- steer clear of programming language specific details – it is possible to bias a design towards a particular language simply because of working habits, but this is not a good design trait, since it limits the range of possible implementations
- postpone the working out of details until you have reached the lower levels of the task description
- formalize each level (keeping to well understood conventions of notation and design)
- verify each level (aim to demonstrate that the current level of design is correct, in that its parts are a true description of the task or sub-task they describe, before moving on to the next one)

For example, you might consider the overall task of writing a formal letter as being:

1. write the recipient's address at the top-left of the paper
2. write the sender's address at the top-right of the paper
3. write the body of the letter
4. write the closure of the letter (e.g. yours truly . . .)

Having created the first level of decomposition, we can then consider each sub-task separately, and deal with them in a similar way:

1. write the recipient's address at the top-left of the paper
   1.1. write the recipient's name
   1.2. write the recipient's street address
   1.3. write the recipient's town
   1.4. write the recipient's post code
2. write the sender's address at the top-right of the paper
   2.1. write the sender's name
   2.2. write the sender's street address
   2.3. write the sender's town
   2.4. write the sender's post code
3. write the body of the letter
   3.1. write the introductory paragraph
   3.2. write the main content of the letter
   3.3. write the concluding paragraph
4. write the closure of the letter
   4.1. if this is a business letter, write 'Yours faithfully'
   4.2. if this is a personal letter, write 'Yours sincerely'
   4.3. if this is a threatening letter, write 'Or else'
   4.4. write the sender's name

Note that the notation has been consistent throughout – a feature that will make this easier to understand when you return to it at a later date. Note also that some of the parts of step 4 in the decomposition are *conditional*, in that one of a number of options will be taken depending on a certain condition (the type of letter being written).

Software task decomposition continues along these lines until the sub- or sub-sub- (or even sub-sub-sub-) tasks are trivial enough to convert directly into program statements. For example, although we could proceed with much of the letter outlined above, we have not decomposed stage 3 sufficiently to allow us to write the whole letter. To do this, we would probably have to concentrate on decomposing step 3.2 (to 3.2.1, 3.2.2 . . . , then possibly 3.2.1.1, 3.2.1.2, etc.) until the actual information required to be in the letter was complete. Note that to do this would involve the introduction of semantic information (meaning) that is not clear from the initial specification. We would have to return to the task of extracting requirements specifications from the customer; no amount of computer programming could add this information. In fact, our inability to complete the letter due to lack of information points to an inadequate requirements specification in the first place.

Figure 1.5 shows pictorially how an overall task (level 1) can be broken down into successive sub-tasks by top-down decomposition.

1.4.1.2 Bottom-up Task Composition

With top-down decomposition, we worked on an algorithm by breaking it down into a number of steps until each step could be translated into equivalent program statements. Sometimes, this approach is so abstract that it is difficult to get started. In some situations it may be that you have access to a range of ready-constructed classes of object that you know will be of use in the current project. In these cases,

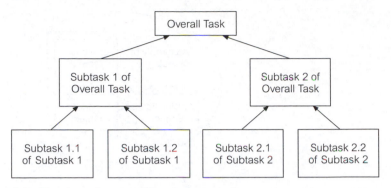

Figure 1.5 Top-down decomposition of a major task

the problem is to identify and describe where the existing objects will fit into the new system. For example, if you are building the communications sub-system of the previously described travel agent's system, you may already have a set of communications objects to work with, but need to know how they will fit into the new system.

We could try to use top-down decomposition with the aim of ending up with low-level sub-tasks that fit exactly with the abilities of the communications objects we have available, but this can be difficult. Instead, *bottom-up* composition is a more suitable approach. The general aim is to start from a number of well-understood low-level system capabilities or already defined objects, and work up towards the construction of sub-sub-systems, then sub-systems, etc.

It is unlikely that an entire system design will be done as a bottom-up composition. For one thing, you are very unlikely to have all of the pre-built objects required to do the job. Top-down is still the preferred method of decomposition, since it is ideal for developing new algorithms and designing new solutions. Bottom-up has some specific features that make it fit well into some problem areas, but these tend to be few. Bottom-up composition is best treated as a way to get past the initial hurdle of the top-level of design. Normally, once you have identified several low-level objects whose services the system can use, you will be in a more comfortable position to proceed with top-level design, aiming to meet the parts constructed by bottom-up composition somewhere in the middle. A typical system would be created by building application-specific classes or objects and combining these with libraries of pre-existing objects, as shown in Figure 1.6.

1.4.1.3 Object-Oriented Design and Task Decomposition

It is worth stressing that the task decomposition methods described will involve objects in many cases. Object-oriented design methods are best used holistically, rather than piecemeal. Although an algorithm, or an individual task, describes a process, the task is likely to be accomplished with the assistance of objects doing some or all of the sub-tasks. This is particularly true when designing for Visual Basic, where a large number of different types of object are used to allow a program to interact with the user.

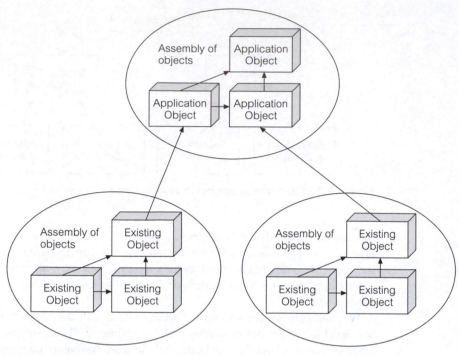

Figure 1.6 Components of a major task

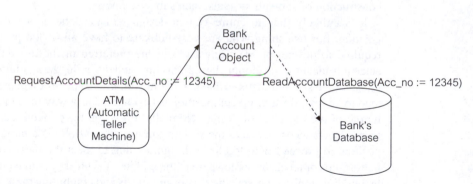

Figure 1.7 A simple object-oriented interaction

Object-oriented programs are most often designed as assemblies of interacting objects, where each object has its own area of responsibility, and objects request services of other objects to work towards an overall goal. A sub-task in a decomposition of some task is likely to be something that some object can do for us. Objects behave like clients (requesting services) and servers (providing them).

In the simple interaction shown in Figure 1.7, a Bank Account object has access to a database of bank account details, and can provide account-specific information as a service to other objects (e.g. the ATM object shown).

Object-oriented design is normally conducted using the following steps:

1. identify the objects and their attributes;
2. determine what can be done to each object;
3. determine what interactions each object can be involved in with other objects;
4. determine the parts of each object that will be visible to other objects – which parts will be public and which will be private;
5. define each object's public interface (the set of procedures that can be called on by clients of the object).

There is much more to object-oriented design and programming than has been described in this brief introduction. When we go on in subsequent chapters to learn the principles of programming, we will work towards an object-oriented style.

1.5 Visual Basic .NET Projects

When we come to create software that implements the requirements we have defined, we need to follow the rules and structure of whatever programming language and platform we are developing for. In the case of VB .NET, applications programs, referred to as *solutions*, are developed so that the best use of the underlying .NET architecture can be applied. One specific feature of .NET is that software is developed in components called *assemblies*. An assembly can be a whole program, or a component that can be used by one or more programs, so we can think of an assembly as a component in a bottom-up task composition. We might depict a typical .NET application program as shown in Figure 1.8.

As the name *assembly* might suggest, one is usually made up of a number of items connected together. These items are referred to as *modules*, which are separate files of program code that perform some function within the assembly. It is useful to create parts of a program in separate modules because we can group thematically

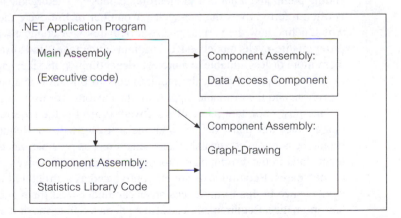

Figure 1.8 A .NET application structure

related code together in a way that might be useful to more than one assembly. For example, within one assembly, we might create code for performing calculations, displaying data on the screen and collecting and validating input data from the user. The code that performs calculations or collecting user-input might be useful in other programs and so developing it as a separate module will make it easy to incorporate into them. With these two levels of component (modules are combined to make up assemblies, and assemblies are combined to make up *solutions*), .NET development is organized to allow the best possible facilities for re-using the work you do on one project for other projects.

When you create a Visual Basic *project*, you are creating a single assembly that can comprise one or more modules, or files of program code. If the assembly is an application program, one of the modules will contain *executive code* that will define how the program starts up (the *entry-point*) – this is often defined as a *sub* (or *subroutine* or *sub-program*) called *Sub Main*, although Visual Basic allows you to define different entry-points for a program; for example, a Windows program (called a WinForms application in .NET) will normally start up by the main *form* (or Window) appearing on the screen.

Microsoft Visual Studio creates solutions, and as their name suggests, these define the complete set of software assemblies for a particular application program. A solution can be a single assembly or several assemblies, one of which will be the main one that contains the entry point. Figure 1.8 depicts the bottom-up composition of a solution and you should notice some similarity between this and Figure 1.6, which depicts a more general composition of an object-oriented program. In either case, the hierarchical structure used promotes flexibility, breaking up the development work into complete sub-assemblies that could be given to separate programmers and simplifying the overall programming task.

1.6 Summary

Software development is often approached as a process with a starting point, an ending point, and a number of identifiable phases. The organization of these phases is often referred to as the life-cycle. A number of life-cycle models exist, most of which define how the various phases articulate to, or connect with, each other. The different life-cycle models have different advantages and disadvantages, making them more or less suitable to a project, depending on its size, nature, the experience of the development team, the requirements information available at the project's inception, and the available input from the customer or user.

The most important phase of a software project is the requirements specification phase, since this phase defines what the software will do. Requirements statements should be as complete, unambiguous and correct as possible, since changes to requirements later in the development process will require expensive reworking through all of the phases. Requirements are often produced as a structured list of English statements, since in this form the customer can understand them and hopefully identify any anomalies. Requirements can also be depicted in terms of the identifiable objects in a system, and the services or operations these objects can provide.

Algorithms are fundamental building blocks of software designs. An algorithm is a step-by-step description of how to complete a task. Since a software system will comprise a large number of tasks, its development will involve the encoding of a large number of algorithms into a programming language. Fortunately, most algorithms are lists of simple instructions for how to accomplish routine operations. Some algorithms are more mathematical, and it is sometimes necessary to prove that a proposed algorithm will actually produce a solution in a finite number of steps (which is a requirement of any algorithm).

In developing an algorithm or a whole software system, it is often necessary to start with a general description of a task and decompose it into a sequence of sub-tasks. There are a number of approaches to this process. Top-down decomposition involves taking the top-level task description (e.g. a requirements statement or a service) and breaking it down into smaller and smaller parts until it is a trivial matter to code each in a programming language. Bottom-up composition involves taking available designs for specific tasks in a system, and combining these into higher and higher levels of task until the system design is built. In most cases, both approaches will have a role to play in a software system's development.

Object-oriented development is a way of building systems by breaking systems down into *objects*. An object is a component that contains data and is associated with specific procedures for manipulating it. Object-oriented designs benefit from a tight association between procedures and data; objects form better models of real-world objects because of it. Object-oriented design involves creating assemblies and other associations of objects. Since objects provide specific services to other objects, the relationship between two collaborating objects is often referred to as a client-server relationship.

In .NET, a single project defines a program or a major component that can be used by other programs, and is known as an Assembly. A solution is a project that can involve one or more assemblies that work together on a task or group of tasks.

Review Questions

1. Indicate which of the following statements about software life-cycles are true and which are false.

   a) The software life-cycle is a system for describing the life of a computer program.

   b) Most of the phases in the software life-cycle are interchangeable.

   c) The Waterfall life-cycle is based on the creation of documents to ease the transition to the next phase of development.

   d) Code-and-fix is an important life-cycle model.

   e) Life-cycle models are best if suited to the type of software being developed and the experience of the developers.

2. Software requirements specification is the most important phase of the life-cycle. Give two reasons why this is so.

3. Write a simple requirements specification for a four-function (+, −, ×, ÷) pocket calculator. Concentrate on what it must do.

4. Write an algorithm for getting cash out of an ATM (i.e. a hole-in-the-wall bank). You should assume that you are directing someone who has never used one.

5. Write an algorithm for looking up a word in the dictionary.

6. Consider the following tasks, and decide whether you would use top-down decomposition or bottom-up composition or both to describe them in detail. Your answers should take into account your experience of the sub-tasks involved. You need not actually create the detailed task descriptions:

   a) making a cup of tea

   b) filling in a tax form

   c) booking a foreign holiday

   d) calculating who pays what after a meal in a restaurant.

Practical Activities

At the end of each chapter of this book, you will find one or more suggested practical activities. These are an important part of the book and should not be ignored if your aim is to learn how to program in Visual Basic .NET. While the body of a chapter will explain a number of topics and describe how they relate to the overall skill of programming, the end of chapter activities will give you a chance to put these topics into practice, experiment with the language and gain essential experience in the use of Visual Studio .NET and Visual Basic.

In the activities for this chapter, we will examine the Visual Basic .Net Integrated Development Environment (IDE), homing in on some of the main features and examining the range of options available for a developer. You will get the most from them by following through the activities at each stage.

Although you can create Visual Basic .NET programs with no more than a copy of Windows Notepad (see Appendix 1), Visual Studio .NET is the best environment for creating VB .NET programs since it provides a full IDE. This enables you to write programs, design user-interfaces, access and extract information from database and web servers and create complex, multi-assembly projects within a helpful environment that protects you from the necessary complexities normally involved.

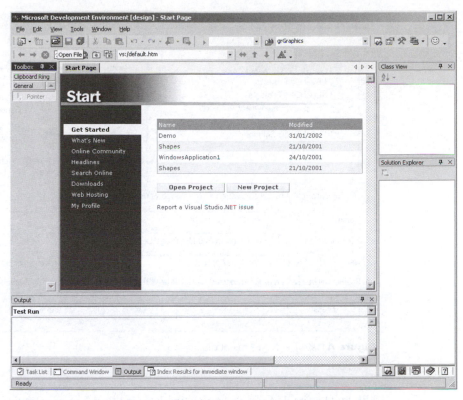

Figure A1.1   The Visual Basic .NET Start Page

Activity 1: Starting up VB .NET and creating a new WinForms Project

When you first start up Visual Basic, you are presented with the Start page (in the centre of Figure A1.1). This shows recently edited projects in a list and gives you options to start a new project or open an existing project that is not in the list (for example a project that you have copied to your PC).

To start a new VB project, click on the New Project button. The IDE will respond by bringing up the New Project dialog box, shown in Figure A1.2.

From this dialog box, you can create a new project using any of the supported languages (Visual Studio .NET can be used to program in Visual Basic, C# or C++) as well as creating a setup package for installing any project you have completed. For our purposes, we will always start one of the Visual Basic project types. The default (for the entire IDE as it is first installed) is to start up a Visual Basic .NET project that is a Windows application, which, as luck has it, is what we will be doing for the first of these activities. We can also create Console applications (applications that work in a Command Prompt window), Class Library projects (for writing code that can be used by a number of other applications), libraries of new Windows controls to place on forms, Web applications and services and a number of other project types. We

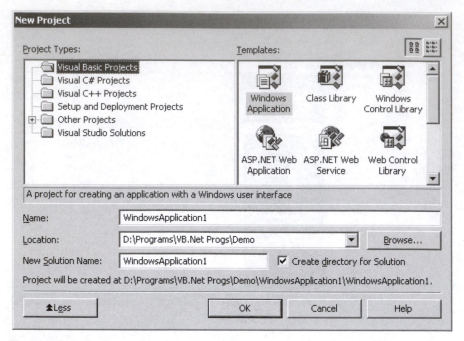

Figure A1.2 The New Project dialog

will build a simple Console application later in this group of activities and look into some of the other options later in the book, but for now we will accept the default Windows application.

The New Project dialog also allows us to specify the name of the project (recommended, since otherwise it will be given a default name that has nothing to do with its purpose), and the folder it will be located in. To create a new Windows application project:

Run Visual Basic from the Windows Start button
From the Start button, select **Start/Programs/Microsoft Visual Studio .NET/ Microsoft Visual Studio .NET**

Select to create a new Visual Basic project
Press the New Project button on the Start page, and when the New Project dialog box appears, change the default project name (**WindowsApplication1**) in the Name box to **Hello**. This will create a project named 'Hello' in a folder called 'Hello' in the default location for Visual Studio projects. We will change this default location in a later activity, but for this first project, Visual Studio's suggested default will suffice. Press **OK** to create the project.

There will be a short flurry of disk activity before Visual Studio places you at the starting point of a new Windows application. The IDE should now appear as shown in Figure A1.3. The default form of the project is shown in the main application workspace (where the Start page used to be). Notice that a new tab has been added

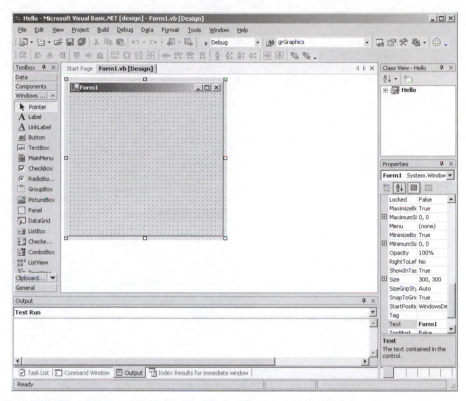

Figure A1.3 A new Windows Application project

to the top of this area specifying the new form's file name (currently **Form1.vb**) and the current development mode (**[Design]**). The Start page is still available by clicking on its tab, and if we add any other component files to the project, these will also get a tab here. *The tabs at the top of this form are one of the most important navigational aids in Visual Studio, allowing quick access to forms, code windows and other designers.*

Activity 2: Changing the appearance of the default form

You will notice that the form that has appeared in the design view has certain settings already applied. For example, its caption is currently **Form1**, it has a grey background colour and buttons to minimize, maximize and close it in the caption bar. Generally, we will want to change some of these as well as other settings for the form, and to do this as the program is being worked on (i.e. in *design* mode), we use the Properties window.

Get to the Properties Window and change the form's caption and Name
If Visual Studio still has its default configuration, the Properties window will be to the right of the IDE (its caption bar is labelled **Properties**). However, if any changes

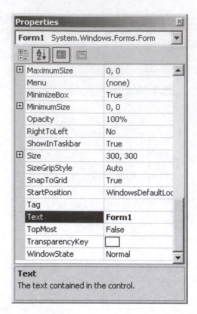

Figure A1.4 The Properties window

have been made, it may be necessary to open and locate the window. If you cannot see the Properties window, press **F4**, or select **View/Properties Window** from the menus. The window should open displaying a list of all of the properties that are available in design mode for the form. This is shown in Figure A1.4.

The Properties window will probably have the **Text** property for the new form already selected, with the property name on the left and its current setting on the right. A form's Text property specifies the text that will appear on its caption bar. Change the current Text property of the form by selecting the current setting and typing a new value. You can select all of the current setting quickly by double-clicking on it. Change it to **Hello VB .Net**. Using the scroll bar on the Properties window, scroll to the **Name** property at the top of the list (it appears as third in the list of properties) and change this to **frmHello**. When naming items that will be referenced in program code, it is sensible to follow a naming convention. We will look into suggested names for Visual Basic objects later in the book.

Add a Button and a Label control to the form
We can change a form in design mode by adding controls from the toolbox and configuring their properties. To add a new Button control to the form, find the **Button** control in the **Toolbox** and double-click on it. The Toolbox window appears by default on the left of the IDE and it can be in permanent view, auto-hidden or closed. If you see a sideways button labelled **Toolbox** to the left of the Form Design window, move the mouse over this and the Toolbox window will appear. If you cannot see the Toolbox at all, select **View/Toolbox** from the menus. Since we are building a Windows Application, the Windows Forms page (Figure A1.5) should

Figure A1.5   The Toolbox, open at the Windows Forms page

already be open, but if not, select this page by clicking on the correct Toolbox Page button.

The Button control will be easy to find as the controls appear in alphabetical order. When you double-click on it, a new button will appear at the top left of the form, as shown in Figure A1.6.

Now add a Label to the form in the same way. Currently both controls will occupy the same location at the top left of the form. Drag each of the controls to a more central location, with the label near the centre of the form and the button below it.

Configure the Button and Label
As with the form, the Button and Label will both have a number of default settings that need to be changed to make it appear and behave as you would wish. The Properties window is again used, but this time, before you change any properties, you must make sure that the correct control is selected (click on a control and *drag-handles* will appear around it). The currently selected control (or if none is selected, the form) is the one that the Properties window will interact with. Change the button's **Name** property to **btnHello**, and its **Text** property to **Hello**. Change the Label's **Name** to **lblHello**, and its **Text** to nothing (i.e. delete the current text – **Label1**, but do not replace it with any text).

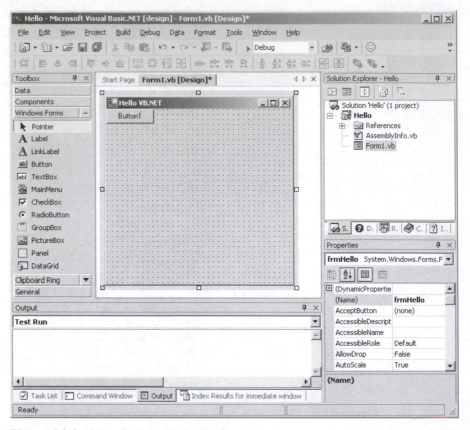

Figure A1.6   A new Button added to the form

As a final tidy-up, you may wish to get rid of a lot of the dead space occupied by the background of the form (i.e. areas that are not occupied by controls). Most Windows users appreciate programs that do not hog screen space unnecessarily. The Label and Button can be moved to occupy a position that will be roughly central in a much smaller form (simply place the mouse pointer over each control, press down the left mouse button and drag the control to its new location). We can then resize the form by clicking on its background (to select the form, making its drag-handles appear) and then dragging the lower right corner handle to resize the form.

These actions (dragging to a new position and resizing) also alter properties of the form and controls (the **Top** and **Left** properties of the controls and the **Width** and **Height** of the form). You can verify this by checking these values in the Properties window before and after the changes. We could also have typed new values into the Properties window, a useful method if you want to specify an exact size or position in pixels, but otherwise dragging to move and resize forms and controls is much easier to do. Once you have changed the size and location of the form and controls, the Designer window should appear as shown in Figure A1.7.

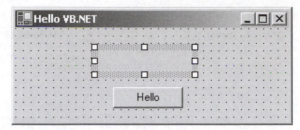

Figure A1.7 The form and controls once properties have been set

Save the changes to the project
Select **File/Save All** from the menus. This will ensure that the project disk files are up to date with the changes made. In general, you should save files after any significant change to a project in case anything causes your work to be lost (such as a power failure or a hardware fault).

Activity 3: Adding program code to the form

Now that the project's form has been configured by changing its properties, all that remains is to write some program code to make it behave as we wish. Note that, for most programs, the phrase 'all that remains is to write some program code . . .' is not really appropriate, since the vast majority of the work required in any real Visual Basic project will be writing program code. For most projects, a developer will spend far more time scripting how the program will do its job than laying out screen forms. However, in this practical session, the main goal has been to gain familiarity with the VB .NET development environment, and programming will play a relatively minor role.

In a Visual Basic Windows application, we normally write programs in such a way that operations are carried out in response to external stimuli, or *events*, such as a mouse button being clicked, a key being pressed or some system generated occurrence (such as a clock tick). An *event-handler* is a program code routine that is executed in response to a specific event. Typically, a Visual Basic program is designed to respond to a range of events so that a variety of scenarios can be initiated. There will be event handlers to respond to a program starting up, the user interacting with it in various ways, other programs or system elements interacting with it and the program closing down.

An event-handler can be anything from a single program statement to thousands of lines of program code, depending on the complexity of what you wish to achieve and the way you organize program code. In this activity, we will create a very simple event handler to illustrate the process. In later activities, more complex event handlers (and more complex program structures) will be used.

Add an empty Event-Handler to the Form
We will create an event-handler to respond to the user of our program clicking on the button on the form with the computer's mouse. Create an 'empty-shell'

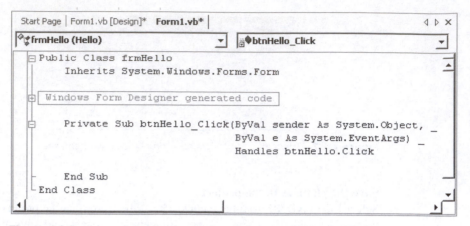

Figure A1.8 An event-handler for a button-click, generated by the VB IDE

event-handler by simply double-clicking on the button on the form while the program is in design mode. VB's IDE will respond by opening up a Code window containing the outline of an event handler as shown in Figure A1.8.

Note I have added line breaks (using the ' _' line continuation sequence, a space followed by an underscore character) to reduce the width of the first line of the event-handler (beginning **Private Sub btnHello_Click...**) to make the code easier to read in this form. Visual Basic generated all of the code up to the blank line before **End Sub** as a single line of code. We will ignore the apparent complexity of this code for now, and simply take its operation for granted. By entering one or more lines of correct program code in the space between the first and last lines of this event-handler, we get to say what will happen when the user generates the event (by clicking on the button). In this case, we will perform a short sequence of actions . . .

1. Ask the user to enter their name.
2. Place a message greeting the user on the screen.

The first of these actions will demand that we have somewhere to store the name the user enters. In a computer program, short-term storage of information is accomplished by assigning the information to a *variable*, which is essentially a piece of computer storage (known as *memory*, since it performs the same function in a program that a human memory does). The type of variable we will use (there are several types, as we will find in later chapters) is a *string* variable, which can store a string (or sequence) of text characters. We warn Visual Basic that we need this storage space by *declaring* the variable.

We can then ask the user to enter their name, *assigning* it to this variable, and proceed to the task of displaying the message, including the user's name. The appropriate lines of code are shown in Listing A1.1.

```
Private Sub btnHello_Click (ByVal sender As System.Object, _
                            ByVal e As System.EventArgs) _
                            Handles btnHello.Click
    Dim Name As String
    Name = InputBox("Enter your name please.")
    lblHello.Text = "Hello " & Name
End Sub
```

Listing A1.1: Code added to the IDE generated event-handler

Enter the three lines of code shown in Listing A1.1

Assuming you have not moved the cursor from where it was placed when you double-clicked on **btnHello**, it will be in the correct location for you to just start typing. If you have clicked the mouse anywhere since the empty event-handler was generated, click it again in the blank line between the line which starts **Private Sub btnHello_Click** and the **End Sub** line. Now simply type the text *exactly* as you see it above. You should notice the VB IDE responding to your typing by formatting the text as you type (changing its colour and capitalization for some words) and popping up boxes full of information. For example, when you type the opening bracket after the word **InputBox**, a box full of information useful to a programmer will pop up under the line you are typing on. For now ignore this and simply continue to type.

Once you have entered all of the program text (be careful with the punctuation in the last line), the program is complete, and you should again select **File/Save All** from the menus or press the Save All button on the toolbar (its symbol is shown to the left of **Save All** on the menu).

Test the program

As a final step, you should run the program to test that it behaves correctly. Select **Debug/Start** from the menus, and VB will proceed to build an executable program based on the form design and code provided. If all is successful, the program will execute and should appear as shown in Figure A1.9.

Figure A1.9   The program as it first appears

Press the 'Hello' button, and a box will pop up allowing you to enter your name (see Figure A1.10).

Figure A1.10 The result of the **InputBox( )** statement – accepting user-input

When you press the OK button on the input-box, the message generated by adding your name after the word **Hello** will be displayed on the label control, as shown in Figure A1.11.

Figure A1.11 The result of assigning a message to a label

You can close the program by clicking on the close-box at the top right of the form (the small button with a 'x' in it) or by selecting **Debug/Stop Debugging** from the menus.

Dealing with Syntax Errors

As you add code to a form, you will occasionally (or frequently if your typing skills are similar to mine) find that Visual Basic will inform you of a *syntax error*. This happens when you enter code that Visual Basic does not recognize as a valid part of the language – for example, by misspelling a name or using incorrect punctuation. In most situations, VB will be able to tell you exactly what it did not understand and therefore lead you directly to the source of the problem. Sometimes though, the error message you get will be difficult to understand, ambiguous or obscure.

For now, in these situations you should check what you have typed carefully. This will in most cases be how you locate errors as you work through the early stages of learning to program using this book. However, as your knowledge of VB and its syntax improves, you will eventually learn how to interpret error messages and trace errors in an efficient and logical way.

Activity 4: Creating a Console Project

For many of the activities in the book chapters, you will build a Visual Basic *console project*. Console projects are used to develop programs that use a standard Console window or Command Prompt window. As Windows programs go, they are simple and provide only very limited options for the user-interaction, centred on the keyboard and a simple, text-mode display. For our purposes, console projects allow us to concentrate on writing programs that define and manipulate objects.

Once you have a good grounding in VB .NET programming, you will almost certainly want to create proper Windows programs, and only occasionally have a need to write a console program. However, in the early stages of learning to use VB .NET you may well appreciate the facility to build a program that performs simple functions without having to worry about the additional complexity of forms and controls.

Start a new project
Select **File/New/Project . . .** from the menus, and from the Visual Basic Projects group, select a Console Application (you may need to scroll down the list of project types in the Templates pane of the New Project dialog) (Figure A1.12).

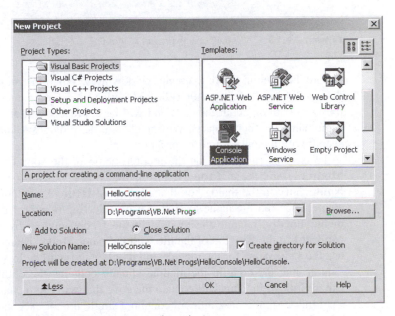

Figure A1.12 Starting a new console project

Enter a name for the project (**HelloConsole**) and, optionally, browse to a folder you wish the solution to be created in. Press **OK** to finalize the project settings and create the project.

Change the name of the module, and the file the module is stored in as shown in Figure A1.13.

By default, the new project will contain a code module (a file that is used to store program code) which will be given the name **Module1**. This Code window will

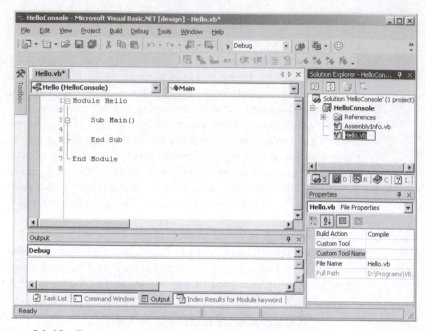

Figure A1.13   The new console project in the IDE

already be open in the IDE's main window area. When the project is saved to disk, this module will occupy a file called **Module1.vb**. These names are not ideal, since they say nothing about the code and will be confused with other modules with the same name in other projects. We can change these names to make them more consistent with the purpose of the program.

To do this, right-click on the module name in the solution explorer (currently **Module1**) and select **Properties** from the pop-up menu. Change the **Assembly Name** entry in the dialog box that appears to **Hello**. To be consistent, you should also change the file name to **Hello.vb** by selecting rename from the same pop-up menu. Finally, rename the module in the Code window by replacing the name **Module1** at the very top of the file with the name **Hello**. There is no need for us to use the same name for the module and its file, but it will be less confusing if we do.

Note that the code in the module already contains the outline of a subroutine, called **Sub Main**. This will contain the code that will run to start off our project.

In this case, the program will contain a single line of executable code, which we will place between the lines **Sub Main** and **End Sub**. Enter the statement as shown in Listing A1.2.

```
Module Hello
    Sub Main()
        Console.WriteLine("Hello VB Console")
    End Sub
End Module
```

Listing A1.2: The code for the Hello console program

Since that is all the code there will be to this program, save the project to disk by selecting **File/Save All** from the menus.

Run the project

When we run a console project, it will normally run to completion within a Console window, and when it comes to the end, will close the window. If we were to run this program without the VB .NET IDE, we would not be able to see the output from it because it would close the Console window down too quickly. Running the program under the IDE will cause the program to run to completion, but an extra line of text, **Press any key to continue**, will be inserted at the end of the output from the program, and the Console window will remain open until we have pressed a key.

Run the program in this mode by selecting **Debug/Start without debugging** from the menus (or pressing **Ctrl+F5**). The program will be compiled, and, if there are no errors, will run in a Console window as shown in Figure A1.14.

Figure A1.14   A running console program

What have we done?

Having completed the activities above and made use of Appendices 1 and 2, you will have examined some of the features of Visual Basic .NET, and should have discovered:

- how to create a new project;
- how to configure a form by changing its properties;
- how to add controls to a form and change their properties;
- how to add an event-handler to a form;
- how to enter program code;
- how to run and stop a program.

We have merely scratched the surface of what we can do in Visual Basic, and as you continue through the book you will find that we have many options to allow us to create professional standard Windows programs. You may find the following additional exercises useful for developing an expertise in using the Visual Basic IDE.

Suggested Additional Activities

To expand on the above practical activities, here are some suggested additional activities.

1. **Change the message displayed**

   It should be an easy matter to alter the message displayed in the label as the WinForms program (Activities 1–3) runs (simply change the text assigned to the label in the last line added to the event-handler). For example, try changing the word **Hello** to **Good day**. You can also change the order in which the text is strung together. For example, instead of adding the user's name after the word Hello, you could attach some other message after the user's name such as **Alistair, welcome to Visual Basic .NET**. Note that in order to do this, we need to change the order that the text assigned to the label appears in – instead of **<Message> & Name**, we would use **Name & <Message>**, replacing <Message> with whatever text we wanted to add.

2. **Change the appearance of the form or controls**

   While we design a WinForms form visually (before we add any code to it) we can make any of a wide range of alterations. Try changing the sizes of the controls added to the form or the form itself, or alter other properties. Experiment with the form in design mode, changing the font and colour properties of the controls or form.

3. **Add new controls**

   You can add additional controls to a WinForms form, and can assign event-handlers to these if required. Try adding a second button to the form (call it **btnGoodbye**) and configuring it (change its Name and Text properties and make it a similar size to the first button). You may wish to move the first button or resize the form to make space for the new one. Once you have done this, add an event-handler to this button (double-click on it) so that when the user clicks on it, they are again asked for their name and an appropriate **Goodbye . . .** message is applied to the label.

Remember to save your work after making any significant change to the program, and especially before you try running the program.

Solutions to Exercises

Exercises 1.1

1. **Life Cycle Terminology**

   Class diagram: design – a class diagram is used to show how various classes (types) of object will be composed and how they will relate to other types in a system.

   Use-case: requirements analysis – a use-case is a description of a scenario in which an end user of a system interacts with the system.

   Validation: testing and maintenance – validation is the process of determining whether a system operates as it was specified to do. Validation should be performed at every stage of the development process, but it is often considered to be specifically a testing phase task.

Configuration management: implementation – configuration management is an activity in which different versions of the components of a system are assigned to specific versions of the system (e.g. the English Language version, the Small Business version, etc.) and the changes in these versions are managed to ensure that incompatibilities and inconsistencies do not creep into a product.

Structure diagram: design – a structure diagram shows how software components are assembled into sub-systems and systems.

Indefinite loop: implementation – an indefinite loop is a software structure in which a sequence of program statements are repeated until some condition becomes true.

Regression test: testing and maintenance – a regression test is a software test that is done to ensure that changes made to a system do not have any adverse side-effects on areas that have been successfully tested already.

Actor: requirements analysis – an actor is a person or system that interacts with a software system in a use-case.

2.   **A loose chronology of programming languages and styles is:**

Imperative programming – the basic principle of programming by issuing instructions to a processor.

Assembly-language programming – programming by writing symbolic instructions that are mnemonic names for specific processor instructions.

Spaghetti programming – a derogatory term used to describe the almost chaotic nature of imperative programs written in a high-level language in which repeated changes and maintenance had made the sequence of instructions confusing and error-prone.

Structured programming – a form of programming introduced in the 1960s (after proposals by Edsgar Dijkstra) to eliminate the confusion and error-proneness of spaghetti programming. Structured programming was the first attempt to bring sound engineering principles into software development.

Object-oriented programming (not asked, but . . .) – a method of programming characterized by the creation of new data types that encapsulate the attributes and behaviour of specific components of a software system.

Visual programming – either programming by creating diagrams that describe the structure and sequence of a task, or (more commonly) building software systems by creating parts of them using a graphical form of interaction that can remove some of the drudgery of developing user-interfaces.

Exercise 1.2

Driving school booking system use-cases:

- register a new customer;
- book a driving lesson;
- book a practice test;
- book a driving test;
- issue a bill.

Note that this is a full answer to the question, which asks only for a list of use-cases. However, descriptions of each use-case will be required for further development (and to make it possible to answer Exercise 1.4.) Therefore, simple elaborations of each use case are:

To register a new customer: The Booking Clerk selects the New Customer command and enters the details for a customer record (Name, Address, Telephone Number, Instructor preferences (e.g. male/female, standard/advanced) and Car preference (e.g. manual shift/automatic)). The clerk then chooses to confirm the new customer entry or to cancel the operation (if the customer decides not to continue).

To book a driving lesson: The Booking Clerk selects the Book Lesson command and enters the booking details (Customer, Date, Time and Duration, plus any special instructions for a lesson). The booking is confirmed if the customer's regular instructor is available at that time and date. If not, the Booking Clerk should offer an alternative Time, Date or Instructor. If the customer accepts a suggested change, the booking details should be amended to suit and the booking confirmed. If not the booking should be cancelled.

To book a practice test: The Booking Clerk selects the Book Practice Test command and then proceeds as for booking a driving lesson.

To book a driving test: The Booking Clerk checks that the customer has obtained a test date and time from the Licensing authority. If a test date and time has been obtained, the Clerk selects the Book Driving Test command and then enters the test date and time. If the preferred instructor is not available for that time, a replacement instructor is booked for the period of the test.

To issue a bill: The Booking Clerk selects the Billing Status command and selects the customer to be billed. The Billing System calculates the amount the customer owes and generates an invoice, detailing the services taken and charges for them. This is then sent to the customer.

Exercise 1.3

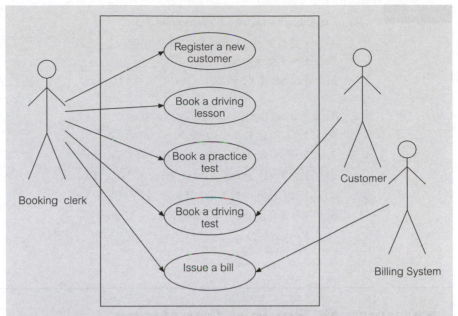

Register a new customer

Book a driving lesson

Book a practice test

Book a driving test

Issue a bill

Booking clerk

Customer

Billing System

Figure Ex1.3

Note that the customer is an actor in this system since he/she is responsible for providing a date and time for an official driving test. This equates to the customer being an external system that provides details necessary for this system to operate.

Exercise 1.4

An initial list of objects taken from the use-cases of the driving school system is:

Booking Clerk, New Customer command, customer record, Name, Address, Telephone Number, Instructor preferences, Car preference, new customer entry operation, Book Lesson command, booking details, Customer, Duration, special instructions, booking, customer's regular instructor, alternative Time, alternative Date, alternative Instructor, suggested change, Book Practice Test command, customer, test date and time, Licensing authority, Book Driving Test command, preferred instructor, replacement instructor, period of the test, Billing Status command, Billing System, amount, invoice, services taken, charges.

Vetting these items for viability as objects in the system, we can reduce the list to:

Customer
Booking
Instructor
Billing Status

All other items are either synonyms (e.g. Customer Record), properties of existing objects (e.g. Date, Time) or external entities (e.g. Licensing Authority).

Exercises 1.5

1. To add sales tax at 17.5% to a purchase:
   1. Let P be the initial purchase price
   2. Let T (tax) = P * 17.5 / 100
   3. Let SP (Sale Price) = P + T

2. To calculate the per-person cost of a meal:
   1. Let Total_Price = 150.00
   2. Let Sales_Tax = Total_Price * 17.5 / 100
   3. Let Total_Price = Total_Price + Sales_Tax
   4. Let Gratuity = Total_Price * 15 / 100
   5. Let Total_Price = Total_Price + Gratuity
   6. Let Cost_Per_Person = Total_Price / 10

Answers to Review Questions

1. Indicate which of the following statements about software life-cycles are true and which are false:
   a) **False – describes the *development* of a computer system**
   b) **False**
   c) **True**
   d) **False – it is not a recommended life-cycle model, but True – many software products are developed in this way. Your answer depends on how you interpret the word 'important'.**
   e) **True.**

2. Software requirements specification is the most important phase of the life-cycle. Give two reasons why this is so. **1. It is impossible to build a piece of software correctly unless you have a detailed specification of what it should do. 2. As it is an early life-cycle phase, subsequent phases will depend on its accuracy. Errors made in the requirements phase are likely to have more impact that those made in later phases and are likely to require more effort to remediate.**

3. Write a simple requirements specification for a four-function (+, –, ×, ÷) pocket calculator. Concentrate on what it must do.

   1. **Allow user to enter first operand**
      1.1. **Reject an invalid entry**
   2. **Allow user to enter an arithmetic operator**
      2.1 **Reject an operator that is not one of +, –, * or /**
   3. **Allow user to enter second operand**
      3.1 **Reject an invalid entry**
   4. **Display result of calculation or an error message**

4. Write an algorithm for getting cash out of an ATM (i.e. a hole-in-the-wall bank). You should assume that you are directing someone who has never used one.
   1. **Insert card into ATM**
   2. **Enter PIN code when prompted**
   3. **Select 'Withdraw cash' option when options are displayed**
   4. **Enter amount to withdraw**
   5. **Retrieve card from ATM**
   6. **Retrieve cash from ATM**

5. Write an algorithm for looking up a word in the dictionary.
   1. **Start by searching the whole dictionary**
   2. **Open the dictionary to a page about $\frac{1}{2}$ way through those pages being searched**
   3. **Examine the range of words on the pages opened**
   4. **If the sought word is within this range go to step 7**
   5. **If the sought word is after this range dismiss all of the pages on the left from the search and return to step 2**
   6. **If the sought word is before this range, dismiss all of the pages on the right and return to step 2**
   7. **Start at the top of the left-hand page**
   8. **If the current word is the sought word, go to step 12**
   9. **Go to the next word**
   10. **If at the bottom of the right hand page, the required word is not in the dictionary. Go to step 12**
   11. **Read the definition of the sought word**
   12. **Stop**

6. Consider the following tasks, and decide whether you would use top-down decomposition or bottom-up composition or both to describe them in detail. Your answers should take into account your experience of the sub-tasks involved. You need not actually create the detailed task descriptions:
   a) Making a cup of tea. **Normally bottom-up, since you probably know how to fill a kettle, add ingredients to a cup, and stir the mixture. Each of these is a sub-task in the bottom-up approach.**
   b) Filling in a tax form. **Probably top-down, breaking the overall task into filling in personal details, employment details, details of income, details of allowances and then continuing by decomposing each of these sections separately.**
   c) Booking a foreign holiday **Bottom-up is likely, since you may already have experience of checking passport and visa details, ordering currency, selecting accommodation, booking flights etc. Any sub-task with which you are not familiar should be approached top-down.**
   d) Calculating who pays what after a meal in a restaurant. **Either way – an individual could work through the bill, calculating the total for each individual and then summing the result. Alternatively, each person could calculate their own sub-total and a delegate could sum the results for the overall total.**

In this chapter you will learn:

- what classes and objects are and how to describe classes of object;
- different types of object interactions;
- how different classes of object can be related to each other;
- how to depict these relationships and interactions in simple diagrams;
- suitable structures for Visual Basic applications.

2.1   Designing Objects, Classes and Applications

In the previous chapter, we described how the process of software development was conducted, and looked at ways in which the requirements of a software system could be stated, decomposed and expressed in a form that made them suitable for rendering in a programming language. We did not consider the actual detailed process of programming or program design. In this section, we will start from the premise that we have fully specified a system and need to develop an object-oriented design that describes how to implement it.

Only the most trivial of computer systems are based on a single type of object or algorithm – many of the early programs you write will implement one type of object, but this is purely for the convenience of learning what objects are and how they work. In real software solutions, we need to be able to describe how objects will interact, sometimes in very complex situations. We will learn how to develop an object-oriented system, including inter-object interactions, to the point where it can be coded in a programming language.

Previously, we looked at algorithms as a form of description that was entirely separate from the way that a computer program would be required to implement it. The key feature in proposing an algorithm was that it should not be encumbered with details of how a specific programming language would be used to implement it. At some point, we need to reconcile the abstract algorithm with the concrete requirements of a computer programming language.

We can picture the development phases of the life-cycle as a progression, from very abstract specifications, through the design stages to a concrete implementation, as shown in Figure 2.1.

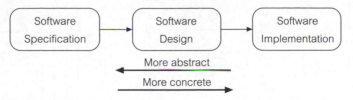

Figure 2.1 Progression through the life-cycle development phases

For our purposes, we can consider these steps in the progression to be as follows:

■ software *specification* is the identification of the objects required by the system to do its job and the services these objects must provide;

■ software *design* is the development of a plan for how the various objects will co-operate on the overall job being done;

■ software *implementation* is the act of realizing a software design as *classes* in an object-oriented programming language.

In the previous chapter we saw how a software requirements description could be analysed so that we could identify the objects required by the system. We can now go on to learn how the objects might be developed to a stage where we could implement them in our chosen language.

2.1.1 Class and Object

Our first requirement is to be able to describe an object, in terms of what information it contains, and what operations it can perform. Visual Basic comes complete with an entire library of pre-defined types of object. Many of these are *controls*, another name for user-interface components, but there are also classes for managing data at run time, dealing with files, 2-D and 3-D graphics, providing services for database access and Internet communications, managing the execution of programs and simplifying the use of the system printer and other resources. All of them share the key characteristics of any software object:

■ they are defined as members of a class, which is simply another way of saying that there are different types of object;

■ they are *encapsulated* – that is, the internal representation of information and operations are protected from users of the objects behind a *public interface*;

■ their capabilities are defined in two ways – *properties*, which are the attributes, or recognizable features of an object, and *methods*, which are the operations a particular class of object can perform.

The notion of a class is one with which you are probably familiar. One very specific use of the word class is to identify a group of students at the same approximate level of learning. However, a more general explanation of the term is that it describes '*a collection or division of people or things sharing a common*

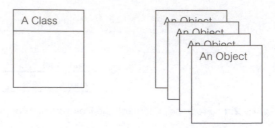

Figure 2.2 Class and object

characteristic, attribute, quality or property'. In terms of object-oriented programming, this description, from the Collins English Dictionary, is ideal.

In object-oriented programming, we aim to develop a program by composing it of objects working together to do some job. In the majority of cases, several objects with similar capabilities would be used to divide up the labour and to represent different, but similar, items. For example, a word processor uses a number of documents. All of these can be displayed on the screen, searched for specific words or phrases, printed and stored on a disk.

With this in mind, we can see that it would be very inefficient to develop object-oriented programs by creating each individual object as a separate programming task. Objects that share capabilities belong to the same class, and the best approach is therefore to develop classes of objects, rather than the objects themselves. Figure 2.2 shows in diagram form a class and several objects of that class.

A class is a template for any number of objects that share the same general characteristics and capabilities. When we develop a class, we describe the types of information that an arbitrary object of the class might contain, and the actions or operations that it can perform.

This does not mean, however, that all objects that belong to a class are identical. In the same way that two word processed documents can be operated on in the same way, even though their text and formatting are completely different, so two objects of a class can contain different information and yet perform the same types of operation. We can make this distinction by saying that two objects of the same class have different *states*. The state of an object is the pattern of data values, or properties, contained in it, so although every object of a class performs exactly the same operations, the operations will have different outcomes because they work with different data.

An example should clarify this. Let's assume that in a given program, we have defined a class of objects that can be displayed on the screen of a computer. All of the objects of the class have the capabilities to display themselves. They all also have a *Colour* property that indicates the colour that an object will display in. In the program, we can create two of these objects, one in white and one in grey, as shown in Figure 2.3.

Figure 2.3 Two objects of the same class with a different Colour property

It should be easy to see that both objects belong to the same class, since they have the same capabilities and store the same *type* of information, but that both are also different, since the colours specified by their Colour properties are different.

2.1.2 Class Notation

If we are to design classes of objects and indicate how they are to be inter-connected, we need some form of notation to save having to use text descriptions repetitively. Software developers tend to work with diagrams, since they make very concise shorthand when describing the structure of systems. Figure 2.4 shows a commonly used form, a UML class diagram, for depicting classes and objects in a system. This can be refined to depict not only the class or object, but also the properties and methods defined for it:

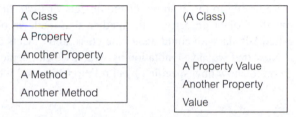

Figure 2.4 Class and object diagrams, showing properties and methods

Figure 2.4 shows a picture of a class (in this case, a generic 'class' class), and of an object of that class. The class diagram shows the properties and methods of the class, while the object diagram shows what class the object belongs to and the specific values taken on by each property. There is no need to indicate the methods in the object, since methods are defined for a whole class. Note that in this form of diagram, we show classes in terms of their *interfaces*. There is nothing in the diagram that indicates *how* information will be stored in an object of the class, or how a particular method actually works.

Figure 2.5 shows a specific class (Appointment) and how its interface is defined. It also shows a specific Appointment object with its property values in place as an example. Note that there is no need to show the names of the class methods (**AddToSchedule** and **SetAlarm**) on the Appointment instance. Since we know that the object is a member of the Appointment class, we are allowed to assume that these methods are available.

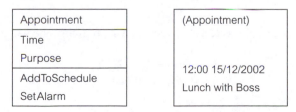

Figure 2.5 An Appointment class and object

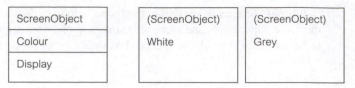

Figure 2.6 The 'ScreenObject' class, with a 'Colour' property and a 'Display' method

As object-oriented programmers, we take it on trust that an object will behave as its interface suggests, and actively avoid bringing in any indication of the detailed workings when we are describing how objects will interact. At another level, we must be able to describe the exact composition and workings of a class. At this *class development* level, we are interested in the specific algorithms used by class methods and the raw information that makes up an object's properties. Class development occurs late in the design phase and in the implementation phase of the life-cycle.

Returning to the example of the objects that can display themselves and have a specific Colour property, if the method that made an object display itself was to be called **Display**, we could depict the class, and objects of it, as shown in Figure 2.6.

Now that we have a notation by which we can depict classes and objects, we can go on to show how specific object relationships and interactions can be described.

Exercise 2.1

Consider a new class that is to be defined for use in a Personal Information Manager program: **DiaryEntry**. Instances of this class will have the following properties:

Date
Time
Text
Alarm

The class will also have the methods:

Display
CheckAlarm

Draw a class diagram for this class, and also draw two instances of the class as diagrams with the following instance data:

25/12/03, 08:00, "Open Xmas presents", Yes
1/1/04, 09:00, "Start new diary", No

In Visual Basic, a class is created in program code within a code module (Listing 2.1).

```
Class Appointment
    'Class definitions go in here...
    '. . .
End Class
```

Listing 2.1: Visual Basic code to define a class

Code to define how the class is composed (properties) and how its operations will work (methods) is placed between the `Class` and `End Class` keywords.

2.2 Object Relationships

There are several ways in which objects can be related to other objects in programs. Among these are:

- *Code inheritance* – a new class can be based on an existing class so that it inherits all of its methods and properties. New methods or properties can be added, and definitions of the existing ones changed for the new class. A new class created in this way is said to *extend* the existing class on which it is based. This form of relationship is defined when a programmer designs new classes. Visual Basic .NET is the first version of the language to provide support for code inheritance.

- *Interface inheritance* – a class can be defined purely in terms of how objects would interact with their properties and methods. An interface is 'empty' – devoid of any data or code to implement behaviour. As such it would be functionally useless, but it does provide the facility that other classes can inherit this *interface* so that objects of the new classes can be guaranteed to be able to communicate with other objects in the same way as the interface class was designed to. This feature allows programmers to define ways of using members of classes that have yet to be created. You could think of the facility as a way of creating 'dashboards' or control panels for objects that have yet to be fully defined.

- *Composition* – in the real-world, most of the things we see around us are assemblies of parts. A spade is a square metal blade attached to a wooden handle; a table is four legs attached to a top, etc. In object-oriented programming, one frequently used method is to create complex objects by combining assemblies of simpler ones. The new object is composed of one or more component objects in such a way that the new object can *delegate* some or all of its behaviour. Since a composite object can also be used as a component in an even more complex composite object, and this can also be used as a component, etc., creating classes by composition is in fact one of the most frequently used and powerful techniques in object-oriented programming.

- *Aggregation* – a member of a class can contain members of the same or other classes, usually multiple members. Methods and properties defined for the new class can delegate some or all of their work to the methods or properties of the *collection* of objects it contains. Again, the programmer designing a class defines this type of relationship, but the actual aggregation relationships are typically formed and modified as a program executes. Visual Basic provides good support for this form of relationship.

- *Message passing* – an object can utilise the abilities of other objects of the same or a different class (server objects) by passing messages to them requesting data or services. This is the main communication method used in object-oriented programming, and simply involves accessing the methods and properties defined in the server object.

Using one, two or all of these mechanisms, objects of one class can be defined in terms of objects of existing classes, or can utilise objects of other classes to distribute the work involved in performing a task. The methods define how most of the interactions that can be implemented in an object-oriented program are implemented.

2.2.1 Code Inheritance

This facility is more correctly referred to as *generalization-specialization*. An existing class, the *generalized* class, is used as a starting point when developing a new class, the *specialized* class. Specialization can be done by adding new properties or methods to the new class, or by changing the way that existing properties or methods work in the new class, or a mixture of both. The new class becomes a specialized version of the existing one. Figure 2.7 shows the standard UML diagram style for depicting code inheritance.

For example, if a generalized class describes **BankAccount** objects which are to be used for managing the transactions of any type of bank account by electronic means, it would be normal to create specializations of this class to deal with specific types of bank account such as investment accounts and cheque accounts. While a general account would have a simple **Withdraw** method for withdrawing cash from it, an investment account would redefine this method so that interest due to the account could be calculated properly, and a cheque account may need a different version of the same method to cope with possible overdraft limits. An investment account would also require the addition of a new method, **PayInterest** that would be used to add interest payments to an account, while a cheque account might need the addition of an **AgreeOverdraft** method. We see these relationships in Figure 2.8.

This type of relationship between generalized and specialized classes is often described as an **Is A** relationship, since the new class is a specialized version of the existing one. An investment account *is a* bank account. In another real-world example, a truck 'is a' vehicle, since 'truck' is a more specialized version of vehicle. A truck has all of the capabilities of a vehicle, plus one or more additional facilities (the ability to carry heavy loads).

Most programming languages that support object-oriented development provide a mechanism that allows new classes to be defined in terms of extensions and alterations to existing classes. This feature allows you to re-use classes you or others

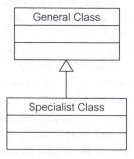

Figure 2.7 Code inheritance

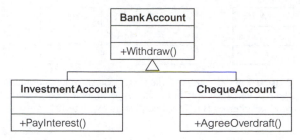

Figure 2.8 An example of code inheritance

have developed by basing a new class on the code of the existing one. If we have the class **ScreenObject**, we can use this as the basis of a new class, say **PrinterObject** that defines much of its behaviour in terms of the existing class. In this case, we would alter the existing method **Display** so that it sent the picture of the object to a printer instead of the display screen.

Defining a class with code inheritance is often easier than defining a new class from scratch, since all of the features of the existing class automatically become features of the new one. The design of the new class is then a matter of adding new properties or methods to it, or changing some of the inherited features. However, since the use of code inheritance suggests a strong **Is-A** relationship, it is important that the designer ensures that this relationship actually exists between the existing class and the class he or she intends to create from it.

For example, a naïve designer may consider that the relationship between circles of different colours, as shown in Figure 2.3, is actually an inheritance. We have a Circle class, and from it we can develop a **WhiteCircle** class and a **GreyCircle** class. This will certainly make it easier to create circles of the specified colour on demand in a program – for a white circle, create an instance of the **WhiteCircle** class and for a grey one create a **GreyCircle** object. However, what if it is later necessary to add a feature to change the colour of a Circle object? Using the inheritance scheme, it will now be necessary to destroy one circle and create another to take its place. Had colour simply been a property of the object as suggested earlier, it could be changed by simply passing a message.

Code inheritance is a double-edged sword, and many programmers have come to consider it a feature that should be used sparingly and with great care. Inheritance relationships are often more complex than as first appears, and while considered use of the facility can result in classes that are easier to develop, maintain and use, badly thought out inheritance relationships are likely to produce classes that are difficult to use and adapt to new circumstances. As an example, consider the inheritance scenario shown in Figure 2.9. Changes to the base class (class A) may or may not affect classes B to E. This may or may not be the intention of the programmer, and requires careful design and coding to control. The changes can affect any applications that use any of the classes, and may introduce subtle errors that are difficult to find.

This problem is not confined to inheritance relationships since it can also affect an aggregation or a composition relationship. Therefore, even languages that do not support inheritance are vulnerable to it. However, since an inheritance relationship is often more subtle, it is more likely that the problem would not be noticed as easily.

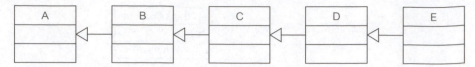

Figure 2.9   Class E inherits from class D, which inherits from class C, which inherits from class B, which inherits from class A. If a method or property of class A is changed in some way, will classes B to E still behave as expected?

Code inheritance is a new feature in Visual Basic, and Microsoft has taken care in its implementation to ensure that programmers using it have control over and are aware of the possible effects it will have on the classes they develop and those that inherit from them. Listing 2.2 shows how one class (a **ChequeAccount**) is made to inherit from another (the **BankAccount class**):

```
Class BankAccount
    'Bank account Properties and Methods...
    '...
End Class

Class InvestmentAccount
    Inherits BankAccount
    'Investment account specialist Properties and Methods
    'go here...
    '...
End Class
```

Listing 2.2: One class inheriting from another

2.2.2 Interface Inheritance

Interface inheritance is a form of inheritance in which a class can be designed so that it has an *interface* that is compatible with some more general class. The difference in this form of inheritance is that only interface elements are inherited. Since there is specifically no underlying code for the interface to connect to, all of the inherited interface properties and methods must be re-coded in the new class – no features are added automatically, and none may be missed out. It may initially seem that interface inheritance is a poor cousin of code inheritance (certainly many C++ programmers among others consider this to be the case). However, interface inheritance is a simpler mechanism that exhibits none of the possible ambiguities of code inheritance. In this form of inheritance, a class is designed so that it has an interface that is compatible with some more general class; interface inheritance acts like a standard plug that enables classes that use it to 'plug into' other software that conforms to the plug's format.

Interface inheritance allows a programmer to create families of classes that are compatible with each other, so that you can replace a member of one class with a member of a compatible one without changing any code that uses the object. This facility supports the powerful object-oriented facility called *polymorphism*. This is a feature that allows the creation of programs that can make use of any of a range of compatible classes. Visual Basic is in good company in providing interface inheritance, which is also a key feature of the languages Ada and Java, and the working principle of Microsoft's Component Object Model, which enables polymorphism between objects from different programs in a Windows environment.

Earlier versions of Visual Basic were considered to be limited by their lack of code inheritance features, and VB .NET has answered the prayers of many VB developers who wanted the language to include 'grown-up features. However, as we have seen, code inheritance does have its pitfalls. The fact remains that Visual Basic programmers did not seem to be unduly hampered by the lack of code inheritance in the past, and it remains to be seen whether its inclusion will be the godsend that many expect it to be. Inheritance is a facility that is plainly useful in reducing the amount of work required to build a complex class hierarchy, as we can see from the entire .NET Common Library Runtime. It is also a feature that can make programs more difficult to understand, and does not provide many capabilities that could not be implemented by other means. In this book, we will use both code and interface inheritance to build class hierarchies. However, they will be used quite sparingly and other styles of relationship between classes, to be discussed below, will often play a more significant part.

A Visual Basic .NET `interface` is composed in a code module as a list of (one or more) method or property definitions within an `Interface..End Interface` block, as shown in Listing 2.3:

```
Interface Sellable
    Property SalePrice()
    Sub Sell()
End Interface
```

Listing 2.3: An interface definition

Any class can be made to conform to this interface by including it in an `implements` statement at the start of the class definition as shown in Listing 2.4. Note that this constitutes a promise by the developer to incorporate definitions of the `SalePrice` property and the `Sell()` method in the new class, and Visual Basic will refuse to accept a class that contains the initial `implements` statement but does not include implementations of the property and method:

```
Class InsurancePolicy
    Implements Sellable
    Public Property SalePrice() Implements Sellable.SalePrice
        'Property definition goes here...
    End Property
    Public Sub Sell() Implements Sellable.Sell
        'Sell method definition goes here...
        '...
    End Sub
```

```
              'Other class Properties and Methods...
              '...
          End Class
```

Listing 2.4: A class that 'Implements' the Sellable interface

2.2.3 Composition/Aggregation

Objects can contain other objects, or references to other objects, and can make use of the capabilities of the objects they contain. Composition is often used as a way to create a new class of object that extends the behaviour of an existing class without the use of code inheritance, which as we have seen, can introduce subtle ambiguities. Aggregation is normally used as a way of assembling complex objects by adding together the capabilities of a number of more simple objects. For example, we might decide to provide our **ScreenObject** class with the ability to display a text caption in a variety of fonts. If we decided to use inheritance, we could design **ScreenObject** as a specialist version of a pre-existing **Font** class. However, it would be wrong to do this as we cannot say that a **ScreenObject** 'is a' **Font**, since then we would be limiting future types of screen object by constraining them to behave like **Font**s. We can, however, use composition to make each **ScreenObject** object contain a **Font** object. This type of relationship is referred to as the **Has A** relationship – a **ScreenObject** 'has a' **Font**. The relationship is conceptually correct.

A composition relationship is shown diagrammatically as in Figure 2.10. The diamond is drawn at the side of the composed object and, in this form, indicates that a **ScreenObject** object has a **Font**.

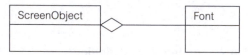

Figure 2.10 An aggregation (**Has A**) relationship

When one object contains multiple objects of the same type, the relationship is more normally described as an 'aggregation'. Often, in an aggregation relationship, we also need to show multiplicity. For example, 'a car has 4 wheels,' and this 'qualified aggregation' relationship can be depicted as shown in Figure 2.11.

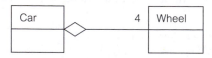

Figure 2.11 A qualified aggregation relationship

Other qualifications can be used to indicate different quantities in aggregations. For example, 'many trucks have 4 wheels, but some types of truck have more than 4 wheels.' This situation can be depicted as shown in Figure 2.12. In a similar way, 0+ is used to indicate zero or more, 1+ as one or more and so on.

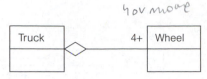

Figure 2.12 A more general qualification

We can use aggregation as an alternative to inheritance when we wish to extend or in some way alter an existing class. More work is involved, since in an inheritance relationship, properties and methods in the existing class automatically become properties and methods in the new class. Using aggregation in lieu of inheritance, it is necessary to recreate all of the methods in the new class, delegating their work to the enclosed version of the existing class.

In a Visual Basic .NET project, composition is done by including a *reference variable* for an existing type in a new class. A reference variable is a name that we incorporate in a class to store a particular type of data or a reference to an object. It is good practice to define the variables that a class is composed of in such a way that they can not be accessed directly from outside the class – the keyword `Private` does this; as shown in Listing 2.5.

```
Class ScreenObject
     Private mvarFont As System.Drawing.Font
     'Other class Properties and Methods...
     '...
End Class
```

Listing 2.5: The `ScreenObject` class, including a `Font` object in its definition

Note that `mvarFont` (`mvar` is a common prefix used to indicate that an item is a *Member Variable* of a class), having been defined as `Private`, will only be accessible to code within the class's own methods. We can make it accessible by adding a definition for a **Font** property, which will include code to define how the `Private` member can be accessed.

2.2.4 Delegation

We can use *delegation* with composition and aggregation relationships as an alternative to code inheritance; a class method can be implemented as a call to a method that performs the same function in one of the objects that make up the class. For example, in the earlier illustration of the use of inheritance, we decided that a **ScreenObject** could be used as the basis of a new **PrintObject** class. If we use composition instead of inheritance, then each **PrintObject** object will contain a **ScreenObject** object. Because we are using composition, we will need to recreate the **Colour** property and the **Display** method.

Since the new class completely redefines the **Display** method, we would treat this no differently as we would in the inheritance situation. However, the **Colour** property will not be automatically available in the new class, and we will have to

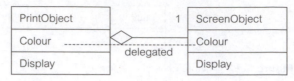

Figure 2.13   The **Colour** property, delegated by the **PrintObject** class to be performed by the enclosed **ScreenObject**

create a new **Colour** property that uses the same property in the class inherited from (see Figure 2.13).

Exercise 2.2

The **DiaryEntry** class from the previous question is to be used as a component of a new class, **DiaryDay**, where one **DiaryDay** object can contain an unlimited number of **DiaryEntry** objects. The appropriate aggregation symbol for this is the infinity symbol – ∞. Draw a diagram that shows how the two classes are related.

2.2.5 Message Passing

The last form of relationship we will consider is where one object accesses the properties or methods of another by 'passing a message' to it. The idea of passing a message is mainly conceptual – we will find it easier to think of objects as collaborating on a task if we can depict this collaboration in a human-oriented way. In fact, any program statement in which a property or method of an object is accessed is considered as passing a message to that object.

Continuing the metaphor, we can think of a class as having a vocabulary, which is the range of properties and methods defined for it. For example, the **ScreenObject** class has a vocabulary consisting of the names of its properties and methods – **Colour** and **Display**.

A message is a call to a method in an object of some class. The key distinction between messages and methods is that the same message can be passed to objects from any class that is capable of interpreting it. Each class may well do something different in response to a message; each will have its own *method* of dealing with it. Classes that share the same vocabulary, or interface, can all respond to the same set of messages.

Messages drive object-oriented programs. Every interaction with an object as a program executes involves passing a message. We can consider messages as having up to three parts. These are:

■ the **name** part of the message;
■ the **parameters** carried by the message;
■ the information returned from, or **result** of the message.

A message is defined for any class of object that has a specific interface. However, a message is always sent to a specific object, and so there is in fact a fourth, implicit part to a message – the **object** to which the message is passed. Not all messages have all of the parts. For example, our **ScreenObject** class has a message, **Display**, which has no parameters and would return no result. Its job is simply to tell the object to display itself on the screen, and no other information is necessary. If we have a **ScreenObject** whose name is **SO**, we can send it the **Display** message with the statement:

```
SO.Display
```

The **Colour** property, on the other hand, defines a message that requires us to pass a parameter. If we wish to change the colour of a **ScreenObject**, we will send it the **Colour** message, stating what the new colour is to be. To change the colour of our object **SO** to red, we use the message:

```
SO.Colour = Red
```

The 'dot' operator used between the name of the object and the message we are sending it is a standard object-oriented way of accessing properties and methods.

Note that we could also define the property **Colour** to *return* the current colour of the object, as shown in the statement:

```
currentColour = SO.Colour
```

Properties as supported by Visual Basic are flexible in this respect, in that they can be defined in several different ways. A property can be defined to pass information into an object to change it in some way and to retrieve the same type of information from the object, as the *current value* of the property. Alternatively, we might define a property in such a way that it is only possible to either retrieve the current value (a read-only property) or to change the current value (a write-only property). Properties are defined in terms of two optional parts – the **Set** part of a property defines how the object will be treated when a statement sets the property to a new value, while the **Get** part defines how the actual value of the property will be retrieved from the object. Missing either part out will make the property read-only (no **Set** part) or write-only (no **Get** part).

We can show message passing in object diagrams by simply using an arrow to indicate which object sends the message and which receives it. The arrowhead is at the receiver end. If we have an object, say **X** that sends a message to a **ScreenObject**, **SO**, to change its colour to red, we can depict this as shown in Figure 2.14.

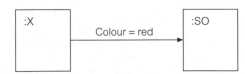

Figure 2.14 **X** sending a message to **SO**

The object **X** could be a form that was being used to edit the **ScreenObject**. Note the colon preceding the object's name in this collaboration. The diagram shows a *specific* object sending a message to another, rather than the more general depiction of an object of one class sending a message to an object of another. If the diagram were to involve a number of objects of different classes, the full syntax, **ClassName::ObjectName** would be used to clarify matters. If we had wanted the object **X** to read the **Colour** property of the **SO** object rather than setting its **Colour** property to a new value, we would have used the simpler expression **Colour** to annotate the message arrow.

Exercise 2.3

A **DiaryDay** object needs to determine the **Time** property of a **DiaryEntry**. Draw a diagram to show this interaction message.

2.3 An Example Class Design

It is worthwhile at this stage to look at an example of a useful class, so that we can try out the various mechanisms that make it work. Note that we will only be *designing* the class for now, although we will go on to implement it in the next chapter.

Let's assume we need a class that we will call **BankAccount**. This will model a simplistic bank account and will include facilities for depositing and withdrawing cash from the account and for determining the current balance. The full requirements specification is given below.

1.   A **BankAccount** will have an indication of the amount of money currently in the account – the **Balance** of the account.
2.   It will be possible to **Deposit** additional cash into the account.
3.   It will be possible to **Withdraw** an amount of cash from the account.
    3.1.   If the amount to be withdrawn exceeds the current account balance, the withdrawal operation will not be allowed.

We can depict this set of requirements as a use-case diagram, as shown in Figure 2.15.

This requirements specification is very simple, and would not be adequate for modelling a real bank account, where each deposit and withdraw transaction would need to be recorded so that an account statement could be generated. We will address this more complex requirement in a later chapter. To design the **BankAccount** class we start by drawing a class diagram containing the name of the class (Figure 2.16).

We can now go on by adding a property to indicate the account balance, and methods to allow the deposit and withdrawal of cash (Figure 2.17).

Since this is a simple class, there is no need for aggregation. We will, however, expect to be able to operate the class by passing messages to it, and so should define the format of these messages. We can use *scenarios*, or use-cases to indicate what each of the properties and methods will be expected to do. Since we only have a

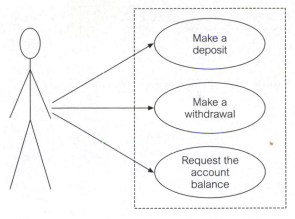

Figure 2.15 A use-case diagram for a simple **BankAccount** model

Figure 2.16 The **BankAccount** class

Figure 2.17 The **BankAccount** class with properties and methods

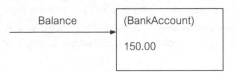

Figure 2.18 Receiving the balance message

single class, we cannot show collaborations with other objects explicitly, but we can show the **BankAccount** end of a collaboration quite easily (Figure 2.18).

Note the use of brackets around the class name to show we have an *instance* of the **BankAccount** class. Note also that the current property value (£150.00) is shown – this is not strictly necessary, and can sometimes cause confusion. The

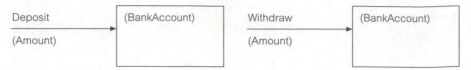

Figure 2.19 The **Deposit** and **Withdraw** methods

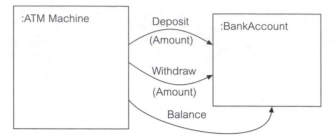

Figure 2.20 A **BankAccount** object and its interactions with an ATM

balance message passed to the account will implicitly retrieve the current account balance (i.e. the *value* of that property).

All we have done with these diagrams is to show what messages an object of the class can respond to, and what information (if any) these messages bring with them. In the case of **deposit** and **withdraw** operations (Figure 2.19), additional information is required to indicate the amount to be deposited or withdrawn. This is, of course, the **Amount** parameter, and is indicated by the word in brackets shown next to the message arrow. We can always describe the action that the messages will have as a short text paragraph to resolve any possibilities of ambiguity.

In designing a single class as we have done here, it is not possible to show full interactions between objects. At some later stage, we will have to incorporate this and other classes into a design diagram that shows the interactions, and shows which object sends a message and which receives it. Figure 2.20 shows a very simple example of this, using specific object instances rather than classes. The object that interacts with the **BankAccount** object is an Automatic Teller Machine (or ATM). The interactions shown are very simple examples, since there are only two objects involved and all interactions are commands directed from the ATM to the **BankAccount** object. Most systems will have to support more complex interactions involving more objects and messages being sent in either direction between them.

Exercise 2.4

Assume the **BankAccount** class has been extended to include information on transaction operations. As a part of this, it is now necessary for a **BankAccount** to determine the **Date** and **Time** that a transaction (deposit or withdrawal) is being made at. It can do this by sending the **Time** and **Date** messages to the **ATMMachine** object. Show the interactions that happen during a withdrawal operation on a diagram.

2.4 Locating Class Code in VB .NET

When you create a new Console or Windows application project in VB .NET, it will be organized so that you will enter program code into a code module, which is a file for containing program text. In the default module supplied with a new console project, initially called **Module1**, you can add new class code by entering class definitions *inside* the module code – that is, between the keywords **Module Module1..End Module**. In this case, you will be creating one or more new classes that are part of the module definition.

In a Windows application, you will find a form module, initially called **Form1** and stored in a file **Form1.vb**. In this file you will find a class definition for the form (initially named **Public Class Form1**). To add a new class to this module, it can be located either inside or outside the form's class definition.

In either type of project, you can also add class definitions to a project by adding a new class module to it. Select **Project/Add Class..** from the menus, and when the dialog box appears, enter the name of the new class (to name the file the class code will be stored in). You can then proceed to add code to the class in the new Code window that appears. In fact, you can add as many different classes as you like to this or any other code file.

When we create an object-oriented program or component, where we locate class code within it is an important issue, since we usually must balance the competing requirements of encapsulation and availability. Encapsulation, which requires us to restrict the accessibility of classes and objects that we wish to maintain precise control over, can be enhanced by hiding classes within other classes; for example, locating a **BankAccount** class within the class definition of a form that will be used as a user-interface for manipulating **BankAccount** objects. Accessibility means being able to create objects of a class or work with them from some other code, and this is restricted when we define one class within another.

Truly independent classes, which can be used from any code in an application without restriction, are best placed in separate class modules. Maximum independence can be realized by placing each class definition in its own file, but this would lead to very complex organizations of files within an application. A better approach is to locate related classes within the same file. For example, we might create the following module (Listing 2.6) as a class library that could be used by applications that dealt with vehicles (note that the actual working code has been omitted from the inside of the definitions).

```
Public Class Wheel
    'Wheel member definitions...
End Class

Public Class Car
    Private mvarWheels(4) As Wheel
    'Other definitions...
End Class
```

```
Public Class Truck
    Private mvarWheels(6) As Wheel
    'Other definitions...
End Class

Public Class BigTruck
    Private mvarWheels(12) As Wheel
    'Other definitions...
End Class
```

Listing 2.6: A Class Library module with four related classes

In a Visual Basic project, all code is stored in files with a **.vb** suffix to their name. In the next chapter, we will look at the syntax rules for Visual Basic .NET, which govern what you can legally add to code modules.

Review Questions

1. Insert the missing words in the following sentences:

    a) Software _____ is the development of a plan of how objects will interact to accomplish a task.

    b) An _____ is an instance of a class.

    c) A _____ is a template for all objects that share the same characteristics.

    d) Classes that have the same set of names for all their properties and methods are said to display _____ inheritance.

    e) A class that inherits the implementation of properties and methods from another is said to exhibit ____ inheritance.

    f) A class that implements a method by calling on a suitable method in a contained object is using the principle of _____.

    g) _____ is used when an object of a class contains a number of other objects.

    h) An inheritance relationship between classes is also known as an ____ relationship.

    i) Objects of classes that are interface-compatible and are therefore interchangeable are said to have the facility of _____.

    j) Objects that interact with others by invoking their methods are said to be passing a _____.

2. Distinguish between a property and a method.

3. In an inheritance relationship, also known as a generalization-specialization relationship, which class (the generalized or the specialized) inherits from which?

4. In terms of classes and objects, how would you describe the relationship between a chapter and a book? What about a car and its engine, chassis, transmission, and body.

5. Distinguish between a message and a method.

6. A new class, **EmailMessage**, has been proposed for use in a desktop communications application. It is to have four properties – **From**, **To**, **Subject** and **Body** – and two methods – **Send** and **Display**. Draw a class diagram for this class.

7. The **MailServer** class and the **MailClient** class interact when an email message is sent. The interaction involves the **MailClient** object passing the **MailServer** object a message, which involves the passing of additional information – an **EMailMessage** object. Show this interaction on a diagram.

Practical Activities

In these practical exercises, you will learn how to:

- create a new class in VB .NET
- add simple properties and methods to the class
- use Sub Main() to create an object of the class and test its properties and methods

The program statements used in this example will be fully explained in the next chapter, so you should concentrate on following the exercises exactly to gain experience in using Visual Studio to create simple Visual Basic code. Our program will be created as a console project.

Activity 1: Add a Class to a new VB Project

We will start this practical session by creating a new project and adding a Class module to it.

Start a new project in Visual Studio
Run Visual Studio, and in the Start page, select **New Project**. In the New Project dialog box, ensure that the Visual Basic Projects folder icon is selected in the Project Types pane, and then select **Console Application**. Change the Name of the application to **BankProject**. You can also at this stage nominate where on your hard disk you would like the project and solution to be saved, by entering or browsing to a suitable location in the Location box. I normally save my Visual Basic projects in a folder on my D: drive (you could use the C: drive instead) called **D:\Programs\Visual Basic.NET Projects**. Using this folder, the New Project dialog should appear as shown in Figure A2.1. Press **OK** to create the new project.

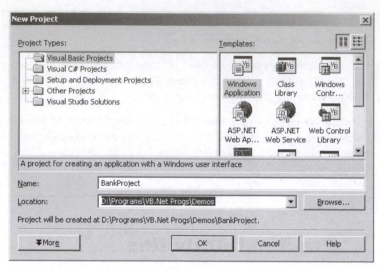

Figure A2.1 The New Project settings for this exercise

Add a Class module to the project

By default, the new project will already contain a module with the name **Module1**. This module will be the main object in our project. Rename the module by changing the first line in the code window to **Module Bank**, and rename the module file to **Bank.vb** in the Properties window.

When it is complete, this program will create a **BankAccount** object and send messages to it to perform various transactions. These messages will be sent from **Sub Main** of the **Bank** module, so the **Bank** module will act as an executive object, starting off the process and directing proceedings. However, we'll start the project by creating our first class. To do this, select **Project/Add Class** . . . from the menus. The Add New Item dialog box will appear (Figure A2.2).

Note that **Class** is already selected as the type of new item to be added (a consequence of our selecting **Add Class** . . . from the menus). The Name box at the bottom of the dialog box gives us an opportunity to name the new module. Type the name **BankAccount** and press **Open**. A new module file, **BankAccount.vb**, will be added to the Solution Explorer, and a Code window will open in the main part of the IDE with the outline of a new class already in place (see Figure A2.3).

Activity 2: Adding code to the class to give it a Property and Methods

Write the code for the BankAccount class

All the code for the **BankAccount** class will be added between the lines **Public Class BankAccount** and **End Class**. This code will define the **Balance** property and the **Deposit** and **Withdraw** methods, plus a special purpose routine, a *constructor*

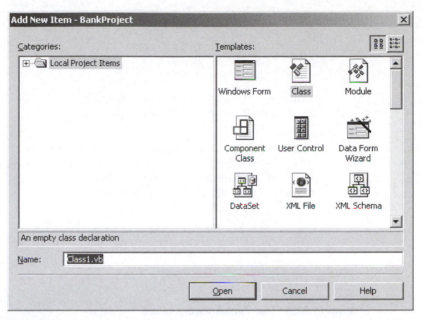

Figure A2.2 The Add New Item dialog box

Figure A2.3 A new class in a Code window and in the Solution Explorer

that will do the job of putting a newly created **BankAccount** into a well-defined state.

The full code for the **BankAccount** class is shown in Listing A2.1. Enter this code between the existing lines in the Code window (do not duplicate the first and last line).

```
Public Class BankAccount
    Private mvarBalance As Decimal

    Public Sub New(ByVal InitialBalance As Decimal)
        mvarBalance = InitialBalance
    End Sub
```

```
      Public ReadOnly Property Balance()
         Get
             Return mvarBalance
         End Get
      End Property

      Public Sub Deposit(ByVal Amount As Decimal)
         mvarBalance += Amount
      End Sub

      Public Function Withdraw(ByVal Amount As Decimal) _
                                         As Boolean
         If Balance >= Amount Then
             mvarBalance -= Amount
             Return True
         Else
             Return False
         End If
      End Function
   End Class
```

Listing A2.1: The BankAccount class

We'll go into the details of how all this works in the next chapter. For now, it is worth knowing that the statement `Private mvarBalance As Decimal` declares (i.e. defines) a *member variable* so that an object of the **BankAccount** class has somewhere to store its current balance, the block of code beginning `Public ReadOnly Property Balance ()` defines the **Balance** property that allows other objects to be able to see what the account's balance is. The two blocks of code beginning `Public Sub Deposit(ByVal Amount As Decimal)` and `Public Function Withdraw(ByVal Amount As Decimal) As Boolean` indicate the start of the **Deposit** and **Withdraw** methods, and the block of code beginning `Public Sub New (ByVal InitialBalance As Decimal)` is the constructor method that defines how a new member of the class will be created.

To test the class, we will need to write some code in **Sub Main** of the **Bank** module that creates and works with a **BankAccount**.

Activity 3: Writing client code

Creating client code

The **Bank** module is a client of the **BankAccount** class. This simply means that it relies on the class to perform services for it; in this case, the services of creating and manipulating a **BankAccount** object. Once an account object has been created, **Sub Main** will send messages to the object to make it perform withdrawals and report on its balance.

Add the code to **Sub Main** in the **Bank** module so that the whole module appears as shown in Listing A2.2.

```
Module Bank

    Sub Main()
        Dim a As New BankAccount(100)
        Console.WriteLine("Current balance : £{0}", _
                          a.Balance())
        If a.Withdraw(150) Then
            Console.WriteLine("Withdrawal successful.")
        Else
            Console.WriteLine('Withdrawal not successful.")
        End If
        Console.WriteLine("Current balance : £{0}", _
                          a.Balance())
        Console.WriteLine("Depositing £80")
        a.Deposit(80)
        Console.WriteLine("Current balance : {0}", _
                          a.Balance())
        If a.Withdraw(150) Then
            Console.WriteLine("Withdrawal successful.")
        Else
            Console.WriteLine("Withdrawal not successful.")
        End If
        Console.WriteLine("Current balance : £{0}", _
                          a.Balance())
        Console.WriteLine("Done")
    End Sub

End Module
```

Listing A2.2: The Bank module, containing client code

What have we done?

In this set of exercises, we have created a class that models a simple bank account. Specifically, we've:

- added a new class to a console project;
- added code to the class to provide it with a property and several methods;
- added a declaration of a **BankAccount** object to the **Bank** module;
- written code that defines how the **Bank** module interacts with the class using messages;
- written statements to output object information to the console.

You should bear in mind that our model is limited in a number of ways, not least in that it does not record the details of any of the transactions (deposits and withdrawals) that are acted on the **BankAccount**. This would make it impossible for a statement to be generated for example. In a later chapter we'll return to the **BankAccount** class and extend it so that it provides a more realistic simulation of a **BankAccount**.

Suggested Additional Activities

1. Changing the initial account balance

   The first statement within **Sub Main** in the **Bank** module sets the initial balance in the account to £100. Try changing this to other values and view the results by re-running the program.

2. Adding other bank accounts

   The **Bank** module declares a single **BankAccount** object (in the statement beginning **Dim**). There is nothing to stop us having as many bank account objects as we wished within **Sub Main**. Simply add another Dim statement for each, giving each new **BankAccount** object a distinct name (**a** is the name used to refer to the **BankAccount** in the exercise). We could then go on to refer to the new bank accounts in the same way as the one in the exercises, sending **Deposit** and **Withdraw** messages and querying the balance. Try adding a second **BankAccount**.

Solutions to Exercises

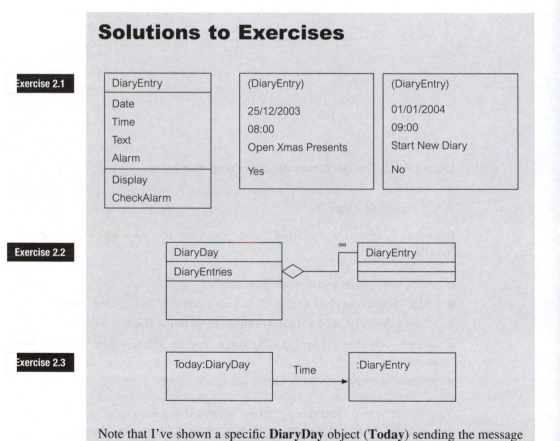

Note that I've shown a specific **DiaryDay** object (**Today**) sending the message to an anonymous (i.e. we do not know or care which) instance of a **DiaryEntry** here. An anonymous **DiaryDay** could have sent the message, and a specific **DiaryEntry** (e.g. one called **CurrentAppointment**) could have received it.

Exercise 2.4

Note the use of sequence numbers ((①,②,③)) to indicate the order that messages are sent in. While not always necessary, these can clear up ambiguities in an object interaction diagram.

Answers to Review Questions

1. Insert the missing words in the following sentences:

   a) Software **design** is the development of a plan of how objects will interact to accomplish a task.

   b) An **object** is an instance of a class.

   c) A **class** is a template for all objects that share the same characteristics.

   d) Classes that have the same set of names for all their properties and methods are said to display **interface** inheritance.

   e) A class that inherits the implementation of properties and methods from another is said to exhibit **code** inheritance.

   f) A class that implements a method by calling on a suitable method in a contained object is using the principle of **delegation**.

   g) **Aggregation** is used when an object of a class contains a number of other objects.

   h) An inheritance relationship between classes is also known as an **Is-A** relationship.

   i) Objects of classes that are interface-compatible and are therefore interchangeable are said to have the facility of **polymorphism**.

   j) Objects that interact with others by invoking their methods are said to be passing a **message**.

2. Distinguish between a property and a method. **A *property* is value that reflects some part of the internal state of an object. A *method* is an operation that an object can perform to modify its own internal state or return some information about its internal state.**

3. In an inheritance relationship, also known as a generalization-specialization relationship, which class (the generalized or the specialized) inherits from which? **The *specialized* class inherits from the *general* or *generalized* class. (e.g. A *truck* is a *specialized* form of *vehicle*, and as such inherits all of the traits of a vehicle but adds *truck*-type specialisms).**

4. In terms of classes and objects, how would you describe the relationship between a chapter and a book? **A *book* is an *aggregation* of *chapters*.** What about a car and its engine, chassis, transmission, and body. **A *car* is a *composition*, since part of its composition is a chassis, engine and body**.

5. Distinguish between a message and a method. **A *message* is a call to an object whose type may be unknown, resulting in the object executing a *method*. i.e. a *method* is a specific piece of code to do a task, a *message* is a request to have a task done by any suitable piece of code.**

CHAPTER
3

The Visual Basic .NET Language

In this chapter you will learn:

- how Visual Basic .NET supports different types of information in the Common Type System;
- what variables are, and how they can be used in programs;
- how different types of variable are used to store different types of information;
- the purpose of identifiers in programs;
- the use of literals, operators and expressions in program statements;
- how blocks of statements behave in a program;
- how to create simple structured data types for use in your programs.

If you were a builder you would take the existence of bricks, mortar, plumbing components and electrical supplies for granted. You would also rightly expect to be able to find tools for doing your job with, and to be able to hire services such as delivery trucks, earth moving equipment and labour to do the work that you did not intend to do yourself. As a Visual Basic .NET programmer, you can assume existence of the equivalent raw materials, components, tools and services.

All of these come as features of the Visual Studio IDE used by Visual Basic programmers. However, much of what you will work with in a Visual Basic project is also available to programmers who use other languages, such as C# or C++. Underlying all programs written for the .NET platform is the .NET Common Language Runtime; an extensive library of data types, classes and pre-built objects that form the core of all software written for .NET.

3.1 The Common Language Runtime

Every computer program has a *platform*; a type of computer that the program has been written for and can run on. In some cases, the platform is an actual type of computer, such as an IBM PC compatible machine or an Apple Macintosh. In others, the platform is an abstraction; a piece of software that acts for all intents and purposes as a type of computer with very specific features and facilities. Such abstractions are created so that it is possible to deploy their programs on a range of different types of computer.

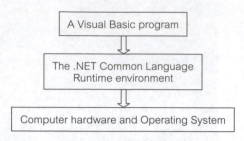

Figure 3.1 The .NET Common Language Runtime environment

Java is a good example of this. Java programs run on the Java Virtual Machine or JVM. Since the JVM is a software construct, a version of it can be written for any suitably featured computer, and so a Java program can be made to execute on an IBM PC compatible, a Macintosh, a micro, mini or mainframe computer running the Unix operating system or a variety of other platforms. Until the release of .NET, this was a trick that Visual Basic programs were incapable of. VB programmers wrote code for the Windows operating system running on an IBM compatible PC and that was that.

The .NET Common Language Runtime (or CLR, or simply the .NET Runtime) (Figure 3.1) acts as a hypothetical computer that runs .NET programs. This has the obvious advantage that once versions of the CLR are developed to run on Macintoshes, etc., any .NET program will be able to run on these machines. It also has the major advantage of being a hypothetical computer designed by programmers. This is important, since the programmers who developed the CLR were able to create an idealized computing platform, providing all the facilities they could wish for in a computer. All .NET programs, regardless of the language they were written in, are converted (or compiled) into Microsoft Intermediate Language (MSIL), which is the native language of the CLR, and can then execute directly on the CLR virtual machine.

However, the biggest advantage of all provided by the CLR is that it can support a wide range of programming languages. Since all of the hard development work has gone into the design of the computing platform itself, and since this has been optimized to make it an easy target for programming language designers, it is a simple matter to create new languages to run on the CLR (of course, the phrase 'a simple matter' is used as a relative term here; I won't be writing any new languages for the CLR – certainly not this week, but for those who find the need to create a new version of their favourite language, .NET must provide the easiest possible route).

3.1.1 The Common Type System

Part of the CLR is the Common Type System, also known as the Common Type Library. This is a range of pre-built data types, built using the best object-oriented programming traditions. The CLR contains fundamental data types for representing numbers, text, logical conditions, dates and currency values. It also contains more sophisticated data types (classes) for use in developing user-interfaces (windows and the widgets on these windows), data systems, file management, graphics, multimedia programs and internet services. Since it is common to all .NET languages, there are no features that are restricted for the use of C++ programmers only (always an annoyance in earlier versions of Visual Basic), and it is possible to extend the facilities of the CLR using any .NET language. (The CLR was built using mostly the C# language, but this does not give C# any additional powers over VB or other languages.) Programmers in Visual Basic, C#, C++ or any of the other languages provided for .NET work with variables and objects from the Common Type System, or with types they have derived from this.

3.2 Variables

Creating and using variables, named storage elements for data, in a VB .NET program is direct and simple. In this chapter we will see a lot of program code examples in which data is created and manipulated, and, to minimize clutter, these will be parts of console applications. Therefore, a common framework for all of the code examples and snippets throughout the chapter is shown in Listing 3.1. Refer back to the practical exercises at the end of Chapter 1 for details of how to create this framework in Visual Studio.

```
Module Module1
    Sub Main()
        'Sample code will go here
    End Sub
End Module
```

Listing 3.1: The framework for all code examples in this chapter

A simple program could be created by adding a number of statements (lines of code) to the framework in Listing 3.1. These statements would be instructions that would be executed at runtime (i.e. when the program is being run), and declarations of variables. Variables are pieces of information stored in the computer's memory and made available to a program. Programs need to store information for a number of reasons:

- data that a user enters into a program from the keyboard or mouse is normally stored until it has been processed;

- the results of calculations and other processing are often stored until a suitable time to display them comes along;

- often, calculations must be done in a number of stages, and so intermediate results must be stored between the stages;

- information in data files on the computer's disk or a CD-ROM can not be used in calculations directly, but must first be read into the computer's memory;

■ information about the current *state* of a program (which item in a list is being worked on, the position a window is to be displayed in, etc.) must be stored if the computer is not to lose track of the task it is currently working on.

In all of these situations and many more, the easiest way to keep tabs on required information is to store it in one or more variables. All programming languages incorporate the notion of a variable, and allow us to take some information and store it in a variable for later use. A variable is simply a named location in the computer's memory into which items of data can be passed and from which the data can later be retrieved. Storing and retrieving an item of data to and from a variable are the most fundamental operations that any programming language will provide.

For example, in a small program for calculating the area of a floor given its length and width (such a program might be useful for someone who has the job of laying tiles), we might use three variables as shown in Listing 3.2.

```
Module Module1
    Sub Main()
        Dim length, width, area As Single
        length = 12.5
        width = 8.75
        area = length * width
        Console.WriteLine("Area is {0}", area)
    End Sub
End Module
```

Listing 3.2: A simple program that uses three variables

The first line inside `Sub Main` in Listing 3.2 *declares* three variables. The entire statement (line of code) states that three variables named `length`, `width` and `area` are to be `Dim`ensioned; that is, space is to be reserved for them.

When a variable is declared, it is given a name (this is often known as its *identifier*), a *type*, which indicates what type of information can be stored in it, and a *scope*, which indicates the parts of the program it can be accessed from. Each of the variables declared here has the same type, `Single` – this indicates that they can be used to store numbers with a fractional part at single precision, which allows for up to seven digits of accuracy. We could store other numbers with a higher precision (*Double* or *Decimal*) or with no fractional part (`Integer`). Since all three are declared at the top of `Sub Main`, which is the entry point of the program (where it starts from), they are all accessible from anywhere in this code routine.

The three lines following the declaration do the work of the program. Simple numeric values are assigned to `length` and `width`, and then the result of multiplying `length` and `width` is stored in the variable `area`. The final line before the line `End Sub` displays the result of this calculation on the computer's screen.

It is useful to notice that the actual calculation done by the program is almost incidental; the value assigned to `area` just happens to be the result of a calculation (multiplying `length` by `width`), and is assigned in just the same way that a simple numeric value would be assigned. The function we perceive as being important in a computer program (in this case the multiplication) is often trivial compared to the way we need to wrap it up in program code to make it work.

VB .NET provides us with a rich set of pre-defined types of variable as the Common Type System. We create and use variables of the supplied types using statements similar to those used in Listing 3.2. What we do with the variables depends on the job our program needs to do. What we *can* do with them depends on which of the various types of variable we decide to use. For example, we would store numbers in one of the numeric variable types (`Single`, `Double`, `Decimal`, `Integer`, `Long`), selecting the type most appropriate for the job required (high or low precision calculations, counting things, storing measurements, etc.). We can also store text (using a `String` variable), dates (the `Date` type), the answers to Yes/No questions (`Boolean` variables) and other forms of data.

Exercise 3.1

Write a short program similar to that in Listing 3.2, that will calculate the area of a circle of a given radius. Define the variables area and radius, and use the formula:

area = 3.14 * radius * radius

to perform the calculation.

3.2.1 Other Simple Variable Types

VB .NET provides us with a wide range of built in types of variable, as Table 3.1 shows.

Using the range of simple data types listed in the table, we can develop programs that can store and manipulate any type of information. In some cases, we may need to be quite ingenious in the way that we use these types to represent some information. For example, we can represent a colour as three numbers, each an indication of the intensity of one of the additive primary colours, red, blue and green, that would be mixed to form the actual colour.

Listing 3.3 shows some examples of various types in use in a program. Note that lines that begin with a '(single quote mark) are comments and are ignored by Visual Basic):

```
Sub Main()
    Dim Name As String
    Dim DateOfBirth As Date
    Dim Gender As Char
    Dim Age As Integer
    Dim Height As Single
    Dim Response As String
    Dim LicencedDriver As Boolean

    Console.WriteLine("ALL ABOUT YOU")
    'First ask for and read the user's name...
    Console.Write("Enter your name: ")
```

Table 3.1 Simple data types in Visual Basic

Type Name	Range	Description
Byte	0 to 255	A small number, equivalent to one unit of storage in computer memory
Short	−32,768 to +32,767	A 16-bit signed number with no fractional part
Integer	−2,147,483,648 to 2,147,483,647	A 32-bit signed number with no fractional part
Long	−9,223,372,036,854,775,808 to 9,223,372,036,854,775,807	A 64-bit signed number with no fractional part
Single	−3.402823E+38 to −1.401298E−45 for negative values; 1.401298E−45 to 3.402823E+38 for positive values	A single-precision floating-point number stored in an efficient binary representation (7 digits of precision)
Double	−1.79769313486231E+308 to −4.94065645841247E−324 for negative values; 4.94065645841247E−324 to 1.79769313486231E+308 for positive values	A double-precision floating-point number stored in an efficient binary representation (15 digits of precision)
Decimal	+/−79,228,162,514,264,337,593,543,950,335 with no decimal point; +/−7.9228162514264337593543950335 with 28 places to the right of the decimal; smallest non-zero number is +/−0.0000000000000000000000000001	A high precision number stored in a direct decimal representation to improve the accuracy of calculations (29 digits of precision)
Boolean	True or False	Used to store simple true/false, on/off, up/down or other 2-state values
Char	0 to 65535	Stores a single alphanumeric character (e.g. the letter 'x', or a digit or punctuation symbol)
String	Up to 2 billion characters	Sequences of text characters, e.g. names, addresses, paragraphs of a document, whole documents, etc.
Date	January 1, 0001 to December 31, 9999	Dates, times and combinations of both. A single date variable stores a point in time (Date and Time)

```
Name = Console.ReadLine()
'Now their birth date...
Console.Write("Enter your date of birth: ")
DateOfBirth = Console.ReadLine()
'Ask if male of female...
Console.Write("Are you male (M) or female (F):")
Response = Console.ReadLine()
'Just in case - convert the response to UPPER CASE...
Gender = Response.ToUpper()
'Ask and read user's height...
```

```
Console.Write("What is your height in metres:")
Height = Console.ReadLine()
'Ask if user has a driving licence...
Console.Write("Do you have a driving licence (Y or N):")
Response = Console.ReadLine()
'Response is a single letter - convert to a Boolean...
LicencedDriver = (Response.ToUpper() = "Y")
'Work out the user's age (from birth date)...
Age = DateDiff(DateInterval.Year, DateOfBirth, Today)
'Now write all this- stuff out to the screen...
Console.WriteLine("Results:")
Console.WriteLine("Name: {0}", Name)
Console.WriteLine("Age: {0}", Age)
If Gender = "M" Then
   Console.WriteLine("{0} is male", Name)
Else
   Console.WriteLine("{0} is female", Name)
End If
Console.WriteLine("Height: {0}metres", Height)
If LicencedDriver Then
   Console.WriteLine("{0} is a licenced driver", Name)
Else
   Console.WriteLine("{0} is not a licenced driver",
   Name)
End If
End Sub
```

Listing 3.3: Different simple variable types in use

The code in Listing 3.3 shows a number of different types of variable being used in a number of ways. The statements beginning `Console.WriteLine` are used to send text and the contents of variables to the screen. Those that end in `Console.ReadLine()` take information from the keyboard and assign it to the variable named on the left of the line. The other statements use variables in some way or other.

There are obvious uses, such as a `String` variable being used to store a name and a `Date` variable being used to store a birth date, and there are also some less obvious uses. A `Boolean` variable can store any piece of information that can have only two possible values; in this case, a person can either be a licensed driver or not, so the two possible values `True` and `False` are ideal for indicating which (we would normally take `True` as meaning 'yes, this person is a licensed driver' in this context).

We could also use a `Boolean` to store someone's gender, but this might lead to a confusing or even contentious usage – does `True` mean Male or Female? Not being a brave enough soul to decide either way, I always find it easier to cop out by using a single character (a `Char` type variable) to store the value 'M' or 'F', although a string could always be used to store the whole word 'Male' or 'Female'.

Since a `Boolean` type will store only the values `True` or `False`, we can also use them to directly store the result of assertions we can make in the program code. For example, the statement:

```
LicencedDriver = (Response = "Y")
```

works by evaluating the validity of the expression 'Response = "Y"'. This can only be True (the value stored in the variable Response is "Y"), or False (it is not "Y"), and so the Boolean variable LicensedDriver will take on one of these two values.

The variable Age takes an Integer value; it would have been possible to use a Short value here, or even a Byte, since the possible range for a human being is well within the range of these types. However, it is quite normal to use an Integer by default for a non-fractional numeric, since an Integer variable corresponds exactly to the size of a number as worked on by a 32-bit processor (the current standard format for microprocessors in desktop PCs). Note that the value in age is calculated as the difference in years between the user's date of birth and today's date, and VB provides a function called DateDiff() to make this calculation.

Once all the required values have been entered by the program's user, results are displayed by a sequence of Console.WriteLine() statements. These work by displaying the text inside the brackets, and incorporating the values of variables from a list after this text if there are any. For example:

```
Console.WriteLine("Name: {0}", Name)
```

will display the text 'Name : ' followed by the contents of the first variable in the list (which in this case is the only one). The sequence '{0}' is interpreted as 'contents of variable number 0', which is the first. If there were three variables to be displayed, a suitable statement would be:

```
Console.WriteLine("Three values: {0}, {1}, {2}", X, Y, Z)
```

which would print the values of the three variables X, Y and Z (X is variable number 0, Y is number 1 and Z is number 2). Note that this scheme of printing or displaying a *format string* into which actual values will be inserted is a common facility in the .NET runtime, and will turn up in a number of different forms.

In the final lines of code, Boolean values have been used again to determine which of two possible messages to display. The statement:

```
If Gender = "M" Then
```

is the start of a code structure that decides which of two sections of code to execute, depending on the outcome of a Boolean assertion. If the value stored in the Gender variable is "M", the statement:

```
Console.WriteLine("{0} is male", Name)
```

will be executed. If not, the alternative statement indicating that the named person is female will execute. In this case, the assertion Gender = "M" is used directly. The second such If..Then construct makes use of the Boolean value stored in the LicensedDriver variable to the same ends.

Exercise 3.2

Select variable types from Table 3.1 to suit the following purposes, and write suitable Dim statements to declare them.

a) A variable, `ProgLang`, to store the value 'Visual Basic .NET'.

b) A variable, `Xmas`, to store the value '25/12/03'.

c) A variable, `Attendance`, to store the number of people present at a football match (assume the stadium has a capacity of 10 000).

d) A variable, `Attendance`, to store the number of students in a classroom which has a capacity of 25.

e) A variable, `Fuel`, to store the exact number of gallons of fuel pumped into a vehicle's tank.

f) A variable, `Category`, to store a value in from the range – 'A', 'B', 'C', 'D' or 'E'.

g) A variable to store the distance in miles from the earth to the moon (approx 250 000).

h) A variable to store the exact time that a customer places an order with an eCommerce website.

3.2.2 Constants

A *constant* is a variable whose value can not be changed. "What use is that?" you might ask. Well, as it turns out, very useful, since there are often situations when we want to make use of a value that will be fixed but is difficult to remember or recognize, or that is generally fixed in a program, but may change infrequently if the program is changed. We can give a value a name and optionally a type by declaring it as a constant, using the keyword `Const`:

```
Const PI = 3.1415927
Const VATPercentRate = 17.5
Const DatabaseName = "SALES.MDB"
```

In the three statements shown, `PI` has been declared a constant since, unless there is a change in the physical laws of the universe, it will always be this value, `VATPercentRate` is a constant because at the time of writing (and for a long period up till now), Value Added Tax in the UK has been set at 17.5%, and `DatabaseName` is a constant because we could be using this file name throughout an application program we are developing.

However, although we will never change the value of PI, we might wish to update our application by altering the `VATPrecentRate` if this is changed in a future budget, and we might decide to use another name for our database file in the final release version of the software. Using constants in these situation means that it will be much easier to find the single declaration in a program and change the value there, than it would be to have to track down and change every instance of the number or text it represents throughout a program.

3.2.3 Identifiers and Literal Values

Note that when we refer to a string variable in program code, its name is used directly, as with any other type of variable. However, when we refer to actual text in code, we must enclose it in double quotes ("). If we did not do this, Visual Basic would find it impossible to differentiate between an identifier for a variable and a string. For example, the statements:

```
Name = Fred
```

and

```
Name = "Fred"
```

differ in that the first assigns the contents of a variable `Fred` to another variable, `Name`, while the second assigns the text 'Fred' to the variable `Name`. We don't have this type of problem when dealing with other data types because numbers, dates and values like `True` and `False` cannot be used as identifiers in program code – a rule defined in the Visual Basic language (and almost every other programming language as well). Microsoft has defined a number of rules you must follow when declaring a name for a variable (or anything else that can be named in a program). Every declared element has a name, also called an *identifier*, which is what the code uses to refer to it. An element name:

- must not be an existing Visual Basic keyword (normally called *reserved keywords*);
- must begin with an alphabetic character or an underscore (_);
- must contain only alphabetic characters, decimal digits, and underscores;
- must contain at least one alphabetic character or decimal digit it if begins with an underscore;
- must not be more than 16 383 characters long.

Some examples of suitable identifiers in programs are:

```
CustomerName
_date
A24
Data_Connection_String
```

While the following are invalid:

```
Date                 (this is a reserved keyword)
24A                  (begins with a digit)
Database'Location    (contains a punctuation symbol)
_                    (underscore only - not allowed)
```

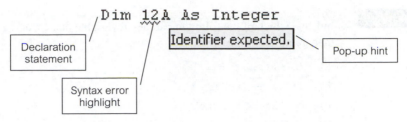

Figure 3.2 How Visual Basic indicates a syntax error (here, an invalid variable name)

Fortunately, Visual Basic will let you know if a name you apply to something does not meet these rules, as shown in Figure 3.2.

In a Code window, once a line of code is completed (by pressing **Enter**), Visual Basic will mark any words or parts of the line that constitute an error by underlining with a blue wavy line (Figure 3.2). If you float the mouse cursor (an I-bar) over the marked text, a pop-up hint will be displayed to describe the problem. This will happen for any type of violation of the rules of the Visual Basic language (syntax errors).

Since variables are used for storing values, and we must sometimes make direct assignments of values to variables in code, we will often have to enter these values directly in code. VB requires us to ensure that these values are easy to tell from the other bits of text in program code – identifiers, and other parts of statements. Due to the rules for identifiers listed above, this turns out to be quite simple, as shown in Table 3.2.

Table 3.2 Rules for literal values in code

Type	Rule	Example
Numeric (Byte, Short, Integer, Long, Single, Double)	Simply state the value directly	12.6 100000 −25
Char	State the value in double quotes	"X" "," (comma)
String	State the value in double quotes	"What, me worry?" "ABCDEFGHIJ"
Date	Enclose in quotes to spell out the date as a string (year part must have all 4 digits). If omitted, time part will be "00:00:00"	"01/01/2003" "25/12/2003 12:30:00"

Exercise 3.3

Indicate which of the following are legal variable names, and state why the ones that are not are illegal:

a) `My Date Of Birth`

b) `My-Date-Of-Birth`

c) `My_Date_Of_Birth`

d) `2ndAttempt`

e) `AttemptNo.2`

f) `Attempt2`

g) `_SystemDirectory`

h) `__SystemFolder`

i) `.NET_Programmer_ID`

j) `#_of_Attempts`

3.2.4 Initializing Variables

A variable without a value is useless. Whenever you declare a simple variable in a VB program, it will have a null value assigned to it. For the simple types such as numbers, dates, etc., this will be the equivalent of a zero value; number variables start with a value of 0 (or 0.0 for one of the types that supports fractional values), strings with a value of "" two double quotes side-by-side signifies the *empty string*, or no text), dates with a value of "01/01/0001 00:00:00" (a date value is entered in a program by enclosing it in double quotes, like a string, and incorporates a time part) and Booleans with a value of `False`. More complex variable types are defined as classes, and for these a null value means 'no object'. We will discuss the ramifications of this later.

These values are assigned automatically by VB (or, more correctly, by the Common Type System) to ensure that a new variable will at least take on some sensible and valid value. However, it is often the case that when we declare a variable, the next thing we will do is assign a specific value to it. Creating a new variable for a specific purpose is therefore a matter of declaring it (which gives it an identifier and assigns a specific type) and then *initializing* it, which assigns a desired initial value. This can be done using two lines of code:

```
Dim myName As String
myName = "Alistair"
```

These individual statements can be one after the other as shown, or a lot of other program statements can come between the first and the second. Sometimes this can lead to unclear programming, where you have to search through the subsequent code to find what value a variable has been initialized to. Visual Basic allows us to perform this compound task in a single line, as follows

```
Dim myName As String = "Alistair"
```

This code does not do anything different from the two line version, but by combining both statements in a single line, it makes it easier to do and therefore less likely that you will omit the initialization step. Also, by not separating the declaration and initialization, it makes it easier to keep track of what you are doing in the program code.

A great many subtle and difficult to find errors in programs have turned out to be caused by creating a variable and not initializing it to a known, safe value. Visual Basic helps to prevent these errors by allowing us to initialize variables before they are used in programs.

Exercise 3.4

What will be the output of the following `Sub Main()` in a console program?

```
Sub Main()
  Dim X As Integer
  Dim Y As Integer = 3
  Dim D As Date
  Dim XMAS As Date
  XMAS = "25/12/2003"
  Console.WriteLine("{0} {1} {2} {3}", X, Y, D, XMAS)
End Sub
```

3.2.5 Variables and Statements

Variables are used to store pieces of data in programs. There are a variety of ways to put the data into them in the first place and to subsequently use these values in calculations of other operations, but all come under the general heading of 'program statements'. A statement is an imperative, instructing the computer to do something, such as work out the result of a calculation, assign a value to a variable or do something with the value stored in a variable, such as display it or store it in a file. Statements are therefore the mechanisms that allow us to manipulate variables.

Simple statements in programs can really only do one of three things:

1. assign a value to a variable;
2. execute a subroutine, which is a separately defined block of statements;
3. control other statements.

There is a fourth type of statement, which executes a special type of subroutine called a function, which calculates some result, and assigns this result to a variable. However, this is really just a combination of 1 and 2 above, and so I won't count it separately.

3.2.6 Assignments and Expressions

You have already met examples of statements that assign a value to a variable, in Listing 3.3. Sometimes the assignment is simple and direct, taking a literal value (like a number) and assigning it directly to a variable:

```
Name = "Fred"
DateOfBirth = "22/10/1974"
ShoeSize = 8
Height = 1.85
```

All of the above are valid assignments of the simplest type. Statements like this are useful in programs, but do not really do much of the work we would expect a computer program to do. We normally expect statements in computer programs to involve calculations, and these again can take the form of assignments:

```
Sum = 11 + 8
Area = Length * Width
Circumference = 2 * PI * Radius
TotalPrice = Price + Price * VAT_Rate/100
FullName = Name & " Bloggs"
```

In all of the above, the stuff on the right of the '=' sign is evaluated and the result assigned to the variable on the left. Note that such assignment can involve variables, literal values and a mixture of both. One interesting example is the last of the above group, where a new string value is calculated by concatenating (adding together) two other strings. Calculations do not always need to involve numbers.

Using some of the built-in functions in Visual Basic, we can also calculate values to store in variables:

```
Square_Size = Sqr(Square_Area)
Age = DateDiff(DateInterval.Year, DateOfBirth, Today)
UpperCaseName = UCase(FullName)
```

The functions shown above are `Sqr()`, which calculates a square root, `DateDiff()`, which calculates the time difference between two dates, and `UCase()` which converts a string into upper case text. The keyword `Today` is also a function call, but in this case does not need any value to work on; it simply calculates today's date.

All of the above examples are examples of assignments to variables. A common feature is that in every case, the value of an *expression* is assigned to a variable. An expression is a combination of literal values, variables and *operators* that can be calculated to produce a single value. The simplest form of an expression is a literal value, such as a number, date or string. More complex expressions involve calculations using arithmetic or some other type of operation (like string concatenation) or calls to functions, or mixtures of both.

3.3 Expressions and Operators

An expression can always be used in the same place as a single value in a statement. For example, the expression 4 + 3 can be used anywhere we could use the individual number 7 in a program. Since either of the numbers in that expression could also be replaced by an expression we can use an expression of any complexity in any place in a program where a value would do. For example 4 + 3 is the same as (2 * 2) + 3 and both are the same as Sqr(16) + 3. In fact, a single value is simply another form of expression.

The notion of an expression in a program is therefore a very powerful thing, since an expression can be of any complexity, and yet can always be used in any situation where we might make use of a value. For example, consider the operation of displaying a single value on the screen of a console program. Looking back to any of the code examples we've seen so far in this chapter, you will see that the general form for displaying a value is:

```
Console.WriteLine("Here comes some value: {0}", value)
```

or

```
Console.WriteLine("Here comes some value: {0}", 42)
```

In the first case, we're displaying the current contents of a variable, `value`. In the second we're displaying a literal value. However, either of these could be replaced by an expression of arbitrary complexity:

```
Console.WriteLine("Here comes some value: {0}", _
            value1 * value2 + value3 / value4)
```

(Note, the sequence of a space followed by a _ at the end of a line allows us to run over on to the next line in a VB program). Replace any of `value1`, `value2`, `value3` or `value4` by another expression and the whole thing is still an expression. We can also do the same in any other place we would normally use a value. For example:

```
y = Sqr(a + b + c)
```

Here the expression `a + b + c` is evaluated as a single value, that is then passed to the built-in Sqr() function. We could even do:

```
y = Sqr(Sqr(256))
```

since the expression `Sqr(256)` evaluates as a single number (16) which can be passed to the Sqr() function. Overall, that statement has exactly the same result as:

```
y = 4
```

Expressions always involve values, either literal ones or values stored in variables. However, they also, except in the case of the simplest expressions (a single value), involve either functions or operators. Visual Basic contains a large number of operators for use in a wide range of situations. Table 3.3 shows most of the available operators.

Table 3.3 Standard operators in Visual Basic

Operator	Meaning	Example	
Arithmetic operators (simple calculations)			
+, −, *, /	Standard arithmetic symbols	i.e. Plus, Minus, Times, Divide	
		e.g. x = (y * z) / 4 (Note that *, not x, is used for multiplication)	
\	Integer division	11 \ 3	Division with integer result (i.e. the fractional part of the result is discarded – here result is 3)
Mod	Modulus – remainder after division	11 mod 3	Result is remainder of 11\3, or 2
^	Exponentiation (power)	X ^ 3	Result is X raised to the power 3
Assignment operators (all assign a new value to the variable on the left)			
=	Simple assignment	X = 3	Assign a new value to variable X
+=	Increment	X += 3	Increases the value of the variable X by the 3
−=	Decrement	X −=3	Decreases the value of the variable X by the 3
*=	Multiply and assign	X *= 3	Multiply the value of the variable X by 3 and assign the result to X
/=	Divide and assign	X /= 3	Divide the value of the variable X by 3 and assign the result to X
\=	Integer divide and assign	X \= 3	Divide the value of the variable X by 3 and assign the integer part of the result to X
^=	Raise to power	X ^= 3	Raise X to the power 3 and assign the result to X
&=	Concatenate	X &= 'abc'	Attach the string 'abc' to the end of the string variable X
Comparison operators (all give a Boolean result)			
<	Less than	X < Y	True if X is less than Y
>	Greater than	X > Y	True if X is bigger than Y
=	Equal to	X = Y	True if X and Y are equal – note, this is distinguished from the assignment = by context
<=	Less or equal	X <= Y	True if X is not bigger than Y
>=	Greater or equal	X >= Y	True if X is not less than Y
Logical operators (used to combine simple Boolean expressions)			
And	Logical And	X And Y	True if both X and Y are True
Or	Logical Or	X Or Y	True if either X or Y is True
Not	Logical inversion	Not X	True if X is False, False if X is true
Xor	Exclusive or	X Xor Y	True if X is True and Y is False or if X is False and Y is True – False otherwise
Concatenation (joining strings)			
&	Concatenation	S1 & X	Joins any two values or expressions to form a String
+	Addition / concatenation	X + Y	Adds two numbers
		S1 + S2	Joins two strings

In addition to these operators, various rules apply in Visual Basic regarding how the operators are applied and the results achieved. In general, an operator is used to provide a specific type of result (e.g. integer, string) and therefore we need to be careful what we do with the result. For example, while the & operator and the + operator can both be used to join strings, sometimes they can produce quite different results when not used with care (Listing 3.4).

```
Sub Main()
    Dim x As Single, y As Single
    x = 3
    y = 6
    Console.WriteLine("x + y gives {0}", x + y)
    Console.WriteLine("x & y gives {0}", x & y)
End Sub
```

Listing 3.4: The + and & operators

The output from the above `WriteLine()` statements will be different, because in the first the + operator will add the two values to give 9, and in the second the & operator will join the 3 to the 6 to give '36'. Obviously, this can matter a lot in a program, so it is necessary to be careful about the operators you make use of in statements. A generally good rule to work by is that you should only ever use an operator that is intended for the variable types it operates on. In the above example, using the '&' operator with the two numeric variables directly is considered bad practice. As we shall see later, Visual Basic provides us with safe ways around this problem.

Exercises 3.5

1. For each of the following, state the value that will be assigned to the variable and the most likely type of the variable where this is not already stated.

   a) `X = 22/11`, where X is an Integer.

   b) `Y = 10/4`, where Y is a Single.

   c) `N = DateDiff(DateInterval.Day, CDate("1/12/2002"), CDate("4/12/2002"))`.

   d) `C = UCase("x")`.

   e) `D = LCase("a")`.

   f) `B = 4 = (2 + 2)`.

   g) `B = 4 = (2 + 3)`.

   h) `Msg = "Welcome " & Name`, where Name is a String that contains your first name.

   i) `Age += 1`, where age originally contains the value 20.

   j) `P += Q`, where P contains 5 and Q contains 3.

   k) `Price *= Markup`, where Price is 10.00, and Markup is 1.10.

   l) `Message &= Name`, where Message is "Hello ", and Name is "Linda".

m) `ChildTicket = Not(Age >= 21)`, where Age is 25.

n) `CanDrive = (Age >= 17) And HasLicence And (Not HasConviction)`, where Age is 28, HasLicence is True and HasConvictions is True.

2. Write simple expressions that will do the following.

a) Assign the number of hours in N full days to the variable `H`.

b) Assign the remainder of the division A/B to the variable `C`.

c) Assign the price including Tax to the variable `Price` when Tax is 15% and `Price` currently contains the price before tax.

d) Square the value in variable `X`, assigning the result to X.

e) Assign `True` to `AdultTicket` if `Age` is 21 or over, `False` otherwise.

f) Reduce the value in `MortgageRemaining` by the amount in `PaymentsMade`.

g) Assign the value of the circumference of a circle to `C`, given its radius is R.

h) Assign the average of N1, N2 and N3 to the variable `N`.

i) Assign the length of the hypotenuse of a right-angled triangle to H, where the other two sides are of length X and Y. The function Sqrt( ) returns the square root.

3.4 Statements and Blocks

In most situations, it will not be possible to do the entire work of a program in a single statement, so we will need to combine multiple statements to get the desired effect. The rule for combining simple statements to get them to collaborate on a single task is refreshingly simple: a simple sequence of statements will be executed in the order in which they appear in the program listing. Note that I've said this is the rule for a simple sequence of statements; there are ways of overriding this rule, but we'll come to them later.

So how would we organize a sequence of statements so that they work coherently together? The key to this is the use of variables to store the *state* of a task from one statement to the next. By the state of a task, we normally mean the current contents of all the relevant variables in combination, and this is important because the next state that the task goes into (after the next statement in a sequence is executed) is a combination of the current state and the effects on it of next statement in the sequence that will be executed.

An example might help here. Consider the task of calculating the price of an item inclusive of tax, when you know the pre-tax price and the tax rate. We would use a sequence of statements to perform this task. These could be executed in the following sequence.

1. Ask the user to enter the price of the item: store the result in a variable – Price.

2. Ask the user to enter the tax rate, say as a percentage: store the result in a variable – Tax.

3. Calculate the total price by applying the expression Price * Tax / 100 + Price: store the result in a variable – TotalPrice.

4. Display the value of TotalPrice.

Now if you examine the sequence closely, you should see that the order in which some of these statements are executed does not matter too much; for example statements 1 and 2, but for others, the sequence is crucial. For example, step 4 will not give the correct answer unless it is the last in the sequence, and it is important that both steps 1 and 2 are executed before step 3 is.

Once we have a group of steps organized into the correct sequence, we would want to define the whole group as an operation within a program, or possibly the whole program. Most programming languages give us the idea of a *block* of statements; a sequence that is organized to operate as a single, indivisible unit. In VB, we have many ways in which we can define a block of statements, but possibly the most fundamental of these is the *subroutine*, or *sub*. A subroutine is simply a block of statements bracketed by the keywords Sub and End Sub and given an identifier, so that we can refer to it in much the same way we can refer to a variable. You have already met subroutines in the preceding examples; so far, all of them have been given the identifier Main. Sub Main takes on the special role of defining the starting point of a Visual Basic console program (although as we'll see later, a VB Windows program normally does not need one).

Let's look at our add-tax task converted into a Visual Basic program (Listing 3.5).

```
Module AddTax

    Sub Main()
        Dim Price As Decimal
        Dim Tax As Single
        Dim TotalPrice As Decimal
        Console.WriteLine("Add Tax to Price")
        Console.Write("Enter item price: ")
        Price = Console.ReadLine()
        Console.Write("Enter tax rate (%): ")
        Tax = Console.ReadLine()
        TotalPrice = Price + Price * Tax / 100
        Console.WriteLine("Price including tax is: {0}", _
                        TotalPrice)
    End Sub

End Module
```

Listing 3.5: A block of statements as a whole program

All of the statements between the keywords Sub and End Sub form a block of code that is also a subroutine. Because this particular subroutine can also be recognized by Visual Basic as the entry point of the program (by its name, Sub Main), it takes on the significance of being the main or executive block of the program (also, in this case, the only one).

Most programs will contain more than a single subroutine – sometimes many. This gives us the power to divide up the overall work of a program into a number of sub-tasks which can be executed in concert. By breaking up the work of a program into separate, smaller tasks, we make the program much easier to design, create and maintain, in much the same way that any large and complex task can be divided into sub-tasks. For example, if you were to build a house, you would normally consider the laying of the foundations as one task, laying the bricks as another, adding a roof as another, doing electrical wiring, plumbing as others, etc. Take any of these tasks and they can again be broken up into a number of sub-tasks. Blocks in programs, particularly named blocks such as subroutines, allow us to treat the overall work of a program as separate tasks and solve each separately.

We can sum up the significance of variables, statements and blocks of statements as follows.

- Variables store items of data that are significant to the job that a program does.
- Statements can operate on variables, performing calculations with their values and assigning the result of these to other variables.
- Blocks of statements can define operations which can manipulate the values in variables in a coherent, scripted way. These can do the work of whole programs, or parts of a program.

We will look into the various ways of creating and organizing blocks of statements in the next chapter.

Exercise 3.6

Create a sequence of statements for each of the following situations.

a) Collect values from the console (ReadLine()) into three variables, a, b and c, and then calculate and display (WriteLine()) their average.

b) Ask the user to enter their name, address and telephone number (use ReadLine() and assign to the variables name, addr and tel), and then display these values in reverse order (use WriteLine()).

c) Calculate and display the volume of a box, using variables Length, Width and Height for the dimensions of the box. Ask the user to enter suitable values using a combination of Write() and ReadLine().

3.5 Structured Variables

All the variable types mentioned so far fall into the category of simple data types. All simple data variables can store a single piece of data; one number, a piece of text, date or time. In some cases, it may appear as if a simple variable was storing more than one piece of data (for example, a Date variable stores all the parts of a date and time – Year, Month, Day, Hour, Minute and Second); however, this illusion is simply a facet of the efficient way that a computer can work with information (a date is a single point in time and can be stored as such by storing the length of a time interval from some reference point in time – the number of seconds that have elapsed since the start of this century, for example). When we need to store more than one piece of data, we have a choice; we can either use more than one variable as was done in Listing 3.2 to store the length and width of a single rectangle in two separate variables, or we can resort to a more complex variable type. The first of these options was once the only one available to programmers, but as programming languages have become more capable, it is now more normal to deal with multiple pieces of data which relate to a single thing (such as a rectangle) in a single variable.

Visual Basic and the underlying runtime system give us several ways of organizing groups of variables into coherent assemblies of data. One option provided by the CLR is that we can create new variable types that can store more than a single value. For example, we can define a new `Rectangle` type that is capable of storing both the `Length` and the `Width` of a rectangle in a single variable. Using this, the code in Listing 3.2 can be rewritten to deal directly with rectangles:

```
Structure Rectangle
      Dim Length As Single
      Dim Width As Single
End Structure
```

In VB .NET, a `Structure` is a definition of a new type of variable that can contain any number of component variables. Once it has been defined, variables of the new type can be declared and used in (almost) the same way as any of the existing types provided by the Common Type System. Of course we need some way of indicating which component variable we want to refer to when we make assignments from simple variables or values, or when we wish to retrieve any of the component values individually. VB provides a simple mechanism using the '.' symbol (dot operator) for this purpose. We can now use this new data type to replace the two separate length and width variables in the earlier program.

```
Module Module1

    Structure Rectangle
        Dim Length As Single
        Dim Width As Single
    End Structure

    Sub Main()
        Dim myRectangle As Rectangle, area As Single
        myRectangle.Length = 12.5
        myRectangle.Width = 8.75
        area = myRectangle.Length * myRectangle.Width
        Console.WriteLine("Area is {0}", area)
    End Sub

End Module
```

Listing 3.6: Making use of the `Rectangle` type

Listing 3.6 shows how the new type would be deployed in a program. The `Structure` definition that appears first defines the component parts of a `Rectangle` – each `Rectangle` has a `Length` and `Width` part. Within `Main`, the variable `myRectangle` is of the new type. Once it has been declared, we can assign values to its component variables (`myRectangle.Length` and `myRectangle.Width`) and later retrieve these values for use in calculations. We could easily have dimensioned and used several rectangles in this program, since the structure `Rectangle` is defined as a new *type* of variable.

Creating new types of variable like this brings several advantages.

- Using structures like this helps us to keep together related items of data, so we can declare a whole `Rectangle` variable in a single statement instead of a number of individual ones.

- We can declare as many of the type as we need in a program (in the same way that we can declare many variables of type `Single`) and assign composite values from one to the other in a single statement. For example, given two `Rectangle` structure variables `R1` and `R2`, we can copy the values from one to the other with the single statement `R2 = R1`.

- It can be clearer to anyone reading the program code what the intentions of the programmer are since the name given to a structure is often self-explanatory. For example, one variable of type `Rectangle` has a more obvious purpose than two individuals of type `Single`.

- While we can't often expect a general purpose programming language to provide us with exactly the range of data types we need to do what we want to in every program, we can easily build task-specific data types, such as rectangles, into our programs.

There is one aspect where it is necessary to exercise care when creating new structured variable types: Visual Basic does not allow us to initialize the elements of a structure when it is declared, so for example, you could not do this:

```
Dim rect As Rectangle = (3, 4) ' This is an error.
```

In this case, the attempt to initialize the `Length` and `Width` parts of a `Rectangle` simply causes the compiler to reject the program.

Exercises 3.7

1. It is possible to create a structure that combines variables of different types (e.g. numbers and dates, strings, etc.). Create structures that could be used to represent the following.

   a) a `Person`, with `Name`, `Address`, `DateOfBirth` and `NumberOfChildren`;

   b) a `Car`, with `EngineSize`, `NumberOfDoors`, `RegistrationDate` and `LicenceNumber`;

c) a CD recording, with Title, Artist, DistributionLabel, IssueYear and NumberOfTracks;

d) a MapReference, with figures for Longitude and Latitude;

e) a window on a PC screen, with Top, Left, Width and Height settings.

2. For each of the above, write sample statements to declare and then assign values to a variable of the appropriate type.

3.6 Enumerations

Structures are new types that we can define as needed in programs: they give us the power to create variables that can contain several pieces of related information. Another way we can define our own variable types is to create variables that have a restricted range of values. *Enumerations* are defined as lists of names, each of which becomes a pseudonym for an integer value. The keyword Enum is used to create one and Listing 3.7 is an example.

```
Enum MusicStyles
     Classical
     Swing
     Jazz
     Pop
     Rock
     Techno
End Enum
```

Listing 3.7: An enumeration (Enum)

With this enumeration, we can now create variables that will be restricted to taking on one of these values and no other. Once an enumeration is defined, Visual Studio will assist you to assign a value to a variable of that type, as shown in Figure 3.3.

Each entry in the MusicStyles list is represented by an integer number – starting by default from 0. This makes enumerations very efficient to work with, since integer numbers are the root of all data in computer programs. In many enumerations, we do not really care what value is assigned to represent a particular entry in an enumeration list. However, an uninitialized enumeration variable will always take on the first value in the range (which will be the zero value).

Enumerations can also be more explicitly defined so that specific entries in the list take on specific integer values – this will affect the default value assigned to an un-initialized variable. We can use this to make the values assigned to members of an enumeration list relate to the names used, as shown, for example, in Listing 3.8.

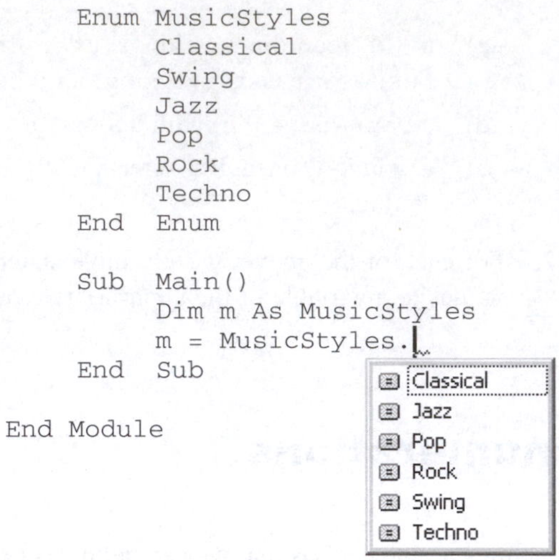

```
                              Enum MusicStyles
                                 Classical
                                 Swing
                                 Jazz
                                 Pop
                                 Rock
                                 Techno
                              End  Enum

                              Sub  Main()
                                 Dim m As MusicStyles
                                 m = MusicStyles.
                              End  Sub

                    End Module
```

⊞	Classical
⊞	Jazz
⊞	Pop
⊞	Rock
⊞	Swing
⊞	Techno

Figure 3.3 Using the `MusicStyles` enumeration

```
  Enum SideCount
       Triangle = 3
       Rectangle = 4
       Pentagon = 5
       Hexagon = 6
       Octagon = 8
  End Enum
```

Listing 3.8: An enumeration with specific values assigned

The `SideCount` enumeration gives us a list of the names of some 2-D figures, but
also sets specific integer values to each member of the enumeration. This gives us
the normal advantage of an enumeration: we have defined a fixed range of 2-D figure
values that can be applied to a variable by name. However, it also ensures that each
of the named values is the actual number of sides that such a figure will have. Note
that it is perfectly legal to have gaps in the list of values (there is no heptagon
{7-sided figure} in the list). We can use this in program code, since the `CInt()`
function (**C**onvert to **Int**eger) lets us access the actual value, as follows:

```
  Dim c As SideCount
  c = SideCount.Pentagon
  Console.WriteLine("Number of sides in a {0} is {1}", _
                                        c, CInt(c))
```

Executing the above code would result in Figure 3.4.

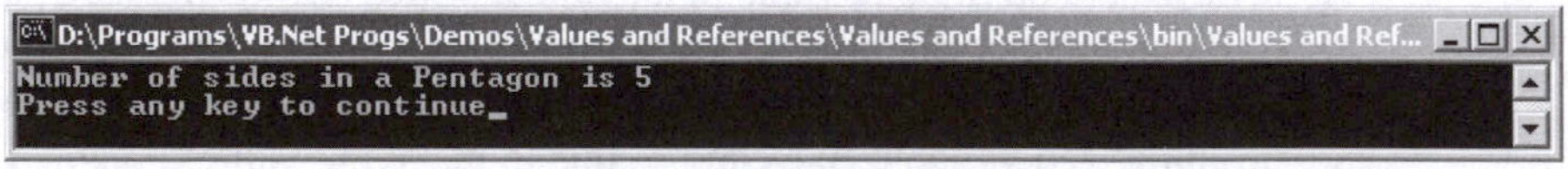

```
D:\Programs\VB.Net Progs\Demos\Values and References\Values and References\bin\Values and Ref... _ ☐ ×
Number of sides in a Pentagon is 5
Press any key to continue_
```

Figure 3.4 The `SideCount` enumeration in use

3.6.1 Advantages of Enumerations

Enumerations are a very useful feature of Visual Basic for a number of reasons.

- They allow us to define variable types with restricted ranges of values that can be assigned to them – it is not possible to assign any value other than the named range. This reduces the possibility of errors in programs dramatically.

- They give us easily memorable names to use in programs, instead of 'magic numbers'. This makes program code more readable.

- The pop-up list provided by Visual Studio when assigning a value to an enumeration variable makes writing code that uses enumerations much easier, since it is not necessary to look up other reference material to discover the legal values that a variable can take on.

- We can easily control the underlying values assigned to the members of an enumeration, and these can be accessed in code easily. The `CInt()` function will always return the underlying value of a member, although the enumeration variable can be used directly in arithmetic expressions.

These advantages make the use of enumerations in programs very attractive. There are many different ways they can be applied. Microsoft makes good use of enumerations when defining the values that can be used in calls to built-in functions. This makes it easier to write calls to these functions without having to refer to manuals or on-line help.

Exercises 3.8

1. Define an enumeration called `Months`, that assigns names to month numbers. Define it so that January is month number 1 and December is month number 12.

2. A motor manufacturer's range includes `TwoDoor`, `ThreeDoor`, `FourDoor` and `FiveDoor` models. Define a suitable enumeration for use in their ordering software.

Review Questions

1. The range of built-in data types and classes in .NET programs is defined in:

    a) the Common Language Runtime

    b) MSIL

    c) the Common Type System

    d) Visual Basic

2. The numeric data type that stores numbers to the highest available precision is:

   a) `Integer`

   b) `Double`

   c) `Decimal`

   d) `Long`

3. An identifier is:

   a) the name given to a variable, structure, enumeration or code block;

   b) line of program code that Identifies some result;

   c) a value that uniquely identifies an operation to be performed;

   d) a tool in Visual Studio for displaying the names of features.

4. Distinguish between a structure and an enumeration.

5. 'An expression can be part of a statement' or 'A statement can be part of an expression'. Which is correct?

6. A structure, `WageRecord`, is defined as shown below:

```
Structure WageRecord
    Dim NormalHoursWorked As Integer
    Dim PayRate As Decimal
    Dim OverTimeHours As Integer
    Dim OverTimeRate As Decimal
    Dim Expenses As Decimal
End Structure
```

   A workers wage is calculated by multiplying `NormalHoursWorked` by `PayRate`, adding the multiplication of `OverTimeHours` by `OverTimeRate`, and adding `Expenses`. Given that a variable of type `WageRecord` had been declared with the identifier `Pay` and has had values assigned to it, write one or more statements that will assign the resulting pay to a variable `Wage`. What would be the most suitable type for this variable?

7. Define an enumeration for the units `Inch`, `Foot` and `Yard` so that the size of each (in inches) is also specified as the enumeration value (12 inches in a foot, 36 inches in a yard).

Practical Activities

This chapter examined the way that variables are defined and used in programs, how statements are formed and how we can create new variable types by aggregating existing types. In this practical session, you will use Visual Basic to create a simple but useful program using variables, sequences of statements and a specially defined structure.

The Decorator's Calculator

The program will help to calculate the amount of materials required to decorate some of a house. It has several limitations that you should be aware of; it uses the assumption that all the ceilings will be painted in one colour with one type of paint, and it repeats this assumption for all of the walls in the house. All of the floors will be covered in a single size of tile. To make the program more accurate for a real house, we should allow for different paints for each room, and so ceilings and walls should be calculated for each room separately. We should also allow for different flooring materials in each room. As an exercise you could alter the program so that it works for your own house.

Activity 1: Define the Room structure

All of the calculations in the program are based on a data structure called Room. This defines a data type with three simple values, these being the Length, Width and Height of a rectangular room. Create a new console project in Visual Studio, and add the Room structure to the project by entering code as shown in Listing A3.1.

```
Module Chapter3
    Structure Room
        Dim Length As Single
        Dim Width As Single
        Dim Height As Single
    End Structure
    Sub Main()
    End Sub
End Module
```

Listing A3.1: A new project with a structure defined

Activity 2: Defining Materials

The program will calculate the quantity of paint required for walls and ceilings, and the number of tiles needed to cover the floors. To perform these calculations, we'll need to indicate the area we can expect a litre of paint to cover, and the area of a single tile.

Amend the code by adding the following declarations (Listing A3.2) to Sub Main():

```
Sub Main()
    'Start by defining the coverage of paint...
    Const PaintCoverage As Single = 12.5  ' Sq. Metres/l
    '...and the size of a floor tile...
    Const TileSize As Single = 0.24     ' Sq. Metres
End Sub
```

Listing A3.2: Defining constants to specify materials

Activity 3: Declaring rooms

With an appropriate data type to represent the various sizes of a room, we can declare variables for the rooms of a house we want to decorate. We'll assume we're decorating one bedroom and the living room. We will also need variables to store the quantities calculated – room areas and materials. Amend the code in Sub Main() as shown in Listing A3.3.

```vb
Sub Main()
    ' Start by defining the coverage of paint...
    Const PaintCoverage As Single = 12.5  ' Sq. Metres/l
    '. . . and the size of a floor tile...
    Const TileSize As Single = 0.24      ' Sq. Metres
    ' Now a variable for each room...
    Dim LivingRoom As Room
    Dim Bedroom As Room
    ' Area of ceilings and paint required...
    Dim CeilingArea As Single = 0
    Dim CeilingPaint As Single = 0
    ' Area of walls and paint required...
    Dim WallArea As Single = 0
    Dim WallPaint As Single = 0
    ' Area of floor and number of flooring tiles required
    '(a whole number - no fractions of tiles)...
    Dim FloorArea As Single = 0
    Dim FlooringTiles As Integer = 0
End Sub
```

Listing A3.3: Defining useful variables

Activity 4: Collecting data

We can now start the process of doing the calculation. The general process is Input→Calculate→Output, so the first stage of the job will be to collect the various room dimensions from the user (see Listing A.3.4).

```vb
Sub Main()
    '
    ' Variable declarations etc.
    '
    Console.WriteLine("Decorator's Calculator")
    Console.WriteLine("======================")
    ' Ask the user to enter dimensions for each room.
    ' Living room first...
    Console.Write("Enter the length of the living room: ")
    LivingRoom.Length = Console.ReadLine()
    Console.Write("Enter the width of the living room: ")
    LivingRoom.Width = Console.ReadLine()
    Console.Write("Enter the height of the living room: ")
    LivingRoom.Height = Console.ReadLine()
    ' Now bedroom...
```

```
        Console.Write("Enter the length of the bedroom: ")
        Bedroom.Length = Console.ReadLine()
        Console.Write("Enter the width of the bedroom: ")
        Bedroom.Width = Console.ReadLine()
        Console.Write("Enter the height of the bedroom: ")
        Bedroom.Height = Console.ReadLine()
    End Sub
```

Listing A3.4: Code to collect input data from the user

Activity 5: Doing the calculations

Calculations for this are simple geometry. The area of a ceiling will be `Length *
Width` of the room, as will the floor area. For the wall areas, the calculation is
`Height * Length` for each long wall, and `Width * Height` for each of the other
two walls. We can simplify this as follows:

```
2 * Height * Length + 2 * Height * Width
= 2 * Height * (Length + Width)
```

To do the overall calculations, simply add the calculated values for each room to
the appropriate variables. The easiest way to do this is to *accumulate* these values
using the += operator. This is shown in Listing A.3.5.

```
Sub Main()
    '
    ' Existing code.
    '
    ' Time to do the calculations.
    ' Ceiling sizes...
    CeilingArea = LivingRoom.Length * LivingRoom.Width
    CeilingArea += Kitchen.Length * Kitchen.Width
    CeilingArea += Bedroom.Length * Bedroom.Width
    CeilingArea += Bathroom.Length * Bathroom.Width
    ' Ceiling paint...
    CeilingPaint = CeilingArea / PaintCoverage
    ' Wall sizes...
    WallArea = 2 * LivingRoom.Height * _
                   (LivingRoom.Length + LivingRoom.Width)
    WallArea += 2 * Bedroom.Height * _
                   (Bedroom.Length + Bedroom.Width)
    ' Wall paint...
    WallPaint = WallArea / PaintCoverage
    ' Floor sizes (easy - same as ceiling)...
    FloorArea = CeilingArea
    FlooringTiles = Int(FloorArea / TileSize) + 1 'Round up.
End Sub
```

Listing A3.5: Doing the calculations

Activity 6: Reporting back the results

The final step is to inform the user of the results of the calculations (Listing A3.6).

```
Sub Main()
    '
    ' Existing code.
    '
    ' Now report this back to the user...
    Console.WriteLine("Total materials required")
    Console.WriteLine("Ceiling paint: {0} litres.",
    CeilingPaint)
    Console.WriteLine("Wall paint: {0} litres.", WallPaint)
    Console.WriteLine("Floor tiles: {0} tiles.",
    FlooringTiles)
End Sub
```

Listing A3.6: Displaying results

Features worth remembering

In this program we have used a number of simple techniques you might use in any program. Several of them are useful enough that you might consider using them in other programs.

■ When asking the user to enter a value at the keyboard, the *prompt* message should use `Console.Write()` rather than `Console.WriteLine()`, since the user's input will then immediately follow the prompt on the screen, rather than appearing on the next line.

■ We can *accumulate* a value over several stages using the += operator. Recall that this adds the value of the expression on the right to the variable on the left, and so by using it a number of times, the variable on the left accumulates a running total.

■ Assigning a number with a fractional part to an integer variable will effectively round the value to the nearest integer, e.g. the assignment:

```
FlooringTiles = FloorArea / TileSize
```

If the calculation resulted in 22.9 tiles, the value assigned to `FlooringTiles` would be 23. However, if the result was 22.1 tiles, the value assigned would be 22. This would leave a 0.1 tile hole in our flooring. We therefore need to make sure to round any fractional result UP to the next biggest integer. The expression:

```
FlooringTiles = Int(FloorArea / TileSize) + 1
```

does this by using the `Int()` function, which always rounds a fractional number DOWN to the next lowest integer, and adding 1. In the case where the division produces an exact integer result, we would of course end up buying one tile too many (although in a real situation we would always need to buy extra tiles anyway to make up for odd bits cut off tiles to fit around pipes, etc.).

Suggested Additional Activity

Using the techniques in this activity, you could create programs that did similar types of calculations for seeding a new lawn, upholstering furniture or building a shed or other structure. In each case some of the details may differ, but the overall approach would be the same.

Solutions to Exercises

Exercise 3.1

```
Module Module1
    Sub Main()
        Dim area, radius As Single
        radius = 8.75
        area = 3.14 * radius * radius
        Console.WriteLine("Area is {0}", area)
    End Sub
End Module
```

Exercise 3.2

a) `Dim ProgLang As String = "Visual Basic .NET"`

b) `Dim Xmas As Date = "25/12/03"`

c) `Dim Attendance As Short`   `'n.b. could be Integer`

d) `Dim Attendance As Byte`   `'n.b. could be`
                                   `Short/Integer`

e) `Dim Fuel As Single`   `'n.b. could be Double`

f) `Dim Category As Char`

g) `Dim EarthToMoonMiles As Integer`

h) `Dim OrderTime As Date`   `'Stores Date and Time`

Exercise 3.3

a) Illegal (contains spaces)

b) Illegal (contains hyphens, interpreted as minus signs)

c) Legal (underscore is ok)

d) Illegal (can not start with a digit)

e) Illegal (decimal point/full stop not allowed)

f) Legal

g) Legal

h) Legal

i) Illegal (decimal point at start)

j) Illegal (# not allowed)

Exercise 3.4

0 3 01/01/0001 00:00:00 25/12/2003 00:00:00

Exercises 3.5

1.

a) 2

b) 2.5

c) 3 (an `Integer` – the number of days)

d) "X" (`Char` – a single character)

e) "a" (`Char`)

f) `True` (Boolean result of 4 = 2 comparison)

g) `False` (Boolean result of 4 = 5 comparison)

h) "Welcome Alistair"   (a `String`)

i) 21 (an `Integer`)

j) 8 (an `Integer`)

k) 11.00 (a `Single` or `Double`)

l) "Hello Linda"

m) `False` (Boolean result of negating (25 >= 21))

n) `False` (Boolean result of an `And` expression where one of the operands is `False` (`Not HasConviction`))

2.

a) `H = N * 24`

b) `C = A Mod B` (Mod operator gives remainder)

c) `Price = Price + Price * 15 / 100`, or `Price *= 1.15`

d) `X *= X`

e) `AdultTicket = (Age >= 21)`

f) `MortgageRemaining -= PaymentsMade`

g) `C = 2 * 3.14 * R`

h) `N = (N1 + N2 + N3) / 3`

i) `H = Sqrt( X * X + Y * Y )`

Exercise 3.6

a)

```
a = ReadLine()
b = ReadLine()
c = ReadLine()
WriteLine((a + b + c)/3)
```

b)

```
Write("Enter your name: ")
name = ReadLine()
Write("Enter your address: ")
addr = ReadLine()
Write("Enter your telephone number: ")
tel = ReadLine()
WriteLine(tel)
WriteLine(addr)
WriteLine(name)
```

c)

```
Write("Enter the length of the box")
Length = ReadLine()
Write("Enter the width of the box")
Width = ReadLine()
Write("Enter the height of the box")
Height = ReadLine()
Volume = Length * Width * Height
WriteLine("Volume is {0}", Volume)
```

Exercises 3.7

1.

a)

```
Structure Person
    Name As String
    Address As String
    DateOfBirth As Date
    NumberOfChildren As Byte 'Could be Short or Integer
End Structure
```

b)

```
Structure Car
    EngineSize As Short        'Allows up to 32Litres
    NumberOfDoors As Byte
    RegistrationDate As Date
    LicenceNumber As String  'Contains letters
End Structure
```

c)

```
Structure CD
    Title As String
    Artist As String
    DistributionLabel As String
    IssueYear As Short
    NumberOfTracks As Short
End Structure
```

d)

```
Structure MapReference
    Longitude As String 'Needed for notation e.g. 10°15'W
    Latitude As String 'Needed for notation e.g. 51°28'N
End Structure
```

e)

```
Structure WindowSettings
    Left As Short
    Top As Short
    Width As Short
    Height As Short
End Structure
```

2.

```
Dim P As Person = ("Fred Bloggs", "1 High St.", _
                  "12/07/1970", 4)
Dim C As Car = (1600, 4, "11/02/2002", "SB51 GGX")
Dim Album As CD = ("The Old Kit Bag", "Richard
                  Thompson", _
                  "Cooking Vinyl", 2003)
Dim Greenwich As MapReference = ("0°0'W", "51°28'N")
Dim WinPos As WindowSettings = (200, 50, 400, 250)
```

Exercises 3.8

1.

```
Enum Months
    January = 1
    February
    March
    April
    May
    June
    July
    August
    September
    October
    November
    December
End Enum
```

2.

```
Enum BodyStyle
    TwoDoor = 2
    ThreeDoor = 3
    FourDoor = 4
    FiveDoor = 5
End Enum
```

Answers to Review Questions

1. The range of built-in data types and classes in .NET programs is defined in:
   a) The Common Language Runtime
   b) MSIL
   c) The Common Type System **Correct**
   d) Visual Basic

2. The numeric data type that stores numbers to the highest available precision is:
   a) `Integer`
   b) `Double`
   c) `Decimal` **Correct**
   d) `Long`

3. An identifier is:
   a) The name given to a variable, structure, enumeration or code block **Correct**
   b) Line of program code that Identifies some result
   c) A value that uniquely identifies an operation to be performed
   d) A tool in Visual Studio for displaying the names of features

4. Distinguish between a structure and an enumeration. **A *structure* is a definition of a package of variables as a type. An *enumeration* is a definition of a range of integer values, giving each a name that describes what the integer represents.**

5. 'An expression can be part of a statement' or 'A statement can be part of an expression'. Which is correct? **An *expression* can be part of a *statement*.**

6. A structure, `WageRecord`, is defined as shown below:

```
Structure WageRecord
    Dim NormalHoursWorked As Integer
    Dim PayRate As Decimal
    Dim OverTimeHours As Integer
    Dim OverTimeRate As Decimal
    Dim Expenses As Decimal
End Structure
```

A workers wage is calculated by multiplying `NormalHoursWorked` by `PayRate`, adding the multiplication of `OverTimeHours` by `OverTimeRate`, and adding `Expenses`. Given a variable of type `WageRecord` had been declared with the identifier `Pay` and has had values assigned to it, write one or more statements that will assign the resulting pay to a variable `Wage`. What would be the most suitable type for this variable?

```
Dim Wage As Decimal
    Wage = Pay.NormalHoursWorked * Pay.PayRate + _
    Pay.OverTimeHours * Pay.OverTimeRate + Pay.Expenses
```

7. Define an enumeration for the units `Inch`, `Foot` and `Yard` so that the size of each (in Inches) is also specified as the enumeration value (12 inches in a foot, 36 inches in a yard).

```
Enum ImperialSizes
    Inch = 1
    Foot = 12
    Yard = 36
End Enum
```

CHAPTER 4

Objects in Visual Basic .NET

In this chapter you will learn:

- how to create a new class of objects in a Visual Basic program;
- how objects are used in object-oriented programs;
- how to use value types and reference types, and how to convert one type to the other;
- how to make use of the properties and methods of a variable or object.

4.1 Classes

A class is a design for a specific type of object. So far in this book, the code examples have made use of pre-defined object types (such as integers, strings, etc.) or have defined types that used simple combinations of these (structures). Classes in Visual Basic (and .NET in general) are the underlying mechanism for defining new types of object that can inherit from existing types – every class in .NET inherits from the `Object` class.

```
Module NewClass
    Public Class BankAccount
        Public AccountName As String
        Private Balance As Integer
    End Class

    Sub Main()
        Dim MyObj As BankAccount = New BankAccount()
    End Sub

End Module
```

Listing 4.1: A class definition, and an object declared in `Sub Main()`

We can create a class easily in VB. The odd syntax of the only statement in `Sub Main` in Listing 4.1 indicates one means that you could use to create an object of the class `BankAccount` (or any other class). In this statement, two things are being done.

1. A variable is being dimensioned to 'hold' a member of the class (`Dim..As..`, much as for any type of variable).

2. A new object of the class is being created (`= New ...`), and assigned to the newly dimensioned variable to initialize it.

This statement points out a fundamental difference between simple variables (*value types*) and class objects (*reference types*). There will be more said about the later in the chapter.

The first thing to notice about the class itself is the use of the keywords `Public` and `Private`. These are used to indicate the accessibility, or *scope*, of the class and the definitions within it. A class definition must be placed within some module of VB code (a file with the extension **.vb**). If a class is defined as having `Public` scope, like this one, it is available for use by code in another module, so the other module can declare and use objects of the class. If, however, a class is given `Private` scope, it can only be accessed within the module it is defined in. Only statements in code within the same module would be able to create variables that belong to a `Private` class.

The `Public` keyword applied to the variable `AccountName` within the class has a similar purpose, making this variable accessible to any code that has access to the `BankAccount` class. However, the `Private` variable `Balance` can only be assigned a value or have its value accessed by code statements inside the class definition. These *scope rules* allow us to create classes and exercise complete control over how objects of the class are used by other program statements. We can include `Private` variables to store information that is useful for how the objects of the class work, but have no significance to other code making use of the class. We can also include `Public` variables that will be able to convey useful information to program statements that use the class.

The term *member variable* is used to describe the `Private` and `Public` variables declared within a class, and signifies that each member (or object) of the class will have its own copy of these variables. We access the member variables of a class in the same way that we access the members of a structure – using the dot notation to indicate which of them we wish to access. Of course, the dot notation will only give us access to a member variable if we are allowed this access. Consider the following alteration to `Sub Main()` (Listing 4.2), which adds a couple of statements that make use of the new `BankAccount` object:

```
Sub Main()
    Dim MyAccount As BankAccount = New BankAccount()
    MyAccount.AccountName = "John Smith"
    MyAccount.Balance = 100 'Error; Private member variable.
End Sub
```

Listing 4.2: Using the class (unsuccessfully)

If you attempt to enter the `Sub Main()` shown in the same module as the class definition, two things will indicate that this code is wrong. Firstly, when you enter the '`MyAccount.`' in the last statement, the pop-up list of class members will not

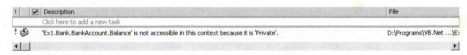

Figure 4.1 The error report from trying to access a private member

offer to provide you with the `Balance` member, indicating that it is not accessible at this point. If you persist, typing the member name manually, Visual Studio will underline the statement with a wavy blue line, indicating that this is a syntax error.

A third indication will appear if you try to run the program – the error report, shown in Figure 4.1.

By making the `Balance` variable in an account object `Private`, we can control access to it, which is of course a useful thing to do with the balance of a bank account, since we can prevent unauthorized access. Of course, if we define a `Private` variable in a class, there must be some way of using it if it is not to be a useless waste of space. For this we need class methods.

Exercise 4.1

Add two new member variables to the `BankAccount` class: one private member variable called PIN (short for Personal Identification Number), and one public member variable called `AccountNumber`.

4.1.1 Class Methods

Classes (and structures) can contain blocks of program statements, organized as subs or functions (of which more later). These are collectively known as the class's methods, and allow us to define how objects of the class can be made to behave in a program.

We can add a method to a class by adding a new `Sub` or `Function`, as shown in Listing 4.3.

```
Public Class BankAccount
    Public AccountName As String
    Private Balance As Decimal
    Public Sub Deposit(ByVal Amount As Decimal)
        Balance += Amount
    End Sub
    Public Function GetBalance() As Decimal
        Return Balance
    End Function
End Class
```

Listing 4.3: Adding methods to the class

We have added two blocks of program statements to the class. The first of these is a sub, `Deposit`, which will add a given amount to the current value in `Balance`. The amount to be added is named in the brackets after the sub's name: this will act as a placeholder for any amount that is given to the `Deposit` method. Any statement calling (executing) the method will have to include an amount, either as a literal value, or in a variable of the correct type (`Decimal`). If a call to the method omits the amount or includes a variable of the wrong type, this will be an error.

The second is a *Function*, `GetBalance`, which will *Return* the current contents of `Balance` (i.e. it will, when called, be equivalent to the actual value specified in the `Return` statement). A function is a special type of method that returns some value to the statement that called it. Since a function is evaluated by Visual Basic as a value of some type (in this case an `Integer`), we could say that a function has the facility of making an object appear as an expression. Any method that is defined as a function within an object can be used in any place a literal value of the same type could be.

Since these methods have access to the `Private` variable `Balance` (it is in their scope), it is ok for them to change and retrieve its value. Since they have been defined with `Public` access, they can be accessed by statements outside the class. The end result is that these methods provide access to information that is `Private` to the class: they are part of the class's *interface* with the outside world.

We can now use the class's methods in any code that works with the class, as shown in Listing 4.4.

```
Sub Main()
    Dim MyAccount As BankAccount = New BankAccount()
    MyAccount.AccountName = "John Smith"
    Console.WriteLine("Account name: {0}", _
                        MyAccount.AccountName)
    Console.WriteLine("Account balance: {0}", _
                        MyAccount.GetBalance)
    MyAccount.Deposit(100)
    Console.WriteLine("Account balance: {0}", _
                        MyAccount.GetBalance)
End Sub
```

Listing 4.4: Using an object's methods

Running the listing will result in the following console output (Figure 4.2).

Since we were only accessing `Public` parts of the `BankAccount` object, the code runs without error, even though this had the effect of accessing `Private` class members via the public methods. This is *encapsulation*, which is the most important feature of object-oriented programming. Encapsulation works as a 'need to know' facility that allows us to maintain control of what is done to the internal state of an

```
D:\Programs\VB.Net Progs\Ch4\Ex1\Ex1\bin\Ex1.exe
Account name: John Smith
Account balance: 0
Account balance: 100
Press any key to continue
```

Figure 4.2 The result of running Listing 4.4

object. Using this principle, an object can have internal workings that are invisible to program code that makes use of the object's capabilities. The power of object-oriented programming lies in our ability to provide controlled access to private data through public methods.

Exercise 4.2

A `Person` class is to have member variables for storing `Name`, `eMail` and `DateOfBirth` of an individual. Write code to define this class, and write a statement in a `Sub Main( )` to create an instance of the class (remember to use `New`). Add a function method that will return the person's age in years (use the `DateDiff` function to return the number of years between `DateOfBirth` and the current date, given by the `Date` function – look these up in Help). Test this method by setting the `DateofBirth` member to some date and using `Console.WriteLine( )` to display the result of the method.

4.1.2 Class Properties

It is easy enough to create methods for a class so that we can access an object of the class's internal variables, for example the `GetBalance()` method of the `BankAccount` example class. The immediate advantage is that it is possible to provide limited access to any internal variables an object has. A member function can be used to return the value of any private member variables in an object. What if we wanted to make it possible to *change* the value in a private member variable? This is an altogether different problem and one that has been tackled in a range of different ways in different object-oriented programming languages. In the .NET environment, the mechanism we need to use is to create a *property* of a class.

A property is a pseudo member variable in a class – something that appears to all intents and purposes as a public member variable like the `AccountName` member in the `BankAccount` example. However, a property is actually a different form of method: one that can provide access to private member variables so that their value can be retrieved, changed or both. For example, in `BankAccount`, we can create a `CurrentBalance` property that would access the `Balance` variable as shown in Listing 4.5.

```
Public Property CurrentBalance() As Decimal
    Get
        Return Balance
    End Get
    Set(ByVal Value As Decimal)
        Balance = Value
    End Set
End Property
```

Listing 4.5: A property definition for `BankAccount`

As that listing shows, there are two parts to this property (although it is not necessary to create both parts). The `Get` part defines how the property value will be retrieved. In this case, the value stored in `Balance` is simply returned, like the result of a function. The `Set` part defines how the value in `Balance` is to be changed. Program statements that use this property look exactly like the program statements that would access a public member variable called `CurrentBalance`:

```
MyAccount.CurrentBalance = 100
Console.WriteLine(MyAccount.CurrentBalance)
```

The above statements would assign 100 to the `Balance` private member variable, and then get the new value to display on the console. To all intents and purposes, this is just like making the `Balance` member variable public. By now you should be thinking "why bother?" – we seem to have gone to a lot of trouble to create a `Private` member variable and make it accessible (under an assumed name) simply to make it appear as if it was a `Public` member variable. The answer (to the question "why bother?") is that we can exercise more control on an internal member variable by hiding it behind a property in this way.

For example, a bank would rightly have a rule that made it impossible for anyone to simply alter the balance in a bank account; otherwise staff with access to the accounts software could commit fraud. This could be prevented in our account by making the `CurrentBalance` property a read-only property, which the following code (Listing 4.6a) does not do successfully:

```
Public ReadOnly Property CurrentBalance() As Decimal
    Get
        Return Balance
    End Get
    Set(ByVal Value As Decimal)
        Balance = Value
    End Set
End Property
```

Listing 4.6a: Creating a read-only property (not quite there)

By adding the keyword `ReadOnly` before the `Property` declaration, we are declaring our intention to make it impossible to use this property name to assign a new value. However, this has the effect of invalidating the property's `Set` part (the blue wavy underline is, as you may recall, VB's way of indicating that all is not right in your code). Well, this is only to be expected, since a read-only property should not have a `Set` part. If we delete the whole `Set` part, VB will be happy again and we will have made the property properly read-only (Listing 4.6b).

```
Public ReadOnly Property CurrentBalance() As Decimal
    Get
        Return Balance
    End Get
End Property
```

Listing 4.6b: Creating a read-only property

It is also possible to create a write-only property (using the keyword `WriteOnly` in place of the current `ReadOnly` one). By creating a property that is either read/write (the default), read-only or write-only, we can provide controlled access to private data members in a class. However, we can do much more with a property than simply access a single variable. We could, for example, create a property that accessed the values of several variables (adding them together or combining them in some other way). A property can also be used to create the illusion of member variables that do not even exist. Consider the following example class (Listing 4.7).

```
Public Class Circle
    Public Radius As Single
    Public Property Diameter() As Single
        Get
            Return 2 * Radius
        End Get
        Set(ByVal Value As Single)
            Radius = Value / 2
        End Set
    End Property
End Class
```

Listing 4.7: Creating a property out of thin air

The listing shows the definition of a new class, `Circle`, which has a single member variable, `Radius`. This member variable is public, so we can access the current value and assign a new value easily. However, a property definition makes it appear as if the `Circle` class also contains a `Diameter` member variable, even though one does not exist. Since there is a simple relationship between the radius and the diameter of a circle, we can use this to provide the illusion of a `Diameter` member variable. Any code that access's a circle's `Diameter` will in fact access its `Radius`, but the `Property Get` will double the value to give the `Diameter` instead. If we change the diameter, we're really changing the radius, and the new value is simply calculated.

We could easily do the arithmetic of this trick directly in the program code that works with a `Circle` object. However, by making the `Circle` class appear as if it has a `Diameter` member, we are improving the class in several ways.

- Users can access and change the value of the diameter easily.
- The `Radius` value can be accessed just as easily as before the `Diameter` method was added
- Members of the class do not need the extra storage space required for a `Diameter` variable. Although this may seem initially to be at best a minor saving – one member variable replaced by a chunk of code – in most circumstances the saving will be very real. Each object of the class will save the space the member variable would have taken up, and yet will require no additional space for the property, which is part of the class, not its objects. A single class can be responsible for a great many objects, and therefore a single property can free up a lot of storage space

■ Most importantly, by *not* storing the diameter as a variable, there is no chance of the member variables having values that are inconsistent with each other – e.g. a radius of 10 and a diameter of 2.

Exercise 4.3

Return to the `Person` class written for Exercise 4.2. Delete the `Name` member variable, and replace it with two other member variables, `FirstName` and `LastName`. Now create a `FullName`, read-only property that combines both first and last names – remember to include a space between first and last names. Test the property in `Sub Main()`.

4.1.3 Constructors

The `Circle` example class used above provides us with a clear picture of one of the most important features of object-oriented programming: no matter how the internal data of a class is organized and stored, it is the public interface that defines how a user of the class (a programmer) will write code to interact with it. We try to simplify the way objects are used by hiding all of the complex data mechanisms behind the class boundaries and exposing only those methods that manipulate objects of the class in such a way as to maintain an internal (and external) consistency.

To make a class truly robust, this consistency must be maintained throughout the entire period that an object is in use. When we create a new object from a class using the `New` operator, it is important that from the word go, the object is in a valid state. The default state of a new object is for every member variable to be null; i.e. numbers to have a zero value, strings to be empty, etc. While this is acceptable for many classes of object, in some situations we need an object to be in a valid but non-null state from the instant it is created.

For example, if we have a `Circle` object, it is a null circle immediately after it has been created. We could say that one essential feature of a circle is that it has a non-zero radius, since otherwise, it is really a point. However, when we create a `Circle` object, we first have to create a circle with a zero radius, and then update the radius. If we are concerned about objects being used consistently, this poses a problem, since, for at least a short period of time, every `Circle` object has to go through an inconsistent state immediately after creation. If a programmer who is unfamiliar with the class was to create a new circle and not set its radius to a non-zero value, this could cause problems.

Visual Basic and .NET provide a way around this possible situation: the class *constructor*. A constructor is a method whose purpose is to build an object in a valid state. Recall that we use the `New` operator to create a new object of any class. We can change the way that `New` works by creating a constructor method for a class. This is a sub that sets up a new class member into a valid state, and is invoked automatically at the point an object is created. Currently, we create a new `Circle` object by using statements like:

```
MyCircle = New Circle
Circle.Radius = 10
```

By adding a Constructor method to the `Circle` class, we can improve on this, by ensuring that it is not possible to insert additional statements in between the creation of the circle and the statement that sets its radius (and therefore makes it valid):

```
MyCircle = New Circle(10)
```

This call to create a new `Circle` includes an *argument*, which is a value passed into a sub, function, or, in this case, constructor, to be used in its code. The argument is dealt with inside the code by defining a *parameter*, which is both a statement of the type of information that can be passed into the code, and an 'alias' for whatever actual value was passed in. The Constructor method that allows us to work with a `Circle` object by accepting an input argument is shown next in Listing 4.8.

```
Public Class Circle
    Public Radius As Single
    Public Sub New(ByVal InitialRadius As Single)
        'This method executes at the point where New
        'creates a Circle (InitialRadius is the Parameter)...
        Radius = InitialRadius
    End Sub
    Public Property Diameter() As Single
        Get
            Return 2 * Radius
        End Get
        Set(ByVal Value As Single)
            Radius = Value / 2
        End Set
    End Property
End Class
```

Listing 4.8: Adding a Constructor method (`New()`)

A Constructor method can therefore serve to set up an object into a safe state as soon as it is created. We can use this facility in the `BankAccount` class also. In this case, we could reason that while it is perfectly valid to have a `BankAccount` with no money in it, we would never create a `BankAccount` that did not have an owner. The constructor should therefore set up the `AccountName` property accepting a suitable argument (a name, or a variable that contained a name) by defining a parameter that could be used to deal with it as shown in Listing 4.9.

```
Public Class BankAccount
    Public AccountName As String
    Private Balance As Decimal
    Public Sub New(ByVal Name As String)
        AccountName = Name
    End Sub
    Public Sub Deposit(ByVal Amount As Decimal)
        Balance += Amount
    End Sub
```

```
        Public Function GetBalance() As Decimal
            Return Balance
        End Function
    End Class
```

Listing 4.9: Adding methods to the class

Now we can create a `BankAccount` that belongs to someone immediately:

```
Dim MyAccount As BankAccount = New BankAccount("Fred
Bloggs")
```

or . . .

```
CustName = "Fred Bloggs"
Dim MyAccount As BankAccount = New BankAccount(CustName)
```

Note that we can invoke the constructor in the same statement as we initialize the reference variable.

We can pass as many arguments as we wish to a constructor, separating each with commas, so it would be possible to have the `BankAccount` constructor accept two values, the `Name` of the account and its initial balance:

```
Public Sub New(ByVal Name As String, ByVal Initial As Decimal)
        AccountName = Name
        Balance = Initial
    End Sub
```

Exercise 4.4

The `Person` class would benefit from a constructor. Create a `New()` method for the class, including first and last names, email, and date of birth as parameters. Test this in a statement in `Sub Main()`.

4.1.3.1 Overloaded Constructors

Overloading is a facility that allows us to define more than one version of a sub or function, where the different versions were distinguishable by the number or types (or both) of parameters accepted. We will look at overloading in detail in the next chapter, but for now, it is worth briefly considering its usefulness for allowing us to create objects flexibly. The constructors described earlier for creating a new `BankAccount` either by name (Listing 4.9) or name and initial balance (above) can coexist in the same class, so that we (programmers) could then choose from the available information which one of them to use. Calling a constructor:

```
Dim MyAccount As BankAccount _
            = New BankAccount("Fred Bloggs")
```

would invoke the constructor defined to accept a `Name` argument, while calling:

```
Dim MyAccount As BankAccount _
          = New BankAccount("Fred Bloggs",100)
```

would invoke the second version that also accepted a value for the initial balance. This can greatly simplify the use of a class in programs.

4.1.4 The Class Interface

A class is defined in terms of its members. Member variables, methods and properties are the elements that make up a class. As we have seen, we can define these to be either `Public` or `Private` (there are a couple of other member access classifications we'll get to eventually – for now, public and private are the significant ones). Since private members are only accessible within the class, and public members are accessible to any statements that use the class, there are two distinct views that we can have of a class. The internal view comprises all of the public and private members (and others). The external view is often referred to as the class *interface*. This term is used to acknowledge that the set of public members is the way in which other objects interact with objects of the class.

Ideally a user of a class (by which I mean a programmer who creates and uses an object in his or her own code) should have virtually no responsibilities, since the class itself exercises control over what can be done to an object. On the other hand, the programmer who creates a class has ultimate responsibility for everything that happens within the class. If I create a class to, say, model a bank account for use in a large banking application, and then hackers who manage to access the system are able to use methods in the class to transfer cash between accounts in the system, it is my responsibility.

Of course, not every class you create will have the potential to enable misuse that could result in unauthorized access to bank accounts. In some software, human lives may depend on the accuracy and dependability of code in classes (although happily most will be more forgiving than this). The designer of a class sets the rules by which objects of the class can be used, and is therefore responsible for what these objects can do. Often, the term *business rules* is used to embody the various controls that the methods of a class implement. For example, consider the situation where someone tries to withdraw £100 from an account that has only £20 in it. As you might imagine, most banks would not be happy to allow this (at least not without some overdraft agreement being hammered out first). A `Withdraw` should allow us to take an amount from an account *provided there is enough in the account to cover it*. This is a simple business rule for the `BankAccount` class.

In short, whenever you create a class for use in a program, it is essential that you design it in terms of its interface. As we'll see later, this will have a happy consequence (for inheritance), although at the time it may seem like an unnecessary burden. A class interface defines all of the ways that objects of the class can be used (or misused).

4.1.5 Responding to Conditions

Between the `Deposit` sub and the `CurrentBalance` property we have almost all the functionality we need to control an account (at least in terms of our computer model) – the interface is almost complete. However, we still need some way of taking money out of the account, and this could be just a little trickier, since there is an implicit business rule in this operation. We need some way of allowing a user to withdraw cash only if there are funds in the account to cover the withdrawal.

VB allows us to exercise this type of control by using a Boolean statement. Recall that a Boolean expression is one that can only take on the values `True` or `False`. VB's `If..Then` structure makes use of a Boolean condition to control another statement or group of statements – if the condition is `True`, the controlled statements are executed, if `False` they are not. Listing 4.10 gives a `Withdraw` method that makes use of this:

```
Public Sub Withdraw(ByVal Amount As Decimal)
    If Amount <= Balance Then
        Balance -= Amount
    End If
End Sub
```

Listing 4.10: Adding a `Withdraw()` method

The first statement in the `Withdraw()` method acts as the start of a control structure that governs one or more other statements. If the enclosed condition (`Amount <= Balance`) evaluates as `True`, the controlled statement is executed. If it is `False`, the controlled statement is ignored. We will go on to look at control structures in more detail in the next chapter.

4.1.6 Class Events

In the above code, we have added control to a class method so that it can respond differently depending on the current circumstances (in this case, the amount being withdrawn and whether the bank balance can cover it). In situations where code is able to adapt in this way, it is often useful to build in a facility that lets us decide later the details of how the different circumstances should be dealt with. In the `BankAccount` class, we might require that any withdrawal should simply proceed, but the bank should be informed if a withdrawal puts the account into the red. This would then allow the bank to decide how to deal with it. Most banks would be happier to allow the excessive withdrawal to go ahead and charge the customer for the overdraft.

We define properties and methods for a class so that we can find out about or change an object's data, or get the objects to do something for us. These mechanisms allow us to tell an object to do something or ask it for information. However, we wish our `BankAccount` to be able to send a signal that something has happened (an overdraft) and allow the rest of the banking system to deal with it as necessary.

For this, we can add events to a class. An event is a signal from within an object, which can be a simple signal that states 'something happened', or a more informative signal that can also provide some data regarding what has happened. An event is a bit like a sub call that does not execute any specific code. Program code can be created to listen for a particular event and respond to it, but there would be nothing wrong in having an event that was ignored. The designers of the `BankAccount` class can decide that an account going into overdraft is something that is important enough to provide a facility for, but that it should be the responsibility of other parts of the banking system to deal with it.

We can add an `Overdrawn` event to the `BankAccount` class, and modify the `Withdraw()` method so that it will send it if a withdrawal results in an overdraft (Listing 4.11).

```
Public Event Overdrawn(ByVal Amount As Decimal)
'Other code . . .
Public Function Withdraw(ByVal Amount As Decimal)
    mvarBalance -= Amount
    If Balance < 0 Then
        RaiseEvent Overdrawn(mvarBalance)
    End If
End Function
```

Listing 4.11: A modified `Withdraw()` method that makes banking sense

In the listing, an event, `Overdrawn`, has been declared. It will incorporate an indication of the amount the account is overdrawn by. When a transaction is made that will overdraw the account, `RaiseEvent` causes the signal to be sent to whatever code is listening for it. If the event is not to be ignored, some sub must 'handle' it. An *event handler* is a sub that has been set up to respond to a specific event. When the event occurs, the event handler will execute as shown in Listing 4.12.

```
Private WithEvents Account As BankAccount
'Other code . . .
Sub DealWithOverdraft(ByVal Amount As Decimal) _
                    Handles Account.Overdrawn
    Console.WriteLine("Account is overdrawn by : {0}", Amount)
End Sub
```

Listing 4.12: An object `WithEvents`, and an event-handler

In the listing, a `BankAccount` object has been declared `WithEvents`. This lets the .NET run time know that it must look out for signals from this object. The first line of sub `DealWithOverdraft` declares that this sub will handle the `Overdrawn` event from that object. This tells the .NET run time to associate the `Overdrawn` signal from `Account` with this sub. The end result is that a `Withdraw` operation that takes more than there is in the account `Balance` will cause the bank account to `Raise` the event, and .NET will in turn use this signal to execute the `DealWithOverdraft` handler – in this case, it writes a simple message on the console.

If at a later date it is decided that an account going into overdraft requires a different type of action, there will be no need to change the coding of the `BankAccount` class, only the event handler.

We now have a full implementation for a class that models a simple bank account, providing methods that allow users of the class to deposit and withdraw money and determine how much is currently in the account. So that you can see the complete picture in one go, the full code for this is reproduced in Listing 4.13.

```vb
Module Bank
    Public Class BankAccount
        Public AccountName As String
        Private Balance As Decimal
        Public Event Overdrawn(ByVal Amount As Decimal)

        Public Sub Deposit(ByVal Amount As Decimal)
            Balance += Amount
        End Sub
        Public Function Withdraw(ByVal Amount As Decimal)
            mvarBalance -= Amount
            If Balance < 0 Then
                RaiseEvent Overdrawn(mvarBalance)
            End If
        End Function
        Public ReadOnly Property CurrentBalance() _
                                        As Decimal
            Get
                Return Balance
            End Get
        End Property
    End Class

    Private WithEvents Account As BankAccount

    Sub DealWithOverdraft(ByVal Amount As Decimal) _
                        Handles Account.Overdrawn
        Console.WriteLine("Account is overdrawn by : {0}", _
                                                    Amount)
    End Sub

    Sub Main()
        Dim Account As BankAccount = New BankAccount()
        Account.AccountName = "John Smith"
        Console.WriteLine("Account name: {0}", _
                        Account.AccountName)
        Console.WriteLine("Account balance: {0}", _
                        Account.GetBalance)
        Account.Deposit(100)
        Console.WriteLine("Account balance: {0}", _
                        Account.GetBalance)
    End Sub
End Module
```

Listing 4.13: The full `BankAccount` class and code to test it

4.2 Object-Orientation and Variables

Unlike in earlier versions of Visual Basic, or in languages such as C++ which are hybrid languages that *support* object-oriented programming, Visual Basic .NET and the other .NET languages are fully object-oriented. As such, their core principle is that everything in a program is an object or part of an object.

Recall that according to the definitions given in Chapter 1, an object is an assembly of data and operations – properties and methods. Whenever you create a variable from the Common Type System, you can expect it to provide properties and methods and use these to manipulate the object and derive information from it.

For example, in `Sub Main()` of a VB .NET console program you can create an *Integer* variable and use it as shown in Listing 4.14.

```
Sub Main()
    Dim i As Integer = 42
    Console.WriteLine("Min value = {0}, Max value = {1}", _
                      i.MinValue, i.MaxValue)
End Sub
```

Listing 4.14: Using an `Integer` variable's methods

Run the program and you will see that the `Integer` variable i has two values associated with it because of the type of variable it is. The `Integer` type comes along with the two properties, `MinValue` and `MaxValue`, along with a number of properties that allow us to manipulate it in ways specific to all integers. We can now see that these properties are a result of some code inside the object that has been given `Public` scope so that they form part of the object's interface. These specific properties tell us the minimum and maximum values we can expect any integer to take on. The properties (and methods) come along as part of the type.

In fact, you will get a strong hint of this relationship between variables and their properties and methods if you run Visual Studio, create a Console application and enter the lines shown into `Sub Main()`. As soon as you enter the '.' (dot) between the name of the variable (i) and either of the properties, VS .NET will pop up a list of object properties and methods as a way of assisting you to write the correct code (see Figure 4.3).

All of the types in the Common Type System come with a set of properties and methods, each appropriate to the type it belongs to. `Integers` have minimum and maximum values; `Strings` have a length (number of characters) and methods that make it easy to convert them to upper or lower case, extract sub-strings, etc.; `Dates` have properties to indicate their `Day`, `Month` and `Year`, etc. and to add a time interval to them to form new dates.

Although everything in VB .NET is an object, you will notice that the objects you work with in programs fall into two broad categories. With some variables, as soon as you define them, they will automatically take on a value, which will be zero, or the equivalent for a non-numeric type (`False` for a `Boolean`, and 01/01/0001 for a

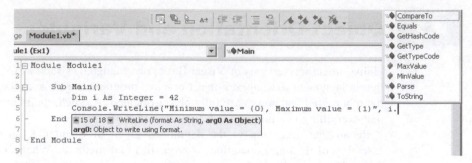

Figure 4.3 Intellisense pop-up code assistance in the Visual Studio IDE.

Date). You can override this zero value by initializing a variable as you declare it, as with the Integer i in Figure 4.3. However, other variable types you declare will not behave in such a straightforward way.

If you declare a variable of type Object and immediately try to reference its GetType method, your program will crash unceremoniously. The first code snippet shown in Listing 4.15 illustrates this.

```
Sub Main()
    Dim i As Integer
    Dim o As Object
    Console.WriteLine(i.GetType())
    Console.WriteLine(o.GetType())'This line causes an error.
End Sub
```

Listing 4.15: Wrong use of an Object type

When the console program that contains the above code is executed, the error message shown in Figure 4.4 is the result. Note that before the error message, the data type of the integer i is properly reported (System.Int32 is the data type in the Common Type System that Visual Basic calls Integer).

```
D:\Programs\VB.Net Progs\Ch3\Ex1\Ex1\bin\Ex1.exe                    _ □ X
System.Int32

Unhandled Exception: System.NullReferenceException: Value null was found where a
n instance of an object was required.
   at Ex1.Module1.Main() in D:\Programs\VB.Net Progs\Ch3\Ex1\Ex1\Module1.vb:line
 29
Press any key to continue
```

Figure 4.4 The result of executing Listing 4.15

The error occurs because the variable o is an Object type. This is the base type of all classes in VB .NET, and the problem occurs because it is necessary to create a *new instance of the class* before we can access its methods or properties. The cure

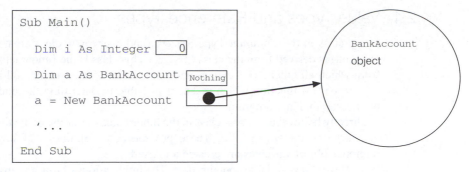

Figure 4.5 A value object (i) and a reference object (a)

for this error is to assign a new object to the variable o before trying to access any of its properties or methods, as shown in Listing 4.16.

```
Sub Main()
    Dim i As Integer
    Dim o As Object = New Object()
    Console.WriteLine(i.GetType())
    Console.WriteLine(o.GetType()) 'No error; the object
    exists.
End Sub
```

Listing 4.16: Proper use of an `Object` type

The difference is that simple variables (sometimes referred to as the *primitive types* or simply *primitives*) are implemented in such a way that a variable directly accesses the memory locations at which it is stored, while other variable types (classes) are used to refer to objects stored separately in an area of memory the CLR reserves for objects. The first type is called a value type object, while the second is a reference type.

Value type objects inherit from the `System.ValueType` class. The key feature of a reference type is that the variable does not *contain* the object, but simply 'knows where to find it' (as shown in Figure 4.5) if one exists. If a reference variable does not refer to an object, it refers to *Nothing*, a valid Visual Basic keyword. Any attempt to access a property or method of a reference variable that refers to `Nothing` will cause a `NullReferenceException` – as described in the error report in Figure 4.4.

Exercise 4.5

Using the `Person` class you created in previous exercises, amend the code in `Sub Main()` so that the keyword `New` is not used to create a `Person` object. Observe the results of this when you attempt to run the code (you should be expecting an error).

4.2.1 Value Types and Reference Types

Every class in the Common Type System (and every new class created in a .NET program) is derived from the class `Object`. This class is the fundamental base class from which all other .NET classes and types inherit. The one method it provides is `GetType()`, a function which makes it possible to determine the underlying type of any variable in a program.

Directly below the `Object` class in the inheritance hierarchy come the two classes `ValueType` and `Reference`. These provide core definitions of how value and reference object variables are created and used.

A `ValueType` variable contains data. The implications of this are profound: every `ValueType` variable is independent of every other one, and since the data is tightly bound to the variable, `ValueType` variables can be operated on very efficiently. When a `ValueType` is created by a `Dim` statement within a sub definition, the memory that stores the variable's value can be accessed directly by the code in the sub (see Figure 4.6).

X as Integer
42

Figure 4.6 A `ValueType` variable

A reference variable on the other hand is stored in memory that is separate from the program code that operates on it. Basically, the variable is an indication of where the data that belongs to it lives – its *address* in memory. To operate on the data, program code must follow the reference to the object (see Figure 4.7). This takes time and therefore reference types are less efficient to deal with. The difference in efficiency is minor, but in a program that deals with a large number of variables, small time differences can mount up.

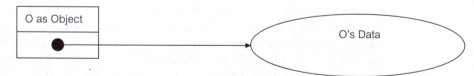

Figure 4.7 A reference variable and its object

Why must we have this distinction between value types and reference types? It all comes down to being able to manipulate variables efficiently in the computer's memory. It is much easier to allocate space to accommodate an object if you know how much memory space it will occupy. All of the value types – numbers, dates, Booleans, characters and structures that contain only other value types are a predictable size and can therefore be allocated space easily at the point of declaration –

when the program is written. No matter what value is stored in them, their size will never change.

On the other hand, the reference types – objects, strings, arrays and collections (both of which we will meet in Chapter 6) – tend to be unpredictable in size. Consider a single string. This can be anything from zero to around 2 billion characters in length. When a `string` variable is declared, the options are to either allocate enough space for *any* string (i.e. 2 billion characters worth), or wait until a string is assigned to it, at which point the required space is known. Over the time that a single `String` variable is used, the space required to store it may change radically. It is therefore much easier to allocate space for it as the program runs, and change the amount of space allocated to it as necessary.

4.2.2 Manipulating Value and Reference Types

There are several consequences of the distinction between value types and reference types that affect the way that we can manipulate them in program code.

- A value type always has a value from the point of its declaration, since a newly created value type variable is automatically assigned a zero value if it is not initialized. Conversely, a reference type is assigned the value `Nothing` when it is declared if it is not initialized – this effectively means 'no object'.
- Value types are processed more efficiently than reference types.
- When a value type is copied by assignment, a new, independent copy is made. When the original value is altered, this has no effect on the copy, which retains the value first assigned until its value is altered specifically. When a reference value is copied by assignment, the new variable is made to refer to the same object as the first. Therefore, any change to either variable's object will be reflected in the other, since there is only one object referred to by two variables.
- When we get to the end of the block of code in which a value type is declared, the variable goes out of scope, which is to say, it can no longer be accessed. When a reference type goes out of scope, the object it refers to may still exist provided some other reference variable refers to it.

For example, Figure 4.8 shows a short piece of program code that manipulates two `Integer` variables.

In the figure, you can see that the variables X and Y are independent of each other: I can copy the value stored in X into Y, but this does not make Y in any sense dependent on X in subsequent code.

In contrast to this, Figure 4.9 shows a similar scenario, but this time using two `BankAccount` variables.

First note it is necessary to use the keyword `New` to create the object the first of these variables is assigned to. Note also the syntax – `Dim ObjectVariable As SomeClass = New SomeClass`. In general we create a new member of a class, and assign it to an object variable. This makes the object variable refer to that object (not contain it).

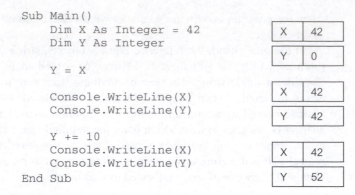

```
Sub Main()
    Dim X As Integer = 42
    Dim Y As Integer

    Y = X

    Console.WriteLine(X)
    Console.WriteLine(Y)

    Y += 10
    Console.WriteLine(X)
    Console.WriteLine(Y)
End Sub
```

Figure 4.8 Working with two `Integer` variables (values)

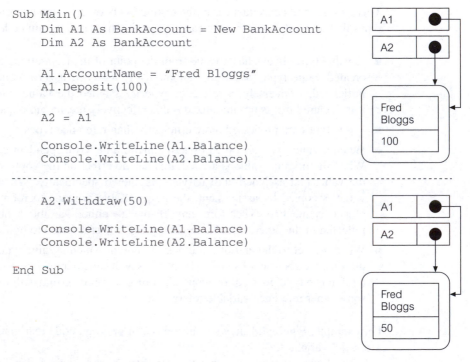

```
Sub Main()
    Dim A1 As BankAccount = New BankAccount
    Dim A2 As BankAccount

    A1.AccountName = "Fred Bloggs"
    A1.Deposit(100)

    A2 = A1

    Console.WriteLine(A1.Balance)
    Console.WriteLine(A2.Balance)

    A2.Withdraw(50)

    Console.WriteLine(A1.Balance)
    Console.WriteLine(A2.Balance)

End Sub
```

Figure 4.9 Working with two `BankAccount` variables (references)

When the assignment `A2 = A1` is made, the variable `A2` now refers to the same object as the variable `A1`. Note that the keyword `New` is not used this time, so no extra objects have been created. Therefore any change made to the object via `A1` will also be seen as a change to the object referred to by `A2`, and *vice-versa*. When £50 is withdrawn from the account via `A2`, the single account object's balance is changed.

4.2.3 Distinguishing Value and Reference Types

Obviously with these pronounced differences in behaviour, it is important to know when you are using a value type and when you are using a reference type. The following are all value types; everything else is a reference type:

- `Numeric` types (`Byte`, `Short`, `Integer`, `Long`, `Single`, `Double` and `Decimal`);
- `Date` variables;
- `Char` variables;
- `Boolean` variables;
- structures, either built-in or defined by a programmer;
- enumerations.

You may find it odd that the `String` type is missing from this list, since we don't need to use the keyword `New` when we create a new string variable. With all of the other reference types, we use `New` to create a brand new instance to assign, and other assignments need to refer to already existing objects, as in the code in Figure 4.9. However, Visual Basic strings are a special form of reference type. They are special in that `New` is not needed to create a string value; an un-initialized `String` variable is given the default value of `Nothing`. Oddly, this equates to an empty string (""), since the result of:

```
If "" = Nothing Then
    Console.WriteLine("Equal")
End If
```

is to display the word 'equal'.

Strings are also special in that when they are manipulated in program code, they *behave* like value types. An example is given in Listing 4.17.

```
Sub Main()
    Dim str As String = "Hello World!"
    Dim strCopy As String = str
    Console.WriteLine("{0} - {1}", str, strCopy)
    strCopy = strCopy.ToUpper
    Console.WriteLine("{0} - {1}", str, strCopy)
End Sub
```

Listing 4.17: Manipulating strings – reference variables?

According to what we know about reference variables, the second `Console.WriteLine()` statement in Listing 4.17 should print out the same upper case string twice. However, Figure 4.10 shows that this is not the case.

What is going on? According to Visual Basic's on-line help, type `String` is a class that 'represents an *immutable* series of characters'. Immutable means 'cannot

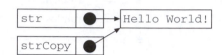

Figure 4.10   These strings are behaving like value types

1. `str` is declared and initialized with "Hello
   World!". "Hello World!" is the string object
   and `str` is made to reference it.

2. `strCopy` is declared, and made to refer to
   the object that `str` references

3. Both reference variables are written out, and so the same object is displayed twice.
   `strCopy` is made to reference the `String` object that is an upper case version
   of the string it currently references. Since a string is immutable, the only way VB can
   manage this is to create a new `String` object, and initialize it to the upper case value

4. Both reference variables are written out,
   this time each referring to a different
   `String` object.

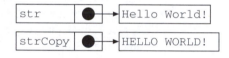

Figure 4.11   Manipulating immutable strings

be altered'. What this is saying is that once we create a `String` object, we cannot
alter it by changing any part of it – we can't convert it to upper case, or replace any
characters in it or any other piecemeal manipulation. If we change a string in code,
the whole string gets replaced!

Look back to Listing 4.17 again and we can now see what is going on (Figure 4.11).

So, we can distinguish between value and reference types quite easily by referring
to the list of value types, but it is not such a simple matter to deduce this from the
behaviour of strings at least. Personally, I hate situations like this where we cannot
simply accept that everything of a particular type behaves in the same way, and usually resent having to learn arcane rules simply because 'it is the way it is!'. However,
there turns out to be a whole raft of good reasons why Microsoft have defined strings
as a wild exception in this way, and given these reasons, I can't say that I would have
done things any differently. We simply need to get used to the idea that strings are
reference variables that don't need to be created with the `New` keyword. Once we
accept this, it is quite easy to forget the details and just get on with programming
with strings (although it is a good idea to keep this difference in the back of your
mind, since there will almost certainly be situations where a string does not behave
as you expect it to in a program).

Review Questions

1. Where must code be placed if it is to be able to access a private member variable of a class?

2. What is the difference between a sub and a function?

3. How is a property different from a sub or a function?

4. How do you create a read-only property?

5. What is a constructor?

6. How does a constructor differ from a normal sub?

7. What is wrong with using these two overloaded constructor definitions in the same class?

    ```
    Public Sub New(CustomerName As String)
      'Code omitted
    End Sub
    Public Sub New(CustomerEmail As String)
      'Code omitted
    End Sub
    ```

8. How does an event differ from a sub?

9. What change is needed to the declaration of an object reference variable if the object must be able to respond to events?

10. How does a reference type variable differ from a value type variable?

Practical Activities

In this chapter, we looked at the detailed composition of simple classes. At its most fundamental level, class building is about adding member variables, methods and properties to classes to provide them with an internal structure (private members) and an external interface (public members). In addition, Visual Basic classes allow the creation of events that can act as signals to the clients of classes (i.e. the program code that creates and uses instances of classes).

In this activity, we will develop a class to do arithmetic – a simple four-function calculator. Although this will be a 'sledgehammer to crack a nut' type of program, it will give us an opportunity to make use of a number of different types of code routine. Before we can get involved in creating the program, we need to consider the details of what the class and system must do.

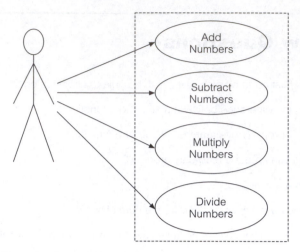

Figure A4.1 Use-case diagram for a simple calculator

Requirements Definition

The requirements definitions for a simple calculator can be expressed quickly and easily by considering the things that you would normally use a calculator to do. We can express these concisely in the use-case diagram in Figure A4.1.

All four use-cases in the above diagram are similar, in that each follows a similar scenario, which can be described as follows:

> To perform an arithmetic calculation, the user enters a number, then the operator, then another number. Provided all three entries are valid, we can calculate and display the result of the operation between the two numbers.

In our program, we will have to accept three inputs and check them for validity. The first and third input should be numbers: if they are not, we can signal an error. The middle input must be an operator, and here we can accept the four standard operators +, −, * and / ('*' is used for multiplication and '/' for divide). Our program will need to be able to distinguish between the four supported functions, which will require that we use a little of the conditional logic that we will look at in detail in the next chapter.

From the use-case diagram and description, we can pick out several items that could be classes or properties of a class. These are 'Calculation', 'Number', 'Another Number', 'Operator' and 'Result'. The names of these items are perhaps a bit odd, and so it would be sensible to change them to "Calculation", "Number1", "Number2", "Operator" and "Result". Quite often we will find that a use-case has been expressed in a language that is couched in vernacular, or expressed in a way that makes perfect sense until we come to analyse it.

Examining the list of items closely, we can see that while '**Calculation**' is likely to be a class, '**Number1**', '**Number2**' and '**Result**' will all be simple numbers that we can express in one of the .NET number classes – **Integer**, **Long**, **Single**, **Double**

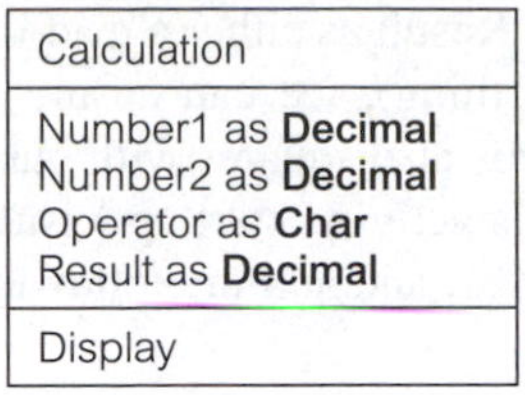

```
┌─────────────────────────────┐
│ Calculation                 │
├─────────────────────────────┤
│ Number1 as Decimal          │
│ Number2 as Decimal          │
│ Operator as Char            │
│ Result as Decimal           │
├─────────────────────────────┤
│ Display                     │
└─────────────────────────────┘
```

Figure A4.2   The **Calculation** class

or **Decimal**. They are also likely to be properties of a calculation. 'Calculate' and 'Display' are verbs describing the operation of the system, and so can be considered as the methods of the **Calculation** class. A Calculate method is likely to be redundant, since **Result**, the result of the calculation, will wholly depend on **Number1**, **Number2** and **Operator**. This suggests that we can make it responsible for performing the calculation as well as returning the result.

In terms of precision, neither **Integer** nor **Long** will suit since they do not provide for a fractional input or result. **Single**, **Double** and **Decimal** are the candidate types, and of these, probably **Decimal** is the most likely since we cannot be sure what precision will be required. The final entity, '**Operator**', is required to store the type of calculation we will be performing: '+', '−', '*', or '/'. A **Char** type variable will hold any of these values.

We can now depict the Calculation class as shown in Figure A4.2.

Since this is a simple class with few properties and methods, we can accept that this diagram provides us with sufficient information to enable us to complete the implementation of it. In more complex systems, we would have to consider the ways that various classes inter-operate and the details of class interfaces in this respect.

Activity 1: Defining the internal class membership

We will need several variables to store the data members of this class:

- Number1 – a **Decimal**;
- Number2 – a **Decimal**;
- Operator – a **Char**; i.e. a single character.

It is tempting to define Result as a member variable as well, since we know that it will be the result of an arithmetic operation between two decimals, which will in turn be a decimal. However, if we consider the need for the members of a class to be consistent with each other, we can see that a Result member variable is likely to be an error. Consider the situation where Number1 and Number2 are both 1.0 and Operator is "+". Result *must* be 2 for the class to be consistent, but with a separate Result member variable, this may not always be the case. An error in our code could leave some inconsistent value in the Result member variable. The easiest way to prevent this type of inconsistency is to ensure that the value returned by Result is calculated as needed.

By defining Result as either a read-only property or a function (which are more or less the same thing), we can ensure that it always returns the true result of the calculation. This also squares with our decision not to have a 'Calculate' method.

To begin this activity, start up Visual Basic, create a new console project, giving it the name `Calc`, and add the following class definition (Listing A4.1).

```
Class Calculator
      Private mvarNumber1 As Decimal
      Private mvarNumber2 As Decimal
      Private mvarOperator As Char
End Class
```

Listing A4.1: The member variables of the `Calculator` class

As private member variables, there is no way that we can access these three members from outside the class. Instead we need to provide some way of passing information into them, and our choices are to provide properties that give read and write access, or a constructor that will allow us to set the three values in a single statement.

Activity 2: Adding Properties to the class

Recall that properties can be read/write (the default), read-only or write-only. These three should be read/write, since we will need to use them to set the internal values (and have no good reason for denying access to the internal values). Listing A4.2 gives the `Number1` and `Number2` properties:

```
Class Calculator
      Private mvarNumber1 As Decimal
      Private mvarNumber2 As Decimal
      Private mvarOperator As Char
      Public Property Number1() As Decimal
          Get
                Return mvarNumber1
          End Get
          Set(ByVal Value As Decimal)
                mvarNumber1 = Value
          End Set
      End Property
      Public Property Number2() As Decimal
          Get
                Return mvarNumber2
          End Get
          Set(ByVal Value As Decimal)
                mvarNumber2 = Value
          End Set
      End Property
      'Operator property required here . . .
End Class
```

Listing A4.2: Property definitions for `Number1` and `Number2`

Exercise A4.1

Define the `Operator` property for the `Calculator` class.

Activity 3: Defining the `Result` method

Now that we have the three input properties, we need to consider the remaining, `Result`, property and the `Display` method. `Result` is the active centre of the class, being responsible not only for returning the result of the calculation, but also performing it. We can define it as shown in Listing A4.3.

```
Public ReadOnly Property Result() As Decimal
Get
      If Operator = "+" Then
          Return Number1 + Number2
      End If
      If Operator = "-" Then
          Return Number1 - Number2
      End If
      If Operator = "*" Then
          Return Number1 * Number2
      End If
      'Code for Divide operation . . .
      '  . . .
End Get
End Property
```

Listing A4.3: The `Result` property

We're using `If..Then` statements to decide which operator the calculation should use; we will look at these in more detail in the next chapter. Here their operation is quite clear: if the expression 'Operator = "+"' evaluates to `True`, then the statement between the corresponding `If` and `End If` statements is executed. If there was more than one enclosed statement, all would be executed. Since there can only be one operator value, only one of these statements will execute to return the correct result.

Note that as a read-only property, there will only be a `Get` part. You should also notice the strong similarity to a function, which suggests that we could easily re-cast this property as a method as shown in Listing A4.4.

```
Public Function Result() As Decimal
      If Operator = "+" Then
          Return Number1 + Number2
      End If
      If Operator = "-" Then
          Return Number1 - Number2
      End If
      If Operator = "*" Then
          Return Number1 * Number2
      End If
      'Code for Divide operation . . .
      '. . .
End Function
```

Listing A4.4: `Result` re-done as a method

These are functionally equivalent. Note that in both cases, the code for the divide method has been omitted.

Exercise A4.2

Add code to the `Result` property or method to perform the `Divide` operation.

Activity 4: A simple test bed

There is now enough code in the `Calculator` class that we can test it out. Add the following `Sub Main()` (Listing A4.5) to the module.

```
Sub Main()
    Dim C As New Calculator()
    C.Number1 = 10
    C.Number2 = 4
    C.Operator = "/"
    Console.WriteLine("Result is {0}", C.Result())
End Sub
```

Listing A4.5: Testing the simple calculator

Provided all is correct (including your definitions of the `Operator` property and the `Result` property/method), executing this program should result in the answer 10/4 being displayed in the Console window. If it does not behave, check your code with the full listing at the end of this walkthrough (Listing A4.8).

You can test the proper operation of the calculator with the other operators by altering the `C.Operator = "/"` statement to assign different operators. Of course this simple test program is not going to satisfy anyone who wants to use the class for real calculations. For that, we will need to make the calculator interactive. This can be done very simply by replacing the values in Listing A4.5 with calls to `Console.ReadLine()` as shown in Listing A4.6. These will be much easier for a user to respond to if they inform the user what to enter:

```
Sub Main()
    Dim C As New Calculator()
    Console.Write("Enter a number:")
    C.Number1 = Console.ReadLine()
    Console.Write("Enter a number:")
    C.Number2 = Console.ReadLine()
    Console.Write("Enter an operator:")
    C.Operator = Console.ReadLine()
    Console.WriteLine("Result is {0}", C.Result())
End Sub
```

Listing A4.6: The simple interactive version

Our program now uses the `Calculator` class to perform calculations interactively. However, I would doubt that any of you would be likely to give up a cheap four-function calculator to use this version, even if it does calculate to very high precisions. One problem with it is that it does the job in very jerky steps. I'm sure if you wanted to multiply 4 by 10, you would prefer to enter a single line: "4*10", followed by the Enter key, to display the result.

To finish this activity, we'll have a brief look at making the calculator behave in a more natural way. First, we need to look at how to take a single string such as "4*10" and break it up into the constituent parts "4", "*" and "10".

Activity 5: Parsing an expression string

There are various methods within the `String` class that allow us to break it into separate sub-strings. The `Chars()` property is an array of single `Char` types, and can be used to access individual characters (such as "*"). However, we need to know the index of a particular character to retrieve it. The `IndexOf()` function can do this for us. Given the expression '4*10', `IndexOf("*")` will return 1 (counting from 0 as the first character of the string).

We could therefore use `IndexOf()` to determine the position of the operator, and from this extract the characters to the left of it (the first number) and the characters to the right of it (the second number). However, at the point where we are trying to determine the position of the operator, we don't know which specific operator will be in the string. A similar method, `IndexOfAny()` can solve this problem for us, since it takes an array of operators, and returns the position of the first occurrence of any of them.

Given the string expression `Expr`, containing '4*10', the following statements (Figure A4.3) will retrieve the two numbers, n1 and n2, and the operator, op:

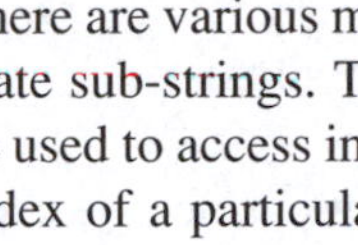

```
Dim operators() As Char = {"+", "-", "*", "/"}
OpPos = Expr.IndexOfAny (operators)
n1 = CType(Expr.Substring(0, OpPos), Decimal)
n2 = CType(Expr.Substring(OpPos + 1), Decimal)
op = Expr.Substring(OpPos, 1)
```

Figure A4.3 Breaking up an expression

Note that `CType()` is being used to convert the number substrings to `Decimal` type directly.

The operation of splitting up an expression into constituent parts is called *parsing*, and is commonly used in programming to break strings into elements that are easier to deal with individually. Now that we have this ability, we can greatly simplify the use of a `Calculator` object by creating a constructor into which we can pass an expression to be evaluated. This is shown in Listing A4.7.

```
Class Calculator
      Private mvarNumber1 As Decimal
      Private mvarNumber2 As Decimal
      Private mvarOperator As Char
      Public Sub New(ByVal Expr As String)
```

```
            Dim OpPos As Integer
            Dim operators() As Char = {"+", "-", "*", "/"}
            OpPos = Expr.IndexOfAny(operators)
            mvarNumber1 = CType(Expr.Substring(0, OpPos),
                                               Decimal)
            mvarNumber2 = CType(Expr.Substring(OpPos + 1),
                                               Decimal)
            mvarOperator = Expr.Substring(OpPos, 1)
        End Sub
        'Other code for the class...
        '...
    End Class
```

Listing A4.7: A constructor for the `Calculator` class

Now our `Calculator` class is much easier to use, since we can assign all of the
input expression in a single statement and then simply display the result. The full
listing of the class and a `Sub Main()` to use it is given in Listing A4.8.

```
    Module Calc

        Class Calculator
            Private mvarNumber1 As Decimal
            Private mvarNumber2 As Decimal
            Private mvarOperator As Char
            Public Sub New(ByVal Expr As String)
                Dim OpPos As Integer
                Dim operators() As Char = {"+", "-", "*", "/"}
                OpPos = Expr.IndexOfAny(operators)
                mvarNumber1 = CType(Expr.Substring(0, OpPos), _
                                                   Decimal)
                mvarNumber2 = CType(Expr.Substring(OpPos + 1), _
                                                   Decimal)
                mvarOperator = Expr.Substring(OpPos, 1)
            End Sub
            Public Property Number1() As Decimal
                Get
                    Return mvarNumber1
                End Get
                Set(ByVal Value As Decimal)
                    mvarNumber1 = Value
                End Set
            End Property
            Public Property Number2() As Decimal
                Get
                    Return mvarNumber2
                End Get
                Set(ByVal Value As Decimal)
                    mvarNumber2 = Value
                End Set
            End Property
```

```
        Public Property Operator() As Char
            Get
                Return mvarOperator
            End Get
            Set(ByVal Value As Char)
                mvarOperator = Value
            End Set
        End Property
        Public Function Result() As Decimal
            If Operator = "+" Then
                Return Number1 + Number2
            End If
            If Operator = "-" Then
                Return Number1 - Number2
            End If
            If Operator = "*" Then
                Return Number1 * Number2
            End If
            If Operator = "/" Then
                Return Number1 / Number2
            End If
        End Function
    End Class

    Sub Main()
        Dim Expr As String
        Console.Write( _
            "Enter an expression (number op number): ")
        Expr = Console.ReadLine()
        Dim Calc As New Calculator(Expr)
        Console.WriteLine("{0} {1} {2} = {3}", _
                          Calc.Number1, Calc.Operator, _
                          Calc.Number2, Calc.Result)
    End Sub
End Module
```

Listing A4.8: The full calculator program

Features worth remembering

In this program we have used a number of methods for dealing with data that you might use in any program. You should consider them as additional tools in your programming tool-bag.

■ Remember that a function and a read-only property are similar in the way that they can be used. Often, it is best to consider how you think of the word being used as the name (e.g. Result) as an indicator of which it should be. Result, as a noun, suggests a read-only property, but a function with a similar job to do might be called GetResult, since that is more like a verb and suggests action.

■ Always consider writing a simple test program like that in Listing A4.5 to try out a class. It is much easier to do this as you go along than to try to locate problems when you add a complex class to a complex program and something does not work.

■ Parsing an expression is a useful technique when it is possible to identify one or more items that will be used as separators between the parts of it. For example, a sentence can be split up into words by recognizing that a space character is used as a separator. Investigate the `Split()` method of the String class, that will take a whole string and return an array of constituent sub-strings. The method takes either one string or an array of strings to define the separators.

Suggested Additional Activities

Several improvements could be made to this calculator program.

1. Currently, the program is not very robust. We will examine ways to deal with problems that occur due to faulty input in the next chapter. One specific problem is that if the second number in a calculation is 0, the Divide operation will cause a crash, since N/0 can not be calculated for any N. Try using an additional `If..Then` statement to get around this problem. If `Number2` has a value of zero, you could return something other than the result of the division operation such as 0.

2. It is possible to add other operations to the calculator. Visual Basic supports the '^' operator (above the 6 key on a standard keyboard) to raise a number to a power, e.g. 2 ^ 3 is 2 to the power 3 or 2 cubed (i.e. 8). It also supports the '\' operator to give an integer result of a division (e.g. 10 \ 3 = 3). Add these to the set of operators – note that you will have to extend the array of operators in the constructor as well as adding other blocks to the `Result` method.

3. You can make the entire calculation process repeat by placing the entire contents of `Sub Main()` inside a *loop structure*. We will look closely at loop structures in the next chapter, but for now, you can try a simple one out. The structure:

```
Do
    'Statements to repeat...
    '...
Loop
```

surrounding all of the statements inside `Sub Main()` will cause them to be repeated until the program is terminated by closing the Console window. Make the calculator behave like this.

Solutions to Exercises

```
Public Class BankAccount
    Public AccountName As String
    Public AccountNumber As Long
    Private Balance As Integer
    Private PIN As Short
    'Other code here . . .
End Class
```

Note that several types could have been used here. A Long integer variable gives a big enough range to cover a bank account number (an Integer, at approx 10 digits long may not). Defining the PIN as a Short integer would do since most bank machines expect a four-digit PIN. However, it could be more efficient to have PIN as an array of four Chars (Private PIN(3) As Char).

```
Class Person
    Public Name As String
    Public eMail As String
    Public DateOfBirth As Date
    Public Function Age() As Integer
        Return DateDiff(DateInterval.Year, DateOfBirth, _
                                            Date)
    End Function
End Class

Public Sub Main()
    Dim P As Person = New Person
    P.Name = "Fred Bloggs"
    P.eMail = "fred@bloggo.com"
    P.DateOfBirth = "22/10/1975"
    Console.WriteLine(P.Age)
End Sub
```

Note the above statements should be placed in a code module to test them. Create a Console application, and enter the code entirely within the pre-defined module (adding the code in Sub Main() to the existing empty definition of Sub Main().)

```
Class Person
    Public FirstName As String
    Public LastName As String
    Public eMail As String
    Public DateOfBirth As Date
```

```
        Public Function Age() As Integer
            Return DateDiff(DateInterval.Year, DateOfBirth, _
                                                Date)
        End Function
        Public Property FullName() As String
            Get
                Return FirstName & " " & LastName
            End Get
        End Property
    End Class

    Public Sub Main()
        Dim P As Person = New Person
        P.FirstName = "Fred"
        P.LastName = "Bloggs"
        P.eMail = "fred@bloggo.com"
        P.DateOfBirth = "22/10/1975"
        Console.WriteLine(P.FullName)
        Console.WriteLine(P.Age)
    End Sub
```

Exercise 4.4

```
    Class Person
        Public FirstName As String
        Public LastName As String
        Public eMail As String
        Public DateOfBirth As Date
        Public Sub New(ByVal FName As String, _
                        ByVal LName As String, _
                        ByVal em As String, ByVal DOB As Date)
            FirstName = FName
            LastName = LName
            eMail = em
            DateOfBirth = DOB
        End Sub
        Public Function Age() As Integer
            Return DateDiff(DateInterval.Year, DateOfBirth, _
                                                Date)
        End Function
        Public Property FullName() As String
            Get
                Return FirstName & " " & LastName
            End Get
        End Property
    End Class

    Public Sub Main()
        Dim P As Person = New Person("Fred", "Bloggs", _
                    "fred@bloggo.com", "12/10/1975")
        'As before...
```

Exercise 4.5

Simply delete New from the previous solution and run the program.

Exercise A4.1

Add this code within the class...

```
Public Property Operator() As Char
    Get
        Return mvarOperator
    End Get
    Set(ByVal Value As Char)
        mvarOperator = Value
    End Set
End Property
```

Exercise A4.2

Amend the result method to include the division operator as shown below:

```
Public Function Result() As Decimal
    If Operator = "+" Then
        Return Number1 + Number2
    End If
    If Operator = "-" Then
        Return Number1 - Number2
    End If
    If Operator = "*" Then
        Return Number1 * Number2
    End If
    If Operator = "/" Then
        If Number2 <> 0 Then
            Return Number1 / Number2
        Else
            Dim Ex As New _
                Exception("Can not divide by zero.")
            Throw Ex
        End If
    End If
    ' Note - added a Power function...
    If Operator = "^" Then
        Return Number1 ^ Number2
    End If
End Function
```

Answers to Review Questions

1. Where must code be placed if it is to be able to access a private member variable of a class? **Within the class definition – i.e. in a *sub*, *function* or *property* definition inside the class code.**

2. What is the difference between a sub and a function? **A *function* does some work and then returns a value to the calling statement. A *sub* does not return a value.**

3. How is a property different from a sub or a function? **A *property* is defined so that a call to it appears as if it is accessing a member variable. Properties are defined as two optional parts – one part (the `Get`) defines how the property returns information from the object's member variables as a value, the other part (the `Set`) defines how object member variables are updated when the property is assigned a value.**

4. How do you create a Read-Only property? **Delete the `Set` part of the definition and add `Read Only` to the first line.**

5. What is a constructor? **A sub that is defined to be called as an object is created, so that the object's member variables can be put into a well defined state.**

6. How does a constructor differ from a normal sub? **A constructor can only be defined for a class, and can be called within a declaration statement.**

7. What is wrong with using these two overloaded constructor definitions in the same class?:

```
Public Sub New(CustomerName As String)
    ' Code omitted
End Sub
Public Sub New(CustomerEmail As String)
    ' Code omitted
End Sub
```

   Both overloaded subs have the same signature, so the compiler could not distinguish between them (and will reject the second definition)

8. How does an event differ from a sub? **An event is a signal sent from within an object, and contains no executable code. An event-handler is a sub that is used to define the response to an event.**

9. What change is needed to the declaration of an object reference variable if the object must be able to respond to events? **The variable should be declared using the `WithEvents` keyword.**

10. How does a reference type variable differ from a value type variable? **A value type variable holds a value directly, while a reference type variable provides access to objects that may hold values. Because of this, assigning a value type to another variable creates a copy, while assigning a reference type to another variable creates a second reference to the same object.**

5

Controlling Program Code

In this chapter, you will learn:

- how to use control structures for executing statements conditionally and repeatedly;
- the need for and use of class constructors;
- how to define and use parameters and arguments;
- error management.

5.1 Control Structures

In the `BankAccount` example class in the previous chapter, we made use of a code control structure to ensure that is was only possible to make a withdrawal from an account if there was enough of a balance in the account to cover it. This is illustrated in Listing 5.1.

```
Public Sub Withdraw(ByVal Amount As Decimal)
    If Amount <= Balance Then
        Balance -= Amount
    End If
End Sub
```

Listing 5.1: Extract from Listing 4.10 demonstrating the use of a control structure

We used this feature again in the `Calculator` class to decide which operation to apply to a calculation. The ability to create statements that can govern other statements like this is one of the most powerful features in programming. The general principle is that a *control structure* is used to bracket any sequence of program statements that we wish to exercise control over – in the above case, the brackets are the statements `If..Then` and `End If`. Using these to surround a section of code (and replacing the . . . with some Boolean condition), we can make the circumstances within the program decide whether the statements are executed or not.

Control structures like this are available for exercising different types of control over program statements:

- executing statements only if a specific condition exists (If..Then);
- selectively choosing between two sequences of statements, depending on whether a condition is True or False (If..Then..Else);
- choosing to execute one of several groups of statements based on the current value of a specific variable (Select..Case);
- executing a group of statements a given number of times (For..Next);
- executing a group of statements repeatedly based on some condition (Do..Loop);
- executing a group of statements for each object in a group of objects (For Each..Next);
- accessing a number of methods and properties of the same object (With..End With).

Between them, these control structures provide us with the tools we need to write code within a class that adapts to the current state of a program, write small sequences of statements that can be executed over a number of different sets of data, and manipulate data items according to the values held in objects. An important feature of the statements in a control structure is that they perform no useful operation in their own right, but are only useful when they are used to modify the behaviour of other program statements.

5.2 Selection Structures

Visual Basic provides a couple of ways of deciding whether to execute a block of code, or which block of code to execute. They come under the general heading of selection structures, and provide the basic mechanisms that can be used to make a program adapt to the circumstances that change as it executes.

5.2.1 If..Then

There are several forms of If..Then structure to choose from in Visual Basic, depending on the type of control we wish to exercise. They are all based on one or more Boolean conditions, that are used to decide which code to execute. The simplest form is shown in Listing 5.2.

```
If <Some Condition> Then
    <Statements to execute>
End If
```

Listing 5.2: The If..Then structure

The phrases in angled brackets are used here to indicate that *some* condition needs to be inserted and *some* statements need to be added – I'm just not being specific about which. For example, we might create a Boolean condition based on the age of the computer user (Listing 5.3).

```
If UsersAge < 17 Then
    Console.WriteLine("You are too young to drive.")
End If
```

Listing 5.3: A example `If..Then` structure

In this case, a user who has previously entered his or her age into the `UsersAge` variable will have the message printed if they are younger than 17, and no message printed if they are 17 or over. The Boolean condition used can be any Boolean expression. That means we can use a comparison expression as shown above, or call a function that returns a Boolean result, or even simply use a `Boolean` variable. This code (Listing 5.4) does exactly the same thing as the code above:

```
Dim TooYoung As Boolean
TooYoung = (UserAge < 17)
If TooYoung Then
    Console.WriteLine("You are too young to drive.")
End If
```

Listing 5.4: Using a `Boolean` variable as a condition

We can of course enclose several statements in the structure (Listing 5.5).

```
If TooYoung Then
    Console.WriteLine("You are too young to drive.")
    Console.WriteLine("Will a bicycle do?")
End If
```

Listing 5.5: Controlling multiple statements

This form of `If..Then` structure simply allows us to choose whether to execute some statements or not. We can extend the structure to select between two different groups of statements (Listing 5.6).

```
If Hour >= 12 Then
    Console.WriteLine("Good afternoon.")
Else
    Console.WriteLine("Good morning.")
End If
```

Listing 5.6: The `If..Then..Else` structure

Again, each section can enclose a number of statements or a single one. We are also allowed to continue the structure by introducing other conditions to be evaluated if earlier ones fail, as shown in Listing 5.7.

```
If Hour < 12 Then
    Console.WriteLine("Good morning.")
ElseIf Hour < 18 Then
    Console.WriteLine("Good afternoon.")
```

```
ElseIf Hour < 22 Then
    Console.WriteLine("Good evening.")
Else
    Console.WriteLine("Good night.")
End If
```

Listing 5.7: A multi-way If structure

Note that in this example, the Else part is used as a default, to be executed if none of the other conditions evaluates as True. In each successive test of a condition, we have already excluded the previous ones (otherwise, if Hour was 10, we would receive in sequence the messages 'Good morning', 'Good afternoon' and 'Good evening'). The overall result is that only one of the possible messages will be displayed on the console.

Using If..Then structures we can choose to execute any of a range of groups of statements. However, what if there are a number of conditions that need to be evaluated before we execute any group of statements. For example, in the UK, someone can only legally drive if a) they are old enough (17 or over), b) they have a valid driver's licence, c) their licence has not been revoked for any reason and d) they are not under the influence of drink or drugs. One way of working to the dictates of all of these conditions is to nest the If..Then structures that would control each of them (Listing 5.8).

```
If Age >= 17 Then
    If HasDriversLicence Then
        If LicenceIsValid Then
            If NotImpaired Then
                Console.WriteLine("You can drive.")
            End If
        End If
    End If
End If
```

Listing 5.8: Combining multiple conditions in a nested If..Then structure

Apart from the first, each of the conditions controlling the above compound structure would be a Boolean variable. For example, HasDriversLicence would have been set to True if the user had a licence, LicenceIsValid would be set to True if the user's licence had not been revoked, and NotImpaired would be set to True if the user was not under the influence.

Exercise 5.1

What will happen as a result of the following code?

```
If X < 5 Then
    If X > 5 Then
        'Controlled statements.
    End If
End If
```

5.2.1.1 Compound Conditions

As you can see from the previous example of the `If..Then` structure, controlling a block of code that is governed by a number of different conditions can get quite complex. Rather than nesting a number of `If..Then` structures, the meaning of the code is sometimes clearer if we group all of the conditions together into one overall complex condition (Listing 5.9). This will save us having to use a lot of individual, nested `If..Then` statements:

```
If (Age >= 17) And HasDriversLicence And _
    LicenceIsValid And NotImpaired Then
                Console.WriteLine("You can drive.")
End If
```

Listing 5.9: Combining conditions with Boolean operators

The `And` conjunction is an operator that joins together two or more Boolean expressions to create a single Boolean expression. As you might guess, the logic is such that the first condition *and* the second condition *and*, etc. all have to be `True` for the overall expression to be `True`. In the above code fragment, all four of the expressions, `(Age >= 17)`, `HasDriversLicence`, `LicenceIsValid` and `NotImpaired` will all need to evaluate to `True` for the 'You can drive' message to be displayed.

There are other logical operators that can be used to join together Boolean expressions (Table 3.3 in Chapter 3 lists the main ones). As a quick summary:

- Using `And`, all of the individual expressions must be `True` for the overall condition to be `True`.

- Using `Or`, any of the individual expressions being `True` makes the overall condition `True` (or, to look at it another way, all of the individual conditions need to be `False` for the overall condition to be `False`).

- `Not` can be used to negate a Boolean expression, making `True` expressions `False` and `False` expressions `True`.

- `AndAlso` can be used instead of `And` to group logical expressions. Using this operator, the partial expressions will be evaluated from left to right only until the overall Boolean result is known. e.g. `If (4 < 3) AndAlso (Age >= 17) Then` would never need to evaluate the second `(Age>=17)` part, since the outcome is already known by the time `(4 < 3)` has been evaluated to `False` (since every part of an `And` expression needs to be true for the whole thing to be `True`).

- `OrElse` can be used instead of `Or` to group logical expressions. This works in a similar way to `AndAlso`, in that the compound expression will only be evaluated as far as necessary to determine the overall condition.

- `AndAlso` and `OrElse` are collectively known as the *short-circuit logical operators*, since they act to limit the number of parts of an expression that need to be evaluated to the minimum required to determine the outcome.

Listing 5.10 gives examples of these.

```
Module BooleanOperators
    Sub Main()
        Dim X, Y, Z As Integer
        If True And True And True Then
            Console.WriteLine( _
                "This will execute (all True=>True)")
        End If
        If True And True And False Then
            Console.WriteLine( _
                "This will not execute (any False=>False)")
        End If
        If False Or False Or False Then
            Console.WriteLine( _
                "This will not execute (all False=>False")
        End If
        If False Or False Or True Then
            Console.WriteLine( _
                "This will execute (any True=>True)")
        End If
        If Not True Then
            Console.WriteLine( _
                "This will not execute (Not True = False).")
        End If
        If Not False Then
            Console.WriteLine( _
                "This will execute (Not False = True).")
        End If
        If Not (False Or False) Then
            Console.WriteLine( _
                "This will execute (Not False = True).")
        End If
        If Not (False Or True) Then
            Console.WriteLine( _
                "This will not execute (Not True = False).")
        End If
        X = 2
        Y = 3
        Z = 5
        If X > Y AndAlso Y > Z AndAlso X + Y = Z Then
            Console.WriteLine( _
                "This will never execute and only X>Y is evaluated.")
        End If
        If X < Y OrElse Y < Z OrElse X + Y = Z Then
            Console.WriteLine( _
                "This will execute and only X<Y is evaluated.")
        End If
    End Sub

End Module
```

Listing 5.10: Demonstrating the Boolean operators

5.2.2 Select Case

In some situations, we might want to select one from a group of blocks of statements depending on a simple outcome – typically the value of a single variable. For example, consider how we might determine how many days are in a given month (we'll make it easy to start with and ignore leap years). Using `If..Then..ElseIf..Else` could give us Listing 5.11.

```
If NameOfMonth = "January" Then
     Console.WriteLine("31 Days")
ElseIf NameOfMonth = "February" Then
     Console.WriteLine("28 Days")
ElseIf NameOfMonth = "March" Then
     Console.WriteLine("31 Days")
ElseIf NameOfMonth = "April" Then
     Console.WriteLine("30 Days")
ElseIf NameOfMonth = "May" Then
     Console.WriteLine("31 Days")
ElseIf NameOfMonth = "June" Then
     Console.WriteLine("30 Days")
ElseIf NameOfMonth = "July" Then
     Console.WriteLine("31 Days")
ElseIf NameOfMonth = "August" Then
     Console.WriteLine("31 Days")
ElseIf NameOfMonth = "September" Then
     Console.WriteLine("30 Days")
ElseIf NameOfMonth = "October" Then
     Console.WriteLine("31 Days")
ElseIf NameOfMonth = "November" Then
     Console.WriteLine("30 Days")
Else
     Console.WriteLine("31 Days") 'This must be December
End If
```

Listing 5.11: A complex multi-way `If` structure

Whew! Of course we could have shortened that code a bit by using the `Or` (or better still, the `OrElse`) Boolean operator, along the lines of Listing 5.12.

```
If NameOfMonth = "September" OrElse _
   NameOfMonth = "April" OrElse _
   NameOfMonth = "June" OrElse _
   NameOfMonth = "November" Then
     ' 30 day months
     ' ..
ElseIf NameOfMonth = "February" Then
     ' 28 day month
     ' ..
Else
     ' 31 day months
     ' ..
End If
```

Listing 5.12: Using Boolean operators to reduce the structure's complexity

This is much neater, but Visual Basic gives us an even better way to do this. The code in Listing 5.13 is clearer and so easier to read.

```
Select Case NameOfMonth
    Case "September", "April", "June", "November"
        Console.WriteLine("30 days in {0}", NameOfMonth)
    Case "February"
        Console.WriteLine("28 days in {0}", NameOfMonth)
    Case Else
        Console.WriteLine("31 days in {0}", NameOfMonth)
End Select
```

Listing 5.13: The `Select Case` structure

In this structure, Visual Basic forms implicit expressions using the variable at the start of the structure (in this example, `NameOfMonth`) and each of the lists of cases given. It then selects from these the statement(s) to be executed. The end result is much more concise.

Given how few lines it has taken to evaluate how many days are in a given month, we can even consider adding statements to check for a leap year (Listing 5.14).

```
Select Case NameOfMonth
    Case "September", "April", "June", "November"
        Console.WriteLine("30 days in {0}", NameOfMonth)
    Case "February"
        If (YearNumber Mod 100 <> 0 And _
            YearNumber Mod 4 = 0) Or _
            (YearNumber Mod 100 = 0 And _
            YearNumber Mod 400 = 0) Then
            Console.WriteLine("29 days in {0}", NameOfMonth)
        Else
            Console.WriteLine("28 days in {0}", NameOfMonth)
        End If
    Case Else
        Console.WriteLine("31 days in {0}", NameOfMonth)
End Select
```

Listing 5.14: Combining `Select Case` and `If...Then` structures

Note how we work out whether the `YearNumber` indicates a leap year. Recall that the `Mod` operator gives us the remainder of a division, so `YearNumber Mod 4 = 0` tells us whether the year number is exactly divisible by 4. You might consider this to be a leap year (many people do), but for a century year to be a leap year, it must be divisible by 400. Our condition therefore becomes a compound expression – either it is not a century year `And YearNumber` is exactly divisible by 4, or it is a century year `And YearNumber` is exactly divisible by 400. Note the brackets used to separate the two groups of compound Boolean expressions; without these, it would be difficult to figure out how we are supposed to combine the individual parts.

Select Case can also be used to select from individual values, ranges of values and individual Boolean expressions. An example is given in Listing 5.15.

```
Console.Write("Enter a number:")
ordNumber = Console.ReadLine()
Select Case ordNumber
      Case 1, 101, 201
          ordinalEnding = "st"
      Case 2, 102, 202
          ordinalEnding = "nd"
      Case 3, 103, 203
          ordinalEnding = "rd"
      Case 4 To 100, 104 To 200, 204 To 300
          ordinalEnding = "th"
      Case Is > 300
          ordinalEnding = " is too big to bother about."
End Select
Console.WriteLine("{0}{1}", ordNumber, ordinalEnding)
```

Listing 5.15: Generating ordinal number endings in a Select Case structure

The Select Case structure above will add an ordinal ending to any integer number entered (up to but not beyond 300), so 1 will be displayed as 1st, 2 as 2nd, etc. As you can see, we can include ranges and even implicit Boolean expressions (e.g. Is > 300) in Select Case, making it a very powerful structure for deciding what block of code to execute.

Exercise 5.2

Assume the String variable CH contains a single character typed from the keyboard. Write a Select Case structure that will determine whether this character is a vowel ("a", "e", "i", "o" or "u"), a digit ("0" To "9") or a consonant.

a)   Assume only lower-case and no punctuation characters have been typed.

b)   Allow for upper and lower-case characters.

5.2.3 Selection Structures within Classes

Of course, the real power of the selection structures, If.. and Select Case.., comes from our ability to use them to make decisions within a class. Effectively, we enable objects to decide on which code to execute based on the conditions in their member variables or elsewhere. The idea is to try to develop classes in such a way that their objects are as autonomous as possible. An object should never be able to perform an operation that did anything contrary to the logic of the class it belongs to.

5.2.3.1 Example: The Bank Account revisited

The BankAccount class is a good example of this, ensuring that cash could only be withdrawn if there was enough in the account to cover the withdrawal. We can extend this behaviour by allowing an account to go into overdraft provided one has been arranged with the bank (Listing 5.16).

```
Module Bank2 ' Updated to allow an overdraft facility

    Public Class BankAccount
        Public AccountName As String
        Public OverdraftAvailable As Boolean
        Private AgreedOverdraftAmount As Decimal
        Private Balance As Decimal

        Public Sub Deposit(ByVal Amount As Decimal)
            Balance += Amount
        End Sub
        Public Sub SetOverdraft(ByVal Amount As Decimal)
            If OverdraftAvailable Then
                AgreedOverdraftAmount = Amount
            End If
        End Sub

        Public Function Withdraw(ByVal Amount As Decimal) _
                                                  As Boolean
            If Amount <= Balance Then
                Balance -= Amount
                Return True
            ElseIf OverdraftAvailable Then
                If Amount <= _
                Balance + AgreedOverdraftAmount Then
                    Balance -= Amount
                    Return True
                End If
            Else
                Return False
            End If
        End Sub

        Public ReadOnly Property CurrentBalance() As Decimal
            Get
                Return Balance
            End Get
        End Property
    End Class

    Sub Main()
        Dim MyAccount As BankAccount = New BankAccount()
        MyAccount.AccountName = "John Smith"
        Console.WriteLine("Account name: {0}", _
                        MyAccount.AccountName)
```

```
                    Console.WriteLine("Account balance: {0}", _
                                MyAccount.CurrentBalance)
            MyAccount.Deposit(100)
            Console.WriteLine("Account balance: {0}", _
                                MyAccount.CurrentBalance)
            If MyAccount.Withdraw(150) Then
                Console.WriteLine("Account balance: {0}", _
                                    MyAccount.CurrentBalance)
            Else
                Console.WriteLine("Withdrawal not allowed")
            End If
            MyAccount.OverdraftAvailable = True
            MyAccount.SetOverdraft(100)
            If MyAccount.Withdraw(150) Then
                Console.WriteLine("Balance (with o/d): {0}", _
                                    MyAccount.CurrentBalance)
            Else
                Console.WriteLine("Withdrawal not allowed")
            End If
        End Sub
    End Module
```

Listing 5.16: The `BankAccount` class modified to allow for overdrafts

In Listing 5.16, the `Withdraw` method has been changed from a `Sub` to a `Function`, so that it can return a `Boolean` result: `True` if the withdrawal was successful, `False` if not. The code in `Sub Main()` now makes two attempts to make a withdrawal; one with no overdraft agreed, and the second, successful, attempt with an agreed overdraft of £100.

Hopefully you can see the power of selection statements, both within a class and in the code that makes use of objects of a class. The trick of replacing a sub with a function that returns a Boolean result is useful when it is possible to allow the class to decide whether or not to perform an operation since, otherwise, the code using the object would not be aware of whether an operation had been successful or not.

Exercises 5.3

1. The `BankAccount` class in Listing 5.16 would benefit from a `Report` function that will return a `String` result based on the following evaluation:

    Balance is positive or zero – "The account is in credit"
    Balance is negative and there is no agreed overdraft – "The account is overdrawn"
    Balance is overdrawn by no more than `AgreedOverdraftAmount` – "The account is within allowed overdraft limit"
    Balance is overdrawn by more than `AgreedOverdraftAmount` – "Account withdrawals have exceeded the agreed overdraft amount"

    Write this function.

2. Write a function that will return the maximum amount that could be withdrawn from the account without exceeding any overdraft limit that existed.

5.3 Repetition

It is often stated that the real power of computers lies in their ability to perform millions of simple operations flawlessly. With the code we have seen so far, we would have to acknowledge that this power is offset by the fact that a human programmer would have to write instructions for these millions of operations; the computer might not make a mistake, but the programmer almost certainly would if each operation had to be individually coded.

Since we are able to write a program so that operations will only be performed if the conditions that govern them are correct, it seems only sensible that we can use a similar mechanism to allow operations to be repeated, again based on some condition. For instance, we might decide that a particular operation was to be executed repeatedly until a certain condition was found to be True: a good example of this would be an operation to locate a specific character within a String variable (Listing 5.17).

```
Console.Write("Enter some text:")
s = Console.ReadLine()
Do
      position += 1
Loop Until s.Chars(position) = " "
Console.WriteLine("The first word was {0} letters long.", _
                  position)
```

Listing 5.17: Using a repetition structure to count the letters in a word

This code contains a Do..Loop that increments a variable until the character at that position in a string matches a single space. The actual repetition structure is as shown in Listing 5.18.

```
Do
      'Code to be repeated.
Loop Until s.Chars(position) = " "
```

Listing 5.18: The repetition structure isolated

It will repeatedly execute the enclosed code until the condition after the Until keyword becomes True. Note that the Chars() method of the String class gives us access to individual characters in the string. It is a little odd because Chars(3) would be the fourth character in the string – characters are counted from position 0 – the first letter.

A feature of this type of loop is that a condition is used to determine whether or not to stop repeating the enclosed statements. Care needs to be taken in using this type of loop because it is easy to specify a condition that will never become true – in effect the program will repeat the enclosed statements forever (or until you get bored and stop it, or until something causes the program to crash). Consider what would happen if the user entered a single word with no following space. Assume the word is four characters long: when the variable position reaches 5, the specified

```
Select D:\Programs\VB.Net Progs\Ch4\Ex1\Ex1\bin\Ex1.exe                    _ □ ×
Enter some text:fred

Unhandled Exception: System.IndexOutOfRangeException: Index was outside the boun
ds of the array.
    at System.String.get_Chars(Int32 index)
    at Ex1.Bank.Test() in D:\Programs\VB.Net Progs\Ch4\Ex1\Ex1\Module1.vb:line 44

    at Ex1.Bank.Main() in D:\Programs\VB.Net Progs\Ch4\Ex1\Ex1\Module1.vb:line 50

Press any key to continue
```

Figure 5.1 The error message given when trying to access the fifth character of a four character string.

condition will try to access the fifth character in a four character string. Visual Basic will respond as shown in Figure 5.1.

Obviously, we need to be a bit careful when creating program loops.

Visual Basic gives us several ways to repeat, or *iterate*, a block of code. There are two general categories.

- Indefinite loops, which are structures that will repeat a block of code until some condition becomes `True` or `False`. Since it is always possible for the condition not to change, this type of loop may never come to an end.

- Definite loops, which are structures that will repeat a block of code a number of times. It should always be possible to work out how many times a definite loop will iterate immediately before it starts.

The `Do..Loop` we've already seen an example of is an indefinite loop (we could have typed in a string that contained no spaces). There are several forms of this type of loop.

5.3.1 `Do..Loops`

The exit condition of a `Do..Loop` can be at the start of the loop (after the word `Do`) or at the end (after the word `Loop`). Exit can be when a condition becomes `True` (`Do Until..Loop`, or `Do..Loop Until`), or when a condition becomes `False` (`Do While..Loop`, or `Do..Loop While`). Table 5.1 shows these variations (using a typical condition – X = Y).

A `Do..Loop` structure can be characterized as performing zero-or-more iterations if the condition is tested at the beginning (`Do While..` or `Do Until..`), or one-or-more iterations if the condition is tested at the end (`Loop While..` or `Loop Until..`). One important facet of this type of loop is that *the enclosed statements must be capable of altering the condition*. This is important, since if the condition can not be altered within the loop, it may never exit. For the example structures in Table 5.1, this means that either X or Y or both must be changed at some point in the enclosed statements, for an exit condition to be possible.

5.3.1.1 Exiting from a `Do..Loop`

Table 5.1 lists the ways that the repeated execution of the code enclosed in a loop can be terminated. `Do..Loop` structures are organized so that it is possible to exit

Table 5.1 Do..Loop structures and their operation

Loop Code	Explanation
Do Until X = Y ' Code to repeat Loop	When the values in X and Y become the same, the code to repeat will not execute any more times. If X and Y are equal immediately before the loop, the enclosed statements will never be executed
Do While X = Y ' Code to repeat Loop	When the values in X and Y become different, the code to repeat will not execute any more times. If X is different from Y before the loop, the enclosed statements will never be executed
Do ' Code to repeat Loop Until X = Y	When the values in X and Y become the same, the code to repeat will not execute any more times. Even if X and Y are the same before the loop starts, the enclosed statements will be executed at least once
Do ' Code to repeat Loop While X = Y	When the values in X and Y becomes different, the code to repeat will not execute any more times. Even if X and Y are different before the loop starts, the enclosed statements will be executed at least once

from the beginning or the end of a loop, providing for zero-or more, or one-or more iterations. It is also possible to exit a loop from anywhere in the middle, using an Exit Do statement. Of course, this is useless on its own, since an unconditional Exit Do would merely serve to create a loop in which only the code up to the Exit Do could ever execute (Listing 5.19).

```
Do
    'First part of the enclosed code
    Exit Do
    'Remainder of the enclosed code (never executes).
Loop
```

Listing 5.19: A Do..Loop with an Exit statement

However, we can enclose the Exit Do statement in an If..Then structure to provide a condition for getting out of a loop in the middle. This makes it possible to form a loop structure that will contain some initial code to set up the potential exit condition, and further code to do something with it. An example is given in Listing 5.20.

```
Do
    Console.Write("Enter a number (0 to quit):)")
    n = Console.ReadLine()
    If n = 0 Then
        Exit Do
    End If
    Console.WriteLine("{0} squared is {1}", n, n * n)
Loop
```

Listing 5.20: Controlled exit from a Do..Loop

Note that this loop does not have a normal exit condition either at the start or at the end – the only possible exit is from the middle of the loop. This turns out to be perfect for this situation – a sequence of statements for getting user-input, followed by the exit condition depending on the user-input, followed by what to do if the quit condition is not met.

It would be possible to have exit conditions in all three locations: at the beginning of the loop, at the end of the loop and also in the middle (in several places if necessary). However, structured programming guidelines (programmers rarely think in terms of rules) are that any loop has a single entry point and a single exit point. Otherwise, the flow of control through a passage of code can become confusing.

While I'm all for reducing the potential for confusion in my programs, I have often found that an occasional breakage of a guideline is necessary to make my code *less* confusing. In some types of loop it seems much more natural to have *two* exit conditions, one for normal situations and one for unusual circumstances.

5.3.1.2 Uses for `Do..Loops`

Often we need to use a condition-based loop in a class to repeat a section of code for some purpose. For example, we might want to ask a user to enter some data and make sure it is valid before continuing. We could do a simple `If..Then` test on the data to validate it, but if the value entered was not valid, what would we do next? A `Do..Loop Until` deals with this nicely (Listing 5.21).

```
Dim n As Integer
Do
     Console.Write("Enter a number between 1 and 10:")
     n = Console.ReadLine()
Loop Until n >= 1 And n <= 10
'By here, n is in range.
```

Listing 5.21: Using a `Do..Loop` to validate user-input

Note that an input error could still occur in Listing 5.21, since the user might enter a value that was not an integer (possibly not even a number). We can always use another `Do..Loop` *inside* the first one to test whether we have a number before testing whether it was in range, as shown in Listing 5.22.

```
Dim Input As String
Dim n As Integer
Do
     Do
          Console.Write("Enter a number between 1 and 10:")
          Input = Console.ReadLine()
     Loop Until IsNumeric(Input)
     'By here, we know that Input is like a number.
     n = CInt(Input) ' Convert it to one.
Loop Until n >= 1 And n <= 10
'By here, n is in range.
```

Listing 5.22: More rigorous validation of user-input

5.3.1.3 Example: Calculating an Average

This is a classic example of the use of a loop in programming. We work out the average of a list of numbers by adding them together and dividing the total by the number of numbers in the list. There are various ways of doing this, but a `Do..Loop` gives us a nicely elegant solution. As each number is entered, we simply add it to a running total, and increment a variable that counts the number of numbers entered so far. When the end of the list is reached (usually the user will be asked to signal this by entering some distinct value after the last in the list), the result is calculated by simple division, and displayed.

We can create a class to do this, with a simple method to do each part of the overall task and this is shown in Listing 5.23.

```
Module Average
Public Class Averager
    Private runningTotal As Single
    Private countOfInputs As Integer

    Public Sub CalcAverage()
        'Get a list of numbers and display their avg.
        GetInputs()
        If countOfInputs > 0 Then
            Console.WriteLine("Average is {0}.", _
                    runningTotal / countOfInputs)
        End If
    End Sub

    Private Sub GetInputs()
        'This method keeps getting input data until
        '"end" is entered.
        Dim input As String
        Dim n As Single
        Do
            input = GetAnInput()
            If input = "end" Then
                Exit Do
            End If
            n = CSng(input)
            runningTotal += n
            countOfInputs += 1
        Loop
    End Sub

    Private Function GetAnInput() As String
        'This method returns either a valid number or "end"
        Dim rawInput As String
        Do
            Console.Write("Enter a number " & _
                    "(or 'end' to end):")
            rawInput = Console.ReadLine()
        Loop Until IsNumeric(rawInput) Or _
                rawInput = "end"
```

```
            Return rawInput
        End Function
    End Class
    Sub Main()
        Dim avg As New Averager()
        avg.CalcAverage()
    End Sub

    End Module
```

Listing 5.23: A class to calculate the average of a list of inputs.

In the `Averager` class, only the `CalcAverage()` method has been made public, since the other methods are only for use within the class. Note how dividing up the functionality of the class in this way makes it easier to understand what is going on, since each method performs a simple task that is easy to describe (`GetAnInput()` gets a valid input from the user, `GetInputs()` collects input data until the user has entered all the values, and `CalcAverage()` calculates the average of a list of input values).

Exercise 5.4

a) The factorial of a number is defined as the product of every integer from 1 up to that number – e.g. the factorial of 3 (written as 3!) can be calculated as $1 \times 2 \times 3 = 6$. Computer programs often use an elegant form of algorithm known as a recursive algorithm to calculate factorials. However, it is possible to calculate the factorial of a number using a `Do..Loop`. Write code that will calculate the factorial of a number N, assuming the number is more than zero.

b) Write code that will display each character of a string on a separate line of the console: you can use the `Chars()` property to determine the character at any position (`Chars(0)` is the first character, etc.), and the `Length()` method to determine how many characters are to be displayed.

5.3.1.4   `While..End While`

Visual Basic provides other ways of repeating a section of code. One is the classic `While` loop, which was initially proposed as the natural structure for repetition in structured programming. This has the form shown in Listing 5.2.4.

```
While <some condition>

End While
```

Listing 5.24: A `While` loop

As it turns out, this exerts exactly the same form of control as a `Do While..Loop` structure, and has really just been included to keep programmers who are used to that form of the structure happy. Since the `Do..Loop` structure does everything that a `While..End While` loop can and more, I find it easier just to stick with the `Do..Loop` form.

5.3.2 Definite Loops

Do..Loops and While..End While loops are Visual Basic's versions of indefinite loops (loops which depend on an exit condition that may or may not occur). However, for years before Do loops and While loops were available in programming languages, BASIC programmers were able to create definite loops using the For..Next structure. This form of loop structure makes use of a *control variable* that it uses to keep count of the number of iterations. The simplest form is the one shown in Listing 5.2.5.

```
For index = 1 To 10
    'Code to repeat.
Next index
```

Listing 5.25: A For..Next loop

In this loop structure, the loop control variable (index) is initially set to the first value in the range given after the '=' operator. At the end of each pass through the enclosed code (at the keyword Next) the control variable is incremented (normally by 1). When the control variable is incremented, if it exceeds the last value in the range, the loop is finished and control passes to the statement after the loop. In short, the loop repeats as the control variable counts through the specified range.

Since the range the control variable is to count through is given at the outset, we can always work out how many iterations will occur, and so this is a definite loop. It does not, however, mean that the range to count through needs to be fixed.

```
Dim index As Integer
Dim start As Integer, finish As Integer
Console.Write("Enter the start of the range:")
start = Console.ReadLine()
Console.Write("Enter the end of the range:")
finish = Console.ReadLine()
For index = start To finish
    Console.Write(" {0} ", index)
Next index
Console.WriteLine()
```

Listing 5.26: Using variables to determine the range of a For..Next loop

In Listing 5.26, the For..Next loop counts through the range start to finish, although the values of these are not known at the time the program was written. Since the user supplies them, the programmer has no way of knowing how many iterations the loop will perform. However, the number of iterations that will be made *is* known immediately before the loop executes (it is finish - start + 1); well, almost. An Exit For statement can be used to break out of a For..Next loop at any point, e.g. Listing 5.27.

```
For index = start To finish
     If index = 0 Then
          Exit For
     End If
     Console.Write(" {0} ", 1 / index)
Next index
```

Listing 5.27: Using an `Exit For` to jump out of a `For..Next` loop

At this point, structured programming purists will be throwing up their hands in horror; pragmatists on the other hand will realize that unusual circumstances occur, even in the middle of definite loops, and so it is sometimes useful to have the option. If you tend towards the purist, simply never use `Exit For` and you need never acknowledge its existence.

The final statement in a `For..Next` loop beginning with the keyword `Next` marks the extent of the loop. Visual Basic allows us to omit the name of the control variable in this line, so that the loop above would work just the same if it was written as in Listing 5.28.

```
For index = start To finish
     If index = 0 Then
          Exit For
     End If
     Console.Write(" {0} ", 1 / index)
Next
```

Listing 5.28: Omitting the control variable's name in the `Next` clause

This makes no difference to a programmer writing a single `For..Next` loop like this, but can make a huge difference to how readable a program is if there are several `For..Next` loops in the same block of code, particularly if these are nested as in Listing 5.29.

```
For outer = 1 To 10
     For inner = 1 To 10
          Console.Write(" {0} ", inner * outer)
     Next inner
Next outer
```

Listing 5.29: Using the control variable names to identify loop endings

Without the control variable name, it can be difficult to identify which `Next` statement goes with which `For` statement, particularly if the block of code contains a large number of lines of code.

5.3.2.1 Changing the Increment Value

A `For` loop does not have to work through a range of values in steps of +1. We might find it useful to create a `For..Next` loop that counts *down* from some value to some

Table 5.2 Counting Options in For..Next loops

For..Next statement	Effect
```For x = 0 To 100 Step 2 'Code to repeat. Next```	Count x up from 0 to 100 in steps of 2
```For y = 100 To 0 Step -5 'Code to repeat. Next```	Count y down from 100 to 0 in steps of –5
```For Z = 0 To 1 Step 0.01 'Code to repeat. Next```	Count z up from 0 to 1 in steps of 0.01 (101 iterations)
```For i = 1 To 12 Step 3 'Code to repeat. Next```	Count in steps of 3 – note that the count will go 1, 4, 7, 10, but will terminate when i exceeds 10
```Limit = 1 For i = 10 To Limit 'Code to repeat. Next```	Repeated code will never execute, because i is made to exceed the limit value at the start

smaller value, or one that counts up or down in bigger or smaller steps. To do this we use the syntax given in Listing 5.30.

```
For controlVariable = initialVal To finalVal Step stepVal
    'Code to repeat.
Next controlVariable
```

Listing 5.30: Counting in a different increment value in a For..Next loop

In this case, the first pass through the loop will assign the value initialVal to controlVariable. At the end of each iteration, controlVariable will have stepVal added to it (if stepVal is negative, the addition will of course decrease the value in controlVariable). If, when stepValue is added, controlVariable becomes more than finalVal for a positive stepVal, less than it for a negative stepVal, the loop will terminate. Table 5.2 gives some example For..Next loops that increment the control variable by values other than one.

5.3.2.2 For..Each loops

Visual Basic provides a variation of the For..Next loop, designed for iterating through all of the members of a collection or array. It will make more sense to describe it once we've looked at these things later in the book.

5.3.3 Uses for For..Next loops

You would use a For..Next loop in any situation where you wanted to perform a series of operations; either setting a variable to each value in a range and performing an operation, or even accessing multiple variables (more on this when we reach data structures). For example, we might want to count through a range of values, operating on each value. One obvious example is a program to generate a 'times table', which might be used in teaching children arithmetic (Listing 5.31).

```
Module TimesTable
Private Class Table
    Private mvarTimesTableValue As Integer
    Private mvarMaxMultiplier As Integer
    Public Property TimesTableValue() As Integer
        Get
            Return mvarTimesTableValue
        End Get
        Set(ByVal Value As Integer)
            mvarTimesTableValue = Value
        End Set
    End Property
    Public Property MaxMultiplier() As Integer
        Get
            Return mvarMaxMultiplier
        End Get
        Set(ByVal Value As Integer)
            mvarMaxMultiplier = Value
        End Set
    End Property
    Public Sub DoTable()
        Dim multiplier As Integer
        Console.WriteLine("The {0} times table:", _
                        mvarTimesTableValue)
        'This For..Next loop works out and displays the
        'multiples of TimesTable...
        For multiplier = 1 To MaxMultiplier
            Console.WriteLine("{0} times {1} = {2}", _
                        mvarTimesTableValue, multiplier, _
                        mvarTimesTableValue * multiplier)
        Next
        Console.WriteLine()
    End Sub
End Class
Sub Main()
    Dim T As New Table()
    Dim tbl As Integer
    T.MaxMultiplier = 12
    'This For..Next loop generates 10 Times-Tables.
    For tbl = 1 To 10
        T.TimesTableValue = tbl
        T.DoTable()
    Next
End Sub
End Module
```

Listing 5.31: A times table program

In this program, a class is used to generate a times table that will display multiplication examples in the following form:

```
1 times 6 = 6
2 times 6 = 12
3 times 6 = 18
4 times 6 = 24
etc.
```

The class has a pair of properties, `TimesTableValue` and `MaxMultiplier`, which provide for setting up the value of the table to be displayed (`TimesTableValue` is 6 in the above example), and the maximum multiplication of it to be shown. Typically this would be set to 10, although higher numbers can be used to generate more difficult tables.

The main operation of the `Table` class is the method `DoTable()`, which works through multiples from 1 to `MaxMultiplier` displaying the arithmetic. In `Sub Main()`, a `Table` object is created and its `MaxMultiplier` is set to 12. This is then followed by a `For..Next` loop that governs the generation of a sequence of multiplication tables (from 1 to 10).

Exercise 5.5

a) Write a `For..Next` loop that will iterate through every allowable value of Integer (hint – look at the available properties for the `Integer` type)

b) The `Asc(s)` function returns the Integer character code of the first (or only) character in a string `s`. The `Chr(x)` function returns the character whose code is x. Write a `For..Next` loop containing code that will display the letters "a" to "z" on the console.

5.3.4 The With Structure

Visual Basic's `With..End With` structure is quite different from the other structures we've looked at so far, in that instead of controlling blocks of program statements, it provides us with a shorthand way to access the available members of a class or structure. In this respect, it is related to the `For..Each` repetition structure, which sets a reference variable to refer to each object in a collection of objects in turn. However, the `With..End With` code structure operates on a single object reference, making all of the public members (properties and methods) easier to access. This ease of access makes it more convenient for the programmer (you), since it removes the need to enter the name of an object reference explicitly in code. It also makes it more convenient for the .NET CLR, which needs to locate an object in memory only once for any number of accesses to properties and methods. For example, consider the program code written in `Sub Main()` in Listing 5.16 and reproduced here as Listing 5.32.

```
Sub Main()
    Dim MyAccount As BankAccount = New BankAccount()
    MyAccount.AccountName = "John Smith"
```

```
Console.WriteLine("Account name: {0}", _
                      MyAccount.AccountName)
Console.WriteLine("Account balance: {0}", _
                      MyAccount.CurrentBalance)
MyAccount.Deposit(100)
Console.WriteLine("Account balance: {0}", _
                      MyAccount.CurrentBalance)
If MyAccount.Withdraw(150) Then
    Console.WriteLine("Account balance: {0}", _
                          MyAccount.CurrentBalance)
Else
    Console.WriteLine("Withdrawal not allowed")
End If
MyAccount.OverdraftAvailable = True
MyAccount.SetOverdraft(100)
If MyAccount.Withdraw(150) Then
    Console.WriteLine("Bbalance (with overdraft): {0}", _
                      MyAccount.CurrentBalance)
Else
    Console.WriteLine("Withdrawal not allowed")
End If
End Sub
```

Listing 5.32: The `Sub Main()` from Listing 5.16

Almost every statement in this sub makes use of the `MyAccount` object reference variable, to the extent where typing the variable's name is tedious and repetitious. The `With..End With` structure allows us to consider the object reference `MyAccount` to be a default object reference, as shown in Listing 5.33.

```
Sub Main()
  Dim MyAccount As BankAccount = New BankAccount()
  With MyAccount
    .AccountName = "John Smith"
    Console.WriteLine("Account name: {0}", .AccountName)
    Console.WriteLine("Account balance: {0}", _
                                      .CurrentBalance)
    .Deposit(100)
    Console.WriteLine("Account balance: {0}", _
                                      .CurrentBalance)
    If .Withdraw(150) Then
        Console.WriteLine("Account balance: {0}", _
                                      .CurrentBalance)
    Else
        Console.WriteLine("Withdrawal not allowed")
    End If
    .OverdraftAvailable = True
    .SetOverdraft(100)
    If .Withdraw(150) Then
        Console.WriteLine("Balance (with o/d): {0}", _
                                      .CurrentBalance)
```

```
        Else
           Console.WriteLine("Withdrawal not allowed")
        End If
     End With
  End Sub
```

Listing 5.33: The same code, reduced by using a `With..End With` structure

In the listing, the amount of code has been reduced by using the `With..End With` structure. Within the `With MyAccount..End With` block, any object reference that begins with a dot operator on its own is taken to be a property or method of `MyAccount`. The result is that the programmer types less code (and in all likelihood endures fewer typing errors because of this), and Visual Basic does not have to keep accessing one of potentially many objects to get to its properties and methods. Within the `With..End With` block, accesses to this one object are therefore much faster to resolve and the code executes more efficiently.

The `With..End With` structure can be used in any situation where the dot operator can be used, so it can also be used with structures and with the built-in objects provided in the .NET framework.

Exercise 5.6

Using a `With..End With` structure, display the type, type-code and hash-code of an `Integer` variable (these are available via the methods `GetType()`, `GetTypeCode()` and `GetHashCode()`).

5.4 Subs, Functions and Parameters

We've already looked at and made use of subs and functions within class definitions. We can refer to them collectively as subroutines (Microsoft uses the word 'procedure' to refer to either subs or functions, but years of programming in Pascal have made me wary of this – in Pascal a procedure is the equivalent of a Visual Basic sub, and as I always remember it that way, I prefer the term subroutine to refer to both sub and function). Subs and functions can also exist in Visual Basic outside of a class definition – in this case they simply become methods of the overall program.

A sub defines a sequence of statements that define some operation as does a function, the distinction being that a function returns some value or object as a result. In themselves, these make important structural elements of a program or a class, since they allow us to create operations that we can execute by simply invoking their name, almost as if we had extended Visual Basic to add new commands that were useful to a class or program.

Subs and functions can optionally be defined so that we can tell them what data to operate on. Consider the two similar subs in Listing 5.34.

```
Sub SetXToZero()
    X = 0
End Sub

Sub SetToZero(ByRef X As Integer)
    X = 0
End Sub
```

Listing 5.34: Two versions of a sub, one with a parameter

The first, `SetXToZero`, does the simple job of setting a variable to zero. For it to work, there must be a variable with the name X, and the sub must be able to access it (it cannot be a `Private` member variable of a different class, or a variable declared with the `Dim` statement inside another sub). This sub has a very limited remit because of this – it can only work on one variable in a program, and only then in a very pre-defined way. We would call it simply by invoking its name in a statement:

```
SetXToZero() 'assign zero to the variable X
```

Note that if it was called and some variable X had not been declared, the subroutine call would fail and the program would probably crash. What we need is some way to generalize the subroutine call so that it can act on any suitable variable.

The second sub, `SetToZero` is defined along with some additional information: the part, `ByRef X As Integer`, indicates that the sub expects an `Integer` variable to be 'passed to it'. `ByRef` indicates that the variable will be passed in such a way that the sub will have the power to access it directly and alter its contents. As a result, the sub `SetToZero` can be used to zero the value in *any* Integer variable. We can call the sub as shown in Listing 5.35.

```
Dim someNumber As Integer = 50
SetToZero(someNumber)
'someNumber now has a value of 0.
```

Listing 5.35: Using a `ByRef` parameter to change a variable

The variable `someNumber` is initialized to have a value of 50. We then pass it to `SetToZero`, and can expect that subsequently it will contain the value zero. *During the execution* of the subroutine call, the variable `someNumber` is referred to within the `SetToZero()` sub as X. X acts as an alias for whatever variable we pass to the sub as it executes.

Note that if we call this subroutine without passing an `Integer` variable to it, this will constitute an error. However, in this case, Visual Basic has a way of checking to see whether the routine has been invoked correctly (by checking the actual variable passed against the type we have defined it to work on). If we pass either no variable, or a variable that is not an `Integer` type, Visual Basic will recognize the error and refuse to compile the program.

So now we can define a sub or function so that we can send data to it for it to work with. We can even pass a whole list of variables to this sub one at a time (Listing 5.36).

```
Dim list(100) As Integer
'Some code here to change the values in list()
For Each value In list
   SetToZero(value)
Next
'All elements of list() are now zero.
```

Listing 5.36: Using a `ByRef` parameter to change a number of variables

In this code fragment, `list` is an array, which is a multiple of individual variables referred to by a single name (`list`, in this case). We will have a detailed look at arrays in the next chapter, but for now it is enough to state that once we have a number of variables in a structured form like this, it is possible to access them all in sequence using a `For..Next` or `For Each..Next` code structure. In the example code, each `Integer` in `List` is sent as a parameter to the `SetToZero()` sub in turn, with the result that all members of the array will be set to zero.

The general name for the variable defined in the first line of the second version of sub `SetToZero()` is a *parameter*. A parameter is a variable used in a sub or function that has been sent to it from the code that calls it (see Figure 5.2). The purpose of parameters is to generalize subroutines by making them work on the data we pass to them, rather than some specific variable or variables.

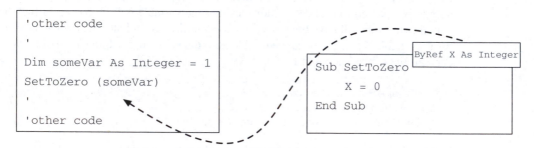

Figure 5.2 A reference parameter acts as an alias for a variable

Consider `Console.WriteLine()`. This is a sub defined within `Console`, and it would be quite useless if we did not have the facility to send items of data to it for display. The statements in Listing 5.37 both make use of `Console.WriteLine()`, but each passes a different piece of data to it. This facility is very powerful, since it allows us to write a generalized subroutine that can act on any data that we decide to send to it, either passively to calculate results, or more actively to change the data in some way.

```
Console.WriteLine("Name: {0}", MyAccount.AccountName)
Console.WriteLine("Balance: {0}", MyAccount.Balance)
```

Listing 5.37: Passing data to the `Console` via the `WriteLine()` parameters

Note that `Console.WriteLine()` in the statements above accepts more than a single parameter – a comma separates the first parameter (a string such as `"Name: {0}"`) from the second (in these cases, the name of a variable). Subroutines can have any number of parameters. A list of parameters defined for a sub or function is matched up with the list of variables passed to it by their position. The first variable passed to a routine is passed 'into' the first parameter, the second into the second parameter and so on.

As an example of how you would define a subroutine with more than one parameter, Listing 5.38 gives a function subroutine that calculates the discounted price of a purchased item, passing both price and discount rate as parameters:

```
Function DiscountedPrice(ByVal Price As Decimal, _
                         ByVal DiscountPercent As Single) _
                         As Decimal
    Return (Price * (100 - DiscountPercent)) / 100
End Function
```

Listing 5.38: A function with two parameters

When this function is called, the first variable in the list passed to it should be the price; the second should be the percentage discount rate. Regardless of the names of the two variables passed, or even if either or both are simply literal values, the first will be referred to within the function as `Price`, the second as `DiscountPercent`. Note that the function's return type (the result passed back to the calling statement) is defined as being of type `Decimal`. Since we are calculating a new price based on an existing price (which is a `Decimal` variable), this is only sensible.

Exercise 5.7

In Exercise 5.3 a) you were asked to write program code that calculated the factorial of a number.

a) Package the code to calculate the factorial of a number as a function that accepts a single `Integer` parameter.

b) Implement the function again, this time using a `For..Next` loop instead of a `Do..Loop`.

5.4.1 `ByVal` and `ByRef`

A parameter acts as a way of assigning a name, or an alias to an input value for use within the subroutine. That saves us having to use variables with the same names as the ones defined as parameter names in the subroutine definition, which would be a serious restriction on the use of a sub or function.

Since the two parameters in Listing 5.38 are passed by value (`ByVal`), we can be sure that no matter what is done with them inside the function, there will be no effect on any variable that is passed as an input – they are 'input-only' parameters. The function simply returns a value calculated from them, e.g. Listing 5.39.

```
Sub Main()
    Dim p As Decimal = 50
    Console.WriteLine("Discounted price: {0}", _
                           DiscountedPrice(p, 10))
    Console.WriteLine("Original price: {0}", p)
End Sub
```

Listing 5.39: A `ByVal` parameter is not changed by a subroutine

Here, the variable p will not be affected, and so the second WriteLine() state-ment will show that p still has a value of 50. What this demonstrates is that when a parameter is passed ByVal (the default), it cannot be affected by the routine it is passed to. This is a very desirable feature as a default, since we can be sure that a subroutine with ByVal parameters will not have any side-effects caused by variables being changed inadvertently. We can always say that ByVal parameters are input parameters.

Parameters that are passed by reference (ByRef) can be affected by the sub-routine they are passed to. Because of this, ByRef is not the default type of par-ameter. By using a ByRef parameter, we are indicating that this parameter will act as an output from the subroutine it is defined for. For example, consider this alter-native way of calculating a discounted price (Listing 5.40).

```
Sub ApplyDiscount(ByRef Price As Decimal, _
                       ByVal DiscountPercent As Single)
    Price -= Price * DiscountPercent / 100
End Sub
```

Listing 5.40: A `ByRef` parameter can be changed by a subroutine

Note that in this case, the Price parameter is passed ByRef (it is necessary to type ByRef when the first line of the sub is entered, otherwise the default, ByVal, will be used). The DiscountPercent parameter is still defined as a ByVal parameter, since there is no intention to change this value, either inside or outwith the sub.

Effectively, Price has been defined as an input/output parameter, while DiscountPercent is purely an input parameter. When the value in Price is changed by subtracting the specified discount (a percentage of Price), this will affect the value in any variable passed into the Price parameter. To use this routine, simply call it passing the price that is to be updated and the discount rate:

```
ApplyDiscount(p, 10)
Console.WriteLine("Discounted price: {0}", p)
```

In the above call, whatever value was in p before the subroutine call will have been reduced by 10% once the subroutine has executed. In this case, p has acted as both an input to and an output from the sub.

Parameters are a general purpose way of sending variables to subroutines, almost as if each parameter was an envelope that could be attached to a subroutine call. Some parameters (those passed by value using the ByVal keyword) act as ways of inputting a value to a sub or function so that it has data to work on. These 'envelopes' are simply deposited into the subroutine so the data can be worked on. Others (those passed by reference, using the `ByRef` keyword) can also take on new values assigned to them within the sub or function, and so act as carriers for data passed back from the routine. These 'envelopes' are returned to the sender once the subroutine has finished executing, with the updated versions of the parameters on-board.

Parameters can seem complex at first, but just keep in mind the following simple rules.

- Parameters are defined in brackets after the title of a sub or function.
- Each parameter has a name and a type.
- A subroutine can have multiple parameters, each with its own name, type and calling style (`ByVal` or `ByRef`). When there is more than one parameter, passed values are associated with parameters by the order in which they appear in the list.
- A parameter that is not specified explicitly as `ByRef` will always be a value (`ByVal`) parameter. If you omit it, Visual Studio will insert the `ByVal` keyword automatically.
- `ByVal` parameters are inputs to a subroutine. If the parameter's value is changed within the subroutine, the change will not be reflected in the value of the variable passed into that parameter.
- `ByRef` parameters are input/output parameters, so any change made to a `ByRef` parameter as the subroutine executes will reflect back in the value of whatever variable was passed into that parameter.
- A function can return a single value as a result. However both functions and subs can be defined to provide any number of outputs by declaring them as `ByRef` parameters.

Exercise 5.8

a) Write a sub that defines two parameters of type `Single`. The subroutine should include code that asks the user to enter values for the `Length` and `Width` of a rectangle, and return these values as outputs. Test the sub.

b) Redefine the sub from part a) as a function. Leave the parameters as originally defined, but make the function return the `Area` of the rectangle as its result. Test the function.

5.4.2 Subroutine Signatures

The combination of a subroutine's name, parameter styles and types and, if it is a function, return type are referred to as its *signature*. Thinking about it, these are the essential bits of information we need to know to call a sub or function. For example, the `ApplyDiscount` sub has the following signature:

```
Sub ApplyDiscount(ByRef As Decimal, ByVal As Single)
```

This tells us that we can use the `ApplyDiscount` routine by passing a `Decimal` and a `Single` parameter respectively, and that the first (`Decimal`) parameter may be changed by the call. We don't need to know the actual parameter names to call the sub (the general case is that variables passed do not match the parameter's names anyway), and so these need not form part of the signature. A *legal* call to a sub or function with parameters only requires that an integer value or variable is passed where an integer parameter is expected, and so on for other data types. Of course, just because we've used the expected types of parameters in the right place does not give us any guarantee that we are calling the subroutine correctly; just because your name and address are both pieces of text, this does not make them interchangeable.

The `DiscountedPrice` function has this signature:

```
Function DiscountedPrice(ByVal As Decimal, _
                         ByVal As Single) As Decimal
```

This tells us that to use `DiscountedPrice`, we need to pass two variables or values, the first a `Decimal` and the second a `Single`, neither of which will be altered by the function. The function will return a `Decimal` result, which we could assign to a `Decimal` type variable. If we wanted to use the `DiscountedPrice` function to *change* the value of some variable containing a price, we could call it thus:

```
ItemPrice = DiscountedPrice(ItemPrice, 10)
```

This will use the original `ItemPrice` value in the calculation of the discounted price, and update it with the new, discounted value on return from the function call.

5.4.3 Overloading Subroutine Names

A subroutine's signature makes it distinctive; it is because of this that Visual Basic can inform you if you have not called a sub or function correctly. This makes it possible to create two subroutines with the same name, provided their signatures differ in some way – for example in the types or number of parameters. For example, we might use a subroutine to display a person's name on the console. Using overloading, we can provide two versions (Listing 5.41).

```
Sub DisplayName(ByVal Name As String)
     Console.WriteLine(Name)
End Sub
Sub DisplayName(ByVal First As String, _
                ByVal Last As String)
     Console.WriteLine(First & " " & Last)
End Sub
```

Listing 5.41: Two overloaded subs

Which sub gets called depends on which matches the signature of the function written in the calling code. For example, a call like:

```
DisplayName("Fred Smith")
```

or:

```
Dim N As String = "Fred Smith"
DisplayName(N)
```

will result in the first version of `DisplayName()` being executed. However, a call like:

```
DisplayName("Fred", "Smith")
```

or:

```
Dim F As String = "Fred"
Dim L As String = "Smith"
DisplayName(F, L)
```

will result in the second version being executed. Overloading subroutines in this way allows us to provide a variety of ways to call on what is effectively one subroutine; at least that is the way we should think of it. However, it is easily possible to misuse subroutine overloading to provide a number of subroutines that, while they share a name, do not do the same job at all, e.g. Listing 5.42.

```
Function Count(ByVal C As Integer) As String
    Do While C > 0
        Console.WriteLine(C)
        C -= 1
    Loop
    Return "Finished"
End Function

Function Count(ByVal S As String) As Integer
    Return S.Length()
End Function
```

Listing 5.42: Not a good example of overloading

In the code in Listing 5.42, two functions with the same name are written to do two entirely different jobs. The first writes messages to the console as it counts down from some number, and then returns a 'Finished' message to the calling code. The second returns the number of letters in a string passed as a parameter. While both of these do a job that fits the name of the function perfectly well, the availability of both in a single program will be confusing. When we overload subroutines, Visual Basic has no way of checking whether the jobs they do are in any way semantically related (do they mean the same thing?). It is our job as programmers to ensure that this is the case.

Bertrand Meyer, one of the pre-eminent gurus of object-oriented programming, has published a paper suggesting that overloading is in fact a bad principle, and that object-oriented programming is far better without it[1]. While he is at odds with many C++, Java, VB. NET and C# programmers, even they would agree that thoughtless use of overloading would be a very dangerous practice.

The notion of a subroutine's signature is important to us as programmers because we need to be aware of what it expects when we call it. If we get any of the bits wrong, the call will be an error and the program will not even compile. It is also important to Visual Basic's compiler, which checks all calls to a subroutine against its signature so that it can check for these errors. Without this information, Visual Basic would not be able to point out errors in your code, and programs would be much more difficult to write.

When we get further down the road of object-oriented programming, the idea of a subroutine's signature will become much more important, due to the flexible way that objects can interact. For now, simply pay attention to the help the editor gives you when entering subroutine calls in your programs, and particularly the errors Visual Basic indicates when you are writing or testing a subroutine call (either to a standard subroutine that is part of .NET, or to any of your own subs, functions or methods).

5.5 Errors and Exception-Handling

We have already covered all of the code structures that you might consider useful in implementing an algorithm in Visual Basic. However, writing a program is seldom as simple as directly implementing algorithms; in particular we will always have to deal with situations in which the program has not progressed as expected – i.e. when errors occur.

As a programmer, you will have to get used to the idea that errors are a fact of life. You will undoubtedly have already met a number of errors if you've been trying out the code examples or exercises on your way through this book. Some of them were possibly simple typing errors, in which case VB would have informed you of the problem and given you a chance to fix it before it would allow you to run the program. These are *syntax errors*.

Others may have been due to errors in the logic of the code – for example you might have wrongly used a < instead of a > operator in an If..Then statement: this would cause the enclosed code to execute under the wrong circumstances. With errors like these, there is not much you can do beyond testing the program thoroughly enough for them to show up in unexpected results. These are *logic errors*.

However, one type of error is unavoidable, and while you can do a lot to prevent it in the way you write a program, you can never remove the possibility entirely. A *run-time error* is an error that occurs while a program is running (obviously) and typically occurs because some external interaction does not happen as expected. For example, assume you have the following section of code (Listing 5.43) in one of your programs.

---

[1] *Journal of Object-Oriented Programming*, Oct/Nov 2001, Overloading vs object technology

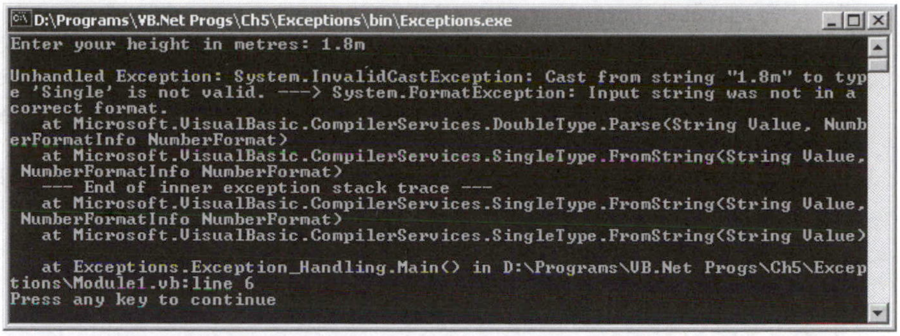

Figure 5.3 The result of a simple typing error

```
Dim H As Single
Console.Write("Enter your height in metres: ")
H = Console.ReadLine()
Console.WriteLine("You are {0} centimetres tall.", H * 100)
```

Listing 5.43: Code that depends on correct user-input

Provided the user is well behaved (and accustomed to using software), you can expect that he or she will enter a number (probably somewhere between 1.5 and 2.0) that will be stored in the numeric variable H. What if the user either deliberately or accidentally enters something that is not a number? This could be a typing error, mischief or perhaps the user was trying to be helpful by entering something like **1.8m**. Either way, the result will be to try to store a non-numeric value in a numeric variable, and Visual Basic will respond in the familiar (and heart-sinking) way shown in Figure 5.3.

Of course this is not a serious problem. The user can re-run the program and enter **1.8** (if they can figure out the bizarre sequence of error messages on the screen). To prevent the crash altogether, we could make the program more robust by assigning the user's entry to a string and testing whether it was a number, using VB's IsNumeric() function before assigning it to H. By doing this in a Do..Until loop, the user's input could be checked until it was Ok, as shown in Listing 5.44.

```
Dim userInput As String
Dim H As Single
Do
    Console.Write("Enter your height in metres: ")
    userInput = Console.ReadLine()
Loop Until IsNumeric(userInput)
H = CSng(userInput)
Console.WriteLine("You are {0} centimetres tall.", H * 100)
```

Listing 5.44: Validating user-input with IsNumeric()

However, there are likely to be many places in a program where the user could enter invalid data. To have to protect every one of them in this way would become a heavy burden, and it could easily become very difficult to pick out the actual algorithm being implemented from the mass of *error avoidance* code that results. That last point is a very important one. As programmers, we struggle to write code that implements an algorithm in as readable a way as possible. Indeed, structured programming constructs like If..Then..Else, Do..Loop, etc. were initially proposed as code features that would maximize the readability of a program at the expense of the freedom of the programmer; it would be a pity to undo all this by making program code more complex than it had to be to do its job.

5.5.1 Exceptions

VB and .NET provide us with a different way to solve problems like this, in fact to deal with any run-time error, whether it is due to errors in the user's input or other problems such as off-line printers, missing files or a host of other input/output related problems. It is direct and elegant – implement the program's algorithm directly, ignoring the potential run-time errors that could occur, but embed it in a structure designed to deal with *any* problems that occur.

When the program runs as expected (the normal condition), our straightforward coding of the algorithm works as we expect. When a run-time error occurs, it is treated as an *exception* to normal operation, and special *exception-handling* code is executed. The exception-handling code can either report the error to the user, or try to fix the problem, or simply ignore it and leave it up to the user to deal with. However, we can ensure that any exceptions to normal operation are dealt with so that the program does not crash. Listing 5.45 shows an exception-handler defined to protect user-input from causing a crash.

```
Sub Main()
    Dim H As Single
    Console.Write("Enter your height in metres: ")
    Try
        H = Console.ReadLine()
        Console.WriteLine("You are {0}cm tall.", H * 100)
    Catch
        Console.WriteLine("Error in input.")
    End Try
End Sub
```

Listing 5.45: A simple exception-handler

In Listing 5.45, the code between Try and Catch is the *nominal path* through the program. Provided all goes well, this code will be executed and the program will end without any error conditions. However, if *anything* goes wrong with this code (between Try and Catch), the error will be caught by the .NET run-time system, and control will automatically transfer to the block between Catch and End Try. In this case, we provide a simple message that something has gone wrong, although we can provide a number of alternative paths depending on what went wrong. Consider the example in Listing 5.46:

```
Sub Main()
    Dim numerator, denominator, quotient As Integer
    Console.Write("Enter two numbers separated by ENTER: ")
    Try
        numerator = Console.ReadLine()
        denominator = Console.ReadLine()
        quotient = numerator \ denominator
        Console.WriteLine("{0}/{1}={2}", numerator, _
                          denominator, quotient)
    Catch
        Console.WriteLine("Error in input.")
    End Try
End Sub
```

Listing 5.46: Code that could cause several types of problem

In the code shown several types of input could cause problems. The user could enter a number for numerator but a non-numeric value for denominator or vice-versa, or the user could enter 0 for denominator. The first two problems would cause errors due to the attempt to enter non-numeric data into a numeric variable. The third would cause a *divide-by-zero* error, since in computer terms (as in mathematics) this is impossible. The way the Catch block is formed in Listing 5.45, the error would be caught and reported and a crash would be averted. However, we could improve the error-handling by telling the user what went wrong, as shown in Listing 5.47.

```
Sub Main()
    Dim numerator, denominator, quotient As Integer
    Console.Write("Enter two numbers separated by ENTER: ")
    Try
        numerator = Console.ReadLine()
        denominator = Console.ReadLine()
        quotient = numerator \ denominator
        Console.WriteLine("{0}/{1}={2}", numerator, _
                              denominator, quotient)
    Catch invalidEx As InvalidCastException
        Console.WriteLine("One entry is not a number.")
    Catch div0Ex As DivideByZeroException
        Console.WriteLine("Attempt to divide by zero.")
    End Try
End Sub
```

Listing 5.47: Explicit handling of specific exception types

The code in Listing 5.46 recognizes that there are two possible sources of input error. The first of these is caused by the user entering a non-numeric value into a numeric variable. This is called an *invalid cast* error, the name coming from the use of a variable to perform a role it is not qualified for. A miscast actor is given a role that is outwith their specialism, like asking W.C. Fields to be a romantic lead. A miscast variable is similarly used to store information it cannot deal with, like passing a string into a numeric variable.

The second error the code deals with is the divide-by-zero problem. In either case, .NET provides a purpose-built Exception class for dealing with it. You can examine the range of Exception classes provided by .NET by looking up Exception Hierarchy in the Visual Studio help system.

Exercise 5.9

The activity at the end of Chapter 4 was to build a simple calculator in which the user enters an expression and this is evaluated. You should now see that there are several situations in which the program will fail or crash, these being:

a) non-numeric input from the user;

b) division by zero;

c) the user entering an operator that is not supported;

d) numeric overflow (operation results in a value that exceeds the range of the variable it is assigned to) or underflow (operation results in a value that is too small for the precision that the variable it is assigned to can store).

For each of the possible error types above, try to enter data into the program to find out how the program will react (i.e. whether it will crash or simply provide a wrong answer). Add exception handling code to cope with the error results.

5.5.2 Structured Exception-Handling

The mechanism used by Visual Basic and .NET to handle run-time errors is known as Structured Exception-Handling (SEH), since the error-handling code is organized as a program structure similar in format to the other code structures we've looked at in this chapter. The general format for an exception-handling structure in Visual Basic .NET is shown in Figure 5.4.

The general outline of exception-handling shown in Figure 5.4 demonstrates the main features of SEH.

- Code is grouped into blocks in SEH, with specific blocks for code that causes exceptions, code that handles exceptions and clean-up code.

- Code between `Try` and the first `Catch` block will execute completely, or until an exception occurs.

- If an exception occurs, .NET will transfer control to the first block that handles the exception. If no block handles the exception that happened, the program will behave just as it would have if no exception-handling was used – most usually, it will crash.

- If a less specific handler for an exception appears in the code *before* a more specific one (e.g. `Catch ex As Exception` occurs before `Catch invalidEx As InvalidCastException`) it will catch the error. Because of this, you must be careful to list exception handlers in order of their specificness to errors. If `Catch ex As Exception` occurs first in the list, none of the others will ever execute.

```
Try
    'some problem here could cause an exception
Catch el As SomeExceptionType
    '
Catch e2 As SomeOtherExceptionType
    'One or more of these blocks will attempt to handle
    'exceptions
Catch e As Exception
    'This will handle any exceptions not yet dealt with

Finally
    'code here will always execute, whether or not an
    'exception happened
End Try
```

Figure 5.4 Outline of the exception-handling structure

■ A `Finally` clause can be entered as the last block in a `Try..End Try` structure. This will mark the start of code that will always run, regardless of whether an exception occurred or not. This is useful, since it allows us to insert 'clean-up code' to perform any program housekeeping that might be necessary. This could be code to close a file that was opened before the exception occurred, or to return a result from a function or any other operation that we need to guarantee will be performed.

The terminology used in SEH might at first seem to be obscure or affected. However, from the standpoint of a programmer dealing with bad things happening in a program as efficiently as possible, they make perfect sense.

An exception, when it happens, is recognized by the program code running; this might be because it is something fundamental (e.g. an attempt to pass a string into a numeric variable) or something specific to your own program code (e.g. an attempt to withdraw cash from a bank account that has a balance of zero). In either case, the problem is easily recognized by the code it happened in; the difficult part is normally figuring out how to proceed once it has happened.

Structured exception-handling is a way of organizing code so that errors can be dealt with at the most appropriate place in a program, in a way that is best suited to the application's job and the person using it. At the point an error occurs, the only available options are to stop the program running because the error is unrecoverable, to ignore the error or to pass information about the error to the application programmer and allow that programmer to decide how to proceed. If an error occurs in your code because the user has entered a negative number when a positive one was expected, you can ask the user to re-enter the number. If, however, the error occurs in code that your program uses, such as the .NET CLR, the only option is to pass the error on to you to deal with as shown in Figure 5.5.

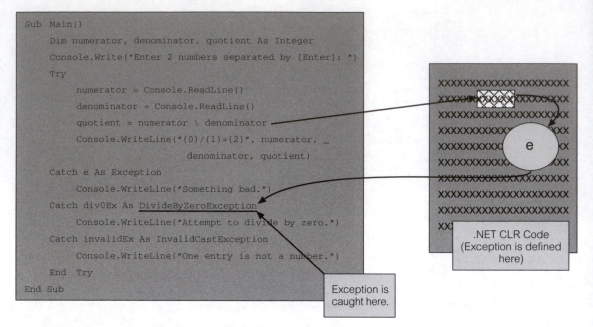

Figure 5.5 An exception – thrown and caught

In .NET, an error that occurs during a call to, say, `Console.ReadLine()`, causes an exception to be *thrown*. That effectively means that it is being passed to whatever code is prepared to catch it. If no code catches it, the only option left will be for .NET to terminate the program. However, if you are prepared for some type of exception, you will have written a `Catch` block that will prevent the program from crashing and allow you to try to recover from it. At the very worst case, if you catch an exception you cannot deal with, you can inform the user with a descriptive message and allow the program to terminate gracefully.

5.5.3 Throwing Exceptions

Generally when an exception can occur in your code, you should write a handler that will deal with it. However, in some situations there would be nothing your code could do with it apart from informing the user and terminating. For example, the following subroutine (Listing 5.48) has the potential for problems.

```
Function Divide(ByVal Num1 As Integer, _
               ByVal Num2 As Integer) As Integer
      Divide = Num1 \ Num2
End Function
```

Listing 5.48: Potential problems in a function

We could deal with the possible divide-by-zero error within this function by using the code shown in Listing 5.49.

```
Function Divide(ByVal Num1 As Integer, _
               ByVal Num2 As Integer) As Integer
    Try
        Divide = Num1 \ Num2
    Catch div0Ex As DivideByZeroException
        Console.WriteLine("Error - Divide by zero.")
        Return 0
    End Try
End Function
```

Listing 5.49: One possible solution – not ideal

The problem that this introduces is that we do not necessarily know where this program code would be called from. The program may not use the console at all (it could be a WinForms program), or it may not be an interactive program, so there will be no user to inform. In a situation like this, we can only deal with the error properly if we know the context of the program it is being used in, so attempting to recover from the error, informing the user of the error or simply ignoring the error may all be inappropriate. The thing to do in this situation is to pass the error to the code that called the function – *throw an exception*. Since we already have a ready-made exception (`div0Ex`), we can simply pass this back. The code in Listing 5.50 re-throws the exception so that it will re-appear in the code from which the function was called. While this may look like we are avoiding the issue, the situation leaves us with no alternatives, and the code that calls the function is much better placed to determine an appropriate response to this error. The code calling the function will of course need to provide an exception-handler, or it will be prone to crashing.

```
Function Divide(ByVal Num1 As Integer, _
               ByVal Num2 As Integer) As Integer
    Try
        Divide = Num1 \ Num2
    Catch div0Ex As DivideByZeroException
        Throw div0Ex
        Return 0
    End Try
End Function
```

Listing 5.50: A more general solution

5.5.4 Exception-Handling Guidelines

Unlike the other program structures that are dictated by algorithm and program design, exception-handling is more a matter of convention. Most software houses impose certain stylistic guidelines on their programmers so that one programmer can easily read and understand the work done by another. Exception-handling is a subject area that different programmers deal with in different ways. However, there are certain aspects of exception-handling that are worth consideration by any programmer.

■ Vet your code for potential errors, and add exception-handling wherever these may occur. As you build and test programs, you will be informed by Visual Studio of errors that caused crashes. When this happens, the name of the exception is provided, and you can use this information to provide exception-handlers.

■ It is tempting to wrap an entire program up in a `Try..Catch e As Exception..End Try` block, since then it will never crash. However, you will never get to know of specific problems in the code (they will be hidden by the exception handling) and will not be able to insert code to recover from otherwise easy to handle errors. Deal with exceptions on a case by case basis; protect blocks where un-validated user-input is passed into variables, where calculations may cause overflows or divide-by-zero errors or where any external device such as a printer or disk drive is used.

■ Don't use exception-handlers to replace good structured programming. For example, you might be tempted to use an exception-handler so that you can write code to attempt to access properties or methods of a reference variable that may not have an object attached to it. It is much more sensible to test if the reference variable is null using `If Not myObject Is Nothing Then...` Exception-handlers should not be used to permit bad coding.

■ You could avoid the issue of error-handling by throwing all exceptions back to the calling code. Two things should stop you doing this: 1) you cannot do this from `Sub Main ()` (or an event-handler which acts as an entry point to a WinForms application the way `Sub Main ()` does to a console program), since there is no calling code to catch it, and 2) it is lazy and defeats the entire principle of SEH, which is to deal with errors at the most appropriate place in program code.

■ Exception-handling is class-based – that is, exceptions are created as objects in code according to the error recognized at the point things are seen to have gone wrong. .NET provides a good range of Exception classes to take care of general problems (e.g. faulty casts, arithmetic problems, bad procedure calls, etc.) and others to take care of specific problems in user-interfaces (WinForms and WebForms), databases, Internet applications, etc. You should use these classes wherever possible, and only derive your own exception classes (by inheritance) when the exception classes provided are inadequate for the purpose (i.e. rarely).

Exercise 5.9

In Exercise 5.6 you were asked to write a function to calculate the factorial of an `Integer` parameter. If you go back and test this function, you will notice that it is very easy to provide a value that will cause an error – the factorial function's result grows very quickly so that even small input values can cause an arithmetic overflow.

a) Test the factorial function with a number of values and determine the exception type that is caused when an overflow occurs (hint – try the factorial of 28).

b) Change the function so that when an exception occurs, it re-throws it to be caught by the calling code (see Listing 5.49).

c) Add exception-handling to `Sub Main()` so that exceptions in the factorial function are dealt with properly.

5.6 Scope

The word 'scope' is derived from the Greek for 'target', and is sometimes used to express the meaning 'range of view'. The scope of an identifier in a program (a variable, constant, enumeration, sub, function, structure or class name in a program) is the range of code that it can be accessed from. Visual Basic and .NET apply very specific rules to determine the scope of an identifier. If you attempt to access an identifier outwith its scope, you either get an error or access to something else with the same name. There are a variety of possible scopes for an identifier, being:

- class scope
- module scope
- namespace scope
- block scope

The member variables and methods in a class have class scope, and this is modified by the visibility modifiers `Public` and `Private` (also `Friend` and `Protected`, which we'll meet in Chapter 7).

5.6.1 Class Scope

Class scope runs from the line immediately following a class identifier (e.g. `Class Rectangle`) to the `End Class` statement. Within this area, all of the members (member variables, subs, functions and properties) can be accessed directly by code within the class methods and properties. Outside the class definition, only the members given the `Public` scope modifier are visible. An example is given in Listing 5.51, in which the members marked `Private` can be accessed only from code inside the class methods or properties. The members marked `Public` can be accessed from an object of the class using the dot operator, e.g. Listing 5.52.

```
Class SomeClass
        Private internalData As String   'Only in class
        Public externalData As String    'Wherever SomeClass
                                         'is in scope
```

```
      Private Sub internalMethod()
          'Only callable from inside a class method
      End Sub
      Public Sub interfaceMethod()
          'Callable from anywhere SomeClass is in scope
      End Sub
  End Class
```

Listing 5.51: Class scope

```
Dim sc As New SomeClass()
sc.externalData = "Test"
sc.interfaceMethod()
```

Listing 5.52: Accessing the `Public` members of a class

All of the above statements are legal within any code to which SomeClass is accessible. To determine where that is, we need to look at Namespace scope. Generally, this means throughout a project, although certain modifications can be applied to hide identifiers that would be in scope within a project from parts of the project. A *namespace* is an area of code that has been marked so that other code must subscribe to it, and for now, we can consider this as being all of the code in any project that we create, plus System scope, which is applied by default to any new project you create in Visual Studio. System scope gives us access to the console, various useful code libraries (such as the primitive data types, collections, strings, maths libraries, etc.) and some debugging facilities.

The point of class scope is to provide encapsulation in code: the facility to hide the internal workings of a class and its objects, but to allow access to an interface, or set of properties and methods that allow us to work with it. We'll see later that we need to modify the simple public/private notion of class scope once we bring inheritance into the picture.

5.6.2 Module Scope

Module scope is similar to Class scope, in that members declared inside a module can be accessed by any code within it, but only members declared as `Public` can be accessed outwith it. While a class behaves as a template for creating many individual objects, a module is a one-off construction. When we declare a `Public` or `Private` variable inside a module, we get exactly one set of the variables declared, rather than one per object as you would expect with a class.

The picture also gets a bit more complex since we are able to create whole class definitions inside a module. Within the module, the scope rules still apply to the class – private variables are visible only within the class, public ones are available outside the class. However, the scope rules apply so that scope is nested, as shown in Listing 5.53 which summarizes the scope rules for code in two or more modules.

```
'This first module declares two classes, one Public, one
'Private. We can test the visibility of these to code in
'this module and in other modules . . .
Module ScopeModule

    Private Class MyPrivateClass
        'Any public member variables, properties or methods
        'declared here will be visible to any code in the
        'module. Private declarations are visible to the
        'class only. Objects of this class can only be
        'declared inside the module, since the class is
        'Private to this module.
        Public ANumber As Integer
        Private AString As String
    End Class

    Public Class MyPublicClass
        'Any public member variables, properties or methods
        'declared here will be visible to any code where an
        'object is visible. Private declarations are
        'visible to the class only. Objects of this class
        'can be declared anywhere in a program which
        'includes this module, since the class is Public.
        Public ANumber As Integer
        Private AString As String
    End Class

    'This sub shows which elements of the above classes are
    'visible (i.e. in scope)..
    Public Sub Test()
        Dim Pri As New MyPrivateClass()
        Dim Pub As New MyPublicClass()
        Pri.ANumber = 2            'OK - ANumber is Public
        Pri.AString = "Hello"      'Error since AString is
                                   'Private
        Pub.ANumber = 4            'Also OK
        Pub.AString = "Hello Again" ' Error - Not possible
    End Sub

End Module

'This module shows which elements of the above module are
'in 'project' scope.
Module ScopeTest

    Sub Main()
        'Declare a member of the Public class . . .
        Dim TPub As New ScopeModule.MyPublicClass()
        TPub.ANumber = 2
        TPub.AString = "Hello"     'ERROR, Member not in
                                   scope,
                                   'even though the class is.
        'Try declaring a member of the Private class.
```

```
                Dim TPri As New ScopeModule.MyPrivateClass()
                ' ERROR - this Class is not in scope
            End Sub
        End Module
```

Listing 5.53: Scope rules for Module and Class scope

5.6.3 Namespace Scope

A namespace is a unit of organization in a .NET program. Every .NET project is automatically organized as a namespace with the same name as the project, so, for example, when you create a new Visual Basic .NET project and leave it with its default name, it will occupy a namespace called `Project1`. The entire assembly, which is all of the files that are component parts of the project, are within the project's namespace. You can also declare other namespaces within a project, which are nested within the overall project namespace.

By declaring a namespace in a project, you indicate that all of the contents (modules, classes, variables, etc.) are placed within a scope that can be explicitly *imported* so that they can be used easily outside of the namespace. To code outside the namespace, identifiers declared within it must prefixed with the namespace's name to be valid, unless the whole namespace is subscribed to using an `Imports` statement. The `Imports` statement effectively says 'I want to incorporate the declarations within the specified namespace into my program'. By importing a namespace, any public declarations within it are accessible without qualification to the code that does the importing, e.g. Listing 5.54.

```
    Imports System.Console
    Module ScopeModule
        Private Class MyPrivateClass
                'etc . . .
```

Listing 5.54: Importing a namespace

The statement immediately before the start of `ScopeModule` in Listing 5.54 indicates that the declarations within the `System.Console` namespace are to be made directly available to the module. Using this statement, all of the declarations within the console namespace can be accessed *without the Console. prefix*. For example, within a sub or function in `ScopeModule`, it is now possible to write code like Listing 5.55.

```
    Public Sub Test()
        Dim n As String
        Write("Enter your name:")
        n = ReadLine()
    End Sub
```

Listing 5.55: Using an imported scope (note, no need for 'Console.')

That is, we do not have to explicitly indicate that these methods are in the console namespace, as we have done previously: `Write()` and `ReadLine()` are now valid substitutes for `Console.Write()` and `Console.ReadLine()`.

We can create a namespace by simply surrounding the required code by the namespace declaration, as shown in Listing 5.56.

```
Namespace MyNamespace
      'Whatever we put in here is part of the namespace.
      'e.g . . .
      Public Class SomeClass
            'Class code . . .
      End Class
End Namespace
```

Listing 5.56: Declaring a namespace

Now, whatever declarations we place in the namespace can only be accessed by prefixing the name with the namespace name, e.g. `Dim   C   As MyNameapace.SomeClass`, or by importing the namespace, using:

```
Imports MyNamespace
```

A namespace does not have to be continuous, which is unusual, since all other code constructs in VB .NET must be. This allows us to write code like that in Listing 5.57.

```
Namespace MyNamespace
'First block of declarations
End Namespace

Class NotInNamespace
'This class is not in the namespace, so code using it does
'not require the MyNamespace prefix.
End Class

Namespace MyNamespace
'Next block of declarations
End Namespace
```

Listing 5.57: A non-contiguous namespace

With the code in Listing 5.57, any declarations within either `MyNamespace` would have to be declared explicitly using the `MyNamespace` prefix. Objects of the `NotInNamespace` class can be declared without this. One useful consequence of this is that we can create a namespace that exists over several diffcrent modules of code, and so can incorporate a number of related constructs (classes, modules, type definitions and variable declarations) within a single namespace, no matter how we have chosen to organize the code into separate files.

Namespaces have nothing to do with algorithms, but have a lot to do with organizing program code so that declarations using similar names in different assemblies do not clash. If we had two namespaces, `Namespace1` and `Namespace2`, and each contained a `MyClass` class declaration, we would be able to distinguish between the two same-named classes by the namespace prefix. Note, however, that if we were to import both namespaces, the declarations would become ambiguous and VB would not allow the code to be compiled if a declaration of `MyClass` was used without a prefix stating which namespace was to be used.

5.6.4 Block Scope

Block scope covers just about every other structural feature of Visual Basic. Recall that a block is a sequence of program statements that are to be considered as an indivisible unit. Every statement in a sub or function is collectively part of a block, as are all the statements inside a `If..Then` structure, or a loop or `With..End With` structure.

Visual Basic allows you to declare a variable anywhere you wish within a sequence of executable program statements. However, once you have declared a variable, its scope is limited to the block in which it is declared. This has fairly profound consequences. For example, if I declare a new variable inside a `If..Then..End If` structure, I am not allowed to refer to it in any statements beyond the end of the structure (or before it either, although you might have expected that). In Listing 5.58, the intention for the `If..` statement might have been to record the fact that `X` had a value of zero at that point in the program. However, the variable used to record this fact (`XWasZero`) would go out of scope as soon as execution has passed beyond the `End If` statement, so the variable effectively would not exist. As a result the code would not compile, except in the circumstances where a different variable with the same name had been declared before the `If..Then` block.

```
If X = 0 Then
    Dim XWasZero As Boolean = True
    'Other statements . . .
End If
'Other statements (including a scope error) . . .
Console.WriteLine("X was zero: {0}", XWasZero)
```

Listing 5.58: Misusing a variable declared in block scope (within the `If..Then` block)

Block scope can be tricky simply because blocks can be nested to any depth.

In Figure 5.6, there are four levels of block scope. Working from the inside out, the variable `I`, declared in block 4 (the `With..End With` block) is only accessible inside this block, although all of the other variables (`X,Y,Z` and `Q`) can also be accessed in it. Code within the `For` loop can access `Q`, declared within the loop, and also `X`, `Y` and `Z`, i.e. those variables declared in the blocks than enclose the `For` loop. The `If..Then` block (block 2), encloses blocks 3 and 4, so variables defined within it are in scope to all code in this block. Finally, the variable `X`, declared at the level of the whole subroutine, is visible throughout the subroutine.

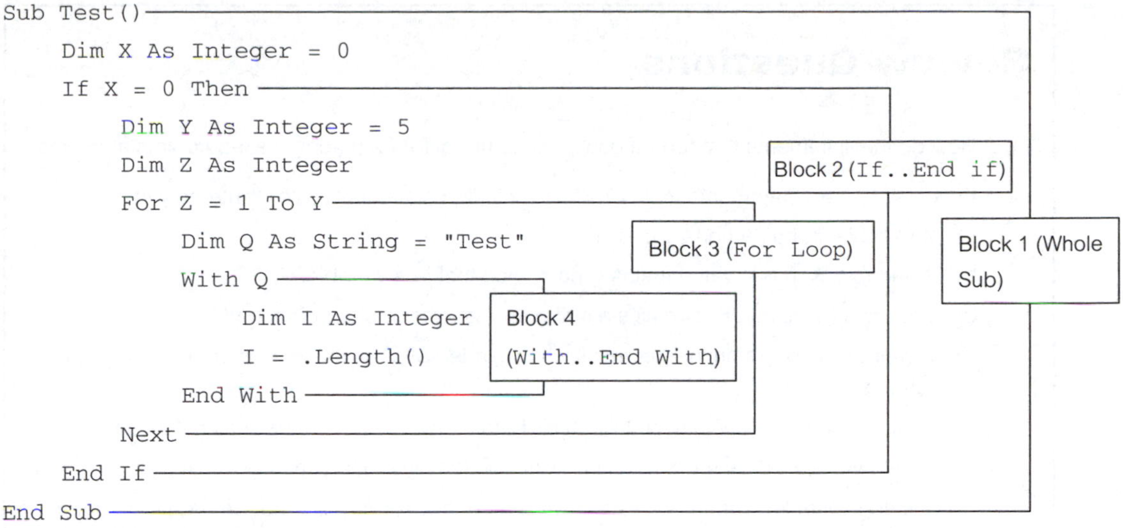

```
Sub Test()
    Dim X As Integer = 0
    If X = 0 Then
        Dim Y As Integer = 5
        Dim Z As Integer                          Block 2 (If..End if)
        For Z = 1 To Y
            Dim Q As String = "Test"          Block 3 (For Loop)        Block 1 (Whole
            With Q                                                        Sub)
                Dim I As Integer    Block 4
                I = .Length()       (With..End With)
            End With
        Next
    End If
End Sub
```

Figure 5.6 Block scope

The general rules for Block scope are:

1. a variable declared within a block can only be accessed within it, and is invisible to code outside the block

2. a variable cannot be declared inside a block with the same identifier as one declared in an outer block

The second rule is important since otherwise it would be possible to inadvertently hide a variable to an inner block of code. Consider Listing 5.59.

```
Dim X As Integer = 100
Dim Y, Z As Integer
For Z = 1 To Y
      Dim X As String = "Hello" 'Not Legal.
      'More code. Note, if this was permitted, X the
      'Integer could not be accessed here.
Next
```

Listing 5.59: Block scope 'hiding' a variable in an outer scope

If this code was legal, statements inside the `For..Next` loop would never be able to access the integer `X`, because the string `X` would mask it. Other languages, for example C and C++, permit this and as a consequence programmers must take care never to use a variable name that is declared further out in the scope hierarchy. The problem would probably never occur in short code sequences as shown Listing 5.59, but is easily possible in long sections of code in which many variables are declared at various levels of Block scope.

Review Questions

1. How do the statements that form a control structure differ from normal executable statements?

2. Write If..Then statements that will allow controlled statements to execute only if:

   a) a variable, X, has a non-zero value;

   b) a variable, X, has a value that is greater than that in a variable, Y;

   c) a string variable, S, contains a string representation of a numeric value;

   d) a variable, X, gives an integer result when divided by 7 (hint: the Mod operator will be useful here);

   e) a date variable, D, contains a date that is before today (given by the system function Date);

   f) a date variable, D, is more than one year ago (assume one year = 365 days);

   g) a string variable, wkDay, contains the name of a week day (i.e. not Saturday or Sunday).

3. What is wrong with the following block of code?

   ```
   If X <> 0 And Y/X < 100 Then
       Console.WriteLine("<Some Message>.")
   End If
   ```

   How could it be corrected?

4. Write a Select Case structure that uses the variable dayNumber (range 1 to 7, with 1 = 'Sunday') to print out the corresponding day name on the console.

5. Select appropriate loop structures (between Do..Loop, For..Next and While..End While) for the following tasks:

   a) to keep getting numeric values from the user, processing them in some way until a 0 is entered;

   b) to keep asking a user to enter a date until a valid one has been entered;

   c) to read items of data from a disk file (using Value = ReadFromFile()) until an item read can be interpreted as a National Insurance number;

   d) to calculate and print out all of the odd numbers in the range up to 1000;

   e) to repeatedly halve the value of a variable until it becomes less than 100.

6. A date variable D holds a specific date. Write a For..Next loop that will assign a sequence of dates starting from D and counting through one year in one-week intervals to a variable incD. (Hint: use a Step value in the For..Next loop.)

7. In Chapter 1 in Section 4.4 on Algorithms, Euclid's algorithm for finding the greatest common divisor of two numbers is given as:

   1. Let quotient = m / n, disregarding any fractional part of quotient

   2. Let Remainder = m-(quotient * n)

3. Let m = n
4. Let n = quotient
5. If Remainder is not zero, go to step 1
6. Greatest-common divisor is m.

    Implement this algorithm in Visual Basic code in a `Sub Main()`.

8. Re-implement Euclid's algorithm as a Visual Basic function which takes two parameters (m and n) and returns the GCD as a result. (Call the function GCD.)

9. Your solution to question 8 should be a function that finds the GCD of two integers. The function can fail if the value passed into the parameter n is zero. Add code to make this function throw an exception (call it `GCDException`) if parameter n is zero.

10. Write a `Sub Main()` that will accept two integer numbers from the console and pass these to the amended CGD function within a `Try..End Try` block.

Practical Activities

The activities for this chapter do not make up a single program, unlike those for previous chapters. Instead, each activity gives you a chance to work with a particular code structure. All of the activities will make use of a program framework in which the required structures will be used within a subroutine (`Sub..End Sub`) designed to demonstrate the operation of that structure. The general format of this will be as shown in Listing A5.1.

```
Module CodeStructures
    Public Sub SomeStructureDemo()
        'Code to demonstrate a specific structure . . .
        '. . .
    End Sub

    Sub Main()
        SomeStructureDemo()
    End Sub

End Module
```

Listing A5.1: Template for the activity exercises in this chapter

You will therefore write a sub that demonstrates a specific feature and then change the single statement in `Sub Main()` to call this sub. Note that for this set of activities, we will ignore the creation of classes and objects in favour of working through simple examples with the minimum of framework. It is as well to bear in mind that as object-oriented programmers, the normal use of these structures will be to provide control within methods of classes.

Activity 1: Create the project framework

Start up a new Visual Basic console project. Use the name **Chapter5** for the project, and change the name of the default module from **Module1** to **CodeStructures**. Having done this, right click on the project entry in the Solution Explorer (Chapter5), select **Properties** from the Context menu and in the general section of the dialog box, change the **Startup Object** setting to **CodeStructures** (it will appear in the drop-down list). This project will house all of the activity exercises for this chapter. The resulting code should appear as shown in Listing A5.2.

```
Module CodeStructures
    'Activity subs go here . . .
    '. . .

    Sub Main()
        'Calls to Activity Subs go here . . .
        '. . .
    End Sub

End Module
```

Listing A5.2: The module framework for these activities

To test out this framework, add a simple sub to the module and call it from `Sub Main()`, e.g. Listing A5.3.

```
Module CodeStructures
    Sub Test()
        Console.WriteLine("Hello World!")
    End Sub s

    Sub Main()
        Test()
    End Sub

End Module
```

Listing A5.3: A sample activity sub and a call to it

Once you have entered this code, execute the program (**Debug/Start Without Debugging**) and make sure it runs properly. In subsequent activities, you will add other subs and change the statement in `Sub Main()` to call the ones you add. Do not delete any existing sub when you add a new one.

Activity 2: Using `If..Then` structures

The first objective for this activity/exercise is to write a sub that will use an `If..Then` structure to differentiate between odd and even numbers. The general form of the sub will be as shown in Listing A5.4.

```
Sub OddOrEven()
    Dim n As Integer
    Console.Write("Enter a whole number: ")
    n = Console.ReadLine()
    If <some condition> Then
        Console.WriteLine("{0} is even.", n)
    Else
        Console.WriteLine("{0} is odd.", n)
    End If
End Sub
```

Listing A5.4: Outline of a sub to distinguish between odd and even numbers

Add the code for this sub to the module, and insert a call to the sub in place of the call to Test() inserted in Activity 1. Note that the If..Then statement is not correct as it stands, since we need to insert a suitable condition between If and Then. There are several ways of formulating this condition, but the easiest will be to check whether the number n divides exactly by 2. If it does the number is even, if not, the number is odd. It is possible to use the Mod operator to determine this.

Exercise A5.1

Insert a condition into sub OddOrEven() that will evaluate to True if n is even, False if it is odd. A suitable condition will use the Mod operator.

The next objective is to compose a condition that will differentiate between digits and non-digit characters. We can determine if a Char type is a digit using a compound condition along the lines of:

```
Ch >= "0" And Ch <= "9"
```

Enter a new sub, coded as shown in Listing A5.5.

```
Sub CharOrDigit()
    Dim ch As Char
    Console.Write("Enter a single character: ")
    ch = Console.ReadLine()
    If <some condition> Then
        Console.WriteLine("A digit")
    Else
        Console.WriteLine("A non-digit.")
    End If
End Sub
```

Listing A5.5: Outline for a sub to differentiate between alpha characters and digits

Exercises A5.2

1. Enter the code in Listing A5.4 and insert a suitable condition that will evaluate to True if ch is a digit.
2. Insert a call to CharOrDigit in Main() and test its operation.

Activity 3: Using the `Select Case` structure

In this activity, we will use a `Select Case` structure to differentiate between various types of character. Enter the following sub definition (Listing A5.6) into the module:

```
Sub ClassifyChars()
    Dim ch As Char
    Console.WriteLine("Enter a single character")
    ch = Console.ReadLine()
    Select Case ch
        Case "0" To "9"
            Console.WriteLine("A digit.")
        Case "a" To "z"
            Console.WriteLine("A lower case letter.")
        Case "£", "$", "€"
            Console.WriteLine("A currency symbol.")
        Case Else
            Console.WriteLine("Unclassified")
    End Select
End Sub
```

Listing A5.6: A sub to classify single characters

Note that `Select Case` allows us to classify items from ranges and lists. Currently the sub will differentiate between digits, lower case characters and currency symbols, with every other character type being unclassified.

Exercises A5.3

1. Add `Case` clauses to Listing A5.5 to allow classification into upper case characters (a range), brackets (a list), punctuation (a list) and arithmetic symbols (a list).

2. Call the `ClassifyChars` routine from `Sub Main()` and test its operation.

Activity 4: Iterating with the `Do..Loop` structure

As the previous exercise has almost certainly made plain, in some circumstances it is extremely useful to be able to repeat a block of code. In the previous exercise, re-running the program over and over again to classify different character is tedious. We can of course use some loop structure to make this a less tedious experience (Listing A5.7).

```
Sub Main()
    Do
        ClassifyChars()
    Loop
End Sub
```

Listing A5.7: Repeating a block indefinitely

Add the `Do..Loop` structure to `Sub Main()` in the previous exercise as shown. Note that as we have defined an indefinite loop, the program will repeat forever. Fortunately, we can terminate a console program by pressing **Ctrl+C**, so once you have checked that the program does indeed repeat indefinitely, terminate it using this key combination.

Since **Ctrl+C** is not a particularly obvious way to terminate the loop, we would be well advised to add some terminating condition. An obvious way to do this would be to display a message (after the call to `ClassifyChars()`) to tell the user what to enter to terminate the program, and then test the user's input against this condition. For example, if we decide the user should enter the lower case letter 'q' to quit, the logic would be as given in Listing A5.8.

```
Sub Main()
    Do
        ClassifyChars()
        Console.WriteLine( _
            "Press 'q' to quit, any other to continue.")
    Loop Until Console.ReadLine() = "q"
End Sub
```

Listing A5.8: Using an extra key-press to terminate the loop

While this will certainly work (try it out), it is perhaps a little cumbersome for the user. One possible alternative would be to amend the `ClassifyChars()` sub itself. If we define a parameter for the sub and pass this as the character to be classified, rather than getting input from the console within it, we can pick up the character to be classified within `Sub Main()` itself, and use this after it has been classified to determine whether to exit to `Do..Loop` or not. This is shown in Listing A5.9.

```
Sub ClassifyChars(ByVal ch As Char)
    Select Case ch
        Case "0" To "9"
            Console.WriteLine("A digit.")
        'Other cases of ch to test . . .
        '. . .
        Case Else
            Console.WriteLine("Unclassified")
    End Select
End Sub
```

Listing A5.9: The `ClassifyChars()` sub altered to accept and classify a parameter

With this alteration of `ClassifyChars()`, the code in `Sub Main()` becomes much less cumbersome for a user (Listing A5.10).

```
Sub Main()
    Dim ch As Char
    Do
        Console.WriteLine("Enter a single character: ")
        ch = Console.ReadLine()
        ClassifyChars(ch)
    Loop Until ch = "q"
End Sub
```

Listing A5.10: `Sub Main()` **redefined to supply the character for classification**

Exercise A5.4

With the changes made to the `ClassifyChars()` sub, the 'quit' character, `"q"` will also be classified before the program exits. Amend the code within the `Do..Loop` so that when the user types `"q"`, this character is not sent to the sub.

Activity 5: Using the `For..Next` structure

In this activity, we will use a different type of loop structure, a `For..Next` loop, to operate on strings of characters. The key feature of a string of characters that makes the `For..Next` structure useful is that a given string has a known number of characters. For example, the string 'Hello' has five characters. A .NET string is able to calculate how many characters it has, and we can use this to write code that works through every character performing some operation.

Breaking up a string

We can work through every character in a string with the `For..Next` loop in Listing A5.11.

```
Sub StringLoop(ByVal s As String)
    Dim index As Integer
    For index = 0 To s.Length() - 1
        Console.WriteLine(s.Chars(index))
    Next
End Sub
```

Listing A5.11: Breaking up a string into individual characters

The sub in Listing A5.10 will print all of the characters of a string on separate lines of the console. Note that since we count from character 0 of the string, a string of length 5 will have individual characters (0) to (4).

While this in itself is not very useful, it does give us access to the individual characters of the string and allows us to perform manipulations on them. For example, we can create a reversed version of a string easily (Listing A5.12).

```
Sub StringLoop(ByVal s As String)
    Dim index As Integer
    Dim newString As String
    For index = 0 To s.Length() - 1
        'Insert the next character BEFORE the previous...
        newString = s.Chars(index) & newString
    Next
    Console.WriteLine(newString)
End Sub
```

Listing A5.12: Reversing a string

Using a similar technique, we could work our way through a string dividing it up into separate words (start a new word after every space), counting specific characters or changing the case of specific characters.

Exercises A5.5

1. Write a function that will return an approximate count of the number of words in a string. This should work by starting a count at 1 and increment- ing it each time a space character is encountered as you iterate through the string. (We are assuming there are no sentence breaks and that there is exactly one space after each word.)

2. Write a function that will return the average word length within a string, where words are counted as above. (Hint – you know the length of the string [s.length()] and can work out the number of words as above; the average should be one less than the average of these [why?].)

3. Write a function that will return a copy of a string from which every space and punctuation mark has been removed and every alphabetical character has been converted to upper case. Your solution to the classification exercise in Activity 3 will be useful here, as will the `ToUpper()` string method.

Recall that a `For..Next` loop can count in steps other than 1 by using a `Step` clause, e.g.

```
For index = 1 To 100 Step 10
```

This gives us ways to count through a string in a variety of ways, including backwards.

Exercises A5.6

1. Write a sub that displays every third character in a string.

2. Write a sub that locates the position of the last space in a string. (Hint: a `For..Next` loop can count in negative steps.)

Features worth remembering

- It is easy to classify data of most types using the `Select Case` structure. This has uses in analysing user-input.

- A `Do..Loop` is a useful mechanism for repeating a whole operation. Coupled with simple user-input, one can be used to allow the user to repeat an operation as often as necessary.

- The `String` class has a range of methods available for finding specific sub-strings or characters, and extracting sub-strings. These can be used with classifying code for transforming strings into another form (e.g. removing punctuation), breaking a string up into useful units (like words) and otherwise manipulating strings.

Suggested Additional Activity

The activities for this chapter have been separate and do not combine to make up a whole program with a single purpose. To execute each exercise you need to continually alter the code in `Sub Main()` to access a particular subroutine.

Add a code to `Sub Main()` to act as a menu for the previous activities so that the user can select which to execute. The general algorithm for this is given in Listing A5.13.

```
Do
    Display a list of options on the console, giving each
    a number to identify it { e.g.
        1. Odd or Even
        2. Alphabetical or Digit
        3. Classify Characters
        4. etc.
        5.
        6.
        7. Quit
    }
    Read number of user's choice
    Select Case number
        Case 1
            OddOrEven()
        Case 2
            CharOrDigit()
        Etc.
        Case 7
            Exit the do loop
    End Select
Loop
```

Listing A5.13: Algorithm for a menu structure in `Sub Main()`

Solutions to Exercises

Exercise 5.1

The controlled statements will not be executed under any conditions.

Exercise 5.2

Unless otherwise stated, I've placed the solution code to exercises into a `Sub Main()`. To try them out, start a new console project and copy the statements *within* the `Sub Main()` shown into the `Sub Main()` in the project.

a)

```
Sub Main()
    Dim CharacterType As String, CH As Char
    Console.Write("Enter a character")
    Console.ReadLine(CH)
    Select Case CH
    Case "a", "e", "i", "o", "u"
        CharacterType = "Vowel"
    Case "0" To "9"
        CharacterType = "Digit"
    Case Else
        CharacterType = "Consonant"
    End Select
End Sub
```

b)

```
Sub Main()
    Dim CharacterType As String, CH As Char
    Console.Write("Enter a character")
    Console.ReadLine(CH)
    Select Case CH
    Case "A", "E", "I", "O", "U", "a", "e", "i", "o", "u"
        CharacterType = "Vowel"
    Case "0" To "9"
        CharacterType = "Digit"
    Case Else
        CharacterType = "Consonant"
    End Select
End Sub
```

Exercises 5.3

1. This function should be placed within the `BankAccount` class code shown in Listing 5.16 (between the end of the property definition for `CurrentBalance` and `End Class`). Note the use of `"Case Is..."` to perform an implicit comparison with the case value (Balance). Add a statement – `MyAccount.Report()` – anywhere in `Sub Main()` where you wish the status of the account to be displayed:

```
Public Function Report() As String
    Select Case Balance
        Case Is >= 0
            Return "Account is in credit."
        Case Is < 0 And AgreedOverdraftAmount = 0
            Return "Account is overdrawn."
        Case Is >= (-AgreedOverdraftAmount)
            Return "Account is within allowed overdraft
            amount."
        Case Is < (-AgreedOverdraftAmount)
            Return "Overdrawn by more than agreed
            amount."
        Case Else
    End Select
End Function
```

2. Again, place this code within the `BankAccount` code, and test by adding `MyAccount.MaxAvailable()` at any point in `Sub Main()`:

```
Public Function MaxAvailable() As Decimal
    If OverdraftAvailable Then
        Return Balance + AgreedOverdraftAmount
    Else
        Return Balance
    End If
End Function
```

Exercise 5.4

a) Factorial calculation:

```
Sub Main()
    Dim n As Integer, f As Decimal, i As Integer
    Console.Write("Enter number to get factorial of:")
    n = Console.ReadLine()
    f = 1
    i = 0
    Do Until i = n
        f *= n
        i += 1
    Loop
    Console.WriteLine("{0} factorial is {1}", n, f)
End Sub
```

Note 1: The result will be *very large* for all but very small integer inputs, therefore the variable that will contain the result and intermediate results should be `Decimal`. Even with this type, the factorial of a number > 27 cannot be calculated.

Note 2: The initial intermediate result (f) must be set to 1, because otherwise it will be 0 and 0 multiplied by anything is still zero.

b) Displaying individual characters of a string:

```
Sub Main()
    Dim Index As Integer
    Dim s As String = "Hello Mum"
    Do Until Index = s.Length()
        Console.WriteLine(s.Chars(Index))
        Index += 1
    Loop
End Sub
```

Exercise 5.5

a)

```
Sub Main()
    Dim index As Integer
    For index = Integer.MinValue To Integer.MaxValue
        'Do something with Index - e.g....
        Console.Write(index)
        'Note - this will take a very long time since
        'index goes through a range of more
        'than 4 billion.
    Next
End Sub
```

b)

```
Sub Main()
    Dim chCode As Integer
    For chCode = Asc("a") To Asc("z")
        Console.Write(Chr(chCode) & vbTab)
    Next
End Sub
```

Note that vbTab is the Visual Basic identifier for a Tab character and so the characters will be displayed spaced out across the Console window.

Exercise 5.6

To read an integer from the keyboard and then display the required values:

```
Sub Main()
    n = Console.ReadLine()
    Console.WriteLine("{0}: {1} {2} {3}", n, n.GetType, _
                        n.GetTypeCode, n.GetHashCode)
End Sub
```

This would display (for an input of 12, for example):

12: System.Int32 Int32 12

a) Factorial function (using a `Do..Loop`). Note that we can do without the additional count variable (i, in the first version) because we can simply count down from N. Since it is a `ByVal` function parameter, changing its value will not affect the actual variable passed to it:

```
Function Factorial(ByVal N As Integer) As Decimal
    Dim F As Decimal = 1
    Do Until N = 1
        F *= N
        N -= 1
    Loop
    Return f
End Function
```

Call this function from `Sub Main()` as:

```
Sub Main()
    Dim num As Integer
    Console.Write( _
            "Enter number to get the factorial of:")
    num = Console.ReadLine()
    Console.WriteLine("{0} factorial is {1}", num, _
                                    Factorial(num))
End Sub
```

b) Factorial function (using a `For..Next` loop). The logic of this is more direct so possibly easier to understand:

```
Function Factorial(ByVal N As Integer) As Decimal
    Dim f As Decimal, Index As Integer
    f = 1
    For Index = 1 To N
        f *= Index
    Next
    Return f
End Function
```

(EXTRA) Factorial function (version b, using recursion):

```
Function Factorial(ByVal N As Integer) As Decimal
    If N = 0 Then
        Return 1
    Else
        Return N * Factorial(N - 1)
    End If
End Function
```

Note: This version of factorial relies on the simple fact that the factorial of any number greater than 2 is that number times the factorial of one less than that number. e.g. the factorial of 4 is 4 times the factorial of 3. Mathematically, the factorial of 0 is defined as 1, so the `If..Then..Else` condition allows us to use this definition to define the function. Confused?

Recursion (a function that calls itself) can do that to people and so I won't be looking at it any further than this example, but try it out and try stepping through the function calls for, for example calculating the factorial of 3 to see how it works.

Exercise 5.8

a) Note that for the parameters to be used as outputs, they *must* be declared as `ByRef`:

```
Sub GetValues(ByRef Length As Single, _
              ByRef Width As Single)
    Console.Write("Enter Length of rectangle")
    Length = Console.ReadLine()
    Console.Write("Enter Width of rectangle")
    Width = Console.ReadLine()
End Sub

Sub Main()
    Dim L, W As Single
    GetValues(L, W)
    Console.WriteLine("Dimensions are {0}, {1}", L, W)
End Sub
```

b) Note that this can work as a function only because the problem has been redefined to state that the function result is a single value – the area of the rectangle:

```
Function GetArea(ByRef Length As Single, _
                 ByRef Width As Single) As Single
    Console.Write("Enter Length of rectangle")
    Length = Console.ReadLine()
    Console.Write("Enter Width of rectangle")
    Width = Console.ReadLine()
    Return Length * Width
End Function

Sub Main()
    Dim L, W, A As Single
    A = GetValues(L, W)
    Console.WriteLine("Dimensions are {0}, {1}", L, W)
    Console.WriteLine("Area is {0}", A)
End Sub
```

Exercise 5.9

Running the project developed at the end of Chapter 4 and attempting to cause errors, you should have found the following.

a) Non-numeric input for any of the numeric values (e.g. Fred * 3) will cause a `System.InvalidCastException`

b) A division by zero input (e.g. 1 / 0) will cause a `System.DivideByZeroException`

c) The user entering an unsupported operator (e.g. 12.3 & 5.2) will cause a `System.ArgumentOutOfRangeException` (since the `IndexOfAny()` method of the string class expects to find one of the Operators array members in the expression

d) Entering an expression that will exceed the range of a decimal (e.g. 1000000000000000000000 * 10000000000000000) will result in a `System.OverflowException`. However, entering an expression that will result in an excessively small result (e.g. 0.00000000000000000001 * 0.0000000000000000001) simply produces a result of zero.

We could deal with all of these exceptions within either of the methods that they could happen in : that would mean having exception handlers in `Sub New()` to deal with the `InvalidCast` and `ArgumentOutOfRange` exceptions and having others in the `Result()` function to deal with overflow and divide by zero. However, we can handle all of the exceptions within `Sub Main()` within one `Try..Catch..End Try` structure:

```
Sub Main()
    Dim Expr As String
    Try
        Console.Write("Enter an expression
        (number op number): ")
        Expr = Console.ReadLine()
        Dim Calc As New Calculator(Expr)
        Console.WriteLine("{0} {1} {2} = {3}", Calc.Number1, _
            Calc.Operator, Calc.Number2, Calc.Result)
    Catch ex As System.InvalidCastException
        Console.WriteLine("Error in numeric input")
    Catch ex As System.ArgumentOutOfRangeException
        Console.WriteLine("That operation is not supported")
    Catch ex As System.DivideByZeroException
        Console.WriteLine("Can not divide by zero")
    Catch ex As System.OverflowException
        Console.WriteLine("The numbers entered are too big")
    End Try
End Sub
```

Exercise 5.10

a) Try it and see.

b) This will require exception handlers to be added to the factorial function and the sub that calls it (e.g. `Sub Main()`):

```
Function Factorial(ByVal N As Integer) As Decimal
    Dim f As Decimal = 1
    Try
        Do Until N = 1
            f *= N
            N -= 1
        Loop
```

```vbnet
                Return f
            Catch ex As System.OverflowException
                Throw ex
                Return 0
            End Try
        End Function

        Sub Main()
            Dim num As Integer
            Try
                Console.Write( _
                        "Enter number to get the factorial of:")
                num = Console.ReadLine()
                Console.WriteLine("{0} factorial is {1}", num, _
                                            Factorial(num))
            Catch factEx As System.OverflowException
                Console.WriteLine("An overflow has occurred")
            End Try
        End Sub
```

Exercise A5.1

```vbnet
Sub OddOrEven()
    Dim n As Integer
    Console.Write("Enter a whole number: ")
    n = Console.ReadLine()
    If n Mod 2 = 0 Then
        Console.WriteLine("{0} is even.", n)
    Else
        Console.WriteLine("{0} is odd.", n)
    End If
End Sub
```

Exercise A5.2

a)

```vbnet
Sub CharOrDigit()
    Dim ch As Char
    Console.Write("Enter a single character: ")
    ch = Console.ReadLine()
    If ch >= "0" And ch <= "9" Then
        Console.WriteLine("A digit")
    Else
        Console.WriteLine("A non-digit.")
    End If
End Sub
```

b)

```vbnet
Sub Main()
    CharOrDigit()
End Sub
```

1.

```
Sub ClassifyChars()
    Dim ch As Char
    Console.WriteLine("Enter a single character")
    ch = Console.ReadLine()
    Select Case ch
        Case "0" To "9"
            Console.WriteLine("A digit.")
        Case "a" To "z"
            Console.WriteLine("A lower case letter.")
        Case "a" To "z"
            Console.WriteLine("An upper case letter.")
        Case "£", "$", "€"
            Console.WriteLine("A currency symbol.")
        Case Else
            Console.WriteLine("Unclassified")
    End Select
End Sub
```

2.

```
Sub Main()
    ClassifyChars()
End Sub
```

The easiest solution to this is to modify the Do loop so that an exit can be made immediately after the character is entered.

```
Sub Main()
    Dim ch As Char
    Do
        Console.WriteLine("Enter a single character: ")
        If ch = "q" Then
        Exit Do
        End If
        ch = Console.ReadLine()
        ClassifyChars(ch)
    Loop
End Sub
```

1. Word count:

```
Function WordCount(str As String) As Integer
    Dim index As Integer, count = 1
    For index = 0 To str.Length() - 1
        If str.Chars(index) = " " Then
            count += 1
```

```
            End If
        Next
        Return count
    End Function
```

2. Average word length:

```
Function AvgWordLength(str As String) As Single
    Return str.length() / WordCount(str)
End Function
```

3. In this exercise, we need to categorize the characters in the string as a space (" "), a lower case character ("a" to "z") or anything else. To create the result string (output), simply add characters one at a time from `str.Chars()` by indexing through the characters. Note the use of the `ToUpper()` method, which is a `Static` method of the `Char` class.

```
Function FixString (ByVal str As String) As String
    Dim index As Integer, output As String
    Dim ch As Char
    For index = 0 To str.Length() - 1
        ch = str.Chars(index)
        Select Case ch
            Case " "
                ' Do nothing
            Case "a" To "z"
                output &= Char.ToUpper(ch)
            Case Else
                output &= ch
        End Select
    Next
    Return output
End Function
```

There is actually a much more efficient way to do this same job, using the `ToUpper()` `String` method (to convert the whole string to upper case) and the `Replace()` `String` method to replace all occurrences of a space (" ") with an empty string (""). However this method does not make use of a loop structure which is part of the exercise. The code for this alternative method is below:

```
Function FixString2(ByVal str As String) As String
    Dim Output As String
    Output= str.ToUpper()
    Return Output.Replace(" ", "")
End Function
```

Exercises A5.6

1. Displaying every 3rd character in a string:

```
Sub DisplayEvery3rd(ByVal str As String)
    Dim index As Integer
    For index = 2 To (str.Length() - 1) Step 3
        Console.Write(str.Chars(index))
    Next
End Sub
```

Note that to display every 3rd character, we need to start with the 3rd character in the string and continue from there (i.e. the starting value for index is 2, skipping characters 0 and 1). Had the loop been from 0 to `str.Length()` - 1 in steps of 3, we would have displayed the 1st, 4th, 7th etc. characters.

2. Locating the position of the last space character in a string:

```
Function LastSpace(ByVal str As String) As Integer
    Dim i As Integer
    For i = str.Length() - 1 To 0 Step -1
        If str.Chars(i) = " " Then
            Return i
        End If
    Next
    Return -1
End Function
```

Note that the function will return either the location (counting from 0) of the last space in the string or −1. It is common practice to use −1 as an indication of no result; since we need to accommodate the possibility that there will be no space in the string, some value must be used to signal this, and a zero value (the obvious choice in most situations) would be indicating that there was a space in the first character.

Answers to Review Questions

1. How do the statements that form a control structure differ from normal executable statements?
   They do not have any effect in their own right, but instead serve simply to modify the flow of execution through other statements.

2. Write `If..Then` statements that will allow controlled statements to execute only if:

   a) A variable, `X`, has a non-zero value

   ```
   If X <> 0 Then . . .
   ```

b) A variable, `X`, has a value that is greater than that in a variable, Y

```
If X > Y Then...
```

c) A `String` variable, `S`, contains a string representation of a numeric value

```
If IsNumeric(S) Then...
```

d) A variable, `X`, gives an integer result when divided by 7 (hint: the Mod operator will be useful here)

```
If X Mod 7 = 0 Then...
```

e) A `Date` variable, `D`, contains a date that is before today (given by the system function `Date`)

```
If CType(D, Date) < D Then...
```

f) A `Date` variable, `D`, is more than 1 year ago (assume 1 year = 365 days)

```
If D + 365 < Date Then...
```

g) A `String` variable, `wkDay`, contains the name of a week day (i.e. not Saturday or Sunday)

```
If Not(wkDay="Saturday") And Not(wkDay="Sunday") Then...
```

3. What is wrong with the following block of code?:

```
If X <> 0 And Y/X < 100 Then
    Console.WriteLine("<Some Message>.")
End If
```

If X is 0 (as the first test checks for), we should not perform the second check since it would result in a divide by zero.

How could it be corrected?

Various ways such as handling a divide by zero exception. However, the most efficient way is to use `AndAlso` in place of `And` between the two Boolean expressions. With this, if the first expression is `False` (i.e. X is 0), the second will not be executed.

4. Write a `Select Case` structure that uses the variable `dayNumber` (range 1 to 7, with 1 = 'Sunday') to print out the corresponding day name on the console.

```
Select Case dayNumber
Case 1
    Console.WriteLine("Sunday")
Case 2
    Console.WriteLine("Monday")
etc, up to . . .
Case 7
    Console.WriteLine("Saturday")
Case Else
    Console.WriteLine("Not a day")
End Select
```

5. Select appropriate loop structures (between `Do..Loop`, `For..Next` and `While..End While`) for the following tasks:

    a) to keep getting numeric values from the user, processing them in some way until a 0 is entered `Do..Loop Until`

    b) to keep asking a user to enter a date until a valid one has been entered `Do..Loop Until`

    c) to read items of data from a disk file (using `Value = ReadFromFile()`) until an item read can be interpreted as a National Insurance number `Do Until <Test here for N.I.Number>`

    d) to calculate and print out all of the odd numbers in the range up to 1000 `For..Next`

    e) to repeatedly halve the value of a variable until it becomes less than 100 `Do While..Loop`

6. A date variable D holds a specific date. Write a `For..Next` loop that will assign a sequence of dates starting from D and counting through one year in 1-week intervals to a variable `incD`. (Hint: use a `Step` value in the `For..Next` loop).

    ```
    For incD = D To D+365 Step 7
    Next
    ```

7. In Chapter 1 in Section 1.4 on Algorithms, Euclid's algorithm for finding the greatest common divisor of two numbers is given as:

    1. Let quotient = m / n, disregarding any fractional part of quotient
    2. Let Remainder = m-(quotient * n)
    3. Let m = n
    4. Let n = quotient
    5. If Remainder is not zero, go to step 1
    6. Greatest-common divisor is m.

    Implement this algorithm in Visual Basic code in a `Sub Main()`

    ```
    Sub Main()
        Dim m, n, quotient, remainder As Integer
        Console.Write("Enter two integer numbers: ")
        m = Console.ReadLine()
        n = Console.ReadLine()
        Do
            quotient = m \ n            'Integer division
            remainder = m Mod n         'Easier than in algorithm
            m = n
            n = quotient
        Loop Until remainder = 0
        Console.WriteLine("Remainder is {0}", m)
    End Sub
    ```

8. Re-implement Euclid's algorithm as a Visual Basic function which takes two parameters (m and n) and returns the GCD as a result. (Call the function GCD.)

```
Function GCD(ByVal m As Integer, ByVal n As Integer) _
                                          As Integer
    Dim quotient, remainder As Integer
    Do
        quotient = m \ n            'Integer division
        remainder = m Mod n         'Easier than in algorithm
        m = n
        n = quotient
    Loop Until remainder = 0
    Return m
End Function
```

9. Your solution to question 8 should be a function that finds the GCD of two integers. The function can fail if the value passed into the parameter n is zero. Add code to make this function throw an exception (call it GCDException) if parameter n is zero.

```
Function GCD(ByVal m As Integer, ByVal n As Integer) _
                                          As Integer
    Dim quotient, remainder As Integer
    If n=0 Then
        Throw GCDException
        Return 0
    End If
    Do
        quotient = m \ n            'Integer division
        remainder = m Mod n         'Easier than in algorithm
        m = n
        n = quotient
    Loop Until remainder = 0
    Return m
End Function
```

10. Write a Sub Main() that will accept two integer numbers from the console and pass these to the amended CGD function within a Try..End Try block.

```
Sub Main()
    Dim num1, num2 As Integer
    Try
        Console.Write("Enter first number:")
        num1 = Console.ReadLine()
        Console.Write("Enter second number:")
        num2 = Console.ReadLine()
        Console.WriteLine("GCD is {0}", _
                                          GCD(num1, num2))
    Catch ex As GCDException
        Console.WriteLine("Cannot calculate for a 0 entry")
    End Try
End Sub
```

6

Data and Object Structures

In this chapter, you will learn:

- how to define multiple elements of data in programs;
- different ways of organizing data;
- how to use arrays and collection classes;
- ways of iterating through the elements in a structure;
- methods of working with aggregations of data.

6.1 Organizing Data

We organize information all the time, often without even realizing it. Organized data surrounds us: a shopping list, the index of a book, the contents of a filing cabinet and an entire library are real-world examples of information that has been grouped, associated, categorized, ordered and cross-referenced. We organize information according to some principle because this will in some way make it easier to use. For example:

- lists of things allow us to group associated items together, for example a shopping list;
- sorting items into order can make it possible to locate a single item from a large collection more quickly, for example, a number from the phone book;
- cataloguing and cross-referencing separate items can make it easy to locate items by various categories, and to perform open-ended searches among them without having to go directly to large numbers of individual items, for example consulting the main catalogue of a library to locate books on Visual Basic programming;
- collecting similar items into groups makes it possible to perform 'batch processing' on them, manipulating each in a similar way, for example, generating an automated mailing list from a list of customers names and addresses;
- categorizing items according to one or other of their attributes simplifies the job of isolating some of them that have something in common, for example, dental patients who have not been for a check-up for more than six months.

To impose some form of organization on a set of data, we need to be able to work with multiple items collectively. Typically, most computerized forms of data organization are based on the idea of lists of items. A number of the methods and constraints we use to organize lists of information work just as effectively in computer systems.

For example, if we want to be able to find an item from a list efficiently, it can help if the list is sorted into some order (e.g. the standard phone book does this). On the other hand, if a list is to be updated frequently, having items necessarily stored in order can make the task of adding an item to a list difficult. Imagine the problem of adding a new item to a 1000 element list, where its natural location is second in the list. Unless some additional free space has been built in to the list, the operation could involve moving 999 of the current list items to make room for the new one.

Another problem that can upset an otherwise efficient system for storing data is that of space allocation. The easiest way to store multiple items of data is to create a 'slot' for each item. For example, we might use pigeonholes on a wall to distribute items of mail to the staff of a company; each person's mail is placed into a separate pigeonhole. However, if the company grows unexpectedly, we may reach a situation where there are more members of staff than there are pigeonholes to store their mail in. In this case, we are faced with the very expensive prospect of adding new pigeonholes to accommodate the new staffs' mail: the analogous computer-based system in which the number of data items outgrows the number of spaces available can be similarly expensive.

It seems that whatever strategy we use to organize data will have some drawbacks: storage speed, retrieval speed, the need to correctly anticipate the maximum number of items; these and other problems make the issue of data organization, and the data structures this depends on, a central issue in computer programming.

Exercises 6.1

1. The standard telephone book may have more than a million entries in a big city or area.

   a) What feature of it makes it possible for you to look up someone's number in a couple of minutes?

   b) What makes it difficult to add or delete an entry in a phone book?

2. Insurance companies, banks and other large service organizations often identify you as a customer by number (e.g. policy number or account number) rather than by your name. Can you think of two reasons why it is more efficient for them to do this?

6.1.1 Multiple Data Items – Individual Variables

Up till now, every program we've looked at has used individual variables to store data and provide operations. For example, in the bank account program in Chapter 4, we used a variable, `MyAccount`, to allow us to create and work with one object of the `BankAccount` class. If we had wanted two `BankAccount` objects, we could have declared a second reference variable. Ten accounts would have required ten reference variables, and since each would have to have a distinct name, would have needed ten sets of similar statements to allow us to manipulate them. Consider a simple program (Listing 6.1) to create and manipulate ten `BankAccounts`:

```
Sub Main()
    Dim Account1 As BankAccount = New BankAccount()
    Dim Account2 As BankAccount = New BankAccount()
    ' Etc..
    Dim Account10 As BankAccount = New BankAccount()

    Account1.AccountName = "John Smith"
    Account2.AccountName = "Mary Green"
    ' Etc..
    Account10.AccountName = "Billy Brown"

    Account1.Deposit(100)
    Account2.Deposit(200)
    ' Etc..
    Account10.Deposit(150)
    ' More operations. . .

End Sub
```

Listing 6.1: Working with multiple individual variables

Considering the power that a computer has to work tirelessly through hundreds, thousands or millions of program statements, this way of working with individual variables seems to be a very limiting constraint. To unleash the full power of computer programs, it would be better if we could work with multiple variables, without having to deal with them on an instance-by-instance basis. Visual Basic provides us with a number of ways of doing this. The simplest of these is the array.

6.2 Arrays

An array is a number of individual variables that all share the same identifier (variable name). We declare an array by indicating in brackets how many elements it will contain, and following this with their type name as if the array was a single variable. For example:

```
Dim Accounts(100) As BankAccount
```

Elements (individual variables) of this array are accessed by combining their name with an index variable or value in brackets. For example, `Accounts(0)` would be the first element of the array of accounts, `Accounts(1)` would be the second element, etc. If we think of a variable as a box for storing a piece of data, we might imagine an array to be a row of boxes, like a single row of pigeonholes, each holding its own piece of data, and each with a number to distinguish it from the others. This is shown in Figure 6.1.

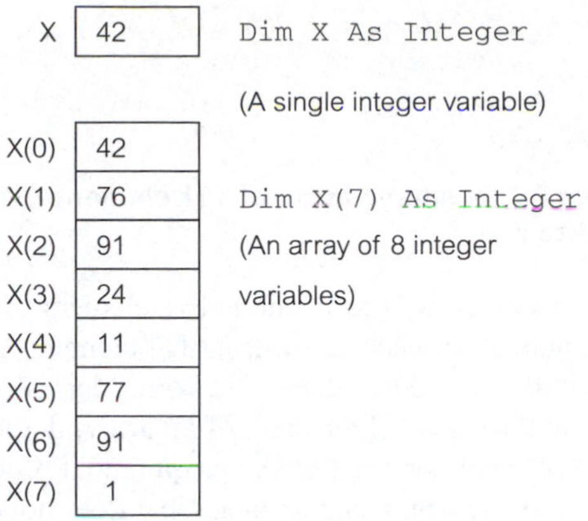

X | 42 | Dim X As Integer

(A single integer variable)

X(0) | 42
X(1) | 76   Dim X(7) As Integer
X(2) | 91   (An array of 8 integer
X(3) | 24   variables)
X(4) | 11
X(5) | 77
X(6) | 91
X(7) | 1

Figure 6.1 A Single integer variable and an array of integers

The combination of an identifier and an index number gives us a simple and elegant way of defining as many individual variables as we could use in a program (almost). However, there is a bit of an oddity to contend with. The declaration of the `Accounts` array (`Dim Accounts(100) As BankAccount`) gives us 101 `BankAccount` reference variables, each of which could refer to an individual object of the `BankAccount` class. Why 101? This is an awkward one to explain and retain any sense of dignity for the computer programming fraternity, but in the C programming language (which we must consider as being the archetype of everything in .NET) arrays always start at element 0. In C, such a declaration would give us an array of integers with exactly 100 elements, numbered from 0 to 99. This in itself is awkward but excusable, because it does at least make it easier to implement arrays in the C language (this is an odd but consistent feature of C).

In older versions of BASIC and Visual Basic, the same declaration would give us 101 elements because there would be elements 0 to 100 (101 inclusive). My understanding is that most people seeing a declaration of a 100 element array would expect 100 elements numbered 1 to 100, and the creators of BASIC decided that this was sensible. Somewhere along the line, the C language went for the pragmatic element 0 approach, and the designers of Visual Basic (and subsequently VB .NET) decided to hedge their bets and go for *both* approaches simultaneously. An array declared like `Dim a(<number>)` gives us <number>+1 elements, starting from element 0 and going up to element <number>. I'm afraid you'll just have to get used to this.

Once we've accepted the odd numbering scheme, working with lots of data elements opens up a whole new way of programming, in which our declarations do not need to impose a limit on the number of items we deal with in our programs. Also, we get to use the arrays we declare very flexibly. For a start, where you would expect to place an index number to indicate a specific element of an array, you can instead put a *variable*! Consider Listing 6.2.

```
Sub Main()
    Dim i(100) As Integer
    Dim index As Integer
```

```
        For index = 0 To 100
            i(index) = index
        Next
    End Sub
```

Listing 6.2: A simple array of 101 elements, and a `For..Next` loop to initialize it

What this does is to create a 101 element array of integers, and then place the index number of each element in that element. `i(0)` will contain 0, `i(1)` contains 1, etc. All of a sudden, the `For..Next` loop takes on a whole new role, as a way of working through each element of an array, getting the enclosed statements to work on each element one at a time. One potential problem with this is that we could refer to an array element using an index that does not exist in the array (e.g. `i(101)`). To get around this potential problem, VB gives us an alternative form of `For..Next` loop (Listing 6.3).

```
    Sub Main()
        Dim i(100) As Single
        Dim value As Single
        For Each value in i
            value = 0.5
        Next
    End Sub
```

Listing 6.3: Using the `For..Each` structure

`For..Each` simply works through every element in the array, and saves us having to know what the upper index bound is. In this case, we end up with an array in which each element is given a value of 0.5. Note that the index variable required by a normal `For..Next` loop is always an `Integer` type, as we are using it to count through the members, while the iteration variable used in a `For Each..Next` loop must be of a type that matches the content of each element of the array: in Listing 6.3, `value` is a `Single`, the same type as the elements in the array `i`.

6.2.1 Initializing Elements of an Array

We can use an alternative type of declaration to initialize the elements of an array of values (Listing 6.4).

```
    Sub Main()
        Dim numbers() As Integer = {10, 20, 30, 40, 50}
        Dim index As Integer
        For index = 0 To numbers.GetUpperBound(0)
            Console.WriteLine("numbers({0}) = {1}", index, _
                              numbers(index))
        Next
    End Sub
```

Listing 6.4: Initializing an array

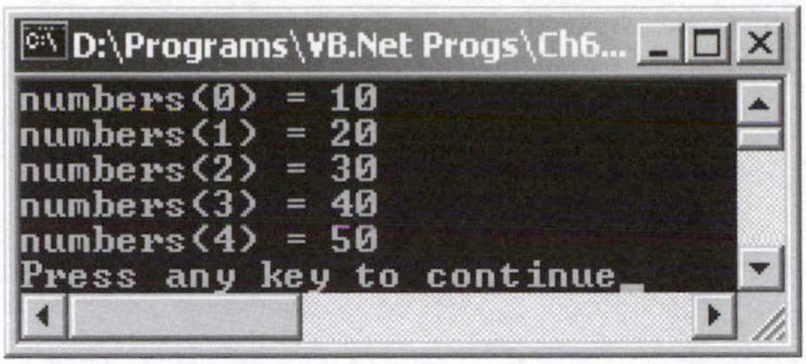

Figure 6.2 Executing Listing 6.4

In this case, the number of elements in the array is implied by the list of values provided in braces {} after it. The `GetUpperBound()` method returns the index of the last array element (in this case 4). Its parameter (0) specifies the dimension of a multi-dimensional array, which we'll look at next – in this case it is specifying the first and only dimension. Executing the code gives a result as shown in Figure 6.2.

Exercises 6.2

1. Create an array that contains the names of the months of the year.
2. Write code to display the names of the months.
3. Create a second array which is related to the first in that it stores the number of days in the corresponding entry in the array of month names (ignore leap-years).

6.2.2 Dimensions of an Array

In the simple arrays we've seen so far, an array has been a list of values. In programming parlance, they have been 1-dimensional arrays. However, Visual Basic also allows us to define 2-dimensional arrays, which are like arrays of arrays, 3-dimensional arrays, which are like arrays of 2-dimensional arrays and so on. While a single-dimensional array can be used as a list of variables, a 2-dimensional (or 2-D) array would be more like a table, with rows and columns, e.g. Listing 6.5 and Figure 6.3.

Row/Column	Column 0	Column 1	Column 2	Column 3	Column 4	Column 5
Row 0	00	00	00	00	00	00
Row 1	00	01	02	03	04	05
Row 2	00	02	04	06	08	10
Row 3	00	03	06	09	12	15
Row 4	00	04	08	12	16	20

Figure 6.3 The 2-dimensional array generated by the code in Listing 6.5

```
Sub Main()
    Dim numbers(4, 5) As Integer
    Dim row, column As Integer
    For row = 0 To 4
        For column = 0 To 5
            numbers(row, column) = row * column
        Next
    Next
    For row = 0 To 4
        For column = 0 To 5
            Console.Write("{0:D2} ", numbers(row, column))
        Next
        Console.WriteLine()
    Next
End Sub
```

Listing 6.5: Creating and using a 2-D array

The first `For..Next` loop initializes the values of all the array elements to the
product of the row and column number, and the second displays the whole array in
a grid or table-like format. Note the use of a number format specifier (`{0:D2}`)
in the `Console.Write()` statement. This indicates that each number should be
displayed as a 2-digit number, with leading zeros where necessary. Note also the use
of a `Console.WriteLine()` statement to force a new line at the end of each row.
The nested `For..Next` loops are ideal for allowing us to access the array by row
and column.

We can again initialize a 2-D array implicitly, as shown in Listing 6.6.

```
Sub Main()
    Dim numbers(,) As Integer = {{5, 12, 17}, {6, 7, 2}, _
                    {3, 3, 6}, {4, 11, 12}}
    Dim row, column As Integer
    For row = 0 To numbers.GetUpperBound(0)
        For column = 0 To numbers.GetUpperBound(1)
            Console.Write("{0:D2} ", numbers(row, column))
        Next
        Console.WriteLine()
    Next
End Sub
```

Listing 6.6: Initializing a 2-D array

The number of dimensions is indicated in brackets after the array name by a comma
– a single comma, as here, shows that two size specifiers are missing, so it is a 2-D
array. `GetUpperBound()` has been used to determine the number of elements in
each dimension of the array – `GetUpperBound(0)` gives the number of rows and
`GetUpperBound(1)` the number of columns. Each row of the array is an array as
well, so in the list of initialization values, whole rows are enclosed in braces, just
like the overall array. Of course, using initialization like this for an array can be quite

a tedious and error prone process, so it would normally only be used for quite small arrays, especially if they have two or more dimensions.

We can also create 3-D, 4-D, etc. arrays, with or without initialization. In theory we can declare arrays with up to 32 dimensions, although Microsoft's Visual Basic documentation on arrays suggests that arrays with more than three dimensions are rare. This is probably because most programmers would have trouble trying to keep track of what they are doing with the elements of, e.g. a 12-D array.

A single-dimensional array is like a list, a 2-D array is like a table, and a 3-D array is like a 3-D matrix of cells – you could picture that as a sort of 'block of flats' arrangement, where the first dimension indicates the floor number, and the second and third dimensions indicate the location of a single flat within a 2-D matrix. However, you might find it difficult to imagine the layout of a 4-D array simply because you have run out of physical dimensions to imagine; a physicist might get by imagining the 4th dimension as the same block-of-flats over a period of discrete time intervals, but by this stage even physicists might have trouble keeping the picture simple enough to work with.

There is another, more immediate reason why high-dimensional arrays are not used much in programs. Let's assume a small application that uses arrays needs each dimension to have 100 elements. For a 1-D array, this is 100 individual variables, for a 2-D array, 10 000, for a 3-D array, 1 000 000. By the time we get to 5-D, there are 100 000 000 elements and we're getting close to filling up the memory of a PC with a generous allocation of memory (currently, 256 Mbytes of memory is pretty normal, and since 100 000 000 integers will occupy 400 000 000 bytes of storage space, this 5-D array would more than fill the memory of a well-specified PC).

You'll find most of the example programs in this book that use arrays stick with the 1-D variety. This is partly because the code in such examples is a little easier, but also partly because we can use classes to manage the complexity of multi-dimensional data structures. Using objects which encapsulate the functionality of arrays (or other list-like data structures) is a useful way of managing this type of complexity, as we'll see later.

6.2.3 Accessing Array Elements in Real-World Situations

Of course, these code examples show us how to work with an array, and although they serve to explain something about accessing array elements, it is an unlikely you will want to do these things in a real program (having an array where each element's value matches its index position in the array, or each element has the same value, or each element's value is already known at the start of the program seems a bit of a waste). On the other hand, Listing 6.7 could be considered useful in many situations.

```
Sub Main()
    Dim names(5) As String
    Dim index As Integer
    For index = 0 To 5
        Console.Write("Enter name:")
        names(index) = Console.ReadLine()
```

```
            Next
        Array.Sort(names)
        For index = 0 To 5
            Console.WriteLine(names(index))
        Next
    End Sub
```

Listing 6.7: Entering and sorting a list of names

This code asks the user to enter a list of names. By using a `Console.ReadLine()` within the loop, we get to assign these with values specified by the user. The next bit is neat: the `Array.Sort()` method is used to re-organize the members of the array into alphabetical order, and these are subsequently displayed with `Console.WriteLine()`. An array is an object that has methods associated with it, so we can expect arrays to be able to sort themselves into order. If we wanted to, we could increase the array size to deal with tens, hundreds or thousands of items of data – not only names. However, with arrays of non-value types, we need to exercise a little care.

Exercise 6.3

An office building has two floors (numbered floor 0 and floor 1), each of which has four offices (numbered 0 to 3). One person occupies each office.

a)   Declare an array that will store the names of occupants of each of the offices.

b)   Store fictitious names in the array declared in a).

c)   Write a short routine (similar to that in Listing 6.6) for printing out the occupants of each office along with the corresponding floor and office number (assumes floors 0 and 1, and office numbers 0 to 3).

6.2.4 Arrays of Reference Objects

Returning to our earlier example, an array of `BankAccount` objects would be defined as:

```
Dim Accounts(100) As BankAccount
```

Of course, this is an array of reference variables, since `BankAccount` is a class. We are therefore not entitled to simply start working with elements of the array immediately, as in Listing 6.8.

```
Dim Accounts(100) As BankAccount, acc As BankAccount
For Each acc In Accounts
    Console.Write("Name of account:")
    acc.Name = Console.ReadLine() 'Error – no account yet
Next
```

Listing 6.8: A problem – array elements need to be created with New first

The statement that dimensions the array does no more than a normal `Dim` statement for a reference variable that does not have an initialization part. Before we can access any of these account objects, we need to create it with the `New` keyword. Also since there are initially no objects in the array, using `For..Each` could cause problems – there may be no object attached to one or more of the reference variables and this will cause the familiar '*Unhandled Exception: System.NullReferenceException: Object reference not set to an instance of an object.*' error message. We'll just have to work our way through the members of the array by index number as shown in Listing 6.9.

```
Dim Accounts(10) As BankAccount
Dim index As Integer
For index = 0 To Accounts.GetUpperBound(0)
    Dim amount As Decimal
    Console.Write("Initial balance:")
    amount = Console.ReadLine()
    Accounts(index) = New BankAccount(amount)
    Console.Write("Name of account:")
    Accounts(index).Name = Console.ReadLine()
Next
```

Listing 6.9: Creating array element objects in a `For..Next` loop

Since there is no account object until one is created with `New`, we can't simply deposit an initial amount into every account in the array. Instead we need to read the initial balance from the console into a temporary variable (`amount`) and use this in the creation of the account with `New`. Once this step has been dealt with for an account, we can go on to assign an account name directly. Note that the array size has been reduced from 101 to 11, to avert the tedium of running this code and then having to enter amounts and names for 101 separate `BankAccount` objects.

6.2.5 Making Objects Sortable

There is another problem with an array of objects. We can expect Visual Basic to know how to sort an array of strings into order, since `String` is a data type that VB knows about (the `Sort()` method sorts an array of strings into dictionary order). However, it would be presumptuous to expect it to re-order an array of `BankAccount` objects without further information: would it be in order of the `Name` property, or possibly the `Balance` in the account? While we humans would probably correctly guess that `Name` order would be expected, we might be wrong, and anyway, Visual Basic programs aren't allowed to guess. If we don't tell it how to do it, it can't do it. For now I'll simply demonstrate the solution to this and leave it to Chapter 7 on inheritance, to explain it in full, gory detail.

To make an array of class' objects sortable, we make the class itself implement a standard interface known as `ICompare`. This has one method, called `CompareTo`. This is a function that returns an integer value: 0 when two compared items are equal, negative when an item is smaller than the one it is being compared to and positive when an item is larger than the one it is being compared to. We'll have a more detailed look into interfaces in the next chapter, but for now I'll simply present the necessary code for the job. With the `BankAccount` class, we need to amend its code as shown in Listing 6.10.

1. Make the class `Implement` the `IComparable` interface ...

```
Public Class BankAccount
    'The following line indicates that elements of this
    'class can be compared to each other..
    Implements IComparable
    etc...
```

2. Create a `CompareTo()` function that compares a member of an object of the class with the same member of another object passed to it as a parameter (note that we do not have to type the long and complex first line of this function, since Visual Studio will create it if we select the `IComparable` interface from the Class Name combo box of the Code window, and the `CompareTo()` method from the Method Name combo box)

```
Public Overridable Overloads Function _
        CompareTo(ByVal obj As Object) As Integer _
        Implements IComparable.CompareTo
'Compare the Name of this object with the Name of the
'Obj parameter...
    If obj.Name = mvarName Then
        'These are the same...
        Return 0
    ElseIf obj.Name < mvarName Then
        'obj is smaller than (comes before) this one...
        Return 1
    Else
        'This one must be smaller...
        Return -1
    End If
End Function
```

Listing 6.10: Making a class sortable

If you add the above code to the `BankAccount` class, the `Array.Sort()` method will have a method it can use to compare two `BankAccount` objects to determine the order they should be in, and will therefore be able to sort the array elements into order (of the `Name` property). An interesting feature of the `CompareTo()` function is that it is unlikely we will ever write any code that calls it directly. The `Sort()` method of the `Array` class will call it however, as it decides how to reorder the items in the array.

6.2.6 Using Arrays of Objects

Once we've defined an array, we can access any of the elements as if they were simple individual variables. Therefore, any rules we need to apply to the use of individual variables will also have to be applied when dealing with any element of an array. For example, we still need to create an object with New before we can access it with a reference variable, whether this is an individual variable or a member of an array of them.

We can use an array to mimic any number of real-world items that deal with multiple pieces of information: lists, tables, queues, pigeonholes, mailboxes and so on. Simply consider what type of variable you would use to house an individual item, and then declare an array with enough spaces to cope with the maximum number of items needed. Since we can make an array of any type of variable, we can use any of the pre-defined types, or a structure or class of our own definition. For example, consider the situation where we need to deal with the names and test marks of a number of students in a class. An individual item is a student and her test mark. We could easily create a class to house one set of this information (see Listing 6.11).

```
Class Student
    Implements IComparable
    Private mvarName As String
    Private mvarMark As Integer

    Public ReadOnly Property Name()
        Get
            Return mvarName
        End Get
    End Property

    Public Property Mark()
        Get
            Return mvarMark
        End Get
        Set(ByVal Value)
            mvarMark = Value
        End Set
    End Property

    Public Sub New(ByVal Name As String, _
                   ByVal Mark As Integer)
        mvarName = Name
        mvarMark = Mark
    End Sub

    Public Sub Report()
        Console.WriteLine("Student: {0} Mark:{1}", _
                          mvarName, mvarMark)
    End Sub

    Public Function CompareTo(ByVal obj As Object) _
                    As Integer _
                    Implements System.IComparable.CompareTo
        'It is possible we are trying to compare this
        'object with a null reference. The following check
```

```
                    'will indicate that 'obj' is less if either its
                    'value is less or it is null...
                    If obj Is Nothing OrElse mvarMark < obj.mark Then
                        Return -1
                    ElseIf mvarMark = obj.Mark Then
                        Return 0
                    Else
                        Return +1
                    End If
                End Function
            End Class
```

Listing 6.11: A `Student` class we can create arrays of (note the `CompareTo()` method)

We can now go on to write a simple array declaration to define a group of students. It is a good idea to try to apply some order to the declaration since this will save some work later. The array itself is the only declaration we really need, but it is useful to keep track of how much of it is in use. Initially, the array as declared will have elements numbered 0 to `.GetUpperBound(0)`. However, none of these elements will contain data when the array is initially declared. We can keep track of how many elements have been filled using a simple `Integer` variable:

```
    Private StudentList(10) As Student
    Private ClassSize As Integer = 0
```

Note that by initializing `ClassSize` to `0`, we have an indication that there are currently no assigned elements in the array. Now, to assign a new element, we can go through the following steps (assume <Name> is a variable containing the new entry's name, and <Mark> the corresponding mark, in code like Listing 6.12):

```
    'Check there is space in the array...
    If ClassSize < StudentList.GetUpperBound(0) Then
        'Assign a student to element number ClassSize...
        StudentList(ClassSize) = New Student(<Name>, <Mark>)
        'Now increment ClassSize to indicate the new entry...
        ClassSize += 1
    End If
```

Listing 6.12: Adding a new student to the `StudentList` array

When we want to do something with each element of the `StudentList` array, we can use a simple `For..Next` loop:

```
    For index = 0 To ClassSize - 1
        StudentList(index).Report()
    Next
```

or for an array that we know to be full . . .

```
For index = 0 To StudentList.GetUpperBound(0)
    StudentList(index).Report()
Next
```

Listing 6.13: Iterating through the array – two ways of getting the upper limit

Listing 6.13 illustrates both methods. Note that we need to make sure not to access element number `ClassSize`, since this has not been allocated yet. Either of the above `For` loops will iterate from the first occupied element of the array to the last.

Having declared an array of `Student` object variables and populated at least some of them with `Student` objects, we can start to do meaningful operations on them: for example, finding out the average class test mark (Listing 6.14), or the students with the highest and lowest marks (Listing 6.15).

```
'Let's now try to work out a few things about the group.
'First the average mark...
Dim index As Integer
Dim total As Integer = 0
For index = 0 To ClassSize -1
    total += StudentList(index).Mark
Next
Console.WriteLine ("Average mark is {0}", _
                   total / ClassSize)
```

Listing 6.14: Calculating the average mark

To get the average mark, we use the same method as we would to calculate an average of anything – add all the marks together and then divide the overall sum by the number of values. To find the students with the maximum mark, guess on some entry as having the maximum mark (usually the first element in the array), and then scan through the rest of the array correcting our guess any time we meet a higher mark. The same technique works for finding the student with the lowest mark, and since the algorithm is nearly the same, we can combine both operations within a single `For..Next` loop.

```
'Find the best and worst students...
Dim min As Integer = 0, max As Integer = 0
'We've started by guessing that StudentList(0) has both the
'highest and the lowest test mark. Now scan through the
'array finding the real highest and lowest...
For index = 1 To ClassSize -1
    If StudentList(index).Mark < StudentList(min).Mark Then
        'Found a student with a lower mark...
        min = index
    End If
    If StudentList(index).Mark > StudentList(max).Mark Then
        'Found a student with a higher mark...
        max = index
    End If
```

```
Next
Console.Write("Lowest marked student is:")
StudentList(min).Report()
Console.Write("Highest marked student is:")
StudentList(max).Report()
```

Listing 6.15: Finding the highest and lowest marked student

Another useful operation would be to be able to find the mark awarded to a particular student. The input to this operation would be the student's name, and the output could be either the student's mark, or some indication that the named student was not found (always a possibility, either because the sought student did not exist in the array, or the student's name was misspelled). This is shown in Listing 6.16.

```
Do
    'Find marks for specific students...
    Console.Write("Enter student's name (none to stop):")
    n = Console.ReadLine()
    If n = Nothing Then
        Exit Do 'No name entered, so we're done.
    End If
    For index = 0 To StudentList.GetUpperBound(0)
        If Not (StudentList(index) Is Nothing) _
            AndAlso StudentList(index).Name = n Then
            StudentList(index).Report()
            Exit For
        End If
    Next
    If index > StudentList.GetUpperBound(0) Then
        Console.WriteLine("No such student")
    End If
Loop
```

Listing 6.16: Looking up a student's mark

In the above code we have a pair of nested loop structures. The outer (main) loop simply iterates the entire process until no name is entered (the exit condition is within the first `If..Then` block). The inner loop (a `For..Next` loop) compares the name sought with the names of members in the list. Note we need to check that a `StudentList()` entry exists at each location in the array before we carry out the name comparison, since otherwise we would be trying to access the name property of an object that did not exist. The use of `AndAlso` ensures that if the first condition fails (there is no `Student` object at that index), the second would not be tested, which would otherwise cause an error (accessing a method of an object that does not exist).

The `For..Next` structure controlling the inner loop ends when index exceeds the upper limit of the loop (`StudentList.GetUpperBound(0)`). This, therefore, gives us a way of checking whether the named entry was found, so we can indicate that the specified name was not located in the list.

Exercise 6.4

Return to the code in Exercise 6.3.

a) Write a sub that will look-up a person's name and display the floor and office that person occupies.

b) Write a function that will take a floor and room number and return the occupant's name.

6.2.7 Encapsulating an Array of Objects

We could go on for some time adding functions to work with this array of Student objects, and as a result end up with some very complex looking code that does a lot of simple things. However, the true nature of object-oriented design is to try to identify types of object that can be encapsulated to make them easy to work with. Each of the array operations we have created could be given a name (such as GetAverageMark, GetMaxMarkEntry, GetMinMarkEntry, FindStudentMark, etc.), and these could become methods of a StudentArray class. We would then be creating an aggregation, as described in Chapter 1; a class that contained multiple instances of another type of object.

The aim in creating an aggregation is to simplify the manipulation of individual elements of the group, and so the various aggregate functions (GetAverageMark, etc.) will perform operations that will involve more than an individual object. It is also worthwhile defining a method to handle adding a new member to the group (Listing 6.17).

```
Class StudentArray
    Private StudentList(10) As Student
    Private ClassSize As Integer

    Public Function AddStudent(ByVal name As String, _
                        ByVal mark As Integer) As Boolean
        If ClassSize < StudentList.GetUpperBound(0) Then
            StudentList(ClassSize) = _
                                    New Student(name, mark)
            ClassSize += 1
            Return True 'A new student was added
        Else
            Return False 'There was no space
        End If
    End Function

    Public Function GetMark(ByVal name As String) _
                                        As Integer
        Dim index As Integer
        For index = 0 To ClassSize -1
            If StudentList(index).Name = name Then
                Return StudentList(index).Mark
            End If
        Next
```

```
        Return -1  'This indicates the name was not
                   'found.
    End Function

    Public Function AverageMark() As Single
        Dim index As Integer, sum As Integer = 0
        If ClassSize > 0 Then 'Check there are marks.
            For index = 0 To ClassSize - 1
                sum += StudentList(index).Mark
            Next
            Return sum / ClassSize
        Else
            Return 0    'Saves a divide by zero.
        End If
    End Function

    Public Function MaxStudent() As Student
        Dim index As Integer, max As Integer
        max = 0 'This is our first guess.
        For index = 1 To ClassSize -1
            If StudentList(index).Mark > _
                StudentList(max).Mark Then
                    max = index     'This updates the guess.
            End If
        Next
        Return StudentList(max)
    End Function

    Public Function MinStudent() As Student
        Dim index As Integer, min As Integer
        min = 0
        For index = 1 To ClassSize -1
            If StudentList(index).Mark < _
                StudentList(min).Mark Then
                    min = index
            End If
        Next
        Return StudentList(min)
    End Function

    Public Function SortedList() As Array
    'This function returns a sorted array of students.
        Dim sortList As Array
        sortList = StudentList
        Array.Sort(sortList)
        Return sortList
    End Function

End Class
```

Listing 6.17: A `StudentArray` class – encapsulating array functionality

In Listing 6.17, all of the previously developed code has been encapsulated into a new class. In doing so, the code has been adapted slightly to create a class interface that is easier to use. Every routine has been made a function that returns some value; this makes it easier to determine if something has gone wrong. For example, an attempt to add a student to a full class will return a `False` result; otherwise, a `True` result will indicate success.

Similarly, the `GetMark()` routine returns a −1 result if the name supplied to the function does not match any names in the list of students. The result here has to be a number since the result returned for a name that does exist will be a number and a result of 0 (zero) could just be the mark given to a student who got no right answers; by choosing −1, we've indicated the function's failure to find the student since no student will have a mark of −1. Of course, this strategy will only work if it is not possible to award a mark of −1 for a student's test.

Care has to be exercised in the `AverageMark` method, since asking for the average mark of a class that has no students would cause a divide by zero error. Hence, we use a `If..Then` structure to test whether `ClassSize` is not zero.

The last three routines are different, in that each returns an object of some type as a result. `MaxStudent()` and `MinStudent()` both return a `Student` object, since this is the most general result for a function of this type. The question they will answer is 'Which student got the lowest/highest mark?' rather than 'What was the lowest/highest mark?', or 'What is the name of the student that got the lowest/highest mark?' Note that the answer to the first of these can supply us with the answer to either of the other two since we can then use the `Student` object's `Name` and `Mark` properties for these.

The `SortedList` method returns an array of `Student` objects. This gives us the ability to provide a sorted list of students on demand without changing the order of the internal list in the class.

By building this class, we can now work with lists of `Student` objects without having to deal with the problems of arrays becoming full, empty arrays or any of the other gotchas that might otherwise cause problems in a program. We also get the ability to work with as many classes of students as we need to, without having to keep track of multiple arrays. The multiple arrays would still be there, but will appear as simple encapsulated variables that do as we ask and provide results on demand. To demonstrate this, Listing 6.18 gives all the code necessary to work with a class of students, calculating statistics and reporting on all of them.

```
Sub Main()
    'Let's enrol a few students...
    Dim Group As StudentArray = New StudentArray()
    Dim n As String, m As Integer
    Do
        Console.Write( _
                "Enter student's name (no name to stop):")
        n = Console.ReadLine()
        If n = "" Then Exit Do
        Console.Write("Enter student's mark:")
        m = Console.ReadLine()
        If Group.AddStudent(n, m) Then
            Console.WriteLine( _
                        "Success adding student {0}", n)
```

```
                Else
                    Console.WriteLine("Class full!")
                    Exit Do
                End If
            Loop
            'Now let's report of the group...
            Console.WriteLine("Statistics:")
            Console.WriteLine("Average mark is : {0}", _
                                Group.AverageMark())
            Group.MaxStudent.Report()
            Group.MinStudent.Report()
            Console.WriteLine("The group in order of marks:")
            'Finally, let's see a sorted list...
            Dim students As Array
            Dim index As Integer
            students = Group.SortedList
            For index = 0 To students.GetUpperBound(0)
                If Not students(index) Is Nothing Then
                    Console.WriteLine("{0}: {1}", _
                        students(index).name, students(index).mark)
                End If
            Next
        End Sub
```

Listing 6.18: Working with the `StudentArray` class

Visual Basic provides a somewhat more elegant way to create an encapsulated array of a specific type of object, based on inheriting the standard array class and amending some of the methods and members to deal with the specified class. We'll come back to this in the next chapter (on inheritance and other object-oriented structuring techniques).

Exercise 6.5

(Major programming exercise)

a) Create a class, `Employee`, that stores the name and phone number of an employee, making both accessible as properties. The class should have a constructor that takes the name and number as parameters.

b) Declare an array similar in dimensions to that used in Exercise 6.3, but make it an array of employees.

c) Create a function to allow an employee's phone number to be looked up, given their name.

d) Create a sub that will return (in output parameters) the floor and room number of an employee given their name.

6.2.8 Changing the size of an array

A limitation of the arrays we have seen so far is that they are declared to have a specific number of elements. If we declare an array for a group of 20 students in a program and then, while using the program, a 21st student comes along to join the class, we seem to have a problem. Visual Basic lets us get around this by *re-dimensioning* an array as a program runs. Consider the example of a shopping list whose size we can not predict (Listing 6.19).

```
Sub Main()
    Const initialSize = 5
    Const sizeIncrement = 3
    Dim list(initialSize) As String
    Dim item As String
    Dim numItems As Integer
    Do
        Console.Write("Enter shopping list item:")
        item = Console.ReadLine()
        If item = Nothing Then
            Exit Do
        End If
        numItems += 1
        If list.GetLength(0) < numItems Then
            ReDim Preserve list(list.GetUpperBound(0) + _
                              sizeIncrement)
            Console.WriteLine("List increased to : {0}", _
                              list.GetLength(0))
        End If
        list(numItems -1) = item
    Loop
    Console.WriteLine()
    For Each item In list
        Console.WriteLine(item)
    Next
End Sub
```

Listing 6.19: Re-dimensioning an array

In Listing 6.19, we start with an array of six strings (`Dim list(initialSize) As String`, where `initialSize` is 5, giving us elements (0) to (5)). Let's assume that this would be the length of our normal shopping list. Items are added to the list as normal (collecting the name of the next entry in the variable `item`, and then assigning this to the array if it is not an empty string). Provided there are six or fewer items, this is all that is needed for the data collection step, and we would go on to print out the list (in the `For..Each` structure).

If we decide to throw a party, we'll probably need to increase the length of our shopping list. The variable `numItems` is keeping count of the number of items in the shopping list. We can test whether `numItems` has reached the maximum the array can cope with using the `GetLength()` method of the array class (we could also have used `GetUpperBound()`, but `GetLength()` returns the actual number, including element 0, so is easier to use in this situation). If the array has no more space, we resize it:

```
ReDim Preserve list(list.GetUpperBound(0) + sizeIncrement)
```

The `Preserve` keyword is optional, and is used to indicate that when the array is changed to its new size, existing elements are kept in the array. Without this keyword, we would be throwing away the array's contents each time we altered its size. In some situations, we might actually want to do that (and the resizing operation is much faster as a result). Most of the time, when we resize an array, we intend to either increase or decrease its size, but keep all of the existing members that will fit in the new size of array.

Note that the array is being resized by three elements at a time. We could have used any number – three was used here simply so that if you try the code out, you won't have to do much typing to see the effect of resizing. We could have resized one element at a time, but this is very inefficient, since each addition beyond the initial size will cause a `ReDim` operation, which will involve moving all of the array reference variables to a new version of the array and then destroying the old one.

When designing a program that relies on resizing arrays, it is often necessary to work out what the most efficient increment in size might be. A number of factors are significant to this: the rate at which the array fills up, how often items are added to the array compared to how often items in the array are accessed, and the initial size of the array compared to the amount of memory available to the program. Some programmers go for a strategy they know has worked in the past – for example, doubling the array size each time it fills up, or adding 10% to its current size. Others will try a number of different strategies in simulations until they find the most efficient one for the application under development. Happily, this is not a problem that you will encounter too often, since .NET provides a lot of other ways of dealing with unknown numbers of data elements.

6.2.8.1 Resizing Multi-Dimensional Arrays

We can also resize arrays with more that one dimension, but in this case, we are only allowed to change the last dimension if the `Preserve` keyword is used, e.g. Listing 6.20.

```
Dim n(2, 3, 4) As Integer
'Code using array at original size
ReDim Preserve n(2, 5, 6)'Illegal – can only change the
                         'last dimension if using Preserve.

Dim n(2, 3, 4) As Integer
'Code using array at original size
ReDim Preserve n(2, 3, 6)'But this is legal
```

Listing 6.20: Limitations in re-dimensioning a multi-dimension array

This limitation comes about because it is relatively easy to change the last dimension of an existing array, but more difficult to change the others (think how confusing it might be to alter a table of data by adding extra columns to it – what happens to all of the rows that had the original number of columns). Of course, if we can throw away the contents and start again, resizing any dimension is as easy as creating the array in the first place.

ReDim cannot be used to change the number of dimensions of an array, but this is probably a good limitation, since otherwise we could never be sure of the number of dimensions an array had and we would have problems writing code to refer to array elements with a variable number of commas.

In general, arrays are good where we can predict the number of items of data we will have to deal with. In such situations, an array is a very efficient way to manipulate multiple items of data. They are also useful where we may need to deal with a number of items of data that only changes infrequently compared to the number of times the existing elements are accessed.

6.3   Other Data Structures

Arrays in Visual Basic are powerful mechanisms for dealing with many data items. However, they have some limitations:

- they are created for a specific number of elements, and require extra code to accommodate situations where the number of elements exceeds expectations;
- they provide only a few built-in methods for manipulating the elements – for example, Sort();
- they do little to make finding specific items or inserting new items in a particular order more efficient;
- they are generally used to accommodate multiples of a single type of variable or class of object (there are ways around this, but these require us to get deeper into object-oriented territory – we will get there, but not yet).

Visual Basic and .NET provide between them a powerful range of data structure types. These are all similar to arrays in that they provide for multiples of an individual variable type, although they all provide alternative methods for organizing the data. Some of them (Collection and Dictionary) rely on inheritance, which we'll look at in the next chapter. The others can be used 'out of the box', and are therefore possible substitutes for the simple array. Collectively, they are referred to as *Collection classes* – see Table 6.1.

We'll look into some of these in some detail.

6.3.1   ArrayList

An ArrayList is similar to an array, but there is no need to specify a size. If we do specify a size, this is used as the initial capacity of the ArrayList. Items are added to an ArrayList using the Add() method, which accepts any type of object as a parameter (including another ArrayList). We can use the Count() and Capacity() properties to determine how many objects there are in the ArrayList and how many it currently has space for. For efficiency purposes, an ArrayList whose initial size is not specified starts off with a capacity of 16 items. Whenever

Table 6.1 Some of .NET's built-in Collection classes (data structures)

Collection Name	Features
ArrayList	This is a smart array that automatically resizes itself as required. We can therefore declare an `ArrayList` and add any number of items to it with no additional programming necessary
BitArray	This is a specialist array type that can only be used to house Boolean (`True` or `False`) data. Its advantage is that a large number of Boolean values can be stored in a very small amount of memory
HashTable	This data structure is used for very fast insertion and retrieval of items where the overall number of items can be very large. It is used mainly for speed
Queue	As its name suggests, this data structure works like a queue – items are added to the end of the queue, and retrieved from the front, so each item in a queue is dealt with in strict order of arrival at the queue – the first added to the queue will be the first removed. Used typically for implementing algorithms where the computer is not always able to deal with items at the rate at which they arrive
SortedList	The `Sort()` operation of an array is used to rearrange the array into a specified order. A `SortedList` works by always inserting new items into the correct place in the first instance, thereby eliminating the need to sort its contents
Stack	Similar to a `Queue` in that items are added to and removed from an end of a strictly ordered list. With a stack, the first item added will be the last to be removed
Collection	This is used to collect data items of a specific type. The core behaviour for dealing with multiple items is inherited (from the `CollectionBase` class) to create a new `Collection` type that deals with a specific class of objects
DictionaryBase	This data structure provides for pairs of specific types of object (typically, a user-defined class and a string), where one item (typically the string) is used as a look-up key for retrieving the other. If you think of how a real-world dictionary works (a single word is used as the key for looking up its own definition), you won't be far off. It is necessary to derive application-specific types of dictionary from the `DictionaryBase` class using inheritance

the capacity is reached, the next `Add()` operation will extend the capacity by doubling it.

Typically, we would use an `ArrayList` in a situation where we did not know how many data items were to be accommodated. For example, the earlier shopping list sample program can be made much simpler using an `ArrayList` (Listing 6.21).

```
Sub Main()
    Dim l As ArrayList = New ArrayList()
    Dim item As String
    Do
        Console.Write("Enter shopping list item: ")
        item = Console.ReadLine()
        If item = Nothing Then
            Exit Do
```

```
            End If
            l.Add(item)
        Loop
        For Each item In l
            Console.WriteLine(item)
        Next
        l.Sort()
        Console.WriteLine("Number of items: {0}", l.Count())
        Console.WriteLine("Current capacity: {0}", _
                                        l.Capacity())
        Console.WriteLine("Sorted:")
        For Each item In l
            Console.WriteLine(item)
        Next
    End Sub
```

Listing 6.21: Using an `ArrayList` for a shopping list

Note that we use the `Sort()` operation very differently with an `ArrayList`. Recall that when sorting a simple array, we used the syntax:

```
Array.Sort(names)
```

where `names` is the array identifier. This indicates that we were actually passing our array to a method of the array class (a shared method) for sorting. With an `ArrayList`, the `Sort()` operation is much more straightforward – simply execute the `ArrayList`'s own `Sort()` method. If we wanted to use an `ArrayList` to manage items of a user-defined class, we could not assume that it would know what rules to apply to sort them into order (as with an array of class objects). In this case, the `Sort()` method would have to use the class's own `CompareTo()` method as with the array sorting example; we would signal this to the `ArrayList` by passing a parameter – the value `Nothing` – to the `Sort()` method.

The `ArrayList` class is a good, general purpose data structure class. I've found it useful in situations where the additional coding required to implement resizable arrays is too onerous.

Exercise 6.6

a) Amend the `Employee` class used in Exercise 6.5, so that the class also stores room number and floor; modify the constructor appropriately.

b) Create an `ArrayList` of employees, and provide functions for looking up phone number, room number and floor number, given the employee's name.

c) Write an `AddEmployee` function that will accept employee data and create and store a new employee. Make the function reject new employees where the supplied phone number, or combination of room number and floor number clashes with those of an existing employee – the function should return `True` if the `Add` operation was successful, `False` otherwise.

6.3.2 `HashTables`

A `HashTable` is a form of `Dictionary`, derived from the `DictionaryBase` class. Dictionary collections store pairs of objects, usually referred to as `Key` and `Value` pairs. In the same way that a real-world dictionary provides us with a way to associate pairs of items (a word and its definition or translation), so a Dictionary collection allows us to associate pairs of objects. Normally, the `Key` object is a value that would be looked up (like looking up a word in the Oxford English Dictionary) and the `Value` object is the object that is returned from the look-up. In this way, we can build complex structures that allow us to collect pairs of objects, where one is used as a way of accessing the other.

Typically, the `Key` of an entry in a Dictionary collection is a string that uniquely identifies the Value object; for example we could use a person's social security number as the key to an object containing other data referring to the person, or a licence number as the key to an object containing a lot of data about a specific car.

A `HashTable` gets its name from the way data is stored and retrieved in it. A hashing function, or hash function, is a function that takes some data, jumbles it up and converts it into a number that is seemingly random. This type of function, fairly useless on its own, is ideal for distributing a lot of key values evenly across a numeric range.

To see why this is useful, consider the job done by a local post office sorting office. Mail is arranged into bins, where each bin contains mail for a particular area. Since the actual areas (normally a postman's 'walk') can be selected by the post office, they are organized so that each area (and bin) will be approximately the same size, and will therefore receive a similar amount of mail. This is organizationally sensible.

Now consider a situation where we cannot predetermine how items would be distributed. Organizing items into bins by the initial letter of someone's surname, for example, would be more haphazard. We call the property or piece of data that we use to identify an item its *key* and although the aim is to have an even distribution of keys, this is unlikely for real-world data. We would not divide the population of a country into 26 groups, where each group is of people with the same initial letter to their surname, and expect each group to be the same size.

If we used the initial letter of a surname, for example, we would have 26 bins, one for each letter A to Z (see Figure 6.4). However, each bin would not be likely to have to accommodate a similar amount of mail. In the UK, names beginning with certain letters are quite unlikely (X and Z for example). These two bins would be nearly

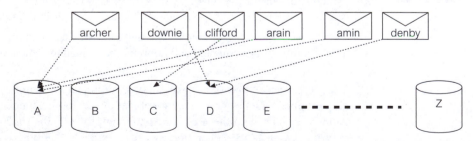

Figure 6.4 Organizing items into bins by initial letter

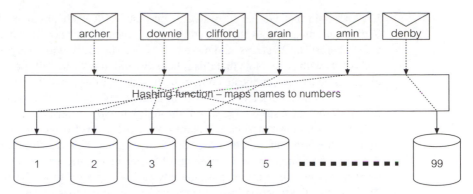

Figure 6.5 Using a hashing function to randomize the distribution of items

empty, and yet the bins for names beginning with the letter S or M would be overflowing. The end result is that, while it will be quite easy and quick to locate a specific item of mail for Mr Xiu because there will be few items in that bin, it will be a much bigger operation to find Mrs Simpson's letter, because the S bin will be very full in comparison.

A hash table works against the same problem with the aim of making each bin equally likely (or as near equally as possible) and therefore reducing the time taken to find an item with a particular value (see Figure 6.5). The hash function takes the key value of an item and calculates from it a numeric value that indicates the 'bin' the item is in. The more bins there are, the smaller the number of items that need to be searched through to find a specific item. Often hash tables are implemented with many more bins than there are items to put in them, and with each bin being able to contain only one item. In this case the hash function is designed to operate so that very similar values might produce very different results; ideally, each item given to the function would produce a unique result and so no two items would end up in the same bin. The result is that no searching is necessary – to find out where an item is; simply apply the hash function to the key value of the item you want, and its location is returned.

While this strategy seems good, there are a number of problems with it.

- A good quality hashing function can be difficult to devise, and no matter how good it is, there is always a likelihood that more than one key value will map to the same location. Better functions reduce the probability of this, but do not reduce it to zero.

- A hashing function that does work well with one set of data may not work well with other sets: the nature of a hashing function is to apparently randomize the keys, but the 'randomness' is an illusion and depends very much on the input key values. In the worst case, we could be very unlucky and have every key map to the same location.

- We need to accept that in all probability, several key values will cause clashes, and so our goal of one item per bin is not very realistic unless there are many more bins than there are items to put in them.

Let's assume that we have 26 arrays, one array for each initial in the alphabet. Without hashing, names that we add to this structure will not in general distribute evenly across the 26 arrays, and there will be certain arrays with many items in them and others with none. Note that this scheme would, however, still speed up access to elements, since we can locate an item by first determining which array it belongs to (using its initial letter), and then searching this array: instead of searching through a list of all the items stored, we search through a much shorter list of items.

Using a hashing function, the names are used instead to generate numbers that indicate the array the item will be stored in. With a well chosen hashing function, there will be a more even distribution of items among the arrays (bins). When we want to retrieve an item, we pass the key (a look-up key) to the hashing function. The result of the function identifies the array the item with that key is in. Since the distribution of items is more likely to be even, there will be comparatively few items in the bin to search through before we find the required one. A hash table can therefore reduce the amount of time taken to find an item among many other items.

6.3.2.1 Advantage of Hash Tables

If the insertion time of a data structure indicates the amount of time it takes to store a new item, and the retrieval time is the time it takes to locate an item, the general rule with simple data structures like arrays is that fast insertion leads to slow retrieval, and vice versa. If we insert an item into an array by simply adding it to the end of the array, it will not be in any pre-determined location and so when we want to retrieve it, we will need to do an exhaustive search, which takes time. If, on the other hand, we insert items into an array in some order, we will generally need to reorganize at least part of the array for each insertion. It might be faster to locate the item, but at the cost of taking time to insert it in the first place.

The more items there are in some data structure types, the more slowly items will be either inserted or retrieved. However, a hash table pulls off the trick of having a fast insertion time and a fast retrieval time almost independently of the number of items in the table. Of course there must be a cost for this; a hash table needs to have a lot of spare space. Depending on the hash function used and the distribution of key values, hash tables working efficiently can typically have 50% or more of the element locations unoccupied.

Hash tables are used in situations where the time taken to add items to a data structure and retrieve them on demand is paramount. For this to be worthwhile, there has to be a significant difference in the time taken to store or retrieve an item, compared to the time taken to store or retrieve the same item from an array or other structure. Generally, this is true only for a large number of items, so in many applications a hash table would be an unnecessarily complex way of organizing data.

For the applications that do benefit from the speed of a hash table, it is a relatively simple algorithm to implement. In Visual Basic .NET it is even more simple because `HashTable` is one of the built-in data collection classes. The various primitive data types (numbers, strings, dates, etc.) have a `GetHashCode()` method that returns a value the `HashTable` would use to locate an item. We can use any of the existing data types as a key or can use one of our own classes or structures to provide key values by devising a `GetHashCode()` method.

6.3.2.2 Example use of a Hash Table

We can use a .NET `HashTable` to store more or less any type of object we wish to, but since any object we add to a `HashTable` must have a `Key` value that allows the hash function to store it efficiently, we would normally use objects that have some property that can be used as a key. We simply need to ensure that the key we use to store an item under will be unique to that item – typical keys in the real world could be social security number (guaranteed to be unique for each person), bank account numbers, car licence numbers, in fact any property that we can say has a unique value for each item of the type. One suitable example might be a system for storing and retrieving data about employees. Each employee can be given a unique employee number, which will then be used as the *hash key* for adding the employee object to a `HashTable`. When we retrieve an employee's data from the table, the employee number will provide us with a fast look-up.

First, we need a suitable data type with the following properties.

- It should contain an amount of data that is large compared to the key used to store and locate it – otherwise, there will be little point to retrieving the information by providing a key value.

- Each item of the type should have some unique piece of data that can act as a 'key' property. The test is simple: the key property must be unique to a specific object, or else it will not be a suitable key value.

- In a normal application there should be potentially many items that need to be stored in a table – otherwise, the overhead of using and managing a hash table will not be worth it.

We can devise a simple `Employee` class that will embody these properties (although we will not test the class in a hash table that contains many objects, we will demonstrate the principle using a few sample objects – we can trust that Microsoft's implementation of the `HashTable` class will scale up to cope with a large number of objects). The class is shown in Listing 6.22.

```
Class Employee
    Public ID As String
    Public Name As String
    Public DOB As Date
    Public Address As String
    Public JobTitle As String

    Public Sub New(ByVal ID As String, _
                   ByVal Name As String, _
                   ByVal DOB As Date, _
                   ByVal Address As String, _
                   ByVal JobTitle As String)
        'Note the use of Me here – this is used to
        'indicate this object's members (ID etc.) to
        'distinguish them from the parameters...
        Me.ID = ID
        Me.Name = Name
```

```
            Me.DOB = DOB
            Me.Address = Address
            Me.JobTitle = JobTitle
      End Sub

      Public ReadOnly Property Key() As String
            Get
                  Key = ID
            End Get
      End Property

      Public Function Value() As String
            Return String.Format("{0}" + ControlChars.Tab + _
                  "{1}" + ControlChars.Tab + "{2}, {3}", _
                  Name, DOB, Address, JobTitle)
      End Function
End Class
```

Listing 6.22: A class that can be used to demonstrate the `HashTable` data structure

Given the class shown in the listing, we can create a hash table that can be used to store items of this class, as shown in the `Sub Main()` in Listing 6.23.

```
Sub Main()
      Dim ht As Collections.Hashtable
      Dim item As Employee
      Dim id As String
      Dim name As String
      Dim DOB As Date
      Dim Address As String
      Dim JobTitle As String
      'First create the hash table..
      ht = New Collections.Hashtable()
      Do
            'Get an employee ID (a unique number or string)...
            Console.Write("Enter ID (none to quit):")
            id = Console.ReadLine()
            If id = Nothing Then
                  Exit Do
            End If
            'An ID was entered, so get the remaining data...
            Console.Write("Enter a name (none to quit):")
            name = Console.ReadLine()
            Console.Write("Enter date of birth:")
            DOB = Console.ReadLine()
            Console.Write("Enter address:")
            Address = Console.ReadLine()
            Console.Write("Enter Job Title:")
            JobTitle = Console.ReadLine()
            'Create the employee...
```

```
            item = New Employee(id, name, DOB, _
                            Address, JobTitle)
            'Display the employee data...
            Console.WriteLine(item.Value)
            'And add the new employee to the hash table...
            ht.Add(item.Key, item)
        Loop
        'We can now look-up individual employees by
        'employee ID...
        Do
            Console.Write("Enter ID (none to quit):")
            id = Console.ReadLine()
            If id = Nothing Then
                Exit Do
            End If
            'Check the id entered is in the table...
            If ht.ContainsKey(id) Then
                'Safe to retrieve this employee...
                item = ht.Item(id)
                Console.WriteLine(item.Value)
            Else
                Console.WriteLine( _
                        "Employee {0} does not exist.", id)
            End If
        Loop
    End Sub
```

Listing 6.23: Building and using a `HashTable` of employees

In Listing 6.23, a `HashTable` of `Employee` objects is built up in the first loop, and we are given the chance to retrieve items from the table in the second loop. The `Employee` class has been given a `Key` property, which is a read-only string. In fact, the `Key` property simply returns the employee ID although we could have used any combination of employee data that would be suitably unique to each employee – using a purpose-defined ID is simply easier. When we create a new employee, it is added to the `HashTable` with the statement:

```
  ht.Add(item.Key, item)
```

The `HashTable`'s `Add()` method takes two arguments: the first is the hash-key to store the item under, the second the item itself. It is essential that the first parameter is a data type that provides a `GetHashCode()` method; otherwise the `HashTable` will not be able to accommodate the object. Strings and other in-built data types in .NET provide this method. If we were to use some alternative (for example, a compound field made up of, say, the `Name` and `PostCode` properties of an object), we would have to provide a `GetHashCode()` method, although there is an easy way to do this by simply concatenating both values to form a string.

When we attempt to retrieve an item from the `HashTable`, it is possible that we could provide a look-up key that did not exist among the items stored. If this is possible, is it safer to check the key exists in the table first, and we can use the `ContainsKey()` method to perform this check. The method returns `True` if the key exists in the `HashTable` and `False` otherwise.

In retrieving an employee from the table (using the `HashTable`'s `Item()` method), the `Employee` class's `Value` function returns a formatted string of employee data, using the `ControlChars.Tab` format character as a separator.

Exercise 6.7

a) Ignoring the improvement in speed that using a `HashTable` will bring to a data structure, state the other advantage that the use of a `HashTable` will bring to even small amounts of data (hint – think of some of the functions you had to write in previous exercises using arrays and `ArrayLists`)?

b) The `StudentArray` class defined in Listing 6.17 uses an array of `Student` objects as a storage mechanism. This has obvious limitations in that the class size is fixed and if it were allowed to become large, finding a specific student could take some time. Amend this class so that it builds and accesses a `HashTable` of `Student` objects instead. You may find it easier to amend the `Student` class so that it has a read-only `Key` property or a `Key()` function (in which you can return the student's name, which being a string, already has the `GetHashCode()` method). You should also note that no two students with the same name can be added to the collection because it uses a `HashTable`.

6.3.3 Enumerators

In the `HashTable` example, there was no code to display the entire table contents. The purpose of a `HashTable` is to allow individual items to be inserted and retrieved quickly. However, a feature of how it does this is that we cannot simply step through all of the items in the table using a `For..Each` loop or a `For..Next` loop with an index value. Since a consequence of hash table storage is that items will not be stored sequentially in adjacent locations, either form of loop would almost certainly try to access unallocated locations in the table and this would result in a *null reference* exception.

To get around this problem, we need some alternative method for iterating over all of the objects stored in a `HashTable`. The Collection classes provided in .NET allow for this by providing an *Enumerator* object, which is an object that can traverse all of the objects in a collection. Arrays and all of the Collection classes listed in Table 6.1 provide the `GetEnumerator()` method, which returns an object specific to the Collection class that will iterate through all of the objects stored in the collection.

For arrays of any type, the returned Enumerator object will simply step through each reference variable in the array, returning its reference in the `Current` property. If there are gaps in the array (null references instead of objects), the array enumerator will return these also, in exactly the same way as using `For..Each` would. This could of course lead to code that tries to access null references and consequent errors.

For the more advanced collection types, the enumerator will only return references that have objects assigned to them. They therefore provide safe access to all of the objects in a collection.

Every enumerator provides one property and two methods to enable you to iterate through the collection it serves. These are:

- `Current` – this property is a reference to the current object in the array or collection class.

- `MoveNext` – this method makes the next item in the collection the `Current` item. The `MoveNext()` method returns a result of `True` if there was a next item, and `False` if not, making it simple to use a `Do While..Loop` structure to iterate over a collection.

- `Reset` – this method places the enumerator before the first item in the collection. An attempt to access the `Current` property immediately after invoking `Reset` will cause a run-time error; `MoveNext` should always be called immediately after a `Reset`.

In addition to these properties and methods, enumerators specific to `Dictionary` classes support the additional properties `Key` and `Value`:

- `Key` – this property returns the `Key` part of the current table entry.

- `Value` – this returns the `Value` part of the object assigned to the table with `Key`.

The Collection classes based on `DictionaryBase` store `Key`/`Value` pairs, and so should provide an enumerator that allows access to these for each entry in the collection.

6.3.3.1 Simple Enumerators

Using these, we can use a bit of standard code to work through every item in any of the built-in collections.

```
Dim myEnumerator As IEnumerator _
    = myCollection.GetEnumerator()
While myEnumerator.MoveNext()
    'Code here can access myEnumerator.Current, but may not
    'alter the collection by adding or removing items.
End While
```

Listing 6.24: Using a simple enumerator

In Listing 6.24, an enumerator is retrieved from the Collection class (which could be an array, an `ArrayList` or any other of the built-in Collection classes except `HashTable` or a `Dictionary` class). The `IEnumerator` reference variable is initialized from the `GetEnumerator()` method of the array or collection. This method is responsible for building a new Enumerator object that reflects the *current contents* of the collection. If the array or collection is modified by adding new items or removing existing items, this enumerator will fail, causing a run-time error. Typically, an enumerator is used to display all the items in a collection, copy them to a database or some other operation that does not affect the membership of the collection.

Problems will occur in the simple enumerator code of Listing 6.22 if the collection is an array in which there are null references (i.e. if any of the reference variables in the array have no object assigned to them). In that case, we would have to check each item returned by the enumerator before accessing it (Listing 6.25).

```
en = myArray.GetEnumerator()
Do While en.MoveNext()
    If Not en.Current Is Nothing Then
        'Code here can access en.Current..
    Else
        Console.WriteLine("Empty")
    End If
Loop
```

Listing 6.25: Safe use of a simple enumerator

Note that this is no different from any code that iterates through every item in an array, using, for example, For Each or a For..Next loop with an index variable. Consequently there is *no advantage* to using a simple enumerator with an array over using a For..Each loop.

6.3.3.2 Dictionary Enumerator

For the Dictionary classes, including HashTables, the dictionary-specific form of enumerator is required, since these classes store key/value pairs. As well as providing a Current property, this form of enumerator also provides Key and Value properties. The equivalent code for enumerating through all of the objects and their keys for a HashTable (which is based on the DictionaryBase class) is given in Listing 6.26.

```
Sub Main()
    Dim ht As Collections.Hashtable = _
                            New Collections.Hashtable()
    ht.Add("One", "First Object")
    ht.Add("Two", "Second Object")
    ht.Add("Three", "Third Object")
    ht.Add("Four", "Fourth Object")
    ht.Add("Five", "Fifth Object")
    Dim dictEnumerator As IDictionaryEnumerator = _
                            ht.GetEnumerator()
    Do While dictEnumerator.MoveNext()
        Console.WriteLine(dictEnumerator.Key & _
                    dictEnumerator.Value)
    Loop
End Sub
```

Listing 6.26: Using a DictionaryEnumerator with a HashTable

This code is only marginally more complex than the code for a simple enumerator. Note however that for a HashTable, there is no other simple way to iterate through its entire collection of objects.

In general, enumerators provide us with a standard way to iterate through all of the objects referenced by a collection object. In most situations we have no need to employ them, since For..Each does a similar job. However, in the special case of a HashTable, we need to use an enumerator to get access to the entire table of objects.

Exercise 6.8

> Implement a ClassList() method for the modified HashTable version of StudentArray from Exercise 6.7. This should use a DictionaryEnumerator to iterate through the objects in the HashTable and call their Report() method.

6.3.4 SortedList

As its name suggests, the SortedList class collects objects (actually Key/Value pairs of objects) and allows them to be accessed in a specific order without the need to sort the list (a time-consuming facility in the other collection classes). The penalty paid for this is that it may take some time to insert an item into a sorted list, since the correct storage location for the key must be found and the existing list may need to be reorganized to accommodate it. The advantages we are paying for are that the list will automatically be in order, which is often necessary for display purposes, it will take less time to retrieve an item than it would by performing an exhaustive search on an array, and it will be easier to determine whether an item exists in the collection, since if it does we will be able to locate it relative to the other items in the collection (e.g. an entry for 'Smith' will be after an entry for 'Roberts' and before an entry for 'Tierney' – if there are no entries between 'Roberts' and 'Tierney', this is no entry for 'Smith').

Microsoft's help pages describe the SortedList class as 'like a hybrid between HashTable and ArrayList'. When an element is accessed using the Item() property, it is retrieved in the manner of a hash table. When accessed using the GetByIndex() method, it is retrieved like an element of a sorted array. We can also use the GetKey() method to retrieve the list of keys in sorted order. The following Sub Main() (Listing 6.27) demonstrates the use of a sorted list for storing simple Key/Value string pairs.

```
Sub Main()
    Dim sl As Collections.SortedList = _
        New Collections.SortedList()
    sl.Add("Charlie", "First Item")
    sl.Add("Delta", "Second Item")
    sl.Add("Alpha", "Third Item")
    sl.Add("Echo", "Fourth Item")
    sl.Add("Bravo", "Fifth Item")
    Console.WriteLine("Using Item() - hashtable access:")
```

```
        Console.WriteLine(sl.Item("Alpha"))
        Console.WriteLine(sl.Item("Charlie"))
        Console.WriteLine( _
                "Using GetByIndex() - sorted access:")
        Dim index As Integer
        For index = 0 To sl.Count - 1
            Console.WriteLine(sl.GetKey(index) & ": " _
                            & sl.GetByIndex(index))
        Next
    End Sub
```

Listing 6.27: Using a `SortedList`

Like a `HashTable` or any other form of Dictionary collection, it is normal to use a string as the `Key` and some other class of object as the `Value` of each entry. In the above example, coding is fairly simple because we use strings for both parts and Visual Basic knows how to deal with strings (sorting them into order and displaying them). If we were to use an arbitrary class for the Value objects, we would not expect to be able to display them so easily, and it would be more usual to use the sorted list as a way of looking up Values in sort order to perform some operation on or with them.

We might also wish to use some other class, not a string, as the `Key` part of entries. In this case, we would need to provide an `ICompare` Interface and a `CompareTo()` method as in Listing 6.9 to properly define the `Key` class. We will look again at this issue in the next chapter.

6.3.4.1 Binary Searches

There are a number of reasons why you might want to keep all of the elements in a list sorted into some order (e.g. alphabetical order), but one of the most compelling is that it is possible to use a very fast algorithm for searching for an item in the list. A *binary search* is a 'divide-and-conquer' algorithm, which works efficiently by repeatedly splitting the list into two equal halves and discarding the half that obviously does not contain the sought item. Since the items in a sorted list are in strict order or key, it is easy to determine which half cannot contain the item you are looking for, and therefore ignore it for the remainder of the search. In a way this is analogous to how you might look up a number in the phone book: open the book half way, check which half the name you are looking up is in by comparing it with the names at the part you have opened, and then repeat with the half that is left.

A binary search algorithm is built-in to the `Array` class and inherited by the `SortedList` class so that you can perform fast look-ups. Since it is only possible to do a binary search on a sorted list of items, care is required when using it with a normal array (typically, use the `Sort()` method first and then `BinarySearch`). No such care is necessary with a `SortedList`.

For a large list, a call to `BinarySearch` is not quite as fast as it would be if we were looking up an entry in a `HashTable`, but since a `HashTable` does not provide a way of retrieving the items in order, a `BinarySearch` on a `SortedList` is a good compromise, giving us a useful combination of ordered data and fast retrieval.

6.3.5 Stacks and Queues

`Stacks` and `Queues` are data structures that require that items are added to and removed from a specific 'end'. Both are useful data structures for managing the way that objects are dealt with when they cannot be processed immediately for some reason.

6.3.5.1 Queues

A `Queue` data structure is sometimes referred to as a 'first-in-first-out' structure, as this is descriptive of the way that items are added to and removed from it. The most obvious analogy for a `Queue` structure is the real queue that you join to receive service at the bank or post office. Every (well mannered) person who joins the line of customers attaches to the end of the queue, and customers leave the queue to get service only after all of the customers before them have left so that they are at the front.

In a bank or post office, if it is a quiet period there may be no queue, since if a customer arrives and there is a free service window they can be served immediately. During busy periods, customers arrive at intervals more quickly than they can be served and in these circumstances a customer who arrives will join the queue, wait until all of the queue members in front of them have been served, and then leave the queue to get service. We can see from this that a queue is a good way of providing fair access to a limited resource (e.g. a bank teller).

Microsoft Windows uses `Queue` data structures in several ways – most notably when dealing with user interactions. Consider the action of a Windows PC that is running several application programs simultaneously. The first thing to be aware of is that a normal PC cannot do more than one thing at once (you can spend a lot on a multi-processor PC so that it *can* do more than one job at a time, but most people's needs would not justify this expense). When you see the computer apparently doing two jobs simultaneously, you are in fact watching it switching so rapidly between the two tasks that you cannot see the join.

Now think of what happens if you select some time-consuming task for your computer to do, such as saving a long text file, or redrawing a complex graphic. While it is busy performing this lengthy task, it will probably appear to ignore your commands. For example, if you click on the Start button to start another program up, the Start menu might not appear immediately. You will most likely notice that after a delay (once it had completed the time-consuming task) the Start menu will pop up. In fact, we are so used to this behaviour in Windows that we tend not to notice unless the delay between initiating some action and the action occurring becomes very long – usually an indication that the computer is stressed.

When you clicked on the Start button, your command was not ignored, but simply placed into a queue until the PC could get round to it. Any other commands that were in front of it in the queue would be processed before your mouse click, but you can be quite sure that, failing crashes, Windows will get around to displaying the Start menu eventually. Typically you will see this behaviour whenever you try to access a printer, open a network drive or deal with some other slow media devices.

The Windows message queue is central to making a Windows computer usable. It ensures that commands are processed fairly in the order that they were issued, and ensures that user interactions are not simply ignored if the computer is currently busy. We can use a short Visual Basic program to simulate this type of behaviour in a few lines of code (see Listing 6.28).

```vb
Sub Main()
    Dim q As Collections.Queue = New Collections.Queue()
    Dim item As String
    Dim command As Integer
    Do
        Console.WriteLine("Queue size is {0}", q.Count)
        Console.Write( _
            "Select 1 to add, 2 to remove, 0 to quit:")
        command = Console.ReadLine()
        If command = 0 Then
            Exit Do
        ElseIf command = 1 Then
            Console.Write("Enter item (a string): ")
            item = Console.ReadLine()
            q.Enqueue(item)
        ElseIf command = 2 Then
            If q.Count > 0 Then
                item = q.Dequeue()
                Console.WriteLine("Removed item is:{0}", _
                                  item)
            Else
                Console.WriteLine("Queue is empty")
            End If
        Else
            Console.WriteLine("Invlaid command.")
        End If
    Loop
End Sub
```

Listing 6.28: A simple queue simulation

In Listing 6.28, once the Queue object has been created, the user is simply given the choices of adding an item to it, removing an item from it or quitting the application. Adding items to the queue is a simple matter of executing the Enqueue() method, which takes a single object as its parameter. If you add a few items in succession, you will see that the queue size increases (the Count property indicates this).

When you select command '2' to remove an item, the item at the front of the queue is removed and displayed, and you will see the queue size reduces by one item. To ensure we do not try to remove an item from an empty queue, a simple check that the queue's Count property is greater than zero is made; this prevents the program from crashing.

We can make use of a queue to deal with situations where it is impossible for a program to keep up with the workload all of the time (although in many situations, the built-in Windows queue will do this for us with no effort on our part). In general, a queue is useful if the average workload a program has to do does not overload the system, but occasional gluts have to be dealt with. Database transaction processing, web services and intensive graphics applications are all types of programs that can benefit from the use of a queue to even out the processing load.

6.3.5.2 Stacks

When you use the word 'stack' in normal conversation, you are probably referring to a pile of items one on top of the other, like a stack of pancakes. In computer terms, a `Stack` is a 'first-in-last-out' data structure; the normal use of the word reflects the computer version provided we only consider removing one pancake at a time from the stack (the first one on the plate will be the last one eaten).

A stack turns out to be a useful structure for dealing with interruptions in the processing of tasks. Imagine you are sitting at your desk working on a new Visual Basic program, when a co-worker arrives to ask you to look over a file they have on a floppy disk. To make sure you don't lose your place in the VB program, you could write the line-number you are working at on a post-it note and stick it on your desk. You then start work on loading and examining the floppy-disk file and have just got part-way down the first page when an email arrives marked 'urgent'. You quickly jot down the page location of where you have reached on another sticky note and place it on top of the first. You read the email, begin a reply and the phone rings – another sticky note with one or two words to remind you of your intended reply and you answer the phone. When the phone conversation finishes, you can remove the top sticky note, remind yourself of what you were writing and complete the reply. Then you can remove the next sticky note, read it, discard it and go back to your colleague's file and finish checking it. Finally you pick up the bottom sticky note and return to the indicated line of the VB program. You have used a stack of information (the sticky notes) to ensure you did not lose the place in any of the jobs that were interrupted.

Computers are doing this all the time. When it is in the middle of a job and it has to suspend it to go off and do a second job, it marks its place by adding status information that indicates where it was in the first job to a stack. That way, when it has completed the second job it can get back to what it was doing by taking the status info for the first off the top of the stack and resuming. If in the middle of the second job, it had to go off to attend to some third task, it could quite safely place status information about the second job on top of the status information about the first (on the top of the stack) and go off to do this third task. It is always able to complete every task that has been interrupted because the appropriate status information remains on the stack until it is removed.

This type of behaviour is built-in to computer hardware, operating systems and programming languages. For example, whenever a sub call is made in Visual Basic (or most other programming languages), information that indicates which line of the program is next to execute and the values of important variables is placed on the system stack so that when the sub call has completed, it can return to the point if left off.

It is less likely that you will make use of a stack very often in normal programs, although there are certain types of processing that can greatly benefit from a `Stack` data structure. Among these are chess playing programs where in order to evaluate a move, the computer has to look ahead several moves with a number of alternative playing strategies – a `Stack` structure is used to allow it to work several moves ahead from one move option, rewind back and then do the same for other move options. In this case, each move option will in turn create a range of response moves, and these another set of move options, so a stack is an ideal mechanism to allow the chess program to work its way through the options in a systematic way.

Card-playing games can also make use of a `Stack` structure. For example, in gin rummy discarded cards are left in a stack face up on the table. Cards can be removed from this stack only from the top (where they are also added). A program that played or simulated this game would almost certainly use a `Stack` structure. Stacks are also useful for implementing various algorithms, such as the next program (Listing 6.29), that is used to reverse the order of words in a sentence.

```
Sub Main()
     Dim s As Collections.Stack = New Collections.Stack()
     Dim sentence As String
     Dim words As Array
     Dim word As String
     Console.Write("Enter a short sentence: ")
     sentence = Console.ReadLine()
     words = sentence.Split(" ")
     For Each word In words
          s.Push(word)
     Next
     Do
          Console.Write(s.Pop & " ")
     Loop Until s.Count = 0
End Sub
```

Listing 6.29: A `Stack` example – reversing a sentence

In Listing 6.29, the user is asked to enter a sentence which is then broken up into an array of individual words (using the `String.Split()` method – the parameter is the character that will be used to indicate the positions in the string that it will be broken at). Once the array of words has been created, each is added to a `Stack` structure in turn. When we remove the items from the stack they are displayed, with spaces re-added between them. Since the last word pushed on to the stack is the first to be removed (popped) from it, we are displaying the sentence from the last word to the first – i.e. in reverse order.

6.4   Choosing Collections

As we have seen, Visual Basic and .NET between them provide a wide range of methods for creating and working with multiple objects, each with their own advantages and disadvantages. This can initially make it difficult to decide which class to choose when building an application that must deal with many items, although

Table 6.2 Data structure classes – advantages and disadvantages

Collection Class	Advantages	Disadvantages
`Array`	Simple, direct, fast	Need to allocate according to an expected capacity – reallocation is time-consuming. Initially filled with null references and so care is necessary when accessing. No specific ordering. Items can be located in a *sorted* array using a binary search (fast)
`ArrayList`	Simple to use, capacity managed automatically, no initial null reference problems	No specific ordering. No method to locate items apart from exhaustive search
Custom `Array`	Tailored to a specific class, so can be made very easy to use. Can provide any combination of aggregate functions	A lot of work required to create data structure before it can be used in a program. May need to change implementation if collected class is changed
`HashTable`	Simple to add and retrieve items – fast for both	Items appear in random order. Need enumerator to get access to all items
`SortedList`	Simple to add and retrieve items. Speed of `HashTable` for retrieval. Items can be retrieved in specified order	Slow to insert items. May need to define an `ICompare` interface for complex keys
`Dictionary`	Can use arbitrarily complex `Value` and `Key` objects	Need to inherit from `DictionaryBase` class, so very application specific
`Stack` or `Queue`	Strict control of the order items are added and removed	Normally used only where an algorithm dictates

experience will soon simplify the selection process. The advantages and disadvantages of each method are summarized in Table 6.2.

Nicklaus Wirth, one of the godfathers of structured programming and a key force in the development of modern object-oriented languages, wrote a book with the title *Programs = Algorithms + Data Structures*. In this, he argued convincingly that the selection of an appropriate data structure for a given purpose is one of the most important decisions a programmer could make. Visual Basic .NET provides the programmer with a set of powerful pre-built data structures encapsulated as objects, thereby making the use of data structures simple and robust. Hopefully the examples in this chapter demonstrate the power and efficiency that a suitably chosen data structure can give a program.

In the remaining chapters of this book, we will make extensive use of the data structures provided by .NET's common type library, and, where necessary, devise a few of our own.

Review Questions

1. How many Integer elements can an array defined as `Dim A(50) As Integer` hold?

2. Which methods or properties of an array can be used to indicate its size and the index of the last item?

3. When iterating through an array of reference objects using `For..Each`, what precaution is necessary before calling a method of any of the objects? Why is this not necessary for an array of value objects?

4. An array of Strings – `Dim A(5,5,5) As String` – needs to be re-dimensioned so that each dimension has a value of 10. Is this possible using `ReDim`? Can the `Preserve` keyword be used to preserve the current contents?

5. An array of Integers, Dates or Strings can be sorted into order using the `Sort()` method. What must be added to a class so that an array of the class' objects can be sorted in the same way?

6. List the advantages of using the `ArrayList` class instead of a simple array.

7. List the advantages and disadvantages of using the `HashTable` class for storing a list of data records.

8. List the properties and methods provided by an `IEnumerator` interface, and the additional properties that the `IDictionaryEnumerator` interface provides.

9. Is it possible to access items from the middle of a `Stack` or `Queue` collection?

10. A program must manage a collection of customer records, with the provisos that an individual customer record must be quickly retrievable by key (the customer number), but It must also be possible to access the entire list of customers in order of customer number. Which is the most appropriate data structure from the .NET collection classes for this purpose?

Practical Activities

The activities in this chapter will work through the complete development process for a simple card game; 21 or Pontoon. Card games are good examples of real-world systems that work well as object-oriented programs, since there are a number of recognizable objects in a card game (Cards, Deck of Cards, Hand of Cards). Before continuing with the development, we should clearly state the rules of a game of 21 and figure out what needs to be done:

Game Description

In the game of 21, there is one dealer and at least one other player (we will confine the game to a single player against the computer as the dealer). The dealer deals two cards from the deck to the player and him/herself. Cards count as their face values (Ace can be 1 or 11, face cards 10), and the value of a hand is the sum of the cards. The player then decides to either *stick* with the current hand or to ask for extra cards (*twist*), one card at a time until either the hand is satisfactory or *bust*, i.e. exceeding a value of 21. If the player is bust, the dealer wins by default. The minimum a player can *stick* with is 16.

The dealer must equal or beat a player's hand to win, and can take extra cards one at a time until the player's hand is beaten or the dealer's hand is bust. If a player has an initial (2 card) hand of 21 (or Pontoon), the dealer can only win by also scoring 21 with 2 cards.

Analysis

We can analyse these rules to determine the objects that will be needed in the program. Picking out the significant nouns:

Dealer, Player, Cards, Deck, FaceValues, Ace, FaceCards, Value (of a hand), Sum (of cards), Hand

Of these, once we remove plurals and synonyms, we can identify several obvious objects (Dealer, Player, Card, Deck, Hand), several items that will be properties of objects (Value of Hand, Sum of Hand), and some that will be simply different values or properties of existing objects (FaceValues, FaceCards). We can also identify that the Dealer and Player both identify specific Hands (a Dealer's Hand and a Player's Hand). The set of classes will therefore be required to represent Cards, a Deck of cards and Hands of cards. Also, a Deck of cards can expect to be sent a message asking for a card to be dealt, and a Hand can expect to have to deal with being dealt a new card. Finally, it might be as well to rename the Hand class to **PontoonHand**, since we might eventually want to add **PokerHand**, **GinRummyHand**, etc. The class relationships are shown in Figure A6.1.

Mediating between objects of these classes will be Sub Main() of the Console application, in response to the user's commands. The details of this will need to be worked out as we decide on the details of the main algorithm for running a game (which is dictated by the initial game description). For example, a main interaction within a game will be for the **CardDeck** to deal a Card to a **PontoonHand**. Since

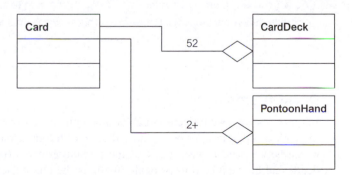

Figure A6.1 The class relationships between Card, Deck and **PontoonHand**

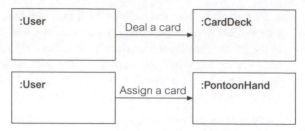

Figure A6.2 Dealing a card from **CardDeck** to **PontoonHand** involves two messages

this interaction will be coded in outwith either class, we will need to depict it as two individual interactions, as in Figure A6.2 (even though the final operation will probably end up as a single statement).

The individual workings of each class must be worked out fully. We can reason out these as follows:

Card Class

A Card must store its value in some way. The most efficient way to do this is to store a single number (from 1 to 52) indicating the card. We can arbitrarily decide which number represents which card, so 1 to 13 could be Hearts, 14 to 26 could be Clubs, 27 to 39 could be Diamonds and 40 to 52 Spades (a range of 13 values per suit). This will make it easy to assign a value to a card, but more difficult to determine its suit, face value (e.g. Ace) or numerical value (e.g. 10 for a Queen). Even so, these calculations are likely to be simple. The **Card** class interface is as shown in Table A6.1.

Table A6.1 Card Class Properties and Methods

Property/Method	Description
New (number)	Create a card (number 1 to 52 indicates the card)
Suit (read-only property): String	The suit of a card (e.g. 'Hearts')
FaceValue (read-only property): String	Name of card rank (e.g. 'Ace', '6', 'King')
Face (read-only property): String	Full name of card (e.g. 'Ace of Clubs')
Value (read-only property): Integer	Worth of a card (e.g. 1 for ace)
AceHigh (read/write property): Boolean	This indicates whether the value of an Ace (if the card is an Ace) is 1 or 11. It will modify the result from the **Value** method

DeckOfCards class

In this class we need to represent a variable number of cards (from 0 to 52), depending on its state (it has just been shuffled or all of the cards have been dealt). In a deck of cards, we need to keep track of the remaining cards (those that have not been dealt) and the next card to be dealt. We must be able to set up a new deck (**New**), randomize the order of the cards (**Shuffle**) and **Deal** a card from the top of the deck. This is shown in Table A6.2.

Table A6.2 DeckOfCards Class Properties and Methods

Property/Method	Description
New()	Create a deck
Shuffle (method)	Randomly mix up the deck of cards
Deal (method/function): Card	Return a card reference from the deck
CardsLeft (method/function): Integer	The number of cards remaining in the deck

PontoonHand class

This class must hold cards that have been assigned to it and be able to calculate their worth. Additionally, it should be able to determine whether a hand is bust (value exceeds 21), allowing for Aces in its collection of cards. See Table A6.3.

Table A6.3 PontoonHand Class Properties and Methods

Property/Method	Description
New()	Create a new hand
Count (read-only property): integer	Indicates how many cards in the hand
NewCard (read/write property): card	This can be a read/write property that will either accept a new card dealt to the hand, or return a reference to the last card dealt
HandValue (method/function): integer	This should indicate the value of the hand according to the rules of 21/Pontoon
CheckBust (method/function): boolean	This is probably the most important function of the class, since it will determine if the hand value exceeds 21, and we can write it to take account of and even adjust the **AceHigh** property of individual cards to maximize the hand's value
HandView (method/function): string	This will return a text listing of the cards in the hand, and will simplify the task of displaying a hand on the screen

Implementing

There is a large number of read-only properties among these classes. Since a read-only property is identical in the way that it works to a function, it is easier to define these as functions and will involve less space on the page and less typing.

Activity 1: The `Card` class

Having fully analysed the game and the classes involved, we can now get on with the task of coding it. The `Card` class is quite simple, although we need to exercise some care in the definition of the methods which evaluate the face value and suit of a card from its number.

Create a new console project, give it the name `CardGame`, and change the name of the project's module to `CardGame`. Now add the class code given in Listing A6.1 to the module (above the outline for `Sub Main()`.

```
Class Card
    'First the member variables to store the card...
    Private mvarNumber As Integer
    '...and whether an Ace is 1 or 11 in value...
    Public AceHigh As Boolean
    'Creating a new card from its number...
    Public Sub New(ByVal number As Integer)
        mvarNumber = number
        AceHigh = True     'Note, initially Ace is 11
    End Sub
    'Work out its Suit from its number...
    Public Function Suit() As String
        Select Case mvarNumber
            Case 1 To 13
                Return "Hearts"
            Case 14 To 26
                Return "Clubs"
            Case 27 To 39
                Return "Diamonds"
            Case 40 To 52
                Return "Spades"
            Case Else
                Return "ERROR"
        End Select
    End Function
    'Within a suit, what number is this card (1 to 13)...
    Public Function CardNumber() As Integer
        Dim cardNo As Integer = mvarNumber
        'Reduce this number into a range of 1 to 13
        'to get the number of the card within a suit...
        Do While cardNo > 13
            cardNo -= 13
        Loop
        Return cardNo
    End Function
    'What type of card is it...
    Public Function FaceValue() As String
        'What is the card's Face within a suit...
        Select Case CardNumber()
            Case 1
                Return "Ace"
            Case 2 To 10
                Return CardNumber.ToString()
            Case 11
                Return "Jack"
            Case 12
                Return "Queen"
```

```
            Case 13
                Return "King"
            Case Else
                Return "ERROR"
        End Select
    End Function
    'How much is it worth...
    Public Function Value() As Integer
        'What is this card worth...
        Select Case CardNumber()
            Case 1 'Note, depends on AceHigh property...
                If AceHigh Then
                    Return 11
                Else
                    Return 1
                End If
            Case 2 To 10
                Return CardNumber()
            Case 11, 12, 13
                Return 10
        End Select
    End Function
    'How would we print it on screen...
    Public Function Face() As String
        'Full description of the card
        '(e.g. Queen of Hearts)...
        Return FaceValue() & " of " & Suit()
    End Function
End Class
```

Listing A6.1: The `Card` class

Now we have a `Card` class that we can incorporate into the `CardDeck` and `PontoonHand` classes. Before going on to create these classes, it is very worthwhile writing a little code to check whether the class behaves as we expect. Add the code given in Listing A6.2 to `Sub Main()` in the module.

```
Sub Main()
    Dim C As New Card(1)
    Console.WriteLine(C.Face)
End Sub
```

Listing A6.2: A simple test of the `Card` class

The code in Listing A6.2 should produce the output given in Figure A6.3. on the console.

It would be worthwhile changing the number passed to the Card constructor (any value between 1 and 52) and running the test several times, to make sure that various cards are depicted properly.

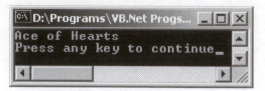

Figure A6.3 The output from a simple test of the Card class

Exercise A6.1

Write code in `Sub Main()` to create new cards with values 1 to 52 in a loop, calling the `Face()` method of each.

Activity 2: The DeckOfCards class

A deck is a simple collection of cards. We could use any of the Collection classes available in .NET for this, but since we know that there will be a maximum of 52 cards, an array seems ideal. A lot of the hard work has been done in the Card class, so the DeckOfCards class can take advantage of this. Apart from creating a whole set of new cards (the numbers 1 to 52 will produce 52 unique cards in the deck), we need to keep track of how many have been dealt, randomize their order and provide a way of dealing them. Note that the array is designated as `mvarDeck(52) As Card`, meaning there will be 53 cards in total. Partly, this is because it is easier to think how to deal with cards numbered 1 to 52. However, the spare (0) card will come in handy in the `Shuffle()` routine. Listing A6.3 shows the DeckOfCards class.

```
Class DeckOfCards
    'A deck of 52 cards...
    Private mvarDeck(52) As Card
    'And how far through it has been dealt...
    Private mvarTopCard As Integer
    'Set up 52 new cards in order...
    Public Sub New()
        Dim no As Integer
        For no = 1 To 52 'Ignore card 0.
            mvarDeck(no) = New Card(no)
        Next
        mvarTopCard = 0
    End Sub
    'Randomize the cards...
    Public Sub Shuffle()
        'The most efficient method is to swap each card
        'with a randomly selected one. Therefore all cards
        'are in a random location...
        Dim no As Integer  'Card we are swapping
        Dim swp As Integer 'Card we swap it with
```

```
                   'A random number generator...
                   Dim rand As New System.Random()
                   For no = 1 To 52
                       'This generates a random number and reduces it
                       'to the range (0 to 51) + 1 (i.e. 1 to 52)...
                       swp = rand.Next() Mod 52 + 1
                       'Now swap them around...
                       mvarDeck(0) = mvarDeck(no)
                       mvarDeck(no) = mvarDeck(swp)
                       mvarDeck(swp) = mvarDeck(0)
                   Next
                   'Having just shuffled, we start dealing from the
                   'top...
                   mvarTopCard = 0
               End Sub
               'Deal one card...
               Public Function Deal() As Card
                   mvarTopCard += 1
                   If mvarTopCard <= 52 Then
                       Return mvarDeck(mvarTopCard)
                   Else
                       Return Nothing
                   End If
               End Function
               Public Function CardsLeft() As Integer
                   Return 52 - mvarTopCard
               End Function
           End Class
```

Listing A6.3: The `DeckOfCards` class

Have a good look at the `Shuffle()` routine and make sure you follow it. You might have thought a suitable algorithm would have been simply to assign cards randomly to each slot in the `Deck` array. However, doing this would then involve checking all of the cards already in the deck before assigning a new one to make sure there were no duplicates. This would be easy enough for the first few cards, but as the deck became full, there would be an increasing chance of assigning a card that was already in the deck and more and more 'tries' to add a card would have to be made before a suitable random card (number from 1 to 52) was found.

Instead, the `Shuffle()` method used does more or less what a human shuffling a deck of cards would do, by swapping the locations of cards already in the deck. We're making good use of the unused card at position 0 in the array, since swapping two objects between two reference variables always requires a third reference variable to use as a temporary store (see the code after the 'Now swap them round . . .' comment).

Again, this class ought to be tested before we use it. Two tests seem relevant. The first will simply create a deck of cards and display them in order (Listing A6.4). The second will create a deck, shuffle them and display the result (Figure A6.4).

Figure A6.4 Results of testing the `DeckOfCards` class

```
Sub Main()
    Dim D As New DeckOfCards()
    Dim C As Card
    Do While D.CardsLeft > 0
        C = D.Deal()
        Console.WriteLine(C.Face)
    Loop
End Sub
```

Listing A6.4: The first test of the `DeckOfCards` – in order

Exercise A6.2

Listing A6.4 is a simple test of the `DeckOfCards` class that creates a deck of cards and then deals cards (into the `Card` reference variable, `C`) until there are none left. To complete testing on it, the `Shuffle()` method should be checked out. Amend the code in Listing A6.4 so that the `Shuffle()` method is called before any cards are dealt and re-test the class. You should expect to see the list of cards in a random order as the result of this test.

Now that we have `Card` and `DeckOfCards` classes, the final class we need is one to represent a hand of cards.

Activity 3: The `PontoonHand` class

The purpose of this class will be to house a collection of cards and collate their information to provide 'collective properties' for them. The `PontoonHand` class (Listing A6.5) is responsible for creating a collection to house individual cards, knowing how many cards are currently in the hand and their total value, accepting new cards dealt to it, being able to check whether hand value exceeds 21 (taking account of the value of aces which may be 1 or 11), and returning a text description of the entire collection of cards.

```
Class PontoonHand
    'Hand for Pontoon/21/Blackjack...
    Private mvarCards As ArrayList
```

```vbnet
'Set up a list to hold the cards...
Public Sub New()
    mvarCards = New ArrayList(5)
End Sub
Public ReadOnly Property Count() As Integer
    Get
        Return mvarCards.Count
    End Get
End Property
'Assign a card/return the most recent dealt...
Public Property NewCard() As Card
    Get
        Return mvarCards(mvarCards.Count - 1)
    End Get
    Set(ByVal Value As Card)
        mvarCards.Add(Value)
    End Set
End Property
'What is this hand worth...
Public Function HandValue() As Integer
    Dim v As Integer = 0, c As Card
    For Each c In mvarCards
        v += c.Value
    Next
    Return v
End Function
'The whole hand as a string...
Public Function HandView() As String
    Dim S As New System.Text.StringBuilder()
    Dim c As Card
    For Each c In mvarCards
        S.Append(c.Face & Environment.NewLine)
    Next
    S.Append("Total hand value is : ")
    S.Append(HandValue())
    Return S.ToString()
End Function
'Check if hand value > 21, and if so, check
'for Ace-high cards whose value can be reduced...
Public Function CheckBust() As Boolean
    If HandValue() > 21 Then
        'Check for aces that can be set to low...
        Dim c As Card
        For Each c In mvarCards
            If c.FaceValue = "Ace" And c.AceHigh Then
                c.AceHigh = False
                Exit For
            End If
        Next
        'Need to check value again...
        If HandValue() > 21 Then
```

```
                        Return True
                Else
                        Return False
                End If
            End If
        End Function
    End Class
```

Listing A6.5: The `PontoonHand` class

Again, we should test this class before we go on to deploy it in a game. Once we create a hand, a suitable set of tests will be to add cards to it, checking on the count and value of the cards as we go and whether the hand is bust. We can also display the hand after each card is dealt. This is shown in Listing A6.6 and Figure A6.5.

```
Sub Main()
    Dim D As DeckOfCards
    Dim H As PontoonHand
    D = New DeckOfCards()
    H = New PontoonHand()
    Console.WriteLine(H.HandView())
    Do
        H.NewCard = D.Deal()
        Console.WriteLine(H.HandView())
    Loop Until H.CheckBust()
    Console.WriteLine(H.HandView())
End Sub
```

Listing A6.6: Testing the `PontoonHand` class

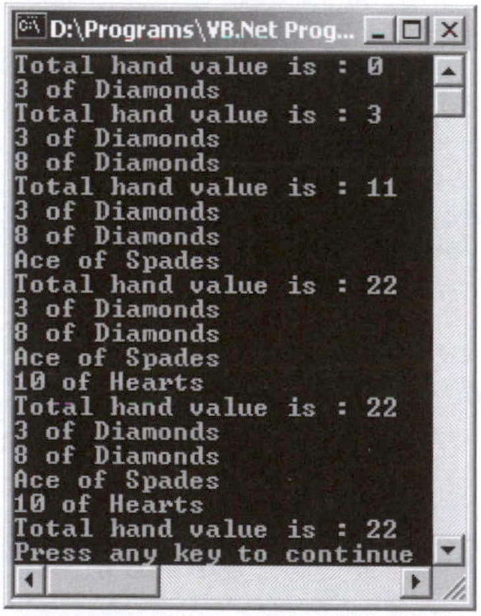

Figure A6.5 Testing the `PontoonHand` class – note how `CheckBust()` has reduced the value of the Ace in the hand (immediately after the dealing of the 10 of Hearts)

The current test code for the `PontoonHand` class adds cards to the hand until the `CheckBust()` method returns `True`; i.e. the hand value exceeds 21. The rules of 21 state that a player may stop adding cards to the hand once it reaches or exceeds a value of 16. Amend the exit condition of the `Do..Loop` in Listing A6.6 so that the hand test follows this rule; i.e. keep adding cards until the hand value is 16 or over. Run this test a few times so that you see the result of hands that are bust and hands that are not.

Activity 4: Playing the game

In this final activity, we will add the code to play a game of 21. A game will involve two hands, the player and the dealer, and will play by the standard rules: the player and dealer are both dealt two cards, the player then accepts his/her hand as it is or takes additional cards until either satisfied or bust. If the player's hand is bust, the dealer wins. If not, the dealer must take cards until the player is beaten or the dealer's hand is bust.

The logic of this game will not require a special class but can be implemented in a single sub, which we can call `Game()`. The logic for a game is a little more complex than the logic within the classes, so we'll go through this a bit at a time.

1. Starting a game

To play a game of 21, we need a `DeckOfCards`, two `PontoonHands` and a variable for collecting the user's response from the keyboard since the user will need to indicate whether or not another card is required. Once the `DeckOfCards` and `PontoonHand` objects have been created, we need to shuffle the deck before beginning the game. The code in Listing A6.7 does this.

```
Sub Game()
    Dim Deck As New DeckOfCards()
    Dim Response As Char
    Dim Player As PontoonHand = New PontoonHand()
    Dim Dealer As PontoonHand = New PontoonHand()
    Deck.Shuffle()
    'More code...
    '...
End Sub
```

Listing A6.7: The variables needed to play a game

The next step (Listing A6.8) is to deal two cards to each hand.

```
Sub Game()
    'Existing code...
    '...
    Player.NewCard = Deck.Deal()
```

```
      Dealer.NewCard = Deck.Deal()
      Player.NewCard = Deck.Deal()
      Dealer.NewCard = Deck.Deal()
      'More code...
      '...
End Sub
```

Listing A6.8: Dealing the initial hands

2. The Player's game

Before we can go any further, the player needs to see their hand and can then decide whether to stay with the hand or take another card. Since this step can repeat as the player takes several other cards, the process should be placed in a loop (Listing A6.9).

```
Sub Game()
      'Existing code...
      '...
      Do
            'Display the hand...
            Console.WriteLine("Player's Hand")
            Console.WriteLine(Player.HandView())
            'Get player's response...
            If Player.HandValue < 21 Then
                  Console.WriteLine("Twist (T) or Stay (S): ")
                  Response = Console.ReadLine().ToLower
            End If
            If Response = "t" Then
                  'Deal the player's second card...
                  Player.NewCard = Deck.Deal()
                  Player.CheckBust()
            End If
      Loop Until Response = "s" Or Player.HandValue >= 21
      'More code...
      '...
End Sub
```

Listing A6.9: Allowing the user to collect extra cards

Note that there are two possible exit conditions from this loop. Either the player has decided not to take any more cards (by pressing 's') or the player's hand has a value of 21 (with which the player can win) or over (in which case the player will lose).

3. Playing the Dealer's game

The dealer's game is simpler than that of the hand played against it. For a start, if the other hand value exceeds 21, the dealer wins by default. If the other player has a hand that is not bust, the dealer has no choice but to beat this hand's value either with the initial two cards or by adding cards. There is no benefit to adding cards to the dealer's hand once it beats the other player's, so a simple loop can add cards to the dealer's hand until either the dealer wins or is bust. Once the dealer's hand has been played, the evaluation for which hand has won is a simple one (Listing A6.10).

```
Sub Game()
    'Existing code...
    '...
    'Now play the dealer's hand...
    If Player.HandValue > 21 Then
        Console.WriteLine("Player is bust - Dealer wins.")
    Else
        Do Until Dealer.HandValue > Player.HandValue _
                 Or Dealer.CheckBust()
            Dealer.NewCard = Deck.Deal()
            Dealer.CheckBust()
            Debug.WriteLine(Dealer.HandView())
        Loop
        Console.WriteLine("Dealer's hand")
        Console.WriteLine(Dealer.HandView())
        If Player.HandValue > Dealer.HandValue _
            Or Dealer.HandValue > 21 Then
            Console.WriteLine("Player wins.")
        Else
            Console.WriteLine("Dealer wins.")
        End If
    End If
End Sub
```

Listing A6.10: Playing the dealer's hand and checking which hand has won

4. Final touches

The final step in this program is to call the `Game()` subroutine from `Sub Main()`. Testing can be accomplished at this stage by running the game and ensuring that the play matches the rules of 21 as stated. This final listing (Listing A6.11) is simply a repeat of all of `Sub Game()` in one place, and the `Sub Main()` that calls it.

```
Sub Game()
    Dim Deck As New DeckOfCards()
    Dim Response As Char
    '        Do
    Dim Player As PontoonHand = New PontoonHand()
    Dim Dealer As PontoonHand = New PontoonHand()
    Deck.Shuffle()
    'Deal player and dealer two cards...
    Player.NewCard = Deck.Deal()
    Dealer.NewCard = Deck.Deal()
```

```
      Player.NewCard = Deck.Deal()
      Dealer.NewCard = Deck.Deal()
      Do
          'Display the hand...
          Console.WriteLine("Player's Hand")
          Console.WriteLine(Player.HandView())
          'Get player's response...
          If Player.HandValue < 21 Then
              Console.WriteLine("Twist (T) or Stay (S): ")
              Response = Console.ReadLine().ToLower
          End If
          If Response = "t" Then
              'Deal the player's second card...
              Player.NewCard = Deck.Deal()
              Player.CheckBust()
          End If
      Loop Until Response = "s" Or Player.HandValue >= 21
      'Now play the dealer's hand...
      If Player.HandValue > 21 Then
          Console.WriteLine("Player is bust - Dealer wins.")
      Else
          Do Until Dealer.HandValue > Player.HandValue _
              Or Dealer.CheckBust()
              Dealer.NewCard = Deck.Deal()
              Dealer.CheckBust()
              Debug.WriteLine(Dealer.HandView())
          Loop
          Console.WriteLine("Dealer's hand")
          Console.WriteLine(Dealer.HandView())
          If Player.HandValue > Dealer.HandValue _
          Or Dealer.HandValue > 21 Then
              Console.WriteLine("Player wins.")
          Else
              Console.WriteLine("Dealer wins.")
          End If
      End If
  End Sub

  Sub Main()
      Game()
  End Sub
```

Listing A6.11: The complete `Game()` routine

Features worth remembering

■ The structure of the 21 game relies on using appropriate ways of collecting objects as necessary. An array of 52 cards makes sense since there are 52 cards in a deck, but in other situations it might be better to use a more flexible structure such as `ArrayList`

- The .NET classes provide simple ways for storing a lot of objects or data values collectively and retrieving them
- While there is a lot of code in this program, breaking it down into easily recognized objects has been central to making it understandable (and was necessary to make it possible to write in the first place). The implementation required a good design to work with.

Suggested Additional Activities

1. The program as it stands plays a single game of 21. To play another game, the program must be re-run. Add a structure to allow the user to choose whether to play another game or not. This will involve a loop of some sort (probably a `Do..Loop`) and some way of asking the user whether or not to play again and collecting a response.

2. Other card games can be coded using the same `Card` and `Deck` classes. Provided you know the rules, there should be no more difficulty to creating a `PokerHand` class, a `GinRummyHand` class or others. The game rules in each case will be different (and possibly more difficult). Try creating a card game of your own choice.

Solutions to Exercises

Exercises 6.1

1. a) Entries in the phone book are sorted into alphabetical order (using surname, then first names, then address). This means we can always work out whether a number being sought is before or after any entry we look at, and can search accordingly.

   b) Because the entries are in strict order, it is not possible to simply add a new entry at the end. Instead, a new entry has to be added at the correct place for the ordering, and this may involve moving all of the entries after it.

2. Firstly, you probably do not have a unique name (very few people do – even with a weird name like McMonnies you will find a good few of them around the world). Since when you add money to your bank account, you want to be sure it will go into *your* account and not that of someone with the same name as you, an account number is essential. Secondly, if banking/insurance records are stored in order of account/policy number, having control of the numbering system can make it easy to ensure that records are in order without having to do a potentially disruptive insert of a new record between two existing ones. Every new record get the next number in the sequence.

Exercises 6.2

1.

```
Dim MonthNames() As String = {"January", "February", _
        "March", "April", "May", "June", "July", _
        "August", "September", "November", "December"}
```

2.

```
Dim month As Integer
For month = 0 To 11
    Console.WriteLine(MonthNames(month))
Next
```

Alternatively:

```
Dim month As String
For Each month In MonthNames
    Console.WriteLine(month)
Next
```

3.

```
Dim MonthLengths() As Integer = {31, 28, 31, 30, 31, 30, _
                    31, 31, 30, 31, 30, 31}
```

Exercise 6.3

a)

```
Private Occupants(1, 3) As String
```

b) Either add initialisation code . . .

```
Occupants(0, 0) = "Bloggs"
Occupants(0,1) = "Jones"
Occupants(0,2) = "Smith"
Occupants(0,3) = "Jackson"
Occupants(1,0) = "Green"
Occupants(1,1) = "Brown"
Occupants(1,2) = "Black"
Occupants(1,3) = "White"
```

or change the declaration to . . .

```
Private Occupants(,) As String = _
    {{"Bloggs", "Jones", "Smith", "Jackson"}, _
    {"Green", "Brown", "Black", "White"}}
```

c)

```
Sub DisplayOccupants()
    Dim floor, room As Integer
    For floor = 0 To 1
```

```
                    For room = 0 To 3
                        Console.WriteLine("Floor{0}, Room{1}:{2}", _
                                 floor, room, Occupants(floor, room))
                    Next
            Next
        End Sub
```

Exercise 6.4

a) This is very similar to the code to display all occupants, but an `If..Then` statement ensures that only a matching name is displayed, and the `Exit Sub` saves continuing through the entire array:

```
Fub LookUpOccupant(ByVal Name As String)
    Dim floor, room As Integer
    For floor = 0 To 1
        For room = 0 To 3
            If Occupants(floor, room) = Name Then
                Console.WriteLine("Floor{0},
                Room{1}:{2}", _
                        floor, room, Occupants(floor, room))
                Exit Sub
            End If
        Next
    Next
End Sub
```

b) Additionally, could add check code to ensure a valid room and floor number (using `If..Then` structures):

```
Function GetOccupant(ByVal floor As Integer, _
                    ByVal room As Integer) As String
    Return Occupants(floor, room)
End Sub
```

Exercise 6.5

a)

```
Class Employee
    Private mvarName As String
    Private mvarPhoneNumber As Integer
    Public Property Name() As String
        Get
            Return mvarName
        End Get
        Set(ByVal Value As String)
            mvarName = Value
        End Set
    End Property
    Public Property PhoneNumber() As Integer
```

```
            Get
                Return mvarPhoneNumber
            End Get
            Set(ByVal Value As Integer)
                mvarPhoneNumber = Value
            End Set
        End Property
        Public Sub New(ByVal n As String, ByVal p As Integer)
            mvarName = n
            mvarPhoneNumber = p
        End Sub
    End Class
```

b) Either we need a lot of initialization code, or . . .

```
Private Employees(,) As Employee
= {{New Employee("Smith", 1234), _
    New Employee("Bloggs", 2345), _
    New Employee("Jackson", 3456), _
    New Employee("Jones", 4567)}, _
   {New Employee("Green", 9876),_
    New Employee("Brown", 8765), _
    New Employee("Black", 7654), _
    New Employee("White", 5432)}}
```

c) Note, 0 is returned if the employee is not found.

```
Function LookUpEmployee(ByVal Name As String) As Integer
    Dim floor, room As Integer
    For floor = 0 To 1
        For room = 0 To 3
            If Employees(floor, room).Name = Name Then
                Return Employees(floor, room).PhoneNumber
            End If
        Next
    Next
    Return 0
End Function
```

d) Note – need to pass floor and room variables `ByRef` (since they are output variables). Also, the values of floor and room are set to −1 if the employee name cannot be found. Otherwise we could conclude that the non-existent employee was in room 0 on floor 0.

```
Sub LocateEmployee(ByVal Name As String, _
                   ByRef floor As Integer, _
                   ByRef room As Integer)
    For floor = 0 To 1
        For room = 0 To 3
```

```
                If Employees(floor, room).Name = Name Then
                    Exit Sub
                End If
            Next
        Next
        floor = -1
        room = -1
    End Sub
```

Exercise 6.6

a) First the modified class code – note that all properties are read-only (saves space here) and that `Floor` and `Room` are also properties now:

```
Class Employee
    Private mvarName As String
    Private mvarPhoneNumber As Integer
    Private mvarFloor As Integer
    Private mvarRoom As Integer
    Public ReadOnly Property Name() As String
        Get
            Return mvarName
        End Get
    End Property
    Public ReadOnly Property PhoneNumber() As Integer
        Get
            Return mvarPhoneNumber
        End Get
    End Property
    Public ReadOnly Property Floor() As Integer
        Get
            Return mvarFloor
        End Get
    End Property
    Public ReadOnly Property Room() As Integer
        Get
            Return mvarRoom
        End Get
    End Property
    Public Sub New(ByVal n As String, ByVal p As
                    Integer, _
                    ByVal f As Integer, ByVal r As
                    Integer)
        mvarName = n
        mvarPhoneNumber = p
        mvarFloor = f
        mvarRoom = r
    End Sub
End Class
```

b) An `ArrayList` of these is easy to declare but cannot be initialized in line:

```
Private EmployeeList As New ArrayList
```

c) Now the modified look up functions (much easier):

```
Function LookUpPhone(ByVal Name As String) As Integer
    Dim E As Employee
    For Each E In EmployeeList
        If E.Name = Name Then
            Return E.PhoneNumber
        End If
    Next
End Function

Function LookUpFloor(ByVal name As String) As Integer
    Dim E As Employee
    For Each E In EmployeeList
        If E.Name = name Then
            Return E.Floor
        End If
    Next
End Function
```

And similar code for `LookUpRoom()`.

d) Finally, the `AddEmployee` function – I've made this return a Boolean to make sure a new employee is not assigned to a room, floor or phone number that is already occupied:

```
Public Function AddEmployee(ByVal Name As String, _
                            ByVal Tel As Integer, _
                            ByVal Flr As Integer, _
                            ByVal Rm As Integer) _
                                        As Boolean
    Dim E As Employee
    For Each E In EmployeeList
        If E.PhoneNumber = Tel Or _
            E.Floor = Flr Or _
            E.Room = rm Then
            Return False
        End If
    Next
    E = New Employee(Name, Tel, Flr, Rm)
    EmployeeList.Add(E)
End Function
```

Testing this class and associated functions in `Sub Main()` is left as an exercise.

a) A `HashTable` includes an automatic look-up method, and so there is no need to write code to search through a list. The `ContainsKey()` method will tell us whether an item exists in the `HashTable`, and the `Item()` property will return an item with a specified key.

b) First, the redefined `Student` class:

```
Public Class Student
    Private mvarName As String
    Private mvarMark As Integer

    Public ReadOnly Property Name()
        Get
            Return mvarName
        End Get
    End Property

    Public Property Mark()
        Get
            Return mvarMark
        End Get
        Set(ByVal Value)
            mvarMark = Value
        End Set
    End Property

    Public Sub New(ByVal Name As String, _
                   ByVal Mark As Integer)
        mvarName = Name
        mvarMark = Mark
    End Sub

    Public Sub Report()
        Console.WriteLine("Student: {0} Mark:{1}", _
                          mvarName, mvarMark)
    End Sub

    Public Function Key() As String
        Return Name
    End Function

End Class
```

And now, the `HashTable` class:

```
Public Class StudentTable
    Private Table As Collections.Hashtable
    Private ClassSize As Integer

    Public Function AddStudent(ByVal name As String, _
                   ByVal mark As Integer) As Boolean
```

```
            If Table.ContainsKey(name) Then
                Return False ' The name was already in the
                table
            Else
                Dim S As New Student(name, mark)
                Table.Add(S.Key, S)
                Return True
            End If
End Function


Public Function GetMark(ByVal name As String) _
                                        As Integer
    If Table.ContainsKey(name) Then
            Dim S As Student
            S = CType(Table(name), Student)
        Return S.Mark
    Else
        Return -1
    End If
End Function


Public Function AverageMark() As Single
    Dim s As Student, k As String
    Dim sum As Integer = 0, count As Integer = 0
    If ClassSize > 0 Then   'Check there are marks.
        For Each k In Table.Keys
            s = Table.Item(k)
            sum += s.Mark
            count += 1
        Next
        Return sum / ClassSize
    Else
        Return 0  'Saves a divide by zero.
    End If
End Function


Public Function MaxStudent() As Student
    Dim s As Student, k As String
    Dim index As Integer, max As Integer
    max = 0 'This is our first guess.
    For Each k In Table.Keys
        s = Table.Item(k)
        If s.Mark > max Then
            MaxStudent = s
        End If
    Next
    'Note - no need for a Return here, as MaxStudent
    '(the function name) will implicitly be returned
End Function
```

```
Public Function MinStudent() As Student
   Dim s As Student, k As String
   Dim index As Integer, min As Integer
   min = 0
   For Each k In Table.Keys
      s = Table.Item(k)
      If s.Mark < min Then
         MinStudent = s
      End If
   Next
   'Note - no need for a Return here, as MinStudent
   '(the function name) will implicitly be returned
End Function

End Class
```

Note that there is now no possibility of obtaining a sorted list (sorting a HashTable is like herding cats – i.e. it is not possible).

Exercise 6.8

Best approach for this is to expose the Table member of the StudentTable class, so that an enumerator can be obtained from it and allowed to work on it.

a) Change the declaration of the Table member to:

```
Public Table As Collections.Hashtable
```

b) Use the enumerator as for any HashTable, from a sub:

```
Public Sub ListStudents(ByVal ST As StudentTable)
   Dim en As Collections.IDictionaryEnumerator = _
                         ST.Table.GetEnumerator()
   Do While en.MoveNext()
      Dim S As Student = en.Value
      S.Report()
   Loop
End Sub
```

Note that this sub uses a parameter of type StudentTable (our encapsulated HashTable).

Exercise A6.1

```
Sub Main()
   Dim C As Card
   Dim index As Integer
   For index = 1 To 52
      C = New Card(index)
      Console.WriteLine(C.Face)
   Next
End Sub
```

Exercise A6.2

```
Sub Main()
    Dim D As New DeckOfCards()
    Dim C As Card
    D.Shuffle()
    Do While D.CardsLeft > 0
        C = D.Deal()
        Console.WriteLine(C.Face)
    Loop
End Sub
```

Exercise A6.3

```
Sub Main()
    Dim D As DeckOfCards
    Dim H As PontoonHand
    D = New DeckOfCards()
    H = New PontoonHand()
    Console.WriteLine(H.HandView())
    Do
        H.NewCard = D.Deal()
        Console.WriteLine(H.HandView())
    Loop Until H.HandValue() >= 16
    Console.WriteLine(H.HandView())
End Sub
```

Answers to Review Questions

1. How many Integer elements can an array defined as `Dim A(50) As Integer` hold? **51, because A(0) is also a valid element.**

2. Which methods or properties of an array can be used to indicate its size and the index of the last item? **`Length()` indicates the number of array elements, while `GetUpperBound(0)` will return the maximum index value of the zero (or only) dimension of the array.**

3. When iterating through an array of reference objects using `For..Each`, what precaution is necessary before calling a method of any of the objects? Why is this not necessary for an array of value objects? **It is necessary to check that the object actually exists, since any element could be a reference variable with no object assigned to it. A suitable check is `"If Not <Element> Is Nothing Then"`. This check is not necessary for arrays of value elements because a value element always exists.**

4. An array of Strings – `Dim A(5,5,5) As String` – needs to be re-dimensioned so that each dimension has a value of 10. Is this possible using `ReDim`? Can the `Preserve` keyword be

used to preserve the current contents? **Yes, it can be redimensioned to the new size. No, `Preserve` cannot be used if any other than the last dimension is being changed.**

5. An array of integers, dates or strings can be sorted into order using the `Sort()` method. What must be added to a class so that an array of the class' objects can be sorted in the same way? **The class must implement the `IComparable` interface.**

6. List the advantages of using the `ArrayList` class instead of a simple array. **No need to specify a maximum number of elements, supports enumerators, it is possible to add a group of items in a single call, no need to worry about `Nothing` references when using `For..Each`, has a `Contains()` method to determine if an object already exists in the list.**

7. List the advantages and disadvantages of using the `HashTable` class for storing a list of data records. **ADV: Fast access to objects. Ability to check for the existence of an object. Can use an enumerator. Can use `For..Each` on the Keys property. DISADV: Cannot be sorted – cannot retrieve objects in any order. Need to use an enumerator to access all objects directly.**

8. List the properties and methods provided by an `IEnumerator` interface, and the additional properties that the `IDictionaryEnumerator` interface provides. **`IEnumerator` provides `Current` property and `MoveNext()` and `Reset()` methods. `IDictionaryEnumerator` also provies `Entry`, `Key` and `Value` properties to access elements directly.**

9. Is it possible to access items from the middle of a `Stack` or `Queue` collection? **No.**

10. A program must manage a collection of customer records, with the provisos that an individual customer record must be quickly retrievable by key (the customer number), but It must also be possible to access the entire list of customers in order of customer number. Which is the most appropriate data structure from the .NET collection classes for this purpose? **A `SortedList` will provide access to items both in a predefined order and directly by key.**

In this chapter you will learn:

- the nature of inheritance in programming;
- what inheritance can do for your programs;
- the differences between code and interface inheritance;
- how you can make classes interchangeable, and how this facility can be put to good use.

7.1 Inheritance in Visual Basic

To many programmers, *inheritance* is the be-all and end-all of object oriented programming, almost as if encapsulation was some way-point on the route to the holy grail of inheritance. Those programmers would certainly have been disappointed by, and even disparaging about, earlier releases of Visual Basic. Visual Basic, up to version 6.0, did not 'do' inheritance.

Or did it? Recall back in Chapter 2, where the various ways that objects could be related to or interact with other objects, that *two* types of inheritance were described. Code inheritance, known simply as 'inheritance' by many programmers, is a facility which allows you to take an existing class and base a new one on it. All of the properties and methods in the existing class automatically became properties of the new class, and any *changes* between the existing and new class were all that it would be necessary to write code for. Interface inheritance, on the other hand, is a way of defining a set of properties and methods that any class that implements the interface must provide versions of. Interface inheritance is like a standard contract that any subscribers (the implementing classes) must adhere to so that they are acceptable (to the VB Compiler), but every class must provide a complete implementation of the code behind the interface.

Visual Basic .NET allows both types of inheritance, but earlier versions of VB (from V5.0 on) supported interface inheritance. As a result, this made Visual Basic 5.0 and 6.0 capable of creating COM components (COM – Component Object Model, Microsoft's prior standard for component-based software). COM was the 'software-bus' technology that made Microsoft office components like Word and Excel automatable, and was widely used not only by Microsoft, but by other applications developers to enable the creation of medium and large-scale applications that supported automation, inter-operation of separately developed sub-systems and distributed systems (i.e. systems which are installed and operate across a range of nodes in a networked environment). Until the upgrade in Visual Basic 5.0 that added interface inheritance, you needed a black-belt in C++ programming to create COM components. Visual Basic 5.0 brought this capability to a large number of ordinary programmers and started an explosion of software functionality for Windows-based systems that continues today.

Compared to code inheritance as provided in VB .NET, the interface inheritance provided by earlier versions of VB was more effort to implement and did not allow you to take easy advantage of work you had already done in classes you had already created. It did provide a way of creating classes that were able to communicate in a pre-defined way with other code, and as a consequence of this, allowed VB to be used to create COM components. Code inheritance has not *replaced* interface inheritance in Visual Basic; it is simply a new way of doing things that can in some circumstances save a lot of development effort.

7.1.1 Inheritance, Extension, Specialization

The name 'inheritance' covers a range of tightly related facilities in programming: inheritance, *extension* and *specialization*. These names describe very distinctive features that just happen to go together well in object-oriented programming.

7.1.1.1 Inheritance

Inheritance itself is a facility that allows you to take an existing class and use it as the basis of a new class. The name is used to suggest an analogy with genetics: you inherit certain physical and mental characteristics from your parents, such as the colour of your eyes or hair, your height and your facility for mathematics, music or juggling (I'm not going to get involved in the nature vs nurture argument here, so if you're not a believer in the ability to inherit some intellectual capabilities, it is best to just accept the analogy for what it is).

The analogy with genetic inheritance is not ideal, because genetically you inherit traits from both your parents, rather than just one of them. This is DNA's method for keeping the population of the world diverse. If you did inherit from a single parent, there would be no genetic melting-pot, and you would be more like a clone than an offspring. In fact this is closer to how inheritance in programming works: a class that inherits from an existing class gets one of everything that existing class has to offer.

Take the example of the `BankAccount` class used in several earlier chapters. Listing 7.1 is an outline definition of a similar class (a constructor, `Sub New()`, has been added to the `BankAccount` code from Chapter 5):

```
Public Class BankAccount
    Public AccountName As String
    Public OverdraftAvailable As Boolean
    Private AgreedOverdraftAmount As Decimal
    Private Balance As Decimal
```

```
        Public Sub New()
            ...
        End Sub

        Public Sub Deposit(ByVal Amount As Decimal)
            ...
        End Sub

        Public Sub SetOverdraft(ByVal Amount As Decimal)
            ...
        End Sub

        Public Function Withdraw(ByVal Amount As Decimal) _
                                              As Boolean
            ...
        End Sub

        Public ReadOnly Property CurrentBalance() As Decimal
            ...
        End Property
    End Class
```

Listing 7.1: The `BankAccount` class defined in Chapter 5

This class is very similar to the one developed in Chapter 5, although a constructor (`Sub New()`) has been added as a prerequisite for inheritance. We can define a new class, based on the `BankAccount` class, as shown in Listing 7.2.

```
    Public Class NewAccount
        Inherits BankAccount
    End Class
```

Listing 7.2: Inheriting from `BankAccount`

Surely, you must be thinking, that's not all there is to it. Well, it is and it isn't. We can create instances of `NewAccount` and use them just as we could with `BankAccount`. However, instances of the new class will be exactly the same as instances of `BankAccount`, which suggests there is not much point in doing it. Recall the earlier statement that code inheritance is a bit like creating a clone. Well here it is; a new class that is functionally an exact copy of the one it inherited from. However, the point to remember is that this new class definition is just a starting point. To make it worth using, we need to give it some capabilities of its own.

7.1.1.2 Extension

Normally, we create a class that inherits code from another class so that we can extend the properties or methods of the existing class; i.e. we can add new properties and/or new methods. For example, let's assume that we want to create an investment account – one that pays the owner some interest on the balance in their account. We can add two facilities to the existing account; an `InterestRate` member variable and an `AddInterest` method (Listing 7.3).

```
Public Class InvestmentAccount
    Inherits BankAccount

    Public InterestRate As Single
    Public Sub AddInterest()
        Deposit(CurrentBalance * InterestRate / 100)
    End Sub
End Class
```

Listing 7.3: Extending `BankAccount`

It's probably best to state up-front that this code is not anything like the code your bank uses to manage interest-bearing accounts, since it deals with the issue of adding interest in a very naïve (not to mention business-bankrupting) way. If you can accept that for the moment, you can, I hope, see that inheritance has allowed us to do something very useful. The `InterestRate` member variable stores the percentage rate on which interest is calculated. The `AddInterest()` method uses this value to calculate the amount of interest to pay (based on the current balance), and deposits this amount. These facilities add to the properties and methods already in `BankAccount`, so we now have two bank account classes. One has no facilities for dealing with interest, but instead sets out the core attributes and capabilities of any bank account. The other is a bank account with all of these core attributes and capabilities, but also the ability to deal with interest payments.

Exercise 7.1

What do you think would happen if you were to try to access the `InterestRate` property of a normal `BankAccount` object, or call its `AddInterest()` method? How does Visual Studio help to prevent you from doing this in your programs (think of what happens immediately before you type a method or property name in the Code Editor window)?

7.1.1.3 Specialization

A class that inherits from another can also contain alternative definitions of the other class's properties and methods. For example, certain types of investment accounts are organized so that interest is only paid if certain conditions have been met, such as there having been no cash withdrawn for a specified period. Again, we need to accept the banking details here are naïve, but we could specify a `SpecialInvestmentAccount` as one that only allowed authorized withdrawals. We could have a special version of the `Withdraw()` method that uses some bank facility to determine if a withdrawal is allowed and returns a `True` result if so.

To make this work, we need to modify the `Withdraw()` method inherited from the `InvestmentAccount` class to incorporate logic to check for authorization. We also need to make a small modification to the `BankAccount` class that will allow us to create a specialized version of `Withdraw()` in a class that inherits from it. The original `BankAccount` class needs this change (Listing 7.4).

```
Public Class BankAccount
    ...
      Public Overridable Function Withdraw( _
                     ByVal Amount As Decimal) As Boolean
      ...
      End Sub
      ...
End Class
```

Listing 7.4: The BankAccount class defined in Chapter 5

The new account class must alter the current definition of the Withdraw() method, and to enable this, it is necessary to mark the method as *overridable*. This has absolutely no effect on the BankAccount class, but makes it possible for a class that inherits from it to provide a specialized version of the method. Now we can create the SpecialInvestmentAccount class (Listing 7.5). For the example, we'll use the simple rule that a withdrawal can only be made from a SpecialInvestmentAccount if the resulting balance is at least £100.00:

```
Public Class SpecialInvestmentAccount
    Inherits InvestmentAccount
    ' Here is the specialized version of Withdraw...
    Public Overrides Function Withdraw(_
                     ByVal Amount As Decimal) As Boolean
       If (Balance - Amount) >= 100 Then
          Return MyBase.Withdraw(Amount)
       Else
          Return False
       End If
    End Function
End Class
```

Listing 7.5: Creating a specialized version of Withdraw()

Note that the SpecialInvestmentAccount class inherits from the InvestmentAccount class, since it will still need an interest rate and method of paying interest. Had it inherited from BankAccount, these facilities would not have been available. Note also that due to this, there are two levels of inheritance going on. InvestmentAccount inherits from BankAccount, and SpecialInvestmentAccount inherits from InvestmentAccount.

One useful feature of inheritance that has been employed here is that our specialized version of Withdraw() has made use of the existing version from the BankAccount class. The special withdrawal rule has been implemented effectively as 'if this withdrawal passes the test for a SpecialInvestmentAccount, go ahead and make a withdrawal using BankAccount's method'. MyBase.Withdraw() is actually a call to InvestmentAccount's implementation of Withdraw(), since this is the *base class* of SpecialInvestmentAccount. However, InvestmentAccount inherits BankAccount's Withdraw() method, so in the end, the new version of `Withdraw()` calls on `BankAccount`'s version to do some of its work.

7.1.2 Vocabulary

We have looked briefly at the three things inheritance brings to object-oriented programming:

1. the ability to create a new class that automatically has all the features of an existing one,
2. the ability to add properties and methods to a class that inherits from another, and
3. the ability to create specialized versions of properties and methods in the new class that makes it a specialist version of the one it inherited from.

As you might imagine, all this power comes at a price to the programmer, and that price is the need to learn how to control the capabilities inheritance brings. As with all things in programming, power comes from the words used and the syntax they are used with, so, like a trainee sorcerer, you need to learn to use the 'spells' of inheritance with care.

There are two different vocabularies you need to be concerned about: the general language of object-oriented programming, which has grown over about 30 years of use in the computing industry, and the specialized form of this language that Microsoft uses in Visual Basic. True, both languages are similar, but you should be aware that Microsoft uses a slightly skewed vocabulary in their documentation on VB. NET; one that a good few experienced object-oriented programmers do not agree 100% with.

7.1.2.1 Lineage

Inheritance relationships are discussed using words that would not be out of place in a genealogists' convention. The class that another class inherits from is called the *parent* class (no need to distinguish between father and mother, since a class can only have a single parent). Similarly, a class that inherits from another is said to be its *child*. The terms *base* class (for parent) and *sub* class (for child) are also commonly used (at least in Microsoft-speak). The term *super* class is also commonly used for Parent class.

A class that inherits indirectly from another (e.g. like `SpecialInvestmentAccount` inherits indirectly from `BankAccount`) is said to be a *descendant* class, while the class it inherits indirectly from is said to be an *ancestor* class. We could also use terms like *grandfather* class (for the parent class's parent class) and *grandchild* class (for a child of a child class), but while this is more precise in indicating a number of levels of inheritance, continuing with that range of terminology to cover, for example, great-grandfather (or great-grandmother) classes can quickly become unwieldy. The important relationships are between parent and child, as shown in Figure 7.1.

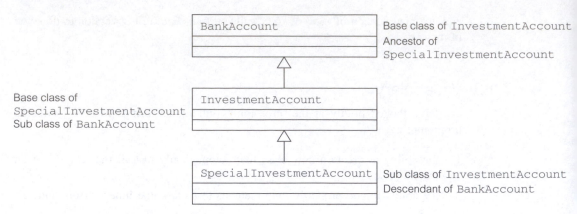

Figure 7.1 Relationships between classes

The term 'base class', as used by Microsoft, is a bit unfortunate, since at least some practitioners of object-oriented programming use the term base class to describe the ultimate ancestor of any class; i.e. the first class that is the start of the inheritance chain that leads to some class. A little thought tells you that this usage of the term base class would not be of much use in .NET, since the object class is automatically the ultimate ancestor of every class in .NET. Microsoft have appropriated the term base class to mean 'the class that is inherited directly from', so we would be well advised to stick with that terminology. In fact, VB .NET provides the keyword `MyBase` as a direct reference to whatever class is named in the `Inherits` statement of a new class.

Inheritance also brings the notion of *abstract* classes and *concrete* classes. An abstract class is one that has been created not to make objects from, but purely to define core behaviour and members that can be inherited by other classes, usually several of them. Classes that can be used to create object instances are sometimes called concrete classes. By using abstract classes, we can define the basic protocol for passing messages to objects even though we have not yet decided how the objects will eventually work when implemented in concrete classes.

7.1.3 Advantages of Inheritance

The obvious advantage of code inheritance is that we can create new classes that contain a lot of properties and methods and yet we do not need to write the code for these. It is far more efficient to inherit existing code and write only new code that is necessary for specific purposes. This advantage of code inheritance is obvious, but it in turn leads to a number of knock-on advantages.

The first of these is that any changes made to a base class will automatically filter through to its Sub classes. This can be a good thing if, for example, you were to discover and fix a bug in a base class, since this bug would also be fixed in all of the classes that inherit from it. The bug might not exist in sub classes if they have created specialized versions of the method that contains the error (i.e. overridden versions of it), but for any methods that exist unchanged in Sub classes, or any that are called by overridden versions, the bugs will also be inherited. If an error is inherited, fixing it in the base class will also fix it in every sub class when these are next compiled.

Another advantage of inheritance is that a sub class is automatically compatible with any Ancestor class in its inheritance chain, a feature known as *polymorphism*. For example, if I write a sub in some code that defines a `BankAccount` object as parameter, then this sub will also automatically accept an `InvestmentAccount` or a `SpecialInvestmentAccount` being passed as an argument, e.g. Listing 7.6.

```
Sub DisplayBalance(ByVal B As BankAccount)
    Console.WriteLine("Balance is " & B.Balance)
End Sub

Sub ShowBalances()
    Dim B As BankAccount = New BankAccount(100)
    Dim I As InvestmentAccount = New InvestmentAccount()
    Dim S As SpecialInvestmentAccount = _
                        New SpecialInvestmentAccount()
    DisplayBalance(B)
    DisplayBalance(I)
    DisplayBalance(S)
End Sub
```

Listing 7.6: Sub classes are compatible with their ancestors

In Listing 7.6, the `DisplayBalance()` sub takes a single parameter, which must be a `BankAccount` object. However, `ShowBalances()` calls this sub three times, passing a `BankAccount` the first time, an `InvestmentAccount` the second time and a `SpecialInvestmentAccount` the third. All three calls will be successful, because `InvestmentAccount` and `SpecialInvestmentAccount` are both type-compatible with `BankAccount`.

Note that this compatibility does not work in the other direction; we could not pass a `BankAccount` as an argument to a sub which defined an `InvestmentAccount` as its parameter. A moment's thought should tell you why this is so. A sub class is always type-compatible with any of its ancestors because it inherits all of the necessary behaviour from them. An `InvestmentAccount` has a `Balance` property and `Deposit()` and `Withdraw()` methods, so it can properly replace any code that uses the interface of a `BankAccount`. However, a `BankAccount` does not have either an `InterestRate` property or an `AddInterest()` method. Passing a `BankAccount` to a sub that expects an `InvestmentAccount` can cause an error because that sub might contain code that accesses the `InterestRate` property, which the `BankAccount` does not have. To prevent this problem, Visual Basic will not compile code when a base class is used where one of its sub classes is expected.

The inheritance relationship is often referred to as an **Is-A** relationship. We can say that an `InvestmentAccount` **Is-A** `BankAccount`, a `SpecialInvestmentAccount` **Is-A** `BankAccount`, and a

SpecialInvestmentAccount **Is-A(n)** InvestmentAccount. However, this does not work the other way round; a BankAccount is not an InvestmentAccount, nor is an InvestmentAccount a SpecialInvestmentAccount.

7.1.4 Disadvantages of Inheritance

The use of inheritance can also have a down-side, since a change made to an ancestor class (either to alter its behaviour or to fix a bug) could cause problems in any descendent classes. If we use encapsulation rigorously, this should not happen; a class interface should not change just because we have made alterations to the implementation. However, as we'll see shortly, we do not always base a Sub class on just the public interface of its parents; sometimes the sub class can have special access to otherwise hidden class members, and so we could make a change to a base class that did not affect the interface but did affect members that a sub class had direct access to. The result could be that the modified internal behaviour of the base class caused problems with the sub class.

Another problem with inheritance (admittedly, not a very profound problem) is simply that over time we can create inheritance relationships to such a depth (i.e. sub-sub-sub-sub . . . -classes) that we could lose sight of the capabilities of the ultimate ancestor class, and therefore lose control of the code. This is a problem that also exists in structured programming, since we can have a sub that calls a sub that calls, etc. to a level of nesting that makes it difficult to follow all of the possible consequences. In structured programming the cure is to be careful not to create call-structures of arbitrary depth; the onus is on the person writing a sub to be aware of the effects of other subs he or she is calling. In inheritance relationships in object-oriented programming, good use of encapsulation and careful consideration of the level of access a class has to its base class is important, and the onus is on the designer of the Base class to provide this. As a developer of a base class, you have a responsibility to make sure inheritors can only access members it is safe for them to access.

Exercise 7.2

Microsoft Visual Studio .NET provides programmers with sources of information and operational cues to ensure that errors are less likely when using inheritance. Start up VS .NET with a new or existing project and examine the following features.

a) Dynamic Help: display the Dynamic Help window (click on the Dynamic Help tab at the bottom of the Properties window if it is not visible) and then enter a private, public or Dim statement that creates a reference variable for an existing class (e.g. DivideByZeroException). Note that a list of help topics appears in the Dynamic Help window – click on one of the top entries (e.g. the DivideByZeroException members entry) and examine the consequent help page

b) Class overview page – note that this help page for any class displays an ancestry chart for that class (always starting from System.Object) and indicating the class, its ancestors and its descendents (note also the Implements list, indicating interface classes this class implements)

c) Class Members page (always at the top of the class overview) – go to this and examine the format that the list of member properties and methods is shown in. Note that only public and protected (explained later) members are listed, and make yourself familiar with the various icons used (hovering the mouse cursor over an icon will reveal its description)

d) Click on a specific class member to go to its definition page. Note that keywords such as `Overridable`, `MustOverride` (described later), `NotOverridable` and others are used to describe the possibilities for using this member in code inheritance

7.2 Code Inheritance

Code inheritance is invoked when a class uses the keyword `Inherits` at the start of its definition. The `Inherits` keyword must be followed by the name of a class that exists in the scope of the module being coded; either a class defined within the same project or within a project to which a reference has been created. Visual Basic .NET will not compile a class that tries to inherit from another class that is not in scope, and Visual Studio will mark the faulty `Inherits` statement with a blue wavy underline.

7.2.1 Access to the Base Class's members

Once a class is properly inherited from, any of its members (variables, properties, subs or functions) that are marked `Public` or `Protected` can be accessed by the sub class. Members that are marked `Private` are hidden from the sub class. The `Friend` access modifier can also be used to indicate members that can be accessed by *any* code in the same assembly; this is a simple way of defining members that are accessible in the project you are coding but not from any other project.

The various access modifiers are there to allow you complete control over inheritance, and operate as shown in Table 7.1.

We use the various access specifiers to create encapsulation. By careful use of these, we can prevent access to sensitive or dangerous members of a class by other code that uses the class while allowing new classes based on it to control access to only those members we decide they will need access to. As a class designer, it is your responsibility to use the encapsulation keywords to protect your code from unauthorized or erroneous access and yet simultaneously provide access to any class that might benefit from it by inheritance.

Note that the `Protected` and `Friend` keywords operate to allow us to break the strict use of encapsulation. In an ideally encapsulated class, there should be no need for any of its subclasses to access `Private` member data; the entire range of

Table 7.1 Access keywords

Scope Keyword	Meaning	Example of Use
Private	Items marked `Private` are visible only to the class or module they are defined in	Use to hide member variables and internal-use only subs and functions from all other code
Protected	Items marked `Protected` are visible to the class they are defined in, and classes that descend from it (i.e. direct subclasses, and their descendants)	Use to create members that are hidden from code that *uses* the class or its descendants, but visible to the descendants
Friend	Items marked `Friend` are visible to all code within the assembly (i.e. the current project), but hidden from code that contains a reference to it	Use `Friend` access to create members that are freely accessible to any and all code in the current project; this allows, for example, two separate classes defined in a project to access each others' member variables. `Friend` access is the default, so providing no access specifier for a member is equivalent to giving it Friend access
Public	Items marked `Public` can be accessed by any code, within the current project and by any other project that has a reference to it.	Generally, use `Public` declarations only to define the Interface for a class or module. `Public` access puts no restrictions on access from code in other classes, modules or even projects
MyBase	Indicates a call to one of a base class's members. The call is only allowed if appropriate access (using one of the scope keywords above) is allowed (e.g. we cannot use `MyBase` to call a `Private` member function)	The `MyBase` keyword is used to indicate that the attached method call is to a method in the base class, rather than to a method with the same name in the class being implemented. For example, a class can use `MyBase.New()` in its constructor to indicate that it should perform the construction work of a base class object as part of its own construction work

behaviour should be accessible via the `Public` interface. However, back in the real world, there are many situations where it is either much easier or more efficient to allow a sub class to access member data that is otherwise kept hidden.

Listing 7.7 demonstrates the use of various access specifiers.

```
Class Parent
    Public MyInt As Integer      ' Available to all
    Protected MySingle As Single ' Available to subclasses
    Private MyString As String   ' Not available outside
                                 ' Parent
    Friend MyDate As Date        ' Available to code in
                                 ' project

    Public Sub New() ' This sub sets up a new Parent object
        MyInt = 0
        MySingle = 3.14
```

```vbnet
        MyString = "Parent String"
        MyDate = Date
    End Sub

    Property TheString() As String ' Default Friend access
        Get                        ' Therefore available to
            TheString = MyString   ' all code in this
                                   ' project.
        End Get
        Set(ByVal Value As String)
            MyString = Value
        End Set
    End Property

    ' Can only be called by methods in Parent...
    Private Function MyFormattedData() As String
        Return MyInt.ToString & "/" & MySingle.ToString & _
                             "/" & MyString
    End Function

    ' Can be called from sub-classes...
    Protected Sub ChangeString(ByVal NewValue As String)
        MyString = NewValue
    End Sub

    ' Available to all code...
    Public Sub ViewData()
        WriteLine(MyFormattedData)
    End Sub
End Class

Class Child
    Inherits Parent

    Public Sub New() ' This sub sets up a new Child object
        MyBase.New() ' by performing a Parent construction
        MyString = "Child String" ' then changing the
                                  ' String value
    End Sub

    Sub UpdateInt()
        ' Ok since MyInt is Public
        MyInt += 1
    End Sub

    Sub UpdateSingle()
        ' Ok, since this is a subclass and
        ' MySingle is Protected
        MySingle += 1.0
    End Sub

    Sub UpdateString()
        ' Can not access MyString directly (Private), so
        ' need to use the Protected method...
        ChangeString("New String Value")
    End Sub
```

```
      Sub ChangeDate()
          ' MyDate is Friend, so no problem...
          MyDate.AddDays(1)
      End Sub
End Class

' This code is part of the module but not class code . . .
Sub Main()
      Dim P As Parent
      P.MyInt += 1                 ' Ok - public
      P.MyDate.AddDays(1)          ' Ok - Friend
      P.TheString = "Hello Mum"    ' Ok - Property is Friend
      P.ViewData()                 ' Only other thing we can do
                                   ' from here

      Dim C As Child
      C.MyInt += 1                 ' Ok - public
      C.MyDate.AddDays(1)          ' Ok - Friend
      C.TheString = "Hello World"  ' Ok - Property is inherited.
      C.ViewData()                 ' Ok - Public
      ' These are all (default) Friend access from Child...
      C.UpdateInt()
      C.UpdateSingle()
      C.UpdateString()
End Sub
```

Listing 7.7: `Private`, `Protected`, `Friend` and `Public` access in code

Exercise 7.3

It is possible to write an entire Visual Basic application without any consideration of scope or the use of the various access keywords; Dim could be used to declare every variable and subs, functions and properties could be declared without access being specified.

a) How would this affect access to classes and members within the same module?

b) How would it affect access to classes and members in a different module?

c) If the project assembly was Imported to a new project, what, if any, parts of the assembly could be accessed by code in the new project?

d) How do any of the available access restrictions affect the user of a program?

7.2.2 Constructors in Inheritance

If we think of Inheritance as a way, principally, of *extending* a class to add data or behaviour to it, it is easy to see why class constructors have a central role to play. Figure 7.2 shows a class inheriting from its base class diagrammatically.

The new class is created by extending an existing class, which suggests that an object of the new class will somehow 'contain' an object of the existing class.

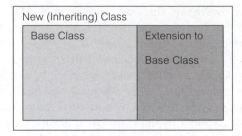

Figure 7.2 Inheritance Extending a Base Class

There is obviously more to the relationship than this, since the interface of the new class includes the interface of the base class automatically by default, something that does not happen if a new class is given a member of an existing class in a composition relationship. However, it is still apparent that to create an object of the new class, the system must first build an object of the base class the new class inherits from.

The role of a constructor is to build a member of a class, and this typically involves packing data values into member variables and possibly creating additional objects that the new object is composed of. When we construct a new member of an inheriting class, much of the construction code has already been implemented in the inherited object; since we cannot remove any members from a class we inherit from, we can always start by building a member of the base class. In the .NET framework, it is a rigid requirement that the constructor of an inheriting class begins with a call to one of the constructors of the class it inherits from. In the example given in Listing 7.7, the constructor for class child was as shown in Listing 7.8.

```
Public Sub New()  ' This sub sets up a new Child object
    MyBase.New()  ' by performing a Parent construction
    MyString = "Child String" ' then changing the String
End Sub
```

Listing 7.8: Constructing an object of a class that inherits from a base class

Every class has a constructor, whether you explicitly define one (or more) or not. In the absence of a coded constructor for a class, the .NET framework will provide a default constructor that takes no parameters and that sets all of the class's member variables up to zero values (i.e. 0, 0.0, "" or `Nothing`). It is therefore always possible (and necessary) to call the base class's constructor.

7.2.3 Overriding

Overriding a member of a class is replacing it with a new definition. Only properties and methods can be overridden, which is sensible since ideally member variables should all be marked `Private` to protect them from being misused. The use of the word *method* to describe a sub or function becomes clearer once we consider the use of overriding, since we can now think of a particular class's method of doing some job. For example, the `BankAccount`'s method of doing a withdrawal was overridden by the `SpecialInvestmentAccount` class, so while both classes have a `Withdraw` function, each had a different method of doing it.

By default, a method in a class can *not* be overridden. This is a sensible approach, since it means that we, as designers of a base class, get to say whether any of its methods can be replaced by alternative code. Since as the designer of a base class we are aware of its implementation details, there is no-one better placed to decide whether a particular method can be overridden or not. If we wish to define a method of a class so that it can be overridden in descendant classes, we use the keyword `Overridable` in its definition (Listing 7.9).

```
Class SomeClass
     Public Overridable Sub SomeMethod()
     'This method can be redefined in a descendant class
     End Sub

     Public Sub SomeOtherMethod()
     'This method can NOT be redefined in a descendant
     'class
     End Sub
End Class
```

Listing 7.9: Making a method overridable

Using the code in Listing 7.9 as a base class, we would find that VB would allow us to override the `SomeMethod()` sub but would prevent us from overriding the `SomeOtherMethod()` sub. Marking a method as overridable is not all that is necessary to allow us to override it in another class. The method's signature, that is the combination of its name and list of parameters, must be the same in the original method and the new method that overrides it. For example, Visual Basic will not allow this (Listing 7.10).

```
Class OtherClass
     Inherits SomeClass
     Public Overrides Sub SomeMethod( _
                          ByVal SomeValue As Integer)
     'This method is not signature-compatible with the one
     'it is overriding, so VB does not allow the override.
     End Sub
End Class
```

Listing 7.10: Overriding a method requires total compatibility (this code does not work)

Once we can override a method, we can provide class-specific ways of doing some job. In our banking example classes, the plain `BankAccount`'s `Withdraw()` method was replaced with a more complex method for a `SpecialInvestmentAccount`. To allow that to happen, we had to mark the plain

`Withdraw()` method as `Overridable`. As a result, each class had the ability to work out for itself how a withdrawal would be made. This is a goal in inheritance; delegate work to classes in such a way that they do the work without us worrying about the details of *how* they do it.

7.2.4 Abstract Classes

As base class designers, we get to be even more specific about the way a class is inherited from than simply indicating which methods can be overridden and which classes or code can access them. We can define a method in a class so that it *must* be overridden in a class that inherits from it. Of course, by doing this, we would also be saying that the class we are defining is not a complete class, since we have deliberately left a hole where the method that must be overridden is.

Why would we do this? One good reason could be that we wanted to create a base class that defined the core behaviour of a family of classes. This would be a class created only for inheritance purposes, and to create it we would also use the `MustInherit` keyword as part of the class definition. For example, let's say we wanted to create a new version of the calculator program developed in the activities at the end of Chapter 4. The new version is to use inheritance to allow a range of different types of calculation on pairs of numbers. Every calculation would involve `Number1` and `Number2`, both of which could be defined as properties or public member variables of *every* calculation class. Every calculation would also have a `Calculate()` method to make it do its job and return a result. However, at this stage, we're more interested in defining what a calculation does than how it works. We can define the core behaviour of a calculation class as shown in Listing 7.11.

```
MustInherit Class Calculation
     Public Number1 As Double
     Public Number2 As Double
     'Here is the function that must be overridden . . .
     Protected MustOverride Function Calculate() As Double
     Public Overridable Sub DisplayResult()
        Console.WriteLine("The result is {0}.", Calculate)
     End Sub
End Class
```

Listing 7.11: A class that must be inherited from

The `Calculation` class shown above cannot be instantiated. We can create a reference variable for the class, such as:

```
Dim C As Calculation
```

but any attempt to actually create an instance will cause Visual Basic to mark the code as an error and refuse to compile it. Note that the method marked `MustOverride` is simply the first line of a method definition and contains no body and no `End Sub`. If we must override the method, there is no point in defining how it works since it will always be overridden. The `Calculate()` method cannot be called by client code since it is protected, but the `DisplayResult()` method will still allow us to show the end result of a calculation.

This class is called an *abstract class* in object-oriented terminology. Having defined it, we have the right to use it as a base class for inheritance (Listing 7.12).

```
Class Add
    Inherits Calculation
    Protected Overrides Function Calculate() As Double
        Return Number1 + Number2
    End Function
End Class

Class Subtract
    Inherits Calculation
    Protected Overrides Function Calculate() As Double
        Return Number1 - Number2
    End Function
End Class

Class Multiply
    Inherits Calculation
    Protected Overrides Function Calculate() As Double
        Return Number1 * Number2
    End Function
End Class
```

Listing 7.12: Three classes that inherit from the abstract `Calculation` class

The three new classes shown in Listing 7.12 benefit from inheriting from their abstract base class since they do not have to individually supply member variables for storing the two numbers to be calculated on or a method for displaying the result of a calculation; these are available through the inheritance. They also have the benefit of all being types of `Calculation` class, and so could be used interchangeably. We could now actually use a reference variable of the `Calculation` class (see Listing 7.13).

```
Dim Calc As Calculation
Calc = New Multiply()
Calc.Number1 = 10
Calc.Number2 = 5
Calc.DisplayResult()
```

Listing 7.13: Creating an instance of a class that inherits `Calculation`

In Listing 7.13, we could have used any of the classes shown in Listing 7.12 as the actual object instance assigned to the `Calc` reference variable. We could obviously create an abstract class that has many more member variables and fully implemented methods or properties, making the inheritance much more worthwhile since we would be inheriting much more ready-built code.

Exercise 7.4

Assume that the code in Listing 7.12 is amended so that the `Multiply` class is given a public function called Product that returns the multiplication result.

a) Do you think this additional method would be accessible in Listing 7.13?

b) How would you amend Listing 7.13 to make the `Product()` method available?

7.2.5 The `MyBase` keyword

Every class except `Object` has a base class. `Object` is the core class developed by Microsoft as the root for all inheritance, a kind of object-oriented version of Adam if you like. Of course, there is no equivalent of Eve in this picture, since a class has only one parent.

The `MyBase` keyword allows access to any `Public`, `Protected` or, in the case of a class within the same assembly, `Friend` method of the parent class. It can only be used *within* class code, since it is access provided to a class, not objects of the class. In many circumstances, the `MyBase` keyword is not necessary since inheritance provides access anyway. However, `MyBase` lets us get around the problem of calling a method in the base class that is also defined in the new class that inherits from it. For example, let's extend the list of classes that inherit from `Calculation` to incorporate a `Divide` class, as shown in Listing 7.14.

```
Class Divide
    Inherits Calculation
    Protected Overrides Function Calculate() As Double
        Return Number1 / Number2
    End Function
    Public Overrides Sub DisplayResult()
        Try
            MyBase.DisplayResult()
        Catch
            Console.WriteLine("Division Error")
        End Try
    End Sub
End Class
```

Listing 7.14: A further `Calculation` class

In the new `Divide` class shown, we have overridden the `DisplayResult()` method to get over the problem of what would happen if `Number2` had the value 0. Normally, this would cause a crash, since there is nothing in the base class to cope with a divide by zero error. However, by placing the code that actually displays the result inside a `Try..Catch..End Try` block, we can change the behaviour by displaying an error if an exception occurs.

Since the base class does the job of displaying the calculation result perfectly well, we call its method (obviously this facility will be even more useful if the base class method contains a lot of lines of code since calling the `MyBase` method will save us from having to repeat all that code. Also, if we decide to change the way the base class does the `DisplayResult()` job, the changes will filter through to the class that inherits the method, which would not happen if we simply did the job again in the new class.

We have elected to use `MyBase.DisplayResult` here because it is generally more efficient. However, you will find one situation where the use of `MyBase` can not be avoided. When a class has only constructors (`Sub New()`) that take parameters, and we inherit from this class to create a new class, Visual Basic will insist that you create at least one constructor for the new class. It will also insist that you use `MyBase.New` as the first statement in the new class's constructor.

This is necessary since we have already told the VB compiler that the base class must be constructed by passing some data to it. When a member of a class that inherits another is created, the first action must be to create a member of the 'inner' class that is inherited, and this must be done according to the rules we have set up for that inner class. This is only necessary when inheriting from a class that does not have a *default constructor*, which is a `Sub New()` that takes no parameters. If this is a default constructor, Visual Basic does not have to be told how to construct a member of the inner class. This is illustrated in Listing 7.15.

```
Class Parent
      Public Sub New(ByVal X As Integer)
           '...
      End Sub
End Class
Class Child
      Inherits Parent
      Public Sub New(ByVal X As Integer)
          'Must call the Base class's constructor...
          MyBase.New(X)
      End Sub
End Class
```

Listing 7.15: A class that inherits from a class with a non-default constructor

7.2.6 Inheritance and Type-Casting

In programming, a *type-cast* is made when we take an object of one type or class and try to assign it to an object variable of a different class. Sometimes it is successful (if I assign the value in an `Integer` variable to a `Double` variable, there is no problem since a `Double` variable can accommodate any value that could be stored in an `Integer`), and sometimes the casting fails (because, for example, the resulting type cannot accommodate all of the information of the original variable – e.g. casting a `Double` as an `Integer`).

With inheritance, there is always the possibility of a type-cast. In the calculation classes, assigning a `Multiply` object to a `Calculation` variable (Listing 7.13) performs a type-cast. The code in Listing 7.13 performs an *implicit type-cast*, so called because we make no mention of the change of type. This cast works because of the inheritance relationship between `Calculation` and `Multiply`. A `Multiply` **Is-A** `Calculation`. Whenever we automatically assign a value of one type to a variable of one of its ancestor classes, we are performing an implicit type-cast.

One problem with implicit type-casts is that it can be difficult to see what is going on. When we write lines of code such as:

```
Dim Calc As Calculation
Calc = New Multiply()
```

we're making use of an inheritance relationship that is defined somewhere else in the code. In the example given with calculation classes, that is not too big a problem. However, consider the situation when a large number of classes with complex inheritance relationships are used in a program. A type-cast is not always obvious, and when this is the case, it is best to do the cast more explicitly: we are letting someone who reads the code know that a) we are aware of the type-cast and it is not simply an error in our code, and b) there is an inheritance relationship between the classes that makes a type-cast possible. Instead of the code fragment above, we can use the `CType()` function to perform a type-cast:

```
Dim C As Calculation
Dim M As New Multiply()
C = CType(M, Calculation)
```

Note that the second parameter in the `CType()` function is a class name. If this is not the name of a class that is compatible, Visual Studio will mark the identifier of the variable we are trying to cast as an error and refuse to compile the code until we have corrected it.

Type-casting works in either direction. We can easily (and implicitly) type-cast a `Multiply` as a `Calculation`. The **Is-A** relationship between these classes makes certain that the cast is always possible. We can also type-cast a `Calculation` as a `Multiply`, but in this case the outcome is not always certain, since the `Calculation` could just as easily be an `Add`, `Subtract` or `Divide` object. In this situation, Visual Studio and the Visual Basic compiler cannot protect us from an invalid cast. It is our job as programmers to be aware of the possibility of casting to an invalid type and to try to prevent it in our code.

Exercise 7.5

The `ArrayList` collection class is defined so that any class of object can be added to an `ArrayList`.

a) Internally, the `ArrayList` class contains an `Array` member. What type is this array?

b) The `Add()` method for `ArrayList` takes a single parameter. What type is this parameter?

c) Assume an `ArrayList` is being used to hold a collection of `BankAccounts`. Write the statements necessary to retrieve a `BankAccount` from an `ArrayList` and assign it to a reference variable of type `BankAccount`.

7.2.7 Shared Members

In Listing 7.3, I show an example of a class inheriting from the `BankAccount` class (`InvestmentAccount`). The code is perfectly acceptable to the Visual Basic compiler as it stands, but there is a potentially damaging inefficiency. The `InterestRate` member variable is an instance variable, which means that every instance of the `InvestmentAccount` class will have its own copy. My bank gives me an interest rate that is the same rate that it gives every other customer with the same type of account, and I'll bet that your bank does the same.

There are two potential problems with the approach used in `InvestmentAccount`. First, each instance of the class contains a member variable that stores the same value; so many instances of the class will contain many copies of the same number, wasting space in all but one account. Secondly, if there is a change in interest rate, it has to be applied to each instance individually, even though only one number has changed. Failing to do this would result in inconsistent interest rates across all of the account objects.

VB .NET has a solution to this in the form of shared members. There are two types of shared members a class can have.

■ *Shared variables* are class member variables defined for the class, rather than individual instances of it. If we declare a variable within a class as shared, then there is a single copy of that variable that is available to every instance of the class and also to the class whether it has an instance or not.

■ *Shared methods* are methods that exist whether there is an instance of the class or not.

The value of shared members is that they can provide facilities that belong to the class itself without need for any instances of the class. We could define the `InvestmentAccount` class as in Listing 7.16.

```
Public Class InvestmentAccount
    Inherits BankAccount

    Public Shared InterestRate As Single
    Public Sub AddInterest()
        Deposit(Balance * InterestRate / 100)
    End Sub
End Class
```

Listing 7.16: A shared member variable

This simple change to the class (adding the keyword `Shared` to the declaration of the `InterestRate` variable) means that now there will be a single copy of the interest rate shared among all of the instances of `InvestmentAccount`, instead of each having its own copy. We can access the shared variable by using the class name:

```
InvestmentAccount.InterestRate = 0.05
```

at which the interest rate member will be set to 5% for every instance of the class.

Shared variables allow us to store values of significance to the whole class and all its members. Shared methods allow us to define behaviour that we can call on whether or not there is an instance of the class. This is useful if you wish to create a library of subs and functions that are thematically related and where there is no need of specific instances. For example, we might define a `Statistics` class to provide us with a range of statistics functions, even though there is no need for any `Statistics` objects (see Listing 7.17).

```
Class Statistics
    Public Shared Function Average( _
                         ByVal list() As Double) As Double
        Dim d As Double, sum As Double
        For Each d In list
            sum += d
        Next
        Return sum / list.GetLength(0)
    End Function

    Public Shared Function Max( _
                       ByVal list() As Double) As Double
        Dim d As Double, mx As Double
        mx = list(list.GetLowerBound(0))
        For Each d In list
            If mx < d Then
                mx = d
            End If
        Next
        Return mx
    End Function

    Public Shared Function Min( _
                        ByVal list() As Double) As Double
        Dim d As Double, mn As Double
        mn = list(list.GetLowerBound(0))
        For Each d In list
            If mn > d Then
                mn = d
            End If
        Next
        Return mn
    End Function
End Class
```

Listing 7.17: A class with shared methods

Here we have a class that contains only shared methods, so there would be no point in creating an instance of the class. We can access all of the methods by simply preceding them with the class name, so, for example, to perform some simple statistics on an array of numbers, we could use the code given in Listing 7.18.

```
Sub Main()
    Dim nums() As Double = {10.0, 12.0, 14.0, 16.0, 18.0}
    Console.WriteLine("Average is {0}", _
                      Statistics.Average(nums))
    Console.WriteLine("Maximum is {0}", _
                      Statistics.Max(nums))
    Console.WriteLine("Minimum is {0}", _
                      Statistics.Min(nums))
End Sub
```

Listing 7.18: Using the shared members

If we had added some instance variables to the Statistics class, the shared methods would not be able to access them. The reason for this is simply that since we can use a shared method without creating a class instance, there would be no way to guarantee that a non-shared member variable existed during the execution of a shared method.

However, we *can* access shared members of a class from any instance of the class. While there is no sensible purpose in creating an instance of the Statistics class from Listing 7.15, it is certain that we would want to create instances of the InvestmentAccount class, and we can access the InterestRate shared member variable from any instance (Listing 7.19).

```
Dim i As New InvestmentAccount()
i.InterestRate = 0.035 '3.5% interest rate
i.Deposit(1000.0)
i.AddInterest()
```

Listing 7.19: Accessing a shared member from a class instance

We have looked at two ways we can make use of shared members in classes. By creating a normal class with some shared member variables and some instance member variables (declared without the keyword Shared), we can arrange it so that information that is the same for all members of the class is stored in a single copy for the whole class. This is good for situations where a value important to a class can vary, but the same value is used for every member; interest rates, maximum and minimum allowable values for variables, the last time any object of the class accessed a database or a count of the number of objects of the class that have been created – these are all good uses for a shared member variable.

Shared methods on the other hand are available so that we can use them without creating a class instance. The most common use for these is in creating libraries of code organized along thematic lines; the statistics library for example. The .NET CLR contains a number of libraries organized in this way; good examples of this are Console, which provides a number of methods for simple screen output and keyboard input and Math which contains a library of standard mathematical functions.

The `Calculation` classes could have been given shared members as the `Number1` and `Number2` member variables.

a)   What restrictions would this have placed on the use of the class?

b)   Can you think of a way that the class could be amended so that it could be used entirely as a shared class (like the `Statistics` class in Listing 7.17)?

7.3   Interface Inheritance

Once you have tried and understood the principles of code inheritance, interface inheritance can at first seem like a poor cousin in comparison. While code inheritance allows you to reuse an existing class and build on it to create new classes, interface inheritance makes you do the work of recreating methods defined in an interface class in any new class that you decide should 'inherit' this interface.

We can already define an interface using code inheritance; the `MustInherit` keyword allows us to define a class that cannot be instantiated. Members of this class marked as `MustOverride` must be fully implemented in any class that descends from it. As discussed earlier, using `MustInherit` and `MustOverride` allows us to create an abstract class, which we cannot create instances of. However, unless *every* method in an abstract class was marked as `MustOverride`, a new class would still inherit the code of any fully implemented methods in the abstract class. An abstract class that contained *only* methods and properties marked `MustInherit` and no member variables would be a bit like an interface class (Listing 7.20).

```
MustInherit Class AbstractVehicle
     Public MustOverride Property NumberOfWheels() _
                                            As Integer
     Public MustOverride Property EngineSize()As Integer
     Public MustOverride Sub PayVehicleTax()
End Class
```

Listing 7.20: A purely abstract class

The abstract class in Listing 7.20 could be used as a base class for a number of concrete `Vehicle` classes: `Bus`, `Car`, `Bicycle`, `AmphibousLandingCraft`, etc. In each, we would need to provide a full implementation of every property and method in the base class.

An interface class is similar to this abstract class but with one important difference. Any class can only inherit the code (even abstract code) of a single class – Visual Basic .NET (and .NET in general) provides what is called *single inheritance*. However, a class can inherit as many *interfaces* as the programmer sees fit. This feature of interfaces makes it possible for us to create classes that can exhibit behaviour compatible with any number of interface definitions. For example, let's say we wanted to create a `Dwelling` class that would represent some form of living accommodation that we could rent out (a house, a cottage, an apartment, a tent, etc.). We might define it as in Listing 7.21.

```
Class Dwelling
    Public NumRooms As Integer
    Public TotalArea As Single
    Private mvarOccupant As String
    Private mvarOccupiedUntil As Date
    Public Sub Occupy(ByVal Occupant As String)
        mvarOccupant = Occupant
        ' Pay the first month's rent...
        mvarOccupiedUntil = DateAdd(DateInterval.Month, _
                                        1, Date.Today)
    End Sub
    Public Sub PayRent()
        ' Pay rent for the next month...
        mvarOccupiedUntil = DateAdd(DateInterval.Month, _
                                        1, Date.Today)
    End Sub
End Class
```

Listing 7.21: A simple `Dwelling` class

Now let's assume that we have decided to branch out in our business by renting out motor homes. We could inherit the `Dwelling` class and add appropriate methods and properties – those of a vehicle, similar to those in the `AbstractVehicle` class. However, that would mean recreating a set of methods that have already been defined as a standard interface in the `AbstractVehicle` class. Recall that one reason we would use an abstract class is to maintain code compatibility among a number of classes – anything that inherits from the `AbstractVehicle` class could be treated in code as if it were an `AbstractVehicle`. It's a pity we can't inherit from both classes; `Dwelling` and `AbstractVehicle`, because our alternative seems to be that we resign ourselves to creating two sets of code for working with vehicle type objects; one for descendants of `AbstractVehicle`, and the other solely for the use of the `MotorHome` class.

Let's redefine `AbstractVehicle` as an interface class (Listing 7.22); after all we're not getting the benefit of inheriting any code from it.

```
Interface IVehicle
    Property NumberOfWheels() As Integer
    Property EngineSize() As Integer
    Sub PayVehicleTax()
End Interface
```

Listing 7.22: An interface class

In keeping with VB .NET convention, we've given the interface class a name starting with the prefix I. All of the standard interfaces defined in .NET follow this convention, making it easy to differentiate between a class and an interface in the pop-up lists of classes provided by the IDE. The first thing to notice about our new interface class is that while it provides the same list of abstract (`MustInherit`) methods and properties as the `AbstractVehicle` class, it takes significantly fewer keywords to do so. Since it is an Interface definition, the `MustInherit` keyword is not necessary since it applies for every property and method. Similarly, there is no need to use the `Public` keyword (in an interface, everything is public) and there would be no need for `Private` or `Protected` either since these would not be allowed in an interface. The interface definition simply states the list of properties and methods that every class that inherits, or *implements*, this interface must provide.

Now we can define the `MotorHome` class (as in Listing 7.23).

```
Class MotorHome
    Inherits Dwelling
    Implements IVehicle 'The class must conform to this
    Public Property EngineSize() As Integer _
                    Implements IVehicle.EngineSize
        Get
            'Code required here
        End Get
        Set(ByVal Value As Integer)
            'Code required here
        End Set
    End Property
    Public Property NumberOfWheels() As Integer _
                    Implements IVehicle.NumberOfWheels
        Get
            'Code required here
        End Get
        Set(ByVal Value As Integer)
            'Code required here
        End Set
    End Property
    Public Sub PayVehicleTax() _
                Implements IVehicle.PayVehicleTax
        'Code required here
    End Sub
End Class
```

Listing 7.23: A class that implements `IVehicle`

The `MotorHome` class inherits from the `Dwelling` class, so we can automatically expect that it will incorporate the members (variables, properties and methods) from that class. It also implements the `IVehicle` interface, and so must provide definitions of the `EngineSize` and `NumberOfWheels` properties and the `PayVehicleTax` method. In the listing, these have not been fully implemented; comments simply show where you would place the code. Note, however, that the Visual Studio IDE was able to provide outlines of all of the `IVehicle` members automatically – the only items of code typed in the methods in Listing 7.23 were the comments.

```
Dim MH As New MotorHome()
MH.
```

Figure 7.3 The Visual Studio IDE providing a list of `MotorHome` members

As a consequence of using an interface, members of this class will now be compatible with both the `Dwelling` class and the `IVehicle` interface. In code that works with objects of the `Dwelling` class, it will behave like a `Dwelling` object because of its inherited behaviour. In code that works with `IVehicle` objects, it will behave like an `IVehicle` because we have provided it with the members every `IVehicle` object provides. VB .NET (and Visual Studio) is aware of both compatibilities. Consequentially, VS can pop up a list of members of `MotorHome` that includes the `IVehicle` interface (see Figure 7.3).

7.3.1 The `IComparable` Interface

As a concrete example of interface inheritance, recall the example in Chapter 6, Listing 6.9, in which an earlier version of the `BankAccount` class was made sortable. The relevant part of the class is reproduced in Listing 7.24.

```
Public Class BankAccount
    Implements IComparable
    ...
    Public Overridable Overloads Function CompareTo( _
                    ByVal obj As Object) As Integer _
                    Implements IComparable.CompareTo
        'Compare the name of this object with the
        'parameter's Name...
        If obj.Name = mvarName Then
            'These are the same...
            Return 0
        ElseIf obj.name < mvarName Then
            'obj is smaller than (comes before) this one..
            Return 1
```

```
        Else
            'This one must be smaller . . .
            Return -1
        End If
    End Function
    ...
End Class
```

Listing 7.24: Using the `IComparable` interface to make a class sort-able

In this case, our `BankAccount` class contains code that makes it compatible with an interface specially defined to allow any objects that implement it to be compared. The `IComparable` interface contains a single method definition (Listing 7.25).

```
Interface ICompareTo
    Function CompareTo(ByVal obj As Object) As Integer
End Interface
```

Listing 7.25: The `IComparable` interface definition

Any class that implements this interface must provide its own definition of the `CompareTo()` method. The reward for this is that an array of objects of the class will be compatible with the `Array.Sort()` method, and can be sorted into an order defined by the programmer's implementation of the method. In the `BankAccount` example, the `Array.Sort()` operation would sort an array of accounts into order of the account name.

The .NET CLR defines a large number of standard interface classes for many different purposes. There is a standard `ICollection` interface, for creating Collection classes that are compatible with the standard collections and interfaces to allow you to define your own encryption classes, connect objects to databases, define new types of events, create formatting classes, interact with web browsers and even extend the features of Visual Studio. Code inheritance allows us to re-use code already written, and therefore put less effort into the development of an application, but interface inheritance is unbeatable as a way of allowing us to hook our own classes into existing code.

Exercise 7.7

a) Interface classes have no need for `Public`, `Private`, `Protected` or `Friend` access scope keywords or the use of `Overridable`, `MustOverride` or `NotOverridable` modifiers for member signatures. Why is this?

b) A number of classes in a complex business application are to be given the ability to collect data from a mail-server. An interface, called `IMailable` is to define two methods – `CheckMail`, a function that will return a Boolean result indicating whether mail is available, and `GetMailData`, a function that will return an `Integer` value. Define this interface.

7.4 Inheriting Data Structures

In the previous chapter on data structures, I mentioned the `CollectionBase` class as being the starting point for creating a *custom collection*; a collection class that would collect only a specific class of object. Microsoft calls this a *strongly typed* collection. The process of creating a strongly typed collection relies on inheritance, and because of this it is very simple to do. The `CollectionBase` class is defined as `MustInherit`, and includes an internal collection based on a protected `ArrayList` member called `List`. It also provides a public `Count` property and a `Clear()` method to remove all items from the collection. The other methods and properties necessary for managing a collection – `Add`, `Remove` and `Item` – must be implemented in the inheriting class.

As an example, assume we wished to create a strongly typed `BankAccountCollection`. The implementation of this is as follows.

1. Create the `BankAccount` class; preferably in a separate class module (we have already met several versions of this). We can add the new Collection class to the same module and therefore guarantee that whenever we use the Collection class, the objects that it collects are already available.

2. Add a new class to the class module called `BankAccountCollection`. This should inherit from `CollectionBase`, which is found in `System.Collections`:

    ```
    Public Class BankAccountCollection
        Inherits System.Collections.CollectionBase
    End Class
    ```

3. Implement a method to add a new `BankAccount` to the collection. A property called `List` is inherited from `CollectionBase`, and it is this collection that we add an account to. Note that because the parameter to the `Add()` method is a `BankAccount`, the collection can only accept `BankAccount` objects (or objects from a class that descends from this):

    ```
    Public Sub Add(ByVal Account As BankAccount)
        List.Add(Account)
    End Sub
    ```

4. Implement a method to remove a `BankAccount` from the collection. The easiest solution is to remove an account by index, since the `List` member provides a `RemoveAt()` method which uses the index of the item to be removed. We need to cater for the possibility that there is no item at the given index, and do so in a way that lets the calling code know whether an item was removed or not. The easiest approach is to implement `Remove` as a function that returns `True` on success:

    ```
    Public Function Remove(ByVal index As Integer) As Boolean
    'Check to see if there is an account at the given index.
        If index > Count - 1 Or index < 0 Then
            'If no account exists, the function failed...
            Return False
        Else
    ```

```
        'We invoke the RemoveAt method of the List object.
        List.RemoveAt(index)
        Return True
    End If
End Function
```

5. Finally, we need to implement the `Item` property. If we make this a `ReadOnly` property, we will prevent a programmer using the collection from trying to assign an item to a given index, thereby by-passing the `Add()` method, which is what makes sure the collection is strongly typed. One problem is that the internal `List` member is *not* strongly typed (it is our collection code that imposes strong typing). When we retrieve an item from this, it will be a member of the `Object` class, but our `Item` property must return a `BankAccount` object. In fact, due to our implementation of `Add()`, there will only ever be `BankAccounts` in `List`. `List` stores these as `Objects`, which is ok since `Object` is an ancestor class of `BankAccount` (and every other class). However, we need to return a `BankAccount` – to do this we *type-cast* the object being returned. The `CType` function takes an object and attempts to cast it as a specified type – in this case a `BankAccount`:

```
Public ReadOnly Property Item(ByVal index As Integer) _
                                    As BankAccount
    Get
        If index > Count - 1 Or index < 0 Then
            Return CType(List.Item(index), BankAccount)
        Else
            Return Nothing
        End If
    End Get
End Property
```

Note that if the item does not exist, we return `Nothing` as a result. We must expect any code that uses the `Item` property to check what has come back from the collection.

As a result of this, we now have a Collection class that is specifically for `BankAccounts`. We can easily use the collection in a program to keep references to any number of `BankAccount` objects (see Listing 7.26).

```
Sub Main()
    Dim A As BankAccount
    Dim Coll As New BankAccountCollection()
    A = New BankAccount(200)
    A.Name = "Fred Smith"
    Coll.Add(A)
    A = New BankAccount(1000000)
    A.Name = "Ritchie Rich"
    Coll.Add(A)
    'etc...
End Sub
```

Listing 7.26: Using the new Collection class

Of course, we can build additional methods and properties into our new Collection class so that it can perform more type-specific behaviour. For example, we could give the `BankAccountCollection` class the ability to return a `BankAccount` by name or account number. Normally we would use account number since someone's name is not necessarily unique, but for the purpose of example, Listing 7.27 shows how we would return an account from the collection given the account name.

```
Public ReadOnly Property NamedAccount( _
            ByVal name As String) As BankAccount
    Get
        Dim a As BankAccount
        For Each a In List
            If a.Name = name Then
              Return a
            End If
        Next
        Return Nothing
    End Get
End Property
```

Listing 7.27: Adding a `NamedAccount` property to the `BankAccountCollection`

Note that again there will be an implicit cast of the returned object as a `BankAccount`.

Exercise 7.8

In the previous chapter (on Data Structures), a new class was created as a collection of students (the `StudentArray` class). List the advantages that the method described above gives to the process of creating type-specific collections?

7.5 Visual Inheritance

This would not be a complete treatment of inheritance if *visual inheritance* was not mentioned. In fact, visual inheritance is a subset of code inheritance, and is only available through tricks performed by Visual Studio. While we can create Visual Basic .NET applications that use inheritance using only a simple text editor like Notepad, we need to use Visual Studio to make use of visual inheritance, since it contains a set of visual development tools, Form Designer windows and the Toolbox, that allow us to manipulate components visually.

Visual inheritance is used to create forms or controls (i.e. visual elements that we can add to and manipulate in a Form Designer window when we are creating a Windows application or component) based on existing forms or controls. It is automatically used whenever we choose to create any Windows application or

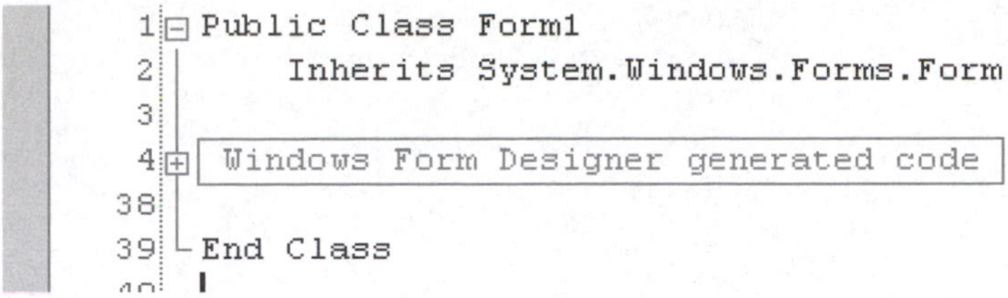

```
 1⊟ Public Class Form1
 2       Inherits System.Windows.Forms.Form
 3
 4⊞ │ Windows Form Designer generated code │
38
39 └ End Class
40   ▌
```

Figure 7.4   The code-view of a new form in a VB Windows application

component, since every form that we create is based on a blank form. When we have a form in a VB project, it inherits from the `System.Windows.Forms.Form` class, which is a standard Windows form with no controls on it. The inheritance is done in code, as we can see from the code that is automatically generated as the definition of a new form (Figure 7.4).

Just as we can create our own base classes to inherit from in code, we can also create our own form designs that can be used as a basis for inheritance. This would allow us to, for example, place a standard company logo on every form in an application, or use a standardized configuration of controls and associated code in every form. The same advantages that inheritance provides to code, reduced effort to create, update and maintain applications software, are also available through visual inheritance to simplify our work in user-interface development. We'll go on to look at visual inheritance and its uses in Chapter 8 on WinForms applications.

7.6   Polymorphism

The term polymorphism is derived from the Greek, and is usually taken to mean 'many forms'. For example, in chemistry, carbon exhibits polymorphism because it can exist in three different forms: graphite, diamond and Buckminster-Fullerenes. In object-oriented programming, polymorphism is used whenever we send a message to an object reference without knowing exactly what type of object it is. For example, in the `Calculation` classes, we could assign either a `Multiply`, `Divide`, `Add` or `Subtract` object to a `Calculation` variable. When we call on the `Calculate` method (or, to put it another way, send the `Calculate` message) of that object, we need not know what actual class of object is being called on to do the calculation. Listing 7.28 illustrates this.

```
Sub Main()
    Dim C As Calculation
    Dim i As Integer
    i = CInt(Int((4 * Rnd()) + 1))
    Select Case i
        Case 1
            C = New Add()
```

```
            Case 2
                C = New Subtract()
            Case 3
                C = New Multiply()
            Case 4
                C = New Divide()
        End Select
        C.Number1 = 10
        C.Number2 = 5
        C.DisplayResult()
    End Sub
```

Listing 7.28: Being unaware of the class in use

In Listing 7.28, the statement `i = CInt(Int((4 * Rnd()) + 1))` generates a random integer number in the range 1 to 4 (look up Microsoft's example in the Help page for the `Rnd()` function). Since we are using a random number to determine what class of calculate object is instantiated, we have no way of knowing what type of object will do the calculation. However, since all of the `Calculation` classes conform to the same interface, Visual Basic allows us to do this.

The scenario given above is not a very realistic situation, and apart from games programming, you would be unlikely to encounter the need for such code. However, as programmers, we often need to work with objects where their type is uncertain. We may need to process a `Deposit` into a `BankAccount`, without knowing the precise type of account (`Deposit`, `Investment`, `SpecialInvestment`, etc.), or we might wish to change the font of every control on a Windows form, no matter what type of control it is.

Polymorphism is the object-oriented way of allowing us to deal with these situations and many others. The only requirement of any object for it to receive a message is that it conforms to a given set of interface methods. As we've seen in this chapter, we have two ways of making that happen: we can either use code inheritance to provide a new class with an interface that has already been fully coded, or we can use interface inheritance, and implement a required interface. In either case, the result is to allow us to create classes that are type-compatible. This in turn allows us to substitute one class for another in a section of code without having to change the code at all.

If you think back to the strongly typed collection class example used earlier, this is an example in which we deliberately limited the range of classes whose objects could be added to an instance of the collection. All of the built-in collections in .NET are widely polymorphic, since they allow us to add objects of any class to them. That can have its advantages, if we need to be able to deal with objects of any type, but that would be an unusual requirement. Instead, we typically wish to create and use a small range of types of object (such as different styles of bank account, or different types of calculation) and use them as flexibly as possible. By creating a strongly typed collection, we are enabling polymorphism by stipulating that any objects added to it must conform to a minimum interface (every type of `BankAccount` provides `Deposit()` and `Withdraw()` methods, and `Name` and `Balance` properties). That allows us to do things like iterating through an entire collection of items of different (but related) classes (Listing 7.29).

```
For Each acc In accountList
    Console.WriteLine("Account: {0} Balance: {1}", _
                                acc.Name, acc.Balance)
Next
```

Listing 7.29: Iterating through a collection

7.6.1 Programming with Inheritance

In later chapters we will make use of inheritance, both code and interface, to allow us to reuse our own code and Microsoft's, and to create polymorphic families of classes that will allow us to write generalized code wherever possible. Whether you inherit from your own classes or those already provided in the .NET common type system, you will find that much of the power of object-oriented programming comes not from what you do, but from what you inherited from.

Review Questions

1. How does inheritance differ from simply adding a reference variable for an existing class as a member in a new class definition?

2. Explain how extension differs from specialization as a way of creating a new class with inheritance.

3. Which does the `MyBase` keyword access in an inherited class – the immediate ancestor (parent class) or the ultimate ancestor (i.e. the first class in the lineage)?

4. A class with a number of methods is given a single `MustOverride()` method. Which of the following is true?

    a. It is possible to create an instance of this class and access all of its methods.

    b. It is possible to create an instance of the class but you must avoid calling the methods marked `MustOverride`.

    c. It is not possible to create instances of this class.

5. Before you can inherit from a class to create a new class, the existing class must have had a `Sub New()` constructor defined. True or False?

6. Some programming languages (e.g. C++) provide for multiple inheritance, which allows a new class to inherit from two or more existing classes. Visual Basic .NET does not support this. What other facility does VB .NET provide to allow you to create classes based on more than one class specification?

7. State the rules for overriding a method in an existing class. How does overriding a method differ from overloading a method?

8. A class, `DataFormatter`, is used as the base class for two other classes, `StringFormatter` and `NumberFormatter`. Which of the following are true?

   a. A `DataFormatter` object can be cast as a `StringFormatter` object.

   b. A `DataFormatter` object can be cast as a `NumberFormatter` object.

   c. A `StringFormatter` object can be cast as a `DataFormatter` object.

   d. A `NumberFormatter` object can be cast as a `DataFormatter` object.

   e. A `NumberFormatter` object can be cast as a `StringFormatter` object.

9. Shared methods cannot be accessed from an instance of a class. True or False?

10. Shared methods are able to access shared variables in a class. True or False?

11. Shared methods are able to access instance variables in the class. True or False?

12. Polymorphism is a facility that allows us to treat an object of a class as a member of a class that inherits from it. True or False?

Practical Activities

In these activities, we will develop a range of classes for calculating sizes and areas for simple geometric shapes. While of little practical use (the scenario you will read shortly is a bit unlikely), the activities will give you a chance to use inheritance in a fairly obvious way and, hopefully, improve your understanding of it.

The flooring calculator

A company prides itself on being able to provide flooring for any shape of building with a minimum of wastage. It is important that the company can calculate the materials cost, based on the area of flooring material (times the cost per square metre of floor) and the perimeter length of the floor (times the cost per linear metre of edging material), for any shape of floor very quickly in response to a telephone enquiry, and so a calculator is necessary to do the cost estimation. It is likely that new shape types will be added to the calculator as these become necessary.

From the above scenario, we can assume that the calculations necessary will be the area of any shape and the distance around (perimeter) any shape. The cost of any shape of floor can be calculated as:

area of floor × cost per square metre of flooring +
perimeter of floor × cost per metre of edging

For example, if flooring costs £12.00 per square metre, edging costs £2.00 per metre and a square floor of 5 m length is to be covered, the total cost will be:

Area × 12.00 + perimeter × 2.00 =
25 × 12.00 + 20 × 2.00 =
£300.00 + £40.00 = £340.00

Activity 1: The abstract class

For any floor, we will need an area calculation, a perimeter calculation and the per-unit cost of the two materials. As we are not yet aware of the types of shape we may need to calculate for, we can create an abstract class that will define the basic calculations (Listing A7.1).

```
MustInherit Class Shape
      Private mvarFlooringCost As Decimal
      Private mvarEdgingCost As Decimal
      Public Sub New(ByVal flooringCost As Decimal, _
                     ByVal edgeingCost As Decimal)
          mvarFlooringCost = flooringCost
          mvarEdgingCost = edgeingCost
      End Sub
      Public MustOverride Function Area() As Double
      Public MustOverride Function Perimeter() As Double
      Public Function TotalCost() As Decimal
          Return Area() * mvarFlooringCost + _
                 Perimeter() * mvarEdgingCost
      End Function
End Class
```

Listing A7.1: The abstract Shape class

The class in Listing A7.1 has been defined as `MustInherit`, meaning we cannot create an instance of it. The two methods `Area()` and `Perimeter()` are the reason why we need a `MustInherit` specification. We cannot code these methods until we decide on a specific shape to be implemented. The constructor is defined to accept the per-unit costs of the two materials and pass these into the appropriate member variables.

Note that although the `Area()` and `Perimeter()` methods are not defined, we are still able to use them in further calculations (in the `TotalCost()` method). This makes the abstract class more useful than an equivalent interface definition, since no calculation and no instance variables could have been defined for an interface.

Activity 2: Creating a simple test shape

The next stage in developing an implementation for this problem is to define a concrete class based on the abstract one: i.e. to create a class that inherits from the `Shape` class that we can create instances of. The obvious starting point is a `Square` class, since the arithmetic will be simple and easy to verify (see Listing A7.2).

```
Class Square
    Inherits Shape
    Private mvarSize As Double
    Public Sub New(ByVal flooringCost As Decimal, _
                   ByVal edgeingCost As Decimal, _
                   ByVal Size As Double)
        MyBase.New(flooringCost, edgeingCost)
        mvarSize = Size
    End Sub
    Public Overrides Function Area() As Double
        Return mvarSize * mvarSize
    End Function
    Public Overrides Function Perimeter() As Double
        Return 4 * mvarSize
    End Function
End Class
```

Listing A7.2: The `Square` sub-class

We can now see the immediate benefit of the `Shape` class – we have no need to calculate the `TotalCost` of a square floor in the `Square` class because this behaviour
is inherited from `Shape`. We can test this class with the calculation done earlier to
see if the answer agrees with the manually calculated answer (Listing A7.3). This
step will give us the confidence to carry on developing new `Shape` classes, knowing
that the base class does its job adequately:

```
Sub Main()
    Dim S As Square
    S = New Square(12, 2, 5)  '£12 per sq.m, £2 per m
                              'and 5 sq.metres
    Console.WriteLine( _
        "Total cost of flooring materials is: £{0}", _
        S.TotalCost())
End Sub
```

Listing A7.3: Testing the `Square` class (and the `Shape` class it is based on)

In Listing A7.3, the numbers assigned are the same as those used for our earlier
manual calculation, so if all is well, we can expect a result of £340.00. Figure A7.1
confirms this.

Now that the general framework checks out, we can go on to create several additional shape classes and demonstrate their operation.

Figure A7.1 Confirmation that our classes are calculating correctly

Activity 3: Adding to the shape library

Exercise A7.1

a) The next most obvious shape class to develop would be a `Rectangle` class, since most rooms will be this shape. A rectangle will require member variables for `Length` and `Width`. You would calculate the `Area()` of a rectangle as length × width and its perimeter as 2 × (length + width). Create and test the rectangle shape.

b) A circle shape (for flooring lighthouses and new age properties) would be useful. A `Circle` class will need a `Radius` member variable to store its size. Area can be calculated as pi × radius × radius, and perimeter (circumference) as 2 × pi × radius. Pi is 3.1415927.

Activity 4: Dealing with complex shapes

Once we have dealt with simple shapes, we can consider extending the system to cope with almost any shape by considering a shape as the sum of several smaller shapes. For example, assume we were given the task of calculating flooring costs for the room shape shown in Figure A7.2.

This shape, although initially appearing complex, is simply the sum of several simple shapes, as Figure A7.3 shows.

By calculating for a single rectangle of 28 m × 20 m, two smaller rectangles of 24 m × 2 m and a circle of 10 m radius, we would be calculating for the overall composite shape. Note there will be a discrepancy due to the additional edging required for the four simpler shapes (four lengths of 24 m, since two lengths are required for each side of the junction between the large rectangle and each of the smaller rectangles), but this will be small compared to the overall cost and the reduction in overall cost easy to calculate manually.

We can extend our library of shapes by adding another shape class, `ComplexShape`, that will allow us to do the cost calculations for shapes such as that shown above. An interesting feature of this shape class is that it will still be a sub-class of the existing `Shape` base class; we will just need to add a new method to add

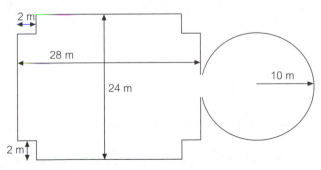

Figure A7.2 A complex shape to calculate

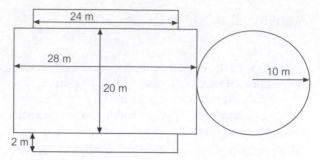

Figure A7.3 The complex shape as the sum of simple shape

individual shapes to a collection of component shapes. The `CompositeShape` class is shown in Listing A7.4.

```
Class CompositeShape
      Inherits Shape
      Private mvarComponentShapes As ArrayList
      Public Sub New(ByVal flooringCost As Decimal, _
                  ByVal edgeingCost As Decimal)
          MyBase.New(flooringCost, edgeingCost)
          mvarComponentShapes = New ArrayList()
      End Sub
      Public Sub AddShape(ByVal S As Shape)
          mvarComponentShapes.Add(S)
      End Sub
      Public Overrides Function Area() As Double
          Dim A As Double = 0
          Dim S As Shape
          For Each S In mvarComponentShapes
              A += S.Area()
          Next
          Return A
      End Function
      Public Overrides Function Perimeter() As Double
          Dim P As Double = 0
          Dim S As Shape
          For Each S In mvarComponentShapes
              P += S.Perimeter()
          Next
          Return P
      End Function
End Class
```

Listing A7.4: The `CompositeShape` class

The code in the `CompositeShape` class is remarkably similar to any of the individual shape classes. It has its own member variable – this time an `ArrayList` to hold the collection of component shapes, and initializes this in the constructor (this time by calling the `ArrayList` constructor).

Among its few differences, it must have one additional method (`AddShape()`) that allows us to add a new shape to the collection, and these component shapes must be incorporated into the overall calculation, which is easily done with a simple `For..Each` loop.

We can test this class for the compound shape in Figure A7.3 (if you have provided the `Rectangle` and `Circle` classes, since these are also involved in the calculation) – Listing A7.5.

```
Sub Main()
    Dim S As Shape, C As CompositeShape
    C = New CompositeShape(12, 2) 'The composite shape
    S = New Rectangle(12, 2, 28, 20) 'The big rectangle
    C.AddShape(S)
    S = New Rectangle(12, 2, 24, 2) 'One of the smaller
                                    'rectangles
    C.AddShape(S)
    S = New Rectangle(12, 2, 24, 2) 'The other smaller
                                    'rectangle
    C.AddShape(S)
    S = New Circle(12, 2, 10) 'The circle
    C.AddShape(S)
    'Now the composite should work out the overall cost
    'for us...
    Console.WriteLine( _
            "Total cost of flooring materials is:
            £{0}", _
            C.TotalCost())
End Sub
```

Listing A7.5: Calculating the costs for a composite shape

You may notice one small anomaly with the `CompositeShape` class, which is that while each of the component shapes has a flooring and edging cost, the `CompositeShape` class also has these. Obviously its per-unit cost values will go ignored in the calculation. We can carry on adding shape classes to our library for as many shapes as we can think of, and deal with more and more complex shapes.

Features worth remembering

■ Inheritance is very useful provided a small amount of ground-work is done. Before considering implementing an inheritance solution, you should identify the common features of the objects you wish to relate and try to factor out a set of core features (such as the per-unit cost variables and `TotalCost` method of the `Shape` class). If these cannot be identified as truly common, the use of inheritance is likely to lead to a bad solution.

■ Consider the use of constructors carefully. Again, core member variables can be set up in the base class to reduce effort in the inheriting classes.

■ Test early and often when you are working on an inheritance solution. Errors in the base class may be difficult to find by the time you have several other classes based on it implemented.

■ Not every complex problem demands a solution based on inheritance. In many cases a simpler solution based on composition, aggregation or simple collaboration between classes will be easier to build and de-bug.

Suggested Additional Activities

1. The activity at the end of the previous chapter was to create a card game. In those activities, a specific game, 21, was created. However, you should now be able to identify the common features between that game and other card games (the `Card` and `CardDeck` classes are more or less complete in their own right and will do fine without any additional work). Try to create a base class that contains all of the features for a hand of any game. The class is likely to contain a collection of cards, a method for evaluating a hand, methods for adding (and possibly removing) cards and a method that will allow a hand to be compared to another to determine if it beats it. (I doubt that this will be a trivial exercise, but it certainly has potential for learning more about using inheritance.)

2. One strong feature that inheritance provides is the facility to deal with a range of different classes as if they belonged to a single class (their base class). This facility allows us to create strongly typed collections of objects even though the objects belong to different classes – simply find a few common features and build a base class from there. Consider the following list as possible contenders for an inheritance tree (and possibly the killer application that will make your fortune).

    a. A Personal Information Manager (PIM) program – typically, a PIM incorporates a diary of appointments, a to-do list, a meeting scheduler, email items (easily possible from VB .NET) and perhaps even an expenses manager.

    b. A program to catalogue a collection of media – CDs, vinyl records, cassettes, video cassettes, DVDs, computer games, etc. Admittedly, you will probably need to spend some time in Chapters 11 and 12 (on files and databases) before you do too much work on this program, but the basic class structure could be mapped out now.

    c. Similar to suggestion b, a suitable program for cataloguing a collection of computer media, such as digital photographs and scanned images, MP3 and other audio files and even digital video files can be created using a base class that factors out the common features of these media types and sub classes to deal with the essential differences.

Solutions to Exercises

Exercise 7.1

The `BankAccount` class does not have an `InterestRate` member or an `AddInterest()` method, so trying to access these would be an error. In Visual Studio, pressing '.' (the dot operator) after the name of a member variable pops up a list of the public members of the class the member variable is declared as, and so these members would never appear in the list. If you were to persist by fully typing the name of a member that was not in the class, Visual Studio will by default mark this as an error in your code with a wavy underline.

Exercise 7.2

These are activity type exercises so there is no set solution. However . . .

a) e.g. with the Dynamic Help pane in view, type `Public ex As DivideByZeroException` at a suitable point in a code window and follow the Members link in the dynamic help links to find out more about the `DivideByZeroException` class. This gives us a quick way to determine the members defined by a class.

b) Once we have access to help on the class either by following dynamic help or by placing the cursor on a class name and pressing **F1**, we can get to the Class Overview page. The top of this page shows the ancestry of the class (e.g. the `DivideByZeroException` class can be seen to inherit from `System.Object`→`System.Exception`→`System.SystemException`→ `System.ArithmeticException`). Click on any of these classes to get to their Help page.

c) Go to the Class Members page to see a list of interface members, organized as separate lists of properties, methods and events.

d) Go to the page for a class member (by following a link from the Class Members page, or placing the cursor on a call in a Code page and pressing **F1**) to see comments on its use and parameters and other info.

Exercise 7.3

a) Using Dim outside a property or method definition will give a member variable `Friend` scope, which means that the member will be accessible anywhere within the project, including the module the declaration is made in . . .

b) . . . and any other module within the project.

c) `Friend` scope limits access to code within a specific assembly (Project), therefore `Friend` declarations in code in an imported assembly would be invisible in the project they were imported into.

d) Not at all. Users of a program have no access to variables, properties or methods, which are for use by programmers only.

Exercise 7.4

a) It would not, since it is a method of the `Multiply` class, and not a method of the `Calculation` class that `Calc` is declared as.

b) If the first line of Listing 7.13 was changed to `Dim Calc As Multiply`, the interface members for the `Multiply` class would be available. Listing 7.13 as it is depends on the fact that `Multiply` inherits from `Calculation`, and so all of the interface elements available in `Calculation` can be executed for a `Multiply` object. In this case, if we want to access an interface element that is specifically a member of `Multiply`, it needs to be done through a `Multiply` interface, which is part of a `Multiply` reference variable.

Exercise 7.5

a) Since we can add *anything* to an `ArrayList`, the member array must be an array of reference variables to class `System.Object`, since every type and class in .NET inherits directly or indirectly from this.

b) Again, `System.Object`, although it is declared as `ByVal Value As Object`.

c) To retrieve a `BankAccount` from an `ArrayList` of `BankAccounts`:

```
Dim B As BankAccount
B = MyArrayList.Item(0) ' Retrieves first item
```

Note, however, that this operation performs an implicit cast, equivalent to:

```
Dim O As Object, B As BankAccount
O = MyArrayList.Item(0)
B = CType(O, BankAccount)
```

Exercise 7.6

a) Since the only member variables of the class would now be shared member variables, we would not be able to create any independent members of the class that would have their own values. Every instance of the class (no matter how many) would have to work with the same pair of values.

b) By making both variables (`Number1` and `Number2`) and *all* of the methods into shared members, the `Calculate` class could become a wholly shared class. However, since we would not be able to add inherited features to work in the same way, we would have to provide instead a set of function methods – `Add`, `Subtract`, `Multiply` and `Divide` so that the class instance provided all of the functionality.

Exercise 7.7

a) The point of an interface class is to define interface (i.e. `Public`) methods, so a `Private` or `Protected Interface` method would be an oxymoron (like a true lie). Also, interfaces are specifically defined so that every class that implements them must be re-coded, so using `Overridable`, `MustOverride` and `NonOverridable` keywords, which are defined to control code inheritance, would make no sense.

b) The `IMailable` interface:

```
Interface IMailable
    Function CheckMail() As Boolean
    Function GetMailData() As Integer
End Interface
```

Exercise 7.8

1. The new class is created using much less code using inheritance.

2. The class will have a standard interface that users of the base class or any of the existing Collection classes will be familiar with.

3. There is less likelihood of an error in the implementation.

4. Changes to the `CollectionBase` class would automatically propagate forward to the new class.

Exercise A7.1

a)

```
Class Rectangle
    Inherits Shape
    Private mvarWidth As Double
    Private mvarHeight As Double
    Public Sub New(ByVal flooringCost As Decimal, _
                   ByVal edgeingCost As Decimal, _
                   ByVal theWidth As Double, _
                   ByVal theHeight As Double)
        MyBase.New(flooringCost, edgeingCost)
        mvarWidth = theWidth
        mvarHeight = theHeight
    End Sub
    Public Overrides Function Area() As Double
        Return mvarWidth * mvarHeight
    End Function
    Public Overrides Function Perimeter() As Double
        Return 2 * (mvarWidth + mvarHeight)
    End Function
End Class
```

b)

```
Class Circle
    Inherits Shape
    Private mvarRadius As Double
    Private Const Pi = 3.1415927
    Public Sub New(ByVal flooringCost As Decimal, _
                   ByVal edgeingCost As Decimal, _
                   ByVal theRadius As Double)
        MyBase.New(flooringCost, edgeingCost)
        mvarRadius = theRadius
    End Sub
```

```
        Public Overrides Function Area() As Double
            Return PI * mvarRadius * mvarRadius
        End Function
        Public Overrides Function Perimeter() As Double
            Return 2 * PI * mvarRadius
        End Function
    End Class
```

Answers to Review Questions

1. How does inheritance differ from simply adding a reference variable for an existing class as a member in a new class definition? **When a class is inherited, public members of the inheriting class automatically become public members of the inherited class. If a new class contains a reference variable to a member of an existing class, an object of the existing class must still be instantiated, and since its public members can only be accessed via the new class's interface, interface members must be created in the new class to delegate to the contained object.**

2. Explain how extension differs from specialization as ways of creating a new class with inheritance. **Extension of an inherited class in a new class involves adding new public members that did not exist in the inherited class to the new class. Specialization involves re-defining selected methods from the inherited class for the new class.**

3. Which does the `MyBase` keyword access in an inherited class – the immediate ancestor (Parent class) or the ultimate ancestor (i.e. the first class in the lineage)? **The `MyBase` keyword is used to access members of the parent (immediate ancestor) class.**

4. A class with a number of methods is given a single `MustOverride` method. Which of the following is true?

    a. It is possible to create an instance of this class and access all of its methods. **False**

    b. It is possible to create an instance of the class but you must avoid calling the methods marked `MustOverride`. **False**

    c. It is not possible to create instances of this class. **True – a class with a member marked as `MustOverride` is a purely abstract class.**

5. Before you can inherit from a class to create a new class, the existing class must have had a `Sub New()` constructor defined. True or False? **False – If `Sub New()` is not defined explicitly, a default constructor (one that sets all member variables to null or zero values) is automatically supplied.**

6. Some programming languages (e.g. C++) provide for multiple inheritance, which allows a new class to inherit from two or more existing classes. Visual Basic .NET does not support this. What

other facility does VB .NET provide to allow you to create classes based on more than one class specification? **While a VB class can only inherit from a single base class, it can implement any number of interfaces.**

7. State the rules for overriding a method in an existing class. How does overriding a method differ from overloading a method? **The new class must inherit from the existing class, and the method that is to be overridden must have been marked as `Overridable` or `MustOverride`. Overloading a method involves providing an alternative version of an existing method with a different signature (parameter list).**

8. A class, `DataFormatter`, is used as the base class for two other classes, `StringFormatter` and `NumberFormatter`. Which of the following are true?

   a. A `DataFormatter` object can be cast as a `StringFormatter` object **False**

   b. A `DataFormatter` object can be cast as a `NumberFormatter` object **False**

   c. A `StringFormatter` object can be cast as a `DataFormatter` object **True**

   d. A `NumberFormatter` object can be cast as a `DataFormatter` object **True**

   e. A `NumberFormatter` object can be cast as a `StringFormatter` object **False**

9. Shared methods cannot be accessed from an instance of a class. True or False? **False**

10. Shared methods are able to access shared variables in a class. True or False? **True**

11. Shared methods are able to access instance variables in the class. True or False? **False**

12. Polymorphism is a facility that allows us to treat an object of a class as a member of a class that inherits from it. True or False? **False – it allows us to treat an object of a class as if it was a member of the class it inherited from.**

CHAPTER

8

WinForms Applications

In this chapter you will learn:

- the way a Windows application is organized;
- how Form Designer windows and associated Code windows interact;
- how to create user interfaces for Windows applications;
- how to build dialog boxes for specific types of user-interactions;
- the different types of control available for Windows applications;
- the event-driven nature of Windows applications;
- what delegate procedures are, and how they are used.

8.1 Application Structure

Console applications like those we've been working on so far have a simple structure that is ideal for when you're learning to program in a new language. The basic console structure: 'get Input, Process it, produce Output', is trivial and easy to imagine as a way of dealing with information. Windows application programs can be more difficult to develop, since they involve a complex system of interaction and control, the possibility of a large number of separate modes of input which can interact in subtle and even unexpected ways, and a structure that is almost like several separate programs simultaneously let loose on a single set of data. By concentrating on the nature of programming and the structure and organization of objects within a piece of software up till now, you should find it easier to work with applications structures of the level of complexity of a Windows program. Graphical user interface software like this can, at its best, create a working environment for the user that is efficient and responsive in ways console-based software can rarely do.

The first thing to realize about a Windows program is that you, the programmer, are no longer in the driving seat. When you choose to develop a Windows-based application, you are effectively saying that the user of the program is in control. A console program is like a script in which you write statements to say what will happen and what order it will happen in. If the user is expected to enter, say, a name, an address and a telephone number for processing, you write statements to collect the data in this order, or whatever order you dictate, and only after collecting the information will you do whatever processing is necessary. In most Windows programs, the user would decide what order to enter the information into the program, and would then decide whether to process the information or cancel the operation.

For a user, this type of interaction is liberating, and provides a more natural and therefore easier to learn way of working with software; data entry can be made more like filling in a form, and complex operations such as manipulating graphics or navigating through a large database can be made more intuitive. For a programmer it makes it more difficult to maintain control of the way a program works, and more likely that the user will leave out important pieces of data or try to perform operations in an order that will not produce the desired result. To write successful Windows programs, a programmer must learn to impose control on the user in more subtle ways than simply dictating the order of input.

8.1.1 An Example User-Interface Task

As an example, consider the way you would elicit input data from a user in a program for calculating income tax. A person's tax liability is calculated from several pieces of information: their annual income, standard tax allowances based on their family circumstances (marital status, number of dependent children), and extra tax allowances based on various types of expenditure that can be offset against tax (professional membership fees, work related purchases, etc.). The actual calculation is based on rates and amounts that vary from country to country. However, in general, a number of values must be used to make the calculation possible. Let's assume the following figures as a basis for tax calculation:

Rates, Limits and Allowances for Income Tax Calculations

(These are not realistic but are for example purposes only)

Single person's allowance: £5000 per annum

Married couple's allowance: £8000 per annum

Child's allowance: £2000 per annum per dependent child

Basic tax rate: 20%

Basic tax limit: £20 000 of taxable income

Higher tax rate: 40% (on all taxable income above £20 000)

In a console style program, we might use a class design for objects that can do the basic calculations, and we would write methods to make sure that all of the necessary data was entered in strict order before using it in the calculation. We would add another method to the tax calculation object for displaying the result, as shown in Listing 8.1.

```vbnet
Module TaxCalc
    Class TaxCalculator
        'Start by declaring the various allowances and rates...
        Public Shared SingleAllowance As Decimal = 5000
        Public Shared MarriedAllowance As Decimal = 8000
        Public Shared ChildAllowance As Decimal = 2000
        Public Shared BasicRate As Single = 0.2
        Public Shared BasicLimit As Decimal = 20000
        Public Shared HigherRate As Single = 0.4
        'Now declare the actual values for a calculation...
        Public GrossIncome As Decimal
        Public Married As Boolean
        Public DependentChildren As Integer = 0
        Public ExtraAllowances As Decimal = 0
        'Methods for the tax calculation...
        Public Function TotalAllowances() As Decimal
            Dim totAllow As Decimal
            If Married Then
                totAllow = MarriedAllowance
            Else
                totAllow = SingleAllowance
            End If
            totAllow += DependentChildren * ChildAllowance
            totAllow += ExtraAllowances
            Return totAllow
        End Function
        Public Function TaxableIncome() As Decimal
            TaxableIncome = GrossIncome - TotalAllowances()
        End Function
        Public Function Tax() As Decimal
            If TaxableIncome() > BasicLimit Then
                Return (TaxableIncome() - _
                        BasicLimit) * HigherRate + _
                        BasicLimit * BasicRate
            Else
                Return TaxableIncome() * BasicRate
            End If
        End Function
        Public Function IncomeAfterTax() As Decimal
            Return GrossIncome - Tax()
        End Function
        'A method to collect the information...
        Public Sub GetData()
            Dim response As String
            Console.Write("Enter gross income:")
            GrossIncome = Console.ReadLine()
            Console.Write("Are you married (Y/N)?")
            response = Console.ReadLine()
            Married = (response = "Y") Or (response = "y")
            Console.Write( _
                "How many dependent children do you have?")
            DependentChildren = Console.ReadLine()
```

```
            Console.Write( _
                "Enter amount of additional allowances:")
            ExtraAllowances = Console.ReadLine()
        End Sub
        'A method to display results . . .
        Public Sub ShowTaxCalc()
            Console.WriteLine("Tax calculation results:")
            Console.WriteLine( _
            "Taxable Income(annual) = {0}", TaxableIncome)
            Console.WriteLine("Total tax (annual) = {0}", _
                            Tax)
            Console.WriteLine(" _
            Annual income after tax = {0}", IncomeAfterTax)
            Console.WriteLine(" _
            Monthly income after tax = {0}",
            Format(IncomeAfterTax() / 12, "£0.00"))
        End Sub
    End Class

    Sub Main()
        Dim TC As New TaxCalculator()
        TC.GetData()
        TC.ShowTaxCalc()
    End Sub
End Module
```

Listing 8.1: A console program to do tax calculations

Listing 8.1 shows a module of code that contains a new class (`TaxCalculator`) and a `Sub Main()` to create an instance of the class and put it to work. I've kept the class code simple by using `Public` member variables rather than properties – not ideal programming but adequate for this example. While the console-based program shown would be perfectly simple to use (see Figure 8.1a), most computer users now expect a more forgiving user interface, such as the Windows form shown in Figure 8.1b.

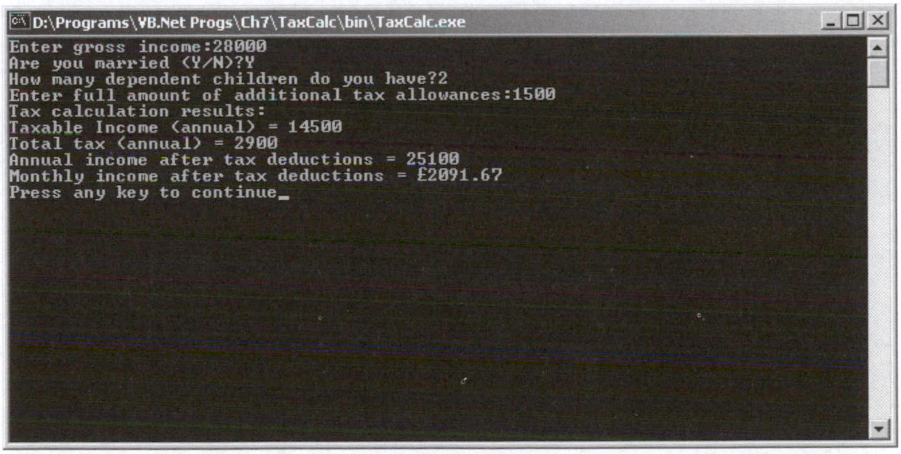

Figure 8.1a The console-based Tax Calculator in use

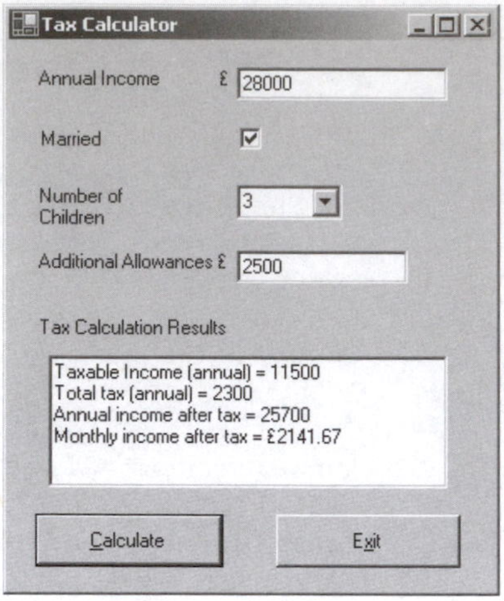

Figure 8.1b A Windows Tax Calculator in use

The console-based version is easy to program, but its operation is at best 'clunky'. However, it does have the benefit of asking for all of the necessary information before performing a calculation. The Windows version, on the other hand, allows the user such latitude in its operation that it is possible to cause the program to fail simply by pressing the Calculate button before all of the necessary information has been entered.

The code for the Windows version of the application is very different, even though an object of the same class is used to collect the various bits of information and do the calculation. It is shown in Listing 8.2.

```
Public Class frmTaxCalc
    Inherits System.Windows.Forms.Form

[+] | Windows Form Designer generated code |

    Private TC As TaxCalculator 'The TaxCalculator object
    Private Sub frmTaxCalc_Load( _
                    ByVal sender As System.Object, _
                    ByVal e As System.EventArgs) _
                    Handles MyBase.Load
        TC = New TaxCalculator()
    End Sub

    Private Sub txtGrossIncome_Validating( _
        ByVal sender As Object, _
        ByVal e As System.ComponentModel.CancelEventArgs) _
                    Handles txtGrossIncome.Validating
        TC.GrossIncome = Val(txtGrossIncome.Text)
    End Sub

    Private Sub chkMarried_CheckedChanged( _
                    ByVal sender As System.Object, _
```

```
                               ByVal e As System.EventArgs) _
                            Handles chkMarried.CheckedChanged
        TC.Married = chkMarried.Checked
    End Sub

    Private Sub cboNumChildren_SelectedIndexChanged( _
                        ByVal sender As System.Object, _
                        ByVal e As System.EventArgs) _
                Handles cboNumChildren.SelectedIndexChanged
        TC.DependentChildren = _
                        CType(cboNumChildren.Text, Integer)
    End Sub

    Private Sub txtExtraAllowances_Validating( _
        ByVal sender As Object, _
        ByVal e As System.ComponentModel.CancelEventArgs) _
        Handles txtExtraAllowances.Validating
        TC.ExtraAllowances = Val(txtExtraAllowances.Text)
    End Sub

    Private Sub btnCalc_Click( _
                        ByVal sender As System.Object, _
                        ByVal e As System.EventArgs) _
                        Handles btnCalc.Click
        Dim report As String
        'Show the results of the tax calculations...
        report = "Taxable Income (annual) = " & _
                TC.TaxableIncome & Environment.NewLine
        report += "Total tax (annual) = " & _
                TC.Tax & Environment.NewLine
        report += "Annual income after tax = " & _
                TC.IncomeAfterTax & Environment.NewLine
        report += "Monthly income after tax = " & _
                Format(TC.IncomeAfterTax / 12, "£0.00")
        txtResult.Text = report
    End Sub
End Class
```

Listing 8.2: Windows code that uses the `TaxCalculator` class

Listing 8.2 shows the code behind the Windows form shown in Figure 8.1b. The first thing I should do here is reassure you by stating that very little of this code had to be entered manually (12 lines of it to be exact). Most of it was generated by Visual Studio as the various *event-handlers* were added to the form. The code that was entered manually was in fact very straightforward, the main difference from the Console application being that:

1. the `GetData()` method was not used since the various bits of the data were picked up from the various Windows controls individually; and

2. the `ShowTaxCalc()` method did not need to be called, since instead of providing console output, the results of the calculations were placed into the textbox immediately above the two buttons on the Windows form.

In Listing 8.2, each source of user-input that the program is set up to handle has a separate event-handler. An event-handler is simply a sub that has been connected by Visual Studio to a signal from Windows. Each control can potentially handle many events, but only those for which event-handlers have been created have any significance.

From the code in Listing 8.2, you can see that different events were used to trigger processing from different controls. The list of events available for each type of control is described in the help pages for each control (accessible via the Dynamic Help window or by selecting a control and pressing **F1**). For most controls, the table listing the available events is quite far down the Help page. Look up the list of events for several of the WinForms controls and in particular read the descriptions of the default events such as the Click event for a button (you can identify the default event for a control by placing the control on a form and double-clicking on it – an event-handler for the default event will be generated in the Code window for the form). The help page for an event contains a link to a page entitled Consuming Events, which provides a good overview of events and event handling.

8.1.2 Event-Handling Code

The main difference between the two versions of the Tax Calculator program is due to the way that Windows handles user-input. In the Console application, the user follows the programmer's prompts as defined in `GetData()` – effectively instructions for how to use the program, including the order that data is to be entered. In the Windows version, the user is free to enter the input data in any order. There would be nothing to stop the user from entering the inputs in reverse order, or from entering one piece of data, running the Windows calculator to make some calculations before entering the next piece, sending an email before entering the remaining pieces and then finally pressing the Calculate button to get the result.

As you might imagine, this would be quite awkward to organize in a Console application. However, in the Windows program, it is a natural consequence of the way Windows deals with input from the keyboard and mouse and any other potential source of input data. Windows programs respond to *events*, which are messages from the operating system indicating that something has happened. In effect, a specially written sub handles each possible type of event.

Windows itself it smart enough to direct events to the program that they were intended for, and the .NET runtime library provides enough additional intelligence to work out which specific control an event was directed at. If the cursor is flashing in a particular text box and the user presses a key, a number of event messages are sent to the form that contains the text box and the form in turn invokes an event-handler that has been created for that text box. If you click on a button, Windows sends a message to the form which can then invoke the appropriate event-handler for a click on that button.

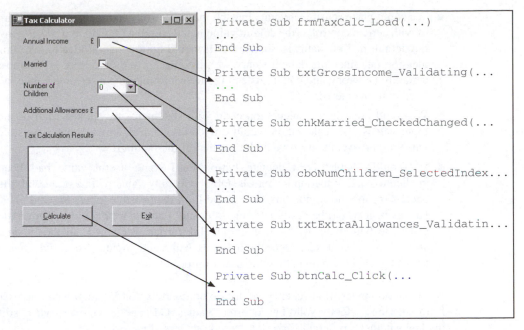

Figure 8.2 Events and event-Handlers

Event-handlers are like little programs. Each event that happens potentially has an event-handler associated with it. If there is no event-handler, the event is ignored by the program. If an event-handler has been created for that event, it is executed from beginning to end. Figure 8.2 indicates how interaction events and event-handlers in this small application are interrelated.

Outlines for the event-handlers are usually created automatically by Visual Studio as you add controls to a form and use the Class Name and Method Name combo boxes in the form's Code window to select events you wish to write response code for. You can also add event-handlers manually by entering the entire code, including the normally generated first and last line, into the form's Code window.

While this structure makes it easy to see how particular user-input occurrences will relate to particular pieces of program code, it does leave us with a problem: how do we do an entire task that would previously have been the work of a program when it is initiated in lots of little steps, or, more specifically, how do we ensure that all of the little steps are done in an order that will produce the correct result?

The answer to this is that we need to design the application program carefully (is there any other way?) and we need to anticipate the user's silliest mistakes. For the Tax Calculation program, we have several options for making sure we get an answer.

■ We could allow null or problem inputs, converting each to the most likely value. For example, if nothing (or nothing valid) was entered into the Annual Income text box, we could assume an annual income of zero. For zero income you would pay zero tax, and so the calculations would still come out as correct.

■ We could place sensible defaults in each input control. This is already taken care of with certain controls – the default value in the Number Of Children box is zero, the default marital status is Single, etc. It would not be a good idea to take this idea too far, since the default salary we place in `txtGrossIncome` will almost certainly be wrong and could mislead the user into thinking a sensible value had already been entered.

■ We could precede the calculation code with statements to validate each of the input values. The calculation would only proceed if all inputs were a sensible value; otherwise, the user would be warned of the input errors.

■ We could disable the Calculate button until some useful value had been applied to each of the input controls. Obviously, any value will be ok in both the check box and the combo box since these limit the possible inputs to valid ones. However, it would be easily possible to ensure that the user could not press the Calculate button by disabling it until valid entries were made in the Income and Allowances boxes. Once both boxes had valid inputs, we could enable the Calculate button and allow the user to proceed.

Note that no matter what scheme we decide on, there is nothing to prevent the user from entering perfectly valid but incorrect values. Garbage-in–Garbage-out is still the law whether a program is console-based or event-driven.

Windows programmers tend to favour the last suggestion from the list above. Good user interface design is about gently guiding the user towards correct usage of a program, and nothing tells a user they have done something wrong more elegantly than simply not allowing them to proceed. A user faced with the inability to press the Calculate button is likely to spot missing or wrong input values quite quickly.

Exercise 8.2

In Listing 8.2 and Figure 8.2, you can see that different pieces of data are picked up from the form using event-handlers for the various controls (e.g. the annual income value is collected using the `txtGrossIncome_Validating()` event-handler). This data could instead have been picked up in the `btnCalc_Click()` event handler, in which case the code for packing the various pieces of data into the `TaxCalc` object would have been placed before the statements that build up the report for display. Write this version of the `btnCalc_Click()` event handler.

8.1.3 Increasing Complexity, and Tiers of Software

As a Windows program becomes more complex, the use of a single form for dealing with all user-input becomes less and less sensible. There are two issues to consider when creating software that by necessity has a complex user-interface: the complexity that the user of the software must contend with, and the increased difficulty in creating the software in the first place.

The usual method of reducing complexity a user perceives in a Windows program is to partition the user-interface into several forms, each with a specific goal or area of the application to deal with. This makes the user's job of working with the software easier, and also makes it less cumbersome to create. Visual Studio itself is a good example of this form of construction, with separate Windows (forms) for providing different views of the current project or parts of it, *dialog boxes* for printing and making changes to the settings of parts of Visual Studio, and a Multi-Document Interface (MDI) so that individual code modules and forms are dealt with separately.

A software developer writing Windows software needs to create not only the classes and structures that perform the software's work, but also a user-interface that makes it easy to use. Because of the way the Visual Studio works, it can be tempting to start with the user-interface and build the code that does the actual work of the software into that; for example, you could place the code to do the tax calculations directly into the event-handlers shown in Listing 8.2. This approach can be successful for a while, but should be avoided for all but the most trivial of software, for a variety of reasons.

- A user-interface is developed to interact with the user. Once the actual missions of an application are built into the user-interface, it becomes difficult to separate one from the other. Changing the user-interface so that the user interacts with it in a different way is likely to have an effect on the way the software works and vice-versa. The ideal is to keep both separate, so that it is possible to change either the user-interface or the workings of the application without these changes affecting the other part.

- Building the core of the software into the user-interface makes both (software design and user-interface design) more complex.

- If an application does its work successfully as a Windows program, it may be desirable to implement it as a web-based application (which would use a browser and Web Forms as its user-interface). If the application software is inextricably linked with the user-interface design, the only solution might be to build the web-based version from scratch. If a design that kept the application core separate from the user-interface had been used, it would be possible to reuse the classes at the core of the application in the web-based one by simply building the web-based user-interface and connecting it to the existing application core.

- Building object-oriented software is about creating classes that perform simple roles in the application well. One obvious simplification of the structure of any part of an application is to create a class to perform some role, and separately create a user-interface component class to work with it. The partition between 'application objects' and 'user-interface objects' is simply good object-oriented design.

These general points are well supported by the notion of 'tiered' or 'layered' software design. A simple two-tier application design is one where the software missions are performed by a set of application objects, and the user controls these objects through a set of user-interface objects. Figure 8.3 is a diagram of a simple two-tier program.

The terms *user-interface tier* or *layer*, and *business tier* or *layer* are often used to describe the separation of the two parts of a simple desktop application (a simple desktop application in this sense is a program that does not utilize connections to

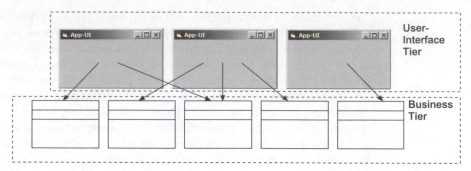

Figure 8.3 A 2-tier application

software on other computers via a network, such as a database server or Internet services). The business tier is the part of the software that does the core work of the application, such as calculating tax; it is the part of the application that specifically implements the software requirements. The user-interface tier is developed to manage user-interactions. At its simplest, that involves accepting user-input, displaying results and accepting commands, although user-interface design can involve much more than this. For example, a well-designed user-interface can display partial results, record user-interactions to allow them to be undone in the event of an error, generate graphical representations of application data, anticipate user actions to simplify input (as Visual Studio does with Intellisense), enable and disable commands as appropriate to reduce the possibility of error and display application status.

One very important benefit to developing the business tier separately is that it makes the workings of the application easier to test and maintain. By allowing a number of different designs of user-interface to be used, it is possible to create a variation of the system where the business model is attached to a very simple user-interface that simply passes established test data into the business tier and examines the results. Whenever any work is done on the business tier, it can be re-tested quickly and easily by building a test version of the application and running the tests.

Exercise 8.3

Identify the separate tiers for business processing and user-interface management for the `TaxCalc` program.

a) Which objects in the program correspond to which tiers?

b) How are the two tiers organized in terms of code modules?

8.2   WinForms Basics

A WinForms application has a user-interface based around forms, which are objects of classes that can be either designed for a particular task in a specific application, or, usefully, designed to perform a common task that might be needed in many applications. Microsoft provides a number of forms which are standard enough to

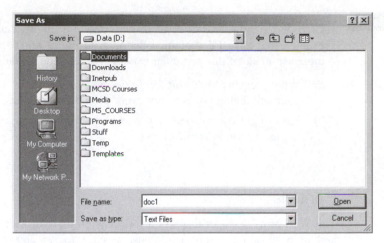

Figure 8.4 The Save File common dialog

be built into the Windows operating system. These *common dialogs* are accessed by either calling on standard functions that are part of Windows itself, known as API (Application Programmer Interface) functions or, more usefully from a Visual Basic WinForms program, by activating them from controls that can be placed on the main form of the VB application. They are available to perform common tasks such as getting the user to enter a file-name and location, selecting a file to load, picking a colour or font, or configuring a printer before a print job is run. Figure 8.4 shows the **FileSaveDialog** in action, and Listing 8.3 shows typical code needed to activate it and collect the file-name entered by the user.

```
Private Sub btnSave_Click(ByVal sender As System.Object, _
        ByVal e As System.EventArgs) Handles btnSave.Click
    Dim fileName As String
    With SaveDlg     'SaveDlg is a control on a form
        .Filter = "Text Files|*.txt"
        If .ShowDialog() = DialogResult.OK Then
            fileName = .FileName
            'Go on to save the file...
        End If
    End With
End Sub
```

Listing 8.3: Using the `FileSaveDialog`

Other forms are either designed specifically for a particular purpose in an application program or designed to be used in a range of applications, in either case using the WinForms designer built into Visual Studio. When you create a new WinForms application in Visual Studio, you are automatically given a blank form which you can then go on to customize by adding controls and setting properties for the form and added controls. You can also add code to a form in the way we have created code for Console applications up till now.

Exercise 8.4

Considering how easy it is to display and use an item as complex as, for example the Save File common dialog, you might think that there would be more use made of this particular way of writing code to interact with the user.

a) What prevents Microsoft from providing you with a wide enough range of common dialog boxes to suit every programming need?

b) How might you try to use this way of working so that your own forms were as easy to use in applications?

8.2.1 Controls

The WinForms designer displays a form design that you can configure using drag and drop to add controls, the mouse pointer to set size and position and the Properties window to change a wide range of properties of 'visual' controls. As you manipulate these controls at design time, the Form Designer adjusts the code behind the form to reflect the changes in settings. Microsoft terminology uses *control* to indicate a visible item on a form that can be manipulated at design time, and *component* to indicate separately built objects that can be added to a program and accessed programmatically using their class interface. A control is a special type of component with a visible design-time presence.

By default, the Form Designer adds controls to a form with `Friend` scope, so that the controls can be accessed from any code within the assembly. It is possible to change a control's scope using the `Modifiers` property, so that it is `Private` (available only within the form's own code), `Protected` (available in the form's code or any forms that inherit from it) or `Public` (available to any code that can access the form). Typically, `Friend` access is adequate, although for complex forms it could be useful to reduce the scope to `Private` or `Protected` for certain controls.

As this suggests, a form design is a class and adheres to all of the rules of scope and inheritance that any other class does. When developing forms for a WinForms application, it is good practice to apply the same object-oriented programming techniques you would apply to classes that you create in code; always use the minimum scope for member variables and methods that you add to a form and use meaningful names for controls, variables, properties and methods.

8.2.2 Windows Focus

All controls in Visual Studio .NET are Windows-based, which means that they can receive the *focus* in an application. A control which receives the focus is the currently 'selected' control on a form. A text box shows a flashing cursor when it has the focus, buttons, check boxes and radio buttons show a dotted-line around their caption, list boxes and combo boxes highlight the selected item and more complex controls indicate they have the focus in a variety of ways (see Figure 8.5). In every case, this indicates that keyboard input will be directed to that control, allowing a user to access everything on a form without having to use the mouse.

Figure 8.5 Various Windows controls with the focus

Focus is controlled by the user clicking on a control to select it, or by the user pressing the Tab key to move around the controls on a form, or by program code. When you design a form, you can set up the order that focus moves in when the user presses the Tab key. Each control has a `TabIndex` property which is a number that indicates what order controls will be selected in using the Tab key; lower numbers come first. Label controls cannot be selected since they are not regarded as input controls, so the `TabIndex` they are given has no effect. If one or more labels are next in the tabbing sequence, the focus will simply jump past them to the next selectable control.

A programmer can programmatically move the focus to a specific control using the `Focus()` method for that control. This makes it possible to direct the user's input to a specific input control even if it is not the next in the normal sequence, which is defined by a control's `TabIndex` property.

Controls are initially given a `TabIndex` set by the order they were put on the form: the first control gets 0, the second 1, etc. At design time the `TabIndex` can be changed by entering a new number for it in the Properties window – select lower for earlier in the list and higher for later. If you give a control a `TabIndex` that is the same as a control already on the form, both controls will share the same `TabIndex`. Tabbing order will then be dictated by the *ZOrder* (or back-to-front order) of the controls; by default controls that were placed on the form later will be selected first as they are on top.

This would all make the job of setting the order that controls were tabbed to quite messy, if it were not for the built-in `TabIndex` reordering tool. Place controls on a form in any order you wish, and then select **View→Tab Order** from the menus. `TabIndex` values will appear as little numbers on the controls in the Form Designer (see Figure 8.6), and you can now set the `TabIndex` by clicking on them in the order you wish. This is a huge leap forward from previous versions of Visual Basic where it was necessary to number the controls individually using the Properties window.

Exercise 8.5

The Windows focus is a very useful mechanism for making the user's interactions with a form easier. Can you think of three specific advantages controlling the input focus might have in simplifying user-interactions? (Hint – think of the order input is collected, what happens when an item of data obviously does not need to be entered, and what could be done if an input error was recognized).

8.2.3 Events

The form you manipulate at design time and all the objects you place on it provide events that act as signals sent to activate procedures on the form. That can seem a

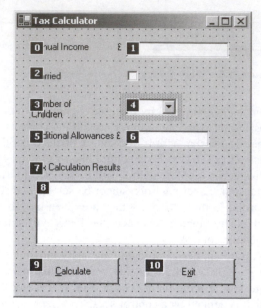

Figure 8.6 Setting the `TabIndex` values for controls

bit odd, a form sending a signal to itself, but it is this that allows for a form's core behaviour to be extended so that it can do things never thought of when the original form class was written by Microsoft. Events are simply notifications from standard signals that Windows and .NET understand, such as mouse clicks and key presses, which are used to execute specially formatted subs that you write. A sub that is executed in response to an event is called an event-handler, and it can take zero or more parameters that give more information about an event. All of the events specified for the controls in VS .NET pass a pair of arguments, which appear to the event-handlers as 1) a reference to the object that sent the event and 2) a reference to an `EventArgs` object (a member of a descendant of the `EventArgs` class) that contains more information about the event. For example, the `TextBox` control sources a `KeyPressed` event, a handler for which appears in outline as shown in Listing 8.4.

```
Private Sub txtName_KeyPress(ByVal sender As Object, _
        ByVal e As System.Windows.Forms.KeyPressEventArgs) _
        Handles txtName.KeyPress
    Dim ch As Char
    ch = e.KeyChar()
    e.Handled = True
End Sub
```

Listing 8.4: An event-handler for the `TextBox.KeyPress` event

When this event fires on a form, the `sender` parameter will be a reference to the `TextBox` object that fired the event. The `e` parameter contains additional information specific to this type of event. In this case the key that was pressed to fire the

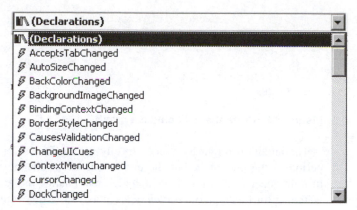

Figure 8.7 Part of the event list for a TextBox control

event (which is being passed into the ch variable within the event-handler), and a Handled Boolean member variable, which can be used in the event-handler to indicate that the key-press has been taken care of. The e parameter varies depending on the event and the control that sent it. For example, a MouseMove event, which is used to indicate that the mouse is moving across a control, passes variables to give the location and button state of the mouse within the e parameter.

Events are coded into a class design in such a way that the Form Designer is able to provide a list of available events for an object at design time. You can write code to add an event-handler to a form manually, but generally you will find it much easier to let Visual Studio generate the outline of an event-handler for you.

All controls have a default event, which is the one that the Form Designer will provide a handler for if you double-click on the control at design time. The default event for a Button is the Click event, for a TextBox the Change event and so on. However, each control can typically source many different events. To get the form designer to generate an event other than the default, simply select the control in the combo box at the top left of the form, and the desired event in the combo box at the top right (see Figure 8.7).

Once an event-handler outline has been generated for a specific event from a particular object, whatever code you place inside it will define the procedure that will be executed in response to the event.

An event-handler can cause other event handlers to fire. For example, several controls have a ... *Changed* event that is caused to fire when the control's content changes in some way; a TextBox has a TextChanged event and this will change if, *for any reason*, the Text in the TextBox changes. Therefore, an event-handler that contains a line of code like:

```
Text1.Text = ...
```

will cause the Text1.TextChanged event to fire. For this reason, the code in Listing 8.5 can cause a crash.

```
        Private Sub txtResult_TextChanged(ByVal sender As
                                System.Object, _
                                ByVal e As System.EventArgs) _
                                Handles txtResult.TextChanged
        txtResult.Text += "."
    End Sub
```

Listing 8.5: Code that will cause a crash

The intention might have been to tidy up the format of the result by adding a period to the end of it, but the effect will be to change the text, which will in turn fire the `TextChanged` event, which will change the text which. . . . It is worth watching for this type of *cascading event* as you write event-handlers.

Exercise 8.6

> From the explanation above, it is obvious that altering a control's contents within a handler for the Changed event can cause problems. Look through the list of events for a `TextBox`, and try to identify a more suitable event for performing the task outlined in Listing 8.5. Write the code that would be placed in the suggested event's event-handler.

8.3 User Interface Code and the Form Designer

User-interface development for a Windows-based application can be done entirely in program code. Listing 8.6 shows a minimal code example of a *Console application* in which a blank form is created and displayed.

```
    Module SimpleForm
        Sub Main()
            Dim F As New Windows.Forms.Form()
            Windows.Forms.Application.Run(F)
        End Sub
    End Module
```

Listing 8.6: A Console application that displays a Windows Form

If you create and run this application (to do so in Visual Studio, you will need to create a Console application and then add a reference to the `System.Windows.Forms` library to make the form class and the application class available), you will notice that as a Console application it still displays a Console window on the screen when it starts up. However, a new blank form is immediately loaded on top of the Console window, which will then do nothing until you close the form, at which it will also close. You can get rid of the Console window by going to the Project Properties dialog box and selecting **Windows Application** as the Output type.

The difficulty with developing a Windows application in this way is that you would now have to change the size of the form, add controls to it and associate them with the form, deal with user interactions and Windows messages and a great many other things, all in Visual Basic code. Fortunately, Visual Studio provides us with designers for Windows applications that take care of all of these details and leave us to get on with writing the application code.

8.3.1 Designer Generated Code

Let's look at a simple Windows form from a new Windows Form application. Selecting **File→New→Project** and selecting to build a Windows Application, you will get a new project that automatically contains a single empty form. This contains the code necessary to set up a Windows form and set it running. Near the top of the form's Code window, you would find a line:

| + | Windows Form Designer generated code |

(e.g. see near the top of Listing 8.2). By clicking on the little + sign at the left, you can open (or unfold) a lot of code that Visual Studio normally hides from you; shown in Listing 8.7.

```
Public Class Form1
    Inherits System.Windows.Forms.Form

#Region " Windows Form Designer generated code "

    Public Sub New()
        MyBase.New()

        'This call is required by the Windows Form Designer.
        InitializeComponent()

        'Add any initialization after the
        InitializeComponent() call

    End Sub

    'Form overrides dispose to clean up the component list.
    Protected Overloads Overrides Sub Dispose( _
                                ByVal disposing As Boolean)
        If disposing Then
            If Not (components Is Nothing) Then
                components.Dispose()
            End If
        End If
        MyBase.Dispose(disposing)
    End Sub

    'Required by the Windows Form Designer
    Private components As System.ComponentModel.IContainer
    'NOTE: The following procedure is required by the Windows
    'Form Designer
```

```
    'It can be modified using the Windows Form Designer.
    'Do not modify it using the code editor.
    <System.Diagnostics.DebuggerStepThrough()> _
    Private Sub InitializeComponent()
        components = New System.ComponentModel.Container()
        Me.Text = "Form1"
    End Sub

#End Region

End Class
```

Listing 8.7: Windows Form Designer generated code for a blank form

Apart from inserting a few line-breaks to make this code fit better on the page, I've made no changes to it. Reassuringly, there is not much in the way of code that we have not met in some form before.

The code for the form is a Class definition, and as you might expect it uses inheritance so that standard properties and methods for all Form classes are already defined. In the earlier example of a simple form, I created an object of the `System.Windows.Forms.Form` class, and here, the Windows Form Designer has created a new Form class by inheriting from the same class. To kick off the design of a new class, the designer has added a constructor (`Public Sub New()`) which makes a call to `InitializeComponent()`. This method is defined later in the class and has the job of creating a Container component for the form, which will hold references to any other components added to the form, and setting the form's caption (the Text property). The only other method defined for the new Form class is the `Dispose()` method, which is used to destroy the collection of objects added to the form (and the form itself) when it is no longer needed in an application.

To keep this code safe from tinkering, Visual Studio places most of it in a code region which by default is hidden. It is worth examining the contents of the region after making some changes to a form to see its effect. For example, if I change the form by adding a Windows control from the toolbox to the form in the Designer window, a new Button reference variable will be added to the Form class, and the code in `InitializeComponent()` will be changed so that the button is properly set up. The button's variable is added with the statement:

```
    Friend WithEvents Button1 As System.Windows.Forms.Button
```

Using a `Friend` declaration for the button makes it accessible by any code within the assembly, so it is easily possible to change the properties of the button anywhere in the project. The `WithEvents` keyword indicates that this control can be a source of events, which in turn tells the Form Designer that it may need to attach matching event-handling code to the form's code.

As a consequence of adding the button to the form, the `InitializeComponent()` method is changed, with statements added to create the Button object and set its initial properties (its location, where it occurs in the tab order of controls on the form and what caption will be displayed on its face). This is shown in Listing 8.8.

```
<System.Diagnostics.DebuggerStepThrough()> _
                        Private Sub InitializeComponent()
    Me.Button1 = New System.Windows.Forms.Button()
    Me.SuspendLayout()
    '
    'Button1
    '
    Me.Button1.Location = New System.Drawing.Point(96, 96)
    Me.Button1.Name = "Button1"
    Me.Button1.TabIndex = 0
    Me.Button1.Text = "Button1"
    '
    'Form1
    '
    Me.AutoScaleBaseSize = New System.Drawing.Size(5, 13)
    Me.ClientSize = New System.Drawing.Size(292, 273)
    Me.Controls.AddRange(New System.Windows.Forms.Control() _
                                {Me.Button1})
    Me.Name = "Form1"
    Me.Text = "Form1"
    Me.ResumeLayout(False)
End Sub
```

Listing 8.8: Code added to the form by Form Designer when a button is placed on it

Note from Listing 8.8 that adding the Button control also makes changes to some of the form's own properties. AutoScaleBaseSize is set to a value if a control with text is placed in the form's main area, and allows size calculations to be done based on the character size of the default font for the form (in this case, the font used in the button's caption text). ClientSize is established for the form so that code can be written to work out the available area for controls and graphics on the form and the form is given a default name. During these manipulations of the form (remember that this sub will be executed at run time to set the form and its controls up), effort is saved in updating the form by calling SuspendLayout(). Once the components are initialized, ResumeLayout() is called, which allows the operations that update the visible appearance of the form to be processed.

A double-click on the button's face in the Form Designer window will generate an outline event-handler for the button (Listing 8.9).

```
Private Sub Button1_Click(ByVal sender As System.Object, _
                    ByVal e As System.EventArgs) _
                    Handles Button1.Click
    'Event handling code goes here.
End Sub
```

Listing 8.9: An event-handler for the button added to the form

Table 8.1 takes the first line of this event-handler step-by-step.

Table 8.1 Breaking down an event-handler's first line

`Private Sub`	The event-handler is a sub that is private to the Form class – i.e. we could not call this event-handler from code outside the class definition. While there is nothing to stop us from changing the declaration from `Private` to any other access type, it could lead to confusing code
`Button1_Click`	The name generated for the handler is simply formed by adding the name of the event handled to the name of the control that handles it. We can change this name if we wish, although generally the name provided is a good reminder of what this sub is for
`ByVal sender As System.Object,`	Sender is a reference variable indicating the actual control that sourced the event. We can if we wish use the same event-handler to respond to a large number of possible events by appending them to the `Handles` list at the end of the line. This parameter allows us to determine which was the cause
`ByVal e As System.EventArgs)`	Any arguments to the event are passed here – for example, the current mouse position for a mouse-related event, the key that has been pressed, etc. The object referenced by e will often be of a class that descends from `System.EventArgs`, since `EventArgs` has no member fields to contain event data
`Handles Button1.Click`	This is the actual link to the object firing the event and the event fired. If the name of `Button1` is changed in the Properties window, the object name here will be changed by the Form Designer, but the sub name will remain unchanged. The `Handles` keyword can be followed by a comma separated list of object events, in which case the event-handler will fire for any of them

In addition to generating code for the form and the objects placed on it, the Form Designer is also responsible for making code changes to reflect any property changes you make as you design a form. An obvious example of this happens if you change the name of a control, since the associated variable declaration must be changed to match, and the `Handles` list of any event-handlers associated with it must also be updated. Other changes to properties will be reflected in the form's `InitializeComponent` sub.

As you can see, the Form Designer takes care of a lot of detail when you build and edit the visual face of a form. While you could do any or all of this coding by hand, Visual Studio and the Form Designer provide an accurate match between visual appearance, property settings and the code that would make this a task of unnecessary drudgery.

8.3.2 Code Attributes

Even for a very simple form with a single button on it, Visual Studio's Form Designer does a lot of work which otherwise you would have to do. As you might expect, there has to be a strong link between the Form Designer and the code to allow this to happen, which brings us to the rather odd statement that you can see in both Listings 8.7 and 8.8:

```
<System.Diagnostics.DebuggerStepThrough()> _
                    Private Sub InitializeComponent()
```

This statement steps out of the bounds of the Visual Basic .NET language as a plain programming language and into a whole new arena – self-describing program code. Visual Basic (and the other .NET languages) supports the notion of *code attributes*, which are parts added to statements that the .NET compiler uses to control the type of code that it generates, or to pass on information that will be of use to other software that works with the code. Attributes in Visual Basic .NET are placed in <> brackets, sometimes at the start of a statement as here, and sometimes within a statement. A range of pre-defined attributes are available within .NET and Visual Studio, and you can define your own attributes to add description to code if you wish. In this case, the `System.Diagnostics.DebuggerStepThrough()` attribute is used to pass on information to the debugger that tells it how to deal with this code (a **Debug→Step Into** operation will not automatically stop in this code unless a breakpoint is placed in it).

Generally, Visual Studio will append one of a range of attributes to code automatically so that it or other software knows how to deal with the code. You can ignore these attributes unless you intend to write programming tools. However, you can devise attributes for your own purposes; for example, to assist in documenting your program code. You will meet attributes again when we come to look at serialization in Chapter 11.

8.4 Tools for Creating a User-Interface

Visual Studio makes building a user-interface as easy as selecting the interaction methods you wish to add and drawing them on a Form Designer window. Of course you need to write some code to make the user's actions manipulate the business-end of your application, which ideally should be objects of classes you have developed for the job, but having created a suitable set of business classes for your application, connecting them up to a user-interface is a minor task.

Generally, when you create a user-interface, the first problem you have is deciding on the ways you want the user to interact with a form. Windows provides a rich set of controls for this purpose, and as a user of Windows and Windows software you already have experience of using these and the kinds of interactions supported. We can consider a user-interface as having two main jobs to do: accept user input and display results. Although Visual Basic .NET comes with a large number of Windows controls as standard, most Windows programs make use of just a few of these controls to create a user-interface. Of these, the most important are those listed in Table 8.2.

A wide range of other controls are available to interact with databases, display the standard Windows dialog boxes for opening and saving files, selecting a font or colour and setting up the printer, choosing a date from a calendar or creating a Windows Explorer-like display of the data in a program. In every case, a control can be configured as you design the form using the Properties window, or certain properties can be altered as a program runs. All controls can also fire events to cause code to be executed as the user interacts with them.

Table 8.2   Some important WinForms controls

Toolbox Icon	Description
	MainMenu control: used to add a structured set of menus to a form, including top-level (main) menus, sub-menus, sub-sub menus and so on. Menu items allow the user to initiate a command and provide a limited form of feedback (a menu item can be made invisible, disabled or a check mark can be placed next to it)
	Button control: standard Windows buttons and are used to initiate commands
	TextBox: this is used to accept typed user-input and display text over one or several lines
	Label: a label control simply displays text in a specific place on a form
	CheckBox: a check box displays a little tick mark or not and allows the user to click to change its state. Typically, the presence of a tick is a reflection of an internal Boolean state
	RadioButton: this gets its name from the type of station selector common in older car radios. Radio buttons are used in groups, only one of which can be selected at a time
	PictureBox: displays pictures and can also be used as a drawing area on a form
	ListBox, **CheckedListBox** and **ComboBox**: these store and display lists of text from which the user can select items. A **ListBox** displays the list (or part of it with the ability to scroll through all of it) and allows for the possibility of a number of simultaneously selected items. A **CheckedListBox** is similar to a **ListBox** but will display a check-mark next to selected items. A **ComboBox** displays only one item at a time but allows the user to select from others in a pop-up list
	Timer: this control can periodically fire an event which is useful for updating displays, checking network connections or acting as a simple stop-watch

Exercise 8.7

Using the Properties window at design time is the normal way of configuring controls on a form. Can you think of any reasons why you might need to change the configuration of a control at run time?

8.5   Dialog Boxes and Other User-Interface Options

Perhaps the simplest type of user-interface to deal with is a dialog box. This is a standard Windows form that provides controls for displaying and/or interacting with the program's objects and also one, two or more buttons which typically initiate the actions of a program or part of it, or cancel the operation. For example, the Tax Calculator form shown in Figure 8.1b is a dialog box which has two buttons; one to initiate a calculation for which data has been entered and the other to cancel the operation.

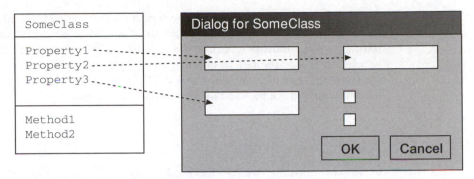

Figure 8.8 A class and an associated dialog box

Most Windows users will be happy with the idea of a dialog box, since they are used throughout Windows and Windows applications. Dialog boxes are generally used to perform a specific task within an application (for example, adding a record to a database), in which case the dialog box is called from a menu or button on another form and, depending on whether the user decides to complete the dialog box or cancel it, will either initiate some action within the program or not. The facility to go on or cancel from a dialog box is an important one, both for the user, who may decide not to complete an operation for any number of reasons, and for the programmer, who needs some standard way of providing a user-friendly interface to a complex operation while giving them the option to back-off from completing the task.

The normal approach is one control per item of data. I work on the principle of a dialog box for a class in most situations. Having pre-defined a class, it is usually a simple matter of creating a dialog box by adding a form to the project and using one control for each property, plus a pair of buttons for OK and Cancel (see Figure 8.8). Extra buttons or menu items can be used to initiate simple class methods, or additional more complex controls such as list or combo boxes for initiating methods where one or more parameters are necessary. This style of dialog box can be used for creating a new member of a class, or for editing an existing object. A bit of careful design and you can use the same dialog box for both purposes.

The dialog box form can also be used as the entire user-interface of a simple application whose job is to perform a single task; for example, logging on to a network or looking up an item of information. In this case, the dialog box will either collect information from the user and then proceed to do the task, or the user will decide to cancel. In either event, once the 'Go' or Cancel button has been pressed, there will be no more interaction with the program.

Visual Basic .NET forms help with the creation of dialog boxes by providing several properties for setting up dialog box style behaviour in a form. The `FormBorderStyle` property can be set to `FixedDialog`, which ensures that the user cannot attempt to change its size and removes extraneous buttons from the form's caption bar. Two additional properties of a form, `AcceptButton` and `CancelButton`, can be set to refer to buttons that will be used to close the form (removing it from the screen) and return an indication of which button was pressed.

Earlier versions of Visual Basic had no specific way of doing this and so programmers were left to write code that sorted the dialog-style behaviour out, including having to pass information back to the code that called on a dialog box to indicate which button was pressed to close it. Now, by simply associating a number of buttons with a specific dialog box action (OK, Cancel, Abort, Yes, No, etc.), this is taken care of without the need to create additional variables.

8.5.1 A dialog box example

For example, assume we had the need to ask a user of a Windows Forms program for their personal information: name, address, gender and phone number. This information could be used to create a new object of a `Person` class; a simple person class definition is shown in Listing 8.10. Note the use of an enumeration to indicate gender, and the use of a constructor `(Sub New)` for setting up a new instance of the class. Typically, such a class would probably have several more methods for manipulating the information.

```
Public Enum GenderType
    gtMale = 1
    gtFemale = 2
End Enum

Public Class Person
    Private mvarName As String
    Private mvarAddress As String
    Private mvarGender As GenderType
    Private mvarTelephone As String
    Public Sub New(ByVal name As String, _
                   ByVal Address As String, _
                   ByVal isMale As Boolean, _
                   ByVal phone As String)
        mvarName = name
        mvarAddress = Address
        If isMale Then
            mvarGender = GenderType.gtMale
        Else
            mvarGender = GenderType.gtFemale
        End If
        mvarTelephone = phone
    End Sub
    'More methods for manipulating the member data...
    '...
End Class
```

Listing 8.10: A `Person` Class

A typical way of creating a new member of this class would be to provide a dialog box that contained controls that would allow the user to enter the information. A suitable new form design has been given an appropriate name (by changing the

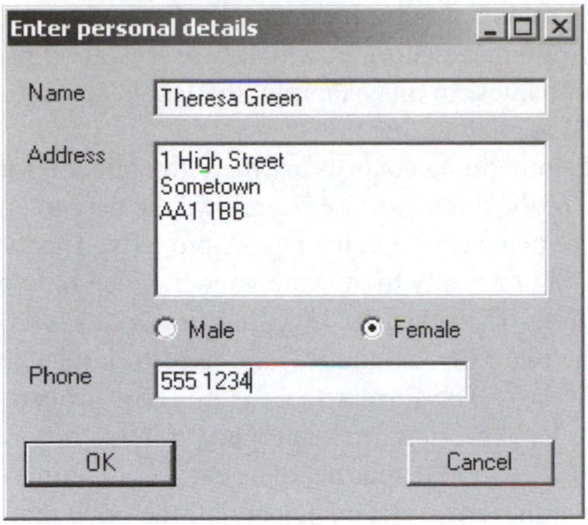

Figure 8.9 A Windows dialog box

Table 8.3 The controls on the dialog box in Figure 8.9

Control Type	Control Name	Purpose
TextBox	txtName	Allow the user to enter their name
TextBox	txtAddress	Allow the user to enter their address over several lines of text
RadioButton	radMale	Indicates the user is Male – mutually exclusive with . . .
RadioButton	radFemale	Indicates the user is Female
TextBox	txtPhone	Allows the user to enter their phone number
Button	btnOK	Indicates the user has completed the dialog box (which therefore contains details for processing)
Button	btnCancel	Indicates the user has cancelled the dialog box (so no details to process)
Label	Label1, Label2, etc.	Various on-screen captions to indicate the purpose of other controls

form's name to dlgPerson in the Properties window). Although frm . . . is a more usual prefix for a form definition, dlg . . . is a sensible prefix to use in the name of a dialog box style form, since it will be used in a different way to a standard form and it is best to make it easy to recognize this in the form's name. The form design appears as shown in Figure 8.9.

This dialog box contains a number of standard Windows controls which are listed in Table 8.3. Each of the controls on the dialog box has a specific purpose. All the Label controls on this form are there purely to indicate the purpose of other controls, and so are not referred to in program code. Label controls can often take a more active role on a form; for example, displaying status information that will change as the program executes, in which case it is good practice to provide them with meaningful names. In this example, the labels are not referred to in code, so names need not be applied to them.

The remaining controls are there to collect information or initiate specific actions. Each of the three TextBoxes allows the user to enter textual information, which can then be picked up from their Text property. The two RadioButtons allow the user an unambiguous way to indicate gender, since only one RadioButton can be selected at a time. The selected RadioButton's Checked property will be set to True.

The two Button controls are used to indicate that the user has finished with the dialog box. The form's AcceptButton property has been set to refer to btnOK, while its CancelButton property refers to btnCancel. Both buttons have been given a _Click event-handler, each containing the single statement: Me.Hide(). In fact, these two statements are all the code that needs to be manually entered into the form – all of the remaining code is generated by the Form Designer.

We can use fairly simple code to create an interaction between the form and the Person class. Typically, the interaction would come from another piece of code intended to create a new Person object – for example a menu item or a button's _Click event-handler. Using this dialog box from another form is a simple matter, as shown in Listing 8.11.

```
Private Sub btnGetInfo_Click(ByVal sender As System.Object, _
                             ByVal e As System.EventArgs) _
                             Handles btnGetInfo.Click
    Dim d As New dlgPerson()
    If d.ShowDialog(Me) = DialogResult.OK Then
        'We can now pick up the data from the dialog box...
        Dim P As Person = New Person(d.txtName.Text, _
                                     d.txtAddress.Text, _
                                     d.radMale.Checked, _
                                     d.txtPhone.Text)
        'Would now go on to do stuff with the new instance
        'of Person...
    Else
        'Cancel was pressed...
        MessageBox.Show("No name supplied")
    End If
    d.Dispose()
End Sub
```

Listing 8.11: Using the `dlgPerson` dialog box

A form in the application has a Button control that has been named btnGetInfo, and the above code is its _Click event-handler. Note that a reference variable, d, for a dlgPerson object has been declared. Deploying the dialog box is a matter of calling a standard form method – ShowDialog(). This method optionally takes a parameter, which is a reference to another form that 'owns' the dialog box. It is a sensible precaution to supply a reference to the owner form if one exists, since this will be considered a 'top-level' window; if for any reason the top-level form is destroyed, it would take the dialog box with it, thereby saving system resources. The easiest way to provide this parameter is to use the keyword Me, which refers to the form that this event handler is part of. If this reference is not supplied, nothing bad will happen unless the calling form crashes, in which case, an 'orphan' form will be left in memory until the application ends or the garbage collector gets it.

The dialog box displays *modally*; that is, once it has been displayed, the user must dismiss it by pressing **OK** or **Cancel** before anything else will happen in the sub the dialog box was called from. Modal behaviour is necessary here since once the dialog box is displayed, we must be sure the user has finished entering information into it before continuing to process this data.

When the dialog box is closed by the user pressing **OK** or **Cancel**, the ShowDialog() method returns a result which is the DialogResult property setting of whichever button was pressed. In this case, our call to the method is check to see if the result was DialogResult.OK. If so, we know we can go on to create the Person object and continue with any other processing that action requires. Since all the controls added to the dialog box have been given Friend scope, all the code in this assembly can access them as if they were properties of the form. We can therefore pass the appropriate properties of these controls straight into the Person constructor.

This is a fairly simple example of the type of job a dialog box would be given to do. We could have effected the necessary interactions in a number of ways; for example, all of the dialog box code could have been added to a method of the Person class itself, thereby making the class responsible for collecting its own information, or we could even have provided the dialog box with a Person reference variable, thereby making the form the master of the object it creates. We'll look into these types of options in the chapter on object modelling.

Exercise 8.8

In the example use of a dialog form in Listing 8.10, the code is executed within the _Click event-handler for a button. Since it is only possible to have a single modal form on display at any one time:

a) how would a second dialog box, say to collect a user's employment details, be dealt with?

b) how has the form that contains the button that initiates this code been displayed?

c) could the dialog box have been displayed from Sub Main() in a Console application?

8.6 Other Form Styles

Dialog boxes represent an easy way of collecting information for a specific action in a program. However, a dialog box has a serious limitation in a Windows program, since its modal behaviour means that only one dialog box can be displayed at a time. Many Windows applications allow the user to display multiple versions of a form, and in the object-oriented way of doing things, each form would display the data from a single object. Because of this, a Windows form can also be displayed non-modally – i.e. once it has been displayed on the screen, other things are allowed to happen.

Without the dialog-style deployment, Windows forms can be more awkward to use since we have no control over the user's interactions with them. Typically, a form will be used to interact with a specific object or set of objects, and we must take care to ensure that an object is dealt with by only one form at a time.

The `Form.Show()` method does the job of placing a form on the screen and then continuing to process the code following the `Show()` statement, leaving the form to process its user interactions from that point on. This is the opposite of the 'modal' behaviour exhibited by a dialog box. If we were to use two separate forms to access the same object, it would become difficult to orchestrate the interactions between forms and object and this would probably result in object data becoming corrupted. For this reason, it is usually best to keep the relationships between forms and business objects direct and simple. One way of doing this is to impose a rule that only one form can be used to access an object at any one time.

Apart from trivial objects, I usually work on the basis that any class I use which requires some form of user-interaction is associated with a specially developed form that will be responsible for working with it. For example, I might have a class that represents a `Customer` object in a database application. It is easy to create a form that allows us to visualize and interact with a single `Customer` object (much like the `dlgPerson` form used earlier with the `Person` class). An easy way of managing the interactions between an object and a form is to make the form wholly responsible for the object by passing the object to the form in its constructor.

For example, members of our `Customer` class could be manipulated by building a `frmCustomer` form which took a reference to a `Customer` object in its constructor. A number of controls on the form would map to the properties of the `Customer` class, and various events for these controls could be used to update the properties. I find it convenient to put the business class and the associated form class into the same module – easiest to add the business class (`Customer`) to the form's module once you have added a new form class and its Form Designer. The code might be something like Listing 8.12.

```
'This is the code module for the Form class.
Public Class Customer
    Private mvarName As String
    'More member variables . . .
    Public Property Name() As String
        Get
            Return mvarName
        End Get
        Set(ByVal Value As String)
            mvarName = Value
        End Set
    End Property
```

```
                'More properties and methods...
                '...
        End Class

        Public Class frmCustomer
                Inherits System.Windows.Forms.Form
                'A Customer reference variable. The object will be
                'created in Sub New...
                Private mvarCustomer As Customer
```

```
 +   Windows Form Designer generated code
```

```
                'This event handler fires when the user clicks on the
                'OK button, indicating that the data entered on the
                'form should be passed into the Customer object. The
                'handler for the Cancel button would simply not pass the
                'data into the object...
                Private Sub btnOK_Click( _
                                    ByVal sender As System.Object, _
                                    ByVal e As System.EventArgs) _
                                    Handles btnOK.Click
                    mvarCustomer.Name = txtName.Text
                    'Update other customer properties from their
                    'controls...
                    '...
                    'Now close the form...
                    Me.Hide()
                End Sub
        End Class
```

Listing 8.12: A Form module with an added business class

In Listing 8.12, both the Customer class and its associated Form class are coded in the same module. Since the Form Designer takes over much of the work of coding forms and interactions for us, it makes sense to add the business class to the form code rather than manually coding the form class in the business class's module. The form is given a business class reference variable (here it is the declaration Private mvarCustomer As Customer) and when it is deployed, a Customer object is passed to this variable.

Each member variable of the business class has an associated control on the form; for example a text box, txtName, is used to collect and display the customer's name. Code in the _Click event-handler for the OK button does the job of passing data from the form into the Customer object. The _Click handler for the Cancel button simply closes the form.

The only remaining change to the Form Designer's generated code is in the hidden region in Sub New(). Since this form is there for the express purpose of working with a Customer object, we can use its constructor to set up the Customer object it will work with. The constructor takes a single parameter, which is a reference to an existing Customer object (the parameter is passed ByRef instead of the default ByVal). As the form is created, the constructor needs to set the various controls on the form to be a true reflection of the properties of the referred to customer (Listing 8.13).

```
Public Sub New(ByRef c As Customer)
    MyBase.New()

    'This call is required by the Windows Form Designer.
    InitializeComponent()

    'Add any initialization after the
    'InitializeComponent() call
    mvarCustomer = c
    'Need to transfer property values on to the form's
    'controls..
    txtName.Text = c.Name
    'Other properties can also be transferred here...
    '...
End Sub
```

Listing 8.13: The modified form constructor

We now have a pair of classes that will always go together since they inhabit the same module. Wherever we make use of a `Customer` object, we will have access to a purpose-built form for making it available to the user. There is one final twist we can add to this (which will simplify coding wherever we use a `Customer` object) – make the form the responsibility of the `Customer` object, by adding a method to the `Customer` class to invoke the form shown in Listing 8.14.

```
Public Class Customer
    'Existing code...
    '...
    Public Sub ShowMe()
        Dim F As New frmCustomer(Me)
        F.Show()
    End Sub
End Class
```

Listing 8.14: Making a `Customer` object autonomous

The result of adding this final method is that we can forget about the details of the customer's purpose-built Form class altogether. Passing `Me` to the form's constructor associates the newly created form with this `Customer` object, which will ensure that updates made on the form will be reflected back to the object. By simply invoking the `ShowMe()` method of a `Customer` object, it will take care of its own display and updating (Listing 8.15).

```
Dim c As New Customer()
c.Name = "Fred Bloggs"
c.ShowMe()
```

Listing 8.15: The customer does all the work

This style of programming with forms will minimize the number of objects you need to keep track of in an application.

It is suggested above that it can be advantageous to place the code for a business class and its associated user-interface (i.e. the Form class) into a single module, so that the form is always available when the class is.

a) Can you see any disadvantage to this approach?
b) What would the advantages and disadvantages of keeping each of the classes in separate modules be?

8.7 Controls Collection

Controls on a form can also be containers for other controls. These inherit from the ContainerControl class, and provide a Controls collection which has properties and methods that allow you to add new controls, remove existing ones and manipulate the contained controls collectively. A form is also a descendant of ContainerControl, and so the same methods can be used to deal with all the controls on a form. For example, the following snippet of code (Listing 8.16) would make every control on the form that it belonged to 10 pixels wider.

```
Private Sub MakeBigger()
    Dim c As Control
    For Each c In Controls
        c.Width += 10
    Next
End Sub
```

Listing 8.16: Resizing all the controls on a form.

Manipulating the controls collection gives us the ability to adapt a form at run-time to the conditions in a program. For example, you can resize controls as the form resizes (although there are easier ways to do this), add new buttons, etc. One very important use for this facility is to add items to a program's menu; something we'll look at in detail in Chapter 10.

8.8 Delegates and Event-Handlers

Events that originate in controls on a form are dealt with by event-handlers in the form's code. To make this possible, the Form Designer must be able to generate the outline of event-handlers that match the events provided by controls on the form. The .NET type system must provide for the ability of a control to execute a piece of code that has not been written yet and may never be written. For example, when you click on a button, the possibility is that an event-handler for that button's `Button.Click` event will have to be called, so the designer of the Button class (or some class in its ancestry) had to provide for the facility to call a sub that may or may not be written.

In .NET, this is provided for by *delegates* – stand-ins for code that may be required. The role they play in a program is to define a *type of* method call, which can then be used to attach an initially unassigned call to a piece of code that matches the delegate. In Chapter 4 we saw code that defined a simple event to signal the occurrence of a particular situation within an object and an event-handler to deal with it. The event was a `BankAccount` going into overdraft. This event-handler was created to match the event generated by the `Withdraw()` method within the `BankAccount`. In fact, the event declaration was a special type of Delegate; one that is declared especially for inter-object communication mediated by the .NET run time system.

A Delegate type is declared almost like the first line of a sub call, except that it is preceded by the keyword `Delegate` and will contain no body of code. Since it is a type, delegate variables of that type can now be created. Once a delegate has been declared, a matching sub can be assigned to it so that calling on the delegate will actually execute the assigned sub.

A simple example should make this clear (see Listing 8.17).

```
'Start by declaring the delegate...
Delegate Sub AlarmCall(ByVal AlarmMessage As String)

'Now a class that will use the delegate...
Class AlarmClock
    Private myTime As Date
    Private myMessage As String
    'Here is the delegate declaration...
    Private myResponse As AlarmCall
    Public Sub New(ByVal AlarmTime As Date, _
                   ByVal Message As String, _
                   ByVal SubToCall As AlarmCall)
        myTime = AlarmTime
        myMessage = Message
        'Assign a Sub to the delegate...
        myResponse = SubToCall
    End Sub
    Public Sub Go()
        Do
            If TimeOfDay >= myTime Then
                'A call to the delegate method...
                myResponse(myMessage)
                Exit Do
            End If
        Loop
    End Sub
End Class
```

```
'Now for some Subs that all match the delegate's signature.
'This one displays a message on screen...
Sub AlarmMessageBox(ByVal aMessage As String)
     MessageBox.Show(aMessage)
End Sub

'This one changes a form's caption...
Sub AlarmCaption(ByVal aMessage As String)
     MainForm.Caption = aMessage
End Sub

'This one sends an email...
Sub AlarmEmail(ByVal aMessage As String)
     SendMail("me@mydomain.com", "Alarm", aMessage)
End Sub

Sub Main()
     'When we create an AlarmClock object, we use its
     'constructor to attach one of the delegate Subs...
     Dim AC As AlarmClock = _
                   New AlarmClock(TimeValue("10:00:00"),_
                   "Go to airport", AddressOf AlarmEmail)
     AC.Go()
End Sub
```

Listing 8.17: A delegate defined and used

In Listing 8.17, a new `Delegate` is declared. Sub `AlarmCall` is not a declaration of a sub (there is no body of code) but of a *kind* of sub – in this case, one which takes a `String` as a parameter. Now that the Delegate type has been declared, we can go on to create a new class, `AlarmClock`, one of whose members is an `AlarmCall` delegate member. Later, an object of the class will be able to use this to indicate what sub to actually call when an alarm is required.

The class's constructor takes three pieces of data – the time for the alarm to go off, the message that is to accompany the alarm, and the *address* of the sub that is to be called. As its name suggests, the address of a sub is where it lives in the computer's memory. If we know this, we can call the sub.

The only other class method is called `Go()`, and this simply executes a `Do Loop` that repeatedly checks the current time (`TimeOfDay`) until it is seen to exceed the alarm time (`myTime`); note this is not a good method for dealing with an alarm since it will hog the PC's processor until alarm time, but it will do for the purpose of demonstration. When the alarm time arrives, the delegate `myResponse` is called, and `myMessage` is passed to it.

Following the class definition comes three different subs, each of which matches the signature of the `AlarmCall` delegate. We can pass the address of any of these three subs into the delegate via the `AlarmClock` class constructor. Now in Sub `Main()`, we can create an `AlarmClock` object, tell it when to generate an alarm, what message to send with it, and what sub to execute.

The point that this simple application is making is that it is possible to call a sub that has been written some time after the code that calls it. That is exactly what an event-handler on a form does, and as you might guess, the delegate mechanism is central to the way that event-handlers work.

8.8.1 Wiring up event-handlers

It is now possible to see how the Form Designer does the job of attaching event-handlers to controls. Recall that a control added to a form is declared using the `WithEvents` keyword:

```
Friend WithEvents Button1 As System.Windows.Forms.Button
```

Also, when you create an event-handler in a form module, the `Handles` keyword is added to its declaration to indicate what events it will respond to (Listing 8.18).

```
Private Sub Button1_Click(ByVal sender As System.Object, _
                          ByVal e As System.EventArgs) _
                        Handles Button1.Click
      'Event handling code goes here.
   End Sub
```

Listing 8.18: A generated event-handler

As you select events within a form's Code window and the Form Designer generates the appropriate outlines for their event-handlers, the code that is generated automatically inserts the addresses of the event-handlers into the control objects to ensure the link between control and event is made. Event-handlers are special Delegate types that are defined for each type of control that can be placed on a form and for the form class itself.

8.9 Visual Inheritance

We've seen how useful inheritance can be in the creation of new classes that can inherit the data and behaviour of existing classes. *Visual inheritance* is analogous to this in form design. To use it, you first create a Class Library that includes a form design and compile this (Visual Studio will create a dll (Dynamic Link Library) file. By then adding this library to a new project, the form design included in the class library will be available as an inherited form in the new application. Any controls of code you added to the form design in the Class Library will be present on the inherited form.

For example, you might decide that every dialog box you create in a new application should have an OK and a Cancel button like the ones used in `dlgPerson` in Figure 8.9; this is a sensible decision since users will have a consistent way of dismissing every dialog box that they meet in the application. Instead of having to add the buttons to every dialog box, set their and the form's properties to configure them and associate them with the form's dialog actions, and then add click event-handlers to trigger the closing of the form, we can create a new form design that is already set up in this way, and inherit from it.

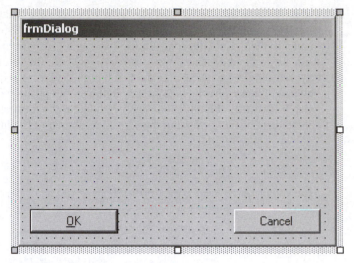

Figure 8.10   A standard form of Dialog Box

The easiest starting point for a Visual Form design that you can inherit from is to start a new WinForms project and configure the default form in this to be the form you will inherit from. The form design shown in Figure 8.10 is that for a simple dialog box with OK and Cancel buttons.

The required property settings are shown in Table 8.4.

Figure 8.10 shows a standard design for a dialog box. Buttons have been given a suitable size and position to be OK and Cancel buttons (Windows users expect these buttons at the bottom of a dialog box, with OK to the left and Cancel to the right),

Table 8.4   Property settings for the `frmDialog` inherited form

Control	Property	Setting
Form	Name	frmDialog
	ContextMenu	(none)
	AcceptButton	btnOK (Note – must add and rename the button before making this setting)
	CancelButton	btnCancel (Note – must add and rename the button before making this setting)
Button	Name	btnOK
	Caption	&OK
	Anchor	Bottom, Left
	DialogResult	OK
Button	Name	btnCancel
	Caption	Cancel
	Anchor	Bottom, Right
	DialogResult	Cancel

and have had their `DialogResult` properties set appropriately. The form has been associated with them by setting its `AcceptButton` and `CancelButton` properties to refer to them. Luckily, controls also have an `Anchor` property that is used to make them stay a fixed distance away from two edges of the form they are on: this property, set to `Bottom, Left` for the OK button, and `Bottom, Right` for the Cancel button will make sure the buttons stay in the proper position relative to the form even when it is resized. Finally, code can be added to the form class to make the buttons able to dismiss the form from the screen, as shown in Listing 8.19.

```
Public Class frmDialog
    Inherits System.Windows.Forms.Form

[+] │Windows Form Designer generated code│

    Private Sub btnOK_Click(ByVal sender As System.Object, _
                            ByVal e As System.EventArgs) _
                            Handles btnOK.Click
        Me.Hide()
    End Sub

    Private Sub btnCancel_Click(ByVal sender As System.Object, _
                            ByVal e As System.EventArgs) _
                            Handles btnCancel.Click
        Me.Hide()
    End Sub
End Class
```

Listing 8.19: The code needed for the `frmDialog` class

Once the form design is complete to your satisfaction, you can test the project to ensure all is ok. When it runs, you should be able to dismiss the form by pressing either of the buttons. Now, to convert this into a form that you can inherit, go to the Project Properties dialog (select the project in the solution explorer and then **Project→Properties** from the menus) and in the Common Properties, General page, change the **Output Type** to **Class Library** as shown in Figure 8.11.

Finally, Build the Assembly (**Build→Build Solution** from the menus) and close the solution down. You can now test the inherited form by creating a new project and Inheriting a form.

Create a new WinForms project. To add the inherited form, right click on the project in the Solution Explorer, and select **Add→Inherited Form** from the context menu. In the dialog box that appears, make sure **Local Project Items** is selected in the left hand pane, and **Inherited Form** is selected on the right hand one. Give the new form a name (e.g. **dlgTest**) and click **Open**. The dialog box that appears now may look initially as if you are being warned of an error, but click on its Browse button and then navigate your way to the folder that contains the project with the dialog box design – choose the DLL file from the BIN folder to reference the Class Library, and select the form design from that project.

A new form matching the design you saved to inherit from will have been added to the project. Controls on the form will be marked with a tiny 'inherited forms' icon

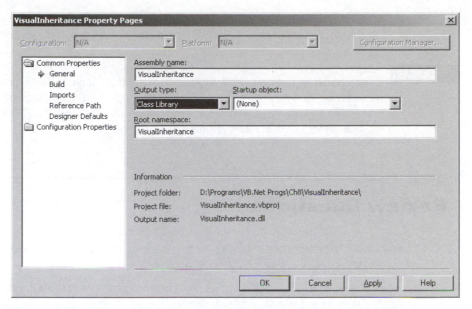

Figure 8.11 Changing the Project Output type

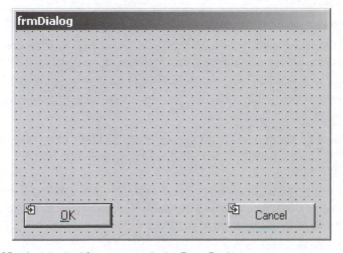

Figure 8.12 An inherited form as seen in the Form Designer

to remind you that you should not try to change them, as shown in Figure 8.12. From here you can continue to add controls, configure their properties and add code as with any WinForms form.

Here we have looked at the fundamentals of WinForms modules, their roots in inheritance and the various mechanisms that the Visual Studio forms designer uses to manage the interplay between visual design and generated code. In the next chapter, we will go on to look in detail at the range of controls that can be added to a form, and strategies for creating interactions between controls and objects.

Exercise 8.10

One good use of visual inheritance is to create a standard look among all the forms in an application – e.g. a corporate logo or version message. Create a new Form class as described above, and add a label that describes it as your form style. Try it in a test program.

Review Questions

1. Creating a WinForms application involves writing code to manage more complex interactions than would be necessary in a Console application. Why is this?

2. It is often preferable to develop a complex WinForms program as a two-tier application. Name and outline the purpose of each tier in such a system.

3. Visual Studio provides a range of common-dialog box forms that can be used in an application. Describe how a typical common dialog form (such as the Save File dialog) differs from a normal Windows form.

4. What is a control, and how does it differ from a software component?

5. What determines the order in which input focus moves around the controls on a form? How can this order be changed at design-time? How can it be changed at run time?

6. Often, event-handler code is written with no reference to the parameters passed to a handler. What are these parameters for? Describe a typical set of information passed in the e parameter of an event-handler sub.

7. What is the quickest way to generate an event-handler for the default event of a control (e.g. a button's _Click event)? How can event-handlers for events that are not the default event be generated?

8. Much of the code generated to configure a form at design time is hidden in a code region in the form's Code window. What is the purpose of this code region? Are you allowed to add code manually to the normally hidden code region?

9. Describe the purpose of the WithEvents keyword.

10. How does a dialog box form differ from a normal WinForm?

11. How is the result of a dialog box returned to a statement that displays it? What other controls are involved and how are these configured to interact with the dialog box?

12. What property of a form allows you to programmatically manipulate every control on it?

13. What is a delegate, and what purpose do delegates play in dealing with events on a form?

14. List the benefits of visual inheritance, and describe how it is related to code inheritance.

Practical Activities

A Words-Per-Minute calculator

In this activity, we'll get a chance to use some of the more common WinForms controls to build a small but practical application. The words-per-minute (or WPM) calculator will time the user as he or she types and produce a continuously updated display of elapsed time, words typed and approximate words-per-minute typing rate. To do this, we'll create a class that will handle the basic calculations and keep track of elapsed time during a test, and link this to a form that will accept user input and display results.

Activity 1: Starting a WinForms project

The first thing we need to do is to create a new WinForms project. Run Visual Studio and select **File/New/Project** . . . from the menus. When the New Project dialog box appears, be sure to select a Windows application and enter a suitable name and location for the program (**WPMCalculator** will describe it well). This is illustrated in Figure A8.1.

Since this will be a single form application, we will add the class code described in the next section to the form module. The default form will be our user-interface.

Activity 2: The `WPMTimer` class

Now we need to figure out how to calculate words-per-minute. In theory, this is very simple, since all we need is a measure of the period of time in minutes and the number of words typed over that time: divide one by the other and we have the

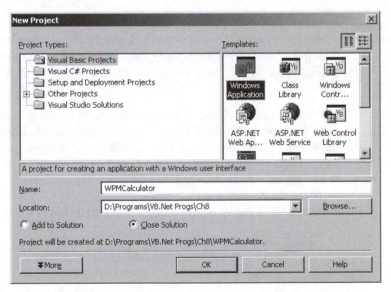

Figure A8.1   Starting the WinForms program

WPM result. In practice, we would need to do a lot of typing to get an accurate measure because whole minutes are quite long periods of time. The measured WPM would be zero for the whole of the first minute, and would only be updated at one minute intervals. To make the calculation provide results in real-time, we can instead measure the number of words continuously and do the calculation based on the elapsed number of seconds. WPM would then be calculated as:

(number of words × 60) / elapsed time in seconds

This will give us a WPM count that can be updated second by second. The next problem is how to calculate the number of words typed. Typing into a `TextBox` control will give us a single string which we need to break up into separate words. Recall from the calculator program done as a practical activity in Chapter 4 that we could use the `Split()` string method to break up a string into substrings, using specified characters to indicate the boundaries to break the string up on. In that exercise, `Split()` was used to convert an arithmetic expression into separate numbers and operators. Here, we can use the same principle to break text into words. We can work out the approximate number of words in a string by performing the operation shown in Listing A8.1.

```
Dim words As Array
Dim separators() As Char = {" "}
words = mvarText.Split(separators)
WordCount = words.Length()
```

Listing A8.1: Working out a word count

Note that we are using a space as the word separator. When there are double spaces (e.g. after a sentence), this method will produce empty cells in the array that will count as extra words. The word count will be inaccurate, but not disastrously so.

Exercise A8.1

We can improve the accuracy in calculating the number of words by working through the words array counting only non-empty word strings. Work out the code for doing this (hint: a `For..Each` loop will be useful).

Working out the elapsed time is made simple by the presence of the `TimeSpan` class available in the .NET framework. This class describes objects for calculating the length of a period of time (e.g. the difference between two dates or times), and so does exactly what we need. The general strategy will be to record the start time (when typing commences) and then periodically calculate a `TimeSpan` from this to work out the elapsed time.

Listing A8.2 shown the class that will do the WPM calculations.

```
Class WPMTimer
    Private mvarStartTime As Date  'Time that calculations start
    Private mvarText As String     'Text containing words
    Public Sub New()
        mvarStartTime = Now        'Record the current time
    End Sub
```

```
                'Text property contains the words...
                Public Property Text() As String
                    Get
                        Return mvarText
                    End Get
                    Set(ByVal Value As String)
                        mvarText = Value
                    End Set
                End Property
                'Work out word count by breaking up the text...
                Public ReadOnly Property WordCount() As Integer
                    Get
                        Dim words As Array
                        Dim separators() As Char = {" "}
                        words = mvarText.Split(separators)
                        Return words.Length()
                    End Get
                End Property
                'Word out how long since this object was constructed...
                Public Function ElapsedTime() As TimeSpan
                    Return Now.Subtract(mvarStartTime)
                End Function
                'Work out the WPM...
                Public ReadOnly Property WPM() As Integer
                    Get
                        Try 'Possible divide by zero error here...
                            Return (WordCount() * 60) / _
                                    ElapsedTime.Seconds
                        Catch ex As OverflowException
                            Return 0
                        End Try
                    End Get
                End Property
            End Class
```

Listing A8.2: The `WPMTimer` class

To perform a WPM calculation, we will simply create an object of the `WPMTimer` class as soon as typing commences, and periodically update its `Text` property to set the words to count. The `ElapsedTime()` function and the `WordCount` and `WPM` properties will then return the results we will display.

Activity 3: Designing the form

The main control on the `WPMCalculator` form will be a `TextBox` with its `MultiLine` property set to `True` so that it can display a large block of text. Apart from this, we will need only buttons to `Stop` and `Reset` a typing trial, and some `Label` controls for displaying results. The form layout is shown in Figure A8.2.

To create this form, add controls and set properties as shown in Table A8.1.

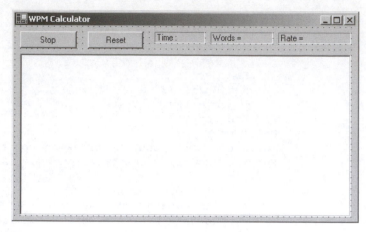

Figure A8.2 Form layout for the WPMCalculator

Table A8.1 Controls on the WPMCalculator form, and their settings

Control	Property	Setting	Comment
Form	Name	frmWPM	Programmatic name for the form
	Text	"WPMCalculator"	Caption on the form
TextBox	Name	txtTypeText	The user's typing area
	Text	" " \<blank\>	The initial text when the control is first displayed
	Multiline	True	Allows text to be entered and displayed over a number of lines
	Anchor	Top, Bottom, Left, Right	Sets the edges of the TextBox so that they stay a fixed distance from the edges of the form (TextBox resizes with form)
Button	Name	btnStop	Used to stop the timer so that WPM count does not continue
	Text	"Stop"	Caption on the button
	Enabled	False	Initially disable the button
Button	Name	btnReset	Used to reset the WPM count by destroying the WPMTimer and disabling the Stop button
	Text	"Reset"	Caption on the button
Label	Name	lblTime	Display element for time
	Text	"Time ="	Initial display text
Label	Name	lblWords	Display element for word count
	Text	"Words ="	Display text
Label	Name	lblRate	Display element for WPM count
	Text	"Rate ="	Display text
Timer	Name	Tick	A Timer control to initiate periodic WPM calculations
	Interval	500	500 milli-seconds, so the timer will fire the Tick event twice a second
	Enabled	False	Initially the timer is disabled (default)

Once you have added and set the controls on the form as per Table A8.1, run the application and make sure the `TextBox` resizes as you would expect it to (it should maintain an even distance to all four form edges as the form is resized). Note that the `Timer` control is configured to fire a `Tick` event every half-second. This will ensure that the seconds count in the elapsed time display is up to date.

We can now go on to the final stage, which is to create event-handlers to perform the operations necessary to manage a WPM count.

Activity 4: Event-handlers for the form

All of the event-handlers on the form will have some effect on a `WMPTimer` object, and so we will need to declare this as a `Private` form member variable. Immediately after the class code (i.e. after `End Class`), add the statement:

```
Private T As WPMTimer
```

This will be the reference variable that will allow access to an instance of the `WPMTimer` class for performing calculations. All of the manipulations of this object will be in response to events from the form controls. The events we need to deal with are:

1. The user presses a key while the `TextBox` is in focus. This will create a new `WPMTimer` object and initiate WPM calculation if the event has not been fired before. Otherwise, it will do nothing. It is much easier for the user to simply start counting at the first key-press than to expect the user to press a button and then start typing. The Stop button should also be enabled so the user can end the WPM timing and calculation

2. The `Timer` control fires a `Tick` event every half-second. This will cause the `WPMTimer` object to recalculate elapsed time, word count and WPM values for display on the form. The appropriate values will be transferred to the Label controls

3. The user presses the Stop button. This should disable the timer to stop WPM calculations from being made and the display from being updated

4. The user presses the Reset button. This should return the program to its initial state, disabling the Stop button and destroying the `WPMTimer` object.

Coding for these (and the `WPMTimer` variable declaration) is shown in Listing A8.3. Remember that you should not enter the first or last lines of an event-handler, but simply double-click on the control that is to fire the event, and for non-default events, select the control and event from the combo boxes at the top of the Code window.

```
    :
Private T As WPMTimer

Private Sub txtTypeText_KeyPress(ByVal sender As Object, _
        ByVal e As System.Windows.Forms.KeyPressEventArgs) _
        Handles txtTypeText.KeyPress
```

```
        If Not Tick.Enabled Then
            T = New WPMTimer()
            Tick.Enabled = True
            btnStop.Enabled = True
        End If
End Sub

Private Sub btnStop_Click(ByVal sender As System.Object, _
                          ByVal e As System.EventArgs) _
                          Handles btnStop.Click
    Tick.Enabled = False
End Sub

Private Sub Tick_Tick(ByVal sender As System.Object, _
                      ByVal e As System.EventArgs) _
                      Handles Tick.Tick
    T.Text = txtTypeText.Text
    lblTime.Text = "Time : " & _
          Format(T.ElapsedTime.Minutes, "00") & ":" & _
          Format(T.ElapsedTime.Seconds, "00")
    lblWords.Text = "Words = " & T.WordCount
    lblRate.Text = "Rate = " & T.WPM() & "wpm."
End Sub

Private Sub btnReset_Click(ByVal sender As System.Object,
ByVal e As System.EventArgs) Handles btnReset.Click
    T = Nothing
    btnStop.Enabled = False
End Sub
```

Listing A8.3: Coding for the event-handlers for the form

Coding for the form is now complete, and you can go on to test the operation of the WPM Calculator program. When the program starts up, the cursor should be flashing in the text box ready for you to type (if it is not, go back to the form in design mode and rearrange the TabIndex values for the controls using **View/ TabOrder** from the menus). The TextBox should have the lowest TabIndex value). As soon as you begin to type, the displays should proceed to update, and will maintain a reasonable estimate of your WPM typing rate until you either stop typing (at which the WPM value will decrease as the number of words remains the same while elapsed time increases) or press the Stop button (at which the various measures displayed on the form will be frozen). In use, the form should appear as shown in Figure A8.3.

This completes the development of the WPM Calculator. Although simple, it demonstrates the type of interactions that you will normally create between business and user-interface objects in an application.

Features worth remembering

- Where possible, you should avoid performing calculations in code on forms. This serves only to tie the functional part of a system to the user-interface, which reduces the scope for maintenance and upgrading.

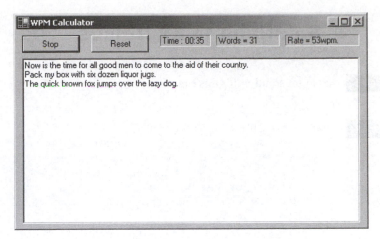

Figure A8.3 The WPMCalculator in use

- The Anchor property is a useful tool for making user-interfaces resizable. While some form styles (particularly dialog boxes) will have no use for this feature, it will improve the professional appearance of forms where the main display elements are such that they can be resized.

- Enabling and disabling controls as appropriate can make things much easier for the user. When a button or other control is disabled (by setting the Enabled property to False), it acts as a cue to the user, effectively saying 'this option is not available just now'.

- Complex calculations, such as the number of words in a string and the time that has elapsed since a particular event, are easily handled by built-in .NET facilities (the the **String/Split**() method and the **TimeSpan** class for these specific examples). It is well worth becoming familiar with the .NET framework to identify classes that perform tasks that you might otherwise do by writing a lot of complex code.

Suggested Additional Activities

1. In Exercise A8.1 it was suggested that you try to write code that would perform a more accurate word count. Try to incorporate this improvement into the application.

2. One useful feature would be to record WPM calculations over a session with the program. There are several ways that this could be done, but perhaps the easiest would be to modify the **WPMTimer** class so that it could be stopped (it would be necessary to record the stop time in a member variable) and then add the object to a collection. This would provide scope for displaying a series of **WPMTimer** objects with settings calculated over a number of trials, and possibly adding a custom dialog box to display and compare these values.

Solutions to Exercises

Exercise 8.1

No set solution for this exercise.

Exercise 8.2

```
Private Sub btnCalc_Click( _
                    ByVal sender As System.Object, _
                    ByVal e As System.EventArgs) _
                    Handles btnCalc.Click
    Dim report As String
    'Place the values from the form controls into the
    'TC object...
    TC.GrossIncome = Val(txtGrossIncome.Text)
    TC.Married = chkMarried.Checked
    TC.DependentChildren = _
                    CType(cboNumChildren.Text, Integer)
    TC.ExtraAllowances = Val(txtExtraAllowances.Text)
    'Now that the TC object has all the relevant data,
    'it can perform the calculations.
    'Show the results of the tax calculations...
    report = "Taxable Income (annual) = " & _
                    TC.TaxableIncome & Environment.NewLine
    report += "Total tax (annual) = " & _
                    TC.Tax & Environment.NewLine
    report += "Annual income after tax = " & _
                    TC.IncomeAfterTax & Environment.NewLine
    report += "Monthly income after tax = " & _
                    Format(TC.IncomeAfterTax / 12, "£0.00")
    txtResult.Text = report
End Sub
```

Note that this approach is much closer to the console program's approach to calculating tax – collect all the data and then process and produce the output.

Exercise 8.3

a) The form and all the components it contains make up the presentation, or user-interface tier. The `TaxCalc` class and the resulting TC object make up the business tier.

b) They are organized so that the user-interface tier is responsible for creating the business tier and initiating all its actions.

Exercise 8.4

a) It would be impossible for Microsoft to anticipate and provide every possible form of user-interface that you might need in applications – in fact the entire point of a development environment like Visual Studio is that you are given the components to build user-interfaces to your own specification. Common dialog boxes perform services that are needed in many applications (i.e. common services – hence the name).

b) The standard common dialog boxes provide a simple and clear interface to what would otherwise be difficult to develop and used services. By mimicking the way Microsoft has organized the programmers' interfaces for these dialogs, you can develop forms for your own applications that are similarly easy to use (within limits, since you are more likely to want to deal with application specific objects rather than simple values such as colour numbers or file names – however, the `PrintDialog` behaviour is a good example of providing a simple interface to a complex user-interface for a complex object).

Exercise 8.5

The windows focus allows a programmer to (1) control the standard order for entering application data into a user interface (by setting a specific tab-order), (2) directly manipulate the focus so that a given action can cause the focus to jump past an un-needed control and (3) cause the focus to return to a control when an invalid value has been entered into it.

Exercise 8.6

Several events can be used to trigger appropriate behaviour for inputs to a control. For a text box, the most useful options are (1) the `Validating` and `Validated` events, (2) the `LostFocus` event and (3) the `KeyPressed` event, since in each case, these events can be used to signal that the user has done something to move from that control to another (`Validating` is triggered when the user chooses to exit from a control and allows code to check that valid data has been entered, `Validated` is triggered once it has been determined that the data in the control is valid according to the code in the `Validating` event-handler, `LostFocus` triggers when the focus (cursor) is moved from a control to another control and `KeyPressed` is triggered by each key-press while the control has the focus (so individual key-strokes can be checked). Of these, the `Validated` event is possibly the most useful, and this could be coded as:

```
Private Sub txtResult_Validated(ByVal sender As Object, _
                        ByVal e As System.EventArgs) _
                        Handles txtResult.Validated
    txtResult.Text += "."
End Sub
```

Exercise 8.7

There are several reasons for altering a control as a program runs. For example, you may wish to enable or disable a control depending on the current state of data in the program (disallowing an application for an overdraft when a customer has reached the overdraft limit, for example), alter the colour of a control to indicate status, change the size of control as the form that contains it is stretched to a new size etc.

Exercise 8.8

a) It would have to be displayed and processed after the first modal dialog has been dealt with.

b) Since this form is displaying modal dialog boxes, it must have been displayed using the standard `Show()` method, which is not modal.

c) Yes it could. It would be necessary to import the Form module in which the dialog was implemented into the console program's main module, but this is easily possible.

Exercise 8.9

a) One disadvantage is that the form code will always be included whenever the business class code is used. Since the business class code can be used with an alternative user-interface (e.g. a console or web-based user-interface), this means that the form code may be taking up memory unnecessarily.

b) The main advantage would be that the form class would always be available when the business class was, making it easy to incorporate user-interactions *in a WinForms application*. However, the main disadvantage is that the form will take up memory unconditionally (as described in a), and that this may in turn make it more awkward to make use of an alternative user-interface. Also, a programmer who wanted to use the business class with the form would need to be aware of the need to reference the form's module separately.

Exercise 8.10

No set solution to this activity-based exercise.

Exercise A8.1

```
Dim S As String
WordCount = 0
For Each S In words
    If s <> "" Then
        WordCount += 1
    End If
Next
```

Answers to Review Questions

1. Creating a WinForms application involves writing code to manage more complex interactions than would be necessary in a console application. Why is this? **In a WinForms application, the user is given the option of which controls to interact with in which order, while in a console program the programmer can control the order of interactions since effectively only one input control (the keyboard) is available.**

2. It is often preferable to develop a complex WinForms program as a two-tier application. Name and outline the purpose of each tier in such a system. **User-interface tier: collects and validates user-input, displays output, initiates commands according to user's interactions. Business tier: models the required system features, provides control structure for operations and properties to represent specific system attributes. Also models the structural relationships between system components.**

3. Visual Studio provides a range of common-dialog box forms that can be used in an application. Describe how a typical common dialog form (such as the Save File dialog) differs from a normal Windows form. **The form is pre-designed and can only manage a set range of interactions.**

4. What is a control, and how does it differ from a software component? **A control is a component in an application that has some appearance on the Windows display and can allow the user to interact with it.**

5. What determines the order in which input focus moves around the controls on a form? How can this order be changed at design-time? How can it be changed at run-time? **The `TabIndex` determines the sequence that controls are naturally processed in. At design time, it is possible to edit the tab order by 1) determining the order to place controls on the form 2) changing the `TabIndex` property of individual controls and 3) invoking the `View-Tab Order` command in the Form Designer.**

6. Often, event-handler code is written with no reference to the parameters passed to a handler. What are these parameters for? Describe a typical set of information passed in the e parameter of an event-handler sub. **The parameters provide a way for the event code to 1) determine which control caused the event-handler to fire, and 2) access specific values that accompany an event, such as the code of the key pressed or the position of the mouse cursor.**

7. What is the quickest way to generate an event-handler for the default event of a control (e.g. a button's-Click event)? How can event-handlers for events that are not the default event be generated? **Double-click on the surface of the control on the Form Designer.**

8. Much of the code generated to configure a form at design time is hidden in a code region in the form's Code window. What is the purpose of this code region? Are you allowed to add code manually to the normally hidden code region? **The code in this region defines the controls on a form (their properties and names) and creates and sets up the form at run-time. Yes – it can be edited and added to, but it is best only to do this advisedly, since otherwise it is possible to break the code.**

9. Describe the purpose of the `WithEvents` keyword. **This keyword indicates that a specific object can fire events that may be received by event-handlers in the containing object (usually a form).**

10. How does a dialog box form differ from a normal WinForm? **A dialog box is displayed modally, which means that it must be removed from the screen before processing can continue beyond the statement that first displayed it on the screen.**

11. How is the result of a dialog box returned to a statement that displays it? What other controls are involved and how are these configured to interact with the dialog box? **The result of the `ShowDialog()` method indicates which control was used to close the dialog box. Several controls can be placed on a dialog box and nominated in the form's properties as generating specific dialog results.**

12. What property of a form allows you to programmatically manipulate every control on it? **The `Controls` property.**

13. What is a delegate, and what purpose do delegates play in dealing with events on a form? **A delegate is a place-holder for a method with a specific signature. An event is designed to call on an as-yet undefined sub by associating it with a matching delegate. At run time (or in the Form Designer) a real code routine can be nominated to handle a specific event provided it matches the event's delegate.**

14. List the benefits of visual inheritance, and describe how it is related to code inheritance. **Visual inheritance makes it possible to pre-define a style of form, with certain controls and code already in place. This can be used to specify common behaviour for a range of forms. It is related to code inheritance since the exact same mechanisms are used to create it – a form is visually designed and as a consequence, the Form Designer's hidden code region has code added to it to specify its look and behaviour.**

CHAPTER

9

WinForms Controls in Detail

In this chapter, you will learn:

- properties, methods and events for the controls you will use most frequently;
- how to use WinForms controls for command input and data entry;
- helping the user to deal with lists and collections;
- how to access the controls on a form collectively;
- adding controls as a program runs;
- adding event-handlers as a program runs;
- how to use graphics in WinForms programs.

9.1   Windows Controls

Since version 1 of Visual Basic, a range of standard controls has been available to allow you to create user-interfaces to enhance the usability of a program. VB has always had a high profile in this area simply because it was the first development environment for Windows that allowed a programmer to create the user-interface graphically; using other programming environments of the time, you would develop a user-interface by writing lines of code to create controls, set their size and position on a form and make any settings that altered their appearance or behaviour.

Visual Studio makes Windows controls, now called WinForms controls, available from the Toolbox, and you normally add them to a form using a drag and drop operation. During the design stages of a WinForms application, you can alter the default settings for a control using the Properties window, and each type of control has its own range of property settings that appear in this window, in addition to a range of settings that are common to most of the WinForms controls you will use.

9.1.1   Common Properties, Methods and Events for WinForms controls

All WinForms controls have properties, methods and events: you might expect this since a control is simply a class that has been given extra functionality so that it can be manipulated at design time using Form Designer windows and the Properties window. Some of the properties, methods and events in a control are specific to that type of control, such as the `Interval` property, `Start` method and `Tick` event of the `Timer` control, while others are common to a range of controls. The most useful of these are described in Tables 9.1 to 9.3.

9.1.2 Common Properties

Table 9.1 Properties common to most WinForms controls

Property	Purpose	Typical Setting
Name	This is the key property of any control. A control's name is used to identify it in program code. Visual Studio provides a unique default name for each control as soon as you add it. It is recommended that you provide controls that you intend to refer to in code with a name that reflects their meaning	**txtUserName** (a text box to accept the user's name) **btnCancel** (a button that acts as a cancel button for a form or cancels an operation)
Anchor	This very useful property allows you to nominate which edges of a form the control will maintain a fixed distance from. It defaults to `Top, Left,` but changing the `Anchor` setting makes creating a form that resizes nicely much easier. See also the `Dock` property	**Bottom, Left** This setting will make sure that when you resize the form, the control will stay a fixed distance from the bottom and left-hand edge of it
BackColor	Sets the background colour of a control. By default, most controls have a light grey `BackColor`, which makes them match the default form colour scheme. The property is a value of type `Color`, which can be one of a range of predefined settings or a ARGB value (Alpha, Red, Green, Blue)	**DarkTurquoise** This setting is a predefined Web Colour. System and Custom colours can also be assigned
BorderStyle	This applies to `TextBox`, `Label` and `LinkLabel` controls, and indicates how these will appear on a form	**Fixed3D** Other possible values are 'None' and 'FixedSingle'
ContextMenu	This property allows a 'right-click' menu to be associated with the control. For example, a `ContextMenu` associated with a `TextBox` might provide `copy`, `cut` and `paste` commands	**mnuEditCommands** This is a reference to a `ContextMenu` object added to the form
Cursor	This property defines the appearance of the mouse cursor as it moves over the control. A range of preset types is provided	**IBeam** This setting would be used with a `TextBox` control to make the cursor appear as an I-beam text cursor
Dock	This property causes a control to attach to the length of one edge of its container (the form or a `Frame` or `Panel` control) or to fill its container's area. There are six available options, these being `None`, `Left`, `Top`, `Bottom`, `Right` and `Fill`.	**Bottom** This setting will make a control dock to the length of the bottom edge of a container

Table 9.1 (cont'd)

Propert	Purpose	Typical Setting
	Using the `Dock` property, a control can be made to resize along with its container	
Enabled	This property sets whether a control will respond to the user's interactions or not. A disabled control will be 'greyed out' to provide a visual cue to the user	**True** The control will respond to the user's interactions
Font	By default, a control will display text in the same font as its container. The `Font` property can be used to make the text in certain controls stand out, or simply to change its size or weight. The `Font` property has a number of sub-properties; `Bold`, `Size`, etc.	**Microsoft Sans Serif, 8.25pt** This setting would be made by setting individual component properties (**Name** is 'Microsoft Sans Serif', **Size** is '8.25', **Unit** is 'Point')
ForeColor	This determines the colour that text or graphics on a control will appear in	**ControlText** This setting indicates that the control will have a foreground colour the same as the text on standard buttons, etc. (normally Black)
Image	This is used to specify a bitmap image (a Windows bmp file or metafile) to display in the control. Typically, small bitmapped images are used to enhance the appearance of a control	**System.Drawing.Bitmap** This text will appear in the Property window for the `Image` property alongside a tiny picture of the image used.
Location	This is a `Point` type (with X and Y components) that indicates the position of the top, left of a control relative to the top, left of its container (`Form`, `Panel` or `Frame`)	**24, 16** The control here would be 24 pixels from the left and 16 from the top of the client area of the form it was on
Modifiers	This indicates the access specifier used in declaring a control, and therefore what objects can 'see' it	**Friend** This is the default setting for a control, so that a control on a form can be accessed from any code within an assembly
Size	This represents the `Height` and `Width` of a control in pixels	**75, 23**
TabIndex	This indicates the position in the tab order that a control has. The first control to receive the focus on a form will have a `TabIndex` of 0	**8**
TabStop	This indicates whether the control can take the focus.	**True**
Text	This is the text that will be shown on the face of a control	**Button1**
Visible	This indicates whether a control will appear on a form or not, and controls its visibility	**True** This setting indicates that the control will be displayed

All of the properties listed above can be set using the Properties window at design time, and most can also be accessed and changed as a program runs. For example, the `Size` property of a control can be set in the Properties window or by statements in program code, and can also be altered while a program is running to resize the control. However, while the `Font` property of a form or control can be accessed by program code so that we can find out style, point size, etc., the font settings cannot be changed at run time.

Most controls also have properties that do not appear in the Properties window at design time, but which can be accessed or altered at run time. There are various reasons why a property might not be available at design time; for example, a `TextBox` has a number of properties to do with selected text (text that has been highlighted for a `Cut` or `Copy` operation) that would have no purpose at design time. These properties are there to be manipulated by code in the same way as the properties we have defined for simple classes.

9.1.2.1 The `Name` Property

Most of the properties in Table 9.1 have some effect on the appearance of a control on a form. Some (e.g. `Anchor`, `Dock`, `TabStop`, `ContextMenu`) will affect the way a control behaves at run time in some way, while others (`Name`, `Modifiers`) are specifically there to affect the way you write code to interact with the control. A control's name is the identifier that you use when referring to it in program code, e.g. Listing 9.1.

```
Private Sub btnGetData_Click(ByVal sender As System.Object, _
                          ByVal e As System.EventArgs) _
                          Handles btnGetData.Click
    Dim address As String
    address = txtAddress.Text
    'go on to process address data
    '...
End Sub
```

Listing 9.1: Accessing a control by name

In Listing 9.1, `txtAddress` is the name of a `TextBox`, and the code will assign the text entered into it to a `String` variable. While this code would work perfectly well regardless of the `Modifiers` setting for the control, the control requires a setting of `Friend` or `Public` to make it possible to access the text box's text from another form, as for example in Listing 9.2.

```
Private Sub btnGetCustInfo_Click(ByVal sender As
                          System.Object, _
                          ByVal e As System.EventArgs) _
                          Handles btnGetCustInfo.Click
    Dim f As New frmCustomer()
    Dim address As String
    If f.ShowDialog(Me) = DialogResult.OK Then
```

```
        address = f.txtAddress.Text
        'go on to process address data
        '...
    End If
End Sub
```

Listing 9.2: Accessing a control on another form by name

The code in Listing 9.2 depends on `txtAddress` being accessible to another module. Since controls added to a form have a `Modifiers` setting of `Friend` by default, this is not a problem.

Exercise 9.1

a) The code in Listing 9.2 retrieves the current text setting from a `TextBox` control on a dialog box. Given that the `Text` property of a `TextBox` is a read/write property, how would you go about setting the text in a text box on the form f to read "Hello"?

b) Assume that the `String` variable `address` currently holds the value "1 High Street". Based on the code in Listing 9.2, how would you go about using the dialog box to allow the user to edit this address?

9.1.2.2 Properties useful for giving the user feedback

Various properties can be used to provide the user of a program with a visual or behavioural cue that indicates whether they are performing an operation properly or not. This is sometimes referred to as 'giving the user feedback'.

The `Enabled` property is an important one since it allows you to stop a control from responding to user interactions (by setting `Enabled` to `False`), and changes the control's appearance to indicate this. This is a rather forthright form of feedback, but is useful where allowing the user to proceed with an operation would result in invalid data. Using the `Enabled` property, you can prevent the user from completing an operation where it would lead to an obvious error; for example, by setting this property for the OK button in a dialog box to `False` initially, and to `True` once the user has entered data into all of the required input controls, we can ensure that the user does not miss entering a value in an *important* field.

Further feedback can be given to the user by changing the `Cursor`, `BackColor` or `Image` properties of controls on a form. Changing the `Cursor` property of a control to `IBeam`, for example, highlights those controls the user is expected to type information into, while setting the `BackColor` of a `TextBox` control to make it stand out can indicate the presence of an input error. Listing 9.3 shows how you could program the `Leave` event of a `TextBox` to set its `BackColor` property and the `Enabled` property of the OK button on a dialog box to make sure the user has entered a valid date:

```
Private Sub txtDate_Leave(ByVal sender As Object, _
                    ByVal e As System.EventArgs) _
                    Handles txtDate.Leave
```

```
              'This event fires when the cursor moves out of the
              'TextBox..
              If Not IsDate(txtDate.Text) Then
                  txtDate.BackColor = System.Drawing.Color.Yellow
                  btnOK.Enabled = False
              Else
                  txtDate.ResetBackColor()
                  btnOK.Enabled = True
              End If
          End Sub
```

Listing 9.3: Using control properties to indicate an error

There are of course many other ways of validating the information entered into a control, but this method is simple and gives the user an easy way to identify errors in input without forcing him or her to correct them immediately.

9.1.3 Common Methods

Table 9.2 Methods common to a number of WinForms controls

Method	Purpose	Example Call
BringToFront	This method puts a control at the front of the ZOrder, which is the setting that indicates whether a control appears behind or in front of others	**imgOnIcon.BringToFront()** This will place an image control on top of any others at the same location on a form
DoDragDrop	Calling this method from a control initiates a drag and drop sequence that will end when the user releases the mouse button over another control	**txtInfo.DoDragDrop(_** **txtInfo.SelectedText,_** **DragDropEffects.Copy)** Starts an operation to drag the text selected in a text box
Hide	This method makes a control invisible and unable to respond to events	**grpEditControls.Hide** Hiding a group box as above will also hide all the controls it contains
FindForm	This method returns a reference to the form that a control is on	**f = txtCustomerName.FindForm** This will set f to refer to the form that the text box is on
Focus	This sets the input focus to (or selects) the control if it is selectable. The input focus of a control makes it respond to keyboard events (for example, placing a cursor in a text box)	**txtOrderDate.Focus** This will place a cursor in the text box

Table 9.2   (cont'd)

Method	Purpose	Example Call

GetChildAtPoint	This will return a reference to any control that is at the given point on a container control, or `Nothing`	`c = grpDataEntry.`
		`GetChildAtPoint(_`
		`    New Point(100,100))`
		This will set `c` to `Nothing`, or make it refer to the control directly under the point 100, 100 within a group box

GetContainerControl	This will return a reference to a control's container control. Often this will be the form that the control is placed on, but can also be a `GroupBox`, `PictureBox` or `Panel` that can contain controls	`c = chkOption1.`
		`GetContainerControl`
		This will return a reference to a `GroupBox`, `Panel`, `PictureBox` or `Form` that contains the control

Invalidate	Causes a `Paint` message to be sent to a control (i.e. fires the `Paint` event), to force a redraw. The call can optionally include an indication of the area that is to be repainted	`frmPaper.Invalidate(New _`
		`Rectangle(100,100,50,50))`
		Forces a 50 × 50 area or the form at location 100, 100 to be redrawn

ResetBackColor, ResetCursor, ResetFont, ResetForeColor, ResetText	These methods will reset the various settings for a control to the default value of the setting (i.e. that assigned when the control is first created)	`txtPassword.ResetBackColor` This will restore the text box's background to white
Show	This method displays a control, and is equivalent to setting the control's `Visible` property to `True`	`btnOK.Show` The button will become visible on a form

SuspendLayout, ResumeLayout	These methods are used to bracket a sequence of updates to a control to suppress the control's appearance being updated multiple times. This speeds up the updating	`lstCustomers.SuspendLayout`
		`For Each C in`
		`CustomerCollection`
		`  lstCustomers.Items.Add(C)`
		`Next`
		`lstCustomers.ResumeLayout`
		This code will add all members of a collection to a list box with only a single screen update

ToString	Returns a String representation of an object. If the base method is not overridden, this method will return the class name as a string	`txtCustInfo.Text =`
		`C.ToString()`
		This will display information on the `Customer` object, `C`, in a text box. If the class has not overridden `ToString()`, it will display the class name

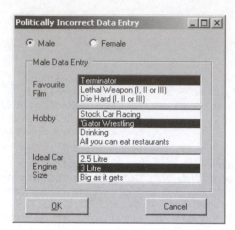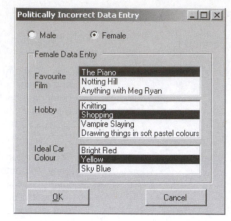

Figure 9.1 Using a `GroupBox` control and the `BringToFront()` method

9.1.3.1 Controlling a control's visibility

The methods shared by most controls allow us to perform generic operations on all or some of the controls on a form. We can, for example, set whether any control is visible on a form by calling its `Show()` or `Hide()` method, or alter the way that controls are stacked on a form using the `BringToFront()` and `SendToBack()` methods. These methods are particularly useful with Container controls (i.e. controls that can contain other controls) since using `Hide`, for example, will make the container plus all of the controls contained by it invisible. This can be used to good effect to provide alternative sets of input controls depending on some feature selected by the user. For example, Figure 9.1 shows a very sexist data input form.

`GroupBox` controls are used to group a number of individual controls together, both to link them visually on a form, and to make it possible to treat them as a group. We can create a 'stack' of group boxes on a form, each containing a set of controls available for various options, by placing them in the same position on the form and making them the same size. Using the `BringToFront` method, we can then quickly bring a specific control to the front. The code to swap between the two `GroupBox` controls that are used to contain the `ListBox` controls shown in Figure 9.1 is short and sweet (Listing 9.4).

```
Private Sub radMale_CheckedChanged( _
                    ByVal sender As System.Object, _
                    ByVal e As System.EventArgs) _
                    Handles radMale.CheckedChanged
    If radMale.Checked Then
        grpMale.BringToFront()
    Else
        grpFemale.BringToFront()
    End If
End Sub
```

Listing 9.4: Switching between two `GroupBox` controls

Note that we only need to bring a group to the front, since any other group will automatically be covered up by it.

9.1.3.2 Controlling updates to the screen

The `Invalidate()` method forces Windows to redraw a control, which is useful if for any reason its graphical content is changed, and the `SuspendLayout()` and `ResumeLayout()` methods can be used to prevent Windows redrawing the contents of a control where a number of changes need to be made. For example, while adding a large number of items to a `ListBox` or a lot of items of text to a `TextBox`, the normal behaviour of Windows to repeatedly update the control's display can greatly slow down a program and make it appear clunky. By bracketing the code that adds the items between `SuspendLayout` and `ResumeLayout` method calls for the control displaying the data, the updates can be made more rapidly and will all appear at once after the `ResumeLayout` call. For example, we can speed up adding a lot of file names to a list box using the code in Listing 9.5.

```
Private Sub ShowFiles()
    Dim f As String
    lstAllFiles.SuspendLayout()
    f = Dir("C:\WINNT\*.*")
    Do Until f = ""
        lstAllFiles.Items.Add(f)
        f = Dir()
    Loop
    lstAllFiles.ResumeLayout()
End Sub
```

Listing 9.5: Using `SuspendLayout` and `ResumeLayout` to speed up updates

Listing 9.5 shows how you would bracket a section of code that performed a large number of screen updates between `SuspendLayout` and `ResumeLayout` to reduce screen update delays. The `Dir()` function will return a list of files that match a specific *file name pattern*, for example "**C:\Documents*.doc**" for all of the document files in the Documents folder on the C: drive. In the first call to it, the file name pattern is passed as a parameter, and all subsequent calls (with no parameter) will return the next file in the list. When the function returns an empty string, there are no files remaining.

The various `ResetXXX` methods (`ResetBackColor()`, `ResetCursor()`, `ResetFont()`, `ResetForeColor()`, `ResetText()`) are useful where a control's appearance is changed at run time to highlight it for some reason, and you then wish to return the control to its normal appearance. Listing 9.3 shows how this can be used.

9.1.3.3 Controlling Drag and Drop operations

The `DoDragDrop` method is used to initiate a drag and drop operation. This is typically used to allow the user to move text or graphics between controls on a form or on different forms. The `DoDragDrop` method is normally executed on a `MouseDown` event of the control form which dragging begins, and the process ends when the form receives a `DragDrop` event from the receiving control. For example, the following code (Listing 9.6) on a form with two text boxes (`txtSource` and `txtDestination`) would allow the user to drag the text from the source text box to the destination one.

```
'This defines what happens when something is 'dropped' ...
Private Sub txtDestination_DragDrop( _
        ByVal sender As System.Object, _
        ByVal e As System.Windows.Forms.DragEventArgs) _
        Handles txtDestination.DragDrop
    txtDestination.Text = _
                e.Data.GetData(DataFormats.Text).ToString
End Sub

'This initiates a 'drag' operation when the mouse button is
'pressed over the text box...
Private Sub txtSource_MouseDown(ByVal sender As
System.Object, _
        ByVal e As System.Windows.Forms.MouseEventArgs) _
        Handles txtSource.MouseDown
    txtSource.DoDragDrop(txtSource.Text, _
    DragDropEffects.Copy)
End Sub

'This provides user feedback by changing the mouse pointer
'while it is dragging over the text box...
Private Sub txtDestination_DragOver( _
        ByVal sender As System.Object, _
        ByVal e As System.Windows.Forms.DragEventArgs) _
        Handles txtDestination.DragOver
    e.Effect = DragDropEffects.Copy
End Sub
```

Listing 9.6: Controlling a drag and drop operation

In Listing 9.6, the user is given visible feedback (`DragDropEffects.Copy`) during the drag and drop operation. While the mouse pointer is being dragged (i.e. with the left button depressed) over the form background and other controls, it will appear as a no-entry sign. When it moves over the destination text box, the pointer will change to a normal pointer with an added '+' sign to indicate that a drop can be made here. Note I have used the explicit control names (`txtSource` and `txtDestination`) instead of the event-handler's name for them (`Sender`) in these events. Either would work, but since `Sender` would be a different control in each event-handler, the controls' names are less confusing.

Drag and drop operations are ideal for moving data from one control to another and can be used between any two controls that support the `DoDragDrop()` method (for the source) and `DragDrop` and `DragOver` events (for the destination).

9.1.4 Common Events

Table 9.3 Events common to a number of WinForms controls

Event	Raised by . . .	Used for . . .
Changed	The 'value' in a control changing	Detecting data updates
Click	The user clicking on a control or form	Command actions, such as a button press or a menu selection
DblClick	The user clicking twice in rapid succession within a small area of a control	Short-cuts to default actions (e.g. used to select a word in a tex tbox)
DragDrop	The user releasing the mouse button while over a control following a drag operation	Copy, cut and paste operations
DragOver	The user moving the mouse over a control during a dragging operation	Providing feedback during a copy, cut and paste operation
Enter	The user moving the focus to a control by mouse or keyboard	Changing the appearance of a control while it is in use (e.g. could change its BackColor to make the current control obvious)
KeyDown, KeyPress, KeyUp	The user pressing a key and releasing it	Reacting to specific key presses or ASCII values
Leave	The user moves the focus from this control to another one	Resetting the appearance of a control
MouseDown, MouseEnter, MouseHover, MouseMove, MouseUp	The user presses on a mouse button (MouseDown), releases a mouse button (MouseUp), moves the mouse cursor on to a control (MouseEnter), holds the mouse cursor over a control (MouseHover) or moves the mouse cursor over a control (MouseMove)	'Tracking' the mouse, e.g. for drawing operations
Paint	Windows raises this event when an area of display including the control or form needs to be redrawn (e.g. after a window has been dragged over it)	Updating the display in program code as needed
Resize	The user changes the size of a form or control, usually by dragging its border	Changing the size or position of items on a form
Validating, Validated	The user is moving the focus to another control (Validating) or all of the validation actions performed in the Validating event handler have completed (Validated).	Checking user input for errors

Every event generated by a WinForms control can be handled by an event-handler in the form's code, and although most controls are capable of generating any of a large number of types of event, in most situations we might decide to handle only one or two of them. Events are most often responses to user interactions, although a line of code manipulating an object can raise an event (e.g. assigning text to a TextBox will raise its Changed() event) and the system can also generate events (e.g. Timer's Tick() events).

9.1.4.1 Events from User-Interactions

From the user we can expect events to do with mouse or keyboard interaction, including events generated by moving a control bar, or pulling down a menu. Mouse events are typically clicks, selections or drags. A user clicks on a button or a menu item to select the command it invokes. Clicking on an input control such as a CheckBox or OptionButton will generally change its selection state, while a click on a ListBox or ComboBox is usually to select an item from the list.

A drag operation is usually done to 'move' data from one control to another, either within the same form or from one form to another. However, you can program a custom type of drag operation to work within a single control, typically a Panel or PictureBox control, for graphical operations. For example, Listing 9.7 below will draw circles on a Panel control on a form.

```
Private Sub Panel1_MouseMove(ByVal sender As Object, _
        ByVal e As System.Windows.Forms.MouseEventArgs) _
        Handles Panel1.MouseMove
    If e.Button = MouseButtons.Left Then
        'Draw a circle radius 10 centred on the cursor
        'position...
        Dim g As Graphics = Panel1.CreateGraphics()
        g.DrawEllipse(Pens.Black, e.X - 10, e.Y - 10, 20, 20)
    End If
End Sub
```

Listing 9.7: Using MouseMove as a drag-style operation to create graphics

Strangely, events are not needed for handling normal keyboard input into a control, since TextBox and similar controls will handle all sorts of user-interactions, including cut, copy and paste, text selection and editing automatically. However, we often need to use keyboard events to filter or validate a user's inputs. For example, Listing 9.8 shows a TextBox event handler that will ensure that only numbers can be entered.

```
Private Sub txtNumber_KeyPress(ByVal sender As Object, _
    ByVal e As System.Windows.Forms.KeyPressEventArgs) _
        Handles txtNumber.KeyPress
    If InStr("0123456789-.", e.KeyChar) = 0 Then
        e.Handled = True
    End If
End Sub
```

Listing 9.8: Using\ the KeyPress event

Note how key-presses are treated in Listing 9.8. The e parameter is specifically for key-press events in this event-handler, and the face value of a key pressed is found in the e.KeyChar member. Using the InStr() function, which tests for the position of one string or character inside another string, we can test for the existence of a numeric key. If a key is not a numeric key, a decimal point or a minus sign, it is marked as being handled, which stops it from being added to the `TextBox`. `KeyDown` and `KeyUp` events are similar except that instead of a `KeyChar` (equivalent to the 'face value' of a keyboard key), the `e` parameter contains key codes. Since several keyboard keys do not have face values (e.g. the function keys and the cursor arrow keys), `KeyDown` and `KeyUp` need to be used to detect these.

Exercise 9.2

A `TextBox` is to be used to accept a user's input of their name. Write a `KeyPressed` event that will allow only alphabetical characters to be entered (note that this should include upper and lower case as well as spaces and the ' character [e.g. O'Brien]).

9.2 Accessing Controls Collectively

Controls placed on a form are added to the form's `Controls` collection. This gives us a simple way to access every control on the form to perform some operation on them collectively. For example, we could write code to change the `BackColor` setting of all the controls on a form (Listing 9.9).

```
Private Sub ChangeColour(ByVal newCol As Color)
     Dim c As Control
     For Each c In Controls
         'Change the BackColor setting of each control...
         c.BackColor = newCol
     Next
End Sub
```

Listing 9.9: Accessing all of the controls on a form

Note that now we have two ways of writing code to manipulate any control on a form. We can access individual controls using the name we have given them at design time (or the default name given when the control was added if we have not since changed it), or we can access controls as part of the `Controls` collection. Of course we can also use selection logic to get the best of both worlds, so that we can choose which members of the controls collection we want to manipulate (see Listing 9.10).

```
Private Sub ChangeColour(ByVal newCol As Color)
     Dim c As Control
     For Each c In Controls
         If TypeOf(c) Is Button Then
             c.BackColor = newCol
         End If
     Next
End Sub
```

Listing 9.10: Accessing particular types of control (including descendants)

In Listing 9.10, the `TypeOf()` function returns a type, which we can test against a specific type using the `Is` keyword to determine if an object is a member of, or is derived from, a given class. This method includes classes related by inheritance (including interface inheritance), so a new class of button derived from the base class `Button` would also have its `BackColor` changed. If we wanted only to affect a single class, we could instead use the `TypeName()` function, which will match a specific class, but not its descendants (Listing 9.11).

```
For Each c In Controls
     If TypeName(c) = "Button" Then
          c.BackColor = newCol
     End If
Next
```

Listing 9.11: Testing for a specific type of control

A subroutine is required to change the foreground colour (`ForeColor`) of every control on a form to a specific colour – `Color.Red`. The form is passed to the sub as the parameter `F As Form`. Write the sub and test it on a simple form design (you can call the sub from a button on the form).

9.3   Command Controls

The simplest controls for providing a way of issuing a command are *buttons* and *menus*. Typically, we use the `Button.Click` event to execute an associated command from a button, although these controls also respond to mouse movements, key-presses, drag and drop and other forms of interaction.

One useful way to get the most from a `Button` control is to make it serve two related and mutually exclusive purposes. For example, a single button can be used to start and stop a `Timer` control. When the timer is currently stopped, the button caption will only be sensible if it says 'start'. Similarly, once the timer has started, a suitable caption is 'stop'. The coding for this is simple and is given in Listing 9.12.

```
Private Sub cmdStartStop_Click(ByVal sender As
                               System.Object, _
                          ByVal e As System.EventArgs) _
                          Handles cmdStartStop.Click
     If cmdStartStop.Text = "Start" Then
          Timer.Start()
          cmdStartStop.Text = "Stop"
     Else
          Timer.Stop()
          cmdStartStop.Text = "Start"
     End If
End Sub
```

Listing 9.12: Using a single button for two related commands

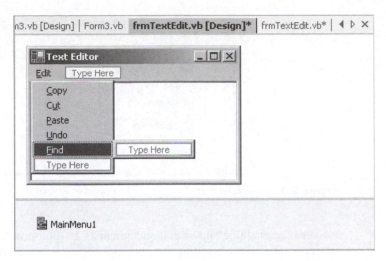

Figure 9.2   A form with a `MainMenu` component (visible in the component tray)

9.3.1 Menus and Menu Design

Menus are just as easy to deal with, although we first need to be able to design a menu structure before we can deal with handling the appropriate events. A `MainMenu` control is added to a WinForms form in the usual way, by selecting it from the Toolbox and dropping it on the form or by double-clicking on it in the Toolbox. Since the `MainMenu` control is not visible at run time (strictly speaking, this makes it a *component*, rather than a control) it appears as an icon in the Component Tray. Figure 9.2 shows a form design to which a `MainMenu` component has been added and the menu editor had been activated.

`MenuItems` are added to the overall menu structure interactively using the in-place menu editor, and configured using properties as with any control. Designing a menu structure is now as easy as clicking on the visible menu item on the Form Designer. It is standard practice to name menu items with a 'mnu' prefix and a name that reflects the hierarchical menu structure. A top level File menu would be called `mnuFile`, while sub-menu items of this would be `mnuFileOpen`, `mnuFileSave`, `mnuFileClose`, etc. Sub-sub-menus would have names that extend this – for example `mnuEditCopyText` and `mnuEditCopyGraphics` might be two sub-menu items of `mnuEditCopy`.

In the Form Designer window, you can create a menu structure simply by clicking on a menu item and entering the appropriate menu item caption. While it would be perfectly functional to simply change the visible captions (i.e. `Text` settings) for the various menu items, it is good programming practice to set up the `Name` and, in some cases, `ShortCut` properties. A menu's name, like the names of other controls, gives us access to it in code, so applying a meaningful name according to the scheme described above is a good idea. A `ShortCut` setting will provide the user with a quick way to fire the menu's `-Click` event-handler without pulling down the menu.

Building a menu structure is simple enough, and adding event-handlers to execute the menu item's command is a simple matter of double-clicking on the menu item in the Designer window. However, proper operation of a menu structure should

Figure 9.3 `Checked` and `RadioCheck` properties in use

also involve enabling and disabling commands as appropriate (using the `Enabled` property), and possibly setting the `Checked` or `RadioCheck` switches for the menu item. A `Checked` menu item typically means that that option is on, and clicking on it will switch it off, while a `RadioCheck` indicates that that item is the selected one of a group. Figure 9.3 shows a menu setup in which the user can switch between **Normal**, **UpperCase** and **LowerCase** text entry (where only one would be selected) and can switch **ScrollBars** on or off for the **TextBox** control. The code to control these facilities is shown in Listing 9.13.

Providing feedback for a menu system is simple enough in principle, but it can be awkward to keep the menu display in synchronization with the settings they control. One good method of arranging this is to set up the various menu item settings as the top-level menu item (e.g. **Edit** and **Modes** in Figure 9.3) is opened – this is signalled by the top-level menu's `Popup` event. Again, Listing 9.13 demonstrates this for a simple text editor (examine the `mnuEdit_Popup` event-handler).

Exercise 9.4

Sub-menu items can be hidden from a menu by setting their `Visible` property to `False`. You can tell whether text in a `TextBox` control has been selected (i.e. highlighted) by checking the `SelectedText` property – e.g. `Len(txtAddress.SelectedText)` will be 0 if no text is selected, >0 if there is some text selected. Write a `Popup` event for a menu called `mnuEdit` which has sub-menu items `mnuEditCut` and `mnuEditCopy`. The `Popup` event should contain code to hide the Cut and Copy sub-menus if there is no selected text in the `TextBox` `txtDocument`, and to show them if text has been selected.

9.4 Simple Input Controls

The main goal in user-interface design should be to make your program as easy to use as possible; this ought to be considered above the secondary goals of making the software easy to develop or making it look good. Most user-interaction with a program will be about entering data. Sometimes this will be text, sometimes a simple selection from a set of options, and sometimes a very simple yes or no type response. You should obviously select controls that provide the best solution for a particular type of data entry, and in many cases, the obvious controls such as `TextBox`, `CheckBox` and `RadioButton` are easiest because the user will be familiar with their operation.

9.4.1 `TextBox` Controls

A `TextBox` is most commonly used for free text entry (i.e. typing) and is the only type of control suitable for many common data entry tasks, such as name and address entry, descriptions, titles, etc. `TextBox`es are also used for numeric input, although for some types of number there are better controls to use. The key program interface elements of a `TextBox` are:

■ `Text` property – this provides programmatic access to the text entered into a `TextBox`.

■ `Multiline` property – a Boolean property that is used to set up a text box so that it can accept a number of lines of text.

■ `Lines` property – a string array that provides line-by-line access to the `Text` contents. Where the `Text` property of a multi-line `TextBox` will contain carriage return characters that indicate where each line ends, the `Lines` property will contain only the text of each line.

■ `AcceptsReturn`/`AcceptsTab` properties – these set up how a text box treats presses of the Enter and Tab keys. If `AcceptsReturn` is `False`, pressing **Enter** while in the `TextBox` will result in the Default button on a form being pressed; if `True`, a new-line will be entered. If `AcceptsTab` is set to `False`, pressing the Tab key will move the focus to the next control in the `TabOrder`; it `True`, the Tab will be entered into the `TextBox`.

■ `CausesValidation` property – if this is set to `True`, the `Validating` and `Validated` events can be used to vet what the user has entered into the `TextBox`.

■ `AppendText` method – this simply adds the string passed in the parameter to the end of the `Text` already in the `TextBox`.

■ `Clear` method – removes all `Text` from the `TextBox`.

■ `Undo` method – removes the most recent typing changes or clipboard operations from the `TextBox`.

■ `Cut`/`Copy`/`Paste` methods – these methods are used to provide the standard cut, copy and paste operations, using the Windows clipboard as the destination for cut/copy operations, and the source of text for a paste operation.

■ `TextChanged` event – this fires when any change is made to the `Text` in the `TextBox`.

Using the listed properties, methods and events along with the generic ones described earlier allows you to apply full programmatic control to a `TextBox`.

Table 9.4 Settings required for the form and controls of the Text Editor

Control	Property	Setting
TextBox	Name	txtEditor
	Multiline	True
	AcceptsReturn	True
	AcceptsEnter	True
	Dock	Fill
MenuItem	Name	mnuEdit
	Text	&Edit
MenuItem	Name	mnuEditCopy
	Text	&Copy
	ShortCut	CtrlC
MenuItem	Name	mnuEditCut
	Text	C&ut
	ShortCut	CtrlX
MenuItem	Name	mnuEditPaste
	Text	&Paste
	ShortCut	CtrlV
MenuItem	Name	mnuEditUndo
	Text	&Undo
	ShortCut	CtrlU
MenuItem	Name	mnuEditFind
	Text	&Find
	ShortCut	CtrlF
MenuItem	Name	mnuModes
	Text	&Modes
	ShortCut	CtrlM
MenuItem	Name	mnuModesNormal
	Text	&Normal
	RadioCheck	True
	ShortCut	CtrlN
MenuItem	Name	mnuModesUpperCase
	Text	Upper Case
	RadioCheck	True
MenuItem	Name	mnuModesLowerCase
	Text	LowerCase
	RadioCheck	True
MenuItem	Name	mnuModesSep1
	Text	- (hyphen - makes a separator bar)
MenuItem	Name	mnuModesScrollbars
	Text	Scroll Bars

Figure 9.4 A Text Editor form with a `MainMenu`

Although the `TextChanged` event seems to be the only specifically useful event defined for a `TextBox`, the generic `KeyPress`, `KeyUp` and `KeyDown` events are ideal for controlling user input.

We can demonstrate a number of `TextBox` features by building a simple text editor. Figure 9.4 shows a suitably designed form containing a `TextBox` and a `MainMenu`. The settings for the form and controls are shown in Table 9.4, and Listing 9.13 shows the code necessary to provide full edit control.

Note that some menu items in the above table do not have shortcuts or accelerator keys. It is normal to provide these only for items that are frequently used.

```
Public Class frmTextEdit
Inherits System.Windows.Forms.Form

+  Windows Form Designer generated code

Private Sub mnuEdit_Popup(ByVal sender As Object, _
                          ByVal e As System.EventArgs) _
                          Handles mnuEdit.Popup
    'This event occurs immediately before the menu appears.
    'It is ideal for setting up the availability of
    'menu items.
    If txtEditor.SelectedText <> "" Then
        'There is text selected, so...
        mnuEditCut.Enabled = True
        mnuEditCopy.Enabled = True
    Else
        'There is no text selected...
        mnuEditCut.Enabled = False
        mnuEditCopy.Enabled = False
    End If
    If Clipboard.GetDataObject.GetDataPresent( _
            (DataFormats.Text) Then
```

```
                'There is text in the clipboard, so...
                mnuEditPaste.Enabled = True
            Else
                'No text in the clipboard...
                mnuEditPaste.Enabled = False
            End If
            If txtEditor.CanUndo Then
                'Provide an undo option...
                mnuEditUndo.Enabled = True
            Else
                'No point in an undo option...
                mnuEditUndo.Enabled = False
            End If
    End Sub
    Private Sub mnuEditCopy_Click(ByVal sender As System.Object, _
                            ByVal e As System.EventArgs) _
                            Handles mnuEditCopy.Click
        'Copy selected text to the clipboard...
        Clipboard.SetDataObject(txtEditor.SelectedText)
    End Sub

    Private Sub mnuEditCut_Click(ByVal sender As System.Object, _
                            ByVal e As System.EventArgs) _
                            Handles mnuEditCut.Click
        'Copy selected text to the clipboard...
        Clipboard.SetDataObject(txtEditor.SelectedText)
        'and then remove the selected text...
        txtEditor.SelectedText = ""
    End Sub

    Private Sub mnuEditPaste_Click(ByVal sender As _
                                System.Object, _
                                ByVal e As System.EventArgs) _
                                Handles mnuEditPaste.Click
        'Paste clipboard contents as the selected text...
        txtEditor.SelectedText = _
                Clipboard.GetDataObject.GetData(DataFormats.Text)
    End Sub

    Private Sub mnuEditUndo_Click(ByVal sender As System.Object, _
                            ByVal e As System.EventArgs) _
                            Handles mnuEditUndo.Click
        'Perform an undo operation...
        txtEditor.Undo()
    End Sub

    Private Sub mnuEditFind_Click(ByVal sender As System.Object, _
                            ByVal e As System.EventArgs) _
                            Handles mnuEditFind.Click
        'Locate text in the editor...
        Static pos As Integer
        Static FindText As String
        'First ask for text to find (previous entry is
        default)...
```

```vb
        FindText = InputBox("Enter text to find.", _
                            "Find Text", FindText)
        'Check something was entered...
        If FindText <> "" Then
            'Try to find it, starting where we left off...
            pos = InStr(pos + 1, txtEditor.Text, FindText)
            'Did we find it?...
            If pos = 0 Then
                'No - let the user know...
                MessageBox.Show("Not Found")
            Else
                'Yes - move the cursor to it and select it...
                txtEditor.Select(pos - 1, FindText.Length)
                txtEditor.ScrollToCaret()
            End If
        End If
    End Sub

    Private Sub mnuModesScrollbars_Click( _
                            ByVal sender As System.Object, _
                            ByVal e As System.EventArgs) _
                            Handles mnuModesScrollbars.Click
        'Sets scroll bars on or off in the textbox...
        If mnuModesScrollbars.Checked Then
            mnuModesScrollbars.Checked = False
            txtEditor.ScrollBars = ScrollBars.None
        Else
            mnuModesScrollbars.Checked = True
            txtEditor.ScrollBars = ScrollBars.Both
        End If
    End Sub

    Private Sub mnuModesNormal_Click(ByVal sender As _
                                System.Object, _
                            ByVal e As System.EventArgs) _
                            Handles mnuModesNormal.Click
        'Sets the TextBox's character case to normal (mixed)...
        txtEditor.CharacterCasing = CharacterCasing.Normal
        mnuModesNormal.Checked = True
        mnuModesUppercase.Checked = False
        mnuModesLowercase.Checked = False
    End Sub

    Private Sub mnuModesUppercase_Click( _
                            ByVal sender As System.Object, _
                            ByVal e As System.EventArgs) _
                            Handles mnuModesUppercase.Click
        'Sets the TextBox's character case to UPPER...
        txtEditor.CharacterCasing = CharacterCasing.Upper
        mnuModesNormal.Checked = False
        mnuModesUppercase.Checked = True
        mnuModesLowercase.Checked = False
    End Sub
```

```
      Private Sub mnuModesLowercase_Click( _
                                ByVal sender As System.Object, _
                                ByVal e As System.EventArgs) _
                                Handles mnuModesLowercase.Click
          'Sets the TextBox's character case to lower...
          txtEditor.CharacterCasing = CharacterCasing.Lower
          mnuModesNormal.Checked = False
          mnuModesUppercase.Checked = False
          mnuModesLowercase.Checked = True
      End Sub
   End Class
```

Listing 9.13: Event-handler code for the Text Editor form

The purpose and operation of most of the code in Listing 9.13 should be quite clear. Interactions with the clipboard are a little awkward because the Windows clipboard can accommodate a range of data types (Text, RichText, Bitmaps, HTML, Colour Pallets, Audio data and a number of custom formats), and can hold a number of these types of data simultaneously. To pick up data from the clipboard, we first have to ask whether it has any data of a suitable format (in this case **DataFormats.Text**) and then call the `GetDataObject()` method specifying the data format we want.

We can use this to our advantage by managing the menu so that it shows only commands that are valid to use. If there is no text in the clipboard, there is no point in making the `Paste` command available. Similarly, if no text in the text box has been selected, there will be nothing to copy or paste. The text box's `CanUndo()` method tells us whether there is any typing for us to undo. We can combine all of these checks, placing them in the `PopUp` event-handler of the top-level menu item, and enabling or disabling menu items as appropriate.

The only other tricky code here is that for the Find command. By using static variables to store the text we wish to find (`FindText`) and the last location where text was found (`Pos`), we can use the `InStr()` function to step through every occurrence of text we are seeking in the editor. Initially, `Pos` is 0, and we start looking in the text box at character number `Pos + 1`. Subsequently, `Pos` will contain the last location that the text was found at, and adding 1 to this will give us the next place to start looking.

The menu item code for the Modes menu takes a slightly different approach. Here, the text box is set up as appropriate by each menu item and the corresponding menu items are `Checked`. Disappointingly, a menu item with a `RadioCheck` setting does not operate as a group with other menu items, so it is necessary to check one item on and the others off in code (bad marks to Microsoft for this).

9.4.2 `CheckBoxes` and `RadioButtons`

Although these controls are similar, they are used for different purposes. A `CheckBox` is a single control that works alone to allow the user to indicate the `True`/`False`, On/Off, 1/0 setting for an item with a Boolean value. For example,

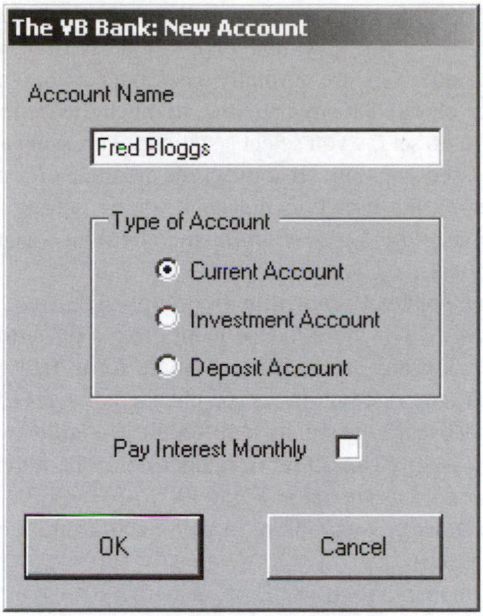

Figure 9.5 Using `RadioButtons` and a `CheckBox`

we could use a check box to allow the user to indicate that they wanted a bank account that pays interest monthly instead of annually (see Figure 9.5).

A check box used in this way allows a user to answer yes or no to a question with minimum effort. At the same time, the result can be determined unambiguously in code. For example, the check box setting in the above can be collected from the `Checked` property using the code in Listing 9.14.

```
Private Sub btnOK_Click(ByVal sender As System.Object, _
                    ByVal e As System.EventArgs) _
                    Handles btnOK.Click
    Dim A As BankAccount()
    If radCurrent.Checked Then
        A = New CurrentAccount()
    ElseIf radDeposit.Checked Then
        A = New DepositAccount()
    ElseIf radInvestment.Checked Then
        A = New InvestmentAccount()
    End If
    A.AccountName = txtName.Text
    A.InterestMonthly = chkMonthlyInterest.Value
    AccountList.Add(A)
    Me.Close()
End Sub
```

Listing 9.14: Collecting the `Checked` property of a `CheckBox` control

RadioButtons are used in a different way, even though each RadioButton has a Checked property that takes on a Boolean value. As their name suggests, RadioButtons are normally used in a group, where only one member of the group can be checked at any one time, in much the same way as preset stations are selected on a radio set (as you select a station by pressing a button, the button that is currently depressed pops up). If a different member of a group of radio buttons is checked, either by the user clicking on it, or by setting its Checked property to True in code, the Checked state of the member that was previously True will automatically go to False.

One apparent problem with groups of RadioButton controls arises if you need to have two or more independent groups of buttons on a form. If all of the buttons for each group are added to a single form, they will in fact be one large group, of which only one button can be checked. To get around this problem, it is necessary to place each group in a different *Container control*. A Panel, GroupBox or PictureBox can all be Container controls, although the obvious one to use is the GroupBox, as shown in Figure 9.5. A GroupBox has the added advantage that you can use its Text property to give each group a caption (like 'Type of Account' in Figure 9.5).

Note that, unlike a MenuItem with the RadioCheck set to True, there is no need to write code to turn check marks on and off in RadioButton controls. The normal user action of clicking on a member of a RadioButton group will turn the checks of the whole group on and off as appropriate.

Exercise 9.5

a) Two forms, F1 and F2, both have TextBox controls txtName and txtAddress on them (each form has both controls). Write statements that will copy the text in these text boxes on F1 to the corresponding boxes on F2.

b) F1 contains a CheckBox control, chkUpperCase. If this box is checked, the text copied to the controls on F2 should be converted to upper case. If not, it should be left in whatever case it is currently in. Amend your answer to a) so that this happens (note – you can get an upper-case copy of the contents of a string S using S.ToUpper().

9.5 List Controls

A RadioButton group is a good way of offering the user one from a small range of options, like the type of account options offered in Figure 9.5. However RadioButtons are limited in that it is impractical to offer a large number of options using them (think of the amount of screen space 50 radio buttons would take up) and it is awkward to add to the number of options as a program runs (although not impossible as we shall see later in this chapter). Instead, we can use one of the available List controls.

There are three types of simple List control: ListBox, CheckedListBox and ComboBox. In addition, the Toolbox offers controls that can display lists of complex items (`ListView` control), hierarchical lists (`TreeView` control) and point and click access to dates and times (`DateTimePicker` and `MonthCalendar` controls).

9.5.1 Adding Items to a List control

The simple List controls are programmed in a similar way, so in most cases what works for a `ListBox` will also work for a `CheckedListBox` and a `ComboBox`. Each has an `Items()` property that is a collection of `Object` type. Since everything in .NET has the `Object` class as an ancestor, you can put anything at all into a list box. This is a significant divergence from earlier versions of Visual Basic, in which the List controls kept a list of `Strings`. It is useful in that it allows you to use a `ListBox` to manage a collection of any class or even a collection of objects of mixed classes. However, it does mean that an object placed in a list box's `Items()` collection must have a method or property defined that will return the information you wish to display for that object.

By default, the `ToString()` method of an object added to the `Items()` collection in a list box defines what is seen in the list. However, you can set the list box's `DisplayMember` property to a string value that indicates what will be seen. This seems to work so that items added to the list will show up according to the current setting of `DisplayMember`, but the text they show does not change if `DisplayMember` is changed; i.e. the setting only affects new members added to the list. Figure 9.6 and Listing 9.15 show a form and code to demonstrate this.

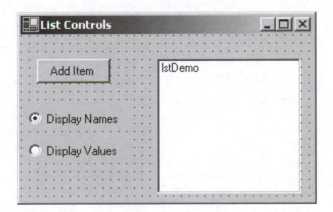

Figure 9.6 A form to demonstrate adding items to a `ListBox`

```
Public Class frmLists

    'Form definition code . . .
    '. . .

    'This class is used to demonstrate how to display
    'items in a listbox . . .
    Class ListItem
        Private ItemName As String
```

```vb
            Private ItemValue As Integer
            Public ReadOnly Property Name()
                Get
                    Return ItemName
                End Get
            End Property
            Public ReadOnly Property Value()
                Get
                    Return ItemValue
                End Get
            End Property
            Public Sub New(ByVal n As String, ByVal v As Integer)
                ItemName = n
                ItemValue = v
            End Sub
            Public Overrides Function ToString() As String
                Return ItemName
            End Function
        End Class

        'This will create a new item and add it to the
        'listbox...
        Private Sub btnAdd_Click(ByVal sender As System.Object, _
                            ByVal e As System.EventArgs) _
                            Handles btnAdd.Click
            Dim n As String
            Dim v As Integer
            n = InputBox("Enter item name")
            v = InputBox("Enter item value")
            Dim LI As ListItem = New ListItem(n, v)
            lstDemo.Items.Add(LI)
        End Sub

    Private Sub radNames_CheckedChanged( _
                    ByVal sender As System.Object, _
                    ByVal e As System.EventArgs) _
                    Handles radNames.CheckedChanged
        If radNames.Checked Then
            'This causes new items added to show the result
            'of their ToString() method...
            lstDemo.DisplayMember = ""
        Else
            'This causes them to show the value held in their
            'Value property...
            lstDemo.DisplayMember = "Value"
        End If
    End Sub
    'End of form class...
End Class
```

Listing 9.15: A class of items to add to a `ListBox`, and code to add and display

Class `ListItem` from Listing 9.15 is a simple class with two member variables – a string `ItemName` and an integer `ItemValue`. Properties are defined to expose these members (`Name` and `Value` read-only properties) and the class also has a constructor and overrides the default `ToString()` member to return the `ItemName` (by default, the `ToString()` member of a derived class returns the class name only).

The handler for the Add button asks the user to enter a name and value (e.g. 'Ten' and 10), and then creates a new `ListItem` initialized to these. The item is then added to the `ListBox`. The two `CheckBox` controls determine how newly added items will be displayed. If 'Display Names' is checked, `lstDemo.DisplayMember` is an empty string, indicating that the `ToString()` member of the `ListItem` will dictate what is seen. When 'Display Values' is checked, `radNames_CheckedChanged` is fired (since its check will be cleared), and `lstDemo.DisplayMember` will be set to 'Value' indicating that the `Value` property of the `ListItem` object will be displayed.

Note that in the above example, the `ListItem` class is defined *within* the Form class. It has default (`Friend`) scope, although it could have `Private` scope in this case since the class is only used from form code. Generally you need a good reason to place one class inside another in this way since we are only able to use the class prefixed with a reference to the form class (`frmLists.ListItem`), or not at all if the scope was made `Private`. However, it is a perfectly respectable thing to do for the purpose of this demo, and is a good use of scope where we know that a class will only ever be used in conjunction with (with `Friend` scope), or wholly within (with `Private` scope) another class or form.

`ListBox` types can also have items added in bulk, which can be useful in a number of ways. For example, we can quickly build a combo box to provide the names of the months of the year (Listing 9.16).

```
Private Sub FillCombo()
    Dim MonthNames() As String = {"January", "February", _
                                  "March", "April", "May", _
                                  "June", "July", "August", _
                                  "September", "October", _
                                  "November", "December"}
    cboMonths.Items.AddRange(MonthNames)
End Sub
```

Listing 9.16: Filling a list or combo box in a single step

Note that in Listing 9.16, the `AddRange()` method of the Items property is used to assign a whole array of strings to the `ComboBox`. A collection object (e.g. an `ArrayList`) can also be used to set the contents of a `ListBox` type, by setting the `Listbox`'s `DataSource` property to refer to the collection, as shown in Listing 9.17.

```
Private Sub FillComboFromCollection()
    Dim DayNames As New ArrayList()
    DayNames.Add("Monday")
    DayNames.Add("Tuesday")
```

```
        DayNames.Add("Wednesday")
        DayNames.Add("Thursday")
        DayNames.Add("Friday")
        DayNames.Add("Saturday")
        DayNames.Add("Sunday")
        cboDays.DataSource = DayNames
    End Sub
```

Listing 9.17: An alternative method for filling a List control

In either case, the text displayed in the list or combo box will depend on either the `ToString()` method of the objects added, or the `ListBox`'s `DisplayMember` setting if one is supplied.

9.5.2 Accessing the Selected Item(s)

The purpose of a List control is to allow the user to select an item or text rather than entering one via the keyboard. Since errors in typing are eliminated, this makes a List control an ideal way of getting the user to enter information where the information is an item from a range.

While a `ComboBox` can only have a single selected item, `ListBox` and `CheckedListBox` controls can be configured via properties so that one or many items can be selected, using the `SelectionMode` property. This can be set to `SelectionMode.One` (only a single item can be selected), `SelectionMode.MultiExtended` (a range of items can be selected if the user holds down the Shift key on the keyboard after the first selection – clicking on a second item will select *all* of the items from the first to the second), or `SelectionMode.MultiSimple` (many individual items can be selected and de-selected by clicking on them). For a List control with the `SelectionMode.One` property setting, a selected item can be accessed using the `SelectedItem` property. If one of the `MultiSelectionMode` properties is set, the `SelectedItems` property returns a collection containing all of the selected items.

To get the single item selected in Figure 9.7, the following code would suffice:

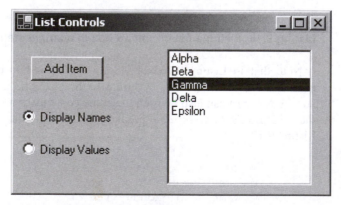

Figure 9.7 A `ListBox` with a single selected item

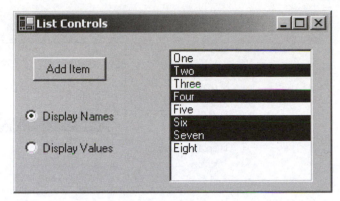

Figure 9.8 A `ListBox` with several selected items

```
Dim O As Object
O = lstDemo.SelectedItem
```

Alternatively, the *index* of the item selected can be found by:

```
Dim I As Integer
I = lstDemo.SelectedIndex
```

Of course, the number returned would be zero-based; the first item has index 0, the second has index 1, etc.

For a multi-selection `ListBox` as shown in Figure 9.8, the `SelectedItem` property will only return the first of the set of selected items. All of the selected items can be retrieved as a collection from the `SelectedItems` property or the `SelectedIndices` property. For example, to work through all of the selected items in a list box:

```
Dim O As Object
For Each O In lstDemo.SelectedItems
    'Code to manipulate O...
    '...
Next
```

or, to work through their indices . . .

```
Dim I As Integer
For Each I In lstDemo.SelectedIndices
    'Code to manipulate indices...
    '...
Next
```

The `SelectionMode.MultiSimple` and `SelectionMode.MultiExtended` settings are not supported by a `CheckedListBox` control, so although this control still has `SelectedItems` and `SelectedIndices` properties, these will only ever

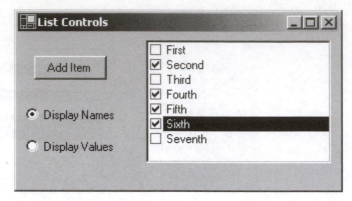

Figure 9.9 A `CheckedListBox`

have a single item in them, and this will match the `SelectedItem` and `SelectedIndex` properties. However, the `CheckedListBox` has instead `CheckedItems` and `CheckedIndices` properties. These work like the `SelectedItems` and `SelectedIndices` properties. Effectively, a `CheckedListBox` is simply a neater version of a standard `ListBox` with the `SelectionMode` set to one of the `multi-` options, so to iterate through the collection of checked items:

```
For Each O In lstDemo.CheckedItems
    'Code to manipulate O . . .
    '. . .
Next
```

Figure 9.9 shows a `CheckedListBox` with several items checked.

9.5.3 More Complex List Controls

The `ListBox`, `CheckedListBox` and `ComboBox` controls are all very well for displaying lists of items, where each item is to be displayed as a single piece of text, but for items where you need to create a list of more complex information, they would not be too suitable. For example, let's say we needed to display bank account details in a list box with the format shown in Figure 9.10.

Account Number	Account Name	Balance
112233445566	Joe Bloggs	1000.00
123456123456	Mary Green	1500.00
. . .	. . .	. . .

Figure 9.10 A format for a list of bank accounts

We could easily place this information into a standard list or combo box by defining a `ToString()` method for the account as in Listing 9.18.

```
Public Overrides Function ToString() As String
    Return Format(Number, "00000000") & vbTab & _
                   Name & vbTab & Format(Balance, "£0.00")
End Function
```

Listing 9.18: Redefining the `ToString()` method for the `BankAccount`

Now, when we add `BankAccount` objects to a list box, they will be displayed as formatted in the `ToString()` method, with a Tab character between the account number and name, and between the name and balance. However, a standard `ListBox` has tabs set up at 10 character intervals, and for information that is more than 10 characters, it will over-run into the next space. This method can therefore not be used to display a neat list unless you can guarantee that every piece of text is less than about 10 characters wide.

If we want to be able to display tidy lists of information, we need to make use of an alternative control. One of the better ones provided with Visual Studio is the `ListView` control. This versatile control can be used to display data in a variety of formats, and can include icons for the items displayed, display items in a tabular format (ideal for bank accounts) and sort items based on some key property. The `ListView` control is used in Windows Explorer windows, and is responsible for the variety of views you can have of files in your system (with the options of Thumbnails, Tiles, Icons, a List or a Details view). For our purposes, it is ideal for displaying a list of items and sub-items; for example a bank account number and a number of associated properties (`Name` and `Balance`). Listing 9.19 shows how we can add a simple method to a class (in this case `BankAccount`) to enable objects to display themselves in a `ListView` control.

```
Public Function LVItem() As ListViewItem
    'This method creates a new ListViewItem with sub-items
    'to display in a ListView control.
    'The Item is the Number of this account . . .
    Dim I As New ListViewItem(Number.ToString)
    'One sub-item is the account Name . . .
    I.SubItems.Add(Name)
    'The other is the Balance . . .
    I.SubItems.Add(Balance.ToString)
    'Finally, we return the main Item . . .
    Return I
End Function
```

Listing 9.19: A method to display an object in a `ListView` control

Note that the method defined for the `BankAccount` class returns a `ListViewItem`. First we create a `New ListViewItem`, initializing it with the account's number converted to a string. Then add each `SubItem` to the `ListView`

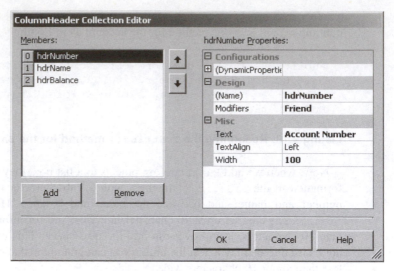

Figure 9.11 The ColumnHeader editor for a ListView control

using `.SubItems.Add()` which takes a `String` parameter. In this case, I've decided that the Item is a `BankAccount`'s `Number` (account number) property, and so `SubItems` are simply the other properties (`Name` and `Balance`). Finally, return the newly created and populated `ListViewItem`.

To set up a `ListView` control to accommodate this data, add one to a form, and select the `Columns` property from the Properties window. This is designated as a (Collection) property, so click on the little ellipsis button (. . .) in the value column to access the `ColumnHeader` property editor:

The `ColumnHeader` editor (Figure 9.11) allows you to add and remove column headings in a `ListView` control, each of which will demarcate a single column in the list of items. Initially there will be no column headings for a new control. Simply press the Add button for each column you want to add and assign values to the (Name), Text (the caption at the head of a column) and Width. I find that the Width property of a `ColumnHeader` is best determined by trial and error initially.

When you have added all of the necessary columns, press **OK** to exit the editor and return to the Visual Studio IDE, where you can examine the results of your labours. You should see the column headings you have set up and can decide whether the column widths you chose were suitable (see Figure 9.12).

Given a collection of bank accounts in an `ArrayList`, we could now add them all to a `ListView` control named `lvAccounts` with the following code (listing 9.20), which could be called from the `Form_Load` event-handler or from some other event.

```
Private Sub FillListView()
    Dim a As BankAccount
    'Select the Details view style . . .
    lvAccounts.View = View.Details
    'Now populate the ListView with account data . . .
```

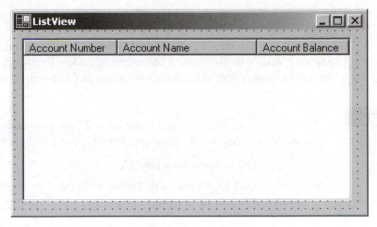

Figure 9.12 A `ListView` control with `Columns` set up

```
      For Each a In AccountList
            lvAccounts.Items.Add(a.lvitem())
      Next
   End Sub
```

Listing 9.20: Using the `ListView` method (`lvAccounts` is a `ListView` control)

This code results in a `ListView` control populated with data as shown in Figure 9.13. Note that the `View` property of the `ListView` control has been explicitly set to `View.Details`. Other `View` options are `View.List`, `View.LargeIcon` and `View.SmallIcon`, corresponding to the views available in Windows Explorer. None of these views would display the `SubItems` added to each Item in the `ListView` and so we would not see an account's `Name` or `Balance`.

For even more complex forms of list, typically lists of items, each with a variable number of sub-items, each of which might have sub-items, etc., we can use the `TreeView` control. This control displays items in a hierarchical list. It is again used

ListView		
Account Number	Account Name	Account Balance
101	Fred Bloggs	1200
102	Sandra Smith	2500
103	James Green	660
104	Paula Wiley	15250

Figure 9.13 A `ListView` control with items added

in Windows Explorer, this time to display the list of drives and folders. The coding for the `TreeView` control is similar to that for the `ListView` control, except that where a `ListView` has a collection of Items, a `TreeView` has a collection of nodes, and each node can also have a collection of nodes. Examples using the `TreeView` control to display hierarchical data are given in Chapters 11 and 12.

An `ArrayList`, `PostCodes`, contains a list of post code data for a city as strings. Write code to add these to a list box, `lstPostCodes`:

a) in the most efficient way possible;

b) so that each post code is displayed in upper case, regardless of how it is stored in the `ArrayList`.

9.6 Manipulating Controls at Run Time

You can add controls to a form as a program executes. There are several reasons why you might want to do this.

- You may want to add `RadioButton` controls to cover a set of options the number of which may change as the program runs.
- You could be designing a form that can be used to collect information for a number of different classes, and this would require a variable number of `TextBox` controls.
- You might want to provide thumbnail pictures of image files (e.g. JPEG files of photographs) in a folder on your computer, and so need to add `PictureBox` controls, one per file, to a form.
- You may want to add items to a menu (e.g. a list of recent files).

In these and other situations, the available options are to have a number of controls of the correct type on a form and make them visible as necessary, or to add new controls as needed. The first option has the limitation that no matter how many invisible controls you add to a form, it is always possible that the number you need exceeds that number. It can also be messy to set up. Since Visual Basic .NET makes it easy to add new controls at run time, it is the preferred option.

9.6.1 Adding controls as a program runs

Controls in a WinForms application are simply objects that inherit from the `Control` class. We can create a new control in the same way that we can create any type of object as a program runs. The only difference is that there are certain things we need to do with a control after we create it before it can be useful. To add a control to a form at run time:

1. Create a control of the required type using the `New` keyword: the type name of each control is the name that you see when you hover the mouse cursor over a Toolbox control.

2. Set the size of the control using the `Size` property. You can copy the size of an existing control (e.g. `newControl.Size` = `existingControl.Size`), or can set the `Width` and `Height` properties explicitly (e.g. `newControl.Width` = `100`: `newControl.Height` = `20`).

3. Set the location of the control relative to the top, left of the container. Typically this will be the top, left of the form, but if you add a control to a `GroupBox` or `Panel` control, it will be the top, left of this. Set either the `Top` and `Left` properties, or create a new location object, assign top and left values to it and assign this.

4. Set the required `BackColor`, `ForeColor` and `Font` properties. A control will automatically take on the `BackColor`, `ForeColor` and `Font` of its container, so you only need to set those properties that you want to be different.

5. Set any `Text`, `Picture`, `Value` or other settings specific to the type of control.

6. Call the control's `Show()` method to make it visible and activate it.

7. Add the control to a Container control: normally this will be a form, but it can be a `Panel`, `PictureBox` or `GroupBox` control. No matter which, the container will have a Controls collection, and the `Add()` method is used to add the new control.

8. Optionally, you can add event-handlers to a control so that it will respond to events by executing a pre-defined sub. The sub must match the signature for the event-handler added (in most cases, it will require two parameters to indicate the sender of the event and the event arguments), and the `AddHandler` statement is used to match up the object's event with the pre-defined handler.

This makes adding a control look quite complicated, but the code to do this is quite straightforward for all but the last step. For example, the sub shown in Listing 9.21. will add a number of `RadioButtons` to a `GroupBox`. The number and text of the options is provided by an array passed to the sub as a parameter.

```
'This Sub is part of a form class.
'As it is private, it must be called from within the form.
Private Sub CreateOptions(ByVal Options() As String)
    Dim item As String
    Dim itemTop As Integer = 10
    Dim itemCount As Integer, itemSpace As Integer
    Dim radItem As RadioButton
    'We can work out how much vertical space to give an item
    'by dividing the available space by the number of
    items...
    itemCount = Options.GetLength(0)
    itemSpace = (grpOptions.Height - 20) / itemCount
    For Each item In Options
        'Create the new control...
```

```
                    radItem = New RadioButton()
                    'Set up its size...
                    radItem.Width = 150
                    radItem.Height = 20
                    'Set up its position...
                    radItem.Left = 20
                    radItem.Top = itemTop
                    'Set the RadioButton's Text property...
                    radItem.Text = item
                    'Make sure only the first one is checked (we
                    'could leave them all unchecked instead)...
                    If itemTop = 10 Then
                        radItem.Checked = True
                    End If
                    'Add the control to a container control...
                    grpOptions.Controls.Add(radItem)
                    'And update to the top of the next item...
                    itemTop += itemSpace
            Next
        End Sub
```

Listing 9.21: Code to create a group of `RadioButtons`

In Listing 9.21, an array of strings is passed as a parameter to the `CreateOptions` sub. We start by working out how many options there will be. The `GetLength()` method of an array does this – the parameter to it is the dimension we want to find the number of items in, 0 for a 1-D array. From this, we can work out the available space for each item. Obviously, the array could have many more items than could be comfortably displayed in the space available, but we'll ignore this limitation since the worst that can happen is that the items will be squeezed too closely together.

The next steps set up the size (by setting `Width` and `Height`) and location of the items. Each `RadioButton` will line up with the others on the left, but they will be arranged in a vertical column, so when we work out the top of the items, we will increment by the amount `itemSpace` as we place each new one. Since the `RadioButton` group is created from an array of strings, we can take the text in each string as the caption for the `RadioButton` (its `Text` property).

Normally we display a set of radio buttons with one of them checked. In this case, the `If..Then` statement operates to set the `Checked` property for only the first one. This is easy to determine from the `Top` property, although we could have used various methods to decide which one was checked, or left all of them unchecked. Now we can add the new control to a group box on the form, and finally, update the `itemTop` value so that the next button, if there is one, will be positioned under the current one.

We could use this sub on any form that had a `GroupBox` called `grpOptions`. Listing 9.22 shows an event-handler for a `Button.Click` event that sets up a suitable array of strings and calls the sub to create a radio button group. Figure 9.14 shows the result.

Figure 9.14 A group of `RadioButtons` created at run time

```
Private Sub btnAddOptions_Click(ByVal sender As
                                System.Object, _
                        ByVal e As System.EventArgs) _
                        Handles btnAddOptions.Click
    Dim a() As String 'This will be our array of strings.
    Dim i As Integer
    i = InputBox("How many options?")
    'Resize the array for the required number of options.
    ReDim a(i - 1)
    'Now collect the text for each option . . .
    For i = 0 To a.GetUpperBound(0)
        a(i) = InputBox("Enter an option caption")
    Next
    'Finally call CreateOptions to build a group.
    CreateOptions(a)
End Sub
```

Listing 9.22: Calling the `CreateOptions` routine

With a group of radio buttons like this, we can always find out which option has been selected by the user by simply examining the `Checked` property of each. Note that `CreateOptions` does not set the `Name` property of the radio buttons, so we would have to identify the selected button by its `Text` property. Code to do this might be something like Listing 9.23.

```
Private Sub btnWhichOption_Click(ByVal sender As
                                System.Object, _
                        ByVal e As System.EventArgs) _
                        Handles btnWhichOption.Click
    Dim C As Control
    Dim R As RadioButton
```

```
        For Each C In grpOptions.Controls
            If TypeName(C) = "RadioButton" Then
                R = CType(C, RadioButton)
                If R.Checked Then
                    MessageBox.Show(R.Text)
                End If
            End If
        Next
    End Sub
```

Listing 9.23: Identifying which of the new controls is `Checked`

The code in Listing 9.23 is quite complex because we need to iterate through all of the controls in the `GroupBox`'s `Controls` collection picking out the `RadioButtons`. If we know for a fact that there will only ever be radio buttons in the group, we could simply iterate through all of them with no need for the `If TypeName..Then` part. However, here I've allowed for the possibility of other controls in the group. We iterate through the `Controls` collection, test each to see if it is a radio button (checking against its `TypeName`), and, if it is, assign it to a `RadioButton` reference variable. We can now test its `Checked` property (a `Control` is not guaranteed to have a `Checked` property, so we must know it is a radio button before doing this test) and, for this example, display its name if it is checked.

All of this might have been much easier if we could simply have attached an event-handler to each button. If we used, for example, a `CheckedChanged` event-handler, we could immediately find out which option had been selected by the user. Fortunately, .NET provides for this possibility with the `AddHandler` statement.

9.6.2 Adding event-handlers as a program runs

Normally we leave it up to Visual Studio to generate the outline of an event-handler for us at design time, and simply add the code to make it do what we want. However, we can attach an existing event-handler to an event in code, and since we are now able to add new controls as a program runs, this is the ideal situation to exploit the capability. `AddHandler` is a statement that allows us to associate an event from a control or other object with a piece of code we want that event to invoke. The format of the statement is:

```
AddHandler <EventToRespondTo>, AddressOf <CodeToExecute>
```

For <EventToRespondTo>, we can specify a generic event-handler that could be applied to handle any type of event. To create an event-handler for a radio button that can be added to a form at run time, we define the handler and a routine that will associate the new button with it. Creating the handler is a simple matter of writing a sub with the following signature:

```
Sub RadioHandler(ByVal sender As System.Object, _
                 ByVal e As System.EventArgs)
```

The two parameter declarations are very important, since this sub will be expected to accept the two parameters that accompany any event. For the new radio button, the .NET runtime will need to call this sub in response to a click, and so it must match the call. If the handler were added at design time, Visual Studio would work out the exact parameters necessary for handling a click on a radio button and specify these as in Listing 9.24.

```
Private Sub RadioButton1_CheckedChanged( _
            ByVal sender As System.Object, _
            ByVal e As System.EventArgs) _
            Handles RadioButton1.CheckedChanged
End Sub
```

Listing 9.24: an event-handler generated at design time

For one we create at run time, the generic declarations for the `sender` and `e` parameters is easier and would allow us to use the code to handle different types of event. However, using a generic parameter like this could cause a problem if the more specific arguments passed to it were not handled properly in the handler's code. For example, coding this handler to handle a `Mouse` event would mean that the `e` parameter would be set up with `X`, `Y` and `Buttons` properties and our code would work with these. If we subsequently tried to use it to deal with a `KeyPressed` event, the properties passed in the `e` argument (`KeyCode`, etc.) would not match and we would get a run time error.

If you were sure that you wanted to handle only one specific type of event, you could always copy the signature of one that was generated at design time (as above), but miss out the `Handles` clause at the end. Then the mismatched event problem would be caught by the compiler and the run time error would never happen.

As en example of adding event-handlers at run time, here is the step by step procedure for adding a group of new `RadioButton` controls to a group box in a form and setting up an event-handler that will change the string variable `SelectedButtonText` to the label of the selected `RadioButton`.

1. Declare the variable to be controlled:

   ```
   Private SelectedButtonText As String
   ```

2. Write a generic event handler that will change its contents at run time:

   ```
   Private Sub RadioButtonChange( _
               ByVal sender As System.Object, _
               ByVal e As System.EventArgs)
       SelectedButtonText = sender.Text
   End Sub
   ```

3. Write code to add the options to be provided by the `RadioButtons`. The list of options can be supplied as an array of strings. The code will need to add one button for each option, and attach each to the event-handler specified in step 2.

4. Use an `AddHandler` statement to add the generic event-handler to controls at run time. Returning to the `RadioButton` example in Listing 9.20, we can add the same event-handler to every radio button created in the `CreateOptions` sub by adding the statements set in bold (Listing 9.25):

```
Private Sub CreateOptions(ByVal Options() As String)
    Dim item As String
    Dim itemTop As Integer = 10
    Dim itemCount As Integer, itemSpace As Integer
    Dim radItem As RadioButton
    itemCount = Options.GetLength(0)
    itemSpace = (grpOptions.Height - 20) / itemCount
    For Each item In Options
        radItem = New RadioButton()
        radItem.Width = 150
        radItem.Height = 20
        radItem.Left = 20
        radItem.Top = itemTop
        radItem.Text = item
        If itemTop = 10 Then
            radItem.Checked = True
        End If
        'This statement assigns an event handler to
        'the radio button . . .
        AddHandler radItem.CheckedChanged, _
                    AddressOf RadioButtonChange
        grpOptions.Controls.Add(radItem)
        itemTop += itemSpace
    Next
End Sub
```

Listing 9.25: Adding event-handlers to a set of option buttons at run time

Note that since we are using a single event-handler to cope with events from a number of different controls, we would need to use the `Sender` parameter of the event-handler to determine the source of the actual event. The short listing under item 2 above shows this.

Generally, adding controls and associated event-handlers at run time is something you will not need to do too often. However, there is one situation in which this technique is commonly used; the addition of new menu items to a menu structure. Many Windows applications provide a Recent Files list in the File menu. These are implemented as controls added at run time.

Exercise 9.7

The following sub has been defined on a form as a generic event-handler for clicking on a `Label` control:

```
Private Sub LabelClick(ByVal sender As System.Object, _
                        ByVal e As System.EventArgs)
    sender.BackColor = Color.Blue
End Sub
```

There are two labels on the form – `Label1` and `Label2`. Write a sub that can be called to assign the above event-handler to handle `Click` events for both of these label controls.

9.7 Graphics in WinForms Programs

One of the great benefits of working with WinForms applications instead of Console applications is the easy availability of graphics. It is possible to write graphical Console applications, but to do this requires a good knowledge of the graphics hardware of the PC the program is running on. Windows has always provided an easier way to work with graphics by having a GDI (Graphics Device Interface), a set of functions and data structures that provide programmatic access to the graphics adaptor on a PC. More recently the addition of the DirectX library to Windows has simplified the use of graphics further by making fairly routine work out of dealing with bitmaps (the dot-by-dot representation of an image on a graphics screen), textures, light and shading and even animation. .NET provides through GDI+ (an upgrade to the earlier GDI) an object-oriented interface to the Windows graphics system, and so provides one of the most powerful and flexible ways that a programmer can create richly graphical application programs.

9.7.1 Graphics Fundamentals

A WinForms application can contain a number of different types of graphic display. We can categorize these as follows.

- Graphics on standard controls: various standard controls in the Toolbox support simple graphics, usually by providing the ability to display a simple bitmap. Many of the standard controls have `Image` and `BackgroundImage` properties. For example, a small graphical item, or *glyph*, can be set as the `Image` property of a standard Button control so that it indicates its purpose with a picture.

- `PictureBox` controls: the `PictureBox` control is provided to allow simple display of graphical images (such as JPG photograph files).

- GDI+ operations: forms and most other controls have a `CreateGraphics()` method that returns a GDI+ device encapsulated as a `Graphics` object that can be drawn into. Once you have obtained a `Graphics` object, you can use its methods to draw lines and shapes, load bitmaps from a variety of file types (Bitmap/BMP, Jpeg/JPG, Graphics Interchange Format/GIF and Windows MetaFile/WMF) and perform graphical transformations (scaling, rotating, skewing and colour operations).

■ `OwnerDraw` for List controls: standard `ListBox` and `ComboBox` controls have a `DrawMode` property that can be set to an `OwnerDraw` mode. With this setting, you need to write code that displays each item in the list, making it possible for each item in a List control to have an icon, or a colour or possibly a font that is specific to the item in the list.

Using pre-defined graphics to embellish controls, as suggested in the first two items above is easy. Programming graphics from scratch to create diagrams or vector graphic drawings is a little more complex (but still quite easy) in VB .NET.

9.7.2 Using Pre-Defined Graphics

In many cases, the graphical effect we want can be created in a drawing program and saved in a file. VB .NET allows us to load a graphic from a file (usually a Bitmap file, but other types are supported) into a control to give it a graphical face. For example, we could create suitable bitmaps as icons to display on the face of `Button` controls. Typically, we would use a program such as Microsoft Paint (supplied free with Windows), Fireworks or Photoshop to create one or more graphic images to use as icons on the face of buttons. Figure 9.15 shows a suitable image to use as an icon on a `Button` control.

Figure 9.15 A bitmap graphic created in Windows Paint

Figure 9.16 The bitmap image on the face of a `Button` control

We can use this icon to give a standard `Button` control a graphical face by simply selecting the Bitmap file to be the `Image` property of the control. To make things as simple as possible, the image can be saved to a bitmap file in the same folder as the VB .NET project (`ClockFace.bmp`). It can then be applied to a button (or any other type of control) by going to the Properties window while the control is selected and clicking on the ellipsis next to the `Image` property. Select the file's name in the dialog box that appears and the bitmap will appear on the face of the `Button` control (see Figure 9.16). The existing text on the button will overlay the image, so to improve the appearance, simply delete the `Text` property.

Displaying static images is a trivial matter as the previous example shows. However, with a little more work, we can load up a selected graphical file at run time to provide graphics that change while a program executes. For example, we can easily create a simple picture viewer. The code in Listing 9.26 shows the code necessary to load a picture into an `Image` control at run time; to use this code, you need to place a `PictureBox` on the form and also a button with the name `btnGetPic`.

```
Private Sub btnGetPic_Click(ByVal sender As System.Object, _
                        ByVal e As System.EventArgs) _
                        Handles btnGetPic.Click
    Dim dlgOpen As New OpenFileDialog()
    'Set up a Filter to allow JPeg, Bitmap, GIF or
    'Metafiles...
    dlgOpen.Filter = "Photos|*.jpg|Bitmap Files|*.bmp|" & _
                    "GIF Files|*.gif Metafiles|*.wmf"
    'Show the dialog box and respond if the OK button was
    'pressed...
    If dlgOpen.ShowDialog(Me) = DialogResult.OK Then
        'Load the selected picture into the picturebox...
        PictureBox1.Image = New Bitmap(dlgOpen.FileName)
    End If
End Sub
```

Listing 9.26: Code to load an image file into a `PictureBox` control

9.7.3 Drawing on WinForms Controls

Most of the WinForms controls provide a `CreateGraphics` method that returns a `Graphic` object. This object provides programmatic access to the 'surface' of a control, allowing you to draw on it using its range of methods. Using this you can write code that draws the face of a control according to your own specification. While most of the controls are capable of being drawn on in this way, the most suitable controls for drawing on are `PictureBox` controls, `Panel` controls and the surface of a `Form` itself.

To draw on a control, all that is needed is to follow the outline sequence shown in Listing 9.27.

```
Sub DoDrawing()
      Dim g As Graphics
      g = <control>..CreateGraphics
      <First in sequence of drawing commands>
      <...>
      <Last in sequence of drawing commands>
End Sub
```

Listing 9.27: General form of code to draw into a control

One small problem in drawing on the face of a control is that the graphics you draw will be 'volatile'. That is to say, anything you draw on the surface of a control will only remain there until that control is obscured, by, for example, another form or program appearing in front of it. When the control is uncovered, its surface will have been returned to the state it was in when it was first displayed. For example, Listing 9.28 (_Click event-handler for the 'Draw' button shown in Figure 9.17) draws a series of circles over the whole area of the `Panel` control shown above the button.

```
Private Sub btnDraw_Click(ByVal sender As System.Object, _
                          ByVal e As System.EventArgs) _
                          Handles btnDraw.Click
    Dim g As Graphics
    Dim x, y As Integer
    g = pnlPaper.CreateGraphics
    For x = 0 To pnlPaper.Width Step 50
        For y = 0 To pnlPaper.Height Step 50
            g.DrawEllipse(Pens.Black, x, y, 40, 40)
        Next
    Next
End Sub
```

Listing 9.28: Code to draw a grid of circles on a `Panel` control

Because of the volatile nature of drawn graphics, opening a window that obscures half of the form and then closing it again results in the display in Figure 9.17.

It is easy to see from Figure 9.17 where a window covered up half of the form: the `Button` control has been redrawn (automatically by Windows) but the graphics on the panel have not. To get around this problem, we need to deal with graphics drawn into controls in a different way.

Each control that can support graphics also has a `Paint` event, and the necessary trick is to do all of the drawing in this event. Windows sends the `Paint` message to forms whenever they need to refresh their surface display, and .NET forms pass this message on as a `Paint` event for each control. A control will automatically re-paint

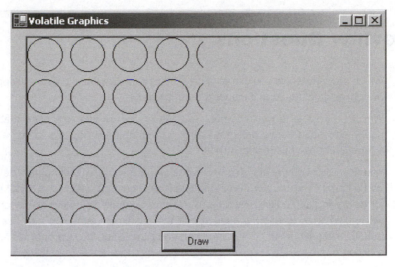

Figure 9.17 A panel with 'volatile' graphics

its standard appearance, for example, the text on the face of a button, but relies on the `Paint` event code to deal with any drawn graphics.

As it turns out, this is easy to deal with. Simply place any drawing code into the `Paint` event of the control, as shown in Listing 9.29.

```
Private Sub pnlPaper_Paint(ByVal sender As System.Object, _
        ByVal e As System.Windows.Forms.PaintEventArgs) _
        Handles pnlPaper.Paint
    Dim g As Graphics
    Dim x, y As Integer
    g = pnlPaper.CreateGraphics
    For x = 0 To pnlPaper.Width Step 50
        For y = 0 To pnlPaper.Height Step 50
            g.DrawEllipse(Pens.Black, x, y, 40, 40)
        Next
    Next
End Sub
```

Listing 9.29: Moving drawing code to the `Paint` event-handler

This has the effect of re-drawing the surface of the control any time it is needed. It also allows us to do away with the Draw button shown in Figure 9.17 since the `Paint` event happens automatically.

A variety of methods are available from a `Graphics` object, for drawing lines, ellipses, rectangles, arcs curves and pie-segments (segments of a circle) as well as for filling areas of a graphic with a pattern, selecting colours and patterns, transforming drawn items (e.g. re-scaling them, rotating them and changing the relative angle between their coordinate axes), filling them with bitmap graphics and writing text. With so many possibilities, it would be impossible to do full justice to the graphics capabilities of .NET controls here.

Review Questions

1. Which property would you use on a control to make sure that it did not disappear off the bottom or right edge of the form if the form were resized?

2. Which property of a control would you alter if you wanted to ensure that the control could not be accessed from a different form in a program (hint: how would you define a variable on a form to impose this restriction)?

3. You have `String` variables (`name`, `address`, `postcode`) that contain details of a customer, and a form (`frmCustomerData`) with text boxes (`txtName`, `txtAddress`, `txtPostCode`) for displaying and editing this data. The form is currently not being displayed. Outline the code you would write to allow a user to edit the customer data. You can assume the form has buttons assigned to its `AcceptButton` and `CancelButton` properties and can be used as a dialog box.

4. A list box is to have 1000 items added to it from a database. Which methods would you use to make sure that the update proceeded as fast as possible?

5. How is the user informed where the drop part of a drag and drop operation can be done on a form?

6. What is the purpose of the `Sender` parameter in a control's event-handlers? What is the purpose of the `e` parameter?

7. The `Controls` collection of a form allows programmatic access to all of the controls placed on the form. What type of code structure would you use to access each control in turn? How would you modify this structure so that you only accessed `TextBox` controls?

8. What options are there for providing information in a menu item apart from the menu text?

9. How do the `Checked` properties of a `CheckBox` and a `RadioButton` differ in the way they are normally used? How does the `Checked` property of a `RadioButton` differ from the `RadioCheck` property in a `MenuItem`?

10. How do you set which property of an item in a `ListBox` is displayed? What are the options and what is the default?

11. List three ways in which items can be added to a `ListBox` or `ComboBox` control.

12. How would you determine the number of a selected item in a `ListBox`?

13. How does the `SubItems` property of a `ListViewItem` object differ from the Items property of a `ListView` control?

14. What is a Container control, and how would you add a new control to one's controls property? What other things would you have to do to the new control before it could be displayed properly on a form?

15. How is the `AddressOf` operator used in assigning an event-handler to a control?

16. How do graphics drawn on a control at run time differ from those added (using the `Image` property) at design time? What event could we use to change this nature of drawn graphics?

Practical Activities

A Simple CAD Program

We can use the graphics facilities described earlier to build a program that allows the user to create drawings on a PC. The Graphics class in VB .NET contains methods for drawing lines, rectangles, circles and ellipses and curves in a range of colours and with defined fill-styles. We can add user-interface facilities to allow the user to select colours from a palette, draw shapes interactively and possibly even edit the graphics created. First we need a brief description of Computer-Aided Drawing (CAD) fundamentals.

CAD and Objects

In computer aided drawing, a user creates shapes on a computer display. We can create drawings in two distinct ways: using bitmapped graphics, as done in Windows Paint and Photoshop, or using object-oriented graphics, as done by Corel Draw and all CAD programs.

Bitmapped graphics are ideal for creating and storing pictures of great complexity, such as photographs and highly detailed images. The reason for this is that each single dot, or pixel, that makes up a bitmapped picture is an object in its own right, with its own colour, and so however complex a photograph is, containing however many separate colours, it can be broken down into a grid of dots and represented as a bitmap. The quality of a bitmap is determined by its resolution, which is related to the number of dots in each row and the number of rows of dots that make up the picture. The limitation of a bitmapped image is that every picture contains a huge number of dots, but no matter how many dots there are if you move in close enough, you can see the individual dots.

An object-oriented or shape-oriented picture is made up of simple descriptions of each figure on it. For example, a picture can be composed of a red circle centred on location 100, 100 with a radius of 50, and a blue rectangle whose top, left corner is at location 150, 400 and that is 200 units wide and 150 units high. This type of picture is usually much simpler than a bitmapped photograph, but for some purposes, illustration and diagrams for example, it is preferable. Pictures like this can be stored as simple descriptions and drawn as necessary, rather than stored as the colour of every single pixel in the picture. They can also be more easily edited, so that a shape can be moved to a different location by changing a number or two, or deleted entirely without affecting the rest of the picture (just try removing a person who strayed into one of your photographs in a program like Photoshop to see how difficult this can be in a bitmapped image). Finally, we can redraw an object-oriented picture at any scale we like by changing the numbers that describe the shapes – doubling each number would double the size of each shape – as we draw it. If we try to re-size a bitmapped image like this, each individual pixel must get bigger, and the picture quality reduces (Figure 9.15 shows how a bitmapped circle drawn at too large a scale would appear).

A CAD drawing is stored as a list of objects, each of which contains numbers to specify its location in the picture, its size and its colour. Different shapes are described by different combinations of numbers. For example, we need three numbers to describe the size and location of a circle (where its centre is in the X and Y directions and what its radius is) but four to describe a rectangle (the location of its top, left corner, its width and its height). We can use objects to hold the numbers that describe each shape, and since all shapes will have some things in common (each will have X and Y coordinates to specify its location, each will have a colour and each will need to be drawn on a display), we can use inheritance to create a basic shape and then inherit this in each new shape we decide to support in the program.

Activity 1: Creating the base class for drawing

To build an object-oriented drawing program, we need first to consider what objects we will want to draw. Inheritance will be a major asset since we can define the core behaviour that all 'drawable' objects should exhibit, and then specialize this for specific 'drawables'.

An abstract Shape class

Try any CAD program and you will almost certainly find that you draw shapes interactively by selecting the shape to draw, selecting a colour and fill-style for it, clicking the mouse button and holding it down at the location of the shape, and dragging the mouse to set the size of the shape. When the mouse button is released, the size and location of the shape will have been set. We'll deal with the problems of displaying an interactive indication of size and shape later, but for now we need to consider how such simple operations can be used to determine all of the necessary information to draw a shape.

Simple geometric shapes can almost always be described by a few numbers. For a circle we need the location of its centre (two numbers) and its radius. We could use the same information to draw a square, pentagon, octagon or any other regular shape. For a rectangle, we need four numbers to give the top, left and bottom, right corner locations. However, we could also use the same four numbers to draw just about any regular shape, since we can inscribe almost any shape within a rectangle, as shown in Figure A9.1.

The core **Shape** class should therefore store the size and location information for any *shape*. It should also contain the data required to describe a shape's outline colour, internal colour and fill-style, since the .NET graphics class allows for these settings. Note that using this scheme may require that we transform the location and size properties of the enclosing rectangle (**X**, **Y**, **Width** and **Height**) in some way to

     Simple

Figure A9.1 Various shapes inscribed in a rectangular outline

```
┌─────────────────────────┐
│ Shape                   │
├─────────────────────────┤
│ X: Integer              │
│ Y: Integer              │
│ Width: Integer          │
│ Height: Integer         │
│ Colour: Color           │
├─────────────────────────┤
│ Draw(g)                 │
│ MoveBy(dx, dy)          │
│ MoveTo(x, y)            │
│ Resize(newX, newY)      │
│ Here(x, y):Boolean      │
└─────────────────────────┘
```

Figure A9.2   The shape class – an abstract drawable shape

match the shape that it actually contains. For example, a line is drawn between two points (X1, Y1, X2 and Y2), and so the coordinates of the second point will need to be calculated (X2 = X1 + width, Y2 = Y1 + height).

When we define the core shape class, we should also consider the core behaviour that every shape will be required to exhibit. The most obvious method to define will be a method to draw a shape. Because we will be using a member of the Graphics class as the venue for a draw operation, the **Draw** method for a shape will need to be given a reference to this object. Other methods for manipulating a shape should be defined to allow it to be moved and resized. Finally, a method that will allow us to interrogate a shape to see if a specific point is within it will be useful if we want a shape to be able to react to mouse clicks. The **Shape** class can be represented as shown in Figure A9.2.

The **Shape** class is abstract. That is, we will not be creating any objects of this class since it is defined only for inheriting from. However, we can create the code for this class now, and it will be a help in designing the rest of the programs since it will provide us with a protocol that the concrete shapes will abide by.

Start by creating a new Visual Basic Windows application project with the name CAD, and add to this a class module with the name `Shapes` and the file-name **shapes.vb**. Add the class code shown in Listing A9.1.

```vb
Public MustInherit Class Shape
    Private mvarX_Pos As Integer
    Private mvarY_Pos As Integer
    Private mvarWidth As Integer
    Private mvarHeight As Integer
    Protected colour As Color

    Public Sub New(ByVal xx As Integer, ByVal yy As Integer, _
            ByVal wid As Integer, ByVal hgt As Integer, _
            ByVal col As Color)
        mvarX_Pos = xx : mvarY_Pos = yy
        mvarWidth = wid : mvarHeight = hgt
        colour = col
    End Sub
```

```vb
Public Property X()
    Get
        X = mvarX_Pos
    End Get
    Set(ByVal Value)
        mvarX_Pos = Value
    End Set
End Property

Public Property Y()
    Get
        Y = mvarY_Pos
    End Get
    Set(ByVal Value)
        mvarY_Pos = Value
    End Set
End Property

Public Property Width()
    Get
        Width = mvarWidth
    End Get
    Set(ByVal Value)
        mvarWidth = Value
    End Set
End Property

Public Property Height()
    Get
        Height = mvarHeight
    End Get
    Set(ByVal Value)
        mvarHeight = Value
    End Set
End Property

Public Sub MoveTo(ByVal newX As Integer, _
                  ByVal newY As Integer)
    X = newX
    Y = newY
End Sub

Public Overridable Sub MoveBy(ByVal dx As Integer, _
                              ByVal dy As Integer)
    X += dx
    Y += dy
End Sub

Public Overridable Sub Resize(ByVal dWidth As Integer, _
                              ByVal dHeight As Integer)
    mvarWidth += dWidth
    mvarHeight += dHeight
End Sub

Private Function Between(ByVal value As Integer, _
                ByVal Lower As Integer, _
                ByVal Upper As Integer) As Boolean
```

```
        If Upper > Lower Then
            Return value >= Lower AndAlso value <= Upper
        Else
            Return value >= Upper AndAlso value <= Lower
        End If
    End Function

    Public Function Here(ByVal xx As Integer, _
                         ByVal yy As Integer) As Boolean
        'xx, yy is 'Here' if the coordinates are within the
        'extents rectangle of the shape . . .
        Return Between(xx, X, X + Width) AndAlso _
               Between(yy, Y, Y + Height)
    End Function

    Public Overridable Sub Draw(ByVal gr As Graphics)
        'Abstract method – implementations will draw on the
        'device referred by mvarDrawDevice.
    End Sub
End Class
```

Listing A9.1: The `Shape` abstract class

Most of the code in the `Shape` class is very simple. The main requirement in defining this class is to use the correct modifiers (`MustInherit`, `Overridable`, `MustOverride`, etc.) to ensure that we can use inheritance appropriately.

A constructor (`New()`) has been added to make creating a new shape a 1-line operation (passing coordinates, sizes and colour to the new shape). Properties for `X`, `Y`, `Width` and `Height` will allow us to find out about a shape's location and size from its interface. Methods to `MoveTo()` a specific location and `MoveBy()` a given distance will simplify using the shape in an overall drawing, as will the method to `Resize()` a shape by adjusting its width and height.

The `Here()` method returns `True` if the specified coordinate location is within the shape's *extents rectangle* (see Listing A9.1). It relies on the private `Between()` function that checks that a single ordinate is between specified limits. Finally, the `Draw()` method is purely abstract: we know it will need to be given a reference to a `Graphics` object to do its work, but beyond that we cannot yet say how it will work since there is as yet no 'shape' to be drawn.

Activity 2: Creating a concrete shape and testing

Before we get too far ahead in this program, it would be a good idea to run a simple test to ensure that the Shape class behaves as expected. To do this, we will need to define a concrete Shape class and test it in a very simple application.

A simple `Line` class (Listing A9.2) will act as a non-threatening inheritor of the `Shape` base class and allow us to test both classes easily. It can go into the `shapes.vb` class module alongside the `Shape` class.

```
Public Class Line
    Inherits Shape
    Public Sub New(ByVal xx As Integer, ByVal yy As Integer, _
            ByVal wid As Integer, ByVal hgt As Integer, _
            ByVal col As Color)
        MyBase.New(xx, yy, wid, hgt, col)
    End Sub

    Public Overrides Sub Draw(ByVal gr As Graphics)
        MyBase.Draw(gr)
        gr.DrawLine(New Pen(colour), X, Y, X + Width, Y +
        Height)
    End Sub

End Class
```

Listing A9.2: The `Line` shape class

Defining the `Line` class is refreshingly simple since we have done all of the groundwork in the `Shape` class. All of the properties are inherited, and the only methods we need to define are the constructor (every class has its own constructor definition) and the `Draw()` method, since this is bound to be different for every shape. We need, of course, to define the `Draw()` method as 'Overrides', but forgetting that would not cause a problem since the compiler would refuse to accept the code until this modifier was added. To draw a line on a `Graphics` object, the `DrawLine()` method takes five parameters – the colour to draw it in, the co-ordinates of the top, left corner (`X`, `Y`) and the coordinates of the bottom right corner (`X + Width`, `Y + Height`).

To test the class, we need a simple form definition with two controls: a `Panel` object to act as the `Graphics` drawing surface, and a button to allow us to create a shape and initiate a draw operation. We can use the default form (`Form1`) of the Windows application project.

Create the form as shown in Figure A9.3. Change the form's name to `frmCAD` and add a button and a panel to it, arranging them approximately as shown opposite. The Line button should have the name `btnLine`. The control that shows as a simple rectangle is `Panel` control, and should be given the name `pnlOutput`. Now double-click on the button to generate the framework for the following event-handler, and add the code shown in Listing A9.3.

```
Private Sub btnLine_Click(ByVal sender As System.Object, _
        ByVal e As System.EventArgs) Handles btnLine.Click
    Dim L As Line
    Dim g As Graphics = pnlOutput.CreateGraphics()
    L = New Line(50, 50, 200, 200, Color.Blue)
    L.Draw(g)
    L.Move(50, 100)
    L.Draw(g)
End Sub
```

Listing A9.3: An event-handler to test the `Shape` and `Line` classes

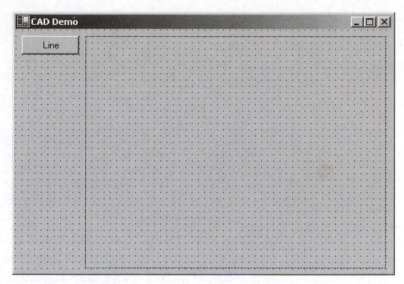

Figure A9.3 A simple form for testing the Shape class

The code in Listing A9.3 is a very simple test of whether we can create a graphics shape and draw it. Because the object variable (L) goes out of scope at the end of the event-handler, we cannot test the interactive Here() method (to determine whether it can tell if a shape's coordinate location is within its extents rectangle), but a test of Draw() and Move() does at least give us the confidence to continue with other classes and the rest of the application. Note how the Graphics object for pnlOutput is created and used. This represents a GDI+ drawing surface and provides a rich set of methods for drawing into a control.

Activity 3: Drawing a shape interactively

Drawing interactively will be necessary if the program is ever to become usable, since no-one would spend much time with a drawing program that required you to calculate and enter drawing coordinates. For the interactivity to be successful, the user must be able to see the location and size of the figure being drawn, and this requires us to draw a shape in a 'rubber-band' mode.

A drawing action will be made up of:

1. selecting the shape to be drawn (for now, a line will have to do);
2. pressing the mouse button at the location of the top-left corner of a rectangle that would enclose the shape;
3. dragging the shape out to the required size (keeping the mouse button pressed), and . . .
4. releasing the mouse button to create the final shape.

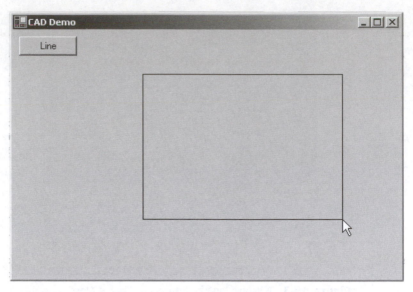

Figure A9.4 Dragging out a shape on the form

During this, we should see the shape drag out to its final size as the mouse moves, as shown in Figure A9.4.

Dragging out a shape on the screen requires us to perform the following sequence of operations.

1. When the mouse button is first pressed (signalled by a `MouseDown` event fired by the `Panel` control), the X and Y coordinates of its current location are recorded in two pairs of variables: `startX`, `startY` will indicate the location of the top, left of the shape to be drawn; `mouseX` and `mouseY` will indicate the current mouse location. Since both pairs of coordinates are the same, they will record the same pair of values.

2. The current state of the graphics inside the panel is recorded as a bitmap. This will be our 'reference' bitmap that we will use to continually return the image on the panel to its initial state during the dragging operation to remove the rubber-band drawing of the shape before replacing it with a new one. The illusion of moving a shape on the display is accomplished by clearing the shape off the display and re-drawing it in a new location. The reference bitmap will allow us to return the display to the way it was before the new shape was drawn

3. As the mouse pointer is dragged across the screen (causing a `MouseMove` event), we continually update the `mouseX` and `mouseY` coordinates. This keeps track of the other corner of the rectangle in which a shape will be drawn. We also draw the shape we want on the panel in its new position, using its `Draw()` method and using the reference bitmap to remove it from its previous position

4. When the mouse button is released (causing a `MouseUp` event), the reference bitmap is copied back to the display for the last time and the shape is drawn on it. We can then destroy the reference bitmap, since having finalized the shape

the whole drawing now includes it. When another shape is drawn interactively, a new reference bitmap, including the shape we have just drawn, will be used.

All of this behaviour will be triggered by events from the `Panel` control that houses the graphics. During the drawing operation, we will need to keep track of the first and current mouse locations within the panel, the `Shape` object being drawn, and the reference bitmap that remembers the state of the drawing before the draw operation started. We will also need to be able to indicate whether we are currently in a drawing operation, since otherwise any time we drag the mouse cursor over the panel will result in a lot of unnecessary work. These values must be available to all of the event-handlers involved in the draw operation, so should be declared as form-scope variables, as shown in Listing A9.4.

```
Public Class frmCAD
    Inherits System.Windows.Forms.Form

[+] Windows Form Designer generated code

    Private mouseX, MouseY As Integer    'Current mouse
                                         'location
    Private startX, startY As Integer    'Initial mouse
                                         'location
    Private s As Shape                   'Reference to
                                         'current shape
    Private background As Bitmap         'Copy of the
                                         'background
                                         'being drawn into
    Private Drawing As Boolean           'Indicates whether
                                         'in a
                                         'drawing operation
    Private g As Graphics                'Graphic 'device' in
                                         'pnlOutput
End Class
```

Listing A9.4: Form scope variables for the CAD form

With the data members declared in Listing A9.4, we will need to do a number of housekeeping operations to keep a drawing up to date and allow 'rubber-band' style drawing of a shape. We will define these as private subs within the form.

- `SaveBackground()`: as soon as a drawing operation commences, we will use this sub to take a snapshot of the current drawing as it appears on the panel's `Graphics` object. To do this, we'll create a new bitmap, `background`, the same size as the panel, create a `Graphics` object for it (like the panel's), and draw into it. This will then be an exact copy of the display at the moment drawing started, and will allow us to replace the display with the snapshot in a single, fast operation.

- `ReplaceBackground()`: every time a `MouseMove` event is fired from the panel, we will need to restore the panel's graphics to the state before drawing started. This sub will overwrite the current state of the panel's graphics with the copy stashed by `SaveBackground()`.

- DoPaint(): we will need to be able to draw graphics shapes, not only on the panel's graphics, but also into the bitmap stashed by SaveGraphics(). This sub will be used to do the drawing into either object passed as a Graphics parameter.

- frmCAD_Load(): this event is fired immediately after the form has been created, and so is a good place to create the Graphics object for the panel. It will be saved into the form-scope variable, g.

These operations are shown in Listing A9.5.

```
Public Class frmCAD
    Inherits System.Windows.Forms.Form
    'Existing code...
    '...

    Private Sub DoPaint(ByVal gr As Graphics)
        gr.Clear(Me.BackColor)
        s.Draw(gr)
    End Sub

    Private Sub ReplaceBackground()
        'Draws the current graphical state back into the
        'panel...
        g.DrawImage(background, 0, 0)
    End Sub

    Private Sub SaveBackground()
        'Create a bitmap to match the panel...
        background = New Bitmap(pnlOutput.Width, _
                                pnlOutput.Height, g)
        'and draw into it...,
        DoPaint(Graphics.FromImage(background))
    End Sub

    Private Sub frmCAD_Load(ByVal sender As System.Object, _
                    ByVal e As System.EventArgs) _
                    Handles MyBase.Load
        g = pnlOutput.CreateGraphics()
    End Sub
End Class
```

Listing A9.5: 'Housekeeping' operations for interactive drawing

Now for the actual drawing operation code: pressing a button to select a shape (for now, we're only dealing with a single line shape) will initiate the operation by creating the appropriate Shape object and assigning it to the Shape variable, s. Note that this is polymorphism in action. We will be drawing a line shape, but as far as the actual drawing code will be aware, it is simply a shape that knows how to draw itself. The panel's MouseDown event will set the initial coordinates and call SaveBackground(), MouseMove will continually clear and redraw the shape in its new size, and MouseUp will complete the drawing operation. This is shown in Listing A9.6.

```
Public Class frmCAD
    Inherits System.Windows.Forms.Form
    'Existing code...
    '...

    Private Sub btnLine_Click(ByVal sender As System.Object, _
                              ByVal e As System.EventArgs) _
                              Handles btnLine.Click
        'Assign a new Line object as the current Shape...
        s = New Line(0, 0, 0, 0, Color.Black)
    End Sub

    Private Sub pnlOutput_MouseDown(ByVal sender As Object, _
            ByVal e As System.Windows.Forms.MouseEventArgs) _
            Handles pnlOutput.MouseDown
        If Not s Is Nothing Then
            startX = e.X    'Record current coordinates
            startY = e.Y
            mouseX = e.X
            mouseY = e.Y
            s.X = startX    'transfer the mouse position
            s.Y = startY    'to the new shape
            s.Width = 0     'currently is it 0 size
            s.Height = 0
            SaveBackground()
            DoPaint(g)      'now draw the shapes
            Drawing = True  'and flag that we're in a
                                  drawing op.
        End If
    End Sub

    Private Sub pnlOutput_MouseMove(ByVal sender As Object, _
            ByVal e As System.Windows.Forms.MouseEventArgs) _
            Handles pnlOutput.MouseMove
        If Drawing Then
            mouseX = e.X    'Get the new size
            mouseY = e.Y
            s.Width = mouseX - startX  'Transfer to the shape
            s.Height = mouseY - startY
            'draw new rubberband...
            ReplaceBackground()
            s.Draw(g)
        End If
    End Sub

    Private Sub pnlOutput_MouseUp(ByVal sender As Object, _
            ByVal e As System.Windows.Forms.MouseEventArgs) _
            Handles pnlOutput.MouseUp
        If Drawing Then
            'The interaction is done...
            Drawing = False
            'So no need to keep the background...
            background.Dispose()
            background = Nothing
```

```
            'Draw the final shape...
            s.Draw(g)
            s = Nothing
      End If
End Class
```

Listing A9.6: Events for drawing a shape interactively

If you test the application at this stage, you should find that you can draw a single
line on to the panel, but this will disappear as soon as you start to draw a new one.
As you draw a line, it should appear interactively, anchored at the point where you
first click on the panel, and stretching out to follow the mouse pointer as you drag it
out to define the length and orientation.

Activity 4: Building a `Shapes` collection

We now need to add the capability to draw more than one line. To do this, we will
need to add some form of data structure to store all of the drawn objects, and amend
the `DoPaint()` code to enable it to draw the whole collection. Whenever a drawing operation ends, the new shape will be added to a collection of shapes and
`DoPaint()` will be called to draw the whole collection.

First the collection: we will use an `ArrayList()` to hold all of the shapes, so this
will have to be declared as a form-scope variable and created in the form's `Load`
event (Listing A9.7).

```
Public Class frmCAD
    Inherits System.Windows.Forms.Form
    'Existing code...
    '...
    Private colShapes As ArrayList
    'Existing code...
    '...
    Private Sub frmCAD_Load(ByVal sender As System.Object, _
                        ByVal e As System.EventArgs) _
                        Handles MyBase.Load
        g = pnlOutput.CreateGraphics()
        colShapes = New ArrayList()
    End Sub
End Class
```

Listing A9.7: Creating the `Shapes` collection

Now we can amend the `DoPaint()` code and arrange for each new shape to be
added to the collection (Listing A9.8).

```
Public Class frmCAD
    Inherits System.Windows.Forms.Form
    'Existing code...
    '...
```

```
Private Sub DoPaint(ByVal gr As Graphics)
    Dim s As Shape
    gr.Clear(Me.BackColor)
    For Each s In colShapes
        s.Draw(gr)
    Next
End Sub

Private Sub pnlOutput_MouseUp(ByVal sender As Object, _
        ByVal e As System.Windows.Forms.MouseEventArgs) _
        Handles pnlOutput.MouseUp
    If Drawing Then
        'The interaction is done...
        Drawing = False
        'So no need to keep the background...
        background.Dispose()
        background = Nothing
        'Add the final shape to the collection...
        colShapes.Add(s)
        'and draw the lot...
        DoPaint(g)
        s = Nothing
    End If
End Sub
'Existing code...
'...
End Class
```

Listing A9.8: Building the `Shapes` collection

The application is now capable of dealing with as many shapes as you want to draw on it, but at the moment, 'any shape as long as it is a line' is a good description of its capabilities. We should now deal with adding to the Shapes library.

Activity 5: Providing more shapes

As you saw in Activity 2 and Listing A9.2, providing a new `Shape` sub-class is a simple matter. For each shape we wish to add, we only need to provide a constructor and a `Draw()` method. We will also need to work out how any particular shape would be drawn given the limitation that the draw operation will need to draw the shape from the sizes of its enclosing rectangle.

Circles and Ellipses

The GDI+ facilities in the .NET framework do not distinguish between circles and ellipses in drawing operations. A circle is simply an ellipse which has equal major and minor axes (see Figure A9.5).

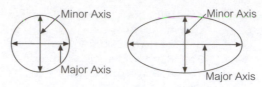

Figure A9.5 A circle is just a specialized ellipse

Fortunately for our application, drawing an ellipse fits in well since the `DrawEllipse()` method of the `Graphics` class takes as parameters the position, width and height of the rectangle that would enclose an ellipse. This matches the `Shape` class definition perfectly, and means we will not need to work out any transformations to do the drawing. The `Ellipse` class is shown in Listing A9.9.

```
Public Class Ellipse
    Inherits Shape
    Public Sub New(ByVal xx As Integer, ByVal yy As Integer, _
            ByVal wid As Integer, ByVal hgt As Integer, _
            ByVal col As Color)
        MyBase.New(xx, yy, wid, hgt, col)
    End Sub

    Public Overrides Sub Draw(ByVal gr As Graphics)
        MyBase.Draw(gr)
        gr.DrawEllipse(New Pen(colour), X, Y, Width, Height)
    End Sub
End Class
```

Listing A9.9: The `Ellipse` class

Add Listing A9.8 to the `shapes.vb` class module. All that will then be required is to add a button to the main form that will create a new `Ellipse` object and assign it to the form's `Shape` variable s. Everything else should be taken care of by the framework we have already built. Creating the new `Ellipse` shape will take just a single line of code, almost exactly the same as for the `Line` class (Listing A9.10).

```
Private Sub btnEllipse_Click(ByVal sender As System.Object, _
                ByVal e As System.EventArgs) _
                Handles btnEllipse.Click
    s = New Ellipse(0, 0, 0, 0, Color.Black)
End Sub
```

Listing A9.10: Event code for the button to add an ellipse

Exercise A9.1

Add a `Rectangle` class to the application, and add a 'Rectangle' button to the form to create new rectangles in a drawing.

Polygon Classes

A polygon is a closed shape made up of straight lines, for example a triangle, rectangle, hexagon and octagon are all polygons. We will need to deal with shapes like these differently (except of course rectangles, which are special cases and handled as such in GDI+). To draw a triangle, we will need to draw three straight line segments that join up. Since the shape must also fit snugly in an enclosing rectangle if we are to create the shape interactively, we will need to take that into account.

There are lots of different types of triangle, but if we stick with regular triangle shapes, we can define a subset that we can add to our shapes library. The two most obvious ones are right-angled and isosceles triangles, which are the two rightmost shapes in Figure A9.1. To draw a right-angled triangle:

```
Draw a line from (X, Y) to (X+Width, Y+Height)
Draw a line from (X+Width, Y+Height) to (X, Y+Height)
Draw a line from (X, Y+Height) to (X, Y)
```

For an isosceles triangle:

```
Draw a line from (X+Width/2, Y) to (X+Width, Y+Height)
Draw a line from (X+Width, Y+Height) to (X, Y+Height)
Draw a line from (X, Y+Height) to (X+Width/2, Y)
```

Since these algorithms are the basis of the `Draw()` method for each of the two triangle types, we can create a class for each type. Listing A9.11 gives the `RightTriangle` class.

```
Public Class RightTriangle
    Inherits clsShape
    Public Sub New(ByVal xx As Integer, ByVal yy As Integer, _
            ByVal wid As Integer, ByVal hgt As Integer, _
            ByVal col As Color)
        MyBase.New(xx, yy, wid, hgt, col)
    End Sub

    Public Overrides Sub Draw(ByVal gr As Graphics)
        MyBase.Draw(gr)
        gr.DrawLine(New Pen(colour), X, Y, X + Width, _
                                    Y + Height)
        gr.DrawLine(New Pen(colour), X + Width, _
                                Y + Height, X, Y + Height)
        gr.DrawLine(New Pen(colour), X, Y + Height, X, Y)
    End Sub
End Class
```

Listing A9.11: The `RightTriangle` class

You can again test the new class in Listing A9.10 by adding a button to the form (`btnRightTriangle`) and coding its `-Click` event-handler as in Listing A9.12.

```
Private Sub btnRightTriangle_Click( _
                          ByVal sender As System.Object, _
                          ByVal e As System.EventArgs) _
                          Handles btnRightTri.Click
    s = New RightTriangle(0, 0, 0, 0, Color.Black)
End Sub
```

Listing A9.12: Drawing a `RightTriangle`

One thing to note about the `RightTriangle` class is that although we have defined a right-angled triangle that is drawn in a particular orientation (with the right angle at the bottom-left), we can draw one in any orientation by simply changing the direction the mouse is dragged in after the initial point has been set.

Exercise A9.2

Create the `IsoscelesTriangle` class, defining the `Draw()` method as described. Add a suitable button to the form and test its operation.

We can continue adding `Shape` classes in this fashion for as many different shapes as we can imagine. You should try adding other shapes to increase the flexibility of the program (e.g. diamond shapes, hexagons, octagons, etc.).

The last embellishment to this program that we'll do as an activity will be to add controls to allow colour to be defined for each shape.

Activity 6: Colour

At the moment, colour is hard-coded into the event-handlers that create the initial shapes. Note that each call to a shape's constructor contains `Color.Black` as its last parameter. We can make it easy to apply any colour we like to a shape by having a `CurrentColour` variable that can be used instead of `Color.Black`. The obvious control for setting the `CurrentColour` value is a `ColorDialog`. We can place a `ColorDialog` control on the form and use it to get the user to pick a new colour as shown in Listing A9.13.

```
Public Class frmCAD
    Inherits System.Windows.Forms.Form
    'Existing code . . .
    '. . .
    Private CurrentColour As Color
    'Existing code . . .
    '. . .
    Private Sub btnColour_Click( _
                        ByVal sender As System.Object, _
                        ByVal e As System.EventArgs) _
                        Handles btnColour.Click
        If ColorDlg.ShowDialog() Then
```

```
              CurrentColour = ColorDlg.Color
              btnColour.ForeColor = CurrentColour
          End If
      End Sub
  End Class
```

Listing A9.13: Defining a `CurrentColour` and code to select it

To complete the application (as far as it will be taken here), you will need to replace the setting of `Color.Black` with `CurrentColour` in each of the `Shape` selection button event-handlers, as in Listing A9.14.

```
  Private Sub btnEllipse_Click(ByVal sender As System.Object, _
                           ByVal e As System.EventArgs) _
                           Handles btnEllipse.Click
      s = New clsEllipse(0, 0, 0, 0, CurrentColour)
  End Sub
```

Listing A9.14: Assigning the `CurrentColour` to a new shape

Features worth remembering

We have covered a lot of ground in this chapter and the end of chapter activities. While different controls will all have their own idiosyncrasies, there are a few general lessons to be learned.

- Always try to find a meaningful name to assign to any control added to a form that will be referred to in text. A three-letter prefix should be used to indicate the type of control (e.g. **txt** for a text box, **lbl** for a label, **btn** for buttons, etc.) and the remainder of the name should indicate its purpose (e.g. **btnColour**, **lblCustomerName**, **txtAddress**, etc.).

- Using the `Enabled` property to disable controls whose use does not make sense in the current state of a program is an easy way to lead the user away from making impossible choices or inappropriate operations.

- Where possible, let a user choose from a list or group of options rather than having to type data into a program. Mistyped entry will only cause problems and it can take a great deal of code to validate data entered from the keyboard.

- Most controls have dozens of events associated with them. While some of these are for exotic uses, many are sensibly provided to allow you to detect changes as they happen to the program. Learn the main events that each control can raise and try to make use of them.

- Use the `Dock` and `Anchor` properties to make controls adjust properly when a form resizes.

- The complex `List` controls (`ListView`, `TreeView`) can be used to display information about whole objects. Build support into classes for these controls by providing methods to return `ListViewItem` and `TreeNode` objects.

Suggested Additional Activities

1. In the activities for this chapter, we worked through the core of an object-oriented graphics program. You can extend this in several ways – adding new `Shape` classes, extending the drawing facilities to handle filled shapes (note the number of `Graphics` methods that begin with `Fill..`) and the user-interface to allow the selection of fill styles and colours.

2. At present, editing the output of the drawing program is not possible. What is needed is a method to select a shape to be deleted or changed. The `Shape` class's `Here()` method is a start in this direction, since you can iterate through each shape to determine which was under the mouse pointer when a click on the panel occurs. Having selected a shape, a dialog box could display its details (coordinates, size and colour) and the user could be allowed to alter any or all of them.

3. In Chapter 11, we will look at methods of saving data to and retrieving it from files. Consider coming back to this application to allow a drawing to be saved to a file and loaded from one.

Solutions to Exercises

Exercise 9.1

a) Simply assign it, as in:

```
f.txtGreeting.Text = "Hello"
```

b) To do this, we need to assign the value in `address` is assigned to the text box *before* the dialog is displayed, then display the dialog and finally copy the updated value back to `address` one the form has been dismissed:

```
Private Sub btnGetCustInfo_Click(ByVal sender As
                                 System.Object, _
                    ByVal e As System.EventArgs) _
                      Handles btnGetCustInfo.Click
    Dim f As New frmCustomer()
    Dim address As String
    f.txtAddress.Text = address
    If f.ShowDialog(Me) = DialogResult.OK Then
        address = f.txtAddress.Text
        'go on to process address data
        '. . .
    End If
    'By here the address will have been edited.
End Sub
```

Exercise 9.2

```
Private Sub txtName_KeyPress(ByVal sender As Object, _
    ByVal e As System.Windows.Forms.KeyPressEventArgs) _
    Handles txtName.KeyPress
    If InStr("abcdefghijklmnopqrstuvwxyz'-", _
                        Char.ToLower(e.KeyChar)) = 0 Then
        e.Handled = True
    End If
End Sub
```

Note that by comparing a lower-case version of whatever character was typed (using `Char.ToLower()`), the handler will allow both upper and lower case characters. I've also provided for a hyphen to deal with names like 'Berners-Lee'.

Exercise 9.3

```
Public Sub ChangeForeColours(ByVal F As Form)
    Dim c As Control
    For Each c In F.Controls
        c.ForeColor = Color.Red
    Next
End Sub
```

Note that this sub can be placed in a code module and called simply by name (`ChangeForeColours(MyForm)`). If however it is a public method of a form, it would have to be prefixed with the form's name (`frmUpdateUI.ChangeForeColours(MyForm)`), unless it was called to change the form it was a public method of (`ChangeForeColours(Me)`).

Exercise 9.4

```
Private Sub mnuEdit_Popup(ByVal sender As Object, _
                        ByVal e As System.EventArgs) _
                        Handles mnuEdit.Popup
    If txtDocument.SelectedText = "" Then
        mnuEditCut.Visible = False
        mnuEditCopy.Visible = False
    Else
        mnuEditCut.Visible = True
        mnuEditCopy.Visible = True
    End If
End Sub
```

Note I've used `txtDocument.SelectedText = ""` instead of checking the length of the selected text. Both methods are valid.

Exercise 9.5

a)

```
F2.txtName.Text = F1.txtName.Text
F2.txtAddress.Text = F1.txtAddress.Text
```

b)

```
If F1.chkUpperCase.Value Then
    F2.txtName.Text = F1.txtName.Text.ToUpper()
    F2.txtAddress.Text = F1.txtAddress.Text.ToUpper()
Else
    F2.txtName.Text = F1.txtName.Text
    F2.txtAddress.Text = F1.txtAddress.Text
End if
```

Exercise 9.6

a) Assign the `ArrayList` directly to the `DataSource` property:

```
lstPostCodes.DataSource = PostCodes
```

b) Here we need to convert each post code to upper case, so members of the `ArrayList` must be dealt with one-by-one:

```
Dim PC As String
For Each PC In PostCodes
    lstPostCodes.Items.Add(PC.ToUpper())
Next
```

Exercise 9.7

```
AddHandler Label1.Click, AddressOf LabelClick
AddHandler Label2.Click, AddressOf LabelClick
```

Exercise A9.1

Note that the class is little different from the `Ellipse` class since an ellipse is drawn in a Windows graphic control by specifying the rectangular outline it is inscribed in.

```
Public Class Rectangle
    Inherits Shape
    Public Sub New(ByVal xx As Integer, ByVal yy As
                   Integer, _
            ByVal wid As Integer, ByVal hgt As Integer, _
            ByVal col As Color)
        MyBase.New(xx, yy, wid, hgt, col)
    End Sub

    Public Overrides Sub Draw(ByVal gr As Graphics)
        MyBase.Draw(gr)
        gr.DrawRectangle(New Pen(colour), X, Y, Width,
        Height)
    End Sub
End Class
```

The button code to create and add a rectangle is then simply:

```
Private Sub btnRect_Click(ByVal sender As System.Object, _
                          ByVal e As System.EventArgs) _
                          Handles btnRect.Click
    s = New Rectangle(0, 0, 0, 0, Color.Black)
End Sub
```

Exercise A9.2

```
Public Class IsoscelesTriangle
    Inherits clsShape
    Public Sub New(ByVal xx As Integer, ByVal yy As
    Integer, _
            ByVal wid As Integer, ByVal hgt As Integer, _
            ByVal col As Color)
        MyBase.New(xx, yy, wid, hgt, col)
    End Sub
    Public Overrides Sub Draw(ByVal gr As Graphics)
        MyBase.Draw(gr)
        gr.DrawLine(New Pen(colour), X+Width/2, Y, _
                                     X + Width, Y + Height)
        gr.DrawLine(New Pen(colour), X + Width,
                                     Y + Height, _ X,
                                     Y + Height)
        gr.DrawLine(New Pen(colour), X, Y + Height,
                                     X+Width/2, Y)
    End Sub
End Class
```

And the code for the button:

```
Private Sub btnIsoscelesTriangle_Click( _
                        ByVal sender As System.Object, _
                        ByVal e As System.EventArgs) _
                        Handles btnIsoscelesTri.Click
    s = New IsoscelesTriangle(0, 0, 0, 0, Color.Black)
End Sub
```

Answers to Review Questions

1. Which property would you use on a control to make sure that it does not disappear off the bottom or right edge of the form if the form were resized? **Either the `Dock` property (to fix the control to specific form edges) or the `Anchor` property (to fix specific edges of a control to remain set distances from a form's edges.**

2. Which property of a control would you alter if you wanted to ensure that the control could not be accessed from a different form in a program (hint: how would you define a variable on a form to impose this restriction)? **The `Modifiers` property can be set to `Private` to prevent external access to a control.**

3. You have `String` variables (`name`, `address`, `postcode`) that contain details of a customer, and a form (`frmCustomerData`) with text boxes (`txtName`, `txtAddress`, `txtPostCode`)

for displaying and editing this data. The form is currently not being displayed. Outline the code you would write to allow a user to edit the customer data. You can assume the form has buttons assigned to its `AcceptButton` and `CancelButton` properties and can be used as a dialog box. **Create the form, place the variables on to the appropriate controls on the form, show the form as a dialog and then, if the dialog result was OK, copy the values on the controls back to the appropriate variables.**

4. A list box is to have 1000 items added to it from a database. Which methods would you use to make sure that the update went as fast as possible? **Either set the `DataSource` property of the list box to an `ArrayList` that contains the data (or a specific column in the database – see Chapter 12), or move the data into an array and use the `AddRange` method of the list box.**

5. How is the user informed where the drop part of a drag and drop operation can be done on a form? **The mouse cursor changes as it moves over controls that can be dropped on – this is controlled by setting the `Effect` property of the `DragEventArgs` argument in a `DragEvent`.**

6. What is the purpose of the `Sender` parameter in a control's event handlers? What is the purpose of the e parameter? **The `Sender` parameter indicates which control raised the event (e.g. which button was pressed). The e parameter provides access to further information, such as the mouse cursor location, key pressed or whatever.**

7. The `Controls` collection of a form allows programmatic access to all of the controls placed on the form. What type of code structure would you use to access each control in turn? How would you modify this structure so that you only accessed `TextBox` controls? **For Each is the most efficient. You could place an `If..Then` block inside the `For..Each` and check the `Type` or `TypeName` of each control, accepting only `TextBox` controls.**

8. What options are there for providing information in a menu item apart from the menu text? **A menu item can be greyed-out (using the `Enabled` property), made invisible (using the `Visible` property), checked or made a visible member of a group of menu options.**

9. How do the `Checked` properties of a `CheckBox` and a `RadioButton` differ in the way they are normally used? How does the `Checked` property of a `RadioButton` differ from the `RadioCheck` property in a `MenuItem`? **A `CheckBox`'s `Checked` property indicates a true or false value that is independent of other controls. In a group of `RadioButtons`, the `Checked` properties are interdependent. In a menu item, the `RadioCheck` property is not interdependent with other menu items and must be switched on and off in code.**

10. How do you set which property of an item in a `ListBox` is displayed? What are the options and what is the default? **Set the `DisplayMember` property of the `ListBox` to nominate a property of items added to the list, or leave this property blank and the list box will display the result of an object's `ToString()` method. The `ToString()` method is the default.**

11. List three ways in which items can be added to a `ListBox` or `ComboBox` control. **Individually, using the `Items.Add()` method, in batches, using the**

`Items.AddRange()` **method, or by setting the** `DataSource` **property to indicate an** `ArrayList` **or an** `ArrayList` **property of some object.**

12. How would you determine the number of selected item in a `ListBox`? **Using the** `Count` **property of the** `SelectedItems` **property – i.e.** `ListBox.SelectedItems.Count`.

13. How does the `SubItems` property of a `ListViewItem` object differ from the `Items` property of a `ListView` control? **Each** `ListViewItem` **can have a list of** `SubItems`. `SubItems` **cannot.**

In this chapter, you will learn about:

- ways of organizing the objects in an application for flexibility and ease of maintenance;
- 3-tier application structures;
- the role that collections play in applications;
- how objects are disposed of;
- class interface design principles;
- software patterns.

10.1 Application Structure

An object-oriented program can involve many classes and many objects of these classes. Each class is a design for objects that have a role to play in the final application. However, in a complex system, the large number of objects in memory at any one time can easily get out of hand. A developer needs some organizational principles to apply to simplify the job of making objects fit together in a way that works and is maintainable.

There are almost as many application structures as there are application programs in use. In some respects, the structure of an application, which is simply the way that the objects fit together to do the work, is what makes it unique. However, we have a limited range of tools to apply to design an application structure, and so we can generally factor out some common design principles. When we approach the design of a new application, we must consider several areas of concern.

- What form will the application take? Will it be a WinForms application, in which there can be several user-interface elements driving the objects, or a Console application with more simple interactive input and output, a simple command driven system or perhaps even a web-based system?

- What is the natural logical structure that associates the main objects in the system with the way that they are processed? For example, a program might be required to deal with a number of independent documents simultaneously, or may allow the user only to work on documents one at a time. In the first of these, the best structure could be to manage a collection of independent objects, each with its own user-interface (Microsoft Word works like this); the second is more easily implemented since there is no need to determine which document is currently active.

- What is the composition of the main objects in the system? We can think of a document as a collection of sections, each of which is a collection of paragraphs, each of which is a collection of sentences, etc. However, a CAD system may be better organized as a single collection of draw-able objects (circles, rectangles, lines, etc.) or as some form of network structure in which the connections between objects define their structural relationships.

- How long will the information contained in the objects be expected to exist? Simple programs may simply accept input, process it, display results and then forget it all. However, you would be rightly upset if your word processor (or even Visual Studio) were to behave like this. Normally, we expect a program to be able to save data to a more permanent storage device (like a disk drive) and be able to retrieve it again later. Depending on the complexity of the information and our needs for accessing it, we may have to save all of the objects to a disk file when a program ends and retrieve them all when it is used again, or we may save individual objects to a database and retrieve them on an as-needed basis.

- How will the user of an application choose which objects to work with? Is their some logical structure that can be mirrored in the application's user-interface (e.g. a spreadsheet is organized as a matrix of cells, and the user selects a cell by clicking on it and entering data or a formula) or will it be necessary to come up with some novel method that allows objects to be manipulated (e.g. a 3-D drawing program will require some way of allowing the user to select a viewpoint from which to 'see' the objects)?

These and other factors could be thought of as individual problems to be dealt with when creating an application. However, it has long been recognized that designing a suitable structure for modelling the information in an application is the key to success in its implementation. Whole libraries of books are dedicated to the subject of *data-structures* in software. In object-oriented design, we more correctly speak of *object-structures* when we consider how the objects in an application are made to fit together.

10.1.1 2- and 3-Tier Application Structures

In the chapter on WinForms applications, we briefly looked at the idea of a 2-tier structure, where the business layer of the program was developed independently of the presentation or user-interface layer. In fact this is a simplification of what happens in most real-world applications, where the 2-tier structure would not be adequate because of the need to make objects persist over time.

In a simple application, we may have no need to store data for later retrieval (for example, calculating someone's tax), and so a 2-tier structure would be suitable for this. However, in most applications we need to store object information from one run to the next (for example a word processor); in such applications, it is possible to use

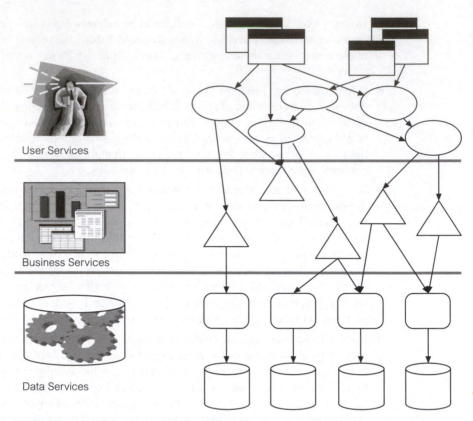

User Services

Business Services

Data Services

Figure 10.1 3-Tier Application Services Structure

a 2-tier structure by making objects responsible for the storage and retrieval of their own data, but it is sometimes organizationally preferable to introduce a 3rd tier to take care of the storage and retrieval of objects. In most business applications, we need to work with a persistent store of object information which may contain the data of thousands or millions of objects (for example, a banking system), and in this case it is necessary to introduce a 3rd tier, responsible for storing and retrieving objects on demand.

Microsoft promotes the idea of *services* in application design, where three distinct application tiers are responsible for *user services* (i.e. the user-interface), *business services* (i.e. the main logic of the application that models the actual requirements) and *data services* (responsible for storing object data in a database and recreating objects from this data as necessary). Figure 10.1 shows this diagrammatically.

In a Visual Basic .NET application, these services are usually developed as separate modules (possibly many in each tier). User services are normally realized as Form classes, possibly with some additional classes to support operations that are only relevant to the job of presenting data (for example, objects that can format data for easier presentation). Business services perform the main work of the application, and are normally realised as classes that define individual business objects (e.g. an email, a customer record or a bank transaction) and Collection classes that organize these into meaningful groups (e.g. an email in-box, a list of customer invoices or all of the transactions in a bank account). Data services may be implemented by standard classes that know how to store data in and retrieve data from a database system (e.g. ADO .NET, which is a set of classes for working with many different forms of database), or custom-built classes that will take care of converting raw data into business objects and storing business objects as raw data.

We will be examining database interactions and the ADO .NET database classes in Chapter 12. For now, it will be enough to accept that a database is a way of storing information with a regular structure that you might conveniently think of as lists of items.

Exercise 10.1

An application program manages multiple bank accounts for multiple users. To create and manage this application, two `ArrayList` collections, `colAccounts` and `colUsers` are instantiated on the Main form of the program and given `Public` scope:

a) Which tier have these collections been allocated to?

b) Which tier do you think they actually belong in?

c) Given that the two collections are only `ArrayList` instances, can you think of a better approach to creating and maintaining them so that they fit better into the tier they belong in?

10.1.2 Appointing Responsibilities

One approach to designing object models is to concentrate on the responsibilities of the objects in the system. In a 3-tier system, we can divide an application's responsibilities as follows.

10.1.2.1 The User-Interface Tier

The very specific requirements for this tier are:

- accept user input to the system (e.g. information to send to a database, or a request for information from a database);
- validate user input to prevent passing on of obviously wrong data to the business layer (e.g. invalid date entries, numbers with alphabetic characters in them, etc.);
- present the user with formatted views of data in the system (e.g. tables of data, bar charts derived from data, forms for data entry or display, etc.);
- provide the user with access to a suitable set of commands and system queries;
- perform all processing that is purely to do with presenting data in some format.

10.1.2.2 The Business Tier

This tier has the following requirements:

- to enforce the business rules regarding the way that information is used and updated in the system – for example, it should not be possible to raise an invoice for a customer who does not have an account record;

- to provide a standard programmatic layer to which a number of different user interfaces can be interfaced – for example an application program for inventory updates, a web browser for customers to examine products, and a WAP phone interface for sales personnel to receive up to date price information from;

- to simplify the development of operations that interact with the corporate database;

- to provide different levels of access to different types of user – for example, customers, managers, shop-floor workers, etc.

10.1.2.3 The Data Access Tier

This tier provides the following services:

- secure access to data services;

- coherent data updates (for example, to ensure that rules for data integrity are maintained);

- access security, via, for example, user identification and verification;

- efficient retrieval of data based on business requirements;

- facilities for data replication (for example, for mobile computer users), data backup and data transformation (e.g. for long-term off-line data storage, sometimes known as data warehousing).

By developing an application as a set of tiers that can perform in these three main areas, we may make it initially more complex, since we will need to deal with three separate sets of class interfaces, and will often need to separate out parts of an operation that might naturally be done together more efficiently. However, the three-tier structure is less about simple expediency in developing a program, and more about planning for expansion and maintainability. Problems in a system can normally be quickly traced to one or other tier by their nature, and the job of fixing a problem is therefore much less difficult when the possible source has been reduced to a single tier.

Changes in an application will be more likely to be required in one or other tier rather than across the board; for example, business rules may change, there may be need for a database system that can cope with a higher volume of data, or it may be necessary to introduce a web-browser based user-interface. All of these situations (and the vast majority of others you can think of) can be dealt with by fixing or upgrading one tier rather than a whole application.

10.1.3 Object Lifetime

One distinguishing feature of object-oriented programming is the way that objects come into existence, are used and destroyed as an application runs. It is useful to

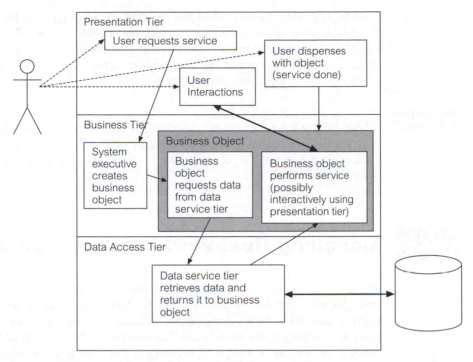

Figure 10.2 Interactions between service tiers

consider an object's lifetime in an application when designing a structure, since different tiers will be more or less important in different stages of the object's time in the computer's memory.

Figure 10.2 shows a typical sequence of interactions between a user and a system. Note that there is a specific point in the sequence when an object is created (system executive creates business object) and another point in the sequence when the object is destroyed (user dispenses with object). From a purely programming point of view, we need to ensure that an object has been created before we can use it; typically, we create a new object immediately before we send the first message to it. From a design point of view, it is also useful to be aware when that object will cease to exist. Objects that take up memory space can become a drain on the system; they will certainly occupy memory and may also take up processing time if they receive events or are included in a search. .NET automatically takes care of objects that we are done with through a process called *garbage collection*. As the name suggests, this involves throwing discarded objects out of memory and so reclaiming their space.

All of the user's interactions (including the creation and destruction of an object) are mediated through the *presentation tier*, all database interactions are done through the *data access tier*, and the business tier acts as a middle-man, interpreting and executing the user's requests and asking for data as necessary.

This picture might change slightly from application to application, but it is easily possible to use this diagram with minor variations to describe a wide range of software systems. You can take almost any piece of software you are familiar with and consider how this diagram describes its way of working. The business object could be a word processed document, someone's bank account or a CAD drawing: Figure 10.2 would require little or no change to depict the object's pattern of creation, use and destruction. As a software designer, you will need to be able to create this and similar application structures for a range of types of system.

Exercise 10.2

Look back at any of the Practical Activity exercises from previous chapters and identify the various stages depicted in Figure 10.2. Where and when are objects created, what interactions do they receive while they are in existence, and when are they discarded?

10.2 Modelling Real-World Object Structures

In an ideal world full of ideal programming languages and environments, you would create software that followed the logical structure dictated purely by the software requirements alone. As we don't inhabit an ideal world and there are no ideal programming languages, we are normally left with the need to implement the idealized application structure in a physical language and environment that imposes its own requirements on the eventual implementation. One approach that is almost universally applicable is to start with the data structure.

The data in an application program always has an ideal logical structure, dictated purely by what the software is required to do with it. In most situations, the logical data structure is a version of the organization of information or entities in the real-world situation that the software is being designed to fit into. For example, consider the Bank Account model that we have used at various points in this book as a platform for describing object-orientation and software. The model used in previous chapters has been a seriously flawed one that no real bank could ever use. The problem with it is due to the very simplified way that deposits and withdrawals are recorded. Simply adding an amount to or subtracting an amount from the account balance is not adequate if, as for any real bank account, it is necessary to provide an audit trail or statement. Have a look at any real bank account statement and you will see that the bank has provided it by keeping a record of every single transaction – how much it was for, what date it was made, what type it was (e.g. deposit, withdrawal, interest payment or charges) and some description of it. A typical bank statement may appear as shown in Figure 10.3.

10.2.1 Example: A Class Model for a Bank Account

The bank statement shown in Figure 10.3 can be analysed to give us a clear picture of the structure of a real bank account. The information at the top (Account Number and Account Name) is items of data that would have to be held for any account, and so we could consider these to be properties of a bank account. However, the

Account Number: 1234567890
Account Name: Mr Wombat Snodgrass

Date	Type	Description	Debit	Credit	Balance
3/10/2002		Carried Forward			1050.28
3/10/2002	Withdrawal	ATM: York Petergate	80.00		970.28
5/10/2002	Withdrawal	Cheque: 0001046	28.65		941.63
7/10/2002	Withdrawal	DD: Home-care Insurance	35.44		906.19
7/10/2002	Charges	Overdraft Charges	15.00		891.19
9/10/2002	Interest			0.94	892.13
10/10/2002	Deposit	ATM: Glasgow W. Nile St		550.00	1442.13
...	...	...	...	...	...

Figure 10.3 A bank statement

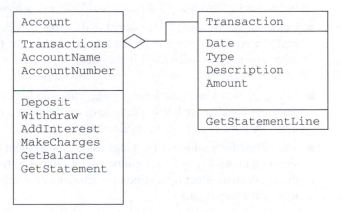

Figure 10.4 A class model for a more functional bank account

remaining information is actually a list (which could be of any length) of other items that belong to the bank account. Each line in the table in Figure 10.3 represents a transaction on the bank account, and so a better representation of structure of a bank account would be that shown in Figure 10.4.

Figure 10.4 shows a class model for a more realistic bank account than those we considered in earlier chapters. You can see that an *aggregation construct* (indicated by the diamond symbol) has been used to show the relationship between an account and its transactions: a bank account **has-a** collection of transactions. The collection appears in the diagram as a property of a bank account, along with `AccountName` and `AccountNumber`. Methods for the account include four separate methods for creating a transaction (`Deposit`, `Withdraw`, `AddInterest` and `MakeCharges` each constitute a form of transaction) plus methods to calculate the account balance (now a more complex operation) and generate a statement.

A `Transaction` has properties to indicate the `Date` and `Type` of transaction (which will be `Deposit`, `Withdrawal`, `Interest` or `Charges`), a textual `Description` of the transaction (important for a statement) and the `Amount` of the transaction. Note that the single `Amount` property takes the place of separate properties for credit and debit, since a positive number will be a credit and a negative number a debit. Note also that a transaction does not include an indication of the account balance, even though the balance is shown at the end of each transaction line in the statement. It is better to calculate the balance for each line of the statement than to store any indication of account balance, especially within a transaction object, since this should not be responsible for information that belongs to the whole account.

If we were to go on to implement this new model of a bank account, we would have to consider how to manage the collection of transactions, since these are central to the account's operation. Referring back to Chapter 6, in which we looked at the various data structures available within .NET, we might decide that an `ArrayList` would be a good structure class to use for this purpose, since:

■ We do not need to specify a maximum capacity, as we would with a simple array: in fact, specifying a maximum capacity would simply place a limit on the number of transactions that an account could support, which could cause problems.

■ Entries in the `ArrayList` are stored in the order in which they are added and can easily be retrieved in that order: there is no need for the list to be organized in any other order, or for individual transactions to be retrievable by some key value, such as a `HashTable` or `Dictionary` would provide.

■ `ArrayList` is a computationally cheap structure to deal with, which is essential since our banking application may have to deal with a great many accounts, and therefore a lot of `ArrayList`s, simultaneously.

■ The coding for working out aggregates (i.e. the account balance and statement) is simple with an `ArrayList`: simply iterate through the transactions computing their collective effect by addition (of amounts or strings of text). A `For..Each` loop will easily do this.

The methods of both classes are quite simple to implement purely because the object model is a good logical picture of the structure of an account; it would have been impossible to generate a statement from our previous model of an account. The single method for a transaction, `GetStatementLine`, simply packs the transaction information into a single string with suitable formatting. This in turn simplifies the `GetStatement()` method of the `Account` class, since it can do the hardest part of its work by asking each `Transaction` object in turn to provide a line of the statement.

The account balance is simply calculated by iterating through each `Transaction`, adding positive transactions (deposits and interest payments) and subtracting negative ones (withdrawals and charges) to form an overall sum. Note that using this method, the actual account balance is *never* stored in the account, but instead is calculated as needed; this prevents the record of account balance getting out of step with the transaction records, which would otherwise be possible if there were coding errors.

10.2.2 Bank Account Classes

We can now go on and implement the improved `BankAccount` class model, starting with the `Transaction` class (Listing 10.1).

```
Friend Class Transaction
    'This will allow us to specify the type of
    transaction...
    Public Enum TransactionType
        Deposit = 0
        Withdrawal
        Interest
        Charges
    End Enum
    'Here are the member fields...
    Private mvarDate As Date
    Private mvarType As TransactionType
    Private mvarAmount As Decimal
    Private mvarDescription As String
    'Here is the constructor...
    Public Sub New(ByVal TrDate As Date, _
                   ByVal Type As TransactionType, _
                   ByVal Amount As Decimal, _
                   ByVal Description As String)
        mvarDate = TrDate
        mvarType = Type
        mvarAmount = Amount
        mvarDescription = Description
    End Sub
    'All of the properties can be read only...
    Public ReadOnly Property TrDate() As Date
        Get
            Return mvarDate
        End Get
    End Property

    Public ReadOnly Property Type() As TransactionType
        Get
            Return mvarType
        End Get
    End Property

    Public ReadOnly Property Amount() As Decimal
        Get
            Return mvarAmount
        End Get
    End Property

    Public ReadOnly Property Description() As String
        Get
            Return mvarDescription
        End Get
    End Property
```

```
'Finally a function to format the transaction
'for a statement...
Public Function GetStatementLine() As String
    Dim trType As String
    Dim len As Integer
    'Specify the transaction type in a string...
    Select Case mvarType
        Case TransactionType.Deposit
            trType = "Deposit     "
        Case TransactionType.Withdrawal
            trType = "Withdrawal "
        Case TransactionType.Interest
            trType = "Interest    "
        Case TransactionType.Charges
            trType = "Charges     "
    End Select
    'Add all the transaction data into one big
    'formatted string..
    Return String.Format("{0} {1} {2,8:£0.00} {3}", _
            mvarDate.ToShortDateString(), _
            trType, mvarAmount, mvarDescription)
End Function
End Class
```

Listing 10.1: The `Transaction` class code

This listing shows all of the code for the `Transaction` class. We will never need to change the various values within a transaction, since a fundamental principle of financial accounting is that accounts' data should never be altered in any way. This makes it sensible for us to store the transaction data in Private member variables and publish them as `ReadOnly` properties.

The class has a constructor even though this is not indicated in the class diagram. Any class that contains data that cannot have a default value should have a constructor, since this will make objects of the class easier to create. `Sub New()` takes four parameters, these being the date of the transaction, the type of transaction it is, the amount it is for and a text description.

Finally, the sole method (apart from the constructor), `GetStatementLine()` does the simple job of packing the transaction data into a formatted string that will represent the transaction on a single line of a statement. Note the way the `Format()` method of the `String` class has been used. This is similar to the way a format can be applied to console output, with the data items indicated by replaceable parameter brackets. Note particularly how the `Amount` field is dealt with: the format string "{2,8:£0.00}" indicates that data value number 2 (3rd in the list) will be given a range of eight character slots (2, 8) and that its format will incorporate a pound sign (£), at least one digit before the decimal point and two digits after the decimal point (0.00).

The `Transaction` class performs all of the storage and data manipulation that we will need for an individual transaction. The remaining functionality resides with the `BankAccount` class. Listing10.2 gives the `BankAccount` code.

```vb
Imports System.Text
'This must be the first line in the module (before the
'Transaction class. It is needed to allow us to use a
'StringBuilder object(see the GetStatement() method.)
'Transaction class code goes here.
'. . .
Public Class BankAccount
    Private mvarTransactions As ArrayList
    Private mvarAccountName As String
    Private mvarAccountNumber As Long
    Public Sub New(ByVal name As String, ByVal number As Long)
        mvarAccountName = name
        mvarAccountNumber = number
        mvarTransactions = New ArrayList()
    End Sub

    Public ReadOnly Property AccountName() As String
        Get
            Return mvarAccountName
        End Get
    End Property

    Public ReadOnly Property AccountNumber() As String
        Get
            Return Format(mvarAccountNumber, "0000000000")
        End Get
    End Property

    Public Sub Deposit(ByVal TrDate As Date, _
                       ByVal Amount As Decimal, _
                       ByVal Description As String)
        Dim T As Transaction
        T = New Transaction(TrDate, _
            Transaction.TransactionType.Deposit, Amount, _
            Description)
        mvarTransactions.Add(T)
    End Sub

    Public Sub Withdraw(ByVal TrDate As Date, _
                        ByVal Amount As Decimal, _
                        ByVal Description As String)
        Dim T As Transaction
        T = New Transaction(TrDate, _
            Transaction.TransactionType.Withdrawal, Amount, _
            Description)
        mvarTransactions.Add(T)
    End Sub

    Public Sub AddInterest(ByVal TrDate As Date, _
                           ByVal Amount As Decimal)
        Dim T As Transaction
        T = New Transaction(TrDate, _
            Transaction.TransactionType.Withdrawal, _
            Amount, "")
```

```
                        mvarTransactions.Add(T)
            End Sub

            Public Sub MakeCharges(ByVal TrDate As Date, _
                                   ByVal Amount As Decimal, _
                                   ByVal Description As String)
                Dim T As Transaction
                T = New Transaction(TrDate, _
                    Transaction.TransactionType.Charges, Amount, _
                    Description)
                mvarTransactions.Add(T)
            End Sub

            Public Function GetBalance() As Decimal
                Dim T As Transaction
                Dim Bal As Decimal = 0
                For Each T In mvarTransactions
                    If T.Type = Transaction.TransactionType.Deposit _
                       Or T.Type =
Transaction.TransactionType.Interest _
                       Then
                         Bal += T.Amount
                    Else
                         Bal -= T.Amount
                    End If
                Next
                Return Bal
            End Function

            Public Function GetStatement() As String
                Dim T As Transaction
                Dim stmt As StringBuilder = New StringBuilder()
                stmt.Append("Bank Account Statement" & _
                         Environment.NewLine)
                stmt.Append("Account Name: " & _
                         mvarAccountName & Environment.NewLine)
                stmt.Append("Account Number: " & _
                         mvarAccountNumber & Environment.NewLine)
                For Each T In mvarTransactions
                    stmt.Append(T.GetStatementLine & _
                             Environment.NewLine)
                Next
                Return stmt.ToString()
            End Function
        End Class
```

Listing 10.2: The `BankAccount` class code

Again, the member variables of the `BankAccount` class have been properly defined with `Private` scope, meaning that they will only be visible within the class code. The class constructor has a little more to do in this class, since in addition to initializing the individual member variables `mvarAccountName` and `mvarAccountNumber`, it also has to create an `ArrayList` object to accommodate the list of transactions.

The four methods for adding new transactions, `Deposit()`, `Withdraw()`, `AddInterest()` and `MakeCharges()`, have parameter lists that will accept enough information to create each type of transaction. Note that while a deposit, a withdrawal or making charges each require a `description` parameter, this has been omitted from the `AddInterest` method, since the transaction type name, `Interest`, is quite self-explanatory. In a real bank statement, deposits, withdrawals and charges all require some further descriptive text. Note also that there is no need to indicate the transaction type among the parameters since this is implicit in the actual method (a `Deposit` operation creates a `Deposit` transaction).

The most interesting code in the class appears in the last two methods, where a balance is calculated and a statement is generated. To calculate the balance of an account, simply work through all of the transactions, adding those credited to the account (deposits and interest payments) and subtracting the debits (withdrawals and charges). A `For..Each` loop is the ideal way to work through the list of transactions for this.

To create all of the text for a statement, we perform a similar operation, this time starting with the simple account information (name and number) and then appending all of the statement lines (generated by each `Transaction` object) and inserting a new line character (`Environment.NewLine`) between each. This text manipulation for this could become a very inefficient operation were we to do it by adding `String` objects together since .NET strings are immutable; for each operation where we appended one string to another, .NET would have to create new strings and throw away the previous ones. However, the `StringBuilder` class comes to the rescue here, since it operates in a far more efficient manner, putting strings together by packing them into a single sequence of characters. Using `StringBuilder`'s `Append()` method, all of the transactions, the new line characters and the statement header are packed into a single object which is finally returned as a `String` at the end of the function (using the `ToString()` method). The use of `StringBuilder` is the reason that the namespace `System.Text` had to be imported at the beginning of the module.

Our `BankAccount` class is now a much more realistic model of a bank account, even though it is no more difficult to use than the simple Bank Account models we created in earlier chapters. The key to this is the way that information has been hidden within the class. A user of the `BankAccount` class need not be aware of the `Transaction` class at all (which explains why it has been declared as a `Friend` Class, accessible from within this assembly but not from any code that imports the assembly). By simply using the `Public` methods of the `BankAccount` class, transactions will be created and managed automatically.

Exercise 10.3

The structure of the `BankAccount` class shown above is much more complex than the previous versions we have worked with. Do you think that as a consequence it will be more difficult to use in a program? As an exercise, try to adapt one of the earlier `BankAccount` programs to use the classes described in Listings 10.1 and 10.2.

10.3 Choices in Modelling Object Relationships

The `BankAccount` code shown in Listings 10.1 and 10.2 is a good example of an **Aggregation** structure. The implementation is straightforward because of the availability of the `ArrayList` class, which takes care of the multiplicity of transactions *owned by* a bank account. In general, we can form composition and aggregation relationships between objects by simply providing one of the objects with one or more reference variables to which other objects can be attached.

In many situations, there can be some doubt about how best to implement a relationship. A common flaw is to use an inheritance relationship instead of a simpler composition relationship. For example, let's say in a real banking system, each account had a corresponding `Customer` object which contained the owner's details – name, address, etc. We might compose a `BankAccount` class with this relationship (see Figure 10.5).

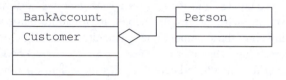

Figure 10.5 A `BankAccount` class that uses composition

The simple 1:1 composition allows us to use a `Person` object as a member field of a `BankAccount` object. In code, it would appear something like Listing 10.3.

```
Public Class Person
    Public Name As String
    Public Address As String
    'etc...
End Class

Public Class CustAccount
    Private AccountNumber As Long
    Private Customer As Person
    Public Sub New(ByVal Number As Long, _
                   ByVal Name As String, _
                   ByVal Address As String)
        AccountNumber = Number
        Customer = New Person()
        Customer.Name = Name
        Customer.Address = Address
        'etc...
    End Sub
    'More methods...
End Class
```

Listing 10.3: Code for the composition structure

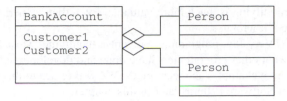

Figure 10.6 BankAccount re-modelled for joint accounts

If we were now to go on to define a JointAccount class, the temptation would be to say that since this is a specialized form of account, we should inherit BankAccount and add in the additional member. However, inheritance is computationally costly in a number of ways, and if we can legitimately avoid using it our program will be more efficient.

The question to ask is whether any of the operations for a BankAccount will need to be significantly changed for a JointAccount. I would answer 'no' to this question, since all of the main operations of an account could deal with either one or two account signatories without any need for inheritance. Instead, the composition relationship could be extended as in Figure 10.6.

Now the code for BankAccount will have to become a little more complex, since we will need to provide a method to optionally add in a second customer, and we will also have to check for a second customer when generating a statement. However, we have saved having to use inheritance, a benefit in itself, and more importantly, we have made it possible to convert any BankAccount into a joint account by simply adding a second customer at any time.

Using inheritance, converting from a standard account to a joint account would have involved a nightmare of code to create the new type of account, copy all of the existing data over to it (including all of the transactions), add in the second customer's information and then destroy the original account. Instead we have replaced an inheritance relationship with a much simpler (and computationally cheaper) composition one. Of course if an unlimited number of signatories were to be possible, we would need to deal with an aggregation of account names, and this might make it worth creating a new class that inherits from BankAccount.

In designing class models, there are always likely to be possible alternative implementations of the ideal situation. The best choice of data structure (e.g. between an ArrayList, a HashTable and a Dictionary) is not always obvious. Similarly, the choice between a simple composition (using reference variables in a class definition) and an aggregation (using one of the Collection class objects) is usually not clear cut. While the best solution is often to choose the most simple and direct approach (e.g. having the space for two Customer objects in a bank account), sometimes this approach can impose a limitation on a class design that will only be apparent later.

Software design is as much an art as a science, and while learning to use the facilities of a programming language is a relatively simple matter, learning how and when these facilities should be employed is much more difficult and comes only with experience. Examining program code, whether from books like this, magazines, journals or on-line is valuable; working with code by copying and modifying is much more valuable. Even then, experienced programmers frequently get it wrong.

Very few programmers invent a technique. Most learn their craft by emulating what other programmers have done and developing a mental catalogue of programming examples and techniques. We will return to this theme when we go on to look at Software Patterns later in this chapter.

> The revised `BankAccount` class in Listing 10.3 allows an account to have one or two customers. Rewrite the `GetStatement()` method from Listing 10.2 to take the variable number of customers into account.

10.3.1 Application Structure and .NET

The aim of software development is to implement the requirements of a system, discovered during the analysis phase at the start of a project. It should always be your aim to start by creating a system design that is purely logical; this is to say that the tools you use and the platform you are writing for influence the design as little as possible. However, it would be folly to think that you can develop whole software systems that are not in any way influenced by these: in the .NET platform, Visual Studio's features and the Visual Basic language itself will all have some bearing on what you finally create.

The object model you design when working on a Visual Basic .NET project is almost certain to contain certain features that were convenient to use because .NET supports them or even provides them. For example, the class model for a bank account discussed earlier in this chapter made use of the `ArrayList` class. While most programming languages and environments will provide some way of organizing an unknown number of objects into a list, they will not all do it this way. The language and environment will influence the design in a number of subtle and not-so-subtle ways.

The .NET environment imposes several design features on an application program. For a start, a .NET application must be an object-oriented program; this should not be a problem for us but it could be a problem to someone who had experience of programming in C or some other structured programming language. Also, any .NET application may automatically incorporate certain parts of the .NET framework: a WinForms application will include the Forms classes plus other components that are expected to be used in that environment; an ASP .NET Web Application will include and require the use of a number of components that interact with a web server, etc. It is usually most efficient to create applications that make the best use of the structural elements imposed by the environment.

For any application, we need to consider a number of things.

■ How does the application start? In a Console application this is always `Sub Main()`, but with a form-based application, the main or start-up form's constructor will be the entry point. This is important, because there will always be a number of things we have to do when an application starts – creating collection objects, setting up status variables, etc. This is often referred to as *initialization*, and can be thought of as the essential groundwork that the rest of the application will expect to have been done. In a Console application, all this work would be done in `Sub Main()`, while in a form-based application, it could be done in the main form's `Form.Load` event-handler.

- What is the main object in the application? An object-oriented program makes use of objects which collaborate on performing the overall task. These need to be created as needed by the application, they need to be sent messages asking them to do work, and the results they produce need to be collated. There should be some executive object in control of this; it can be the start-up form of the application, or where we have a `Sub Main()` defined, it is the application itself. (Microsoft has fudged this a little in Visual Studio. Using the Project Properties dialog box, you can set the start-up object in the project to be any form in a WinForms project or `Sub Main()`. `Sub Main()` is a procedure, not an object, and what Microsoft has omitted to tell us is what class/object this belongs to. I like to think of `Sub Main()` as a method of the whole program, and so consider a Console application to have an executive object with a `Sub Main()` method).

- What information should be globally available? If a project is stand-alone, then everything in it with a `Friend` declaration can be considered global. If, however, a project is being built as a component or library that can be used in other projects, only reference variables marked as `Public` will be visible to the applications that use the project. Good software design suggests that we should have as few global variables (or objects) as possible in a program.

- What are the 'ownership' relationships between objects? For example, a `BankAccount` with a number of transactions can be said to own the transactions, since without the `BankAccount`, there would be no transactions. An object that owns other objects will have certain responsibilities for them – creating them either when it is created or on request, and disposing of them cleanly when it is destroyed.

- Which classes in a project are *product* classes, and which are *system* classes? A Product class is a definition for the *business* objects of an application, while the classes that are developed purely to aid in their manipulation (such as user-interface classes, collection classes, utility classes) are system classes.

Answers to these questions will strongly suggest the best ways of organizing the objects in a running application, and will therefore influence the classes developed for it.

Exercise 10.5

Go back to look at some of the programs you have created as exercises (look at both console and WinForms programs):

a) Can you identify the first line of code to be executed in each case?

b) Is it always this line that is executed first?

c) How do user-interactions affect the order that things are done in?

10.3.2 System and Product Classes

Simply put, the business objects (those that collectively make up the business tier) in an application are product classes. These classes and the objects that they produce will make up the logical structure of the application; the idealized assembly of objects that will come out of analysing the use-cases defined at the requirements specification stage. We can call them Product classes because they are the ultimate product of the application. In a sales-ordering system, they will be classes that represent customer, orders, products, order-lines, and invoices. In a CAD system, they will represent 'drawable' objects, and in an email system, they will represent emails and entries in the address book.

System classes are all of the other classes that are not specifically product classes. These will be form designs, controls on forms, collection classes, data access tools and any class that does not fit nicely into the logical model of the application. Typically, these classes will form the top and bottom tiers of a three tier application, although some system classes will occupy the middle, business tier as well.

No matter whether a class works as a product or a system service, it is necessary to consider its lifetime within the application. When will it be created and when will

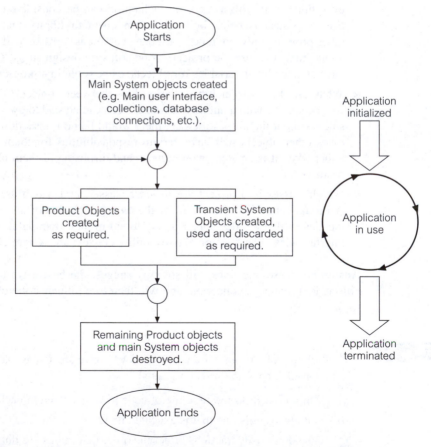

Figure 10.7   Lifetimes of product and system objects

we be able to dispense with it? Typically, product classes are created on demand (e.g. by the user clicking on a menu item or other control) and are destroyed when the user no longer needs them or when the program ends. System classes will normally either be created when an application starts and destroyed when it ends (e.g. a collection, a database connection or the main user-interface) or will be created to perform a specific task and discarded when the task is completed. Figure 10.7 shows this diagrammatically.

10.4 Managing Scarce Resources

Objects take up memory, memory is a limited resource, and the .NET framework is designed to make sure that once we are done with an object, it will be cleanly removed from memory and the space it occupied restored to the 'heap' of available memory in the system. For most applications, we can simply create objects as and when they are needed and leave it up to .NET to deal with clearing up after them. Microsoft's guidelines on this are pretty specific. To quote the help page: "For the majority of the objects that your application creates, you can rely on the .NET Framework's *garbage collector* to implicitly perform all the necessary memory management tasks".

However, some resources that we can make use of in programs cannot be automatically cleaned up by the .NET runtime system. These are called *unmanaged resources*. Say, for example, you have a class in which each object creates and opens a disk file as it is constructed, and writes data to this file throughout its lifetime. Pretty obviously, when you are done with this object the disk file should be closed; it is an unmanaged resource because the .NET framework will not automatically close the file as the object that uses it is destroyed.

In a C++ program that contained an object like this, you would create a class *destructor*, which as its name suggests is a routine that undoes what the constructor did. In the destructor, you would place code to close the file and therefore release the scarce resource that would otherwise be a drain on the operating system. In Visual Basic .NET, the nearest we have to a destructor is the `Finalize()` method. If a class is given a `Finalize()` method, it will be called automatically when the object is destroyed. This would be the place to put the code to close the file the object was holding open.

However, in a C++ program, the programmer must explicitly call on a class's destructor by deleting the object (actually, this is only necessary for non-local objects declared outside any function, but we don't need to bother about these details here), whereas in Visual Basic .NET, we are warned (by Microsoft) to ignore the `Finalize()` method and leave it up to the garbage collector to call it for us.

That's right; the part of the system that deals with discarded objects is called the garbage collector, and it acts like its namesake in that it has the job of collecting together all of the discarded objects and reclaiming their memory: it is more like a recycler really. While it is doing its job, if it clears up any objects that have a `Finalize()` method defined, it executes this method. We are therefore guaranteed that the file held open by our object will eventually be closed.

There is a limitation to the effectiveness of the garbage collector; it decides when to compact the memory taken up by discarded objects (collect the garbage) based on the amount of available space left, how frequently objects are being created to fill it up and other factors. In some systems with a lot of memory, it could take hours for the garbage collector to decide a tidy-up was necessary, and during this time, our object's file will remain open. Leaving a file open for a long time beyond the time we need it for is not good practice. If the system crashes, someone trips over the computer's power cord or some other spanner falls into the works, the file will be corrupted and probably its contents will be lost for good.

For similar reasons, there are a number of resources that you might use in a program that it would be best not to trust to the unpredictable operation of the garbage collector. Leaving a modem connection open, not freeing the system printer after a printing session or hanging on to a connection to another program after data has been transferred to it are all situations where a program can hog a scarce resource and cause system problems. The upshot of this is that, like in a C++ program, we need to take care of our own resources if they are not managed by the .NET run-time system for us.

10.4.1 Garbage Collection

Every object that you create in a program occupies some system memory. Objects are created in an area of memory called the 'heap', which, as its name suggests, is a fairly unorganized section of memory. We create objects and assign them to reference variables so that we are able to access their properties and methods, and these reference variables act as our link to objects in heap memory.

When an object is created, .NET must first request the memory it will occupy from the operating system. When the request for memory has been granted, .NET will then call the object's constructor which will store the object's data in the memory, and return the reference to the object to be assigned to a reference variable in your program. Figure 10.8 shows a number of objects referred to by reference variables in a program.

The heap is a block of memory allocated to an application for storing objects in. When a new object is created, the CLR allocates some space in the heap by simply taking the next free area beyond the space it allocated to the previous object. Pretty obviously if a program runs for long enough and creates new objects periodically as it does, the heap will eventually fill up. However, during the period the program has been running, objects will also have been discarded by the program, and the space that was taken up by them will be 'holes' in the area of the heap assumed to be in use.

Garbage collection takes place periodically so that the CLR can reclaim all of the discarded blocks of memory that were once objects (e.g. objects 9 and 10 in Figure 10.8). Once the garbage collector has worked on the heap, all of the objects still in use occupy one contiguous block of memory. The memory that was once occupied by discarded objects has been collected into a single block so that the free heap space is also collected together. The result is that the heap once again has a large contiguous block of free memory from which it can allocate space for new objects.

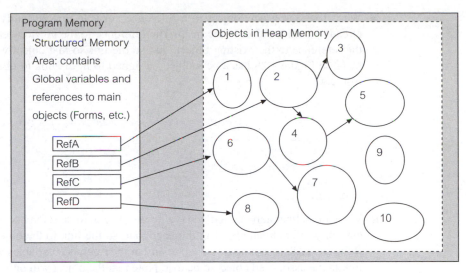

Figure 10.8 References to objects in 'heap' memory

The main benefit of garbage collection is that you, the programmer, do not have to worry about the way you use and discard objects because an invisible servant follows you around clearing up the mess you have made. Since the collection of discarded memory into easily usable blocks is automatic, your program will generally run more efficiently without you having to do anything.

The down-side of this is that the garbage collector takes time to do its work, and when it does your application will be put on-hold while it does it. This can appear as an unresponsive user-interface, or even, for some types of resources (e.g. a database connection), act as a block on further processing. However, unless you write memory hogging programs which allocate lots of objects only to discard them shortly afterwards, or which allocate very large objects (e.g. to store pictures or video clips) frequently or make use of very scarce resources, you are unlikely ever to experience a garbage collection delay.

From a programming perspective, an object is discarded whenever the link between the object and the reference variable that refers to it is broken. There are a number of ways in which the link to an object in heap memory can be broken.

■ The reference variable referring to the object may be a local variable in a sub or function. At the end of the sub or function, the values or references in local variables are discarded. Therefore, if a local variable holds a reference to an object in the heap, the link to that object will be lost. In Figure 10.8, if the variable RefA goes out of scope, the link to object 1 in the heap will be lost, e.g.

```
Sub W()
    Dim RefA As SomeClass = New SomeClass() 'Object 1
    'Object is used...
    '...
End Sub 'RefA out of scope here, so Object 1 is lost.
```

■ We can assign a new object to a reference variable that currently refers to an already existing object in the heap. The reference to the new object will replace the reference to the existing object, and so the link to that object will be lost. If `RefD` in Figure 10.8 has a new object assigned to it, the link to object 8 will be lost, e.g.

```
Sub X()
    Dim RefD As SomeClass = New SomeClass() 'Object 8
    'Object 8 is used...
    RefD = New SomeClass() 'Discards Object 8
    'New object is used...
    '...
End Sub
```

■ We can deliberately assign the value `Nothing` to a reference variable that currently refers to an object in the heap, and so the link to the object to be lost. If Figure 10.8, assigning `Nothing` to any of the reference variables will cause the link to the associated object to be lost. Note that the object will only be destroyed if there are no other references to it in the program (for example, if it had been added to a collection, it would not be destroyed), e.g.

```
Sub Y()
    Dim RefA As SomeClass = New SomeClass() 'Object 1
    'Object 1 is used...
    RefA = Nothing 'Discards Object 1
    '...
End Sub
```

■ If an object in the heap references another object in the heap, and the link to the first object is destroyed by one of the above methods, then the link to the object it references will also be destroyed

```
Sub Z()
    Dim RefC As SomeClass = New SomeClass() 'Object 6
    RefC.SomeObject = New SomeOtherClass() 'Object 7
    'Combination of objects is used...
    '...
    RefC = Nothing  'Now Objects 6 and 7 are both
                    'discarded
End Sub
```

In all of these cases and many other situations, losing the last reference to an object means that the object can no longer be reached by any program code. .NET is smart enough to realize whether an object is reachable or not and when its garbage collector runs it clears up these unreachable objects. If the garbage collector finds an unreachable object, it marks it for removal and subsequently returns the memory it occupied to the operating system.

10.4.1.1 Pre-empting the Garbage Collector

Garbage collection is built into the .NET framework. It kicks in periodically when an application's heap memory is becoming scarce and new objects are being allocated at a frequency that will make it run out soon. New objects are allocated space from the block of memory that does not contain either current or discarded objects, and as an application runs, this block is continually reducing in size.

In effect the garbage collector has two jobs to do. Its primary job is to figure out which memory blocks are no longer in use and mark these as available for use. Once it has done this for every block in heap memory it can get on with its second job, which is to shuffle all of the memory blocks still in use into a single, contiguous area, thereby freeing up the memory for use by new objects. Since the garbage collector's work can be intensive, we can assume it will not be brought into action more often than is necessary.

We can make use of the garbage collector's knowledge of every object's `Finalize()` method. This protected method is defined in the object class, which is the ultimate ancestor of all classes in .NET. When we allocate an unmanaged resource such as opening a file or database connection to an object in its constructor, it is recommended that we make sure that it is de-allocated (i.e. closed) in the `Finalize()` method. However, the `Finalize()` method should never be called directly. Microsoft suggest that if you define one you should give it protected scope to prevent other users of your class from calling it directly, and also that you should never call it directly yourself. If you do, you run the risk of the garbage collector calling it again to free up resources that have already been freed, and thereby causing a run-time error.

Here is our dilemma:

■ we can de-allocate scarce resources in the `Finalize()` method, which we are not allowed to call directly, and so must then leave their de-allocation up to when the garbage collector gets around to doing it for us – potentially a long time;

■ alternatively we can de-allocate resources in some other sub (e.g. a public sub called `Close()` or `Deallocate()`), and leave it up to the user of the class to call it when resources are no longer needed.

The first alternative gives us the certainty that resources will be freed, at the price of not knowing when. The second would make it certain that resources would be freed in a timely manner, but only if we remembered to use it. Ideally, we could do with the best of both.

10.4.1.2 The `Dispose()` Method

The `Dispose()` method provides us with a way out of this dilemma. `Finalize()` is a protected method and so cannot be called directly. If we want to be able to invoke it, we can define a `Public Dispose()` method that can be called by code in our application when we know the object can be dispensed with (see Listing 10.4).

```
Class SomeResourceUsingClass
    'Other class code...
    '...
    Protected Overrides Sub Finalize()
        'Put code to release any resources here.
        'e.g. Close files, network connections, Database
```

```
                'connections, unload forms, or release memory
                hogging
                'resources like graphic bitmaps.
        End Sub

        Public Sub Dispose()
            GC.SuppressFinalize(Me)
            Finalize()
        End Sub
    End Class
```

Listing 10.4: The `Finalize()` and `Dispose()` methods

In `Sub Dispose()`, we need to do two things: firstly we need to tell the garbage collector that it should not call `Finalize()` because we will do it in our own code, and secondly, we must then call `Finalize()`. The overall result of this is that we will have released scarce resources earlier than the garbage collector would have done most of the time. We can now arrange that when an object of a class has done its job, we can release it and any resources it makes use of immediately. For example, suppose we needed to implement a `Data Logging` class that keeps a file open to write data to frequently. The `Finalize()` and `Dispose()` methods would be responsible for ensuring the file is closed.

```
    Class DataLogger
        Dim F As IO.StreamWriter
        Public Sub New(ByVal LogFileName As String)
            F = New IO.StreamWriter(LogFileName)
        End Sub
        Public Sub WriteLog(ByVal Message As String)
            F.WriteLine(Message)
        End Sub
        Protected Overrides Sub Finalize()
            F.Close()
        End Sub
        Public Sub Dispose()
            GC.SuppressFinalize(Me)
            Finalize()
        End Sub
    End Class
```

Listing 10.5: Using the `Dispose()` method to clear objects out of memory

The class in Listing 10.5 makes use of a `StreamWriter` object that can send text to a file in the computer's hard disk. There will be a full explanation of files and the associated classes in Chapter 11. For now, you simply need to be aware that while a file is open, it is using a scarce system resource.

If we remember to call `Dispose()` once we are done with a `DataLogger` object, the file will be closed. If we don't, the garbage collector will do it for us eventually. Note that the space occupied by the `DataLogger` object will still need to wait for the garbage collector to reclaim it.

One final warning on the use of `Finalize()`. You might assume from the explanation above that `Finalize()` is an important method and therefore you should define it for every class along with a `Dispose()` method. However, the garbage collector has to do extra work in dealing with a class that has a `Finalize()` method other than the default one inherited from the object class. While the garbage collector can deal easily with objects that rely on the object class's version of `Finalize()`, it must take extra care in getting rid of objects that use any other `Finalize()` method, and so will not destroy the object the first time it meets it. Objects from classes with a non-default `Finalize()` method therefore hang around for longer. Therefore, you should only ever define `Finalize()` and `Dispose()` for a class where you know it is necessary.

10.4.2 Managing Ownership Relationships

You should now see that the way that relationships between objects are implemented can have an impact on the efficiency of an application and on how easy it is to maintain it. Possible relationships between objects in a running application are:

■ an object owns other objects (composition or aggregation);

■ an object is owned by another object, or is a member of an aggregation owned by another object;

■ an indirect ownership relationship can exist – e.g. an object owns another object which owns a third object;

■ an object collaborates with other objects via messages.

The key to managing these relationships is in being aware of where responsibilities should lie. An ownership relationship suggests that the owner object is in some way responsible for the owned objects. Normally this is implemented so that the owner object is responsible for creating the owned objects and disposing of them, although garbage collection is normally used to take care of disposal automatically. By implementing `Finalize()` and `Dispose()` methods for a class, we are taking responsibility for clearing up unmanaged resources. An object that owns other objects can dispose of them when they are no longer needed. For example, consider an application that uses two classes, `DataLogger` and `DataLoggerCollection`. The `DataLoggerCollection` class has a collection of `DataLogger` objects, each of which hangs on to an unmanaged resource. We might implement the ownership relationship by giving the `DataLoggerCollection` class a method to create a `DataLogger` object on demand, in which case, it should also be responsible for getting rid of the collection of `DataLogger` objects.

```
Public Class DataLogger
    'See listing 10.5 for definition.
End Class

Public Class DataLoggerCollection
    Private Loggers As ArrayList   'A collection of owned
                                    objects
```

```
        Public Sub New()               'Constructor - creates the
            Loggers = New ArrayList() 'collection
        End Sub
        Public Sub Add(ByVal fileName As String)
                                                  'Add a DataLogger
            Dim Logger As = New DataLogger(filename)
            Loggers.Add(O)
        End Sub
        Protected Overrides Sub Finalize() 'Finalize destroys the
            GC.SuppressFinalize(Me)        'owned objects
            Dim L As DataLogger
            For Each L In Loggers
                L.Dispose()
            Next
        End Sub
        Public Sub Dispose()
            Finalize()
        End Sub
    End Class
```

Listing 10.6: An owner-owned relationship

The object model in Listing 10.6 shows how you would define product classes in a program so that they could be disposed of automatically. However, unless explicit use is made of the `Dispose()` method of the `DataLoggerCollection` class, this work will still be left up to the garbage collector. To manage the disposal of the collection of objects on demand, we need to call the `Dispose()` method explicitly, which means we need to be aware when the `DataLoggerCollection` and its collection of `DataLogger` objects is no longer needed. In a WinForms application, we might make use of the `DataLoggerCollection` and its collection in one particular form. We can therefore use the `Form.Load` event-handler to create the owner and `Form.Close` to dispose of it. This is shown in Listing 10.7.

```
Private DataLoggers As DataLoggerCollection
Private r As Random
Private Sub Form1_Load(ByVal sender As System.Object, _
            ByVal e As System.EventArgs) Handles MyBase.Load
    DataLoggers = New DataLoggerCollection()
    r = New Random()
End Sub

Private Sub btnAdd_Click(ByVal sender As System.Object, _
            ByVal e As System.EventArgs) Handles btnAdd.Click
    Dim FileName As String
    FileName = "C:\LogFiles\Log" & r.Next().ToString() &
    ".log"
    DataLoggers.Add(FileName)
End Sub

'Code here to write text to log files in the collection...
'...
```

```
Private Sub Form1_Closed(ByVal sender As Object, _
          ByVal e As System.EventArgs) Handles MyBase.Closed
       DataLoggers.Dispose()
End Sub
```

Listing 10.7: Using the `Dispose()` method in a form

It is worth emphasizing that you can leave all of this work to the garbage collector provided the objects in your application program do not make use of any limited resources such as database connections, files, forms, etc. It is possible to impair the efficiency of a program by giving the garbage collector extra work to do.

Exercise 10.6

The `Finalize()` method is a good tool for informing you when objects are actually destroyed in a VB .NET program. Go back and add the following `Finalize()` method to some classes in programs you have written (note you can only add it to a class definition, not as a separate method in a code module):

```
Protected Overrides Sub Finalize()
    MessageBox.Show("I've been finalized.")
End Sub
```

Now run the program and create and use objects. It may be useful to also display some data from the object that you've given the finalize method to, so you can identify exactly which object has been finalized.

10.5 Software Patterns

Objects give us the ability to create new types of variable and use them in a range of applications. Object structures add the facility to create collections of objects organized to optimize aspects of efficiency such as speed of access. We can deal with individual entities and collections of similar entities using the techniques described so far in this book.

However, applications programs are rarely composed entirely of homogeneous collections of objects that can be modelled in a single collection or hierarchy. When developing a collection, we are more likely to be confronted by the need to connect together a wide variety of objects in a less orderly way. This can lead to the belief that each application has a unique structure that must be crafted individually. In particular, we can be left with the impression that re-use of program code is an ideal that can only be realized for individual classes and very simple structures.

One aspect of why we still find it difficult to re-use elements of programs we created last week in new programs this week is that object-oriented programming can only partially address the problem of structure in programs. Structure is the framework of software, and, in most cases, goes beyond what can be accomplished by a single object or class, or by a specific form of collection. If we wish to build an application that models a complex view of reality in software, we will probably need to model the interconnections between all of the components of the real-world system (i.e. the objects) as much as the software components themselves.

Object-oriented programming shows us how to create classes and collections of objects, but we are left to assume that these alone will form the basis of our software model of a real world system. *Software design patterns*, or simply *patterns*, provide the next step. Once we have a methodology for constructing models of the components of the world we wish to model, we have need of a model for connecting them together in assemblies, and this is provided by patterns.

Christopher Alexander proposed the idea of design patterns in a book in 1977[1]. To quote a passage of this, "Each pattern describes a problem which occurs over and over again in our environment, and then describes the core of the solution to that problem, in such a way that you can use this solution a million times over, without ever doing it the same way twice". In Alexander's discipline of architecture, the patterns were structures such as entrances, mezzanines and town squares. In software, we can use much the same approach to generalize the design of specific algorithms, ways of constructing objects and data structures. The core text in this area is *Software Patterns*, by Gamma, Helm, Johnson and Vlissides, and this has become a key text in computer science since its publication in 1994.

In this chapter, we will examine specific examples of software patterns and implementations of them in Visual Basic. Gamma *et al.* divides software patterns into three groups: *Creational Patterns*, *Stuctural Patterns* and *Behavioural Patterns*. These describe ways of creating objects in programs, ways of forming connections and collaborations between objects and organizations of objects that define operations or algorithms. We have already used some of these patterns in the example programs of earlier chapters, so the key point of this chapter is that we should be able to recognize a pattern and therefore apply it to a variety of situations. The important feature of using patterns is the philosophy, which takes us a step beyond objects and into the next phase of software development.

Exercise 10.7

In previous chapters we have examined the idea of structures in object-oriented software: Data structures and Object structures. How do you think the idea of software patterns differs from a structure?

10.5.1 Creational Patterns

This type of pattern is used to generate objects conforming to a specific super-class or interface. It allows us to separate the mechanism used to create objects from the logic of the application in which they are created. A typical non-pattern method of doing this is to have a separate method defined to create each type of object – e.g. in an event-handler on a form. This is then used to create a specific class of object (the *product* class) given a specific cue (e.g. a button press, menu or Toolbar selection).

---

[1] (Christopher Alexander, Sara Ishikawa, Murray Silverstein, Max Jacobson, Ingrid Fiksdahl-King and Shlomo Angel, *A Pattern Language*)

10.5.1.1 The Factory Method Pattern

Our simple CAD program in the previous chapter used an event-handler for each type of drawn object to be created, as shown in Listing 10.8.

```
Private Sub btnLine_Click(ByVal sender As System.Object, _
                          ByVal e As System.EventArgs) _
                          Handles btnLine.Click
    s = New Line(0, 0, 0, 0, CurrentColour)
End Sub

Private Sub btnEllipse_Click(ByVal sender As System.Object, _
                          ByVal e As System.EventArgs) _
                          Handles btnEllipse.Click
    s = New clsEllipse(0, 0, 0, 0, CurrentColour)
End Sub

Private Sub btnRightTri_Click(ByVal sender As System.Object, _
                          ByVal e As System.EventArgs) _
                          Handles btnRightTri.Click
    s = New RightTriangle(0, 0, 0, 0, CurrentColour)
End Sub
```

Listing 10.8: Several methods for creating a shape object

As an improvement to this way of doing things, we can define a Factory Method function, that will create an object based on some other cue from the user-interface. Normally, this function is created as a method of a Factory class (Listing 10.9).

```
Public Class ShapeFactory
    Public Shared Function NewShape( _
                          ByVal ShapeName As String, _
                          ByVal col As Color) As Shape
        Select Case ShapeName
            Case "Line"
                Return New Line(0, 0, 0, 0, col)
            Case "Ellipse"
                Return New Ellipse(0, 0, 0, 0, col)
            Case "Right Triangle"
                Return New RightTriangle(0, 0, 0, 0, col)
        End Select
    End Function
End Class
```

Listing 10.9: A `ShapeFactory`

The `NewShape()` method in the `ShapeFactory` class is a function whose job is to create objects. We pass the function a value that indicates the type of object we want, and it returns an object of the required type. This function is known as a *Factory Method* and is one of the standard patterns described by Gamma *et al.*

In a call to the shared `NewShape()` method, `ShapeName` is a string that indicates the name of the class that is to be instantiated. This could be the text of a menu item, the caption of a button or the selected item in a `ListBox`, and so it can be made very easy to extend the user interface to deal with new shapes as they are added. The event-handlers that created instances of the `Shape` objects were, in the CAD application, subs in the user-interface form. However, it would be better practice to place the factory code in the separate module with the `Shape` classes, since whenever we add a new `Shape` class, we will want to amend the Factory Method to be able to deal with it.

The Factory Method pattern has the following benefits.

■ Objects are created at a central location (the Factory Method) of the application, and so object creation and the user-interface operations that lead to object creation are kept distinct. This makes the user-interface and object creation features easier to test in isolation.

■ We can add new product types (e.g. new `Shape` classes) to the application more easily, since apart from the new class, we simply need to amend the Factory Method's `NewShape()` function.

■ Use of the Factory Method enforces polymorphism, since the method has only a single return type (`Shape`), and so all classes of object that it can return must inherit from the `Shape` class.

■ We can use the Factory Method to perform some other useful tasks in setting up a new object once it has been created but before it is returned to the application.

The Factory Method is a useful pattern in programs where a variety of 'product' objects of compatible types are required. By centralizing the creation of the various product classes, we can simplify the development and maintenance required by the program and improve its logical structure.

10.5.1.2 The Prototype Pattern

The Factory Method used in the CAD example still requires a certain amount of the main application logic to be altered. It is not possible to leave main application logic untouched entirely when adding new product classes, since we would need to amend the way that the type of new product objects are selected by a user. In the CAD application as it was, we would need to add a new Button control to the form for each new product class, for example `Rectangle`, and provide an event-handler so that the type identifier could be set to indicate that type (`ShapeName = "Rectangle"`). In this type of application, it would not be too difficult a task to provide this.

However, it should always be a design goal to minimize the number of changes required in an application when we augment its functionality. Typically, new product classes need to be linked into an application and routes to their constructors provided.

Using the Factory Method, it is necessary to update the code in the `NewShape()` function whenever a new product class was introduced to the application. It is also necessary to add control methods to allow us to choose instances of the new classes to instantiate. Although not a particularly onerous set of requirements for the provision of an extensible range of products, it is always worth looking for ways to reduce the update burden.

The *Prototype pattern* has a similar objective to the Factory Method pattern; allowing us to delegate the creation of new objects to a structure that is well suited to the job. However, it is often the case that the best way of creating a new object is to copy an existing one. The Prototype pattern hinges on a requirement that all objects of product classes are able to *clone* themselves. Clones are autonomous copies of objects of their own class. The cloning process creates an *exact copy* of the prototype in the state it is in at the point of creation.

We could make use of this facility in the CAD application as a way of encapsulating the colour and fill style of an object. Using the Factory Method explained previously, a shape is created by a statement like: Return New Line (0, 0, 0, 0, col), where `col` is the colour of the shape. To make shapes more varied, it would be better to include in each a set of outline and fill specifications that incorporated outline line style, width and colour and internal fill style and colour. Ideally, we would define a class to store these settings, and add to each `Shape` object an instance of this class (Listing 10.10).

```
Public Class DrawStyle
    Private mvarOutline As Pen
    Private mvarFill As Brush
    Public Sub New()
        mvarOutline = New Pen(Color.Black)
        mvarFill = Brushes.White
    End Sub
    Public Sub New(ByVal P As Pen, ByVal B As Brush)
        mvarOutline = P
        mvarFill = B
    End Sub
    Public Property Outline() As Pen
        Get
            Return mvarOutline
        End Get
        Set(ByVal Value As Pen)
            mvarOutline = Value
        End Set
    End Property
    Public Property Fill() As Brush
        Get
            Return mvarFill
        End Get
        Set(ByVal Value As Brush)
            mvarFill = Value
        End Set
    End Property
    Public Function Clone() As DrawStyle
        Dim MyClone As New DrawStyle(Outline, Fill)
        Return MyClone
    End Function
End Class
```

Listing 10.10: DrawStyle settings for a Shape object – a Prototype class

The first thought when looking at this class is that it is bound to increase the complexity of the CAD application hugely, since each shape will need to have an individual member of the class, and this would have to be set up at the point where a shape were created. However, this class has been specially created to implement the Prototype pattern, and as such is designed to minimize the effort required to create many objects of the class.

To start with, the changes required in the `Shape` classes are minor. In the `Shape` class itself, replace the declaration of the `mvarColour` variable with one for a `DrawStyle` member, `mvarDrawStyle`. Now amend the constructor of every `Shape` class to accept this as a parameter (you could use **Edit/Find** and **Replace** to do this), as shown in Listing 10.11.

```
Public Sub New(ByVal xx As Integer, ByVal yy As Integer, _
            ByVal wid As Integer, ByVal hgt As Integer, _
        ByVal style As DrawStyle)
    mvarX_Pos = xx : mvarY_Pos = yy
    mvarWidth = wid : mvarHeight = hgt
    mvarDrawStyle = style
End Sub
```

Listing 10.11: Amending the `Shape` constructor to accept a `DrawStyle`

Finally for the `Shape` classes, amend the `Draw()` methods of all the closed shape classes (rectangles, ellipses, etc.) to use the appropriate `FillXXX()` method to fill the shape that has just been drawn. This should only be done for closed shapes. For example, to draw filled rectangles, the `Draw()` method of the `Rectangle` class becomes the code shown in Listing 10.12.

```
Public Overrides Sub Draw(ByVal gr As Graphics)
    MyBase.Draw(gr)
    gr.DrawRectangle(mvardrawstyle.Outline, _
                X, Y, Width, Height)
    gr.FillRectangle(mvardrawstyle.Fill, _
        New Rectangle(X + 1, Y + 1, Width - 2, Height - 2))
End Sub
```

Listing 10.12: Drawing a filled rectangle

Note that the `FillRectangle()` method of the `Graphics` object is given the position, width and height of a rectangle that is inside the outline rectangle (X + 1, Width − 2, etc.). Otherwise, the filled rectangle will draw over the left and top lines of the outline.

Now to implement the Prototype pattern, we can have a single `DrawStyle` object variable declared and instantiated on the main form, and use its `Clone()` method to create new instances for each shape we draw. Any change we make to the colour, line style or fill style of this object will be reflected in the clones it creates. The CAD application's main form code is as shown in Listing 10.13.

```
Public Class frmShapes

    Inherits System.Windows.Forms.Form
    'Other member variables...
    '...
    Private CurrentDrawStyle As DrawStyle

    Private Sub frmShapes_Load(ByVal sender As
                              System.Object, _
                              ByVal e As System.EventArgs) _
                              Handles MyBase.Load
        'currentColour = Pens.Black.Color
        Dim P As Pen = New Pen(Color.Black)
        Dim B As SolidBrush = New SolidBrush(Color.White)
        CurrentDrawStyle = New DrawStyle(P, B)
        grGraphics = pnlOutput.CreateGraphics()
    End Sub

    Private Sub btnColour_Click(ByVal sender As
                               System.Object, _
                               ByVal e As System.EventArgs) _
                               Handles btnColour.Click

        With colDlg
            .Color = CurrentDrawStyle.Outline.Color
            .ShowDialog(Me)
            CurrentDrawStyle.Outline.Color = .Color
            btnColour.ForeColor = .Color
        End With
    End Sub

    Private Sub btnFillColour_Click(ByVal sender As
                                   System.Object, _
                                   ByVal e As System.EventArgs) _
                                   Handles btnFillColour.Click
        With colDlg
            .Color = CurrentDrawStyle.Fill.Color
            .ShowDialog(Me)
            CurrentDrawStyle.Fill.Color = .Color
            btnFillColour.BackColor = .Color
        End With
    End Sub
    Private Sub NewShape(ByVal ShapeName As String)
        s = ShapeFactory.GetShape(ShapeName, 0, 0, 0, 0, _
                                  CurrentDrawStyle.Clone())
    End Sub

End Class
```

Listing 10.13: Using the Prototype pattern to simplify drawing settings

Beyond declaring the reference variable for the `DrawStyle` object, we need to create an instance of the class (in `Form_Load()`), provide user-interface methods to change its settings (`btnColour_Click()` and `btnFillColour_Click()`) and amend the code used to create a new shape so that it uses the `Clone()` method of the `DrawStyle` instance to generate a new `DrawStyle` object for each shape created (`NewShape()`).

We could also have used the Prototype pattern to create the `Shape` objects in the first place, by using a collection of prototype shapes in conjunction with a Factory Method. A major advantage of this is that instead of a case statement that would need to be updated with the addition of each new type of `Shape` object, we could keep a collection containing one of each concrete `Shape` class and use the Factory Method to iterate through the collection until it finds a matching prototype to identify itself (Listing 10.14).

```
Public Class ShapeFactory
    Private Shared colPrototypes As
    System.Collections.Hashtable _
                   = New System.Collections.Hashtable()

    Public Sub AddPrototype(ByVal Name As String, _
                         ByVal Proto As clsShape)
        colPrototypes.Add(Name, Proto)
    End Sub

    Public Shared Function GetShape(ByVal ShapeName As String, _
                          ByVal X As Integer, _
                          ByVal Y As Integer, _
                          ByVal Width As Integer, _
                          ByVal Height As Integer) _
                          As Shape
        Dim Prototype As Shape
        If colPrototypes.ContainsKey(ShapeName) Then
            Prototype = colPrototypes.Item(ShapeName)
            Return Prototype.Clone(X, Y, Width, Height, _
                          Style)
        Else
            Return Nothing
        End If
    End Function

    Public Shared Function PrototypeList() As String()
        Dim Keys() As String
        colPrototypes.Keys.CopyTo(Keys, 0)
        Return Keys
    End Function

End Class
```

Listing 10.14: Using the Prototype pattern in a Factory Method pattern

Now, instead of having to amend the Factory Method code whenever we add new prototypes, we can simply add the prototype to the collection (using `AddPrototype()`). Note, however, that a new method would have to be added to the `Shape` class. The `ShapeName()` method would be required to return unique identifier, in this case a string that was different for each class that implements the interface. Note also that the ShapeFactory class now provides a PrototypeList() method that returns the keys of all of the prototypes as an array of strings. This would make it a trivial matter to add a list of available prototypes to a list box or some other user-interface element (see Listing 10.15).

```
Dim S As String
For Each S In ShapeFactory.PrototypeList
    lstShapes.Items.Add(S.ShapeName)
Next
```

Listing 10.15: Adding a list of prototype names to a listbox

Now whenever we wish to amend the range of Shape classes that can be used, we can leave the code on the user interface unaltered and make the changes in the module that contains the class definitions and the class factory.

10.5.1.3 Other Creational Patterns

Gamma *et al.* specify five creational forms of pattern. In addition to those described here, there are:

- *Abstract Factory*, which provides an interface for creating *families* of related or dependent objects without specifying their concrete classes;
- *Builder*, which separates the construction of a complex object from its representation so that the same construction process can generate different representations;
- *Singleton*, which ensures that only a single instance of a class can be created and provides a global point of access to it.

In all but the last of these, the specific goal is to separate the creation of product objects from the application in which they are managed. This allows the use of polymorphism to be maximized. The Singleton pattern is used when only a single object of a class can be allowed. For example, Visual Basic provides a PrintDocument class. Typically you would want to limit the number of PrintDocuments to one, since usually there is a single system printer.

Exercise 10.8

a) Creational patterns are used in programs where objects are created interactively by the user. Explain the key feature that a creational pattern would bring to the design of this type of application.

b) How does a Prototype pattern differ from a Factory Method?

10.5.2 Structural Patterns

Structural patterns are concerned with the mechanics of building complex structures in software while maintaining the general goal of promoting reusability and abstraction. This can be used to allow incompatible classes to inter-operate, complex hierarchical structures of objects to be maintained uniformly within an application, or for a variety of other reasons where the clean structure of an application would be compromised by a proliferation of classes or objects.

10.5.2.1 The Adapter Pattern

A typical use of structural patterns would be to integrate an existing class into an application where a similar but different class would fit more easily. For example, we could have a class that accepts a member of the `ArrayList` class as a parameter – perhaps to perform some calculation on the values of all its members. Assume the class contained a member function with the following signature:

```
Public Function CalculateTotal(ByVal A As ArrayList) As Decimal
```

We need to pass an `ArrayList` to this method. Now assume we need to be able to pass some other collection of items to this method – an array, the `Items()` property of a `ListBox` or `ComboBox` or some custom collection based on the `CollectionBase` class. The only option would seem to be to create a new `ArrayList` object and add all of the objects in the incompatible collection to it. However, the `ArrayList` class provides a shared method, `Adapter()`, which will take almost any collection object and make it work like an `ArrayList`. Its use is shown in Listing 10.16.

```
Dim AR() As Integer = {1, 2, 3, 4, 5, 6, 7, 8, 9, 10}
Dim AL As ArrayList
AL = ArrayList.Adapter(AR)
'We can now go on to work with AL as if it was an
'ArrayList
Dim T As Integer
T = CalculateTotal(AL)   'AR has been made to look like
                         'an ArrayList
'...
```

Listing 10.16: Using an `Adapter()`

Microsoft has incorporated the Adapter pattern into the .NET framework because it is the ideal way to deal with this particular situation. The Adapter pattern is used to make a member of one class appear as if it was a member of another class. Since the class interface is an all-important feature of object-oriented programming, and since we spend so much time making sure that interfaces will only accept objects of a particular type to make classes robust, the Adapter pattern comes along as a particularly useful feature when we need to create inter-operations between objects of two incompatible classes.

In general, the Adapter pattern allows us to mix and match objects of classes from a wide range of applications and interfaces, without the need to make any alterations to any of the existing classes.

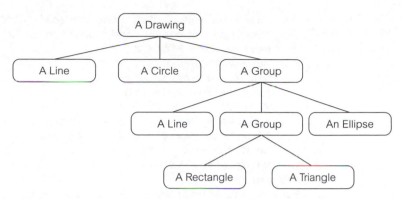

Figure 10.9 A drawing made up of composite elements

10.5.2.2 The Composite Pattern

This pattern allows us to work with complex hierarchical structures of objects in the same way that we would work with single objects. It is based on a hierarchical tree structure.

In the earlier example of a graphics application, we may decide to implement a Group command so that we can compose a number of graphics primitives into a single object. The resulting complex object should be addressable as a single object for the purposes of editing, moving deletion, copying, etc. The structural requirements are shown in Figure 10.9.

Items in this drawing structure are either *primitives* or *groups*. However, we will be making the drawing and editing code in the application unnecessarily complex if we make it necessary to distinguish between these two types of drawn item. The Composite pattern allows us to avoid making the distinction by preserving the compatibility of both single items and groups. We can do this by sub-classing the Shape class to create a shape that can contain other shapes, as shown in Listing 10.17.

```
Public Class CompositeShape
    Inherits clsShape
    Private mvarChildren As ArrayList
    Public Sub New()
        MyBase.New(0, 0, 0, 0, New DrawStyle(Pens.Black, _
                                      Brushes.White))
    End Sub
    Public Sub AddShape(ByVal S As clsShape)
        'We should only create the ArrayList if it is needed.
        'If a Shape has no Children, the ArrayList object
        'would just take up memory unnecessarily
        If mvarChildren Is Nothing Then
            mvarChildren = New ArrayList()
        End If
        mvarChildren.Add(S)
        'To make the composite object include S, we will
```

```
                    'need to ensure that the enclosing rectangle
                    'includes the size and location of S...
                    Me.X = Math.Min(S.X, Me.X)
                    Me.Y = Math.Min(S.Y, Me.Y)
                    Dim X1, Y1 As Integer
                    X1 = Me.X + Me.Width
                    Y1 = Me.Y + Me.Height
                    X1 = Math.Max(X1, S.X + S.Width)
                    Y1 = Math.Max(Y1, S.Y + S.Height)
                    Me.Width = X1 - Me.X
                    Me.Height = Y1 - Me.Y
                End Sub
                Public Sub Remove(ByVal S As clsShape)
                    Dim Item As clsShape
                    For Each Item In mvarChildren
                        If Item Is S Then
                            mvarChildren.Remove(S)
                        End If
                    Next
                End Sub
                Public Function GetChild(ByVal Index As Integer) As
                clsShape
                    If Index <= mvarShapes.Count - 1 Then
                        Return mvarChildren.Item(Index)
                    Else
                        Return Nothing
                    End If
                End Function
                Public Overrides Sub Draw(ByVal g As Graphics)
                    Dim S As clsShape
                    For Each S In mvarChildren
                        S.Draw(g)
                    Next
                End Sub
            End Class
```

Listing 10.17: The Composite pattern added to the abstract Shape classes

Since a CompositeShape is a shape by inheritance, we can add CompositeShape objects to a CompositeShape, which results in a very flexible way of creating and manipulating complex assemblies of Shape objects. We can create a composite shape by grouping other shape items together, or by deliberately assembling them in code (see Listing 10.18).

```
    Public Function NewTriangle() As Shape
        Dim C As CompositeShape
        Dim L As Line
        C = New CompositeShape()
        L = New Line()
```

```
        L.X = 500
        L.Y = 0
        L.Width = 500
        L.Height = 1000
        C.Add(L)
        L = New Line()
        L.X = 0
        L.Y = 1000
        L.Width = 1000
        L.Height = 0
        C.Add(L)
        L = New Line()
        L.X = 0
        L.Y = 0
        L.Width = 500
        L.Height = 1000
        C.Add(L)
        Return C
    End Function
```

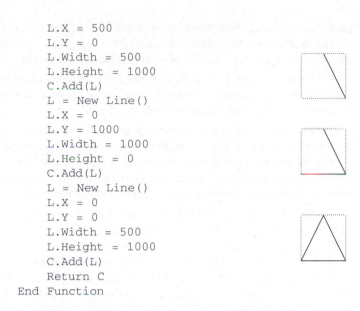

Listing 10.18: Creating a `CompositeShape`

Of course, the method shown above for creating a new triangle shape is not very useful, since it is not interactive. However, by allowing multiple items to be selected and the selected items to be grouped, we could provide a way for user-defined composite shapes to be built as the CAD program runs.

The Composite Pattern is used extensively in CAD, but is also a feature of many types of interactive software. For example, multiple documents can be combined to form composite documents, and groups of database records can be formed so that a common operation can be performed on each member.

10.5.2.3 Other Structural Patterns

The set of structural patterns described by Gamma *et al.* covers the range of possibilities for building flexible software structures and maximizing the use of object-oriented programming principles. Among these are:

- *Bridge*, that allows us to use a range of abstractions (e.g. abstract base classes) with a range of implementations (concrete classes) in such a way that a given concrete class can be appointed a *different* abstract class. In effect, two separate class hierarchies are maintained: one for abstractions and another for concrete implementations. By enclosing a member of the base implementation in the base abstraction, it becomes possible to make generalized changes to the abstract classes that proliferate throughout the implementation classes.

- *Decorator*, that allows us to extend an object dynamically, by attaching a member of a helper class. The Decorator pattern allows us to avoid sub-classing in the case where we wish to extend the functionality of specific objects. The example given in Gamma *et al.* is the addition of `Border` and `Scrollbar` objects to a plain `TextViewer`. By creating `Border` and `Scrollbar` as `Decorator` classes, we can avoid having to create a sub-class of the `TextViewer` class, and also have the ability to apply `Decorator` objects to other viewer classes.

- *Façade*, which allows us to provide a single uniform interface to a complex set of interfaces. For example, we might consider a Visual Basic form with added properties to access the data in controls as a Façade pattern.

- *Flyweight*, which allows a large number of small items to share a single object. An example of this is the use of *Flyweight* objects to represent any of a large number of characters in a word processor. Each character has font, size, style, colour, etc. attributes, but instead of occupying an object each, a single flyweight object can act as the interface to a large number of characters.

- *Proxy*, which is a way of making one object act as a surrogate for another to provide control access. For example, we could use a proxy instead of dealing directly with a `Printer` object. Since the `Printer` object may have to access the network and verify the on-line, etc. status whenever it is accessed, the proxy could be used to maintain a copy of the printer status and allow us to control the printer. Meanwhile, the proxy would only contact the real `Printer` object when it was necessary for printing.

Exercise 10.9

In almost every case, the structural patterns described result in code that has a more complex structure than you might have used to do the same job. Why is this and what advantage do the structural patterns bring to software (you may be able to think of several)?

10.5.3 Behavioural Patterns

So far, we have examined patterns that provide for the flexible creation of objects and optimization of software structures. Behavioural patterns are about the generalization of algorithms and the assignment of responsibilities among objects. The behavioural patterns codify how objects communicate with each other in a way that can assist our understanding of control flow in a program. Instead of managing control flow, you deal with object inter-connections; this in turn manages control flow.

Behavioural patterns are the most diverse group. This is probably because the history of computing has concentrated more on algorithms than on structures. Structure is a feature that supports good algorithms, but algorithms make the data work.

10.5.3.1 The Observer Pattern

This is also known as *Subject-Observer*, since it allows us to define the interaction between an object (the subject) and another object that is interested in its state (the observer). The purpose is to set up an automatic interaction between subject and observer so that updates need not be performed by the application code. Visual Basic is particularly suited to the pattern because a number of the built-in user-interface controls are potential subjects or observers.

Assume, for example, that we wish to make sure that all of the controls that are currently displaying state information about a specific object are kept up to date. We might, for example, have displayed two or more forms, each of which displays specific properties of an object, and these forms might also allow us to edit the object.

The Observer pattern allows us to keep the two or more observer forms in synch with the current state of the object by providing a `Notify()` method. The subject class keeps a list of all of its current observers, and dispatches the `Notify()` message to each whenever its state changes. The end result is an automatic update of all observers, without any need to code the updates into the application program. For example, a simple `Subject` class is shown in Listing 10.19.

```
Public Class Subject
    Private mvarWidth As Integer       'Width of an image
    Private mvarHeight As Integer      'Height of an image
    Private mvarGraphicFile As String 'Picture file name
    Private mvarObservers As ArrayList 'The list of observers

    Public Sub New(ByVal W As Integer, ByVal H As Integer, _
                ByVal F As String)
        'Set up the sizes and picture file...
        mvarWidth = W
        mvarHeight = H
        mvarGraphicFile = F
        'And create the observer collection...
        mvarObservers = New ArrayList()
    End Sub

    Public Property Width() As Integer
        Get
            Return mvarWidth
        End Get
        Set(ByVal Value As Integer)
            mvarWidth = Value
            Update() 'Update Width in all observers
        End Set
    End Property

    Public Property Height() As Integer
        Get
            Return mvarHeight
        End Get
        Set(ByVal Value As Integer)
            mvarHeight = Value
            Update() 'Update Height in all observers
        End Set
    End Property

    Public Property GraphicFile() As String
        Get
            Return mvarGraphicFile
        End Get
```

```
            Set(ByVal Value As String)
                mvarGraphicFile = Value
                Update() 'Update file in all observers
            End Set
        End Property

        Public Sub AddObserver(ByVal Obs As ObserverForm)
            'Add a new observer to the list...
            mvarObservers.Add(Obs)
            'Update it...
            Obs.Notify(Me)
        End Sub

        Private Sub Update()
            'Update all observers...
            Dim Obs As ObserverForm
            For Each Obs In mvarObservers
                Obs.Notify(Me)
            Next
        End Sub

        Public Sub Dispose()
            'Object is going, so destroy all its observers...
            Dim Obs As Form
            For Each Obs In mvarObservers
                Obs.Dispose()
            Next
        End Sub
    End Class
```

Listing 10.19: A `Subject` class – part of the Subject-Observer pattern

With the `Subject` class able to maintain a list of observers (in this case forms, but an `Observer` object does not need to be visible), we can now turn to the creation of `Observer` objects. The only pattern requirement for these is that they must implement a `Notify()` method and have some way of accessing the subject's state. With that in mind, it is a good idea to create an abstract base `Observer` class that we can use to define the `Notify()` method protocol (see Listing 10.20).

```
Public Class ObserverForm
    Inherits System.Windows.Forms.Form

[+] | Windows Form Designer Generated Code |

    Public Overridable Sub Notify(ByVal S As Subject)
        'Base class declares the Notify method.
        'Sub-classes must define how they behave.
    End Sub

End Class
```

Listing 10.20: An `Observer` base class – a form

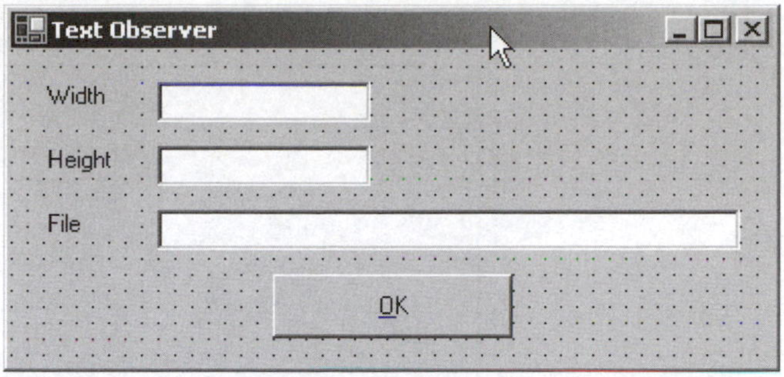

Figure 10.10 The `TextObserver` form, with controls to display the subject's data

Note that the `Observer` base class above was created by adding a form to a WinForms project, and adding the empty `Notify()` method. No controls were added to the form, although any controls added would have been inherited by classes that inherited this form and this may have been useful in some circumstances. Ideally, `ObserverForm` would be abstract (defined with the `MustInherit` keyword), and `Notify()` would be defined as `MustOverride`. However, changing the definitions to make this so upsets the Form Designer and so we must simply remember to override the `Notify()` method for each observer (with a proper abstract class, the Form Designer reminds you and will not compile code in which abstract methods have not been property overridden).

With a form definition to inherit from, the next step is to create some concrete observer forms. You can either build the assembly as it is (without any concrete observers) to enable visual inheritance, or simply change the inherits statement at the top of the new forms to reference `ObserverForm`. I find this was much faster and easier. To demonstrate the principle, we need two observer forms, since the point of the Observer Pattern is that the subject only needs to know there is an observer, not how it does its job. The first will display the subject information as text in three text boxes (`txtWidth`, `txtHeight` and `txtFile`) Figure 10.10 and Listing 10.21.

```
Public Class TextObserverForm
    Inherits ObserverForm

[+]  Windows Form Designer Generated Code

    Public Overrides Sub Notify(ByVal S As Subject)
        txtWidth.Text = S.Width.ToString()
        txtHeight.Text = S.Height.ToString()
        txtFile.Text = S.GraphicFile
    End Sub

    Private Sub btnOK_Click(ByVal sender As System.Object, _
            ByVal e As System.EventArgs) Handles btnOK.Click
        Me.Hide()
    End Sub
End Class
```

Listing 10.21: The code behind the `TextObserverForm`

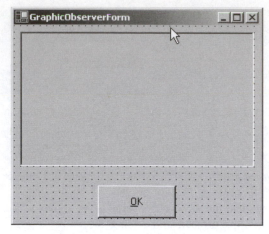

Figure 10.11 The GraphicObserverForm, with a PictureBox to display the subject

The second observer will display the picture in the specified picture file at the specified Width and Height, so it will only require a PictureBox control to do this Figure 10.11 and Listing 10.22.

```
Public Class GraphicObserverForm
    Inherits ObserverForm

 +  Windows Form Designer Generated Code

    Public Overrides Sub Notify(ByVal S As Subject)
        If Not picObserver.Image Is Nothing Then
            picObserver.Image.Dispose()
        End If
        picObserver.SizeMode = _
                    PictureBoxSizeMode.StretchImage
        picObserver.Width = S.Width
        picObserver.Height = S.Height
        picObserver.Image = New Bitmap(S.GraphicFile)
    End Sub

    Private Sub btnOK_Click(ByVal sender As System.Object, _
            ByVal e As System.EventArgs) Handles btnOK.Click
        Me.Hide()
    End Sub
End Class
```

Listing 10.22: Code behind GraphicObserverForm

The Notify() code in GraphicObserverForm makes sure that the PictureBox control will resize the picture to fit its specified dimensions (PictureBoxSizeMode.StretchImage) and load the specified image file into it. Note that in each observer, we simply pass a reference to the subject directly to the observer's Notify() method. However, this may require us to break encapsulation

Figure 10.12 The main form to control the observer demonstration

in some cases, and then more specific parameters would need to be defined for the `Notify()` method.

As a final step, we need some way of creating a subject and adding observers to it. We can return to the default form of the WinForms application (renamed as `MainForm`) and add a few buttons to it, as shown in Figure 10.12.

Code on this form (Listing 10.23) does as it says on the button captions.

```
Public Class MainForm
    Inherits System.Windows.Forms.Form

[+] Windows Form Designer Generated Code

    Private S As Subject
    Private Sub btnCreate_Click(ByVal sender As
                             System.Object, _
                          ByVal e As System.EventArgs) _
                          Handles btnCreate.Click
        S = New Subject(0, 0, "")
        UpdateSubject()
    End Sub

    Private Sub UpdateSubject()
        If Not S Is Nothing Then
            S.Width = InputBox("Enter width of subject", _
                            "Picture Width", 100)
            S.Height = InputBox("Enter height of subject", _
                            "Picture Height", 100)
            Dim dlg As OpenFileDialog = New OpenFileDialog()
            With dlg
                .Filter = "JPeg Files|*.jpg|All Files|*.*"
                If .ShowDialog = DialogResult.OK Then
                    S.GraphicFile = .FileName
                End If
            End With
            dlg.Dispose()
            dlg = Nothing
        End If
    End Sub
```

```
                Private Sub btnUpdate_Click(ByVal sender As
                                    System.Object, _
                              ByVal e As System.EventArgs) _
                              Handles btnUpdate.Click
            UpdateSubject()
        End Sub

        Private Sub btnAddObserver_Click( _
                      ByVal sender As System.Object, _
                      ByVal e As System.EventArgs) _
                      Handles btnAddObserver.Click
            Dim F As ObserverForm
            If MessageBox.Show("Text Observer?", _
                "New Observer", _
                MessageBoxButtons.YesNo) = DialogResult.Yes Then
                F = New TextObserverForm()
            Else
                F = New GraphicObserverForm()
            End If
            S.AddObserver(F)
            F.Show()
        End Sub

        Private Sub btnDestroy_Click(ByVal sender As
                                System.Object, _
                          ByVal e As System.EventArgs) _
                          Handles btnDestroy.Click
            S.Dispose()
            S = Nothing
        End Sub
    End Class
```

Listing 10.23: Code behind the main form creates subject and adds observers

Note that to save duplicating code, a sub, UpdateSubject(), has been defined. This lets the user change Width and Height (using InputBox() calls) and provides a OpenFileDialog() so the user can select a new graphic file. It is called from both the Create Subject and Update Subject buttons.

The end result is that we can now create as many observer forms as we wish (multiple copies of each type is perfectly acceptable), and all will stay in step with changes to the subject (see Figure 10.13).

Subject-Observer is a very simple method for keeping a number of objects in synchronization. In Visual Basic, it is ideal for providing a number of alternative views of a single object or structure, but it can also be used as a method for keeping objects in touch with each other.

10.5.3.2 The Iterator Pattern

This pattern exists to allow us to work our way through the items in a collection without knowing or caring what form the collection takes. We met the Iterator pattern in Chapter 6 on Data Structures, although there it was called an *enumerator*.

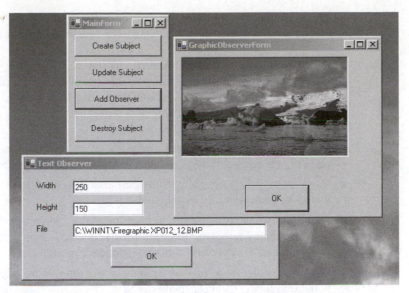

Figure 10.13 Two observer forms and the main form in operation

Regardless of name, an iterator/enumerator is useful for stepping through all of the members of a collection. Using an iterator/enumerator allowed us to use a standard code structure to access each object in a collection (see Listing 10.24).

```
Dim myEnumerator As IEnumerator = myCollection.GetEnumerator()
While myEnumerator.MoveNext()
     'Code here can access myEnumerator.Current, but may not
     'alter the collection by adding or removing items.
End While
```

Listing 10.24: Using an Iterator to step through a collection

The advantage of using an Iterator Pattern is that the same code structure can be used to step through all of the objects of any type of collection. If you decided to change a collection in an application from, say, an array to a `HashTable`, then the usual `For..Each` loop you might have used would not work and you would need to recode these. If an enumerator-based loop was used, then the code structure for stepping through the collection could stay the same.

As usual with a pattern, the software you write is slightly more complex than the most obvious method, but is worthwhile for keeping solutions as general as possible. The Iterator pattern is one that .NET provides for specifically because of this advantage.

10.5.3.3 Other Behavioural Patterns

The behavioural patterns section of the Gamma *et al*. book is the richest collection. These patterns are there to simplify and generalize algorithms in some way, and are all recognizable as ways of keeping to the abstract solutions devised for a system design during the implementation stages. The remaining ones are:

- *Chain of Responsibility*, which separates an operation from the request for it, thereby providing for a range of possible operations in response. The example given by Gamma *et al.* is of a context-sensitive help system, in which a request for help starts at the specific context of the request and works up a hierarchy until the most specific available level of help is found.

- *Command*, which encapsulates a request for an operation as an object, thereby allowing the request to be parameterized with respect to client, stored or logged.

- *Interpreter*. This pattern allows the grammar of a language to be represented so that syntax can be easily maintained.

- *Mediator*, which is a pattern for defining the interactions between different objects, thereby removing the need for the interacting objects to refer explicitly to each other. This preserves the independence of either end of the interaction.

- *Memento*, which is a way of keeping a snapshot of an object's internal state without violating its encapsulation.

- *State*, which is a pattern for allowing an object to vary its behaviour when its internal state changes. The object appears to change class depending on its state.

- *Strategy*. This pattern allows a range of algorithms to be used interchangeably, allowing different algorithms to be used in different situations.

- *Template Method*, which defines skeletal algorithms, steps of which are delegated to sub-classes to enable an algorithm to be used in a wider range of situations without change.

- *Visitor*, which represents a generalized operation to be performed on the elements of an object structure. The operation can be changed without changing the class of the elements operated on.

Exercise 10.10

Behavioural patterns allow us to encapsulate algorithms within re-usable classes. How do such patterns differ from subroutines and functions that allow us to implement an algorithm in code?

Review Questions

1. What are the three tiers in a 3-tier application?

2. What does Microsoft call the tiers in an application?

3. Which tier in a 3-tier application would have the responsibility of validating input data?

4. Which tier would provide different levels of access for different types of user?

5. In a program that is used for cataloguing music CDs, three classes are used. The `Track` class stores data about and performs operations on individual tracks on a CD, the `CD` class stores data about the CD and performs operations related to CDs and collections of tracks, and the `Catalogue` class keeps track of a collection of CDs and performs operations on the collection. Identify the classes that should be made responsible for: a) calculating the length of a whole CD; b) adding a CD to the collection; c) indicating who wrote a particular track; d) searching for a song when you know the title but not the CD it appears on.

6. List the situations in which an object would be marked for destruction by the garbage collector. Does setting an object reference to `Nothing` always cause the object to be destroyed?

7. When should you define a `Finalize()` method for a class? What can you do to prevent a discarded object hanging on to a resource while it waits for the garbage collector to call its `Finalize()` method?

8. What is the purpose of the Prototype pattern? What makes it more useful than a constructor in some circumstances?

9. If, in a program, it was necessary to add a `Fish` object to a collection that was designed to accept only objects based on the `Mammal` class, what pattern could you use to make this possible? How would the pattern do this?

10. What is the other name for the Observer pattern, and how is this name more descriptive of the overall pattern's operation? Which class in the Observer pattern implements the `Notify()` method?

Practical Activities

In this activity, we will build a program that produces a number of different types of clock faces. Since there is only one correct time (at least in a given time zone), there will be only one timekeeper, which will be an instance of the Singleton pattern (which provides for only one object of a class). The `Timekeeper` class will also be the subject of an Observer pattern (so that it will be able to keep each `ClockFace` instance up to date). Creating a new clock face will involve instantiating a new object of one or other class, and the Factory Method pattern will be useful for this.

More that anything else, this activity will be an exercise in connecting objects together in established patterns (subtext – it will be of little real use apart from providing examples of the patterns it demonstrates).

Activity 1: Creating a `Timekeeper` class

The main requirement of this class will be to provide a point of access for the time of day. It will implement the Singleton pattern for this, which allows for only one instance of the class (since there is only one time of day), and will also implement the subject end of the Subject-Observer pattern, so that observing `ClockFace` objects can be notified of the current time.

We will also need to implement the observer end of the Subject-Observer pattern so that there are objects to notify that the time has changed. These will be forms, although they could be of any type of class. Since we wish all the observer forms to conform to the observer side of the pattern, we could use code inheritance to create a common interface. However, each clock face (observer) will implement the `Notify()` message in a different way, so code inheritance will not save us from doing any work. Instead, we will use interface inheritance: each form (or other class) that implements the `ITimeObserver` interface can be added to the timekeeper's list of observers.

The Timekeeper Class

There is no need to wear two watches provided they are both set to the same time zone. Similarly, there will be no need for there ever to be more than a single `Timekeeper` object. This will simply check the time periodically and broadcast this as part of the `Notify()` message to update any observers.

The Singleton pattern is easy to implement in Visual Basic .NET. Having developed a class that performs some useful function, we simply add a small amount of code to it to prevent there ever being more than one instance of it. There are a number of ways of doing this, but the most common solution is to keep a single Shared `Instance` variable within the class. To prevent any external code from creating its own objects of the class, we can make the constructor a private member (in most circumstances, this would be weird behaviour since it prevents members of the class from being created – in this case, that is what we want). Since we need a way of getting to the single instance of the class, we provide an `Instance()` method, which creates the single instance if it has not been created already, and returns it to the caller. The code (Listing A10.1) is easier to follow than the abstract explanation.

```
Public Class Timekeeper
    'A Single instance of this class...
    Private Shared theInstance As Timekeeper
    Private mvarObservers As ArrayList
    Private t As System.Threading.Thread

    Private Sub New()
        'This is for the collection of Observers...
        mvarObservers = New ArrayList()
    End Sub

    'This function implements the Singleton pattern.
    'Since the constructor is private, this is the only
    'way to create an instance of the class, and it will only
    'create a single instance...
    Public Shared Function Instance() As Timekeeper
        If theInstance Is Nothing Then
            theInstance = New Timekeeper()
```

```
            End If
            Return theInstance
        End Function
        'More code to come...
        '...
```

Listing A10.1: Code for the Singleton pattern

The first member variable in Listing A10.1 is the variable that will refer to a single instance of the class. The constructor does its normal work (in this case preparing a new `ArrayList` for use by the Observer pattern), except that it is `Private`. If external code wants access to the `Timekeeper` object, it does so by calling the `Instance()` shared method, which returns a reference to `mvarInstance`. Note that the code here checks whether `mvarInstance` currently refers to a `Timekeeper` object, and will only create one if it does not.

Client code wishing to use a `Timekeeper` object simply uses the call:

```
TK = Timekeeper.Instance()
```

and can continue to use its methods and properties as usual.

The timekeeper must implement two methods to fulfil its duty as a subject in the Subject-Observer pattern (Listing A10.2).

```
'Update all observers...
Public Sub Update()
    Dim o As ITimeObserver
    For Each o In mvarObservers
        o.Notify(theInstance)
    Next
End Sub

'Add a new observer...
Public Sub AddObserver(ByVal o As ITimeObserver)
    mvarObservers.Add(o)
End Sub
```

Listing A10.2: The timekeeper methods for implementing Subject-Observer

The `Update()` method simply sends the `Notify()` message to each observer in the collection. If there are no observers, `Notify()` will never be called. `AddObserver()` can add any object that implements the `ITimeObserver` interface (defined later).

The remainder of the `Timekeeper` class is involved with keeping track of and reporting the time and updating itself periodically. Keeping track of the time is straightforward enough (see Listing A10.3).

```
Public Function TheTime() As String
    Return DateTime.ToString("hh:mm:ss")
End Function
```

```
Public Function DateTime() As Date
    Return Now
End Function
Public Function Hour() As Integer
    Return DateTime.Hour()
End Function
Public Function Minute() As Integer
    Return DateTime.Minute()
End Function
Public Function Second() As Integer
    Return DateTime.Second()
End Function
```

Listing A10.3: Timekeeper methods for returning the time of day

By providing the time both as a string (`TheTime`) and as separate integer values for `Hour`, `Minute` and `Second`, we will make it easier to implement any style of observer we wish. We now need to consider how to update the observers at regular intervals. The most simple (but flawed) approach would simply be to call `Update()` in a loop, as shown in Listing A10.4.

```
Do
    theInstance.Update()
Loop
```

Listing A10.4: Not a good way of updating observers

While this approach would work, it would waste all available processor time, since the loop never gives any other processing a chance to happen. At worst, this would lock up the system. If the `Timekeeper` class were a Form class, we could use a `Timer` control to call `Update()` at defined intervals. We could also do this by creating a `Timer` control in code. However, this approach would involve setting up an event handler for the `Timer` control we created – not difficult, but there is a better approach, using the .NET `Thread` class.

Threads – a word of warning

A *thread* is a separate processing path that can run concurrently with others on a multi-tasking computer system. Generally, concurrency is considered one of the black arts of programming, and rightly so since misusing concurrency can create problems that are difficult to diagnose and can cause a system to lock up or crash. The problem stems from two separate pieces of code executing more-or-less simultaneously (in fact they execute one at a time in turns, but the change from one section of running code to another is performed so rapidly that it appears that they are executing side by side). If both pieces of code operate using only variables and resources they have exclusive access to, there is usually no problem. If, however, both threads of execution try to change the value of a shared variable, the outcome is unpredictable and could leave a variable in an unknown state.

Various strategies can be used to allow simultaneous threads of code to access shared data, but these introduce their own problems. Whole university courses are run on the subject of concurrency in computer systems because of the subtle pitfalls that can occur. The upshot of this is that when programming with threads, it is a very good idea to take great care to follow approaches that you are confident in, and usually this means using techniques that have been well tried by many people.

In the `Timekeeper` class, using a thread does not pose any particular problem because we will not be sharing a set of data between two or more threads. The entire purpose of a thread in this class is so that we can set it up to call the `Update()` method periodically. Even so, take care that you follow the code and explanations carefully before you try this for the first time, and always save your project before trying to execute the program.

With a thread, we have three things to consider: starting it, giving it a job to do periodically, and stopping it. Giving it the job to do periodically is simple (Listing A10.5).

```
Public Sub TickTock()
    Do
        theInstance.Update()
        t.Sleep(1000)
    Loop
End Sub
```

Listing A10.5: The code to update observers, controlled by a thread

The `TickTock()` sub is almost the same code as Listing A10.4. The variable `t` was declared at the top of the `Timekeeper` class (Listing A10.1) as `System.Threading.Thread`. This is the `Thread` object, and its purpose here is to go to sleep, or lie dormant, for 1000 milliseconds (1 second). This is not a statement that says 'do nothing for 1000 mS'. Rather, it says 'don't take up any processor time for 1000 mS'. During this time, other programs and threads can continue doing their work with no hindrance. Getting the thread started in the first place is only a little trickier (Listing A10.6).

```
Public Sub Go()
    t = New System.Threading.Thread(AddressOf Me.TickTock)
    t.Start()
End Sub
```

Listing A10.6: Starting up a thread

The `Thread` object is created as usual with a call to its constructor. However, the parameter we pass to `Sub New()` uses the `AddressOf` operator. This, as its name suggests, tells us the location of the `TickTock()` method (`Me.TickTock()` since it is a sub in the same class), and this we pass on to the `Thread` object. Knowing where it lives, the thread is now capable of calling `TickTock()` for us. This we then instruct it to do by calling the thread's `Start()` method. From here, the thread will execute separately from the rest of the program. Since whenever it calls `TickTock()`, it is then sent to sleep for a second, we can be sure that `TickTock()` will not be executed during this time since it is being executed on the thread that has just gone to sleep.

The overall result of this is that all observers of `Timekeeper` will be updated once a second or so (1 second of sleep time plus the tiny amount of time that it takes to `Notify()` all the observers). The final thing we need to do is to make sure we can stop the clock ticking. Left to its own devices, the thread will continue to execute forever, until the computer is shut down, or more likely, until it tries to interact with an object that no longer exists (which it will do when it calls notify if the rest of the program has stopped running). Stopping a thread is as simple as calling its `Abort()` method, but since the thread is a resource, we will need to make sure there are no circumstances where `Abort()` is not called (or is left up to garbage collection to be dealt with). To deal with this, we can implement a `Dispose()` method for the `Timekeeper` class that takes care of stopping the thread. This is shown in Listing A10.7.

```
'Existing code...
'...
Public Sub StopClock()
    t.Abort()
    t = Nothing
End Sub
Public Sub Dispose()
    StopClock()
    Dim o As ITimeObserver
    For Each o In mvarObservers
        o.Kill()
        o = Nothing
    Next
End Sub
End Class
```

Listing A10.7: Stopping the thread and cleaning up

`StopClock()` simply ends the thread, and so `TickTock()` will not be called again once this has happened. To get rid of the timekeeper we should stop the clock and get rid of all of the observers. Since an observer can be any class, we need to make sure the appropriate action is taken, whatever that action is. For a form observer, we would close and dispose of it, for other `Observer` objects we might want to dispose of them or simply disconnect them from the subject. To make sure some appropriate action is taken, `Sub Kill()` has been added to the `ITimeObserver` interface.

The ideal place for this interface is in the same class module as the `Timekeeper` class, since it would never be used without a `Timekeeper` object. The interface is simple (Listing A10.8).

```
Public Interface ITimeObserver
    Sub Notify(ByVal T As Timekeeper)
    Sub Kill()
End Interface
```

Listing A10.8: `ITimeObserver` – `Observer` objects will need to implement this

All that this interface does is to ensure that any class that implements it must have a `Notify()` method and a `Kill()` method with matching signatures.

Activity 2: Implementing `TimeObservers`

From here we simply need to create one or more classes that implement the above interface and display the time notification sent by the timekeeper. A digital clock is very easy to create. Add a new form to the project, give the file the name **DigitalTimeObserver.vb**, and set it up as shown in Figure A10.1 and Table A10.1.

Figure A10.1 `DigitalTimeObserver` – an observer for the `Timekeeper` class

Table A10.1 Property settings for the `DigitalTimeObserver`

Control	Property	Setting	Description
Form	Name	DigitalTimeObserver	The name we will address the form by in code
	ControlBox	False	Removes any buttons from the form's caption. This prevents a user from closing the form
	Text	DigitalTimeObserver	The form's caption
Label	Name	lblTime	The label that will show the time of day
	Text	"00:00:00"	This setting will allow you to adjust the font size of the label for best appearance
	TextAlign	MiddleCenter	Make sure the label text appears central
	Font	Choose any you like	The text appearance

The `DigitalTimeObserver` form contains a single `Label` control, `lblTime` which has been given a size and font that will make it display the time of day clearly. Note that several settings have been applied to the `Form` and the `Label`.

Code for the digital clock simply implements the two `ITimeObserver()` methods as necessary (see Listing A10.9).

```
Public Class DigitalTimeObserver
    Inherits System.Windows.Forms.Form
    Implements ITimeObserver
```

```
+  Windows Form Designer Generated Code
```

```
Public Sub Notify(ByVal T As Timekeeper) _
                Implements MultiClock.ITimeObserver.Notify
    lblTime.Text = T.TheTime()
End Sub
```

```
Public Sub Kill() Implements
MultiClock.ITimeObserver.Kill
    Me.Close()
    Me.Dispose()
End Sub
```

```
End Class
```

Listing A10.9: Code for the digital clock form

Start by adding the `Implements` statement near the top of the code listing (`Implements ITimeObserver`). You can then add the `Notify()` and `Kill()` methods that define how the form does the jobs specified in the interface.

The `Notify()` method takes the string returned by the timekeeper's `TheTime()` method and places it in the label's `Text` property. Since it has been formatted by the `Timekeeper` object, there is only a simple assignment required. The `Kill()` method closes then disposes of the form. Note that when you add these implementations of the `ITimeObserver` interface, Visual Studio will write the first and last line of each for you. Simply select `ITimeObserver` from the Class Name drop down box at the top-left of the form's Code window, and each method in turn from the Method Name box at the top right, as shown in Figure A10.2.

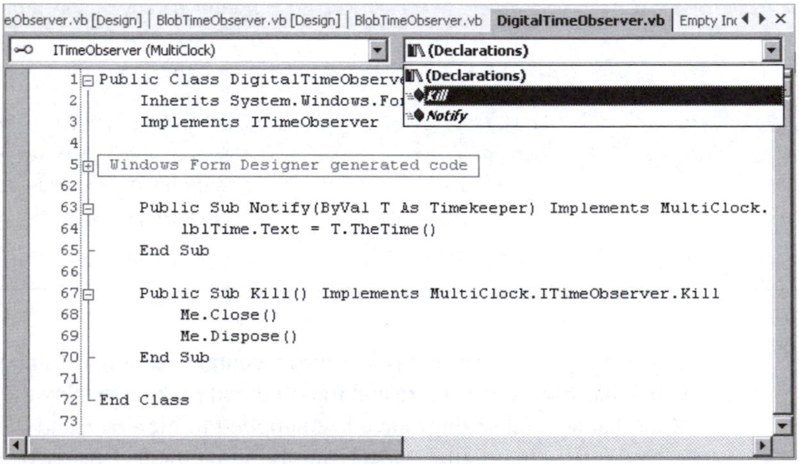

Figure A10.2 Adding the interface methods

Testing the `Observer` class

We can now test the `Observer` (and the `Subject` class, timekeeper). First, go to the main form in the project, i.e. the default form that was created with the new project and give it the name `frmMain` (if you changed the original main form to make it the `DigitalTimeObserver` form, simply add a new form and name it `frmMain` before proceeding). Now add a single instance variable to the Form class (Listing A10.10).

```
Public Class frmMain
    Inherits System.Windows.Forms.Form

    [+] | Windows Form Designer Generated Code |

    Private TK As Timekeeper
End Class
```

Listing A10.10: Adding a timekeeper to `frmMain`

Add a `form_load` event-handler to create the single instance of timekeeper (double-click on the background of the form to generate the outline) (Listing A10.11).

```
Private Sub frmMain_Load(ByVal sender As System.Object, _
                         ByVal e As System.EventArgs) _
                         Handles MyBase.Load
    TK = Timekeeper.Instance()
    TK.Go()
End Sub
```

Listing A10.11: Creating the timekeeper instance

Now add a button to the main form, and give the button the caption 'Digital Clock' and the name `btnDigital`. Code the `_Click` event-handler shown in Listing A10.12 for it.

```
Private Sub btnDigital_Click(ByVal sender As System.Object, _
                             ByVal e As System.EventArgs) _
                             Handles btnDigital.Click
    Dim face As New DigitalTimeObserver()
    TK.AddObserver(face)
    face.Show()
End Sub
```

Listing A10.12: Creating and adding an observer

Run the program and press the button. A new form displaying a digital clock should appear and continue to update. Press the button a few more times, and each press should create an instance of a digital clock. The important feature to remember is that all of the clocks are getting the time from the `Timekeeper` object via `Notify()`.

When the main form is shut down, the digital clock faces should close also. However, you will find that the program is still running, since the `Timekeeper` object has not been destroyed. Shut the program down by selecting **Debug/Stop Debugging** from the menu. We can fix this by calling timekeeper's `Dispose()` method as the form closes. Add the code shown in Listing A10.13 to the main form's `Closing()` event-handler.

```
Private Sub frmMain_Closing(ByVal sender As Object, _
        ByVal e As System.ComponentModel.CancelEventArgs) _
        Handles MyBase.Closing
    TK.Dispose()
End Sub
```

Listing A10.13: Disposing of the timekeeper cleanly

We now have a fully working Subject-Observer based clock. However, we are not constrained to having only one implementation of the `ITimeObserver` interface.

Activity 3: Creating alternative observers

Add another form to the project, giving it the name `AnalogTimeObserver`. Make the form roughly square in shape, remove its control buttons by setting the `ControlBox` property to `False`, and add a single `Panel` control to the form. Name the `Panel` control `pnlClock`, and, instead of changing its size, set its `Dock` property to `Fill` (the middle setting in the drop down box in the Properties window). Again this form will need to implement the `ITimeObserver` interface, so add the appropriate `Implements` statement. Implement the methods using the code in Listing A10.14.

```
Public Class AnalogTimeObserver
    Inherits System.Windows.Forms.Form
    Implements ITimeObserver

[+] [Windows Form Designer Generated Code]

    Public Sub Notify(ByVal T As Timekeeper) _
             Implements MultiClock.ITimeObserver.Notify
        UpdateFace(T.Hour, T.Minute, T.Second)
    End Sub

    'This is called in response to a Notify message..
    Public Sub UpdateFace(ByVal hh As Integer, _
                          ByVal mm As Integer, _
                          ByVal ss As Integer)
        Dim hAngle, mAngle, sAngle As Single
        Dim hX, hY As Single
        Dim mX, mY As Single
        Dim sX, sY As Single
        Dim cX, cY As Single
```

```
    Dim hLength, mLength, sLength As Single
    'Calculate the lengths of the hands...
    hLength = pnlClock.Width * 0.35
    mLength = pnlClock.Width * 0.4
    sLength = pnlClock.Width * 0.45

    'Work out the angle for each hand...
    hAngle = (Math.PI / 2) - ((hh / 6) * Math.PI)
    mAngle = (Math.PI / 2) - ((mm / 30) * Math.PI)
    sAngle = (Math.PI / 2) - ((ss / 30) * Math.PI)

    'Work out the end-points of the hands...
    sX = sLength * Math.Cos(sAngle)
    sY = -sLength * Math.Sin(sAngle)
    mX = mLength * Math.Cos(mAngle)
    mY = -mLength * Math.Sin(mAngle)
    hX = hLength * Math.Cos(hAngle)
    hY = -hLength * Math.Sin(hAngle)

    'Get the centre of the Panel...
    cX = pnlClock.Width / 2
    cY = pnlClock.Height / 2

    Dim gc As Graphics = pnlClock.CreateGraphics
    gc.Clear(Me.BackColor)
    Dim r As New Rectangle(0, 0, _
         pnlClock.Width, pnlClock.Height)
    gc.DrawEllipse(New Pen(Color.Black, 2), r)
    'Draw the second hand...
    gc.DrawLine(New Pen(Color.Black, 1), cX, cY, _
                                  cX + sX, cY + sY)
    'Draw the minute hand..
    gc.DrawLine(New Pen(Color.Black, 2), cX, cY, _
                                  cX + mX, cY + mY)
    'Draw the hour hand..
    gc.DrawLine(New Pen(Color.Black, 4), cX, cY, _
                                  cX + hX, cY + hY)
End Sub

Public Sub Kill() Implements MultiClock.ITimeObserver.Kill
    Me.Close()
    Me.Dispose()
End Sub

'This is needed to ensure the clock face stays square...
Private Sub AnalogTimeObserver_Resize( _
            ByVal sender As Object, _
            ByVal e As System.EventArgs) _
            Handles MyBase.Resize
    'Need to keep a square aspect...
    If Me.Width > Me.Height Then
        Me.Width = Me.Height
    Else
        Me.Height = Me.Width
```

```
        End If
    End Sub
End Class
```

Listing A10.14: An observer with an analogue clock face

Most of the code in Listing A10.14 simply works out the sizes and positions of the clock hands. Most computer languages (including VB .NET) have a geometry system that calculates angles in radians. 0 radians is at 3:00, and angles increase in an anti-clockwise direction. Therefore 12:00 is at an angle of +90% or PI/2 radians. Working out the angle of an hand is a matter of working out how much of a rotation it has gone through (2 * PI is a full circle) and subtracting this from PI/2. For example, 6:00 is 6/12ths of 12 hours (since 12 hours make a full rotation) and the angle is (PI/2) − (6 * 2 * PI)/12 = PI/2 = PI = −PI/2. In general, any given hour will be at an angle of:

(PI / 2) − ((hour / 6) * PI)

A given number of minutes will be at:

(PI / 2) − ((mm / 30) * PI)

and the same calculation for seconds. Calculating the end positions of hands from these angles is a matter of a bit of trigonometry. Once all these calculations have been made, it is a matter of creating a `Graphics` object for the panel, and using the various `Draw()` methods to draw a clock face. All of the code to do this is in the `UpdateFace()` method, which is called from the `Notify()` method. The only remaining routines are one to implement the `Kill()` interface method (exactly as for the digital form) and a `Resize()` event-handler that will keep the form roughly square in shape.

Exercise A10.1

Add a new button to the main form, give it the name `btnAnalog` and the caption "Analog Clock". Now add code to cause it to create an `AnalogTimeObserver` and attach it to the `Timekeeper` object (the code will be very similar to the code to attach the digital clock).

Activity 4: Anything that ticks

Just for fun, the code shown in Listing A10.15 can be placed on another form that has controls and properties exactly like the `AnalogTimeObserver` (remove the control box from the form, give it a name (`BlobTimeObserver`), and a panel with the name `pnBlobs`, and set its `Dock` property to `Fill`). It will produce an unusual clock face for anyone who is bored with easy time-telling. Having added the form, remember to add a button to create instances of it.

```
Public Class BlobTimeObserver
    Inherits System.Windows.Forms.Form
    Implements ITimeObserver
    Private x_6 As Integer, x_2 As Integer, x_5_6 As Integer
    Private y_2 As Integer
```

```
Public Sub Notify(ByVal T As MultiClock.Timekeeper) _
              Implements MultiClock.ITimeObserver.Notify
    Dim hourBlob As Rectangle, hourSize As Size
    Dim minBlob As Rectangle, minSize As Size
    Dim secBlob As Rectangle, secSize As Size
    Dim xs, ys As Single
    SetSize()
    xs = x_6 * T.Hour / 12
    ys = y_2 * T.Hour / 12
    hourBlob = New Rectangle(x_6 - xs, y_2 - ys, _
                               xs + xs, ys + ys)
    xs = x_6 * T.Minute / 60
    ys = y_2 * T.Minute / 60
    minBlob = New Rectangle(x_2 - xs, y_2 - ys, _
                               xs + xs, ys + ys)
    xs = x_6 * T.Second / 60
    ys = y_2 * T.Second / 60
    secBlob = New Rectangle(x_5_6 - xs, y_2 - ys, _
                               xs + xs, ys + ys)
    Dim g As Graphics = pnlBlobs.CreateGraphics()
    Dim drawFont As New Font("Arial", 16)
    Dim drawBrush As New SolidBrush(Color.Black)
    Dim textRect As New RectangleF(x_6 - 20, _
                                    y_2 - 10, 40, 20)
    g.Clear(Color.White)
    g.FillEllipse(Brushes.Blue, hourBlob)
    g.DrawString(T.Hour.ToString("00"), drawFont, _
                drawBrush, textRect)
    g.FillEllipse(Brushes.Yellow, minBlob)
    textRect.X = x_2 - 20
    g.DrawString(T.Minute.ToString("00"), drawFont, _
                drawBrush, textRect)
    g.FillEllipse(Brushes.Red, secBlob)
    textRect.X = x_5_6 - 20
    g.DrawString(T.Second.ToString("00"), drawFont, _
                drawBrush, textRect)
End Sub

Private Sub SetSize()
    x_6 = pnlBlobs.Width / 6
    x_2 = pnlBlobs.Width / 2
    x_5_6 = pnlBlobs.Width - x_6
    y_2 = pnlBlobs.Height / 2
End Sub

Public Sub Kill() Implements MultiClock.ITimeObserver.Kill
    Me.Close()
    Me.Dispose()
End Sub

End Class
```

Listing A10.15: Another `ITimeObserver` form

Figure A10.3   One timekeeper, several observers

The resulting application is shown in Figure A10.3, with four observer instances in operation.

Features worth remembering

In this chapter, we've looked at a range of areas that broadly address the ideal of building object models. In programs that you go on to create, you should consider the following.

- Patterns are templates for code devised by experts. On your way to becoming an expert, you should always be on the lookout for established ways of doing things. The book on patterns mentioned earlier in the chapter is an important resource to very many professional programmers, and there are lots of websites which now contain material specifically on patterns in Visual Basic.

- The code in an application will only be as good as the structure it is applied to. While it is possible to create a program that has a badly thought out structure and get it working, it will always be much more difficult to maintain that type of program. Learn the established structures and what situations they are used in.

- Managing resources in .NET is easier than in most programming environments, since garbage collection takes care of most of the objects you will ever create. However, you should be aware that some resources (usually external resources such as files, database, network connections, etc.) are not managed by .NET and you should keep the general approach to the `Dispose()` method in your armoury for when you need to release resources in a timely manner. Beware though, that you should not normally deal with managed resources in this way since that could make your application less efficient.

Suggested Additional Activities

1   The activities in this section were to introduce you to design patterns. You should consider looking back through the programs earlier in the book and identifying situations where patterns would be useful.

2   Look up some components you have used in .NET programs in the help system (e.g. `ArrayList`), and read the section on Thread Safety. Look up the `Thread` class and read the help pages on that. Be aware that threads are there to improve the overall throughput of information in programs, but in most software will simply be an unnecessary and dangerous addition. Look up a some Internet resources on concurrency and find out what the good and bad features are.

Solutions to Exercises

Exercise 10.1

a)   The business tier.

b)   Here we need to distinguish between `colUsers` – a collection of bank account `User` objects or account holders – and application users, who would communicate with the business objects using the presentation tier. It would be feasible to create `ApplicationUser` objects which managed purely user-interface data and interactions and place these in the presentation tier, although even here, these objects would probably need to manage some aspects of the business rules of the application, such as security access rights, and so might be better placed in the business tier. However, the bank account `User` objects stored in `colUsers` are certainly implementations of business rules for bank account management and so undoubtedly belong in the business tier.

c)   A better approach to constructing and managing collections of business tier objects in an application would be to build a strongly typed collections, as described in the chapter on inheritance, using `CollectionBase` as a starting point.

Exercise 10.2

For example, we can look at the CAD program done in the practical activity at the end of the previous chapter. Objects are created in response to event-handlers (button clicks) in the presentation tier. Once an object is created, it is positioned and sized in response to user-interactions in the presentation tier, although the actual re-sizing and positioning is done in methods of the drawn objects – i.e. in the business tier. Objects are finally destroyed in response to the main form closing down – a presentation tier event. In this application, as in many highly interactive programs, the interactions between business objects and user-interface objects make the division of the application into specific tiers complex. However, the identification of tiers is straightforward enough – drawn objects and the collections they are managed in form the business tier, and the user-interface and associated event-handlers are the presentation tier.

Exercise 10.3

Because of the care taken to preserve the class interface of the earlier forms of bank account, using this more complex form of account will be no different and in fact illustrates one of the most significant benefits of object-oriented programming.

Exercise 10.4

```
Public Function GetStatement() As String
    Dim T As Transaction
    Dim stmt As StringBuilder = New StringBuilder()
    stmt.Append("Bank Account Statement" & _
                Environment.NewLine)
    stmt.Append("Account Name: " & Customer1.Name)
    If Not (Customer2 Is Nothing) Then
        stmt.Append(" and " & Customer2.Name)
    End If
    stmt.Append(Environment.NewLine)
    stmt.Append("Account Number: " & mvarAccountNumber & _
                Environment.NewLine)
    For Each T In mvarTransactions
        stmt.Append(T.GetStatementLine & _
                    Environment.NewLine)
    Next
    Return stmt.ToString()
End Function
```

Exercise 10.5

There is no set solution to this exercise. You can find the first statement executed in an application by stepping into the application using **Debug→Step Into** instead of the **Run** command in the IDE.

Exercise 10.6

There is no set solution to this exercise. It is worth performing the activity on a range of programs to discover how and when objects are disposed of.

Exercise 10.7

Structures in software indicate how objects are connected together (e.g. to form lists, collections or compositions). Patterns in software are less specific, in that they can indicate elements of structure, algorithms or simply well tried techniques and methods.

Exercise 10.8

a) A creational pattern is used to decouple the application logic from the creation of objects (particularly business objects) to simplify or make routine the way that objects are created in response to user-interactions. Generally, it is used to remove any need to deal with the complexities of how objects can be brought into existence.

b) A Factory Method is a function call that returns an object of a class (specified in a parameter of the method). The Prototype pattern is based on giving each class a facility to allow objects to create clones of themselves, and tends to be more suitable to use when objects with a predefined state are needed, since a generator object can be placed into a specific state immediately before the cloning process. The Prototype pattern can be used within the Factory Method pattern.

Exercise 10.9

Patterns are used to make the wealth of experience of programmers available in a recipe-like way. Solutions based on patterns are therefore more likely to be robust and simpler to incorporate into an application, even though they themselves are more complex. Advantages include – routine implementation of complex facilities in programs, patterns are well known and other programmers are more likely to be able to understand the implementation, less likelihood of fundamental problems due to proven design, easier adaptation.

Exercise 10.10

An algorithm based on a pattern is never likely to be implementable as a single sub or function in such a way that it will be generally useful. Behavioural patterns tend to incorporate data structures (that will exist outwith any specific sub or function), and interactions that go beyond a single routine process.

Exercise A10.1

```
Private Sub btnDigital_Click(ByVal sender As System.Object, _
                          ByVal e As System.EventArgs) _
                          Handles btnDigital.Click
    Dim face As New AnalogTimeObserver()
    TK.AddObserver(face)
    face.Show()
End Sub
```

Answers to Review Questions

1. What are the three tiers in a 3-tier application? *Presentation, business and data access* **(covered in Chapter 12).**

2. What does Microsoft call the tiers in an application? **Services or service layers.**

3. Which tier in a 3-tier application would have the responsibility of validating input data? **The presentation tier.**

4. Which tier would provide different levels of access for different types of user? **The presentation tier.**

5. In a program that is used for cataloguing music CDs, three classes are used. The Track class stores data about and performs operations on individual tracks on a CD, the CD class stores data about the CD and performs operations related to CDs and collections of tracks, and the Catalogue class keeps track of a collection of CDs and performs operations on the collection. Identify the classes that should be made responsible for: a) calculating the length of a whole CD, b) adding a CD to the collection, c) indicating who wrote a particular track, d) searching for a song when you know the title but not the CD it appears on. **a) CD class, b) Catalogue class, c) Track class, d) Catalogue, CD and Track classes together (Track allows name to be matches, CD gives access to a list of tracks, Catalogue provides access to all CDs.**

6. List the situations in which an object would be marked for destruction by the garbage collector. Does setting an object reference to Nothing always cause the object to be destroyed? **Object is attached to a Local variable which goes out of scope, object is attached to an object (including collections) that is destroyed, object is explicitly set to Nothing. No – Nothing is assigned to a specific reference variable. If the object is also referenced by one or more other references (including membership of a collection), it will not be marked for destruction.**

7. When should you define a Finalize() method for a class? What can you do to prevent a discarded object hanging on to a resource while it waits for the garbage collector to call its Finalize() method? **When an object holds on to a resource such as a file, network or database connection which must be released. Provide a Dispose() method.**

8. What is the purpose of the Prototype pattern? What makes it more useful than a constructor in some circumstances? **Create new objects that are exact copies of a prototype object. It is sometimes easier to create a new object in a specific state if a prototype can be used as an indicator of the required state.**

9. If, in a program, it was necessary to add a Fish object to a collection that was designed to accept only objects based on the Mammal class, what pattern could you use to make this possible? How would the pattern do this? **The Adapter pattern. By providing a Mammal class wrapper that contained (by Composition) a Fish reference variable.**

10. What is the other name for the Observer pattern, and how is this name more descriptive of the overall pattern's operation? Which class in the Observer pattern implements the Notify() method? **Subject-Observer. The Subject class.**

CHAPTER
11

Files, Streams and Serialization

In this chapter you will read:

- why persistence is an important issue in programming, and why .NET provides so many competing persistence mechanisms;

- how to store application settings or data into the Windows Registry;

- what files are and the core mechanisms that a programmer can access to deal with file storage and retrieval;

- about different types of file and ways of creating, writing to and reading from files;

- what a stream is, and how objects can be serialized on to a stream for storage or transport;

- what XML is, why it is a central mechanism that .NET relies on, and how to create, read and write XML data.

11.1 Storing Application Data

11.1.1 Off-Line Storage

Computers would be reduced to the level of mere machinery if it were not for the availability of *off-line storage*, the mechanisms that allow programs to be stored for later use and the mechanisms for storing their data to and retrieving it from storage devices. Computer main memory, the type that programs run in, is volatile. If the computer's power is switched off, it forgets everything in its main memory (in almost all computers, a small amount of memory, no more than a few variables' worth, is used to store settings that must persist while the power is off).

When you use a word processor or a spreadsheet program, you expect that the documents you created yesterday will be available for editing and printing. In fact all but the most trivial programs that you use would be completely useless were it not for the facility to retrieve data that you had previously created, or move data from another source on to your computer.

A generic name for the facility to store data off-line (i.e. while the computer is switched off) and retrieve it again is *persistence*, and in a modern PC there are often several mechanisms that make this possible. The PC I am working on as I write this has a floppy disk drive that can accommodate a fairly small amount of data by today's standards, a fixed disk drive (or hard disk drive) that can cope with a huge amount of data (which in a few years time will almost certainly be considered to be a trivial amount), and a CD read/write drive that allows me to store significant amounts of data on to removable media. It also has a small memory-card reader that I use to transfer photographs from my digital camera, and I use a small 'data-pen' type device to make quick backup copies of documents I'm working on to transfer to a laptop PC.

While these devices are based on widely different storage technologies, my PC recognizes all of them as file-storage devices and mostly treats them as equals in terms of how to read data from them and write data to them. Obviously, the computer's operating system is doing a lot of work on my behalf to make it as easy as possible to store data off-line and retrieve it again.

A program often needs to store several types of data to do its work. A quick look at Visual Studio should convince you of that. Every program that you create will occupy several files on your computer's hard disk drive. These files will hold the program code and form designs, translated versions of these for use by the .NET framework, plus any settings that have been made for the program, such as the name of the start-up form. In addition, Visual Studio stores data for its own purposes; how you have set up VS in the Tools/Options dialog box, which add-ins have been made available, how you have the various windows organized on the screen, etc.

Any non-trivial program that you write will create data that you will need to store off-line to save the user having to re-enter it the next time the program is run. All of this data can be saved in files, and can be retrieved either automatically or on demand when the program is run at a later date.

11.2 Computer Files

The word 'file' is heavily overloaded in the English language. Look it up in a dictionary, and you will find several definitions:

1. a folder or box used to keep documents or other items in order;
2. the documents kept in this way;
3. documents or information about a specific subject;
4. a line of people in marching formation;
5. any of the eight vertical rows of squares on a chess board;
6. a block of data that can be accessed . . . from a storage device.

Version 4 in the above list is of interest because it tells us something about the way things are organized in files. A file of any type of items will be organized so that the items occur in some order. The order could be alphabetical, or by number or even random, but the order of items within the file stays the same unless the file is deliberately altered in some way. If a line of soldiers on a parade ground is set to march around the ground, the person at the front of the line will always be at the front of the line unless the line is reorganized. Files in a filing cabinet are placed in a specific order so that it is easy to find them again. Computer files are sequences of data items that are written to a storage device in a particular order. When a computer file comes to be read into a program, the order that the items are read will be the order that they were first written in.

This feature of files, that they maintain the order originally applied to them, is important, because it allows us to store quantities of data in such a way that they can be retrieved predictably. If you consider how your local telephone directory is ordered, and how the alphabetical index of names makes it possible for you to look up someone's telephone number from among several hundred thousand in around two minutes, you can see that ordering data is a powerful technique that can have many uses in data manipulation and management.

There are four specific operations that a program can perform on a file.

1. A file can be opened to make its contents available to the program: there is some overhead in computer memory and time to opening a file, so the natural state of a file is closed, reducing the load on the computer. A file is also vulnerable to corruption while it is open, so files are only opened when access to their contents is required.

2. An item of data can be read from a file: typically, the item read is the next available item, and the act of reading it will make the following item become the next available item.

3. An item of data can be written to a file: normally, the item written will be placed at the end of the file.

4. A file can be closed: this frees up computer memory and places the file into a state that is much less vulnerable to corruption.

These four operations are fundamental to any file-storage system. In all of them, the computer operating system does the majority of the work and so the operations are very easy to do in a program. File handling in a program is usually more about organising the information, so that it is stored in a sequence that makes it easy to work with.

11.2.1 Application Settings

Application settings are the incidental pieces of information that govern how the program operates. For example, I find it easier to work with a program if when I run it its main form appears on the screen at the same size and position that it had the last time I was using it. The four numbers that determine the form's size and position (width, height, top and left) can be stored off-line when the program exits, and retrieved when the program starts up again, therefore saving me having to drag the form to its usual position and resize it to the size I normally prefer.

Other information, such as the most recently used files, my preferences for font or colours, or even personal data such as my name, address or email address can be stored as application settings so that I do not have to type them in each time I use a program.

Generally, I consider the facility to save application settings in a program I use as a convenience. While this facility does not have a big effect on what the program can do, it does pre-dispose me towards a program so that, all other facilities being equal, I prefer it over other programs that do the same job but do not save settings.

11.2.2 Object Model Data

This is a much bigger subject area than the simple storage and retrieval of application settings, and will occupy most of this chapter and all of the next one. The object-model within a program holds the main data. Typically, this data is the reason the program is there in the first place. Word-processed documents, spreadsheets, computer-aided drawings, photographs, and Visual Basic Program Code are all things that a user would consider to be the core data of their respective programs, and in an object-oriented world, would reside in the object-model of the program as it executed. A user will rightly expect the programs to allow their object-model data to be stored off-line so that the object-models can be recreated during a subsequent run.

Some programs, such as word processors, spreadsheets, programming languages and drawing programs will need the ability to create any number of files so that the user can work on different documents at different times. Other programs, such as address-book software, web browsers and games may only work with a single file or set of files, storing the latest state of the object model whenever they are shut down and retrieving it the next time they are run. In either case, the ability to save to and retrieve from a file will be similar.

The significant difference between these types of program is in whether the users are given the option to create new files or not. In a program that allows the user to create new files and store them by name, we think of the program as being a producer of documents.

11.3 The Windows Registry

The Windows Registry is a repository of information necessary for the correct operation of the operating system and application programs that must maintain 'settings' over a period of time. Since it contains data for just about every program you will use on a regular basis, you can rightly expect that the registry takes up a lot of space and that the smooth running of a computer depends on it.

This makes it unsuitable for storing large amounts of data from any single program. For example, it would not be sensible to store your entire address book in the registry, since if every program decided to store that level of information, the registry would become excessively large with the result that operations to retrieve or store data in it would take too long to process.

Therefore, the registry should be used for storing a few application settings, rather than the information contained in a whole object model. The .NET framework includes classes that make it easy to write data to and restore data from the registry, as the example (Listing 11.1) to persist the size and position of a form between runs of the program demonstrates.

```
Public Class frmRegistry
    Inherits System.Windows.Forms.Form

[+] | Windows Form Designer generated code |

    Private Sub frmRegistry_Load( _
                        ByVal sender As System.Object, _
                        ByVal e As System.EventArgs) _
                        Handles MyBase.Load
        Me.Left = CInt(GetSetting("RegDemo", "Position", _
                            "Left", CStr(Me.Left)))
        Me.Top = CInt(GetSetting("RegDemo", "Position", _
                            "Top", CStr(Me.Top)))
        Me.Width = CInt(GetSetting("RegDemo", "Size", _
                            "Width", CStr(Me.Width)))
        Me.Height = CInt(GetSetting("RegDemo", "Size", _
                            "Height",
CStr(Me.Height)))
    End Sub

    Private Sub frmRegistry_Closing(ByVal sender As Object, _
            ByVal e As
System.ComponentModel.CancelEventArgs) _
            Handles MyBase.Closing
        SaveSetting("RegDemo", "Position", "Left", _
                            CStr(Me.Left))
        SaveSetting("RegDemo", "Position", "Top", _
                            CStr(Me.Top))
        SaveSetting("RegDemo", "Size", "Width", _
                            CStr(Me.Width))
        SaveSetting("RegDemo", "Size", "Height", _
                            CStr(Me.Height))
    End Sub
End Class
```

Listing 11.1: Saving an application's setting in the registry

All data stored in the registry is textual (i.e. data that would normally be stored in a `String` variable). Listing 11.1 shows how the `Form_Load` and `Form_Closing` events can be used to save application settings in the registry. `Form_Load` is likely to be the first event processed by a form, and `Form_Closing` will be one of the last events it will process, so between them these event-handlers are ideal for saving form data and restoring it again. The program introduces two new functions for saving settings to and retrieving settings from the Windows registry. `GetSetting()` takes three or four arguments, all strings, as follows:

```
<Value> = GetSetting(<AppName>, <SectionName>, <KeyName>, _
                <DefaultKeyValue>)
```

The `<AppName>` argument is the name given to the application, and is included so that all of the settings that belong to one program are situated in one part of the registry (this makes it easy to find and extract all of the settings for a program). The `<SectionName>` argument is a string that indicates the section or category under which you want the information to be stored. In Listing 11.1, there are two sections, `"Position"` and `"Size"`. `<KeyName>` is the name given to a specific setting. Since the registry is not guaranteed to have a value stored for any particular setting, the final argument, which is optional, is a string that indicates the value to be returned if a value is not found in the registry matching all of the `<AppName>`, `<SectionName>` and `<KeyName>` parts. The function returns a string that is either the value for the specified key, or the default value, or, if no default value is provided, an empty string ("").

`SaveSetting()` takes four string arguments:

```
SaveSetting(<AppName>,<SectionName>,<KeyName>,<KeyValue>)
```

which correspond to the application name, section, key name and the value for that key. Note that the code used in Listing 11.1 converts all values passed into both `GetSetting()` and `SaveSetting()` to strings if necessary, and that the values returned from `GetSetting()` must be converted to a suitable data type (`Integer` for the individual position and size values of a form). You can examine the values stored in the registry using the Windows Registry Editor (**RegEdit.exe**) and using the Edit→Find menu item to locate the <AppName>, as shown in Figure 11.1. Note that using the Registry Editor on a casual basis is not recommended because it is possible to corrupt the registry files and therefore cause the operating system to be corrupted.

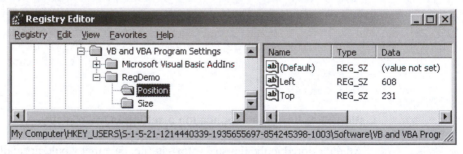

Figure 11.1 The registry editor (**RegEdit.exe**) showing the settings made in Listing 11.1

Using the registry like this, we can save any type of data belonging to an application provided it can be converted to a string for saving and converted back from a string to its normal type on retrieval. As mentioned earlier, the limitation is that it is not sensible to store a large number of values (or indeed a single large value like a picture or a very long string) in the registry, since it is a resource that many applications use; a greedy application that stores a lot of data in the registry will simply slow things up for the operating system and other applications.

Exercise 11.1

Many Windows programs save the names of the last few files accessed as a Most Recently Used, or MRU list (e.g. Word, Visual Studio [see File/Recent Files and Recent Projects on the menus), Excel, etc. Assume you are working on a program, called 'LetterWriter', and wish to store the two most recently used file names (stored in variables `File1` and `File2`) when the program closes down and retrieve them to add to the File menu when the program re-starts. They are to be kept in a section called 'Recent Files' under the names 'MRU1' and 'MRU2'. Write a sub that will store these file names (available in `String` variables `mruFile1` and `mruFile2`). Also write the sub to restore the setting into their variables. Default names (for if there are no entries under these settings) are both '(none)'.

11.4 **File Storage**

The registry is good for saving a small amount of data from an application. Typically, it is used for values that will provide the program with some long-term memory, such as a number of the most recently used file-names, the location of windows or various other configuration settings. The actual data created in a program is likely to be more than a few simple values, and it is therefore necessary to look to some other method that will not cause the registry, which is a central operating system resource, to become overfilled with information.

Visual Basic has always had the capabilities necessary for saving information directly into files and retrieving it again. It has also always had ways to make it easy for the user to identify an existing file for loading information from, and to specify a name and location for a new file that a program will create. In the .NET environment, these facilities have been greatly improved over previous versions of Visual Basic.

11.4.1 Streams

A *stream* is a class of object designed for reading data from and writing data to a storage device. In .NET, a characteristically flexible interpretation is applied to this since a storage device can be a disk file, a large string, the Internet or even an area of the computer's main memory. The name 'stream' comes from the way that data flows into and out of it. If you drop a number of (floating) items off a bridge into a stream or river, they will flow downstream in the order in which you drop them. If someone at the next bridge along picks the items out of the stream, they will be picked out in exactly the order you dropped them in.

In a similar way, data items sent to a stream from a program will arrive at its destination in the order they were sent in. If another stream is used to retrieve the data, the data will arrive in the order in which they were originally sent into the first stream.

The support for streams in .NET is strong, with a number of classes defined to deal with streaming data to and from storage devices: look up *Streams, Fundamental*

Operations in the help index for details and descriptions of these. In most cases, you will use the `StreamReader` and `StreamWriter` classes to get data from and send data to a stream. As their names suggest, these provide methods for reading data from and writing data to a stream. By using them in conjunction with the `File` class, it is a simple matter to store and retrieve information. All three classes exist in the `IO` namespace. The first example program (Listing 11.2) shows how the contents of a `TextBox` can be sent to a file using a `StreamWriter`.

```
Sub SaveText()
      'In this sub, the text in the text box txtFileInfo
      'is saved to a text file...
      Dim fileName As String
      Dim outStream As IO.StreamWriter
      fileName = "C:\Data\TextFile.txt"
      outStream = New IO.StreamWriter(fileName)
      outStream.Write(txtFileInfo.Text)
      outStream.Close()
End Sub
```

Listing 11.2: Writing text to a file using a `StreamWriter`

In Listing 11.2, the first step is to define a file-name. In this case, the full path of a file is given so that the file, named `"TextFile.txt"`, will be saved in a folder called `"Data"` on the C: drive. This is fine for a simple test program but we will examine some better solutions for deciding where a file should be stored later. Note that this step was not strictly necessary, since we could instead have simply passed the literal file-name in quotes to the `StreamWriter`'s constructor. Declaring a `fileName` variable like this can make it easier to write code that adds flexibility to the operation of opening a file, which we'll look at later.

Once we have a file-name, creating the file is a simple matter: create an instance of a `StreamWriter`, passing the file-name as an argument. Note that if this file does not already exist, it will be created; if it does exist, it will be replaced with a new version. For this reason, it is important to take care not to use the name of a key system file or some other file you would not want to have overwritten. Now that the file has been created or opened for writing, a single `Write` statement will take care of the entire contents of the text box. Since a `TextBox` with its `MultiLine` property set to `True` can display and accommodate up to 2 GBytes of text, the single write statement can deal with as much text as you might want to save in one go.

The final step is to call the `StreamWriter`'s `Close()` method, which will place the file into a safe state. If a file is not properly closed once all the information has been written to it, it may remain open until the program exits. Since this could be a long time, the file is more likely to be corrupted; you could, for example trip over the computer's power cord, lightning could strike at your electricity supply or some key computer component could fail. With operations for reading and writing files, the accepted safe practice is to have as short a time as possible between opening and closing a file.

Reading the text back from a file into a text box is almost as simple, as shown in Listing 11.3.

```
Sub LoadText()
    'In this sub, we check whether a file exists.
    'If it does, the file is loaded as a block
    'of text into txtFileInfo...
    Dim fileName As String
    Dim inStream As IO.StreamReader
    fileName = "c:\data\TextFile.txt"
    If IO.File.Exists(fileName) Then
        'Open the file...
        inStream = New IO.StreamReader(fileName)
        'Read contents as a block and add to text box...
        txtFileInfo.Text = inStream.ReadToEnd()
        inStream.Close()
    Else
        MessageBox.Show(fileName & " does not exist.")
    End If
End Sub
```

Listing 11.3: Reading text from a file using a `StreamReader`

In addition to the steps of getting a file name and creating a `StreamReader` object, we have one other check to perform if the program is to be robust. While a `StreamWriter` will create a new file if one does not exist to write to, a `StreamReader` expects the file-name passed in its constructor to be the name of an existing file, and the code will cause a crash if this is not so. The `File` class gives us a method for checking to see if the named file exists before the `StreamReader` is constructed. If the `Exists()` method of the `File` class (all of the methods of this class are `Shared`, so we do not need to create an object) returns `True`, we can go on and create the stream. If not, a suitable error message can be displayed.

The `ReadToEnd()` method of the `StreamReader` class will return the entire contents of the file, which can be passed directly to the `Text` property of the `TextBox`. Again, the stream is closed immediately to place the file into a safe state.

11.4.2 Safe File Operations

All operations that deal with bringing data into a program from some device or writing data to a device are likely to cause problems. When a program tries to read from a device, the device name could be wrong, the device might not exist, or might be switched off, or the information on the device might be in a different format from what is expected; all situations that will cause the read operation to fail. Similarly, an attempt to write data to a device can fail because the device is missing, or cannot be written to, or has failed in some other way. Compared to moving information around inside a program, moving data to or from a storage device is fraught with danger.

When writing code to interact with some storage device, it is necessary to be aware of the potential pitfalls, and optimally, to deal with them when they arise. Fortunately, the .NET framework gives us a catch-all way of dealing with such problems; exceptions, described in-Chapter 5, are tailor-made for coping with the types of run-time error that can occur while trying to move data to or from files.

Recall that run-time error-handling is about stopping a program from crashing simply because some situation that cannot be dealt with in the normal flow of an algorithm arises. For example, we might try to open a file and read data from it. If it all works, the program can continue to do its nominal work. If, however, the file fails because it is corrupt or because of some other physical problem, the default behaviour of a VB. NET program is to exit with a terse error message. If we were to deal with the unavailable file safely, we might inform the user that the expected data was not available, and try to tidy up before continuing without the expected information. Generally it is a good idea to try to close a file, and perhaps even provide some default information to take the place of what we expected to read from the file.

In VB. NET, we can use a `Try..Catch..Finally` block to provide a safety net (Listing 11.4).

```
Try
    inStream = New IO.StreamReader(fileName)
    txtFileInfo.Text = inStream.ReadToEnd()
    lstFileLines.Items.AddRange(txtFileInfo.Lines)
Catch ex As Exception
    MessageBox.Show(ex.Message)
Finally
    If Not inStream Is Nothing Then
        inStream.Close()
    End If
End Try
```

Listing 11.4: Using a `Try..Catch..Finally` block to deal with file errors

Now, if the stream object cannot gain access to the named file for any reason, the `Catch` block will tell the user and the `Finally` block will ensure that the stream is not left open.

It is important to be aware that every file operation involving opening, reading or writing has the potential to cause a program to crash, and so every file operation ought to be enclosed in an exception-handling structure in this way. Later in this chapter we will look at more structured files and this will introduce a whole new category of potential problems to deal with – exception-handling will save us from becoming bogged down in code written solely to work around the potential problems that might occur.

11.4.3 Interacting with the File System

In many of the programs you write, you will want to give the user the opportunity to provide a file with a meaningful name, in much the same way as Word, Excel and even Visual Basic do. We could simply expect the user to type the fully qualified file name, such as:

"c:\Documents and Settings\Default User\My Program\My Data.dat"

into a `TextBox` control or an `InputBox` statement, but this is error prone and is not the Windows way of doing things. Where possible, the user should be able to *select* a file for input, or select a folder to write a file to. The `SaveFileDialog` and `OpenFileDialog` controls exist to give us this capability with only a small amount of programming. Both are available as controls from the WinForms Toolbox in Visual Studio. However, both can also be used very easily by writing a few lines of code within an event or a sub on a form. For example, the code in Listing 11.5 will load a file that the user chooses from the file system in response to a click on the File/Open menu.

```
Private Sub FileOpen()
    Dim dlgOpen As OpenFileDialog = New OpenFileDialog()
    dlgOpen.Filter = "Text Files|*.txt|All Files|*.*"
    dlgOpen.InitialDirectory = Application.ExecutablePath
    If dlgOpen.ShowDialog = DialogResult.OK Then
        fileName = dlgOpen.FileName
        'Open and read file here...
        ' ...
    End If
End Sub
```

Listing 11.5: Using the `FileOpen` dialog box

In this code, we first create a new `OpenFileDialog` object (not necessary if you are using an `OpenFileDialog` control from the Toolbox), set its filter so that it will show only Text files (with the file extension ".txt") or any file (".*") depending on which the user chooses from the `Files Of Type:` combo box, and then show it as a dialog box.

Note the format of the `Filter` property. This is organized as pairs of sub-strings separated by the '|' character (shift+'\' on my keyboard). The first substring in a pair is the name of the file type (e.g. Text files) and the second is a wildcard description of the file type that the operating system will understand. We can specify any text file as "*.txt", meaning a file whose name ends in the extension ".txt". Any file is "*.*". If the user selects a file and presses the OK button we can then retrieve the file-name from the control and go on to open it.

Note that I've used a bit of sleazy code in Listing 11.5, by setting the `InitialDirectory` property of the `OpenDialog` control to be `Application.ExecutablePath`. Strictly speaking, this is the full path to *and file-name* of the executable program (e.g. **c:\VBNETPrograms\FileDemo\bin\ filedemo.exe**) and so includes a name for a file. However, the `OpenDialog` control expects only a directory, and will simply ignore the file name part, returning **c:\VBNETPrograms\FileDemo\bin** or whatever folder the program is running from. I find it much easier to store the files belonging to an application in the application's own folder, since if I ever decide to move the program, I can move the folder and the files will come too. If you're slavishly following Microsoft's guidelines on where to store data files, the `Application` property to use in place of `ExecutablePath` is one of:

```
Application.CommonAppDataPath()
Application.LocalUserAppDataPath()
```

both of which will return a folder in the **My Documents** area of the main disk drive that Windows is installed on.

Saving a file to a chosen location is very similar to Listing 11.6.

```
Private Sub FileSaveAs()
    Dim dlgSaveAs As SaveFileDialog = New SaveFileDialog()
    dlgSaveAs.Filter = "Text Files|*.txt|All Files|*.*"
    If dlgSaveAs.ShowDialog = DialogResult.OK Then
        fileName = dlgSaveAs.FileName
        'Open and save the file...
        FileSave()
    End If
End Sub
```

Listing 11.6: Using the `SaveFileDialog` dialog box

Note that in a program that allows the user to choose the name to save a file as, there are normally two menu options for saving, as shown in Figure 11.2.

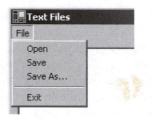

Figure 11.2 File saving options

The File/Save menu item behaves in one of two ways: if the current document has already been saved under a given name, it will be saved again with the same name, overwriting the previously saved version. If it has not been saved, the user will be given the `FileSaveAs` dialog box so that a name can be specified. The File/SaveAs . . . menu item will *always* ask the user to enter a file-name, so that the current document can be saved under a new name leaving the first saved version undisturbed. Coding for this (Listing 11.7) is very simple from the `_Click` event-handler of the `mnuFileSave` menu item.

```
Private Sub mnuFileSave_Click(ByVal sender As System.Object, _
                        ByVal e As System.EventArgs) _
                        Handles mnuFileSave.Click
    'fileName is a module-scope variable...
    If fileName = "" Then 'Save the file with a new name...
        FileSaveAs()
    Else  'Save the file with the existing name...
        FileSave()
    End If
End Sub
```

Listing 11.7: Coding the Save menu option to ask for a file name if necessary

Exercise 11.2

Write a short sequence of statements or a sub that will use an `OpenFileDialog` to ask the user to specify a file name and location. The dialog box should open in the programs My Documents folder, given by the application setting:

```
Application.LocalUserAppDataPath()
```

11.5   Structured Data

As you can see, the actual operation of saving any amount of text in a string to a file is almost trivial. For more complex organizations of data, we have to do a bit more work, but the `StreamReader` and `StreamWriter` classes we've already used to load and save text are still up to the job. Remembering that the desirable feature of a stream is that data that goes into it in a set order will also come out of it in that order, we can send complex sequences of data into a stream and, provided we are careful to read the individual items back in the same order that we sent them into the stream, can reconstruct the original data from it.

There are a number of ways we can use to send sequences of variables into a text stream, but all of them involve being able to disentangle the individual variables when we read them back. For example, if we were to write the contents of five integer variables with the values 10, 20, 30, 40 and 50 to a stream one after the other, they would end up as a sequence of digits 1020304050. This could be interpreted as one big integer (just over 1 billion), or 10 single digit integers.

To make it possible to separate the original items back out of a stream, it is normal to send a *delimiter* character between each item. A comma (,) is most commonly used, resulting in a file format known as Comma Separated Variable, or CSV. However, we could easily use a space, a semicolon, a carriage return or just about any other character or control code we choose. For example, the five numbers we wished to store could be stored in a CSV file, which, if we opened it using a plain text editor such as Windows Notepad would appear as:

10,20,30,40,50

The only limitation of this scheme is that normally we should not include the delimiter character (a comma) in the data we wished to store. Consider the situation where we use a CSV file to save someone's name and address, where the actual data being stored is:

Name: Joe Bloggs

Address: 25 High St., Sometown

PostCode: SO1 1AA

Note the presence of the comma between the street name and the name of the town. We would save this data into a comma delimited file as:

Joe Bloggs,25 High St., Sometown,SO1 1AA

The additional comma in the address will certainly confuse the operation that would be used to read the data back from the file, since it now appears that the data has four distinct variable values instead of the three that were originally saved.

We can get around this problem by replacing any instances of the delimiter in the original data with some other character that will not appear in it, but now we have simply substituted some other character so that we cannot use it instead. In most cases this will not be a problem. I've been known to use a tilde character (~) as a delimiter simply because I know there is no chance of it appearing anywhere else in the data that I'm saving to a file – can you think of a situation where this might appear in data in a program that you have written? If the choice of delimiter is likely to be a problem, we can get around it by replacing any instance of the delimiter character with two delimiters in a row, and watching for this when we read the data back from a stream.

Listing 11.8 shows how a sequence of names and addresses (stored in two string arrays) would be saved to a CSV file. The assumption is made that while no-one's name is likely to contain a comma, addresses may well do so.

```
Private Sub SaveList(ByVal fileName As String)
    Dim names() As String = {"Fred Bloggs", "Mary Green", _
                             "Peter Jones", "Linda McCabe"}
    Dim addresses() As String = {"1 High St.", _
                                 "15 Bishop's Close, Meadow", _
                                 "5 Clive Way", _
                                 "77 Foundry Lane, Lampton"}
    Dim index As Integer, address As String
    Dim outStream As IO.StreamWriter

    outStream = New IO.StreamWriter(fileName)
    For index = 0 To names.GetUpperBound(0)
        address = addresses(index).Replace(",", "~")
        '~ is unlikely to appear in an address
        outStream.WriteLine("{0},{1}", names(index), _
                                        address)
    Next
    outStream.Close()
End Sub
```

Listing 11.8: Saving data into a comma delimited file.

The code in Listing 11.8 uses the format string `"{0},{1}"` to indicate how the two variables following it will be written to a file with a comma delimiter between them. Because we expect a comma could occur within an address, the `Replace()` method of the `String` class is used to replace "," with "~" (a tilde character), therefore storing a modified version of an address in the variable address. The data written to the file is:

Fred Bloggs,1 High St.

Mary Green,15 Bishop's Close~ Meadow

Peter Jones,5 Clive Way

Linda McCabe,77 Foundry Lane~ Lampton

Note that there are actually two delimiters used in this file. A comma is used to separate a name and address in a single line of the file, but each entry of a name and address pair has a line to itself because we've used a `WriteLine()` statement. The lines in a text file are separated by *carriage-return line-feed* sequences in a Windows PC. We can ignore the details of this since the `WriteLine()` method that was used to write out each name and address pair automatically includes this. The `StreamReader` class gives us a method (`ReadLine()`) to read the data back line by line.

When we read this data back from the file, commas will separate a name from an address, and tilde characters will represent what were originally commas. We can therefore retrieve the original data, as shown in Listing 11.9.

```
Private Sub LoadList(ByVal fileName As String)
    Dim names(3) As String 'We know there are 4 entries
    Dim addresses(3) As String
    Dim index As Integer, buffer As String, data() As String
    Dim inStream As IO.StreamReader
    inStream = New IO.StreamReader(fileName)
    For index = 0 To 3
        buffer = inStream.ReadLine()
        data = buffer.Split(",")
        names(index) = data(0)
        addresses(index) = data(1).Replace("~", ",")
    Next
    inStream.Close()
    'We would now go on to use the data...
    '...
End Sub
```

Listing 11.9: Recovering data from a comma-delimited file

Note that the most straightforward way of reading comma-delimited text from a stream is to read the stream a line at a time, and then break up the line at points indicated by the commas. The `Split()` method of the `String` class performs this operation for us, returning the separated parts of the line as a string array: `data(0)` will contain the first part (the name) and `data(1)` will contain the second (the address). We again use the `Replace()` string method to translate tilde characters back into commas.

Exercise 11.3

A text file contains two lines of text. The first is a list of the names of the days of the week. The second is a list of the names of the twelve months. Both lines use a semicolon character (;) as a delimiter. Write a sub that takes the name of the file as a parameter and reads the data into two arrays – `Weeks()` and `Months()` – both of which are the correct size for the number of data elements they will store.

11.6 Serialization

Of course, as object-oriented programmers, we will rarely need to persist individual variable values as we've seen done in the previous examples in this chapter. We will, however, need to be capable of sending whole objects to a stream at will, and, just as importantly, we will need to be able to bring them back in one piece. The process of taking a whole object model and sending it to a storage device or across a communications network (which, like a file, will only accept data a byte at a time) is called *serialization*.

We are lucky since the .NET framework provides an in-built mechanism that makes trivial work of this. However (working on the adage 'no pain, no gain'), we should first have a look at how serialization works at a fundamental level. Then, if things go wrong in the automated Microsoft way of doing things, we will be better placed to discover what the problem is.

In essence, serialization involves sending an object model that may include large data items (strings, arrays and collections of other objects) across a narrow channel by deconstructing the object model into a sequence of bytes (the fundamental storage element of a PC). Not only that, but we also need to be able to reconstruct the original model, in all of its complexity, from a serialized stream of bytes at the other end. As far as PC architecture is concerned, the byte is the fundamental unit of communication and so memory, storage devices (disks) and communications devices (modems and networks) all deal with bytes of data. Although the true fundamental unit of data is the binary digit, or bit, personal computers have always been built around hardware that groups these into bytes. Fortunately, we will never even have to consider the bytes that make up an object's data members, and will be able to deal with the various data types directly (Integers, Doubles, Strings, etc.).

When we serialize an object model, we are really only interested in the data members of all of the objects in the model. The code that defines the various objects' methods exists in class modules and compiled byte-codes, and we assume that these will be available at both ends of the channel. For persistence, the channel will usually be a stream, at either end of which is a copy of the program sending or receiving the serialized data. This can be two programs running simultaneously, one transmitting and one receiving the data, or one program at different times, having sent the serialized data to storage at one time and retrieved it an another.

As with the data file of names and addresses previously, our program or the .NET framework will need to be able to separate out the parts of an object sent across a stream. In Figure 11.3, these are the two strings that make up the name and address

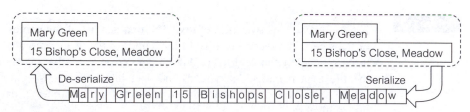

Figure 11.3　Serializing an object

members of a person object. Again, delimiters can be used, but with an object model, things can get much more complicated. For a start, individual member variables in an object can be strings, numbers, dates or even any type of object an application already knows about, so placing a comma between these items might not be enough. Secondly, we might want to serialize an object that contains a collection of other objects (e.g. a `BankAccount` and all its `Transactions`). Working out where one object ends and the next starts can be a bit of a problem.

There are two ways around this. We can use delimiters between objects and between the member variables within each object, much as was done with the name and address data, where a comma separated a name from an address and a carriage-return line-feed sequence separated the different entries. We could call this *coded serialization* since the job of inserting delimiters at one end and extracting the separate member variables from the stream at the other end must be done entirely in code we write for a class. While this is easy to do, it does require that the builder of a class model takes care in how data is interleaved with delimiters and how it is reconstructed at the other end. In some situations this is a perfectly reasonable way to go, but can involve quite a lot of effort on the part of the programmer.

Alternatively, we can send a *header* before each item of information to identify its type and, if necessary, its size. This is the method that .NET uses when automatically serializing data. For each item that is serialized to a stream, .NET first sends a block of descriptive information that effectively says "the next thing you will read will be a string of 57 characters" (for example). The headers are in a standard format that guarantees the .NET will not get them tangled up with the data itself, and since the .NET framework has access to information that describes the detailed format of every class, even those that you have written, the entire process can be automatic.

11.6.1 Coded Serialization

As an example of this, we'll return to the `BankAccount` classes; specifically the `BankAccount` object model in which a `BankAccount` incorporates an aggregation of `Transaction` objects described in the previous chapter. To serialize this object model, we can use the algorithm in Listing 11.10.

1. Send BankAccount member variables to the stream
2. Send the count of Transactions belonging to this account
3. For Each Transaction in the Account
4. Send Transaction member variables to the stream *
5. Next

Listing 11.10: Serializing a `BankAccount`

De-serializing this object model is only a little more complex (Listing 11.11).

1. Retrieve BankAccount member variables from the stream
2. Retrieve the Count of Transactions this account should have
3. For Index = 1 To Count

4. Create a New Transaction object
5. Retrieve its member variables *
6. Add this Transaction to the Bank's Transactions collection
7. Next

Listing 11.11: De-serializing a `BankAccount`

The two statements marked with an asterisk in Listings 11.10 and 11.11 are of interest because there are two ways we could go about doing this. We could have a line of code in the `BankAccount`'s serialization method that saved off the member variable values contained in each `Transaction` object, and a couple of lines in the de-serialization method that retrieved these values and passed them into a new `Transaction` object. However, this approach breaks encapsulation (a class should not need to know the internal composition of another class to work with it) and leads to inelegant code that is awkward to maintain. If, for example, we decided to change the way a transaction's date was stored, we would need to change the `Transaction` class, and also the `BankAccount` class responsible for serializing and de-serializing it.

The second, and better approach, is to give each class that will be serialized a pair of methods, one to serialize it and the other to de-serialize it. In deference to years of programming habit, I usually call these methods `Save()` and `Load()`, although `Serialize()` and `DeSerialize()` would probably be more appropriate. Listing 11.12 gives the part of the `Transaction` class that includes its member variable declarations and its `Save()` and `Load()` methods. Note that I've omitted exception-handling code in this to make it easier to follow – generally, you should always include exception-handling when dealing with files.

```
Class Transaction
    'This allows us to specify the type of transaction...
    Public Enum TransactionType
        Deposit = 0
        Withdrawal
        Interest
        Charges
    End Enum
    'Here are the member fields...
    Private mvarDate As Date
    Private mvarType As TransactionType
    Private mvarAmount As Decimal
    Private mvarDescription As String
    'Here is the normal constructor...
    Public Sub New(ByVal Type As TransactionType, _
                   ByVal Amount As Decimal, _
                   ByVal Description As String)
        mvarDate = Now
        mvarType = Type
        mvarAmount = Amount
        mvarDescription = Description
    End Sub
```

```vbnet
'This second constructor lets us create a Transaction
'directly from a stream...
Public Sub New(ByRef R As StreamReader)
    Load(R)
End Sub

'Missed out code - Property definitions etc.
'...
'...
Public Sub Save(ByRef W As StreamWriter)
    Dim Data As String
    Data = String.Format("{0}, {1}, {2}, {3}", _
                         mvarDate, _
                         CType(mvarType, Integer), _
                         mvarAmount, mvarDescription)
    W.WriteLine(Data)
End Sub

Public Sub Load(ByRef R As StreamReader)
    Dim Data As String
    Dim members() As String
    Data = R.ReadLine()
    members = Split(Data, ",")
    mvarDate = members(0)
    mvarType = CType(members(1), TransactionType)
    mvarAmount = CType(members(2), Decimal)
    mvarDescription = members(3)
End Sub
End Class
```

Listing 11.12: The `Transaction` class, with methods to `Save` to and `Load` from a stream

Note that a second constructor has been added to the `Transaction` class. This takes a reference to a `StreamReader` as a parameter, and calls the `Load()` method. We can use it from the `BankAccount`'s `Load()` method to combine the separate actions of creating a new transaction and retrieving its member variables. The `Save()` code depends on being passed a stream that is ready to have a transaction serialized into it, and the `Load()` code depends on being passed a stream that is positioned at the start of a serialized `Transaction` object. The corresponding code in the `BankAccount` class takes care of these requirements, and is shown in Listing 11.13.

```vbnet
Public Class BankAccount
    'Here are the member fields...
    Private mvarTransactions As ArrayList
    Private mvarAccountName As String
    Private mvarAccountNumber As Long
    'This is the normal constructor for a new account...
    Public Sub New(ByVal name As String, _
                   ByVal number As Long)
```

```
                mvarAccountName = name
                mvarAccountNumber = number
                mvarTransactions = New ArrayList()
        End Sub
        'This to retrieve one from a stream...
        Public Sub New(ByRef R As StreamReader)
                mvarTransactions = New ArrayList()
                Load(R)
        End Sub

        'Missed out code - Property definitions etc.
        '...

        Public Sub Save(ByRef W As StreamWriter)
                Dim T As Transaction
                W.WriteLine(mvarAccountName)
                W.WriteLine(mvarAccountNumber)
                W.WriteLine(mvarTransactions.Count)
                For Each T In mvarTransactions
                    T.Save(W)
                Next
        End Sub

        Public Sub Load(ByRef R As StreamReader)
                Dim T As Transaction
                Dim Count, Index As Integer
                mvarAccountName = R.ReadLine()
                mvarAccountNumber = R.ReadLine()
                Count = R.ReadLine
                For Index = 1 To Count
                    T = New Transaction(R)
                    mvarTransactions.Add(T)
                Next
        End Sub
    End Class
```

Listing 11.13: The `BankAccount` class with serialization code

Again an overloaded constructor is used to pass a `StreamReader` to a new `Account` object, which then calls `Load()` to de-serialize the object model.

This is an example of how you might use serialization in an application in which we are only interested in persisting the data from a single object model. The main form that starts up the `BankAccount` object model has the `Form_Load()` and `Form_Closing()` event-handlers shown in Listing 11.14.

```
    Private Sub frmBank_Load(ByVal sender As System.Object, _
                        ByVal e As System.EventArgs) _
                    Handles MyBase.Load
        Dim fileName As String = "c:\Data\Account.dat"
        If File.Exists(fileName) Then
            Dim R As StreamReader = New StreamReader(fileName)
            Account = New BankAccount(R)
```

```
            R.Close()
      End If
End Sub

Private Sub frmBank_Closing(ByVal sender As Object, _
      ByVal e As System.ComponentModel.CancelEventArgs) _
      Handles MyBase.Closing
   Dim fileName As String = "c:\Data\Account.dat"
   Dim W As StreamWriter = New StreamWriter(fileName)
   Account.Save(W)
   W.Close()
End Sub
```

Listing 11.14: Using the `BankAccount`'s overloaded constructor

An advantage of using code like this to serialize an object-model is that it results in a text file that a human can read without difficulty. Figure 11.4 is an example of the file resulting from a test run of the above code.

```
Fred Bloggs
1234
8
19/12/2002 13:22:01, 0, 250,    Cash
19/12/2002 16:11:25, 0, 1500,   Cheque
20/12/2002 09:17:05, 1, 50,     ATM
20/12/2002 11:47:33, 1, 200,    Cheque#12345
20/12/2002 14:56:02, 0, 25,     Cash
21/12/2002 00:00:01, 2, 2.55,
21/12/2002 00:00:01, 3, 12,     Overdraft interest
23/12/2002 20:18:46, 1, 125,    Debit Card
```

Figure 11.4 Serialized output from the `BankAccount` model

The above file text has the account name on the first line and the account number on the second. This is followed by the number of transactions (8), and then a line per transaction, containing the date and time, the transaction type (0 is Deposit, 1 is Withdrawal, etc.) and the description.

We could continue to use this strategy to deal with a hierarchy of any size. For example, a bank can have many branches, a branch many customers, a customer many bank accounts and a bank account many transactions. Provided we are careful to provide suitable `Load()` and `Save()` methods for each class, remembering that a class that contains objects or a collection must also serialize\de-serialize these (using almost identical code to that used in the `Load()` and `Save()` methods of `BankAccount`), the strategy will work perfectly well.

11.6.2 .NET Automated Serialization

Having closely examined the carefully coded method of serialization in the previous example, we can now go on to look at the .NET automated version of the same approach. We'll use the same BankAccount class model.

```
<Serializable()> Class Transaction
    'This will allow us to specify the type
    'of transaction...
    Public Enum TransactionType
        Deposit = 0
        Withdrawal
        Interest
        Charges
    End Enum
    'Here are the member fields...
    Private mvarDate As Date
    Private mvarType As TransactionType
    Private mvarAmount As Decimal
    Private mvarDescription As String
    'Code continues here, but there are no Save()/Load()
    'methods defined and no constructor that works with a
    'StreamReader object.
    '...
End Class

<Serializable()> Public Class BankAccount
    Private mvarTransactions As ArrayList
    Private mvarAccountName As String
    Private mvarAccountNumber As Long
    'Code continues here, but again no Save()/Load()
    'methods defined and no constructor that works with a
    'StreamReader object.
    '...
End Class
```

Listing 11.15: BankAccount classes marked as <Serializable()>

In Listing 11.15, the most surprising feature is that no special code is added to save or load a bank account or transaction to or from a stream. In fact, .NET serialization requires no extra code to deal with persistence. The only change to the original class described in the object-modelling chapter is the addition of the two class attribute markers, <Serializable()>. An attribute in the .NET framework is a marker that you use to describe some aspect of your code to the run-time system. Attributes can be used to describe types, member fields, properties, specific methods or whole classes as here.

When an attribute is used with code, it allows the .NET runtime to interact with the code in ways that are not specifically built in to the language you are using (Visual Basic in this case). The <Serializable()> attribute is used to mark classes that we want the run-time system to be able to persist for us. You might think that rather than use a special purpose attribute for this, it would be easier just to build the feature into every class. However, there will generally be a lot of information in a program that you would not want to persist from run to run, and there are certain types of information that cannot automatically be persisted by the .NET run time (for example, data that comes from software components not developed in a .NET language such as old-style Visual Basic components from an earlier version). There is also an overhead in that a serializable class must incorporate extra code. It is easier to allow a programmer to opt-in to a scheme than to have to opt-out of all the ones that will not be used, so serialization must be specifically chosen by the programmer. When you see the reduction in the amount of work you have to do, I think you'll agree it is a good deal.

To serialize the whole object model, we simply add some code to an object best placed to serialize and de-serialize it at run time; typically one that will be available as soon as a program starts to execute. Normally, this will be the start-up form, so we would write the code shown in Listing 11.16.

```
Private Sub frmBank_Closing(ByVal sender As Object, _
        ByVal e As System.ComponentModel.CancelEventArgs) _
        Handles MyBase.Closing
    Dim fileName As String = "c:\Data\BinAccount.dat"
    Dim str As New IO.FileStream(fileName, _
                                 IO.FileMode.Create)
    Dim b As New _
  Runtime.Serialization.Formatters.Binary.BinaryFormatter()
    b.Serialize(str, Account)
    str.Close()
End Sub
Private Sub frmBank_Load(ByVal sender As System.Object, _
                     ByVal e As System.EventArgs) _
                     Handles MyBase.Load
    Dim fileName As String = "c:\Data\BinAccount.dat"
    If IO.File.Exists(fileName) Then
        Dim str As New IO.FileStream(fileName, _
                                     IO.FileMode.Open)
        Dim b As New _
  Runtime.Serialization.Formatters.Binary.BinaryFormatter()
        Account = CType(b.Deserialize(str), BankAccount)
        str.Close()
    End If
End Sub
```

Listing 11.16: Serializing a serializable class model

The key to serializing an entire class model like this is the `BinaryFormatter` class, found in the `RunTime.Serialization.Formatters.Binary` namespace. Basically, this class's `Serialize()` method stores each member variable of the specified object (`Account` here) in turn as a binary image of its data in memory. Where a member variable is in fact a non-value member, it stores an image of each member variable of that owned object and so on until the entire object model has

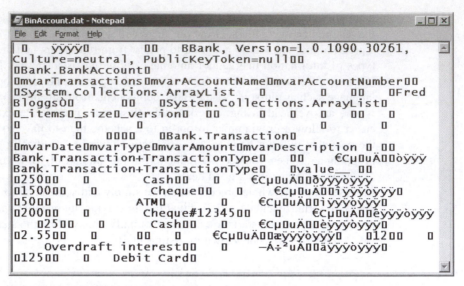

Figure 11.5 Data serialized by .NET

been persisted. For it to be able to do this, every class in the object model must be marked with the `<Serializable()>` attribute. Fortunately, most of the .NET collection classes (including `ArrayList`, used here) are already marked as serializable, and so our entire object model was. The result is a file of binary data that can be used to reconstruct the object model. Unlike the data saved by the manually coded version, most of this data will not be readable by humans (although as you can see from Figure 11.5, you can still pick out the text strings from among the other data).

When bringing an object model back from serialization, the .NET runtime will happily reconstruct all of the data that was the original object model, placing it back into memory in its original format. However, we need to cast the resulting object model to the correct type to complete the de-serialization operation, which is why the `CType()` call was necessary before assigning the result of `b.Deserialize()` back to the `Account` variable.

To recap, serialization in this way is only possible if:

■ the top-level object passed to the `BinaryFormatter` object is from a class marked as serializable;

■ all of the member variables included in the top-level object are also from classes marked as serializable, and all of the member variables of these classes and so on;

■ every variable that you want to include in the serialization is reachable from the top-level object.

Since almost every class that is part of the standard .NET framework meets these criteria, we only need to be careful to mark our own classes as serializable and to call the serialization method passing an object that includes in its object model all of the other objects to be serialized.

As you can see, this scheme makes it easily possible to make any information in a running program persist until the program is run again. Very little effort is required to implement this form of serialization, but if for some reason the serialized data was to become corrupted, there would be little you could do to recover it.

Given the simplicity with which new .NET classes can be made serializable, why would it still be useful to create serializable classes by writing the serialization code, as in Listings 11.12 to 11.14?

11.7 XML

The serialization examples we've been looking at so far have been ideal ways of saving data that a single program or a set of related programs is able to retrieve. These programs store their data in a proprietary format, so the data saved is stored or transmitted efficiently, using a small amount of disk space or bandwidth and taking little time to retrieve it. However, it is often the case that data that originates in one program may need to be loaded into a different one. For example, we might want to store sales data accumulated in a program used as a point-of-sales terminal and retrieve it into a different program that does financial analysis for accounting purposes.

Using the schemes we've looked at so far, this is possible, but would involve placing compatible load and save code in both applications. This in turn suggests that both programs originate from the same source (for example a software company or an in-house IT department). Moving a set of proprietary data between two applications that come from different sources is more awkward, since the application that originates the data needs to make its format known to the other one. This difficulty has hampered the easy movement of data between applications for almost the entire history of electronic data storage.

The eXtensible Mark-up Language, or XML, is a development designed to eliminate these problems. It does this by storing data in a text format, in which each piece of information is enclosed by a pair of markers, or tags, that describe it. For example, Figure 11.6 shows a part of a XML document that contains information about a

```
<customer ID="12345">
        <name>Fred Bloggs</name>
        <address>
                <street>25 Glen Road</street>
                <town>Ayr</town>
                <postcode>KA11 1BG</postcode>
        </address>
        <lastorderdate>17/12/2002</lastorderdate>
        <email/>
</customer>
```

Figure 11.6 A part of a XML document

customer of some company. Even if you have never met XML before now, I would bet that you can figure out what information about this customer has been included:

All information in a XML document is either enclosed in pairs of descriptive tags whose name appears in <> brackets, or is a named attribute appearing in quotes within an opening tag. For example, the ID number of customer Fred Bloggs is "12345". This attribute value must appear enclosed in quotes (single or double). Each opening tag must end with a matching closing tag which has a "/" prefix to the name given in the opening tag. If a tag is empty, this can be relaxed so that a single tag is used to indicate an empty item, for example, "<email />", indicating the customer data does not include an email address: <email /> and <email></email> are equivalent. We refer to a pair of tags and its contents as a node.

There are five simple rules that dictate what makes a proper XML document.

1. Each opening tag must have a matching closing tag, or a single empty tag must be used if there is no data.

2. Opening and closing tags must be properly nested so that one tag pair is completely enclosed by another (e.g. <A><B> . . . </B></A>, not <A><B> . . . </A></B>).

3. Apart from a standard XML document header and comments, an XML *document*, no matter how complex, must appear as a single element, called the *root element*, and must be enclosed in a single tag pair. Within the root element, a document can contain any number of tag pairs. The XML document in Figure 11.6 is the entire <customer> .. </customer> tree.

4. XML tags are case-sensitive. <doc> and <DOC> are treated as two different tags.

5. attributes within an opening tag must be given a name and the associated value must appear in single or double quotes.

If a document adheres to these rules, it is said to be *well-formed*, and will cause no problems with any program designed to cope with XML. Specific *types* of XML document in which certain tags are required are governed by a XML *schema*, which is a XML document that describes the tags and attributes used, and the way they can be combined. A document that meets the requirements of a given schema is said to be a *valid* XML document. A XML schema is also a valid XML document.

The .NET framework incorporates XML, which is used extensively within all .NET programs for storing and communicating application information, transporting information to and from sites on the World Wide Web, and even to provide descriptive information about classes within a .NET assembly. We can therefore expect that the .NET framework will include XML management classes that we can use within our own programs.

11.7.1 XML Structured Data

The key factor that indicates how useful XML will be in an application is structure. XML was developed to deal with information that had an inherent structure, and this

Table 11.1 A set of student data

Matric	Name	Subject Code	Title	Mark
js021234	James Smith	COMP1014	Introduction to Programming	64
		COMP1102	Information Tools	68
		COMP1122	Internet Information Gathering	53
lm023311	Liz McCabe	COMP1014	Introduction to Programming	47
		COMP1332	Database Fundamentals	66
		COMP1822	Data Analysis	59
		LANG1103	Introductory Spanish	77
af013341	Alex Farlowe	COMP1332	Database Fundamentals	52
		COMP2011	Data and Abstraction	62

is guaranteed by the five rules described above. XML can be written by an application program using the `XmlTextWriter` class, which takes care of the well-formedness of a document. As a programmer, you are required to ensure that each opening tag has a matching closing tag, but the `XmlTextWriter` will take care of tag names and formatting.

As an example, consider a program that manages the assessment data for a list of students. A student has a Name and a Matriculation number. Each student can attend several classes (I'll refer to them as Subjects to save confusion with Visual Basic Classes), and each Subject has a Title, a Code and the student's Mark. The data for a group of students might appear as in Table 11.1.

In XML this data would appear as in Listing 11.17.

```
<?xml version="1.0" encoding="utf-8" ?>
<Students>
    <Student Matric="js021234">
        <Name>James Smith</Name>
        <Subjects>
            <Subject Code="COMP1014">
                <Title>Introduction to Programming</Title>
                <Mark>64</Mark>
            </Subject>
            <Subject Code="COMP1102">
                <Title>Information Tools</Title>
                <Mark>68</Mark>
            </Subject>
            <Subject Code="COMP1122">
                <Title>Internet Information Gathering</Title>
                <Mark>53</Mark>
            </Subject>
        </Subjects>
    </Student>
    <Student Matric="lm023311">
        <Name>Liz McCabe</Name>
        <Subjects>
```

```
            <Subject Code="COMP1014">
                <Title>Introduction to Programming</Title>
                <Mark>47</Mark>
            </Subject>
            <Subject Code="COMP1332">
                <Title>Database Fundamentals</Title>
                <Mark>66</Mark>
            </Subject>
            <Subject Code="COMP1822">
                <Title>Data Analysis</Title>
                <Mark>59</Mark>
            </Subject>
            <Subject Code="LANG1103">
                <Title>Introductory Spanish</Title>
                <Mark>77</Mark>
            </Subject>
        </Subjects>
    </Student>
    <Student Matric="af013341">
        <Name>Alex Farlowe</Name>
        <Subjects>
            <Subject Code="COMP1332">
                <Title>Database Fundamentals</Title>
                <Mark>52</Mark>
            </Subject>
            <Subject Code="COMP2011">
                <Title>Data and Abstraction</Title>
                <Mark>62</Mark>
            </Subject>
        </Subjects>
    </Student>
</Students>
```

Listing 11.17: The XML version of Table 11.1

Examining the listing, you can see that there are two XML components. The first is the single line:

```
<?xml version="1.0" encoding="utf-8" ?>
```

which specifies the XML version used and the text encoding method. This makes the document recognizable to different operating systems and even different (e.g. later) versions of XML. The second is the entire data hierarchy, between the top-level tags <Students> and </Students>. Within this, each next-level tag pair (<Student>...</Student>) encloses the data for a single student, which is the name and a list of subjects taken by that student. The matriculation number (matric) for a student is specified as an attribute within the opening <Student> tag since this is the key identifier for a specific student (students need not have unique names, but must have a unique matriculation number).

The repeated list of `<Subject>` and `</Subject>` tags is enclosed within a single tag pair `<Subjects>` and `</Subjects>`, just as was done for the list of students. Again, each `<Subject>` opening tag has an attribute, the subject code, which uniquely identifies a class.

This structure could be repeated up to a higher level (for example, all of the students within a course group) or down to a lower one (for example each individual assessment for a particular subject) by simply extending the same encoding scheme. The end result is a document structure that is self describing (you can always figure out what a particular data element is), highly structured, and, most useful to us, simple to produce from a computer program and easy to read into a computer program. Listing 11.17 could easily be the output of a simple program that contained a collection of `Student` objects, where each student had a collection of modules.

11.7.2 Generating XML in code

We will now go on to construct this program, using methods very similar to those that allowed us to serialize an object model. The System.Xml namespace contains a number of classes to make working with XML documents simple. The important class for creating (writing) a XML document is the `XmlWriter` class, which includes methods to create the start and end of a compound node (`WriteStartElement()`, `WriteEndElement()`), to add an attribute to a node (`WriteAttributeString()`), to write simple elements (`WriteElementString()`), add comments to a document (`WriteComment()`) and to write the XML header node (`WriteStartDocument()`). An algorithm for writing out a whole XML document of the `Students` object model is:

1. Open a new XML document for writing
2. Write the document header
3. Write the start of the Students node
4.   For Each Student in the Students collection
5.   Write the start of a Student node
6.   Write the Student's Matric attribute
7.   Write the Name element
8.   Write the start of the Subjects node
9.   For Each Subject in the Student's Subjects collection
10.   Write the start of a Subject node
11.   Write the Subject's Code attribute
12.   Write the Title element
13.   Write the Mark element
14.   Write the end of a Subject node
15.   Next Subject
16.   Write the end of the Subjects node
17.   Write the end of a Student node

18.   Next Student
19.   Write the end of the Students node
20.   Close the XML document

To read the XML document created by the above algorithm and reconstruct a `Students` object model, the corresponding algorithm is:

1.   Load the XML document
2.   Create a Students collection (a HashTable will allow us to us the Matric as a key)
3.   Extract the Students node from the document
4.   For each Student node in Students
5.   Read the Student's Matric attribute
6.   Extract the Name element
7.   Create a new Student object, using Matric and Name values
8.   Create a Subjects collection (an ArrayList will do here)
9.   For Each Subject node in Subjects
10.   Read the Subject's Code attribute
11.   Extract the Title element
12.   Extract the Mark element
13.   Create a new Subject object, using Code, Title and Mark values
14.   Add the Subject to the Subjects collection
15.   Next Subject
16.   Add the Student to the Students collection
17.   Next Student node

Note that the algorithm to read back data from a XML document to an object-model contains fewer steps. This is simply because while writing XML it is necessary to finish a compound element by writing its closing tag, while in reading the XML back, an entire node, including its closing tag, is extracted in one step.

11.7.3 Coding XML operations in Visual Basic

While the above algorithms are perfectly straightforward, you could not always expect to write or read an object-model in such a small number of steps; the more complex the object-model, the more complex the code to write or read it in its entirety. However, we have already seen that we can deal with this type of complexity within an object-model by observing the principle of encapsulation. To create one lump of code that was able to write out the entire hierarchy of a complex object-model, we would have to give every member variable of every class `Public` or `Friend` scope. This would not be good encapsulation (it would not be encapsulation at all). As usual in this situation, a better approach is to make each class responsible for its own management, including methods to write an object into a XML stream and to extract a new object from a XML node.

The `Subject` class shown in Listing 11.19 is 'XML stream aware', having a constructor to create an object from a XML node, and a method to write member variables into an `XmlWriter` stream.

11.7.4 The `StudentModel` Module

We can put the entire class model into a single VB module. This will accommodate the `Subject` class, the `Student` class and code to manage a collection of `Student` objects.

All of the code for dealing with subjects, students and a collection of students will need access to the System.Xml namespace, so this must be imported to the module using the code in Listing 11.18.

```
Imports System.Xml   'Makes the XML classes available.

Module StudentModel
    'Here we'll add classes, instance variables
    'for the collection, and code for managing
    'the collection
    '...
End Module
```

Listing 11.18: A module for accommodating the `Student` object model

11.7.5 The `Subject` Class and XML awareness

We start as usual with the smallest item (i.e. the one lowest in the object model hierarchy), which is the `Subject` class. This class needs to be able to generate XML descriptive data from an object, and build an object from an XML node. It is shown in Listing 11.19.

```
Class Subject
    'Member variables for a subject...
    Private mvarCode As String
    Private mvarTitle As String
    Private mvarMark As Integer
    'Normal constructor for a new subject...
    Public Sub New(ByVal code As String, _
                   ByVal title As String, _
                   ByVal mark As Integer)
        mvarCode = code
        mvarTitle = title
        mvarMark = mark
    End Sub
    'Construct a subject from a XML node...
    Public Sub New(ByVal subjectNode As XmlNode)
        Dim Code As String, Title As String, Mark As Integer
```

```
              'Can add a new order to the customer...
              mvarCode = subjectNode.Attributes("Code").Value
              mvarTitle = subjectNode.Item("Title").InnerText
              mvarMark = _
                CType(subjectNode.Item("Mark").InnerText, Integer)
          End Sub
          'Return a TreeNode of this Subject's data...
          Public Function TreeItem() As TreeNode
              Dim item As New TreeNode(mvarCode)
              item.Nodes.Add(mvarTitle)
              item.Nodes.Add(mvarMark.ToString())
              Return item
          End Function
          'Write out this subject to a XML stream as a XML node...
          Public Sub WriteXML(ByVal writer As XmlWriter)
              With writer
                  .WriteStartElement("Subject")
                  .WriteAttributeString("Code", mvarCode)
                  .WriteElementString("Title", mvarTitle)
                  .WriteElementString("Mark", _
                                            mvarMark.ToString())
                  .WriteEndElement()
              End With
          End Sub
      End Class
```

Listing 11.19: The 'XML aware' `Subject` class

All of the member variables in a `Subject` object are simple value members. The `WriteXML` method inserts these values with suitable tag names (`"Code"`, `"Title"` and `"Mark"`) into a stream by using the `XmlWriter`'s methods. An object of the class will become an entire XML node, for example:

```
<Subject Code="COMP1014">
    <Title>Introduction to Programming</Title>
    <Mark>64</Mark>
</Subject>
```

`WriteStartElement()` starts a new node and gives its tag the specified title (`"<Subject>"`), while `WriteEndElement()` automatically closes off the most recently started element with a matching closing tag (`"</Subject>"`). Between these calls to open and close a new XML node, we use `WriteAttributeString()` and `WriteElementString()` to fill the node with encoded data. `WriteAttributeString()` inserts an attribute name and value pair into the node's opening tag; we use the subject `"Code"` value since this is a good member for identifying a specific subject. `WriteElementString()` is used to insert the remaining values. These must be strings, and so the `ToString()` method of any numeric, date or other type should be used.

Going in the other direction to create a new subject from a XML `<Subject>` node is best done by creating a constructor to which we pass the node. The constructor code simply has to unpack the member variable values from the node using attribute values and the `InnerText()` values from any simple nodes. Where the information returned from the inner text of a node (the text between its opening and closing tags) is not to be a string, we can use the `CType()` function to cast the data to the appropriate type; for example the `"Mark"` sub-node of a subject has its value cast back to an integer before it is assigned to the class member variable:

```
mvarMark = CType(subjectNode.Item("Mark").InnerText, Integer)
```

Note that I've also added a `TreeItem()` method to the class so that it can return a `TreeNode` object containing a copy of the object's data. A `TreeView` control displays `TreeNode` items in a useful hierarchical way (like the left-hand pane of a Windows Explorer window), and we will be able to make use of this to provide a flexible user-interface for the `Student/Subjects` object model.

11.7.6 The `Student` class and managing a compound XML Node

The `Student` class is created similarly, except that since a student is composed of its own member data plus a number of instances of the `Subject` class, the operations to write an object as a XML node and to construct a new student by extracting object data from a XML node are a little more complex – similar to the tasks of sending a compound object to a stream or retrieving one from a stream. However, using the methods already described for the encapsulated subject class limits the complexity of these operations. The `Student` class in shown in Listing 11.20.

```
Class Student
    'Member variables for a student...
    Private mvarMatric As String
    Private mvarName As String
    'Must include the collection of subjects...
    Private mvarSubjects As ArrayList
    'Normal constructor...
    Public Sub New(ByVal matric As String, _
                   ByVal name As String)
        mvarMatric = matric
        mvarName = name
        mvarSubjects = New ArrayList()
    End Sub
    'Construct a student from a XML node...
    Public Sub New(ByVal studentNode As XmlNode)
        mvarMatric = studentNode.Attributes("Matric").Value
        mvarName = studentNode.Item("Name").InnerText
        mvarSubjects = New ArrayList()
        'Now extract the Subject nodes and add them to
        'the mvarSubjects collection...
        Dim subjectNode As XmlNode
        Dim subjectCollection As XmlNode
        subjectCollection = studentNode.Item("Subjects")
```

```
                Dim S As Subject
                For Each subjectNode In subjectCollection.ChildNodes
                    S = New Subject(subjectNode)
                    AddSubject(S)
                Next
            End Sub
            'Write a whole student out into a XML stream...
            Public Sub WriteXML(ByVal writer As XmlWriter)
                Dim S As Subject
                writer.WriteStartElement("Student")
                writer.WriteAttributeString("Matric", mvarMatric)
                writer.WriteElementString("Name", mvarName)
                writer.WriteStartElement("Subjects")
                For Each S In mvarSubjects
                    S.WriteXML(writer)
                Next
                writer.WriteEndElement()
                writer.WriteEndElement()
            End Sub
            'Return a TreeNode of this student, including the
            'collection of subjects...
            Public Function TreeItem() As TreeNode
                Dim item As New TreeNode(mvarMatric)
                item.Nodes.Add(mvarName)
                Dim S As Subject
                For Each S In mvarSubjects
                    item.Nodes.Add(S.TreeItem)
                Next
                Return item
            End Function
            'Add a new subject from data...
            Public Sub AddSubject(ByVal Code As String, _
                                  ByVal Title As String, _
                                  ByVal Mark As Integer)
                Dim S As New Subject(Code, Title, Mark)
                AddSubject(S)
            End Sub
            'Add a new subject object...
            Public Sub AddSubject(ByVal S As Subject)
                mvarSubjects.Add(S)
            End Sub
            'Property definitions...
            Public ReadOnly Property Matric()
                Get
                    Return mvarMatric
                End Get
            End Property
        End Class
```

Listing 11.20: The 'XML aware' Student class

The `WriteXML()` method for a student does all of the same things that the subject's version did, except that when dealing with the contained subjects collection, it must write an enclosing tag pair (`<Subjects>`...`</Subjects>`) and insert each `Subject` node between these. Inserting a `Subject` node is now trivial, since each member of the `Subject` class makes use of the class's `WriteXML()` method. Note that the `Student`'s `WriteXML()` method ends with two `WriteEndElement()` calls, the first to close the `<Subjects>` node and the second to close the `<Student>` node.

The XML aware constructor for the `Student` class takes a whole `Student` node of the form:

```
<Student Matric="af013341">
    <Name>Alex Farlowe</Name>
    <Subjects>
        <Subject Code="COMP1332">
            <Title>Database Fundamentals</Title>
            <Mark>52</Mark>
        </Subject>
        <Subject Code="COMP2011">
            <Title>Data and Abstraction</Title>
            <Mark>62</Mark>
        </Subject>
    </Subjects>
</Student>
```

and extracts a `Student` object hierarchy from it. As with the `Subject` class, first we extract the node's attribute (`"Matric"`) and then the value from the `Name` element using the `InnerText()` property. Beyond this, we need to deal with the complex `<Subjects>` node, by extracting this entire node in one step (`studentNode.Item("Subjects")` does this). This node has a number of child nodes (i.e. nodes entirely within an outer node), and we can iterate through these with the `For..Each` structure:

```
For Each subjectNode In subjectCollection.ChildNodes
    'deal with subjectNode...
Next
```

From here it is again trivial, since we can send each `subjectNode` directly to the Subject constructor to retrieve an instance of the class, and then simply add this to the `mvarSubjects` collection.

The class has also been given an overloaded pair of `AddSubject()` methods, one to add a subject constructed from raw data (code, title and mark) and the other to add an instance of the `Subject` class to the collection (the latter makes it easier to add a subject that has been constructed from a XML node). Again, a `TreeItem()` method has been defined to make it easy to display the whole of a student's information, including each subject, in a `TreeView` control.

11.7.7 Managing the collection

The overall result of this is that an entire collection of `Student` objects can be easily passed to a user-interface element for navigation and view. Both of these classes have been added to a new class module, where their default `Friend` scope will make them accessible to forms and other code within an assembly. However, we will need code for adding a student, storing the whole collection (in XML form) and retrieving the collection from a XML document.

First we need a suitable collection for students; a `HashTable` is useful, since we can retrieve individual students from this by key (their matriculation number). An individual `Student` variable will also be useful:

```
Private students As Hashtable
Private currentStudent As Student
```

Next, we will need methods to write an entire collection to a XML document, and to populate a collection from a XML document (see Listing 11.21).

```
Friend Sub WriteXmlStudentData(ByVal fileName As String)
    'Need to use the XmlTextWriter class...
    Dim writer As XmlTextWriter = _
                New XmlTextWriter(fileName, Nothing)
    Dim S As Student
    'This will make the document easier for
    'a human to read...
    writer.Formatting = Formatting.Indented
    'Write the document header...
    writer.WriteStartDocument(False)
    'Start the main node...
    writer.WriteStartElement("Students")
    'Then write out each Student...
    For Each S In Students.Values
        S.WriteXML(writer)
    Next
    'Then close the main node...
    writer.WriteEndElement()
    'This will ensure that all data is written...
    writer.Flush()
    writer.Close()
End Sub

Friend Sub ReadXMLStudentData(ByVal fName As String)
    Dim doc As XmlDocument = New XmlDocument()
    Dim studentCollection, studentNode As XmlNode
    Dim name As String, matric As String
    Dim S As Student
    doc.Load(fName)
    'The first (0) node is the XML header, so the whole
    'collection of students is element(1)...
    studentCollection = doc.ChildNodes(1)
```

```
        students = New Hashtable()
        'Now can iterate through students...
        For Each studentNode In studentCollection.ChildNodes
            Dim subjectCollection, subjectNode As XmlNode
            'Create a student from a XML Node...
            S = New Student(studentNode)
            'Add the new student to the collection
            '(HashTable)...
            students.Add(S.Matric, S)
    Next
End Sub
```

Listing 11.21: Subs for writing and reading the collection in XML

We've already done most of the work necessary to display students in a `TreeView` control, but a sub (Listing 11.22) is needed to display the entire collection.

```
Friend Sub DisplayStudentCollection(ByVal tv As TreeView)
        'The HashTable stores generic Objects...
        Dim o As Object
        Dim s As Student
        'Start by emptying out old content...
        tv.Nodes.Clear()
        'Now iterate through the objects in the HashTable...
        For Each o In students.Values
            'Need to cast each back to a student type...
            s = CType(o, Student)
            'And can now add them to the TreeView...
            tv.Nodes.Add(s.TreeItem)
        Next
End Sub
```

Listing 11.22: A sub to display the entire collection in a `TreeView` control

Lastly, there should be methods to add a new student to the collection, and to add a new subject to a student, given the student's identifying matric number. This is given in Listing 11.23.

```
Friend Sub AddNewStudent()
        Dim S As Student
        Dim n As String, m As String
        n = InputBox("Enter student's name:")
        m = InputBox("Enter student's matriculation number:")
        S = New Student(m, n)
        Students.Add(S.Matric, S)
End Sub

Friend Sub AddSubject(matric As String)
        Dim t As String, m As Integer, c As String
        Dim CurrentStudent As Student
        c = InputBox("Enter subject code:")
```

```
            t = InputBox("Enter subject title:")
            m = CType(InputBox("Enter mark:"), Integer)
            CurrentStudent = Students(matric)
            CurrentStudent.AddSubject(c, t, m)
    End Sub
```

Listing 11:23: Code to extend the Student/and Subject collections

11.7.8 Providing a User-Interface for the Object Model

We now have all of the code in place to perform operations that will allow us to work with the Student object model, adding new students, appending subjects to a student and persisting the entire collection in XML format. The last stage ought to be trivial since the object-model has been developed to take care of all the hard work of collection management and XML persistence. First, the design for the form (see Figure 11.7).

The form shown has been given the name frmXMLStudents. It includes only four controls (Table 11.2).

Figure 11.7 A form for managing the Students collection

Table 11.2 Controls and properties on the student form

Control Type	Property	Value
TreeView	Name	tvStudents
Button	Name	btnNewStudent
	Text	New Student
Button	Name	btnAddSubject
	Text	Add Subject
Button	Name	btnExit
	Text	Exit

As well as responding appropriately to clicks on the various buttons, we also need to provide code to respond to the form being loaded (to load up data from a XML stream) and the form closing (so that the up to date collection can be persisted to XML). The entire form code is shown in Listing 11.24.

```
Public Class frmXMLStudents
    Inherits System.Windows.Forms.Form

+  Windows Form Designer Generated Code

    Private Sub frmXMLStudents_Load( _
                    ByVal sender As System.Object, _
                    ByVal e As System.EventArgs) _
                    Handles MyBase.Load
        'First work out a file path and name...
        fileName = Application.ExecutablePath
        fileName = fileName.Substring(0, _
                        fileName.LastIndexOf("\")) _
                        & "\Students.xml"
        'Reconstruct the object model from XML...
        ReadXMLStudentData(fileName)
        DisplayStudentCollection(tvStudents)
    End Sub

    Private Sub frmXMLStudents_Closing( _
        ByVal sender As Object, _
        ByVal e As System.ComponentModel.CancelEventArgs) _
        Handles MyBase.Closing
        'Write the new version of the XML document...
        WriteXmlStudentData(fileName)
    End Sub

    Private Sub btnExit_Click( _
                        ByVal sender As System.Object, _
                        ByVal e As System.EventArgs) _
                        Handles btnExit.Click
        Me.Close()
    End Sub

    Private Sub btnNewStudent_Click( _
                        ByVal sender As System.Object, _
                        ByVal e As System.EventArgs) _
                        Handles btnNewStudent.Click
        AddNewStudent()
        DisplayStudentCollection(tvStudents)
    End Sub

    Private Sub btnAddSubject_Click( _
                        ByVal sender As System.Object, _
                        ByVal e As System.EventArgs) _
                        Handles btnAddSubject.Click
        'First establish that a node has been selected...
        If tvStudents.SelectedNode Is Nothing Then
```

```
                       MessageBox.Show( _
                                 "Need to select a student first.")
            Else
                'Get the selected node...
                Dim n As TreeNode = tvStudents.SelectedNode
                'The user could have clicked on any item in
                'the treeview, so if necessary, work up to find
                'the top level node...
                Do Until (n.Parent Is Nothing)
                  n = n.Parent
                Loop
                AddSubject(n.Text)
                DisplayStudentCollection(tvStudents)
            End If
        End Sub
    End Class
```

Listing 11.24: Form code for working with the `Students` collection

Most of the code in Listing 11.24 is pretty self explanatory since mostly it calls on the module code for managing the collection. The method of working out a file-name for the XML file (in `frmXmlStudents_Load`) is a little different. `Application.ExecutablePath` was used earlier to prime the `FileOpenDialog` control with a start-up location. That worked because the control was smart enough to work out the location from the full file-name and path. Here, we need to provide our own code to remove the file-name from the end of the string returned by `Application.ExecutablePath` so that we have the name/location of a disk folder, and then append the actual file-name.

We start this by getting the full path and name from the `Application` object, and then removing everything from the last '\' character. The `String.LastIndexOf()` method will return the last position in a string where the given character occurs. Using this with the `String.SubString()` method, we can extract everything up to the last backslash character, and then simply append a file-name:

```
fileName = fileName.Substring(0, _
          fileName.LastIndexOf("\")) & "\Students.xml"
```

The only other odd code occurs in the `_Click()` event-handler for the Add Subject button. After a check to see if any node in the `TreeView` control has been selected, we need to find the student that a new subject is to be added to. However, as you can see in Figure 11.8, the selected node could be any node, from the top-level (matric) down to one of the details of an individual subject.

The `AddSubject()` method needs to pass the matric value of a student, which is always a top-level node in the `TreeView`. The code:

```
Dim n As TreeNode = tvStudents.SelectedNode
Do Until (n.Parent Is Nothing)
    n = n.Parent
Loop
AddSubject(n.Text)
```

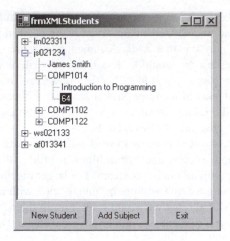

Figure 11.8 The `TreeView` control with a detail selected

starts at the selected node and, if necessary, works up from node to node in the hierarchy using the `Parent` property of a node until the node has no parent, at which point it must be a top-level node. The required matric value is then the `Text` property of this top-level node.

There are still many features that could be added to this application to make it genuinely useful, such as the ability to edit a student or a subject or make deletions. However, it is more likely that you would want to re-use the methods used here in other applications, and particularly the ways of handling XML. Because of the way the classes have been built using encapsulation, it would be no more difficult to extend the hierarchy further to produce very complex data models and stream these to and from XML documents.

11.7.9 XML vs simple serialization

As you have seen, XML is simply a format that is useful because the values stored in a document are accompanied by their own descriptions. In this respect, they are an improvement on straightforward serialized object data since it will always be possible to examine a XML document and work out an appropriate object-model. However, the penalty for this is that a XML document is much bigger than one saved to a binary stream due to the overhead of the tags. It is quite common for a XML document to be several times the size of the same information serialized as plain text or binary data.

For this and other reasons, XML is most useful for moving data between systems rather than as a way of storing data. In fact, all forms of serialized data (in which we can include XML) have one very serious limitation. When we de-serialize data from a storage device, it is normally an all or nothing operation. It is usually quite awkward to read only a part of a XML document or any serialized data, because these storage methods rely on a structure that involves a whole hierarchy. While for many types of application, this is a perfectly acceptable limitation, there are many more applications where the data stored is the most important and biggest component.

We may create a XML document that represents a single class of students in a college, but we would be less likely to write a single document that contained all the data for every student, subject and exam result for a whole college. Working with objects in memory on that scale is neither efficient nor desirable; it would be a bit like taking an entire row of filing cabinets home because you want to work on one customer's sales records.

Once we start needing to work with large data sets, thousands of students, tens of thousands of customers or millions of orders, the methods we've examined in this chapter will all run out of steam. The larger the data set, the more likely that the computer we are using will not be able to cope with all of it in memory at one time, and the less likely that we would want it to. In the next chapter, we will go on to look at the subject of databases and how Visual Basic .NET can be used to work with them.

Exercise 11.5

a) The very first example program in this chapter showed how to store the size and location of a form in the Windows Registry. Write this code so that instead, it stores size and location in a XML document stored in the file `FormData.xml` in the executable application's folder. Also write the code to read the data back from XML.

b) Why do you think that it would be a bad idea to store the Windows Registry in XML format?

Review Questions

1. What do you need to do before reading data from a file or writing data to a file?

2. List the four parameters of the `GetSetting()` function. Which of these may not be needed? What is returned from the function?

3. What test would you perform before trying to open a file to read data from it in a program given the file-name? Why is this test unnecessary if the file-name has come from an `OpenFileDialog`?

4. What do you call the character that is used to indicate the end of one data item and the beginning of the next in a file? Why can this sometimes cause a problem?

5. How do you enable a class you have written to be serialized by serialization classes in the .NET framework? Why might this not work properly?

6. What two things are wrong with this XML node: `<Data ID=1234>Fred Smith</data>`?

7. What class is used to write data into a XML document?

8. A person's name, date of birth and social security number is being read from an XML document into Visual Basic variables of the most appropriate types. Explain what may have to be done to the data as it is extracted from the XML document.

9. What is the main limitation of XML as a format for storing large amounts of data?

10. Where does Microsoft suggest you save application data files on a Windows computer? What are the alternatives?

Practical Activities

A Photograph Album

In this activity we will make use of a variety of Windows controls and a couple of classes to create a Photograph Album. This could be used to catalogue and display your collection of digital photographs, and we will add facilities to allow descriptive text to be added to a picture and pictures to be grouped into related categories; holiday snaps, pictures of your relatives, landscapes, etc. The overall aim will be to produce an application in which data is persistent using one or more of the methods described in this chapter.

Analysis and design details

As a starting point, we should decide what facilities we need to provide in the program, what information we will need to incorporate and how we will organize the classes to make it all work. Typically, a catalogue of items contains references to the items rather than the items themselves. For example, an old-style library catalogue normally contains small index cards containing the details of books in the collection (Title, Author, Publication Date, Publisher, etc.) and an indication of where to find them (which room, rack, shelf, etc). Our picture catalogue will also work this way, containing whatever descriptive details of photographs we decide to store plus an indication of where it is on the computer's hard disk. As a first cut at the things we want this catalogue to do, we can start with a use-case diagram (Figure A11.1) describing the operations it will support.

Use-cases

From the use-case diagram in Figure A11.1, we can create a scenario description for each individual use-case, and from there determine the object we will need.

- Add picture to catalogue: the user selects the option to add a picture, and then must indicate the picture to be added by choosing a picture file on the system's hard disk. Having selected a picture file, the user should give the picture a title, category name, a description of the picture. This data will then be added to the catalogue along with a reference to the picture

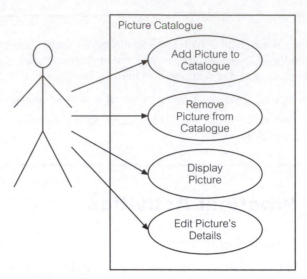

Figure A11.1 A use-case diagram for a simple picture catalogue

- Remove picture from catalogue: the user selects a picture from the displayed list of pictures in the catalogue, and selects the option to delete it. After confirmation, the picture is removed from the catalogue

- Display picture: the user selects a picture from the list of pictures in the catalogue and selects the option to display it on screen

- Edit picture's details: the user selects a picture from the list of pictures in the catalogue and selects the option to edit the details for it stored in the catalogue. After being presented with the details for editing, the user confirms to update the catalogue.

There are possibly more use-cases that could be described for this system to add detail, but as we implement these fundamental ones, we can adapt our decisions to take into account any features whose usefulness may become apparent. Note that there are no use-cases describing the saving and loading of data to and from files. The user need not be aware of these operations even though they are central to the proper operation of the program.

Classes and Properties

From the elaborated use-cases above, we can identify a number of potential classes and properties of them.

- **Picture**: an obvious class, this should contain the catalogue details for a picture file.

- Picture file: this is the data that a **Picture** object must store to keep track of a picture on the system's hard disk. As a file-name and location can be stored in a simple string, this will be a property of the **Picture** class.

- Title, category name, description: like Picture file, these are properties of the **Picture** class.

- **Catalogue**: this is the overall program, but could also refer to the overall collection of pictures, in which case it is a collection of **Picture** objects. We can use a **Dictionary** class to allow pictures to be listed by **Title** or some other attribute.

- Reference to the picture: a synonym for Picture file.

- Displayed list of pictures: we will need to provide a method for the user to identify a picture in the catalogue. A list of titles may suffice. Since .NET is well equipped with methods of displaying lists of information, this class is likely to turn out to be one of the built-in list mechanisms.

- Picture details: this is simply a collective name for the individual properties already identified for a **Picture**.

Although not mentioned in any of the use-cases, a rudimentary knowledge of digital imaging tells us that each digital photograph has a date and time stamp that indicates when the picture was taken. We can incorporate this information into the **Picture** class and this may allow us to do sophisticated searches or filtering of the catalogue list. From this information, we can create a class diagram for the system (see Figure A11.2).

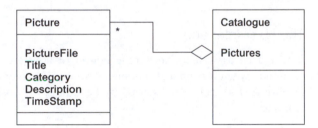

Figure A11.2   A class diagram showing properties and methods

Operations and Methods

To add more detail to the class diagram, we need to consider the operations required by the program, and decide which class should be responsible for them.

The Picture class
We need to be able to create a **Picture**, add information to it, display it, save the data to file (not the picture, since this will already be stored in a file in some location of the system's hard disk) and load the data back from file. In creating a picture, we will need to locate the actual image file and store its name and path within the object. The user will need to add **Title**, **Category** and **Description**, but the **TimeStamp** member can be determined from the date and time on the Picture file.

The Catalogue class
The **Catalogue** will require methods to add a picture, remove a picture, retrieve a **Picture** object from the collection (by **Title**), and load and save the whole collection.

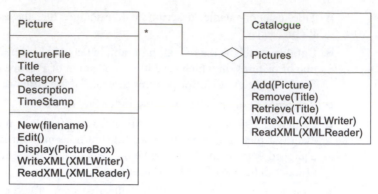

Figure A11.3 The class diagram with methods

File formats

There are several formats we could use in this application, but XML is likely to be a good choice since it is human readable, and flexible enough that if our application outgrows serialized file storage, we will be able to import the data into a database.

From this information we can create the more detailed class diagram shown in Figure A11.3.

The User-Interface

It would be as well to have some notion of how the user will interact with the catalogue when it is up and running. A simple drawing of a suitable user-interface (Figure A11.4) can get us started by becoming the basis for the prototype of the real one.

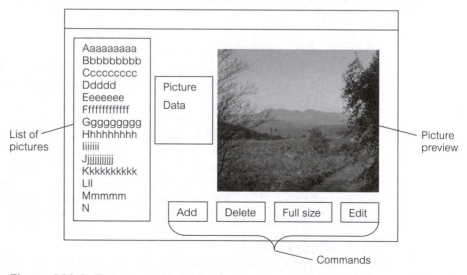

Figure A11.4 The main application form

The simple drawing of the main form indicates key features of how the user will interact with the program. Selecting a picture from the list on the left will make that picture appear in the preview panel on the form. The various buttons will allow us to **Add** new pictures, **Delete** existing ones, display the current one **Full Size** (or as large as the PC screen can accommodate) and **Edit** the various descriptive fields associated with a picture.

From the class diagrams, we can also see how these will interact with the object-model. For example, the Add button will need to initiate two consecutive operations, one from the **Picture** class and the other from the **Catalogue**: create a **Picture** (which will involve finding a picture file-name and adding other information) and add it to the **Catalogue**. The Delete button will remove a picture reference from the **Catalogue**, etc.

Activity 1: Creating the `Picture` class

Since most of the `Picture` properties are text, it presents little difficulty. For now, we'll provide an `Edit()` method that simply asks the user to respond to `InputBox()` calls. Later we can add a custom form for the class. Listing A11.1 shows the `Picture` class.

```
Imports System.Xml

Public Class Picture
    Private mvarTitle As String
    Private mvarFile As String
    Private mvarCategory As String
    Private mvarDescription As String
    Private mvarDateStamp As Date

    Public Sub New(ByVal FileName As String)
        'FileName refers to a JPG picture file...
        mvarFile = FileName
        Edit()
    End Sub

    Public Sub New(ByVal pictureNode As XmlNode)
        ReadXML(pictureNode)
    End Sub

    Public ReadOnly Property Title()
        Get
            Return mvarTitle
        End Get
    End Property

    Public ReadOnly Property Category()
        Get
            Return mvarCategory
        End Get
    End Property
```

```
Public Sub Edit()
    'For now, we'll use a clunky InputBox method...
    mvarTitle = InputBox("Enter a title:", _
                         "New Photo", mvarTitle)
    mvarCategory = InputBox("Enter a category name:", _
                         "New Photo", mvarCategory)
    mvarDescription = InputBox("Enter a description:", _
                         "New Photo", mvarDescription)
    If IO.File.Exists(mvarFile) Then
        mvarDateStamp = IO.File.GetCreationTime(mvarFile)
    Else
        MessageBox.Show("Image file missing")
    End If
End Sub

Public Sub Display(ByVal P As PictureBox)
    If IO.File.Exists(mvarFile) Then
        P.Image = New Bitmap(mvarFile)
    Else
        MessageBox.Show("Image file missing")
    End If
End Sub

Public Sub WriteXML(ByVal writer As XmlWriter)
    With writer
        .WriteStartElement("Picture")
        .WriteAttributeString("Title", mvarTitle)
        .WriteElementString("File", mvarFile)
        .WriteElementString("Category", mvarCategory)
        .WriteElementString("Description", _
                             mvarDescription)
        .WriteElementString("DateStamp", _
                             mvarDateStamp.ToString())
        .WriteEndElement()
    End With
End Sub

Public Sub ReadXML(ByVal pictureNode As XmlNode)
    mvarTitle = pictureNode.Attributes("Title").Value
    mvarFile = pictureNode.Item("File").InnerText
    mvarCategory = pictureNode.Item("Category").InnerText
    mvarDescription = _
                pictureNode.Item("Description").InnerText
    mvarDateStamp = _
     CType(pictureNode.Item("DateStamp").InnerText, Date)
End Sub
End Class
```

Listing A11.1: The `Picture` class

Note that whenever an operation involving the actual Picture file is used, we're checking that the file actually exists. This is always a potential problem with an application of this type, since the catalogue refers to Picture files that can be deleted or moved to a different folder from Windows Explorer, so that an entry in the catalogue no longer exists where it is expected to be. The class has two constructors, one of which creates a new catalogue entry while the second reconstructs an entry from an XMLNode. The `Title` and `Category` properties have been defined as `ReadOnly`. `Title` will be needed by form code when adding a picture to the `HashTable` collection, since this will be the collections `Key` property. `Category` may be useful if we decide to expand the program to allow categories of pictures to be displayed independently. All other data will be managed entirely within the class.

Activity 2: Creating the `Catalogue` class

The `Catalogue` class is simpler than the `Picture` class, since its main purpose is just to manage the collection. The `WriteXML()` and `ReadXML()` methods are a little more tricky because of the structured XML and the use of a `HashTable`, but not significantly different from Listing 11.21 earlier in this chapter. Listing A11.2 shows the `Catalogue` class.

```
Public Class Catalogue
    Private mvarPictures As Hashtable

    Public Sub New()
        mvarPictures = New Hashtable()
    End Sub

    Public Sub New(ByVal fileName As String)
        mvarPictures = New Hashtable()
        'Now load it all up...
        ReadXML(fileName)
    End Sub

    Public Sub Add(ByRef P As Picture)
        mvarPictures.Add(P.Title, P)
    End Sub

    Public Sub Remove(ByVal Key As String)
        mvarPictures.Remove(Key)
    End Sub

    Public Function Retrieve(ByVal Key As String) As Picture
        Return mvarPictures.Item(Key)
    End Function

    Public Sub ListCatalogue(ByRef L As ListBox)
        Dim Key As String
        Dim P As Picture
        L.Items.Clear()
        Dim dictEnumerator As IDictionaryEnumerator = _
                        mvarPictures.GetEnumerator()
        Do While dictEnumerator.MoveNext()
            L.Items.Add(dictEnumerator.Key())
        Loop
    End Sub
```

```
Public Sub WriteXML(ByVal fileName As String)
    Dim writer As XmlTextWriter = _
                New XmlTextWriter(fileName, Nothing)
    Dim P As Picture
    writer.Formatting = Formatting.Indented
    writer.WriteStartDocument(False)
    writer.WriteStartElement("Pictures")
    'Then write out each Picture.
    'Note, as it is a hashtable, we need to use a
    'DictionaryEnumerator for this (see Chapter 6 and
    'Chapter 10)...
    Dim dictEnumerator As IDictionaryEnumerator = _
                    mvarPictures.GetEnumerator()
    Do While dictEnumerator.MoveNext()
        P = dictEnumerator.Value()
        P.WriteXML(writer)
    Loop
    writer.WriteEndElement()
    writer.Flush()
    writer.Close()
End Sub

Public Sub ReadXML(ByVal fileName As String)
    Dim doc As XmlDocument = New XmlDocument()
    Dim pictureCollection, pictureNode As XmlNode
    Dim reader As XmlNodeReader
    Dim P As Picture
    doc.Load(fileName)
    pictureCollection = doc.ChildNodes(1)
    mvarPictures = New Hashtable()
    For Each pictureNode In pictureCollection.ChildNodes
        Dim subjectCollection, subjectNode As XmlNode
        P = New Picture(pictureNode)
        mvarPictures.Add(P.Title, P)
    Next
End Sub
End Class
```

Listing A11.2: The `Catalogue` class

We can now get on to the job of building the user-interface and testing our classes. We can start with the main form (Figure A11.5), since this will allow us to check all of the main functionality of the class model.

The form layout is more or less as designed. One useful feature of .NET forms and controls is the `Anchor` property, which allows controls to be attached a distance from any or all of the form sides. Once the controls are laid out, anchors are set to make resizing easy: the list box anchors to the `Top`, `Left` and `Bottom`, so will resize in height with the form, the buttons anchor to the `Bottom` and `Right`, so will stay along the bottom of the form, and the picture box anchors to all four sides, and so it will resize along with the form.

Property setting for the controls are shown in Table A11.1.

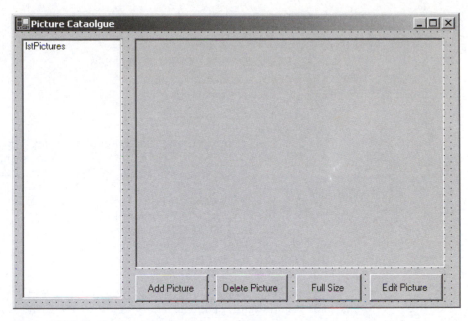

Figure A11.5 The PictureCatalogue form

Table A11.1 Control settings for the PictureCatalogue form

Control	Property	Setting	Description
Form	Name	frmCatalogue	Name to refer to it by in code
	Text	Picture Catalogue	The form's caption
ListBox	Name	lstPictures	
	Anchor	Top, Left, Bottom	Keeps the list box snug along the left of the form
PictureBox	Name	picViewer	
	SizeMode	StretchImage	Resizes the picture to fit the box
	Anchor	Top, Left, Right, Bottom	The picture box grows with the form
Button	Name	btnAdd	
	Text	Add Picture	Add a picture to the catalogue
Button	Name	btnDelete	
	Text	Delete Picture	
Button	Name	btnFullSize	Allows the picture to be displayed as big as possible
	Text	Full Size	
Button	Name	btnEdit	For editing the picture data
	Text	Edit Picture	

The code for the form is shown in Listing A11.3.

```
Public Class frmCatalogue
    Inherits System.Windows.Forms.Form

    'The picture catalogue object...
    Private Cat As Catalogue

    'Create a catalogue, and read the XML data file if
    'one exists...
    Private Sub frmCatalogue_Load(ByVal sender As _
                                            System.Object, _
                            ByVal e As System.EventArgs) _
                            Handles MyBase.Load
        Cat = New Catalogue()
        If IO.File.Exists(FileName) Then
            Cat.ReadXML(FileName)
            Cat.ListCatalogue(lstPictures)
        End If
    End Sub

    'This works out the filename for a data file in the same
    'folder as the program. See text explaining listing
                                                11.24...

    Private Function FileName() As String
        Dim fn As String
        fn = Application.ExecutablePath
        fn = fn.Substring(0, fn.LastIndexOf("\")) & _
                                "\Catalogue.xml"
        Return fn
    End Function

    'Add a picture...
    Private Sub btnAdd_Click(ByVal sender As System.Object, _
                        ByVal e As System.EventArgs) _
                        Handles btnAdd.Click
        'Get a picture file using the OpenFileDialog...
        Dim dlg As OpenFileDialog = New OpenFileDialog()
        dlg.InitialDirectory = "d:\Media\Photos"
        dlg.Filter = "Photographs|*.jpg|All Files|*.*"
        If dlg.ShowDialog() Then
            'A picture has been selected.
            'Create it..
            Dim P As New Picture(dlg.FileName)
            'Display it...
            P.Display(picViewer)
            'Get the user to edit details...
            P.Edit()
            'Add it to the catalogue...
            Cat.Add(P)
            'And update the list...
            Cat.ListCatalogue(lstPictures)
        End If
    End Sub
```

```
'The user has clicked on an item in the list box.
'Display this picture...
Private Sub lstPictures_SelectedIndexChanged( _
                ByVal sender As System.Object, _
                ByVal e As System.EventArgs) _
                Handles lstPictures.SelectedIndexChanged
        If lstPictures.SelectedItem <> "" Then
            Dim P As Picture
            P = Cat.Retrieve(lstPictures.SelectedItem)
            P.Display(picViewer)
        End If
End Sub

'The user has chosen to delete the current selection...
Private Sub btnDelete_Click( _
                ByVal sender As System.Object, _
                ByVal e As System.EventArgs) _
                Handles btnDelete.Click
        If lstPictures.SelectedItem <> "" Then
            If MessageBox.Show( _
                "Delete the current picture?", _
                "Delete Picture", _
                MessageBoxButtons.YesNo) = _
                DialogResult.Yes Then
                    Cat.Remove(lstPictures.SelectedItem)
            End If
        End If
End Sub

'Closing now, so write out the data file...
Private Sub frmCatalogue_Closing( _
            ByVal sender As Object, _
            ByVal e As System.ComponentModel.CancelEventArgs) _
            Handles MyBase.Closing
        Cat.WriteXML(FileName)
End Sub

End Class
```

Listing A11.3: The code for the `PictureCatalogue` form

Features worth remembering

In this exercise, we've used a number of different techniques for file handling and user-interface creation.

- The `Anchor` property is very useful for allowing forms to be easily resized without controls disappearing or going into odd configurations

- `IO.File.Exists()` can be used to stop problems happening because an expected file has been deleted or moved. Check for it, then open it

- Structured XML is best dealt with from a structured collection of objects. Each object can deal with its own instance data, while the collection manager simply calls on them to load and save

- There are a range of ways for persisting data, some are better suited to particular purposes than others. Always consider the wider implications of a format you decide to use – can it be repaired if it becomes corrupted? (difficult with .NET streams), is it easy to pass into other software? (XML is ideal), etc.

Suggested Additional Activities

1. There are a number of glaring omissions in this application while the core of it works adequately. A full-size picture view will require you to create another form with a picture box and load the picture into it. If you set the picture box's `SizeMode` setting to `AutoSize`, the picture box will grow to fit the image. You can then use it's `Resize` event to change the size of the form to either the full picture size or the screen size, whichever is smaller.

2. The `Category` property of the `Picture` class is currently unused, but could be used to allow groups of pictures to be displayed. Examine the `ListCatalogue()` method of the `Catalogue` class. This can be amended to include a given category name as a parameter so that only the matching pictures were added to the list.

3. The picture data really needs a custom form for entering picture details. A call to this form would be placed in the `Edit()` method of the `Picture` class – pass the details to controls on the form, show the form (as a dialog), and retrieve the details when the dialog is closed.

Solutions to Exercises

Exercise 11.1

```
Sub SaveMRU()
    SaveSetting("LetterWriter'', "Recent Files", _
                                  "MRU1", File1)
    SaveSetting("LetterWriter", "Recent Files", _
                                  "MRU2", File2)
End Sub

Sub LoadMRU()
    File1 = GetSetting("LetterWriter", "Recent Files", _
                                  "MRU1", "(none)")
    File2 = GetSetting("LetterWriter", "Recent Files", _
                                  "MRU2", "(none)")
End Sub
```

Exercise 11.2

```
Private Sub FileLoad()
    Dim dlgLoad As OpenFileDialog = New OpenFileDialog()
    dlgLoad.Filter = "Text Files|*.txt|All Files|*.*"
    dlgOpen.InitialDirectory =
    Application.LocalUserAppDataPath
    If dlgSaveAs.ShowDialog = DialogResult.OK Then
        fileName = dlgSaveAs.FileName
        'Open and load the file...
        '. . .
    End If
End Sub
```

Exercise 11.3

```
Sub ReadWeeksAndMonths(ByVal FileName As String)
    Dim Days(6) As String
    Dim Months(11) As String
    Dim buffer As String, data() As String
    Dim index As Integer
    Dim inStream As IO.StreamReader
    inStream = New IO.StreamReader(FileName)
    buffer = inStream.ReadLine()
    data = buffer.Split(";")
    For index = 0 To 6
        Days(index) = data(index)
    Next
    buffer = inStream.ReadLine()
    data = buffer.Split(";")
    inStream.Close()
    For index = 0 To 11
        Months(index) = data(index)
    Next
    For index = 0 To 6
        Console.WriteLine(Days(index))
    Next
    For index = 0 To 11
        Console.WriteLine(Months(index))
    Next
End Sub
```

Exercise 11.4

As demonstrated, the file that is created as a result of .NET's built-in serialization is a binary file. This format is efficient in storage terms and speed of operation, but does make the data impossible for a human to read. While text-based serialization is much less efficient, this is often not an issue where small amounts of data are concerned, and the readability of the data can make the file more accessible to other programs, and the software easier to debug.

a) These subs could be placed in a code module so that they could be used by a form in any application. Note that if more than one form was to be saved, it would be necessary either to use a separate file per form or to provide another level of hierarchy in the XML file so that each form had its own XML node (which could be identified by form name):

```
Sub WriteXmlWindowSettings(ByVal fileName As String, _
                           ByVal F As Form)
    Dim writer As XmlTextWriter = _
                    New XmlTextWriter(fileName, Nothing)
    writer.Formatting = Formatting.Indented
    writer.WriteStartDocument(False)
    writer.WriteStartElement("WindowSettings")
    writer.WriteElementString("Left", _
                          CType(F.Left, String))
    writer.WriteElementString("Top", _
                          CType(F.Top, String))
    writer.WriteElementString("Width", _
                          CType(F.Width, String))
    writer.WriteElementString("Height", _
                          CType(F.Height, String))
    writer.WriteEndElement()
    writer.Flush()
    writer.Close()
End Sub

Sub ReadXmlWindowSettings(ByVal FileName As String, _
                          ByVal F As Form)
    Dim doc As XmlDocument = New XmlDocument()
    Dim Reader As XmlNodeReader
    Dim XmlSettings As XmlNode
    doc.Load(FileName)
    XmlSettings = doc.ChildNodes(1)
    F.Top = CType(XmlSettings.Item("Top").InnerText, _
                                            Integer)
    F.Left = CType(XmlSettings.Item("Left").InnerText, _
                                            Integer)
    F.Width = _
        CType(XmlSettings.Item("Width").InnerText, _
                                            Integer)
    F.Height = CType( _
        XmlSettings.Item("Height").InnerText, Integer)
End Sub
```

b) The Windows Registry is a very large database of entries which are stored in a proprietary binary format for efficiency. Using XML as a file format for the registry would lead to a much larger set of registry files that would take much longer to process. It would also make it difficult for the Windows system to access individual settings in the registry.

Answers to Review Questions

1. What do you need to do before reading data from a file or writing data to a file? **A file must be** *opened* **before it can be read from or written to.**

2. List the four parameters of the `GetSetting()` function. Which of these may not be needed? What is returned from the function? **`ApplicationName`, `SectionName`, `KeyName` and `DefaultKeyValue`. Of these, the `DefaultKeyValue` will not be necessary if the `Key` is known to exist in the registry. The value that was stored for a specific key (setting), or the default value if none was.**

3. What test would you perform before trying to open a file to read data from it in a program given the file-name? Why is this test unnecessary if the file name has come from an `OpenFileDialog`? **You should check that the file exists (using the `File.Exists()` method). The test is unnecessary for a file-name returned from an `OpenFileDialog` because either the user has selected a file (which must exist) or, if no file has been selected, the file name will be an empty string.**

4. What do you call the character that is used to indicate the end of one data item and the beginning of the next in a file? Why can this sometimes cause a problem? **A** *delimiter*. **If the delimiter character or code is used within the data items in the file, there can be a problem since it will appear to the program as if an extra piece of data (for each stored delimiter character or code) is in the file.**

5. How do you enable a class you have written to be serialized by serialization classes in the .NET framework? Why might this not work properly? **Mark the class with the `<Serializable>` attribute. If a class that has been marked as serializable contains member objects (in a composition structure) which are not themselves serializable, the serialization process will fail.**

6. What two things are wrong with this XML node: `<Data ID=1234>Fred Smith</data>`? **1) The attribute value (1234) is not enclosed in single or double quotes and, 2) The closing tag name does not match the opening tag name (XML tags must match exactly – including character case).**

7. What class is used to write data into a XML document? **`XMLWriter`**

8. A person's name, date of birth and social security number is being read from an XML document into Visual Basic variables of the most appropriate types. Explain what may have to be done to the data as it is extracted from the XML document. **As data is extracted from the XML document, it may have to be cast to an appropriate type (e.g. `Date` for the date of birth value), since XML contains only text data.**

9. What is the main limitation of XML as a format for storing large amounts of data? **The main limitation is that in many situations, an entire XML document must be read into memory, even if there is only a small amount of data required from it. Also, XML data is space inefficient because of the amount of text in the tags. (Note that it is actually possible to**

partially read a XML document, using an implementation of XML known as SAX (Simple API for XML). However, this still requires that a XML file is read up to the point where the required data has been found, and this is a severe limitation compared to other available methods.)

10. Where does Microsoft suggest you save application data files on a Windows computer? What are the alternatives? **Application.CommonAppDataPath or Application.LocalUserAppDataPath. It is also possible to use Application.ExecutablePath, or a custom folder (e.g. D:\MyData) to store data in.**

While streams are a perfectly good persistence mechanism for saving and restoring the complete state of an object-oriented system, this is often not required, and for some systems may not be possible. Consider, for example, the database system for a large company. It is likely that there will be millions, or even billions of records of data, each of which corresponds to the state of a single object. To load the state of the entire system into an object-model would require a huge amount of computer memory, and would probably take a very long while to do. Systems of this scale tend to work on the basis of manipulating single data records, small sets of data records or aggregate information about a lot of data records (for example the total number of customer accounts, or the average of all today's customers' total purchases).

We would neither be able to nor wish to develop a system that would create an object model of the entire system in cases like these. Database systems work with large amounts of information, most of which is stored *off-line*, on a disk or some other form of permanent storage. Information is brought into main memory to be processed, and then sent back to off-line storage. New data records are created in main memory and sent to disk when their data has been entered in full.

12.1 Object-Oriented Database Systems

In contrast, objects are kept in the computer's main memory, and so far, we have only considered permanent storage to be a useful way of keeping information when a program is not actually running. However, there is an entire class of object-oriented program that is required to work with larger amounts of data than could be maintained as an on-line object model. These *object-oriented database* programs work on the principle that an object is reconstructed from a disk record if and when it is required. Matters get complicated when the objects in the object model in use are highly interconnected. In this case, reconstructing an object from a disk record may then have the knock-on effect of forcing the reconstruction of all of the objects that the first refers to, and in turn all of the objects that they refer to, and so on. Various strategies are used to minimize the impact of these types of interconnections in object databases.

Object-oriented databases tend to be large and complex systems purpose-built for strategic purposes: large-scale Computer Aided Design and Manufacturing (CAD/CAM) systems, telecommunications data management systems and similar applications with massive data requirements. We will not consider them further here.

12.1.1 Relational Database Systems

The most common way of storing and maintaining medium or large sets of data for use by one or more programs is a *relational database*. There are a variety of these available, from the simple desktop variety like Microsoft Access or Borland Paradox, to major systems that can be accessed simultaneously by many users in a networked environment such as SQL Server, Oracle and DB2. Visual Studio .NET in the Professional and Enterprise versions is supplied with a size-limited version of SQL Server called the Microsoft Database Environment or MSDE for short. MSDE is also shipped along with Microsoft Office Professional and Microsoft Access.

The .NET framework includes classes for working with most of the available database types including Access, Oracle, SQL Server, MSDE and others. Currently, the components provided for working with SQL Server and MSDE are favoured since they have been developed to connect to these database types in a more direct way than the generic components that allow connection to the other types. It is expected that this will change as other manufacturers develop their own classes for establishing a direct connection between a .NET application and their database format.

The `System.Data` namespace in the .NET framework contains a number of classes that we can use to write coded methods for getting data from and inserting data into a database. Visual Studio .NET also contains components for accessing databases, tools for examining the content of database servers, wizards for generating forms for accessing data and controls to make the presentation of data on a form a simple matter. Before we go on to look at these, we should have a look at the underlying theory of databases and relational databases.

12.1.1.1 Flat-File Databases

In the previous chapter we used streams to move data from object models into files. In one example, information was stored in a comma-delimited file as rows of information. Each row had a similar composition (e.g. a name, address and telephone number) so that the data stored in the file was effectively a table.

A flat-file database is similar to this with one necessary exception. Since it is important that a database system can retrieve an item of information as quickly as possible, it is important that each row in the data table takes exactly the same amount of storage space as every other row. Then, an operating system feature that makes it possible to jump directly to any location within a file and read the data from that point on can be used to gain direct access to *any* record in a table.

For example, Table 12.1 shows data that could be stored in a flat-file database. In the table, each row (apart from the first, headings row) contains a *record* of data. Each column specifies a *field*, which is an atomic item of data (one that contains a single piece of information in the context of the record). During the specification of a table, each field is described in terms of the type of data it may contain (number, textual characters, date, etc.), and its format or maximum size (e.g. numeric floating point, numeric integer, maximum of 40 characters, etc.). Since this type of decision fixes the amount of storage space that a field will fit into, it has the advantage of making a table of data a very efficient structure to store and to work with.

Table 12.1 A table of data

Name	Address1	Address2	PostCode	Telephone	Date of Birth
Joe Bloggs	1 Acacia Ave.	Glasgow	G11 3XX	041 123 4567	22/11/65
Annette Curtin	2 High St.	Stewarton	ST1 2EW	123 5678	12/3/62
Neil Doon	3 Low Rd.	Kingussie	KG2 QQQ	234 4567	3/9/70
"	"	"	"	"	"

Table 12.2 Field structure for the table in Table 12.1

Field	Type	Size in bytes
Name	Character	60
Address1	Character	40
Address2	Character	40
PostCode	Character	9
Telephone	Character	16
Date of Birth	Date	8

For example, assume that the fields in Table 12.1 are organized as shown in Table 12.2.

Each record in the table will take exactly 173 bytes of storage space, found by adding together the byte size of each of the fields. Note that the size of each character field would be chosen by a database developer, while the date size is standard for a given database engine. Given the fixed record size, a routine to access it will be able to do its work very fast. Record 1 will occupy bytes 1 to 173, record 2 bytes 174 to 346 and so on. For example, the 31st record of data will be located from byte number $(30 * 173 + 1)$ to byte number $(31 * 173)$ in the file. Any computer-based random-access filing system (such as the Windows FAT or NTFS filing systems) can access and return this information very quickly.

The limitation is of course that every record must take up exactly the same amount of space. If someone's name is only 10 characters long, 50 characters of space will be wasted. If they have only one line of address, the entire field for the second line will be wasted. The most obvious alternative scheme of placing a marker at the end of every field in the table (for example, a comma) will allow data of any size to fit snugly in a field but would slow things up by forcing the filing system to count through each marker of each record to access a particular record, since no simple calculation could work out where a given record started.

Using a system like this, a flat-file database can store and retrieve simple information quickly. Provided care has been taken in deciding on the length of the variable-width fields (usually strings), the system can also be acceptably efficient in its use of space. Given the current standard of multi-gigabyte disk drives, the wasted space can be considered to be trivial.

Table 12.3 A Flat-File Orders Database

Invoice-No	Date	Cust-ID	Cust-Name	Cust-Addr	Item-Code	Description	Quantity	Unit Cost	Total Cost
0123	12/02/03	0011	Green	1 Acacia Ave . . .	0001	1/2″ Bolt	100	0.04	4.00
0123	12/02/03	0011	Green	1 Acacia Ave . . .	0082	6ba Wingnut	80	0.12	9.60
0123	12/02/03	0011	Green	1 Acacia Ave . . .	0144	6″ Driver	5	1.25	6.25
0124	14/02/03	0035	Brown	5 Main St . . .	0001	1/2″ Bolt	5000	0.04	200.00
0124	14/02/03	0035	Brown	5 Main St . . .	0322	100cl Oil	2	0.85	1.70
0124	14/02/30	0035	Brown	5 Main St . . .	1136	Circlip × 100	50	1.08	54.00
0125	17/02/03	0046	Blue	11 High St . . .	0006	1/4″ Bolt	500	0.04	20.00
0126	17/02/03	0058	Black	15 River Ave . . .	0081	4ba Wingnut	100	0.16	16.00
0126	17/02/03	0058	Black	15 River Ave . . .	0082	6ba Wingnut	200	0.12	24.00
0126	17/02/03	0058	Black	15 River Ave . . .	0144	6″ Driver	2	1.25	2.50
0126	17/02/03	0058	Black	15 River Ave . . .	2242	Hammerite	0.5	4.22	2.11
0126	17/02/03	0058	Black	15 River Ave . . .	3881	Rubber feet	10	0.60	6.00
0127	19/02/03	0035	Brown	5 Main St . . .	1172	2.5mm cable	50	1.43	71.50

Exercise 12.1

Using Table 12.2 as an example, define a flat-file structure for a table of `BankAccount` transactions. You should aim to use the most suitable field types from `Character`, `Date` and `Number` for each field, and should carefully consider the best size for any text fields you define.

12.1.1.2 Limitations of Flat-File Databases

The flat-file storage system can easily be applied to simple data systems. However, a limitation soon becomes apparent; in the real world, few systems contain information of only one type. For example, consider a simple ordering database system. This will contain information on customers, products for sale, items ordered and invoices for billing purposes; a minimum of four separate types of information. To create a flat-file database from this information would involve constructing a large table in which each row would contain all of the information for any single purchase. An example of this is shown in Table 12.3, and will be referred to later in the section on Relational Database Principles.

The first thing to notice about the table is that each row contains data on each of the different types of information; it should actually be four tables rather than one (a table for customers, one for orders, one for ordered items and one for products). The second thing to notice is that various records (rows) contain repeated groups of information. For example, in the first three records, the first four fields contain the same data. This is confirmation that there is more than one table of data here. It is also an indication of data *redundancy*. To improve on this, we need to move to the *relational* database model.

12.1.1.3 Relational Database Principles

The problem with flat-file databases is that they are no more than a conversion of a good model for storing data manually (e.g. in card indexes) to a computer format.

Computer systems can deal with this model with no trouble, but many of the possible advantages that could be gained from using a computer model cannot be fully realized, due to the deficiencies of the model.

Take the example of a card index system that you might use to catalogue your tapes or CDs. If each card represents a musical artist or group, there will be a maximum number of albums that could be fitted on a card. Say each card has space for 15 lines of text. One line each for the artist's or group's name and some comments, plus one line per CD, allowing a maximum of 13 titles (ok, it is possible to use the back of the card, but the argument remains with just some changes in the numbers). If we now wanted to list all of the tracks on each CD there would only be room for one, or at the most two albums per card.

One way around the physical limitations of the card formats would be to have two sets of index cards, one containing artist details and the other containing CD details. To match artists to CD, it would be simple to add a cross-reference on each CD card, giving the name or even just a number that refers to the matching artist card. We could take this a stage further, by creating a card index for record companies, with each artist card referring to the appropriate company card. An example of this scheme is shown in Figure 12.1.

Note that there is an immediate improvement in efficiency, both for storage and for *insertion*, the act of adding a new CD to a database. In storage terms, each artist card does not need to have the name of the record company explicitly on it, so there is more room for artist information. If an artist changes record companies, it will be a simple matter to update the cross-reference on the card (although this can cause an

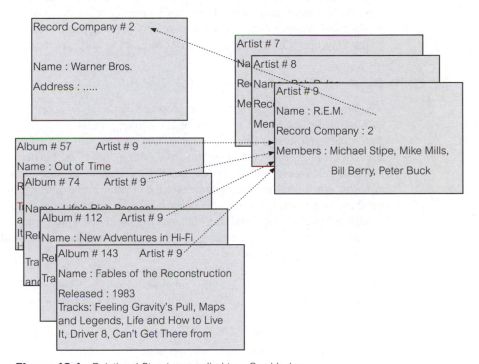

Figure 12.1 Relational Structure applied to a Card Index

awkward anomaly as we'll see later). Insertion wise, adding a new record for a CD by an artist for whom there is an existing card will involve only listing the album specifics – Name, Artist Reference Number, Date, Tracks.

Of course, adding a new CD by an artist who is not already listed will involve completing two new cards, one with CD information and one with artist information. If the record company were not already listed, a third new index card would be necessary. However, even having to add all three cards for a new entry does not have many overheads compared to writing the same information on a single card. Also, we would normally hope that this type of operation would be the exception.

Where inefficiency creeps in is in *retrieving* the information about a specific artist or CD, since we will now have to search through several card indexes to find all of the relevant information. However, this is what computer database systems excel at, particularly where some system of indexing has been set up for a table of data.

It is worth noting that there is a severe flaw in the above representation of a structured tape and CD index card database. What if an artist, after releasing several CDs on one label, changed record companies? If we were to update the artist card with the number of the new record company, then it would look as though all of the artist's CDs were released under the new label. This would complicate matters if you were to give this information to someone who wished to place an order for a copy of one of their earlier CDs.

A more efficient way to structure this database would be to refer to the record label on each *CD* card, rather than on the artist's. This type of problem occurs often in databases (think of a customer/order database where a customer changes their billing address – using this scheme would make it look as if all orders ever sent to the customer went to the new address before they even occupied it), and often results in structural changes to an entire database system being made at great effort and cost to the developers. Database design takes care, effort and experience.

12.1.1.4 Relational Database Theory: E.F. Codd

The cross-referenced storage format proposed in the above example is the essence of relational databases. A true relational database will have a data structure created following a number of rules designed to maintain the *integrity* of the database (i.e. prevent the cross-referencing system from failing) and to eliminate redundancy.

These rules were first proposed by Dr E.F. Codd, who developed a *relational calculus* as a formalized mathematics for the creation and manipulation of relational database structures. Central to his proposals for relational databases was the use of a RDBMS (Relational DataBase Management System), which would act as a layer of software hosted by an operating system that allowed tables to be created, updated, *queried*, altered and destroyed.

The paper, 'Is Your DBMS Really Relational?' by Dr Codd, explains 12 rules that govern a RDBMS[1]. Many so-called relational database systems ignore the majority of these rules, but use the tag 'relational' anyway. In fact few of the large number of

---

[1] These rules can be found in various websites.
e.g. http://www.cis.ohio-state.edu/~sgomori/570/coddsrules.html

available 'relational' database systems are truly relational, in that they break some or many of Codd's rules. However, the power of the relational database model shines through, even in products, which have compromised the rules. In most cases, the rules have been side-stepped for purely pragmatic reasons.

12.1.1.5 A Relational Example

Going back to the customer/orders database originally depicted as a flat file in Table 12.3, we could structure this database as a set of four tables as shown in Figure 12.2.

Note that each Invoice belongs to one Customer and is made up of a number of Orders. Each Order is for a quantity of a particular Item. In general, cross-references direct from the *detail* end to the *master* end. Therefore, Orders contain a reference to Items (since one type of item can appear on many orders) and to Invoices, since one invoice can have a number of orders on it. Customers contain a reference to Invoices, since one customer can have any number of invoices.

Note also that each table has one or more particular columns that have been highlighted. This column or columns contains values that are unique to each record in the table. For example, we can arrange it so that each Customer, Invoice and Item in their tables are given a unique ID number; one that we can guarantee not to use in any other record in the same table. In the Orders table, the two fields Invoice-No and

Item-Code	Description	Unit Cost
0001	1/2" Bolt	0.04
0006	1/4" Bolt	0.04
0081	4ba Wingnut	0.16
0082	6ba Wingnut	0.12
0144	6" Driver	1.25
0322	100cl Oil	0.85
1136	Circlip × 100	1.08
1172	2.5mm cable	1.43
2242	Hammerite	4.22
3881	Rubber feet	0.60

Items Table

Invoice-no	Item-Code	Quantity
0123	0001	100
0124	0001	5000
0125	0006	500
0126	0081	100
0123	0082	80
0126	0082	200
0123	0144	5
0126	0144	2
0124	0322	2
0124	1136	50
0127	1172	50
0126	2242	1/2
0126	3881	10

Orders Table

Invoice-No	Date	Cust-ID
0123	12/02/03	0011
0124	14/02/03	0035
0127	19/02/03	0035
0125	17/02/03	0046
0126	17/02/03	0058

Invoices Table

Cust-ID	Cust-Name	Cust-Addr
0011	Green	1 Acacia Ave . . .
0035	Brown	5 Main St . . .
0046	Blue	11 High St . . .
0058	Black	15 River Ave . . .

Customers Table

Figure 12.2 The Customer-Orders system from Table 12.3 as a relational database

Item-Code will be a unique combination for each order (since an invoice will contain a list of orders for *different* items). We call this field or combination of fields the *primary key* of a table, since it can be used to unambiguously identify each record in the table. If we refer to Item-Code 0006, it can only ever be a reference to a $\frac{1}{4}$" bolt. Similarly, Customer no 0035 is always Brown of 5 Main St and Order 0123-0082 will always refer to an order of 80 6ba Wing-Nuts on an Invoice for Customer no 0011 generated on 12/02/03.

Primary keys make cross-referencing between tables possible and efficient. The value of a primary key should **never** change, since that would break the integrity of the database by breaking the link between the record whose primary key it is and other records in other tables. When a cross-reference in made by inserting the primary key field from one table into another table, it is referred to as a *foreign key* or *secondary key* in the other table.

12.1.1.6 Relationships

A relationship is a link between one item in a table and another item in the same or a different table. We describe the relationships between items in terms of how many items there can be at either end. For example, a single customer can have a number of invoices (as shown for Customer no 0035 in Figure 12.2), which we would call a *one-to-many* relationship. Similarly, one invoice would normally contain more than one employee (e.g. Invoice-No 0126). However, if we included a table of credit limits into our orders database, one customer would be related to one credit limit record, and vice-versa – a *one-to-one* relationship.

There is a third form of relationship, in which many items in one table can be related to many items in another. This form of relationship does not come up too often, but needs to be catered for in some circumstances. For example, a publisher's database could contain a table of Authors and a table of Books. One author could be responsible for writing any number of books, but also a single book could have been written by a number of authors (computer books are often written in this way). Unfortunately, this form of relationship cannot be dealt with by having the relationships directly between the two tables, since a relationship is always a one-way link. We can add an AuthorID column to the Books table and a particular author's id could appear in any number of rows to show what books that author had written, but if we try to reverse the relationship so that a BookID could appear in a number of author entries, the picture gets confused: has the author written the one book whose ID is in his table entry, or the many that have his ID in the Books table?

The way around this to create true *many-to-many* relationship is to add a third table, which holds only *links* between authors and books. For example, the table excerpts shown in Figure 12.3 are from Microsoft's Biblio database, supplied as an example database with copies of Access, SQL Server and MSDN. Three tables itemize authors ('Authors'), books ('Titles') and the many-to-many link between authors and books ('Title Author'). The link table in the middle shows that the author with AuthorID 2340 has contributed to two books (in fact many more than this) since that author's ID appears in two rows. The book with ISBN 0-2011173-4-7 was written by two authors (2340 and 7707). The result is that the link table can be used to relate many items in one table with many items in another.

Packages   *Packages-PrSup*   *Prod-Sup*

AuthorID	Author
...	...
2340	Shelly, Gary B.
7707	Garrison, C.
...	...

Author Table

AuthorID	ISBN
...	...
2340	0-1345787-0-8
2340	0-2011173-4-7
7707	0-2011173-4-7
...	...

Link Table (Author Title)

ISBN	Book Title
...	...
0-1345787-0-8	Inductive Logic
0-2011173-4-7	dBASE III: Ready Reference Manual
...	...

Title (Book) Table

Figure 12.3 A table set showing a many-to-many relationship

Tables and relationships are the defining components of a relational database, and every database system benefits from the meticulous design of these. By carefully considering the entities that appear in tables (rows), and the primary as foreign key fields required to relate them appropriately, a developer can create a foundation that will support a complex data management system through many different versions of the operating software.

Exercise 12.2

Devise a table structure for dealing with bank accounts and transactions, using the descriptions given in Chapter 10. You will need select or provide a primary key field and a foreign key field for creating the link between the tables.

12.1.1.7 Normalization

Given a well-organized table structure with key fields to define relationships between records as discussed in the previous section, we can quite easily build up a database system. It should be obvious that a certain amount of optimization can be performed on a set of data to minimize the amount of space used and to improve its logical structure (and thereby simplify any changes that may need to be imposed on it in the future). Working from a set of entity descriptions, and carefully checking to ensure that there are no hidden relationships between values in fields (attributes) can result in a well-organized structure. Many database designers and programmers work out a table structure for a database almost intuitively, and manage to produce totally logical and maintainable structures in this way.

However, it is difficult to teach this approach to database design since generally it is based on experience gained over a long period in database development. This usually includes much experience gained by doing it wrong and having to apply a lot of effort to recover from a structural disaster (possibly the most effective form of experience). It also depends on the designer being able to work from the ground up, allocating descriptions for the items that will appear in the database and assigning fields to tables as necessary. Often, data already exists and a suitable structure must be created to fit it.

There is a more realistic approach to database design which, with a little effort, will generally lead to an optimal data structure. The process is known as *normalization*, and involves organising *existing* data into optimal table structures by grouping attributes to form entities of an efficient size and composition. The eventual goal of this is to eliminate the storage of duplicated information and to create the best structure for accommodating future changes to the data. A full description of normalization is beyond the scope of this book. Almost any decent book on database design (e.g. *Database Systems, A Practical Approach to Design, Implementation and Management*, by Connolly and Begg) will describe the technique more than adequately.

12.1.2 SQL: An Implementation of Relational Calculus

There are many DBMS systems in operation in the world, and many of these use proprietary languages for creating databases, populating them with data, and extracting specific sets of information from them. Most use the notion of *sets* of data explicitly, and these languages are therefore characterized as *set-oriented*. Of all of the available languages for RDBMS operation, Structured Query Language (SQL), originally defined by IBM in the 1970s is regarded as a standard; the *lingua franca* for relational database management.

SQL was developed from Sequel, IBM's first attempt at a RDBMS language. There are two distinct parts to SQL, both of which are necessary to form a language that obeys Codd's rule 5, which relates to the facilities necessary for a RDBMS. These parts are a Data Definition Language (DDL), which allows the structure of databases to be defined and altered, and a Data Manipulation Language (DML), which allows data to be entered into a database, altered and extracted from it.

Using the two components of SQL, a database developer can construct SQL statements to manipulate the structure or content of a database. SQL can be used to perform three types of operation:

1. queries can return *views* of a database (DML);
2. SQL updates can *update* a database contents (DML);
3. other SQL statements can *modify the structure* of a database (DDL).

Of these, the query is the type of SQL statement that is used most often. SQL has been implemented in one form or another by just about every software company that has claims to producing DBMS systems. Some products have only a DML component while others incorporate both components. Some with a DML component only usually make use of some form of Graphics User Interface (GUI)-based data definition tool for defining and altering tables.

Few of the available implementations of SQL are fully compatible with the standard language. (A definitive version was published in 1992 by two related authorities; a 580 page specification published by ANSI as American National Standard X3.135-1992 and one by ISO/IEC as International Standard 9075:1992. The two specifications are word-for-word identical.) A command-line environment (Oracle, Ingres) fronts some SQL implementations. These usually include optional GUI tools. Others are implemented as *embedded* languages, which are hosted by other programming languages. As we shall see, the .NET framework takes this approach, while Visual Studio .NET incorporates functional GUI tools as well.

12.1.2.1 The Structure of a SQL statement

A SQL statement is made up of three parts:

1. a verb, such as CREATE, MODIFY, SELECT, INSERT or UPDATE;
2. a predicate part that specifies a field set to the query (e.g. *, Titles.Au_ID);
3. a prepositional clause that indicates the tables involved (e.g. Authors, Publishers).

Typical queries are . . .

```
SELECT * FROM Authors;
INSERT INTO Customers SELECT [New Customers].* FROM
[New Customers];
```

The .NET framework does not specify or preclude any specific form of SQL, since it is an express requirement that *any* database format can be used with it. The various *database drivers* available to a Visual Basic program define how the program communicates with a database, and any specific SQL that a programmer needs to embed in a piece of Visual Basic code must conform to that which the database expects. For many, probably most, .NET database programs, this will be Transact-SQL, the implementation used by Microsoft's SQL server and MSDE.

12.1.3 Relational Databases and Object-Orientation

From our perspective as object-oriented programmers, a relational database is made up of tables, each of which can contain the member data for all of the objects of a specific class. Compared to a true object-oriented database, this is an inadequate system since each class's methods have been separated from the object data in a very non-object-oriented way. However, we can make use of a relational database as a persistence mechanism. Provided we use the information in tables as simply the data from which objects can be reconstituted, the relational database model works well in supporting object-oriented systems, particularly those in which objects are not required to be available on-line at all times.

12.2 .NET Support for Relational Databases

Microsoft provides in the .NET framework a solid object hierarchy for the management of relational databases. The range of classes for database work is found in the System.Data namespace. For classes which must deal directly with a database server (a program that manipulates a database on behalf of other programs), there are currently two categories; those that are optimized for use with SQL Server and MSDE, and those that can use Open DataBase Connectivity (ODBC) via Object Linking and Embedding (OLE) to provide access to a wide range of other database types including Microsoft Access, dBase III and IV, Oracle, DB2 and Paradox. These are differentiated by a prefix, either 'Sql' or 'OleDb' in the class name. Classes in the `System.Data` namespace without either of these prefixes can be used for working with data from either version.

A few classes are used to establish access to databases to support database working sessions (`SqlConnection`, `OleDbConnection`) while others provide ways of sending commands to a database server and retrieving the results (`SqlCommand`, `OleDbCommand`). Also important are the classes that encapsulate information retrieved from a database (`SqlDataReader`, `OleDbDataReader`) and those that allow that information to be updated (the `SqlDataAdapter`, `OleDbDataAdapter` and `Dataset` classes). These are backed up by a range of classes that provide detailed access to tables (`DataTable`), rows (`DataRow`), columns (`DataColumn`) and relations (`DataRelation`). The on-line help provided with Visual Studio .NET is a comprehensive guide to these classes and their use.

12.2.1 Three-Tier Application Support in .NET

Recall that the components of an application can be usefully organized into three separate tiers or layers. This organization provides a good solution to the compromises often encountered in complex application design when considering the sometimes conflicting goals of organizational complexity, application flexibility, component re-use and maintenance.

We can build application-specific and user-interface specific code on top of the standard database classes to make it easy to manage data in programs. The result is a *three-tier* application, the tiers being:

■ The *data-access* layer, that deals with forming a connection with and getting information to and from the actual database. Typically, the `Sql/OleDbConnection` classes, the `Sql/OleDbDataReader` classes and the `Sql/OleDbDataAdapter` classes perform this function.

■ The *business-object* or *business-logic* layer that forms a set of business-objects from the information in the database so that certain *business rules* can be imposed on the way the information is handled. An object model tailored to the system requirements is the most likely form of this layer.

■ The *user-interface*, or *presentation* layer, that deals with presenting the business objects and allowing the user to interact with them. Forms and controls are used to implement this layer.

This three-tier approach gives us a very flexible way of presenting a database to a user while imposing business rules on the way that the database is used. The benefits of this approach are the same benefits that object-orientation can provide to any type of application, but have additional purchase in database style applications.

- Objects can be used to manage all of the database-specific operations within the application, thereby making the application code itself easier to create and maintain. These are the *data access objects* that make up the data access layer.

- Changes to the underlying database need not affect the application code since they can be made to the classes that provide database access.

- Changes to the business rules can be localized to the business-object layer, so that it is often possible to avoid making changes to the database structure or access layer.

- The way that the information in the database is used and updated can be tightly controlled by the middle, business-logic layer. The business objects in this layer know how to interact with the data-access layer but impose rules as to how this data can be used and changed, from the perspective of the environment they are used in. For example, *business rules*, such as a rule that makes it impossible for a customer to withdraw money from a bank account that has a zero balance, would be coded in this layer.

- We can make the information in a database appear as though it was a simple object model to the user-interface. Data access and business logic can be given an interface that provides apparently continuous access to every element in a large database even though only a few objects may be in memory at any one time, thereby simplifying the design of the user-interface layer. This layer simply handles events from the user and presents information from the lower layers.

- Once the two bottom layers are built, we can create a range of applications based on the same database and object model. This makes it possible to develop applications that are optimized for particular users within a larger organization. For example, applications for data entry and recall might be important in the front office of a company, while others might provide for the analysis of all of the information in the database to enable executives to make strategic decisions.

By developing an object model to act as an access layer between the application and the database, we will effectively be making on-the-fly translations from the relational data model to an object model and back again, as shown in Figure 12.4.

In object-oriented programming terms, most of the classes in `System.Data` would be used in only the data-access layer of an adequate object-oriented database solution. However, the `DataSet` class is powerful and flexible enough that it has functions to offer both the data-access layer and the business layer.

Generally, a complex database application will benefit from the separation of data access and the implementation of business rules, and normally we would encapsulate the business rules in a business-objects layer. However, for many systems the business rules may be simple enough that we can create a `DataSet` that will implement them, in which case there may be no need for a separate object model to build around the business rules. Of course for system engineered around highly functional classes that interconnect in complex ways, a proper object model will still provide the best solution. The deciding factor should be based on whether the data in database tables is simply stored and updated as a form of record-keeping system, or whether that data is to be used to reconstruct an object model that does significant work in its own right.

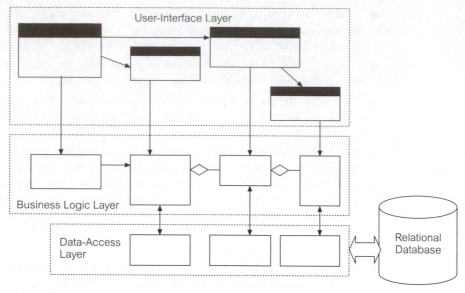

Figure 12.4 Three tiered application structure

12.3 Data Access in a Three-Tiered System

Since database design and development is a major undertaking that would at present get in the way of our real goal of developing Visual Basic .NET code to access databases, we will make use of one of Microsoft's existing database examples to describe a three-tiered approach to database applications programming. The Biblio example database has been provided with versions of Microsoft Access, Visual Studio and Visual Basic over several versions, the most recent being Biblio2002 (see Figure 12.5). This is a database containing related tables of Publishers, Authors and books (Titles), and includes one link table (Title Author) to take care of the many-to-many relationship between authors and books (one author can have written many books, one book can have many authors) as described earlier (see Figure 12.3).

If you have installed a version of MSDE then you will be able to access this database using the classes in the System.Data.SqlClient namespace. If not, you should have the Access equivalent database file (Biblio2002.mdb). Alternatively, almost any earlier version of the Biblio.mdb Access database should be adequate for the program examples here.

One useful thing to notice about Figure 12.5 is that although it was drawn to show the relationships between database tables in the Biblio database, it is in fact a UML class diagram and can be used to infer the class model of an application program for working with this database. When we come to writing code to manipulate the database later in this chapter, we will create a rationalized version of this model (there will be no need for a link table in the object-oriented world). Before that, we should have a look at a simpler situation where we can access the information in one of the tables.

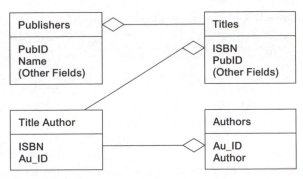

Figure 12.5 The structure of the Biblio (Biblio2002) database

12.3.1 Connections and Connection Strings

The first requirement to enable us to access a database from a .NET program is to establish a connection to it, for which we use a connection class. Version 1.0 of Visual Studio .NET provides two types of connection class: SqlConnection and OleDbConnection. The first is for use with Microsoft SQL server and MSDE database environments and provides a very efficient connection to either of these database servers. The second type is a generic database connection class that uses OleDb, which stands for Database Object Linking and Embedding. OleDb is an earlier database connection model used extensively in Visual Basic 6.0 programs to access database engines. Because the OleDb connection class must connect to a database using an additional layer of code running in a separate process, it is far less efficient than the direct access route that the SqlConnection class provides.

To create a connection, the Connection object must be given a *connection string*. The connection string is simply a piece of text that contains the database access details. For a SqlConnection, this includes the name of the server, the catalogue (database) to open, the security protocol by which the object is to be granted access, the name of the workstation from which the database program is running, etc. A connection string for an OleDbConnection will vary in format depending on the database server that it is to access. A connection to an Access database file can be quite simple compared to some of the server-based variants. A typical connection string (the one that connects to the example databases on my laptop PC) is shown broken into sections in Table 12.4. Note that the sections shown would be joined into a single string, with semicolon delimiters between sections.

Creating a connection string can be a complex business if you want to write it yourself, but fortunately Visual Studio gives us an easy way to generate one. Using the Server Explorer window (which normally inhabits the same location in the Visual Studio IDE as the Toolbox, on a separate tab) you can 'drill down' to a specific server and drag the required database element on to a form. This will create two components in the form's component tray: a Connection object and a Data Adapter object. You can then determine the connection string from the properties of the connection. Appendix 2 shows you how to create connections and

Table 12.4 A connection string deconstructed

Connection string section	Description
`data source=CIS-LAP2002;`	The name of the database server installation.
`initial catalog=Biblio2002SQL;`	The database to connect to.
`integrated security=SSPI;`	The data access security model used.
`persist security info=True;`	Whether a secured connection will work over multiple operations.
`workstation id=CIS-LAP21;`	The workstation used to access the server.
`packet size=4096`	The maximum number of bytes extracted per access.

connection strings for SQL Server and OleDB databases, and how to manipulate these in code.

Exercise 12.3

If you have an available database system installed on a PC, use the guidelines in Appendix 2 to create a connection string for it (you would need a separate connection string for each database, so select one). Once you have created a suitable connection string, copy it and paste it into Windows Notepad or some other text editor, and save it to a file on your PC (use a memorable name, such as `BiblioConnString.lnk`). Using the .lnk file-name extension will make it easier to make use of this connection string in database programs.

12.4 Reading and Writing Data

Having connected to a database, the next obvious requirement is to access the data. Reading data from a database is relatively simple and can be done using a number of different classes. Writing data back to a database generally involves a little more effort, and provides more scope for errors. We will look at how to read data first.

12.4.1 The `DataReader` Class

As you might expect, a class whose name includes the term `DataReader` is tailor-made for the purpose of reading information from a database. It is used in a situation where we want to examine the data of an entire table or a subset of this data but have no need to update it. The `DataReader` classes provide very fast read-only access to sets of data. There are presently: `SqlDataReader` (from the `Data.SqlClient` namespace) and `OleDbDataReader` (from the `Data.OleDb` namespace).

We use a `DataReader` object to extract information from a database, but in order to do so we must first establish a connection to the database (using either the `SqlConnection` class or the `OleDbConnection` class) and issue a command that says what data we want to access (using either the `SqlCommand` or the `OleDbCommand` class). One or other version of the code in Listing 12.1 can be called from the `Form_Load` event-handler for a form or anywhere we want to get read-only access to the contents of the "Titles" table of the Biblio database.

```
Private Sub ReadTitles()
    Dim dbConn As SqlClient.SqlConnection
    Dim dbCmd As SqlClient.SqlCommand
    Dim DataReader As SqlClient.SqlDataReader
    Dim SQLText As String = "Select * From Titles;"
    'The next line uses a connection string stored in
    'CONNSTR...
    dbConn = New SqlClient.SqlConnection(CONNSTR)
    dbCmd = New SqlClient.SqlCommand(SQLText, dbConn)
    dbConn.Open()
    DataReader = _
        dbCmd.ExecuteReader(CommandBehavior.CloseConnection)
    'We would now go on to display data from DataReader.
    'For example . . .
    With DataReader
        Do While .Read()
            Debug.WriteLine(String.Format("{0}, {1}, {2}", _
                .Item("Title"), _
                .Item("Year Published").ToString(), _
                .Item("ISBN")))
        Loop
    End With
End Sub

Private Sub ReadTitlesOleDb()
    'These are OleDb versions of the Connection,
    'Command and DataReader objects . . .
    Dim dbConn As OleDb.OleDbConnection
    Dim dbCmd As OleDb.OleDbCommand
    Dim DataReader As OleDb.OleDbDataReader
    Dim SQLText As String = "Select * From Titles"
    dbConn = New OleDb.OleDbConnection(CONNSTR)
    dbCmd = New OleDb.OleDbCommand(SQLText, dbConn)
    'From here, code is the same . . .
End Sub
```

Listing 12.1: Using a `DataReader` (2 versions for Sql and OleDb connections)

The code in Listing 12.1 looks imposing, but a step by step explanation should make its operation clear. We need a Connection object (`dbConn`) to form a connection to the database server (in the first sub, this will be either SQL Server or MSDE, since we are using the `SqlConnection` class, using the second sub, it would be an

Access database), and this is instantiated passing a connection string to it. We also need a Command object (dbCmd) to indicate what information we want the database to provide. The SqlCommand constructor used takes a string containing the SQL text that specifies what data to extract, and a Connection object that gives it access to the database server. The data to be extracted is specified in the SQL statement "Select * From Titles", which says 'Retrieve every row of complete records (*) from the "Titles" table'.

Having set up a connection and command, the connection is opened, and then a DataReader object is created by calling the command's ExecuteReader() method. This is set by the CommandBehavior.CloseConnection parameter to run so that once the data has been read the connection will automatically be closed. Alternatively, the connection could be left open so that you could issue other commands after this one (CommandBehavior.Default). Various other settings can be applied to ExecuteReader() to achieve different ends; see the on-line help for details.

The DataReader object will now provide access to rows of data from the "Titles" table. Each Read() operation makes the next row available as the Item() property and returns True until after the last item has been read, when a False result is returned. To access any column in the current row, we simply pass the column name into the Item() property.

In this example, the database information is simply printed in the Debug window, but with a very small amount of effort we can add the rows of data to a list box or, even better, to a ListView control. If we add a ListView control to the form and give it the name lvAuthors, we can display the entire table with the code in Listing 12.2.

```
'Clear out the current ListView stuff . . .
lvAuthors.Clear()
'Set it to show details in columns . . .
lvAuthors.View = View.Details
'Add and configure three columns: we need to specify a Title,
'Width and Alignment for each column . . .
lvAuthors.Columns.Add("Au_ID", 60, HorizontalAlignment.Right)
lvAuthors.Columns.Add("Author Name", 150, _
                                    HorizontalAlignment.Left)
lvAuthors.Columns.Add("Year Born", 80, _
                                    HorizontalAlignment.Right)
'Now read the data and add it to the ListView . . .
With DataReader
    Dim lvItem As ListViewItem
    Do While.Read()
        lvItem = New ListViewItem(.Item("Title"))
        lvItem.SubItems.Add(.Item("Year
                                    Published").ToString())
        lvItem.SubItems.Add(.Item("ISBN"))
        lvAuthors.Items.Add(lvItem)
    Loop
End With
```

Listing 12.2: Displaying retrieved data in a ListView control

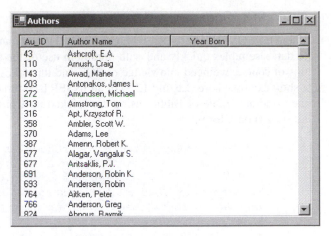

Figure 12.6 The result of the code in Listing 12.2

This code results in a table-style view of the entire contents of the "Authors" table (see Figure 12.6), including a scroll bar for access to items far down the list. One useful feature of this is that if a row of the `ListView` is selected by clicking on it with the mouse cursor, the `SelectedItems()` property will include it (`SelectedItems()` is a collection property). If a single row is selected, `SelectedItems(0).Text` will return the value in the left-hand column, which for the view shown is the primary key column of the table. This will be useful when dealing with related tables (for example, if we wished to add a new item to a table related to this one).

Exercise 12.4

a) Create a sub to display every title in the Biblio database using a `DataReader` object

b) Amend the sub so that it saves the list of titles to a text file using a `StreamWriter` object

c) Amend the sub to add the list of titles to a `ListView` control.

12.4.2 Gaining read-write access to data

The `DataReader` control does not allow changes to be made to data. Its purpose is to collect a set of data as rapidly as possible and return it to a program. As soon as you want to apply changes to the data, you are left with a choice: whether to work in SQL directly or to use a `DataSet`. The `DataSet` class allows you to extract an entire set of data from multiple tables, specify relationships between the data in the tables, add new rows, delete rows or edit the existing data, and then write all of the changes back to the database. As you might expect, a `DataSet` object is complex, can contain large amounts of interrelated data and involves quite a bit of programming effort. Before we go on to examine the `DataSet` class, we'll have a look at some much simpler ways of changing the content of a database.

12.4.2.1 Using SQL Commands directly

Using the SQL INSERT, DELETE and UPDATE commands, we can make changes to database tables quickly and with minimum use of the system's resources. To do this of course, we need knowledge of SQL and this takes time to develop. I'll give a short example here (Listing 12.3) of an INSERT command to add a new record to the "Authors" table of Biblio, using data picked up from text boxes (txtAuthor, txtBorn) on a form.

```
Private Sub btnAdd_Click(ByVal sender As System.Object, _
                         ByVal e As System.EventArgs) _
                         Handles btnAdd.Click
    If txtAuthor.Text = "" Or txtBorn.Text = "" Then
     MessageBox.Show("Need to enter name and year of birth.")
    Else
        'First define the command text...
        Dim Sql As String = _
            "INSERT INTO Authors(Author, [Year Born])" & _
            "VALUES (@Author, @Year);"
        'Declare and create Connection...
        Dim dbConn As OleDb.OleDbConnection
        dbConn = New OleDb.OleDbConnection(CONNSTR)
        'Declare and create Command object...
        Dim dbCmd As New OleDb.OleDbCommand(Sql, dbConn)
        'We need to add a parameter for each value inserted.

        'The Author's name...
        dbCmd.Parameters.Add("Author", txtAuthor.Text)
        '... and year of birth...
        dbCmd.Parameters.Add("[Year Born]", _
                             CType(txtBorn.Text, Integer))
        'Open the connection and execute the command...
        dbConn.Open()
        dbCmd.ExecuteNonQuery()
        'Refresh the ListView so we can see if the insertion
        'has worked...
        UpdateView()
    End If
End Sub
```

Listing 12.3: Inserting a record into a table

As you can see, inserting a new record can be quite involved. However, the programmer has more control over the process, and it represents the most efficient way of adding data to a database. You may be wondering why only two of the fields of the "Authors" table have been given values (Figure 12.6 shows it has three fields). The reason for this is that the Au_ID field of the "Authors" table in Biblio has been designated as an Identity field (in Access, it is called an AutoNumber field). With this type of field, each new row added gets the next number in the sequence automatically. This guarantees that each row of a table will have a different value in this field, and so it is suitable to use as a primary key field. The results can be

Figure 12.7 After adding a new record to the "Authors" table

seen in Figure 12.7, where I've added my own details to the table (well, I'm writing this book!).

12.4.2.2 SQL Commands and Parameters

Using SQL commands (passed to the database using a Command object) is the most direct and efficient way of updating a database. However, it can take a lot of coding to build the appropriate commands and populate them with data. In particular, setting up the parameters for a command, as in the code segment in Listing 12.4, can be tedious and therefore error-prone.

```
'These statements create the basic SQL command...
Dim Sql As String = _
            "INSERT INTO Authors(Author, [Year Born])" & _
            "VALUES (@Author, @Year);"
Dim dbCmd As New OleDb.OleDbCommand(Sql, dbConn)
'But we still need to add a parameter for each value
'inserted...
'The Author's name...
   dbCmd.Parameters.Add("Author", txtAuthor.Text)
'... and year of birth...
   dbCmd.Parameters.Add("[Year Born]", _
                            CType(txtBorn.Text, Integer))
```

Listing 12.4: Code to insert parameters into a command

The block of code in Listing 12.4 is an extract from Listing 12.3, and is required because of the use of place markers (@Author, @Year) in the SQL command for the data we wish to insert. If we entered the SQL directly into a command line for a database server, and wished to add the same data, the command would be simply:

```
INSERT INTO Authors(Author, [Year Born])
              VALUES('McMonnies', 1955)
```

An alternative method to do this in Visual Basic code would be to build the command string above by joining the contents of the text boxes to the basic command. We could define a function to return the result of joining all of the necessary fragments of text together. Within the function, the String.Format() method would be ideal for doing the job of concatenating the parameter values and punctuation required.

12.4.2.3 Coding SQL Parameters

```
Private Function AddCommand(ByVal Name As String, _
                        ByVal YearBorn As Integer) As String
    Dim SQL As String
    SQL = "Insert Into Authors(Name, [Year Born]) "
    SQL &= String.Format("Values('{0}', {1})", _
                            Name, YearBorn.ToString)
    Return SQL
End Function
```

Listing 12.5: Generating a SQL string to insert data

In Listing 12.5, note how the Name parameter was enclosed in single quotes (string delimiters in SQL). Generally, we need to exercise care in this type of code to make sure that all the necessary opening and closing marks are put in the right place. There is no such requirement for the integer value YearBorn. We could now use this to create a much less complex sub for inserting data from text boxes into the table (see Listing 12.6).

```
Private Sub btnAdd_Click(ByVal sender As System.Object, _
                    ByVal e As System.EventArgs) _
                    Handles btnAdd.Click
    If txtAuthor.Text = "" Or txtBorn.Text = "" Then
        MessageBox.Show("Need to enter name and year of birth.")
    Else
        Dim Sql As String = AddCommand(txtAuthor.Text, _
                                txtBorn.Text)
        Dim dbConn As OleDb.OleDbConnection
        dbConn = New OleDb.OleDbConnection(CONNSTR)
        Dim dbCmd As New OleDb.OleDbCommand(Sql, dbConn)
        dbConn.Open()
        dbCmd.ExecuteNonQuery()
        UpdateView()
    End If
End Sub
```

Listing 12.6: Using the generated SQL text (see Listing 12.5)

Other types of SQL commands (SELECT, DELETE, UPDATE) can be built and deployed using the same techniques. However, if we are coding a large and complex database with many tables, the use of these techniques can require you to write a great deal of program code. The `DataSet` class contains a few tricks that can simplify much of this.

Exercise 12.5

The SQL DELETE command uses a `Where` clause to indicate the record(s) to delete. Normally this would use the primary key as an identifier, and a typical SQL delete would be of the form: `"DELETE * FROM SomeTable WHERE PrimaryKey=1234"`. Write a sub that will execute the SQL DELETE command on an author, given the author's primary key value was available in the parameter `AuID` (a `Long` integer).

12.4.3 Using a `DataSet`

The `DataSet` class allows multiple tables of related data to be manipulated simultaneously. It does this by providing two internal collections, `Tables` and `Relations`, which are used to hold individual tables of data and relationships between them. Microsoft describes the `DataSet` class as a class for managing an in-memory cache of data.

Working with a `DataSet` usually involves three steps.

1. a `DataSet` is created, filled with tables from `DataAdapters` that are connected to the database, and has `Relations` defined to indicate how the tables are linked. It then disconnects from the database.

2. The user views, adds to, deletes from and edits the data in the `DataSet`. During this stage, the `DataSet` can be persisted to XML and reloaded without reference to the actual database so that there can be breaks in working on it.

3. `DataAdapters` connected to the database are updated, using the altered tables in the `DataSet`, and this passes any updates back to the database.

For example, using the Biblio database, we could create a `DataSet` object and populate it with each of the four tables (Publishers, Authors, Titles and [Title Author]) and four relation objects to describe the links between them (Publishers to Titles, Publishers to Authors, Titles to [Title Author] and Authors to [Title Author] – the last two of these form the many-to-many link between Authors and Titles). Having done so of course, we would have a `DataSet` object that contained all of the data for an entire database, which is not a very desirable thing (remember we are using a database to save having to store an entire object model in memory at one time).

Much more useful would be to load smaller subsets of data from the database for off-line working; a table containing a single Publisher row and another containing all of the Titles published by that publisher, or a table containing all of the Titles published in 2002 and another containing only the Publishers of these titles. SQL is easily capable of extracting subsets of database tables like these and so we can create a `DataAdapter` to bring these into our `DataSet`.

12.4.3.1 Filling a `DataSet`

`DataAdapter` objects are used to quickly connect to a database, fill a `DataSet` with data from the database and then disconnect from the database. For example, assume we needed to display all of the Publishers listed in Biblio, and for each publisher, a list of Titles they have published. The `GetDataSet()` function in Listing 12.7 builds and returns a Publishers/Titles `DataSet`.

```
Private CONNSTR = "..."     'Code omitted - see Appendix 2.
Private dbConn As SqlClient.SqlConnection
Private ds As DataSet
Private daTitles As SqlDataAdapter
Private daPublishers As SqlDataAdapter
Private pubMover As CurrencyManager

Private Function GetDataSet() As DataSet
    Dim sqlPub As String = _
                "Select Name, PubID From Publishers"
    Dim sqlTitles As String = _
                "Select Title, ISBN, PubID From Titles"
    'Create the connection and adapters...
    dbConn = New SqlClient.SqlConnection(CONNSTR)
    daPublishers = New SqlDataAdapter(sqlPub, dbConn)
    daTitles = New SqlDataAdapter(sqlTitles, dbConn)
    'Create a new datset...
    Dim ds As DataSet = New DataSet()
    'Fill the dataset with tables...
    daPublishers.Fill(ds, "Publishers")
    daTitles.Fill(ds, "Titles")
    'Now configure the dataset's relationships...
    Dim dcPublishers, dcTitles As DataColumn
    Dim dr As DataRelation
    dcPublishers = ds.Tables("Publishers").Columns("PubID")
    dcTitles = ds.Tables("Titles").Columns("PubID")
    dr = New Data.DataRelation("PubsTitles", _
                            dcPublishers, dcTitles)
    ds.Relations.Add(dr)
    Return ds
End Function
```

Listing 12.7: Filling a `DataSet` with data, using `DataAdapters`

In Listing 12.7, we necessarily use a lot of objects to build our `DataSet`. The first requirement is simply to extract the necessary data from the database, for which we make use of a connection and two `DataAdapter` objects. A `DataAdapter` object is used whenever we wish to get data from a database into a `DataSet`, or send updates from a `DataSet` back to the database.

Each `DataAdapter` is constructed from a SQL query string that describes the data we want and the connection, which says where it comes from. Note that instead of grabbing the entire table, the SQL queries in this example specify only the columns that are required. As a result, the queries will execute and return data much more quickly, and will not return any data that would take up space but go unused. The `DataAdapter.Fill()` method does the job of extracting the data as a table and adding it to the `DataSet`'s `Tables` collection.

The data retrieved, we now go on to tell the `DataSet` how the two tables are related. The Publishers table has a column, 'PubID', which acts as its primary key. The Titles table also has a 'PubID' column, which is the foreign key that indicates which item in the Publishers table describes the book's publisher. To build the relationship, we need to identify these columns:

```
Dim dcPublishers, dcTitles As DataColumn
dcPublishers = ds.Tables("Publishers").Columns("PubID")
dcTitles = ds.Tables("Titles").Columns("PubID")
```

and then create a `DataRelation` object, giving it a name (`"PubsTitles"`) and indicating the column in the master table (Publishers) and the related one in the detail table (Titles):

```
Dim dr As DataRelation
dr = New Data.DataRelation("PubsTitles", _
                            dcPublishers, dcTitles)
```

Finally, the `DataRelation` is added to the `DataSet`'s `Relations` collection:

```
ds.Relations.Add(dr)
```

Now our `DataSet` contains two tables of data and an object that indicates how they are related, as shown in Figure 12.8.

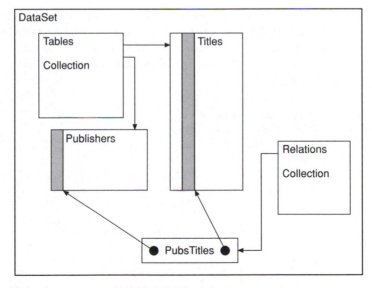

Figure 12.8 A `DataSet` with tables and a relation

Having built our `DataSet`, we can manipulate the information in it directly. This has a major advantage in that making changes to the `DataSet` does not involve the database which is currently disconnected from the program (note that there is no `dbConn.Open()` statement in Listing 12.7. The `DataAdapter.Fill()` calls opened the connection to get the data and then closed it again). We can add records to tables, delete records from tables and edit records to update their content. Any changes made can be sent to the database via the data adapter by calling its `Update()` method, provided an appropriate command to perform the operation has been defined for it.

12.4.3.2 `DataSet` Flexibility

Using a `DataSet` is complex because it is much more than a simple embodiment of data tables. During much of the time a `DataSet` is in use, it is disconnected from the database. This can have huge advantages in performance (no constant traffic of data to and from a server across a network), convenience (having filled a `DataSet` with the required subset of a database from whatever source, the data can be viewed, edited, added to and deleted from entirely in the memory of a PC before being written back to the database in a single operation) and flexibility (a `DataSet` can be saved as a XML document in local storage on a laptop, so that it can be worked on over a period when the laptop is unable to access the server).

This flexibility is why setting up a `DataSet` is such a complex business. With no on-line database to work with, all of the information in the `DataSet` has to be organized to mimic its structure (or at least the structure of the part of the database that is currently in the `DataSet`).

12.4.3.3 Viewing data from a `DataSet`

A `DataSet` that contains one table is no more difficult to deal with than the data returned from a `DataReader`. We can easily extract a table from a `DataSet` to display in a `ListView` control as we did with the `DataReader`. For example, using the `DataSet` created in Listing 12.7, we can populate a `ListView`, `lvPubs`, as shown in Listing 12.8.

```
Dim r As DataRow
Dim item As ListViewItem
lvPubs.Clear()
lvPubs.View = View.Details
lvPubs.Columns.Add("Name", 160, HorizontalAlignment.Left)
lvPubs.Columns.Add("PubID", 50, HorizontalAlignment.Left)
For Each r In dsBiblio.Tables("Publishers").Rows
    item = New ListViewItem(r.Item("Name").ToString())
    item.SubItems.Add(r.Item("PubID").ToString())
    lvPubs.Items.Add(item)
Next
```

Listing 12.8: Displaying a table from a `DataSet` in a `ListView` control

If, however, we wish to display related data from a `DataSet`, we will need to make use of more flexible controls or combinations of controls. The `TreeView` control is ideal, since we can use it to show up a master-detail structure (for example, Publishers and each Title published by them). The code in Listing 12.9 fills up the `TreeView` control `tvPublishers`.

```
Private Sub FillTree(ByVal d As DataSet)
    Dim pRow, tRow As DataRow
    Dim Publisher, Title As String
    Dim PubID As Integer
    Dim n As TreeNode
    tvPublishers.BeginUpdate()
    tvPublishers.Nodes.Clear()
    Try
        For Each pRow In d.Tables("Publishers").Rows
            Publisher = pRow.Item("Name").ToString()
            PubID = CType(pRow.Item("PubID"), Integer)
            n = New TreeNode(Publisher)
            n.Tag = PubID
            For Each tRow _
                In pRow.GetChildRows _
                            (d.Relations ("PubsTitles"))
                n.Nodes.Add(tRow.Item("Title").ToString())
            Next
            tvPublishers.Nodes.Add(n)
        Next
    Finally
        tvPublishers.EndUpdate()
    End Try
End Sub
```

Listing 12.9: Displaying master-detail information from a `DataSet`

The outer loop in the listing (`For Each pRow In d.Tables("Publishers") .Rows`) is similar to any loop you would use to iterate through the rows of any `DataTable`. We use this to pick up Publisher information (`"Name"` and `"PubID"`) and insert it into `TreeNode` objects instead of `ListViewItem` objects. A `TreeNode` is a line in a `TreeView` control that has its own collection of `TreeNodes` (each of which in turn can have its own collection of `TreeNodes` and so on). Note the way data has been added to the `TreeNode` for each publisher:

```
Publisher = pRow.Item("Name").ToString()
PubID = CType(pRow.Item("PubID"), Integer)
n = New TreeNode(Publisher)
n.Tag = PubID
```

Having created a new `TreeNode`, using the text we want it to display as a parameter to its constructor, we can use the `Tag` property to store another, related object. We can use this property to store the primary key of the publisher row (`"PubID"`), which will be useful if we need to add another title to this publisher's node.

Each Publisher row in the Publishers table (pRow) has associated with it a number of rows from the Titles table. This is as a result of adding the relation to the `DataSet` that indicated how the two tables were linked. To populate each Publisher's node in the `TreeView` with sub-nodes (one for each of the Titles published), the inner loop makes use of the publisher `DataRow`'s `GetChildRows()` property. This returns a collection of rows related to the publisher, and we can iterate through these in a second, inner loop:

```
For Each tRow In pRow.GetChildRows(d.Relations("PubsTitles"))
    n.Nodes.Add(tRow.Item("Title").ToString())
Next
```

The variable n is the `TreeNode` that holds the publisher information, so we add to its own `Nodes` collection a node that contains the title published. Finally, this node is inserted into the `TreeView` control (`tvPublishers.Nodes.Add(n)`) before looping back to deal with the next publisher and its titles. Note that all of the code that adds information to the `TreeView` control is bracketed between calls to the `TreeView`'s `BeginUpdate()` and `EndUpdate()` methods. This suppresses screen updating while the data is being added, since otherwise, the face of the `TreeView` would be redrawn at each addition of a node, which would be grossly inefficient. Note also the use of a `Try..Finally` block to make sure that whatever happens, the `TreeView` control is eventually updated on the screen. The result of all of this code is a `TreeView` control that contains a list of publishers, each of which has a list of Titles (see Figure 12.9).

Note that the form shown in the figure contains a group of controls for adding a new Title to the `DataSet`. The operation to insert a new record or row into a `DataSet` is described next.

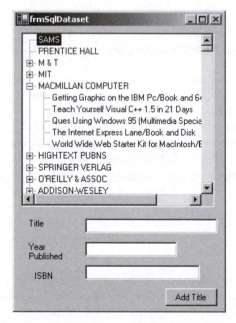

Figure 12.9 The `TreeView` of Publishers and Titles built by Listing 12.9

12.4.3.4 Binding data to controls

The `TreeView` built in Listing 12.9 allows us to display an entire `DataSet`, but has no direct connection to the actual tables and rows in the `DataSet`. To gain more direct access to the data in a `DataSet`, we can *bind* the information from the tables to individual controls. For example, by binding the Name column of the Publishers table in the `DataSet` to the Text property of a text box, `txtPublisher`, we can use the statement:

```
txtPublisher.DataBindings.Add( _
              New Binding("Text", ds, "Publishers.Name"))
```

The `Binding` object added to the `txtPublisher` control's `DataBindings` collection is constructed using the name of the host control's property that is to display the data (`"Text"`), the data source to be used (the `DataSet ds` in this case) and the data member to be displayed (using a string `"TableName.ColumnName"`). We can bind several controls to various columns in the `DataSet`'s tables to provide a view of whole or partial records (rows) in the set. As a result, information in a row/column will be displayed in the control and if the control is editable (e.g. a `TextBox`), changes made will be reflected in the `DataSet`.

12.4.3.5 Navigating and the (oddly named) `CurrencyManager`

Of course, columns bound to controls like this can only display the value in one record at a time, so to make the bound controls usable we need to provide some way of moving from record to record (row to row). For this we need to make use of the bizarrely named class, `CurrencyManager`. I'll freely admit here that when I first encountered this class, I assumed it was something to do with monetary values: perhaps some smart foreign currency exchange calculator or interest evaluator. In fact, the `CurrencyManager` class is used to select and indicate the 'current' record or row of a table in a data source (hence its name). Fortunately, it is very easy to set up and use.

We need to declare a `CurrencyManager` reference variable for use throughout a form, create the `CurrencyManager` configuring it for the correct data source and table, and then provide event-handlers (usually button `.Click()` events) to move to the first, last, next and previous positions in a table. Associating the `CurrencyManager` with the data source and table requires the use of the form's `BindingContext` property, which will return a `CurrencyManager` object given the name of the data source and table to be navigated. This is shown in Listing 12.10.

```
'Declare a navigation manager for access within this form...
Private pubMover As CurrencyManager
Private Sub LoadDataSet()
    'Code to load up a dataset (ds)...
    '...
    'Create and set up the navigation object...
    pubMover = Me.BindingContext(ds, "Publishers")
End Sub
```

```
'Four navigation buttons...
Private Sub btnFirst_Click(ByVal sender As System.Object, _
                          ByVal e As System.EventArgs) _
                          Handles btnFirst.Click
    pubMover.Position = 0
End Sub

Private Sub btnLast_Click(ByVal sender As System.Object, _
                          ByVal e As System.EventArgs) _
                          Handles btnLast.Click
    pubMover.Position = pubMover.Count - 1
End Sub

Private Sub btnPrev_Click(ByVal sender As System.Object, _
                          ByVal e As System.EventArgs) _
                          Handles btnPrev.Click
    pubMover.Position -= 1
End Sub

Private Sub btnNext_Click(ByVal sender As System.Object, _
                          ByVal e As System.EventArgs) _
                          Handles btnNext.Click
    pubMover.Position += 1
End Sub
```

Listing 12.10: Setting up navigation with a `CurrencyManager`

12.4.3.6 Viewing the master-detail relationship

Given the ability to bind data from a table in a `DataSet` to one or more controls and to navigate through rows in the table, there is one further requirement that we need to deal with for viewing this `DataSet`. Navigating from publisher to publisher will be more effective and useful if we can view the titles published by each publisher we navigate to. We have already seen code to display a collection of rows in a `ListView` control. Now we simply need to provide this facility for the set of child rows owned by each Publisher row (Listing 12.11).

```
Private Sub DisplayTitles()
    Dim pubRow As DataRow
    Dim pubView As DataRowView 'As returned by a
                               'CurrencyManager
    pubView = pubMover.Current 'Currently visible item
    pubRow = pubView.Row       'The associated row
    lvTitles.Clear()
    lvTitles.View = View.Details
    lvTitles.Columns.Add("ISBN", 80, HorizontalAlignment.Left)
    lvTitles.Columns.Add("Title", 250,
                                  HorizontalAlignment.Left)
    Dim tiRow As DataRow
    Dim item As ListViewItem
    For Each tiRow _
        In pubRow.GetChildRows(ds.Relations("PubsTitles"))
```

```
            item = New ListViewItem(tiRow.Item("ISBN").ToString())
            item.Tag = tiRow    'Useful for updates.
            item.SubItems.Add(tiRow.Item("Title").ToString())
            lvTitles.Items.Add(item)
    Next
End Sub
```

Listing 12.11: Displaying the (detail) Title records associated with a (master) Publisher

Note that the `Tag` property of each `ListViewItem` is set to refer back to the `DataRow` that populated it. The `Tag` property is very useful for stashing a piece of information that might be of use later, and in this case is ideal for keeping a reference to a `DataRow` that we might want to refer to later. Now, whenever we change the `CurrencyManager`'s `Position` property, we simply call `DisplayTitles()` to update the associated titles in a `ListView`, as shown in Figure 12.10.

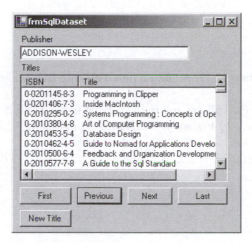

Figure 12.10   A master-detail view

12.4.3.7   Inserting new data into a `DataSet`

Adding a row to a table in a `DataSet` is a three step process.

1. Call the `DataTable`'s `NewRow()` method. You can access the `DataTable` as a component of the `DataSet` (`DataSet.Tables(TableName)`) or assign a table to a `DataTable` reference variable and use it.

2. Assign the various values to the `Item()` properties of the `DataTable`. `Item(ColumnName)` references a specific column.

3. Call the `DataTable`'s `Rows.Add()` method.

The danger here is in step 2, since it is necessary to make sure that the data assigned is of the correct type for the column it is added to. Data picked up from text boxes, list boxes or most of the WinForms controls is likely to be in the form of a `String`, so it is usually necessary to use the `CType()` function to convert this to an appropriate type.

For example, to add a new Title to the Publishers/Titles `DataSet`, we will need to add values for the Title, ISBN and PubID columns. Title and ISBN will be supplied by a user (the details of the new book entry), while PubID would be the currently displayed publisher (in the form shown in Figure 12.10). It is sensible to do the update in a sub (see Listing 12.12).

```
Private Sub AddTitle(ByVal Title As String, _
                     ByVal ISBN As String, _
                     ByVal PubID As Integer)
    'Insert this data into the Titles table...
    Dim tbl As DataTable, newRow As DataRow
    tbl = ds.Tables("Titles")
    newRow = tbl.NewRow()
    newRow.Item("Title") = Title
    newRow.Item("ISBN") = ISBN
    newRow.Item("PubID") = PubID
    tbl.Rows.Add(newRow)
End Sub
```

Listing 12.12: Adding a new Title into the `DataSet`

We can call this sub from an event-handler (e.g. for the New Title button shown in Figure 12.10), and this is illustrated in Listing 12.13.

```
Private Sub btnNewTitle_Click(ByVal sender As
                                        System.Object, _
                        ByVal e As System.EventArgs) _
                        Handles btnNewTitle.Click
    Dim pubRow As DataRow
    Dim pubView As DataRowView
    Dim pubID As Integer
    'First identify the correct publisher ID
    '(from the CurrencyManager's current record)...
    pubView = pubMover.Current
    pubRow = pubView.Row()
    pubID = CType(pubRow.Item("PubID"), Integer)
    'Now get the remaining data...
    Dim t As String, isbn As String
    t = InputBox("Enter the new title:")
    isbn = InputBox("Enter the new title's ISBN number")
    Try
        AddTitle(t, isbn, pubID)
        DisplayTitles()
    Catch ex As Exception
        MessageBox.Show(ex.Message)
    End Try
End Sub
```

Listing 12.13: Calling the `AddTitle` sub and updating the display

This listing contains rudimentary exception-handling so that we are informed if the insertion to the table has gone wrong in any way. Note that while Title and ISBN are collected using `InputBox()` calls here, we would normally use a custom form or additional controls on the form containing the data-bound controls. PubID is collected as previously by retrieving it from the `CurrencyManager`'s current row's `Item()` collection. Care is necessary in that it has to be cast to an Integer since the data values in the `Item()` collection can be of any type.

12.4.3.8 Deletions and edits

Deleting a row from a table in a `DataSet`, or changing some of the details in one are both simpler operations than adding a new one. To delete a row in a `DataSet`, we simply need to get a reference to it and call its `Delete()` method. If you refer back to Listing 12.13, you will see that the code to fill the `TreeView` with Title data included a line to store a reference to each title in the `ListViewItem`'s Tag property. We can use this to enable a delete or an edit. For example, the code in Listing 12.14 will delete all titles selected in the `ListView` control.

```
Private Sub btnDelete_Click(ByVal sender As System.Object, _
                            ByVal e As System.EventArgs) _
                    Handles btnDelete.Click
    Dim item As ListViewItem
    For Each item In lvTitles.SelectedItems
        Dim tiRow As DataRow
        tiRow = CType(item.Tag, DataRow)
        tiRow.Delete()
    Next
End Sub
```

Listing 12.14: Deleting titles selected in the `ListView`

Note the necessary cast of the selected item's Tag property to a `DataRow`; without this, the call to `Delete()` would cause an error. Listing 12.15 shown how to edit a title.

```
Private Sub btnEdit_Click(ByVal sender As System.Object, _
                          ByVal e As System.EventArgs) _
                  Handles btnEdit.Click
    If lvTitles.SelectedItems.Count = 0 Then
      MessageBox.Show("You need to select a Title to edit")
    ElseIf lvTitles.SelectedItems.Count > 1 Then
      MessageBox.Show("You can only edit a single title.")
    Else
        Dim tiRow As DataRow
        tiRow = CType(lvTitles.SelectedItems(0).Tag, DataRow)
        tiRow.Item("Title") = InputBox("Enter new title:", _
              "Edit Title", tiRow.Item("Title").ToString())
        'Could edit other items but this would mess with
        'data integrity
    End If
End Sub
```

Listing 12.15: Editing a title

Note that in the listing we are allowing a single selected title to be edited. It would probably not be wise to edit multiple selections, and if no item was selected there would be nothing to edit. Again we rely on casting to retrieve the appropriate `DataRow` and in this example only the Title column is being offered to be edited. The `InputBox()` call here sets the default to be the existing title, since with this a simple spelling mistake could be edited without typing the entire title again. The only other columns in the Titles data table are the ISBN and the PubID, both of which relate to other tables, so it would generally be considered very wrong to allow a user to change these.

12.4.3.9 Committing changes to the database

Although we can insert new rows into the `DataSet`, delete rows and edit the values in existing rows, there is currently no provision for reflecting these changes back to the database. What we are doing is modifying the in-memory dataset, and to make the changes permanent, we will have to provide the code to enable the `DataAdapters` for Titles and Publishers to write these changes back. `DataAdapters` do not come pre-configured with the ability to do this for a number of reasons. We might not need to pass changes back to the database at all since we may be using a dataset purely as a way of viewing complex information while we are disconnected from the database. We might only be interested in editing existing records, or deleting records from the set, in which case the additional code to add new records is unnecessary. Finally, the database updates could be much more complex than simply adding new records to a table. In many database systems, an insertion operation must insert records into more than one table, perhaps to perform some form of security or cross-referencing, or perhaps because the tables we have in memory in the `DataSet` are an amalgam of two or more tables in the real `DataSet`.

For all of these reasons, `DataAdapters` do not come fully equipped with facilities for sending changes back to a database, but we can add these easily, using a `CommandBuilder` object. We can add simple commands to INSERT new records, DELETE existing records and UPDATE any changes to records individually, so that the `DataAdapter` contains only the required facilities. The best time to do this is when the `DataAdapter` object is first created (i.e. within the code in Listing 12.16):

```
'Create and configure a DataAdapter...
daTitles = New SqlDataAdapter(sqlTitles, dbConn)
'Create a CommandBuilder for configuring this...
Dim cmdBuilder As New SqlCommandBuilder(daTitles)
'And add only the required commands - these are new lines.
'Add an Insert command...
daTitles.InsertCommand = cmdBuilder.GetInsertCommand()
'And a Delete command...
daTitles.DeleteCommand = cmdBuilder.GetDeleteCommand()
'And an Update command...
daTitles.UpdateCommand = cmdBuilder.GetUpdateCommand()
```

Listing 12.16: Adding database update commands to a `DataAdapter`

If we had any complex requirements for sending data back to the database, we would not use the `CommandBuilder` but would instead develop Command objects incorporating SQL command strings to deal with them. For insertions to a single data table, this is not necessary.

With fully equipped `DataAdapter` objects, we could now easily send changes to the `DataSet` back to the database either on demand (at the press of a button or click of a menu item), or when the form closes or even when the application terminates, using the code in Listing 12.17.

```
Private Sub frmSqlDataset_Closing(ByVal sender As Object, _
        ByVal e As System.ComponentModel.CancelEventArgs) _
        Handles MyBase.Closing
    Dim dsChanges As DataSet
    dsChanges = ds.GetChanges()
    If Not dsChanges Is Nothing Then
        Try 'data update
            daTitles.Update(dsChanges, "Titles")
        Catch ex As Exception
            MessageBox.Show(ex.Message)
        End Try
    End If
End Sub
```

Listing 12.17: Committing changes in the `DataSet` (Titles table only) to the database

Listing 12.17 is the `Closing()` event of the form that contains the `DataSet` and related declarations, this being a good place to perform database updates. We first check whether there have been any changes to the database, since otherwise we would be performing an unnecessary connection to the database (managed automatically by the `daTitles DataAdapter. GetChanges()` will return a new `DataSet` from an existing one, containing only indications of alterations to the original `DataSet`. If there are none, `GetChanges()` will return nothing and we can use this to decide whether we need to issue an update at all. The `Try..Catch..End Try` block will simply inform us if the update operation did not work, which could be for various reasons such as the database server being off-line.

Exercise 12.6

a) Create a form for displaying Author details from the Biblio database. In this, use a `DataSet` to create an internal data model containing the Authors table and the [Title Author] table.

b) Use a `CurrencyManager` to allow backwards and forwards movement through the Author details.

c) Add code to display the ISBNs of each title written by an author in a list box.

12.5 Data Object Modelling

In all the code examples so far, we have been using the `DataSet` class as a pre-built object model. In fact most database applications will use this strategy, since data storage, retrieval and simple editing are the bread and butter operations of the vast majority of database programming. However, if we want to build an object-oriented application in which a database is used for persistence of a more functional object model, we necessarily will have more work to do. The object model we create will be the business layer, and ideally we would build it so that persistence was automatic and did not need to be considered from the presentation layer.

Of course an application of this type can become very complex if we consider high degrees of interconnection and object interactions. Each interaction with an object could change its state, and the change in state would need to be reflected back to the database.

We could use any number of strategies for doing this, but two obvious ones are:

1. make each individual class responsible for the retrieval of object member data from and update of object member data to the database;
2. retrieve objects from and return objects to a `DataSet`.

The first strategy has the advantage of being simple and direct and, working on an object-by-object basis, retrieving only the required data from the database and sending it back again. However, it may be inefficient, requiring many 'round-trips' to the database to fetch individual objects. The second has all the advantages of `DataSets`; disconnected operation and persistence to XML while the database is unavailable, in-memory editing and built-in relationships. Also, a `DataSet` can be created that holds the member data values for many objects using a minimum number of database accesses.

As an example of the first type, assume you needed to be able to work with individual `Book` objects, where the `Book` class retrieved the associated object from the database as required and updated changes to the database when required. The `Book` class ought to contain relationships with members of an `Authors` class and a `Publishers` class to persist the database model fully, but that can be managed by storing only primary keys for these items. Listing 12.18 is a simplified `Book` class where I've missed out much of the detail data.

```
Public Class Book
    Private mvarTitle As String
    Private mvarYearPublished As Integer
    Private mvarISBN As String
    Private mvarPubID As Integer
    Private mvarAuthors As ArrayList
    Private mvarChanged As Boolean = False
    Private mvarBrandNew As Boolean = False

    'Properties for Title, YearPublished, ISBN (read-only)
    'PubID and the Authors collection go here...
```

```
'This is a 'nearly new' book - retrieved from the database...
Public Sub New(ByVal ISBN As String)
    mvarAuthors = New ArrayList()
    Dim r As SqlClient.SqlDataReader
    r = GetReader("Select * From Titles Where ISBN = '" _
                  & ISBN & "';")
    r.Read()
    mvarTitle = r.Item("Title")
    mvarYearPublished = r.Item("Year Published")
    mvarPubID = r.Item("PubID")
    r = GetReader( _
            "Select * From [Title Author] Where ISBN = '" _
            & ISBN & "';")
    Do While r.Read()
            AddAuthor(r.Item("Au_ID"))
    Loop
    mvarChanged = True
    mvarBrandNew = False
End Sub

'This is a 'brand new' book - not yet in the database...
Public Sub New(ByVal ISBN As String, ByVal Title As String, _
               ByVal YearPublished As Integer, _
               ByVal PubID As Integer)
    mvarAuthors = New ArrayList()
    mvarISBN = ISBN
    mvarTitle = Title
    mvarYearPublished = YearPublished
    mvarPubID = PubID
    mvarChanged = True
    mvarBrandNew = True
End Sub

'As it is an Authors collection, need to be able to add
'multiples...
Public Sub AddAuthor(ByVal Au_ID As Integer)
    mvarAuthors.Add(Au_ID)
    mvarChanged = True
End Sub

'Call this sub when the object is no longer needed...
Public Sub UpdateDatabase()
    Dim updSQL As String
    If mvarBrandNew Then
        'Add a new database record . . .
        updSQL = String.Format( _
                "Insert Into Titles(Title, " & _
                "[Year Published], ISBN, PubID) " & _
                "Values('{0}', {1}, '{2}', {3})", _
                 mvarTitle, mvarYearPublished, _
                mvarISBN, mvarPubID)
```

```
            If CType(ExecuteCommand(updSQL), Integer) = 0 Then
                MessageBox.Show("Insert Title did not work.")
            End If
            Dim A As Integer
            For Each A In mvarAuthors
            updSQL = String.Format( _
                    "Insert Into [Title Author] " & _
                    "(ISBN, Au_ID) " & _
                    "Values('{0}', {1})", ISBN, A)
                If CType(ExecuteCommand(updSQL), Integer) _
                                                    = 0 Then
                    MessageBox.Show("Insert Author #" & _
                                A.ToString() & " did not work.")
                End If
            Next
        ElseIf mvarChanged Then
            'Update data fields in existing record...
            updSQL = String.Format( _
                    "Update Titles Set Title='{0}', " & _
                    "[Year Published]={1}, PubID={2} " & _
                    "Where ISBN='{3}'", mvarTitle, _
                    mvarYearPublished, mvarPubID, mvarISBN)
                If CType(ExecuteCommand(updSQL), Integer) = 0 Then
                    MessageBox.Show("Update command did not work.")
                End If
        End If
    End If
End Class
```

Listing 12.18: The Book class, incorporating database persistence

The proper working of the Book class relies on two external functions (they are not part of the class because they will be of use to any class that uses the database in a similar way – e.g. Authors and Publishers). GetReader() is a function that takes a SQL Select string and returns a data reader with the corresponding data from database tables. We can retrieve all of the information from a row of the Titles table with the SQL query:

```
Select * From Titles Where ISBN = <some ISBN string>
```

The GetReader() function creates and opens a database connection and retrieves the DataReader so that individual columns can be extracted from it.

The ExecuteCommand() function is used to execute a SQL command on the database. Typically this will be used for non-query commands (INSERTS, DELETES and UPDATES), although the function can also execute a SQL Select command and return a result. Two different ways are used to execute the command, depending on whether it includes the word 'Select' or not. If there is no Select part to a command, the ExecuteNonQuery() method is used since this will return a count of the number of rows in the database affected by the query. If there is a Select part to the command, it should be sent by the ExecuteScalar() method, which can return a single item of data. This is useful if we are executing an INSERT command where there is an identity field in the database, since an added Select statement (shown later) can return this. The result (if the SQL string is properly constructed) is an update to the database and a single `Object` result, which must be cast to a type that matches the type of data you expect to be returned. `GetReader()` and `ExecuteCommand()` are as shown in Listing 12.19.

```
Private CONNSTR = "<usual connection string stuff>"
Private dbConn As SqlClient.SqlConnection
Private dbCmd As SqlClient.SqlCommand
Private dbRdr As SqlClient.SqlDataReader

Function GetReader(ByVal SQL As String) _
                              As SqlClient.SqlDataReader
     Dim rd As SqlClient.SqlDataReader
     dbConn = New SqlClient.SqlConnection(CONNSTR)
     dbCmd = New SqlClient.SqlCommand(SQL, dbConn)
     dbConn.Open()
     rd = dbCmd.ExecuteReader( _
                    CommandBehavior.CloseConnection)
     Return rd
End Function

Function ExecuteCommand(ByVal SQL As String) As Object
     Dim result As Integer
     dbConn = New SqlClient.SqlConnection(CONNSTR)
     dbCmd = New SqlClient.SqlCommand(SQL, dbConn)
     dbConn.Open()
     If InStr(SQL, "Select", CompareMethod.Text) > 0 Then
         result = CType(dbCmd.ExecuteScalar(), Integer)
     Else
         result = dbCmd.ExecuteNonQuery()
     End If
     dbConn.Close()
     Return result
End Function
```

Listing 12.19: Functions for fetching and storing data

The `Book` class has two constructors. The first takes an ISBN string and uses it to retrieve the corresponding book's record. I've omitted any error-handling code for clarity but there should certainly be some, at the very least to indicate where a supplied ISBN string is not in the database. Code in this constructor would be very simple but for the need to retrieve a possible list of Author identifications from the [Title Author] table. Note the use of the `AddAuthor()` method to append the author ids to an `ArrayList` of authors.

The second constructor is simpler, since it just takes the supplied parameter data and assigns it to the various member variables. Note that author ids are not included in this list since we would never know how many to deal with (I've seen some computing books with more than a dozen authors names on the jacket). Each author is added individually using the `AddAuthor()` method.

Having been the product of one of these two constructors, a `Book` object would now be used normally, assigning and retrieving values from the properties and executing methods as required. When the object has fulfilled its purpose, the `UpdateDatabase()` method should be called. Its purpose is to send only new or changed information back to the database. To help it decide whether the data is unchanged, altered or new (to the database), two member variables, `mvarChanged` and `mvarBrandNew`, are used to track any changes to the object. `mvarBrandNew` is only set to true from the second constructor.

Adding a new Title to the database requires that a row is inserted into Titles, plus one row for each author into the [Title Author] table. SQL queries are built to do the inserts (using the `String.Format()` method, which is ideal for inserting variable values into an otherwise literal string). The SQL strings used for these inserts are:

```
Insert Into Titles(Title, [Year Published], ISBN, PubID)
Values('<>', <>, '<>', <>);
```

and

```
Insert Into [Title Author](ISBN, Au_ID) Values('<>', <>);
```

The `String.Format()` method simply makes it easier to handle the lists of variable names, inserting quotes (' ') around the string fields.

Using a `Book` object from a form is a simple matter, as the code to retrieve a `Book` object from the database using a ISBN entered into a text box (Listing 12.20) shows:

```
Private Sub btnGetBook_Click(ByVal sender As System.Object, _
                             ByVal e As System.EventArgs) _
                             Handles btnGetBook.Click
    If txtISBN.Text <> "" Then
        Dim B As New Book(txtISBN.Text)
        txtTitle.Text = B.Title
        txtYear.Text = B.YearPublished
        Dim A As Object
        For Each A In B.Authors
            lstAuthors.Items.Add(A)
        Next
    End If
End Sub
```

Listing 12.20: Retrieving a book's data from the database

Inserting a new book is similarly trivial (see Listing 12.21).

```
Private Sub btnAddBook_Click(ByVal sender As System.Object, _
                             ByVal e As System.EventArgs) _
                             Handles btnAddBook.Click
    Dim B As Book
```

```
      B = New Book(txtISBN.Text, txtTitle.Text, _
                  CInt(txtYear.Text), CInt(txtPubID.Text))
      Dim A As Object
      For Each A In lstAuthors.Items
          B.AddAuthor(CType(A, Integer))
      Next
      B.UpdateDatabase()
   End Sub
```

Listing 12.21: Inserting a new `Book` object into the database

Note that the various member fields for the new book have been entered into text boxes and converted as necessary. Author ids have been taken from a list box.

We can do the same for the Authors table so that an author can be retrieved from the Au_ID number and information updated as necessary (Listing 12.22).

```
Public Class Author
      Private mvarName As String
      Private mvarAuID As Integer
      Private mvarYearBorn As Integer
      Private mvarChanged As Boolean = False
      Private mvarBrandNew As Boolean = False
      'Properties for Name, YearBorn, AuID(read-only)
      'go here...
      Public Sub New(ByVal AuID As Integer)
          mvarAuID = AuID
          Dim r As SqlClient.SqlDataReader
          r = GetReader( _
                  "Select * From Authors Where Au_ID = "& _
                  AuID & ";")
          r.Read()
          mvarName = r.Item("Author").ToString()
          mvarYearBorn = Val(r.Item("Year Born").ToString())
      End Sub

      Public Sub New(ByVal Name As String, _
                  ByVal YearBorn As Integer)
          mvarName = Name
          mvarYearBorn = YearBorn
          'To get a AuID value, we'll need to send this to the
          'database now...
          Dim Sql As String
          Sql = String.Format("Insert Into Authors(Author, " & _
                      "[Year Born]) Values('{0}',{1});", _
                      mvarName, mvarYearBorn)
          'We need a Select part to this query to retrieve the
          'AuID value...
          Sql &= "Select Au_ID From Authors " & _
                          Where (Au_ID = @@IDENTITY)"
          mvarAuID = ExecuteCommand(Sql)
      End Sub
```

```
Public Overrides Function ToString() As String
    Dim s As String
    s = mvarName
    'Best to account for null birth year values...
    If mvarYearBorn > 0 Then
        s &= ", " & mvarYearBorn.ToString()
    End If
    Return s
End Function

'Other methods here...
'...
End Class
```

Listing 12.22: The `Author` persistent class

As a result of these two classes and the associated database functions, we can easily work with persistent `Book` and `Author` objects that can be sent to and retrieved from the database at will. Use the code in Listing 12.23 to retrieve a Book and details of its authors.

```
Private Sub btnGetBook_Click(ByVal sender As System.Object, _
                             ByVal e As System.EventArgs) _
                             Handles btnGetBook.Click
    If txtISBN.Text <> "" Then
        Dim B As New Book(txtISBN.Text)
        txtTitle.Text = B.Title
        txtYear.Text = B.YearPublished
        Dim A As Object
        For Each A In B.Authors
            lstAuthors.Items.Add(New Author(A).ToString())
        Next
    End If
End Sub
```

Listing 12.23: Using the `Book` and `Author` classes

The main problem with the approach used in these listings is the inefficiency of forming and closing database connections on an object-by-object basis. The code could be altered to maintain a single, shared connection for use by the class, but this could result in a database connection being held open over a long period of time whether or not it was necessary.

One approach to a strategic solution would be to implement the classes to work with a `DataSet`, since the normal working mode would then be disconnected. However, using and defining a `DataSet` would bring its own problems: how to determine how many records to retrieve and which ones, how to deal with multiple objects accessing the same `DataRows`, etc. The techniques shown here do no more than provide an example of how you would create and use an object model with database persistence, and they need to be applied with care to make the most effective use of the database.

Exercise 12.7

Create a `Publisher` class (ignore most of the fields, implementing only the `PubID` and `Name` members as properties). Add code to Listing 12.23 so that the Publisher's name will appear on the form when a title is clicked on.

12.6 Summary

In this chapter we've covered a lot of ground, from database and relational database theory to database facilities in .NET, using connected and disconnected databases and database-persistent object modelling. The more you look into .NET's database support, the more you find and the more ways you can think of using it. If it all seems complex and confusing just now, it is worth remembering that databases and Visual Basic has always been more complex than Visual Basic itself. However, with .NET, the database facilities are now logical and comprehensive.

Review Questions

1. A flat-file database manager is able to go directly to any record in a database given the record number. What prevents us from implementing the same type of mechanism in a comma-delimited file of the type we looked at in Chapter 11?

2. What is a field that is used to store a reference to a record in a different table called?

3. How is a many-to-many relationship created in a relational database?

4. What is the language used to alter the structure of a database called?

5. How does a `SqlConnection` object differ from a `OleDbConnection` object?

6. Which type of Connection object (from Q5) would you use to connect to a MSDE database?

7. Which class of object is used to send SQL strings to a database?

8. What type of SQL query is used to change the values in existing records in a database table?

9. What class of object is used to get data into a `DataSet` object? Which method of the class is used to get data into the dataset?

10. List the three steps necessary to add a new item to a `DataTable` inside a `DataSet`.

11. What is a `CurrencyManager`?

12. It is necessary to add commands to a `DataAdapter` to enable changes made to a `DataSet` to be sent back to the database. Which class of object can be used to generate simple, single-table commands?

Practical Activities

While concentrating on code for manipulating databases in this chapter, we've missed out on perhaps one of the most useful features of Visual Studio .NET in its relation to databases. The Data Form Wizard is a built-in utility that will automatically generate a form for accessing a database, including the code required to perform common operations. By answering a few questions about the database to access and the data you want to manipulate, Visual Studio can quickly create a new form class that will be an instant user-interface to the selected data, providing view, add, delete and update facilities with code that is robust and well organized.

In general, this approach can be used to create 'standard' forms for data access, and can allow you to rapidly put together a user-interface to demonstrate the capabilities of a prototype application, or even a final version of a simple application. The code is not organized into individual tiers, and the user-interface is based on standard controls; no `ListView` or other exotic user-interface elements, so in many cases the resulting form would be used as a starting point for an application. In particular, breaking the functionality of a Wizard-designed form into separate presentation, business and data-access tiers could end up being a complex and messy business.

Activity 1: Getting the database

Again, we will make use of the Biblio sample database, since this is widely available and properly structured as a relational database. Which version you use will depend on which copy of Visual Studio you have installed and whether you also have SQL Server version 7.0. If you do have SQL Server V7.0 installed either on your development PC or somewhere on a network that you are connected to, you will already have a copy of Biblio. If not, you have the options of either installing MSDE, or making use of Biblio.mdb, Biblio2000.mdb or Biblio2002.mdb, the Microsoft Access versions of this database. In general, you should opt for a SQL Server or MSDE version if possible, because these offer greatly improved performance over the Access version.

Installing MSDE

If you have a purchased copy of Visual Studio .NET Professional, setup files for MSDE will have been copied to your system by default when you installed Visual Studio. On my system, these were installed in C:\Program Files\Microsoft Visual Studio .NET\Setup\MSDE. If you chose to install Visual Studio to a different location, you will find the setup files in a different location. If you chose not to install the SQL Server Desktop Engine, you will need to go through the Visual Studio .NET process again to install them. To install MSDE, find **Setup.exe** in the **\Setup\MSDE** folder and execute it. It will install several databases, including Biblio. Checking for the existence of Biblio will be different for different versions of Biblio.

Locating Biblio for MSDE or SQL Server

If you have installed SQL Server or MSDE on your computer (hereafter, I'll just say SQL Server to cover both of these products), it will be best to use this version. To check for this on SQL Server:

1. Open the Server Explorer and click on the Services sub-tree to open it. At the bottom of the list of services, you should find SQL Server (it will be named this whether you are using the actual SQL Server or the free MSDE version). If not, SQL Server is not installed on your machine. You can install a copy of MSDE from your Visual Studio Professional CDs, or from a copy of the Microsoft Office Professional CD, the Microsoft Access CD or some earlier versions of Visual Basic, Visual Studio or Office Professional, or you can skip to the next section to check for the Access version.

2. Biblio2002 should be visible as a node when you open the SQL Server sub-tree. If your copy of SQL Server is currently running, this will be displayed as a little database icon with a connection (plug and cable) as shown in Figure A12.1. If it is not, it will be displayed as a database icon with a red cross (as shown for some of the other database icons).

3. You should be able to 'drill down' to show tables, and further to show the columns in each table.

To check for an Access version of Biblio:

4. Go to the Windows Start button, select **Search**, and choose **For Files and Folders . . .** In the box 'Search for files or folders named', enter **Biblio*.mdb**.

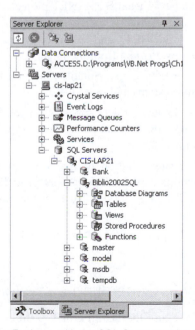

Figure A12.1 The Server Explorer, with the SQL Server version of Biblio open

The asterisk at the end of Biblio serves as a wild-card so that **Biblio.mdb**, **Biblio2000.mdb** and **Biblio2000.mdb** will all be found. Press **Search Now** and wait to see whether any copies of the database turn up. If any results do appear in the Search Results window, *take a note of the path to the file* (on my system, **Biblio.mdb** and **Biblio2000.mdb** both appear in a folder: **C:\Program Files\Microsoft Visual Studio\VB98**)

If you have neither version of Biblio available on your system, all is not lost. Microsoft provides some versions as a free download from their developer's website:

5.   Visit msdn.microsoft.com, enter **Biblio.mdb** into the Search box, and select **Downloads** from the combo box below this. The resulting page will contain a link to allow you to download a copy of the **Biblio.mdb** access database

6.   Press the link to download, fill in any information that Microsoft asks you for, and when the Download box appears, browse to a folder to save the downloaded version of Biblio in. I would suggest a folder inside the folder where you keep your .NET programs.

Activity 2: Creating the application

Now we can start putting together an application for accessing this database. Since we may eventually create several database access forms, it will be a good starting point to build a simple shell application that we can add the forms to later.

Create a new Visual Basic .NET project.

1.   Run VB .NET and choose **New Project** from the Start page, or **File/New/Project** from the menus.

2.   Enter or browse to a suitable folder for the project files, enter the project name (**BiblioSystem**) and press **OK.**

3.   When the new project appears, rename **Form1** to **frmMain** and rename its file to **frmMain.vb**. Change the Text property so that the form's caption shows as **Main Form**.

4.   Add a single button to the form, give it the name `btnPublishers`, and change its caption (Text property) to **Publishers**. Later, we will add code to use this button to open the Publishers form that we build using the data form wizard.

5.   Save the project files before proceeding to Activity 3.

Activity 3: Generating a master-detail form

We can now use the Data Form Wizard to create a table for accessing the set of Publishers and the books they publish.

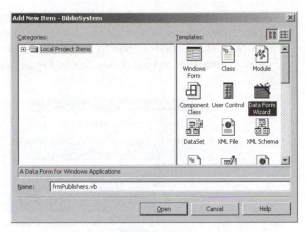

Figure A12.2   Starting the Data Form Wizard

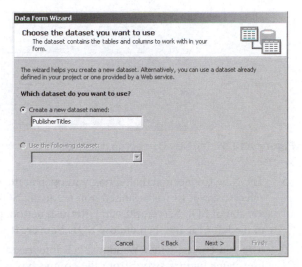

Figure A12.3   creating a new `DataSet`

1. Select **Project/Add Windows Form** from the menus, choose **Data Form Wizard**, and enter the name **frmPublishers.vb** in the **Name:** box. Click on **Open**. The process is shown in Figure A12.2.

2. The Data Form Wizard's welcome page will appear, and from here you will be directed through the various stages to specify the data you want the form to access. Press **Next**.

3. In the first page, you are given the options to create a new dataset or to select an existing one. The option to select an existing one will be disabled since your project does not yet contain a dataset. Enter a suitable name for the dataset (**PublisherTitles** will be an accurate description), being careful not to have any spaces in the name. Press **Next**. This is shown in Figure A12.3.

4. On the next page, you can select from existing connections (as you add new connections, they will be added to this list so that they can be reused) or press the New Connection . . . button to create a new database connection. Press **New Connection** and the dialog box in Figure A12.4 will appear:

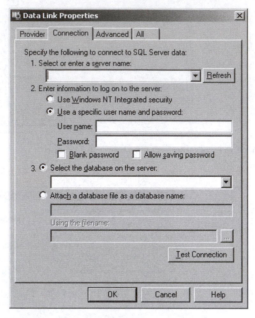

Figure A12.4 The New Connection dialog box

5. The New Connection dialog box will open at the second page ready for you to select a server (it has assumed you are using SQL Server). If you are using a version of SQL Server, press the Refresh button, pull down the combo box list to the left of it and then choose **SQL Server**. If you are not, go to Step 9.

6. You can choose either Windows NT Integrated Security or to use a specific user name and password from the combo boxes below the server name. The first option will then use your Windows NT login to authenticate access to the database (which is the most secure option), the second will expect to find the user name and password provided specified in the connection string. For this simple demo, either will do.

7. Select the Biblio database from the "Select the database on the server" combo box – this could be called **Biblio**, **Biblio2000**, **Biblio2002** or another, similar name for a later version.

8. Finally, press **Test Connection**. A message box should appear indicating the success of the connection. Now go on to Step 13.

9. If you are using an Access copy of Biblio, press the Provider tab at the top, left of the dialog box. When the list of providers appears, choose the Microsoft Jet 4.0 OLE DB Provider (this is the most up to date version for Access databases on my system – you may have a later version) and press **Next**. This is shown in Figure A12.5.

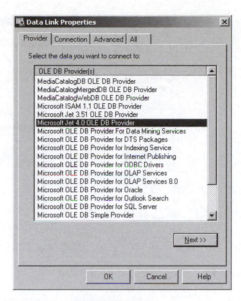

Figure A12.5 Choosing the Access (JET) Provider

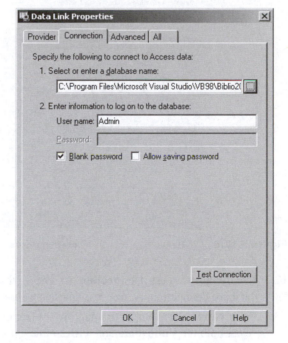

Figure A12.6 Specifying the location of the Access database file

10. In the Connection page, press the Ellipsis (. . .) button to the right of the database name box and browse to the folder you found in Activity 1 as the location of the Biblio database file, and select the file. Press **Open**.

11. Leave the user name as **Admin** and leave the Blank password box checked (see Figure A12.6).

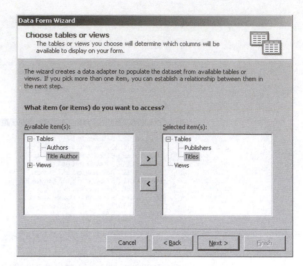

Figure A12.7 Selecting database tables

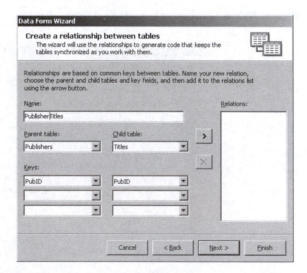

Figure A12.8 Creating the relationship between tables

12. Finally, press **Test Connection** to check that everything is ok with the database connection. A 'Success' message should appear.

13. Press **Next** to step on to the page for selecting database tables. In this box, select both the **Publishers** and **Titles** tables, pressing the '>' button after each selection (see Figure A12.7).

14. Step on to the next page by pressing **Next**. This page allows you to set up a relationship between the tables selected. Enter a name for the relationship (**PublisherTitles**), select the Parent table (**Publishers**) and the Child table (**Titles**), and select matching key fields in the top two boxes of Keys (**PubID** for both). This is shown in Figure A12.8.

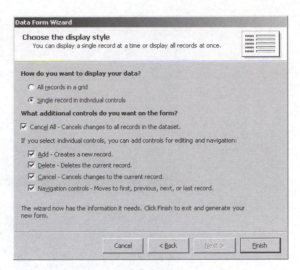

Figure A12.9 Choosing a layout for the form and database controls

15. Finally, press the '>' button to establish the relationship, and press **Next** (note that the '>' button is disabled unless a suitable name (with no spaces) is entered for the relationship).

16. Choose the tables and fields you wish to appear on the form. The default of both tables and all fields is fine. Press **Next**.

17. The final page of the Wizard lets you choose how the master-detail data will be displayed. The main choice is between all the master records in a grid or on separate controls. A grid will display a number of rows of the master table, while individual controls will show only one record at a time. Choose individual controls. The child records in the Titles table can only be displayed in a grid format.

18. You can select only the additional controls you need on the form – these allow records to be added, deleted, etc. (see Figure A12.9) Leave the default (all additional controls selected).

19. Press **Finish**, to complete the Wizard. It will now go on to create the form and populate it with code (see Figure A12.10).

This form is fully functional and so can be integrated immediately with other forms in the project. To do this, we need to add only the two statements in Listing A12.1 to the `btnPublishers` (added in Activity 2) event-handler.

```
Private Sub btnPublishers_Click(ByVal sender As
                                      System.Object, _
                           ByVal e As System.EventArgs) _
                           Handles btnPublishers.Click
    Dim F As New frmPublishers()
    F.ShowDialog()
End Sub
```

Listing A12.1: Code to load the Publishers form

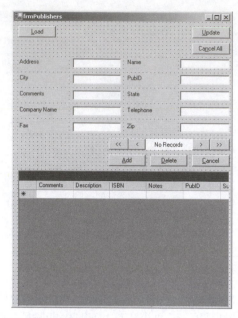

Figure A12.10   The Wizard-build data access form

Test the program at this stage and you should find that once the main form has loaded, pressing the Publishers button will load the Publishers `DataForm`. You need to press **Load** to show the `DataSet`, but having done this you will be able to skip from record to record using the navigation buttons added to the form.

Activity 4: Changing the master-detail form

The Wizard-generated form is fully functional, but the design is not ideal. For one thing, the default sizes of the master table's `TextBox` controls for viewing are mostly too small. You can resize these but will also need to resize the form to accommodate them. The grid at the bottom of the form is also too narrow to show the child records. It is also a bit unnecessary to have to press the Load button to load up the `DataSet` since having opened this form, its only purpose is to view data. The easiest fix for this is to cut the code from the Load button's event-handler and paste it into a `Form_Load()` event-handler.

1. Double-click on the form's background to generate a `Form.Load()` event-handler.

2. Locate the `btnLoad_Click()` event-handler and select all of the code within it (but not the first and last lines). Cut this code from the event-handler (press **Ctrl+X**).

3. Go back to the `Form_Load()` event-handler, place the cursor between the first and last line, and paste the code into it (**Ctrl+V**).

4. You can now remove the Load button, and the vestiges of its -Click event-handler sub.

5. Rearrange the other controls on the form to be less wasteful of space – having removed the Load button, the Update and Cancel buttons can be moved to occupy less space; the text boxes can be widened and the label controls reduced in width to give them space.

6. Set the Anchor property of the grid control to Top, Bottom, Left, so that it resizes with the form without covering the other controls. The re-shaped form could appear as shown in Figure A12.11.

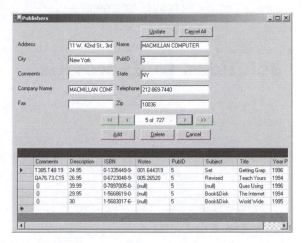

Figure A12.11   The re-organized form

Note that the form will take a little longer to open now because the data loading stage is included as it opens. This completes the activities for this chapter and the book.

Features worth remembering

■ The Data Form Wizard produces a lot of code as well as laying out a form to provide access to a set of data. It is worth examining this code, since it will be robust (Try..Catch..End Try is used copiously) and can suggest ways that you can add your own database code to forms.

■ You can mix and match an application with custom, hand-designed forms and Wizard-generated ones to provide the best set of features for your applications.

■ The Practical Activities concentrated on the use of a Wizard, so remember that this does not generate an ideal design where the system is organized as separate tiers for presentation, business and data services. Since generating data forms by Wizard is so quick and easy, it is as well to use it to develop rapid prototypes. In the end though, the power and flexibility of object orientation make it sensible to work using tiered application design and, particularly, business classes, since the result will be to create an application based on flexible and re-usable components.

Suggested Additional Activities

1. Create additional Wizard-generated forms for Titles alone and Authors and Titles (more complex because of the many to many join). These can be wired up to the main form via a pair of additional buttons and will provide a fully usable application for managing the Biblio database. You can apply the same techniques to your own databases.

2. Try incorporating a different set of data viewing controls into a Wizard-generated form. Once the form has built all of the data access components, you can use the techniques outlined in the chapter to place master-detail data sets into a `TreeView` control for example.

Solutions to Exercises

Exercise 12.1

Field	Type	Size in bytes
AccountNumber	Long Integer	8
Name	String	60
Address1	String	40
Address2	String	40
PostCode	Character	9
TransactionDate	Date	8
TransactionType	Character	1
Amount	Decimal	16
Description	Character	60

Note – guesses must be made for the maximum number of characters that might appear in Name, Address and Description fields. The sizes chosen are adequate for most situations in the UK, but may be totally inadequate in other locales. The Transaction Type field is set as a single character, since we can use "D" for Deposit, "W" for Withdrawal, "C" for Charges and "I" for Interest. Note that the Numeric format chosen has been Long Integer for an account number and Decimal for cash values, since these match the .NET data type most commonly used to represent primary keys and monetary values. However, a database environment is likely to have its own numeric formats, and Number, plus some indication of precision is more normal.

Exercise 12.2

Account table:

Field	Type	Size
AccountNumber	Long Integer	8
Name	String	60
Address1	String	40
Address2	String	40
PostCode	Character	9

Transactions table:

AccountNumber	Long Integer	8
TransactionDate	Date	8
TransactionType	Character	1
Amount	Decimal	16
Description	Character	60

Note that the `AccountNumber` field is a suitable primary/foreign key to match accounts with transactions.

Exercise 12.3

No set solution to this exercise.

Exercise 12.4

a) The following code places the list of titles into a `ListBox` control,

```
Private Sub ReadTitles()
    Dim dbConn As SqlClient.SqlConnection
    Dim dbCmd As SqlClient.SqlCommand
    Dim DataReader As SqlClient.SqlDataReader
    Dim SQLText As String = "Select * From Titles;"
    'The next line uses a connection string stored in
    'CONNSTR...
    dbConn = New SqlClient.SqlConnection(CONNSTR)
    dbCmd = New SqlClient.SqlCommand(SQLText, dbConn)
    dbConn.Open()
    DataReader = _
    dbCmd.ExecuteReader(CommandBehavior.CloseConnection)
    'We would now go on to display data from DataReader.
    'For example...
    With DataReader
        Do While .Read()
            lstTitles.Items.Add(.Item("Title"))
        Loop
    End With
End Sub
```

b)

```
Private Sub ReadTitles()
    Dim dbConn As SqlClient.SqlConnection
    Dim dbCmd As SqlClient.SqlCommand
    Dim DataReader As SqlClient.SqlDataReader
    Dim writer As IO.StreamWriter
    Dim SQLText As String = "Select * From Titles;"
    'The next line uses a connection string stored in
    'CONNSTR...
    dbConn = New SqlClient.SqlConnection(CONNSTR)
    dbCmd = New SqlClient.SqlCommand(SQLText, dbConn)
    dbConn.Open()
    DataReader = _
    dbCmd.ExecuteReader(CommandBehavior.CloseConnection)
```

```
            writer = New IO.StreamWriter("d:\Titles.txt")
            With DataReader
                Do While .Read()
                    Writer.WriteLine(.Item("Title"))
                Loop
            End With
            writer.Close()
        End Sub
```

c)

```
    Private Sub ReadTitles(ByVal lv As ListView)
        Dim dbConn As SqlClient.SqlConnection
        Dim dbCmd As SqlClient.SqlCommand
        Dim DataReader As SqlClient.SqlDataReader
        Dim lvi As ListViewItem
        Dim SQLText As String = "Select * From Titles;"
        'The next line uses a connection string stored in
        'CONNSTR...
        dbConn = New SqlClient.SqlConnection(CONNSTR)
        dbCmd = New SqlClient.SqlCommand(SQLText, dbConn)
        dbConn.Open()
        DataReader = _
        dbCmd.ExecuteReader(CommandBehavior.CloseConnection)
        With DataReader
            Do While .Read()
                lvi = New ListViewItem(.Item("Title")
                lvi.SubItems.Add(.Item("Year Published"))
                lvi.SubItems.Add(.Item("ISBN"))
                lvi.SubItems.Add(.Item("PubID"))
                lvi.SubItems.Add(.Item("Description"))
                lvi.SubItems.Add(.Item("Notes"))
                lvi.SubItems.Add(.Item("Subject"))
                lvi.SubItems.Add(.Item("Comments"))
                lv.Items.Add(lvi)
            Loop
        End With
        writer.Close()
    End Sub
```

Exercise 12.5

```
Private Sub DeleteAuthor(ByVal ID As Long)
    Dim SQL As String
    Dim dbConn As OleDb.OleDbConnection
    Dim dbCmd As New OleDb.OleDbCommand(Sql, dbConn)
    SQL = "DELETE * FROM Authors WHERE Au_ID = " & ID
    dbConn = New OleDb.OleDbConnection(CONNSTR)
    dbConn.Open()
    dbCmd = New OleDb.OleDbCommand(Sql, dbConn)
    dbCmd.ExecuteNonQuery()
    dbConn.Close()
End Sub
```

```vb
'Note, this code should go on a form, and the form should
'Import the System.Data.SqlClient library.
Private ds As DataSet
Private dbConn As SqlClient.SqlConnection
Private auMover As CurrencyManager

Private Sub CreateDataSet()
    'a)   Code to create the DataSet (ds, declared above)...
    Dim sqlAuthors As String = "Select * From Authors"
    Dim sqlTitles As String = _
                        "Select * From [Title Author]"
    Dim daAuthors As SqlDataAdapter = _
                New SqlDataAdapter(sqlAuthors, dbConn)
    Dim daTitles As SqlDataAdapter = _
                New SqlDataAdapter(sqlTitles, dbConn)
    Dim ds = New DataSet()
    daAuthors.Fill(ds, "Authors")
    daTitles.Fill(ds, "Titles")
    Dim dcAuthors, dcTitles As DataColumn
    Dim dr As Data.DataRelation
    dcAuthors = ds.Tables("Authors").Columns("Au_ID")
    dcTitles = ds.Tables("Titles").Columns("Au_ID")
    dr = New DataRelation("AuthorsTitles", _
                                dcAuthors, dcTitles)
    ds.Relations.Add(dr)

    'b)   Code to set up a CurrencyManager (auMover)...
    auMover = Me.BindingContext(ds, "Authors")
End Sub

'b)contd. Four navigation buttons...
Private Sub btnFirst_Click(ByVal sender As System.Object, _
                        ByVal e As System.EventArgs) _
                        Handles btnFirst.Click
    auMover.Position = 0
    DisplayTitles()
End Sub

Private Sub btnLast_Click(ByVal sender As System.Object, _
                        ByVal e As System.EventArgs) _
                        Handles btnLast.Click
    auMover.Position = auMover.Count - 1
    DisplayTitles()
End Sub

Private Sub btnPrev_Click(ByVal sender As System.Object, _
                        ByVal e As System.EventArgs) _
                        Handles btnPrev.Click
    auMover.Position -= 1
    DisplayTitles()
End Sub
```

```vb
Private Sub btnNext_Click(ByVal sender As System.Object, _
                          ByVal e As System.EventArgs) _
                          Handles btnNext.Click
    auMover.Position += 1
    DisplayTitles()
End Sub

'c) Code to display all titles for an author in a ListBox.
' Note - this is called each time the CurrencyManager
' moves our view to a new Author...
Private Sub DisplayTitles()
    Dim auRow As DataRow
    Dim auView As DataRowView 'As returned by a
                              'CurrencyManager
    auView = auMover.Current  'Currently visible item
    auRow = auView.Row        'The associated row
    lstTitles.Items.Clear()
    Dim tiRow As DataRow
    For Each tiRow _
        In auRow.GetChildRows(ds.Relations("AuthorsTitles"))
        lstTitles.Items.Add(tiRow.Item("ISBN").ToString())
    Next
End Sub
```

Exercise 12.7

```vb
Public Class Publisher

    Private mvarName As String
    Private mvarPubID As Integer
    Private mvarChanged As Boolean = False
    Private mvarBrandNew As Boolean = False

    'Properties for Name, PubID(read-only)
    'go here . . .
    Public Sub New(ByVal PubID As Integer)
        mvarPubID = PubID
        Dim r As SqlClient.SqlDataReader
        r = GetReader( _
            "Select * From Publishers Where PubID = " _
            & PubID & ";")
        r.Read()
        mvarName = r.Item("Publisher").ToString()
    End Sub

    Public Sub New(ByVal Name As String)
        mvarName = Name
        Dim Sql As String
        Sql = String.Format( _
                    "Insert Into Publishers(Publisher)" _
                    "Values({0});", mvarName)
        Sql &= "Select PubID From Publishers " & _
                            Where (PubID = @@IDENTITY)"
```

```
        mvarPubID = ExecuteCommand(Sql)
    End Sub

    Public Overrides Function ToString() As String
        Return mvarName
    End Function

    'Other methods here...
    '...
End Class

'Amending listing 12.23...
Private Sub btnGetBook_Click(ByVal sender As
                                        System.Object, _
                    ByVal e As System.EventArgs) _
                    Handles btnGetBook.Click
    If txtISBN.Text <> "" Then
        Dim B As New Book(txtISBN.Text)
        txtTitle.Text = B.Title
        txtYear.Text = B.YearPublished
        Dim A As Object
        For Each A In B.Authors
            lstAuthors.Items.Add(New Author(A).ToString())
        Next
        Dim P As Publisher = New Publisher(B.PubID)
        'P object now has all of the Publisher properties...
        lblPublisher.Text = P.Name
    End If
End Sub
```

Answers to Review Questions

1. A flat-file database manager is able to go directly to any record in a database given the record number. What prevents us from implementing the same type of mechanism in a comma-delimited file of the type we looked at in chapter 11? **Records in a comma-delimited file are likely to be different lengths, and so no simple algorithm can calculate where a specific record will begin.**

2. What is a field that is used to store a reference to a record in a different table called? **A Primary Key field.**

3. How is a many-to-many relationship created in a relational database? **An extra table is created which has two columns – one for the primary key of the Master table, another for the primary key of the Detail table.**

4. What is the language used to alter the structure of a database called? **The Data Definition Language or DDL.**

5. How does a `SqlConnection` object differ from a `OleDbConnection` object? **A `SqlConnection` object is optimized to create a connection to a SQL Server or MSDE database. `OleDBConnection` can form a connection to any database which has a (standard) ODBC driver, and so is used to access non-native databases. `OleDbConnection` technology is much slower in operation.**

6. Which type of connection object (from Q5) would you use to connect to a MSDE database? **`SqlConnection`.**

7. Which class of object is used to send SQL strings to a database? **A *Command* object – either `SqlCommand` or `OleDbCommand`.**

8. What type of SQL query is used to change the values in existing records in a database table? **An Update query.**

9. What class of object is used to get data into a `DataSet` object? Which method of the class is used to get data into the dataset? **A `DataAdapter` object (`SqlDataAdapter` or `OleDbDataAdapter`).**

10. List the three steps necessary to add a new item to a `DataTable` inside a `DataSet`. **Call the `NewRow()` method, set the various `Item()` values, and then call the `Rows.Add()` method, passing the new row object as a parameter.**

11. What is a `CurrencyManager`? **An object that is used to update Form controls to show the values of current row in a `DataSet`.**

12. It is necessary to add commands to a `DataAdapter` to enable changes made to a `DataSet` to be sent back to the database. Which class of object can be used to generate simple, single-table commands? **A `CommandBuilder` object.**

VB .NET Programming without Visual Studio

Visual Studio includes a comprehensive set of programming tools that provides a deluxe environment for programmers. As well as hosting the various .NET language compilers (Visual Basic, C#, C++ and other, add-in languages), it contains a tailored code editor, a Visual Form Designer for Windows and Web applications, the Server Explorer for creating links to databases and other server-based components, tools to configure an application and create links between components and other utilities and features almost too numerous to list.

However, it is possible to build Visual Basic (and C#) projects without a copy of Visual Studio installed. The .NET Framework, which must be installed on a computer before you can run any .NET programs, comes complete with compilers for Visual Basic .NET and C#. A compiler is a tool that translates source code, the text form of a computer program which is what a programmer writes, to object code, the program in a form that can be executed on a computer. Once a Visual Basic program is written in text format, it is saved to a file (normally one with a .vb extension on the end of its name). This file-name is then given to the compiler, which produces a new file, one with a .exe extension, that can be executed on the target computer.

The .NET Framework

This is freely available from Microsoft, and can be downloaded from the MSDN.Microsoft.com website. It has also been distributed as a cover mount disk by a number of programmer's journals and magazines, and by Microsoft at publicity events. Check the MSDN.Microsoft.com website and look up '.NET Framework' for instructions on how to obtain a copy. If you have a broadband Internet connection, you can download the framework from the site, but if not you can order a copy from Microsoft (any charge made will be purely for copying and distribution costs).

Once you have the .NET Framework, either as a download or on CD, you can install it on your PC and begin Visual Basic or C# programming immediately. It is worthwhile keeping a copy of the most up to date release of the framework to hand, because you will have to install it on any computer you intend to run your programs on. Microsoft intends to incorporate the framework in future versions of Windows, starting with a service release of Windows XP. However, early versions of XP, all versions of Windows 2000 and Windows 98 and Millennium-based computers will need to have the framework installed to make .NET programs work.

Creating a .NET programming environment

To create .NET programs, you must have one of the following operating systems installed on your PC:

- Windows XP Home, Professional or Server edition
- Windows 2000 Professional or Server edition
- Windows NT 4.0
- Windows 98
- Windows ME

In addition, you must have the .NET Framework installed. Beyond this, your only crucial requirement is a text editor. Both EDIT.COM (a clunky but perfectly workable DOS-mode editor) and Notepad are installed on every Windows system by default. However, most programmers prefer to work with a text editor designed specifically for programmers, of which a huge number are available. Several very good programmers' (and web-designers') editors are available as freeware. Among these, my favourite is the excellent PFE (Programmers File Editor), developed by Alan Phillips of Lancaster University. To obtain a copy of PFE, visit http://www.lancs.ac.uk/people/cpaap/pfe, from where it can be downloaded.

Once you have installed the .NET framework on a suitable PC and chosen and installed a suitable editor, there are a few configuration tasks you should perform to create a well-organized programming environment where the tools work easily and seamlessly together. The first thing that is necessary is to set up the .NET compilers so that they will work on your program files wherever they are on your system.

Typically, programmers need to be able to invoke the compiler and any other required tools from a folder that does not contain the tools. One way of doing this is to include in the statement that executes the compiler its location on the computer. The Visual Basic compiler is in a file called **VBC.EXE**, and this is normally installed in the following location on a Windows PC in which the .NET Framework has been installed:

```
C:\Windows\Microsoft.NET\Framework\v1.0.3705\VBC.EXE
```

or

```
C:\WINNT\Microsoft.NET\Framework\v1.0.3705\VBC.EXE
```

depending on your operating system. Note the version number, that is the name of the folder the compiler is found in, will change from version to version of the framework.

If I have Visual Basic .NET program code in a file called **Test.vb** in the Programs folder of my C: drive, and wish to compile it into a Visual Basic executable, I can execute the command:

```
C:\WINNT\Microsoft.NET\Framework\v1.0.3705\VBC Test.vb
```

(on a Windows 2000 or NT system). Note, we can miss out the .EXE extension to the file-name. Having to include the full path to the compiler is not only tedious, but also error-prone and does not make for a streamlined programming session since I may need to compile a file many times to eliminate bugs and make changes to the way it works.

There is an alternative to this, which is to set up the PATH environment variable on your system to include the folder that contains the Visual Basic compiler. Environment variables are like variables in a program, in that they are names given to areas of memory that store data. These, however, are available to the operating system and are used to configure various aspects of it. The PATH environment variable contains a list of paths to folders which you would like the operating system to look up whenever you enter a command or the name of an executable file. We can add the location of the .NET tools to the PATH environment variable using the following command-line statement (in a Command Prompt window):

```
path=%path%;C:\Windows\Microsoft.NET\Framework\v1.0.3705
```

The `%path%` at the start is the existing value of the PATH environment variable, and the addition of the .NET Framework folder is made after a semicolon. Now, to compile the same Visual Basic program file, simply enter the command:

```
VBC Test.vb
```

Since we would want to use both the compiler and the editor in the same way (entering just the name of the program to execute it), you can either copy your editor to the .NET Framework folder, or can include it in your PATH setting by adding another `path=` statement:

```
path=%path%;C:\Windows\Microsoft.NET\Framework\v1.0.3705
path=%path%;C:\Program Files\PFE
```

Now, both edit commands (PFE32 **Test.vb**) and compile commands (VBC **Test.vb**) will work from any folder in the computer's hard disk. Since these commands to set the environment variables are themselves long and arcane, it would be better if we could store them somewhere in the computer so that they could be replayed at will. For this, we can create a batch file that we can then invoke by double-clicking on it. A batch file is simply a text file that contains commands you would normally type into a Command Prompt window. The batch file listed in Figure Appx1.1 can be typed into Windows Notepad or another text editor and will set up a Command-line environment for programming with Visual Basic .NET or C#, incorporating the PFE editor as a command tool.

Note that two additional statements have crept into the batch file. The statement beginning 'CD' is a Change Directory command, and is being used to change the Command Prompt's current working directory to the one named (**C:\VB.NET Progs**), which is where I keep all of my Visual Basic .NET programs written in this way. The last line opens a Command Prompt window, ready for me to start work in.

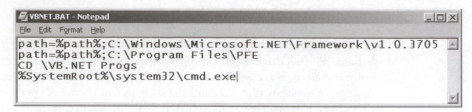

Figure Appx1.1 A Notepad file (**VBNET.BAT**) that sets up a command environment for programming

Create this batch file tailored to your own system and tools (you may need to change the folder locations in the PATH commands, and the name of the folder you will use for your Visual Basic programs) and save it as **VBNET.BAT** in a suitable folder on your computer (in the .NET Framework folder beside the compiler is ideal). Then open Windows Explorer, locate the file and, using the right mouse button, drag it to your desktop or the Windows Start button. When you release it, select **Create shortcut(s) here** from the context menu. Now, when you want to start a programming session, you can simply double-click on the batch file to get going.

Writing a Visual Basic .NET Program

Having set up a programming environment, we are now ready to begin programming. As usual, the first program I would write in this environment is one that displays a 'Hello World' message on the terminal, since if this works I can be confident that the system is behaving properly. The simplest option is to create a console program.

Double-click on the **VBNET.BAT** shortcut on your desktop to get started. You should have a Command Prompt window on your screen as shown in Figure Appx1.2.

Figure Appx1.2 A Command Prompt session

Figure Appx1.3 Creating and moving to a new folder, ready for a new program

To start programming, I simply need to invoke the editor and enter code. However, it is good practice to create each new project in a separate folder, so I would normally start by entering a couple of commands to create and then move into a new folder (Figure Appx1.3).

Now, it is time to start the editor and create the program. To run Notepad and create the new program file, enter the command **Notepad Hello.vb**. You will be asked if you want to create a new file (**Hello.vb**) to which you should answer **Yes**. Now enter the code in Listing Appx1.1.

```
Imports System

Module Hello

    Public Sub Main()
        Console.WriteLine("Hello World")
    End Sub

End Module
```

Listing Appx1.1: The full code of the Hello.vb program

Select **File/Save** from the Notepad menus to save the program file. If you have a different editor, e.g. PFE, the only real difference should be in the command that you enter to begin editing a file. For PFE, the command is **PFE32 Hello.vb**.

Now you can try compiling the program. Note that there is no need to exit from Notepad or PFE or any other editor to do this. Simply enter the compile command: **VBC Hello.vb**, and wait for a second or two while it does its job. If the compilation is successful, you will see the Microsoft trademark and copyright messages on the screen and nothing else. If there is an error in your code, you will get a detailed description of the error and its location in the file. For example, missing the closing bracket from the `WriteLine()` statement results in a display like that in Figure Appx1.4.

Once you have compiled the program successfully, the final stage is to try it out. To run the program resulting from a source code file with the name **Hello.vb**, simply enter the first part of the name (you can if you wish tack a '.exe' on to the end of the file-name, since the actual executable file created will be **Hello.exe**). This is shown in Figure Appx1.5.

Figure Appx1.4 The Visual Basic Compiler issuing an error message

Figure Appx1.5 Executing a compiled program

Writing a Windows Program

The process for creating a Windows program is the same in almost every respect to that of creating a console one. Of course, it is necessary to incorporate all of the usual Windows object instances into the program, and import the System.Windows.Forms.Form namespace, but the actual code and compile process is almost exactly the same.

As an example, enter the short Windows program shown in Listing Appx1.2.

```
Imports System.Windows.Forms.Form

Module WinProg

    Public Sub Main()
        Dim F As Form
        F = New Form()
        F.Text = "Hello Windows"
        Application.Run(F)
    End Sub

End Module
```

Listing Appx1.2: The full code of a simple WinForms program

We need to do a little extra to compile this program, because the compiler needs to be made aware of the library files that it will find the various component classes in. We get a big clue from the Imports statement at the top of the

Figure Appx1.6 Compiling a WinForms program

listing, since `System.Windows.Forms` is located in the library file `System.Windows.Forms.dll` (dll stands for Dynamic Link Library). We also need to incorporate the System.dll library. These are added to the compilation using the /r (reference) switch as shown in Figure Appx1.6.

If you compile then execute this program for the Command Prompt window, it will behave as you expect. However, if you find the executable (**HelloWin.exe**) and double-click on it, you should notice that the program executes as normal, but that a new Console window opens behind it, and stays on the screen until the Windows form is closed. To get around this, you need to compile with the **/target:winexe**, or **/t:winexe switch**, as shown in Figure Appx1.7. This contains an implicit instruction to the compiler not to generate code to open a Console window:

Figure Appx1.7 Compiling a Windows-only executable (note the /t:winexe switch)

With the tools and configuration described above, you can write any Windows program that you could with Visual Studio, although in most cases it would involve a huge amount of additional effort since there is no Intellisense pop-up help, you cannot use the Windows Forms Designer, etc. In the end, most programmers would go for the more expensive but convenient route of using Visual Studio, but the free availability of the .NET Framework is a boon to learners or those who would like to dip their toes in the water of .NET programming.

Connections

Making a Connection to a Database

This operation will be similar whether you connect to a server-based database system like SQL Server or Oracle, or a file-based system like Access or Paradox. The first requirement is that you know what database you intend to connect to, for which you can use the Server Explorer.

Figure Appx2.1 shows the Server Explorer window in Visual Studio .NET. Typically, this will show all of the servers (network, mail, database, etc.) that the PC currently has access to. In the case of the explorer shown, the PC is a laptop that is not currently connected to a network and shows that there are two sources of data. At the bottom of the tree view is the CIS-LAP21 SQL Server (which is actually an installation of MSDE). This provides access to a number of databases, and the screen-shot shows that the **Bank**, **Biblio2002**, **master** and **tempdb** databases are live, having been accessed in the current session. The others are marked with a (red) cross which indicates that they are currently 'off-line'.

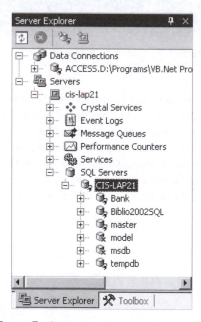

Figure Appx2.1   The Server Explorer

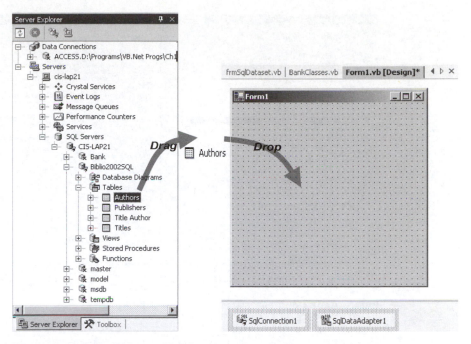

Figure Appx2.2   Adding a database connection to a form

To create a connection to any of these databases from a Visual Basic WinForms program, you need to 'drag' a database resource from the Server Explorer to a form. Open up any of the database nodes to access the resources. If, for example, I wished to use the Authors database table from a Visual Basic form, I could simply drag it from the explorer and drop it on the form, as shown in Figure Appx2.2. This has the effect of adding a `Connection` object and a `DataAdapter` object to the hidden controls tray for the form, as shown.

We could now go on to use the Connection and the DataAdapter from code within the form. The drag and drop operation also instantiates a number of Command objects for use with the database. Command objects allow us to perform operations on the database, and individual commands are instantiated and set up to allow selections, insertions, updates and deletions to be made to the database table dropped on the form. These objects will also be linked into any 'data-aware' controls that are added to the form to create interactions between the controls and the database automatically.

Connecting to an Access Database file

At the top of the Server Explorer window in Figure Appx2.1, you can see that Visual Studio has also been connected to an Access database (the full path and name of the database is too long to display in the window at its current width, but this is not important since it will be different for different databases). The server-based databases are added to the Explorer window automatically when you run Visual

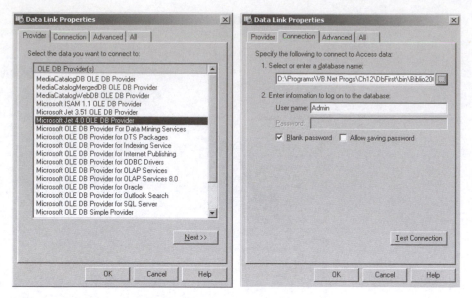

Figure Appx2.3 Connecting to an Access database file

Studio, but an Access-based one must be connected to explicitly, using the **Tools/Connect to Database** ... menu item. This menu item allows you to connect the Server Explorer window to a specific Access database file using the dialogue box shown in Figure Appx2.3. Note that this is a multi-tabbed dialog box, and it should first appear with the 'Connection' tab selected.

To make a connection to an Access database:

1. Select the **Tools/Connect to database** ... menu item.

2. Click on the 'Provider' tab and select one of the entries for a Microsoft Jet Provider (JET is Joint Engine Technology, the name Microsoft gave to the Access database engine that provided the facility to connect to a wide range of different underlying database software. The Jet 4.0 OLE DB Provider is the most up to date Access database connection and should be selected unless you have good reason to choose an earlier version of the driver).

3. Press **Next** to move to the 'Connection' page of the dialog box.

4. Using the small ellipsis button under the label '1.Select or enter a database name', locate and choose a suitable database.

5. Press the Test Connection button to check that the options you have chosen are valid. You will be informed of any problems, or, provided all is ok, that the connection succeeded.

Visual Studio .NET version 1.0 provides very few Access Database files and these are intended to demonstrate web access to databases. The Biblio database is available as an Access file (**Biblio.mdb**, **Biblio2002.mdb**) supplied with earlier copies of

Visual Basic, Microsoft Access, Visual Studio and Microsoft Office Professional. It may also be available as a download from Microsoft's website. Examples in Chapter 12 use the Biblio database, either as an Access database or from MSDE.

Once you have connected to an Access database, you can proceed to work with it just as if it was a SQL Server or MSDE database. There is a penalty in performance due to the OleDb connection and the fact that Access is not designed for client-server operation. There will also be some limitations on the code that you can write for accessing the database and the database facilities you can expect (Access does not support Stored Procedures for example), but for many applications, these will not be serious limitations. For all of the examples shown in Chapter 12, an `OleDbConnection` to an Access database will behave no differently to a `SqlConnection`.

Extracting and Manipulating a Connection String

Ultimately, the actual database connected to and the form of the connection (what types of commands it will allow and how it will convey security information to the database server) is embodied in the `ConnectionString` property of the Connection object. We can copy this string and paste it into a VB class, form or code module, to allow us to create a connection programmatically. We can even store it in the Windows registry, or a file in plain text or XML form so that the connection details are not 'hard-wired' into a database program; this would allow us to alter the connection setting without having to change the program at all.

We can retrieve the connection string from a Connection object (either `SqlConnection` or `OleDbConnection`) from its `ConnectionString` property, shown in Figure Appx2.4.

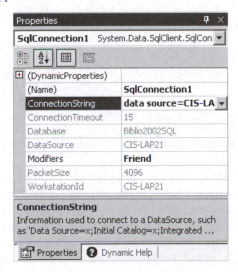

Figure Appx2.4 The `ConnectionString` property of a database connection

To extract this as text, click to the left of the start of the string (the words 'data source') and select the whole line (hold down the Shift key and press the End key on the keyboard). Now copy the text (**Ctrl+C**) and you can paste it into a code module or a text editor such as Notepad. I would normally place the ConnectionString text into a string constant at the top of a code module or near the top of a Form class. In Listing Appx2.1 shown below, I've broken the string up into separate lines, adding quotes, string concatenation operators (&) and line continuations so that all of it is visible but this is unnecessary: a typical connection string will disappear off the right of the code window but will still work perfectly well.

```
Public Class Form1
    Inherits System.Windows.Forms.Form

    Private Const CONNSTR As String = "data source=CIS _
                                    LAP21;" & _
                    "initial catalog=Biblio2002SQL;" & _
                    "integrated security=SSPI;" & _
                    "persist security info=True;" & _
                    "workstation id=CIS-LAP21;" & _
                    "packet size=4096"
```

[+] Windows Form Designer Generated Code

```
End Class
```

Listing Appx2.1: Placing a ConnectionString in a string constant

Listing Appx2.2 shows a ConnectionString for an OleDbConnection to an Access database added to a Visual Basic module. Note that to make it more generally useful a Friend declaration is used, and so I would be able to make use of it from any part of the VB application. The ConnectionString shown in Listing Appx2.1 would be usable only from that form.

```
Module Module1
    Friend Const CONNSTR =
                    "Provider=Microsoft.Jet.OLEDB.4.0;" & _
            "Data Source=D:\Programs\Databases\Biblio2002.mdb;"
End Module
```

Listing Appx2.2: A ConnectionString for an Access database

By storing only part of this connection string as a constant and adding the location of the database file to it at run time, it is possible to make the program connect to the database even when you are not aware where it will be stored on the system that an application will be deployed on. While this is less useful for server-based databases (a database server is accessed via the server's name, not the location of a file on a disk), it is ideal for Access databases that you want to distribute with an application.

Place the Access file in the same folder as the executable program, and form the connection string as shown in Listing Appx2.3.

```
'This part of a connection string indicates the database
'type...
Private Const CONNSTR = "Provider=Microsoft.Jet.OLEDB.4.0;"

'This function adds the location of the Access file...
Friend Function DbConnectionString() As String
    Dim fileName As String
    fileName = Application.ExecutablePath
    fileName = fileName.Substring(0, _
                        fileName.LastIndexOf("\")) _
                        & "\Biblio2002.mdb"
    Return CONNSTR & fileName

End Function
```

Listing 3: Building a connection string at run time

Once you have retrieved or built a connection string (or added a Connection object to a form as described earlier, gaining access to data from a database is simply a matter of using the correct classes. See Chapter 12 for details on the various database classes in .NET.

Style may seem like a bizarre word to apply to the coding of a computer program, but one of the key factors that makes the work of one programmer unintelligible and another readable is the style in which the program code is written. Most software houses require a set of stylistic conventions from their programmers; naming conventions for variables and components, standard forms for the layout of program code and specifications for in-program comments. By imposing the use of these conventions, companies are making sure all the programmers in a team can read each other's code. This makes it easier to change or debug software, even in the absence of the original programmer. It also makes it easier to introduce new programmers to the projects a team is working on.

Rigorous use of a well-thought out programming style has other benefits. In many projects, particularly in sub-contracting work, customers may well look through the code to get a feel for its quality. Consistent code looks professional and looks as though it has been the product of a mature and stable life-cycle. Code that is written to a well-defined style can also be easier to construct analysis tools for, often a key component of a quality assurance programme. Finally, well-written program code tends to be self-documenting, requiring less in the way of additional explanatory text to expose its algorithms, assumptions and limitations.

In this appendix, I will describe a small number of conventions that can be applied to the creations of program code. One point that will hit you in the eye a number of times as you read through it is that I am not very diligent at following my own style guide. From this you can conclude either that I am a bad author, or a hypocrite, or, I hope, that programming in a professional environment must be different from the work of creating small example programs for educational purposes. While writing this book, I did frequently agonize over the way that code was being laid out. The main requirement was to demonstrate programming techniques in a way that would encourage new programmers. While I have used several of the techniques described here in the program examples in the book, I shied away from several of them simply because they might make the code look more technical and therefore less clear to non-programmers. Maybe as an exercise you could go through the book 'marking' my code examples.

General Principles

Several things you should always aim for when writing program code:

- Apply your chosen formatting rules as you go along – writing code with the intention of going back over it to make it look nice later is never satisfactory because in general you are unlikely to go back over it immediately, and when (if) you do get around to it, you may already need the extra help the nicely formatted code gives you to be able to read it.

- Try to get it right first time. As an adage we would all like to adhere to always, this might seem a tall order. However, code that you lash up to do a quick fix or experimental code may just end up becoming the core of the final version. If you skimp at the point where you create code, that code will be harder to convert into 'well-formed' code later. If the code you write does not end up in a final version, nothing has been lost, and you might thank yourself for making it easy to read when you go back to borrow from it later.

- Develop a coding style that you are comfortable with – if you have to struggle to remember how to apply a naming convention or look up a manual to see how you are supposed to format the heading comments for a procedure, you are more likely not to do it.

Elements of Program Style

There are three major elements that make up style in program code:

1. the way the code is laid out;
2. the choice of identifiers for constants, variables, subs, functions, objects and classes, and the way they are typed;
3. the use of comments as in-code documentation.

None of these elements will make any difference to the way that the code works. If you choose to give all variables a single letter name and never add any comments, the program will in theory work exactly the same. In practice, humans write program code and less than perfect humans (i.e. all of us) need to be able to read what they write before adding to it, changing it or using it in another context.

Laying out Program Code

There are several aspects to this.

- Indenting – making the structure of your code visible by varying the left margin of passages of it. This is a trivial thing to get right if you are using Visual Studio

.NET, because it indents code as it is entered. If you are working without the benefit of Visual Studio, either by choice (because you prefer your own code editor) or for some other reason, you will need to take care of this aspect as you type code.

- Including extra spaces – blank lines make code more readable by making logically separate groups of statements distinct.

- Breaking up long lines – apart from saving the reader from having to scroll a Code window to the right to read long statements, this also has the benefit of preparing code for hard copy, since code that goes beyond the right-hand margin of a printed page will automatically wrap to the start of the next line making a mess of any other formatting you have carefully applied.

Indenting

The general principle here is to show which lines of code are enclosed or governed by which others by offsetting their left margin. Visual Studio's 'Smart' indentation is quite standard in its approach to code layout. One extra level of indentation is added for each level of enclosure, highlighting the following code constructs.

Subs and Functions

Every statement in a sub or function or property is indented.

```
Public Sub SomeSub()
    Dim someVariable As Integer
    ...
    ...
End Sub

Private Function MyFunction() As Integer
    Dim MyLocal As Integer
    ...
    ...
End Function
```

If..Then and If..Then..Else blocks

Indent the statements controlled by an If..Then or If..Then..Else block.

```
If x = 0 Then
    ...
End If

If name = "" Then
    ...
Else
    ...
End If
```

Select Case blocks

Everything between Select and End Select is indented so that all of the lines that begin with the Case keyword are indented and their contents are indented one more level. In earlier versions of Visual Basic, my preference was to indent the `Select Case` and `End Select` statements to the same level as the `Case` labels, reasoning that the extra level of indentation added to each `Case` label (and on to further indent the statements for each `Case`) led to code that disappeared too quickly off the right hand edge of the Code window. Visual Studio is to my mind over-enthusiastic in this respect, but with no choice, we will just need to put up with its version.

```
Select Case customerCreditLevel
    Case 0
        ...
    Case 200
        ...
    Case 1000
        ...
    Case Else
        ...
End Select
```

Loops

`For`, `While` and `Do` loops are treated the same as with `If..Then..Else` blocks.

```
For count = min To max
    ...
Next

While someCondition
    ...
Wend
Do
    ...
Loop Until someCondition
```

Multiple Level Indenting

Indentation is hierarchical. Where one enclosing structure appears within another (a `For` loop inside a sub, for example), its contents are indented to two levels, and so on. This can lead to heavily indented lines of code where structures are nested to several levels deep. However, it is a good idea to try to break up code into sub-procedures before you get to too many levels of structure, so very heavily indented lines might just be an indication of over-complex code that should be redesigned.

You can control the amount of indenting that pressing the Tab key introduces in Visual Basic by changing the **Tab Size** and **Indent Size** settings on the **Tools/Options/Text Editor/All Languages** dialog box setting, as shown in Figure Appx3.1. The standard setting is 4, where a single tab press moves in four spaces, but I have found 2 to be adequate, 3 to be optimal. You can use the **Text Editor/All Languages** page of the **Tools/Options** dialog box to control indenting, choosing to turn it off (**None**), choose **Block** indentation (which will simply make each new line indent automatically to the same level as the previous one so that you need to press Tab to indent a level), or **Smart** (which automatically indents language constructs).

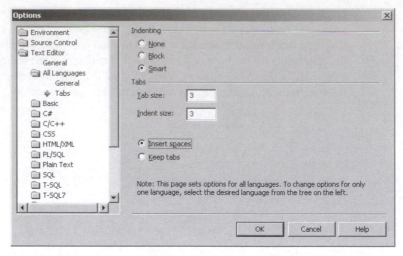

Figure Appx3.1   The **Text Editor/All Languages** page of the **Tools/Options** dialog box

Introducing Extra Space in Code

White space is a very valuable commodity in program code. It can be used to visually indicate the logical sub-divisions of an algorithm or to highlight certain sections, as well as to simply make the code look neater. Visual Basic will automatically introduce extra spaces in lines of code (for example, on either side of a '=' sign), and will also resist any attempt you make to add or remove any of the spaces within a syntactically correct line of code. It will also, if set to Smart indenting (see above), insert white space at the start of each line (indent it) to indicate code structure. It has its own opinion of how space characters in code should be used, and in this, we can assume it knows best. However, when it comes to the amount of space *between* lines, you are in control.

I have generally skimped on blank lines in the exercises in the book, since every blank line is a bit of a page than could be used to add explanatory text. In production code, I am lavish with extra blank lines.

It is sensible to leave at least one blank line between each sub or function in a code module (oddly, the Visual Basic editor does not enforce this automatically), but extra blank lines within subs should be used to indicate logical groupings.

Use blank lines to separate:

■ The declarative statements at the beginning of a procedure and the executable statements in it:

```
Public Sub MySub()
    Dim myInteger As Integer

    myInteger = GetInteger()
    ...
    Print myInteger

End Sub
```

- Logical sections of a procedure:

```
Sub LoadText(ByRef T As TextBox)
   Dim dlgOpen As OpenFileDialog = New OpenFileDialog()

      'In this sub, we check start by getting a file name...
      dlgOpen.Filter = "Text Files *.txt All Files *.*"
      dlgOpen.InitialDirectory = Application.ExecutablePath
      If dlgOpen.ShowDialog = DialogResult.OK Then
         fileName = dlgOpen.FileName

         'We now know the file exists, and its location.
         'Open it and read its contents into the specified
         'text box...
         Dim inStream As IO.StreamReader

         inStream = New IO.StreamReader(fileName)
         T.Text = inStream.ReadToEnd()
         inStream.Close()
      Else

         'Something went wrong...
         MessageBox.Show("Error reading " & filename & ".")
      End If

   End Sub
```

- Logical groups of variable declarations in the General Declarations section of a module:

```
Option Explicit
Private dataFileName As String      ' Variables for file
                                    ' handling
Private dataFileHandle As Integer
Private dataPath As String

Private dataElements() As Double    ' Data variables
Private dataCount As Integer
Private dataMin As Double
Private dataMax As Double

Private lastDataError As ErrObject ' Error reporting
Private errorCount As Integer
```

- Any sections of code that you wish to distinguish from others.

Breaking Up Long Lines

Long lines are almost inevitable in program code. Definitions of and calls to subs and functions that take a number of parameters will often go beyond the width of a Code window, even when it is maximized. Statements that combine a number of logical sub-expressions using `AndAlso` and `OrElse` tend to get lengthy, as do statements containing complex arithmetic. Very long lines are an annoyance because they cannot be viewed without scrolling on a screen, and they do not print properly. Apart from this, it is often difficult to follow the logic of a single line that is made up of a number of terms, while one that has been broken down into logical units can be perfectly clear in its intentions.

For these reasons, Visual Basic Code windows allow the use of the line continuation sequence; a space followed by an underscore, ' _', to allow a line of code to be broken and continued on the next screen line. As diligent coders, it is up to us to make sure that lines are broken at an appropriate point and that subsequent lines are indented to best indicate the logical flow.

Breaking up lines that define a procedure and its parameters
The most effective format for this is easy to deal with:

```
Public Sub myProcedure(ByVal intParameter As Integer, _
                       ByVal strParameter As String, _
                       ByVal dateParameter As Date, _
                       ByVal numParameter As Double, _
                       ByVal curParameter As Currency)
```

Breaking up this type of line as shown above brings the advantage that all of the parameters and their types appear as columns in a table – an immediate boon to readability. This format also makes it possible to add end-of-line comments to indicate the purpose of the parameters:

```
Public Function LoanPayments(ByVal capital As Currency, _
                                              'Amount borrowed
             ByVal term as Integer, _         'No of months
             ByVal interest As Single, _      'Rate of loan
             ByVal frequency As Integer, _    'Payment interval
             ) As Currency
```

A function definition line written in this way is its own documentation. By aligning the left of each 'column', we again produce a tabular and easy to read structure.

Breaking up lines that contain long combinations of numbers or strings
This type of line breaks up naturally:

```
errorMessage = "Error: " & ex.Message & _
                Environmant.NewLine & _
                "Location: " & ex.Source & _
                Environmant.NewLine & _
                "Do you want to try to recover?"
diagonal = Sqr((right - left) * (right - left) + _
               (top - bottom) * (top - bottom))
```

Breaking up lines containing a long procedure call
Some of the visual basic graphics methods (for `PictureBoxes` and `Forms`) can get quite long due to the large number of potential parameters:

```
With pnlOutput.GetGraphics()
    .DrawPie(Pens.Blue, _          ' Colour of graphic
             pieX, pieY, _         ' top-left of box.
             pieWidth, pieHeight   ' Size of pie chart
```

```
              segmentStartAngle,      ' Starting angle
              segmentSweepAngle)      ' Size of pic-slice
End With
```

By combining these techniques for adding readable space to programs, it is very possible to write code that is both easy to read and professional in appearance.

Choosing Identifiers

All truly professional programming teams use naming conventions. They clarify program code in a way that no other formatting measure can, turning lines that are intended to be followed by a dumb machine into expressive statements of the intention of programming code. Read the following block of code:

```
If (a < 65) Then
    Y = 65 - a
Else
    Y = 0
End If
```

To know what is happening here, you need to be aware of what the identifier 'a' represents, the relevance of the number 65 and the purpose of the identifier 'y'. It is so much easier to interpret:

```
If (age < RETIREMENT_AGE) Then
    yearsStillToWork = RETIREMENT_AGE - age
Else
    yearsStillToWork = 0
End If
```

Basically, you should not use a single letter variable or an obscure combination of letters and numbers in place of a meaningful term. The only time an exception should be allowed is when a single letter or abbreviated variable name is used frequently enough that it will not be misunderstood. For example, using the letter 'i' as a counter in a `For..Next` loop, or the identifier `msg` to hold a message string. Keep to a well-defined set of these 'standard' identifiers and no-one will be surprised by them. The rule should be, if anyone who needs to read the code has to have it explained, it should not be used.

Beyond this obvious simple rule, several equally obvious conventions can be applied.

Use the names that are used in the application domain

If you are writing code for a user who refers to his customers as 'Clients', use `Client` instead of `Customer`. Years ago I had to write a database application for a driving school proprietor who referred to his clients as 'pupils'. I decided this sounded silly and used the term 'Student' in the database. At a later date the driving school proprietor introduced me to a new requirement – he was introducing a student discount scheme to encourage new young drivers. This caused so many misunderstandings as we discussed the new requirements that eventually I had to give up and replace all instances of the word 'Student' with the word 'Pupil'. In situations like this, the customer is always right and his or her terminology is the best terminology to use.

Avoid abbreviations

Some programmers and designers still advocate the use of whole words with all of the vowels removed as variable names. I was even party to a book that made this suggestion in the early 1990s – although it was for C++ programmers who never use three keystrokes when two will do. Even so, I am now ashamed of the suggestion and my association with it. It is generally a bad idea, since code written in this way is difficult to read out loud and can lead to an ambiguous situation if two such abbreviations clash. Write your code so that if you need to, you can read it to a colleague over the phone. Remember that on today's hard disks, the extra space taken up by additional characters is virtually free.

Break up words with Capitals

Using more than one word squashed together to form a variable, sub or function name is almost essential to get meaning into the identifiers you use. Unaided, this can result in identifiers that need to be decrypted laboriously by the reader. For example:

```
Private datatablename As String
Public customeridentitynumber As Long
Public customercreditlimit As Currency

Public Sub Enrolnewcustomer()
   . . .
```

These long and tortuous sequences of characters can easily be made readable by the strategic introduction of capitals at the start of each new word:

```
Private dataTableName As String
Public customerIdentityNumber As Long
Public customerCreditLimit As Currency

Public Sub EnrolNewCustomer()
   . . .
```

It's not that it is very difficult to read the first version; just that it is so much easier to read the second. Note that I use a starting capital for a procedure name, but start variable names with a lower case letter. This can be a matter of choice, since it does not affect the way that capitals break up the words within an identifier. However, more and more programmers are using this convention so it probably makes sense to conform. One very persuasive reason for using this convention in Visual Basic is that the editor will make sure once you have introduced an identifier for the first time that every subsequent time you use it, the case will automatically be made to match the first use. Essentially, type it right the first time and ignore the shift key from then on.

Use Plurals

Arrays and collections exist to keep several things of a similar type together. For example:

```
Private Cards(1 To 52) As Card
Public Players As ArrayList
```

You should always use the plural form for these, and for any classes or types that you create that manage more than one of anything. For example, the user-defined type . . .

```
Structure InvoicePrintSettings
    LeftMargin As Single
    RightMargin As Single
    TopMargin As Single
    BottomMargin As Single
    LinePitch As Single
End Structure
```

. . . contains, not an array, but a number of related items that will be dealt with in the plural, so it makes sense to make the type name a plural.

Use UPPERCASE to define constants

C programmers have used this convention successfully for many years. It pays to be able to pick out constants from other identifiers, since otherwise you might be tempted to try to assign values to them. Refer back to the RETIREMENT_AGE code fragment for an example.

Documentation

Program code is the culmination of the development life-cycle, of which the only other evidence that exists is the documentation – specifications, diagrams, etc. As you will probably have noticed throughout this book, program code can be expressive, but still tells only part of the story. While a subroutine can be written in a style that spells out quite clearly what is happening, there are other aspects that go beyond the code: the assumptions that have been made, the conditions under which the code can be expected to run (and fail), the place a piece of code has in the grand scheme of things.

To make a piece of code tell the whole story, extra documentation is necessary. Within a program, this comes in the form of comments.

What Comments are used for

Comments in program code play several distinct roles:

1. to state the purpose of a class or routine in plain words;
2. to describe the conditions required for a routine to run properly;
3. to indicate the effects that a procedure will have on variables and objects within its scope;
4. to state any known limitations of a piece of code;
5. to describe significant changes that have been made to program code;
6. to indicate who has written a module or procedure and when.

Styles of Comment

I tend to use three forms of comment in test and production code. These are:

- in-line comments, placed at the end of statements to further describe their purpose;
- single-line comments, normally placed immediately before a statement or block of code I wish to clarify;
- block comments, normally placed at the start of a module, before blocks of variable declarations, at the start of a procedure (sub, function or property) and in front of any passage of code that I think needs significant clarification.

In-line comments are placed at the end of a line to explain it:

```
Private Sub mnuFileSave_Click(ByVal sender As
                                       System.Object, _
                        ByVal e As System.EventArgs) _
                        Handles mnuFileSave.Click
    If fileName = "" Then 'fileName is a module variable.
        FileSaveAs() 'Save the file with a new name.
    Else
        FileSave()    'Save the file with the existing name.
    End If
End Sub
```

Single line comments are used to describe the following section of code:

```
'Then write out each Student...
For Each S In Students.Values
    S.WriteXML(writer)
Next
```

Block Comments are used to provide a 'heading' for a significant structural item, a class, Sub, Function or Property:

```
'In this sub, we check whether a file exists.
'If it does, the file is loaded as a block
'of text into txtFileInfo...
Sub LoadText()
    Dim fileName As String
    Dim inStream As IO.StreamReader
    fileName = "c:\data\TextFile.txt"
    ...
```

Commenting out blocks of code

You can temporarily remove a block of Visual Basic code from a program by commenting it out – preceding each statement with a comment character (apostrophe). You can either do this laboriously a line at a time, or use the Comment Block command, available only from the Edit toolbar (select **View/Toolbars** and check the **Edit** toolbar). Select the text you want to temporarily disable and press the Comment Block button (hover the mouse pointer over buttons to see their names). All of the selected lines will be preceded with a comment character. To remove the comments and restore the code, select the commented out lines and press the Uncomment Block button.

General Commenting Principles

Use comments to spell out your intentions
Describe your intentions for a procedure in comments, and then fill in the program code, leaving the comments in place. For example:

```
Sub LoadText(ByRef T As TextBox)
    'Get the file name from an OpenFile dialog box
    'Open the file and read the contents
    'Close the file and transfer the contents to the text box
    'If something goes wrong, report it
End Sub
```

Now that the required process has been adequately described, it is a simple matter to 'fill-in the blanks' and create the sub, either immediately or at a later date:

```
Sub LoadText(ByRef T As TextBox)
    Dim dlgOpen As OpenFileDialog = New OpenFileDialog()

    'Get the file name from an OpenFile dialog box
    dlgOpen.Filter = "Text Files | *.txt | All Files | *.*"
    dlgOpen.InitialDirectory = Application.ExecutablePath
    If dlgOpen.ShowDialog = DialogResult.OK Then
        fileName = dlgOpen.FileName
```

```
        'Open the file and read the contents
        Dim inStream As IO.StreamReader
        Dim fileText As String

        inStream = New IO.StreamReader(fileName)
        fileText = inStream.ReadToEnd()
        'Close the file and copy the contents to the text
        'box
        inStream.Close()
        T.Text = fileText
    Else

        'If something goes wrong, report it
        MessageBox.Show("Error reading " & filename & ".")
    End If

End Sub
```

Do not simply repeat the code in comments

If comments do not add something to the expressiveness of your code, there is no point in having them. Avoid comments such as:

```
' Add 1 to x...
x = x + 1

' Get the first character of customers(x)...
ch = Left(customers(x), 1)
```

Instead, try to use comments to *describe* what you are actually doing:

```
' Move to the next customer and get the initial...
cust += 1
ch = Left(customers(cust), 1)
```

Write comments in the active voice

Program code is an active medium – as a programmer, you do not have things done to your variables; *you* do things to them. e.g.:

```
'Close the file and transfer the contents to the text box
inStream.Close()
T.Text = fileText
```

and not:

```
'The file is closed and the contents moved to the text box
inStream.Close()
T.Text = fileText
```

Keep comments and code in synch

Finally, the most heinous crime imaginable is to change program code without updating the comments that describe it. This looks shoddy when it is obvious, and can cause a lot of wasted effort when it is not.

If you are writing a program for a customer, it pays to apply a little quality assurance to the job before you finally deliver it. The code will look better, you will find it easier to change and fix, and if the customer does look at it, you will be making a much better impression. You can apply the following checklist to almost any program to produce an objective measure of how well written it is, both stylistically and technically. Each *No* answer indicates a shortfall in quality.

Routines (Subs and Functions)

■ Does each routine's name describe exactly what it does?

■ Does each routine perform a single, well-defined task?

■ Have all parts of each routine that would benefit from being put into their own routines been put into their own routines?

■ Is each routine's interface obvious and clear?

■ Have functions been used when a routine has a useful result?

■ Do the routines in a module perform related tasks?

Data names

■ Are type names descriptive enough to help document data declarations?

■ Are variables meaningfully named?

■ Are variables used only for the purpose for which they're named?

■ Are loop counters given informative names (i.e. *not* i, j, n)?

■ Are well-named enumerated types used?

■ Are named constants used instead of *magic numbers*? (e.g. 3.1415926 is a magic number – PI is a good identifier).

Classes

■ Have classes been used to model real-world objects in the application domain?

■ Have the relationships between real-world objects in the application domain been modelled in the program?

- Are class interfaces defined to expose only necessary interface properties and methods?
- Has inheritance been used appropriately (can you say that a sub-class object Is-A(n) instance of a super-class object)?
- Are method names action words?
- Do property names describe attributes of the class?
- Do parameters have descriptive names and appropriate types?

Data Organization

- Are extra variables used for clarity when needed?
- Are references to variables close together and to the variable definitions?
- Are data structures simple so that they minimize complexity?
- Is complex data accessed through abstract access routines (abstract data types or classes)?

Control

- Is the nominal path through the code clear?
- Are related statements grouped together?
- Have relatively independent groups of statements been packaged into their own routines?
- Does the normal case follow the `If` rather than the `Else` in an `If..Then..Else` structure?
- Are control structures simple so that they minimize complexity?
- Does each loop perform one and only one function?
- Is nesting minimized?
- Have variable expressions been simplified by using additional variables, Boolean variables and Boolean functions?

Layout

- Does the program's layout show its logical structure?
- Are blank lines used to indicate logically distinct segments of code?
- Are long lines broken in suitable places so that they can be read easily on-screen and in hard copy?

Design

- Is the code straightforward and does it avoid cleverness?
- Are implementation details within a routine or class hidden as much as possible from statements that use the routine or class?

■ Is the program written in terms of the problem domain (e.g. finance) as much as possible rather than in terms of computer-science or programming language structures?

Documentation

■ Does each module have a headline comment block that describes its overall purpose?

■ Does each sub and function have a heading comment to describe its purpose?

■ Are necessarily complex algorithms adequately described in comments?

■ Are comments used to describe the purpose of all significant public, private and local variables?

■ Are all comments up to date with the program code?

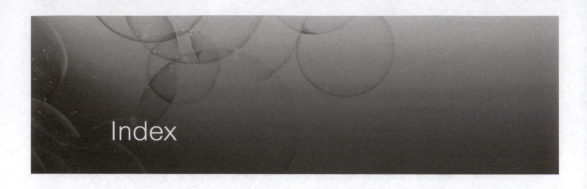

Index